Why Do You Need this New Edition?

If you're wondering why you should buy this new edition of *Families and Their Social Worlds*, here are 8 good reasons!

1 Coverage of the most current topics, including the effects of the recession and health care reform on families.

2 Updated discussions of trends such as the increase in cohabitation, the rise in unemployment, and the fluctuation in teen birthrates.

3 The statistics have been updated throughout, using the most current data available from the U.S. Census Bureau, CDC, United Nations, Population Reference Bureau, and other government and international organizations.

4 An increase in global content to show the importance of globalization and its effect on families.

5 A reorganization of the chapter on violence and abuse and a more contemporary approach that recognizes a wider variety of intimate partner violence.

6 A more explicit and expanded focus on family strength and resilience.

7 An expanded discussion on communication in relationships.

8 "What Do You Think?" questions that are strategically placed in chapters to help us to think critically, integrate material from other chapters, and apply the information to our own lives.

PEARSON

SECOND EDITION

Families

AND THEIR SOCIAL WORLDS

Karen Seccombe
PORTLAND STATE UNIVERSITY

Allyn & Bacon

Boston • Columbus • Indianapolis • New York • San Francisco • Upper Saddle River
Amsterdam • Cape Town • Dubai • London • Madrid • Milan • Munich • Paris • Montreal • Toronto
Delhi • Mexico City • Sao Paulo • Sydney • Hong Kong • Seoul • Singapore • Taipei • Tokyo

Executive Editor: *Karen Hanson*
Associate Editor: *Mayda Bosco*
Editorial Assistant: *Christine Dore*
Executive Marketing Manager: *Kelly May*
Marketing Assistant: *Janeli Bitor*
Senior Production Project Manager: *Patrick Cash-Peterson*
Manufacturing Buyer: *Debbie Rossi*
Editorial Production and Composition Service: *PreMediaGlobal*
Photo Researcher: *Lisa Jelly Smith and Poyee Oster*
Cover Designer: *Kristina Mose-Libon*

Credits appear on page 534, which constitutes an extension of the copyright page.

Many of the designations by manufacturers and sellers to distinguish their products are claimed as trademarks. Where those designations appear in this book, and the publisher was aware of a trademark claim, the designations have been printed in initial caps or all caps.

Library of Congress Cataloging-in-Publication Data
Seccombe, Karen, 1956–
   Families and their social worlds / Karen Seccombe.—2nd ed.
     p. cm.
   Includes bibliographical references and index.
   ISBN-13: 978-0-205-79774-5
   ISBN-10: 0-205-79774-1
  1. Families. I. Title.
   HQ503.S38 2011
   306.85—dc22

                         2010044055

10 9 8 7 6 5 4 3 2 1 RRD-OH 15 14 13 12 11

**Allyn & Bacon
is an imprint of**

ISBN 10:   0-205-79774-1
ISBN 13: 978-0-205-79774-5

Brief Contents

PART I   UNDERSTANDING FAMILIES AND THEIR SOCIAL WORLDS

CHAPTER 1   *Families and the Sociological Imagination* *2*

CHAPTER 2   *Families Throughout the World: Marriage, Family, and Kinship* *38*

CHAPTER 3   *Families Throughout History* *66*

CHAPTER 4   *Sex, Gender, and Families* *90*

CHAPTER 5   *Social Stratification, Social Class, and Families* *118*

CHAPTER 6   *Race, Ethnicity, and Families* *148*

PART II   NEGOTIATING FAMILY RELATIONSHIPS

CHAPTER 7   *Courtship, Intimacy, and Partnering* *182*

CHAPTER 8   *Marriage: A Personal Relationship and Social Institution* *218*

CHAPTER 9   *Becoming a Parent* *254*

CHAPTER 10   *Raising Children* *286*

CHAPTER 11   *Families and the Work They Do* *314*

CHAPTER 12   *Aging Families* *344*

PART III   SOCIAL PROBLEMS AND FAMILIES

CHAPTER 13   *Violence and Abuse* *378*

CHAPTER 14   *Divorce, Repartnering, and Remarriage* *410*

PART IV   WHAT HAVE WE LEARNED?

CHAPTER 15   *Summing It Up: Families and the Sociological Imagination* *442*

Contents

Preface   xiii
About the Author   xxv

PART I
UNDERSTANDING FAMILIES AND THEIR SOCIAL WORLDS

CHAPTER 1
Families and the Sociological Imagination   2

Chapter Preview   3
What Are Families?   5
  The Political Reality: Why Definitions
    Are Important   5
The Sociological Imagination   8
  Comparative Perspective   9
  An Empirical Approach   10
  ■ EYE *on the World:* Comparative Infant Mortality
  Rates, 2009   *12*
  Theory: Helping Us Make Sense of the World   15
Families and Social Change   17
  A Snapshot of American Families Today
    and How They Have Changed   18
  Family Change as a Political Issue   19
The State and Family Policy   22
  Selective versus Universal   22
  Family Policy and Family Values   24
Themes of This Book   26
  Families Are Both a Public Social Institution
    and a Private Personal Relationship   26
  Social Inequality Has a Powerful Influence
    on Family Life   28
  ■ USING *the Sociological Imagination:*
  Ideology of "Family" Shapes Perceptions of
  Immigrant Children   *28*
  An Expanded Strengths-Based Perspective Can Improve
    Family Resiliency   29
  ■ FAMILIES *as Lived Experience:* Meet Nathan
  Cabrera   *31*

Family Policies Reflect Historical, Cultural, Political,
  and Social Factors   32
Understanding Families in the United States Requires
  a Comparative Perspective   33
  ■ OUR *Global Community:* Adolescence
  Among the Maasai   *35*
Conclusion   36
Key Terms   36
Resources on the Internet   37

CHAPTER 2
Families Throughout the World: Marriage, Family, and Kinship   38

Chapter Preview   39
Functions of the Family: Variations and Universals   40
  Regulation of Sexual Behavior   41
  Reproduction and Socializing Children   42
  Property and Inheritance   42
  Economic Cooperation   42
  Social Placement, Status, and Roles   42
  Care, Warmth, Protection, and Intimacy   42
Differences in Marriage and Family Patterns   43
  ■ OUR *Global Community Marriage:* Among
  the !Kung San of Southern Africa   *44*
  Marriage   45
  ■ EYE *on the World:* Comparative
  Marital Patterns   *46*
  ■ FAMILIES *as Lived Experience:* Imagination:
  A Personal Ad from Adolph, Mary, and Megan   *50*
  Patterns of Power and Authority   51
  ■ OUR *Global Community:* Fistulas Are a Hidden
  Epidemic   *52*
  Patterns of Kinship, Descent, and Inheritance   54
  Patterns of Residence   55
Modernization Theory: Social Change
  and Families   55
  The Loss of Community: Gemeinschaft and
    Gesellschaft   56
  World Revolution and Family Patterns   56

World Systems Theory: Social Change and
Families   57

Families Around the World: India, Japan,
and Sweden   58

Developing Nations, Example: India   58

Cultures in Transition, Example: Japan   60

Toward Equality, Example: Sweden   62

Conclusion   64

Key Terms   64

Resources on the Internet   65

CHAPTER 3
Families Throughout History   66

Chapter Preview   67

Why Study Family History?   68

■ **USING** *the Sociological Imagination:* Piecing
Together the History of Family Life   **70**

Families in Preindustrial Societies   72

Family Life as Hunter-Gatherers   72

Family Life in Horticultural and Agrarian Societies   72

Family Life in Preindustrial United States   73

Native Americans   73

Colonial America: European Settlers   74

Colonial America: African Americans and Slavery   77

Mexicans   78

American Families in the Nineteenth Century   79

The Changing Nature of the Economy: Industrialization
and Urbanization   79

Demographic Changes: Immigration   80

Families in the Twentieth Century: The Rise
of the "Modern" Family   82

National Events: World Wars and the Great
Depression   82

■ **SOCIAL** *Policies for Families:* The Nineteenth
Amendment Is Ratified   **83**

Post–World War II: The Unique 1950s   84

■ **FAMILIES** *as Lived Experience:* Coming
of Age in the Depression   **85**

Social Change and the 1960s and 1970s   86

Recent Family Issues and Their Historical
Roots   86

An Example: Families and the Recession   87

Conclusion   88

Key Terms   89

Resources on the Internet   89

CHAPTER 4
Sex, Gender, and Families   90

Chapter Preview   91

Sex and Gender: What's the Difference?   93

Gender Is Socially Constructed   93

■ **USING** *The Sociological Imagination:* Getting to
Know Yourself   **94**

Sex Differences   95

Incongruence Between Sex and Gender   96

■ **USING** *the Sociological Imagination:* Transgender
Experience Leads Scientist to Critique Sex and Gender
Differences   **97**

Where Do We Learn Gender?   98

Family Members   98

Toys   99

Schools   100

Peers   101

■ **FAMILIES** *as Lived Experience:* The Sexualization of
Young Girls   **102**

The Mass Media   103

How Do Race, Ethnicity, and Class Shape Gender
Socialization?   104

The Pitfalls of Masculinity   104

Institutional Sex Discrimination: Patriarchy   105

Female Genital Cutting   105

The Power of Education   107

Does Patriarchy Exist in Western Nations?   107

■ **EYE** *on the World:* Comparative Literacy Rates—
Literate Women as a Percentage of Literate Men
Worldwide Between 15–24 Years, 2000–2004   **108**

What's in a Name?   110

Implications for Families   111

How Sex and Gender Matter: Income and Earnings   111

Social Policy and Family Resilience   114

Family Planning Can Make a World of Difference   114

Conclusion   116

Key Terms   116

Resources on the Internet   117

CHAPTER 5
Social Stratification,
Social Class, and Families   118

Chapter Preview   119

Social Class and Family Relationships   121

What Is Social Stratification?   123
   Caste and Class Systems in a Comparative Perspective   123
   Example: Social Class in Great Britain   124
Social Class in the United States   125
   The Upper Class   126
   ■ **USING** *the Sociological Imagination:* The *Social Register*, Class or Caste?   **127**
   The Upper Middle Class   128
   The Middle Class   128
   The Working Class   128
   The Working Poor   129
   The Underclass   129
   Social Mobility: Fact or Fiction?   130
Families in Poverty   131
   What Do We Mean by "Poor"?   132
   Who Is Poor?   133
   Comparative Studies   133
   ■ **SOCIAL** *Policies for Families:* Making Ends Meet on a Poverty Budget   **135**
   ■ **OUR** *Global Community:* "Nalim" in Bhutan   **136**
   Causes of Poverty   137
   ■ **EYE** *on the World:* A Comparative Look at Purchasing Power Parity, in U.S. Dollars, 2008   **138**
   Consequences of Poverty   142
Social Policy and Family Resilience   146
   Example: Earned Income Tax Credit   146
Conclusion   147
Key Terms   147
Resources on the Internet   147

CHAPTER **6**

Race, Ethnicity, and Families   **148**

Chapter Preview   149
Increasing Diversity in the United States   151
   Immigration   151
   Illegal Immigration   153
   ■ **SOCIAL** *Policies for Families:* Arizona's Immigration Law   **153**
Defining Basic Concepts   155
   Race   155
   Ethnicity   155
   Minority Group   156
   Racism: A Pervasive Problem that Affects Families   156

   Who Counts as "Them"?   159
   ■ **FAMILIES** *as Lived Experience:* Loving Across the Color Line: A White Adoptive Mother Learns About Race   **159**
   ■ **EYE** *on the World:* Comparative Ethnic and Racial Diversity   **160**
Hispanic Families   162
   A Tapestry of Cultures   162
   Hispanic Families Today   163
   Family Focus: Bilingual Education   164
Black Families   166
   Black Families Today   168
   Family Focus: Blacks and Extended Families   168
Asian American Families   170
   Asian American Families Today   171
   ■ **OUR** *Global Community:* One Child's Very Special First Fourth of July   **172**
   Family Focus: Generational Tension   174
American Indian and Alaska Native Families   175
   American Indian Families Today   175
   Alaska Natives   176
Interracial and Interethnic Families   177
Social Policy and Family Resilience   179
   Example: Affirmative Action   179
Conclusion   180
Key Terms   180
Resources on the Internet   181

PART II
NEGOTIATING FAMILY RELATIONSHIPS

CHAPTER **7**

Courtship, Intimacy, and Partnering   **182**

Chapter Preview   183
Courtship and Mate Selection   185
   What's Love Got to Do with It?   185
   ■ **USING** *the Sociological Imagination:* The Historical Relationship between Love and Marriage   **185**
   India   187
   United States   188

Love   193

■ **FAMILIES** *as Lived Experience:* "Living in Mania" **195**

Sex Differences in Loving   195

Sexuality   196

Sexual Orientation   197

■ **OUR** *Global Community:* Fourteen Years of Hard Labor **200**

Sexual Scripts   201

Sexually Transmitted Infections   205

Heterosexual Cohabitation   207

Who Cohabits?   208

Cohabitation and Marriage   209

Cohabitation and Children   211

Gay and Lesbian Intimate Relationships   212

Gay and Lesbian Commitment and Cohabitation   213

Social Policy and Family Resilience   214

Example: Civil Unions versus Same-Sex Marriage   214

Conclusion   216

Key Terms   217

Resources on the Internet   217

CHAPTER **8**

Marriage: A Personal Relationship and Social Institution   **218**

Chapter Preview   219

The Universality of Marriage   220

Wedding Ceremony   221

■ **EYE** *on the World:* Percentage of Women Aged 20–24 that Were Married/in Union Before the Age of 18   **222**

■ **OUR** *Global Community:* Iraqi Marriages: "It's Safer to Marry a Cousin Than a Stranger"   **224**

The Changing Nature of Marriage   226

Marriage Rates   226

Delaying Marriage   228

Racial and Ethnic Intermarriage   228

■ **SOCIAL** *Policies for Families:* Antimiscegenation Laws   **229**

Same-Sex Marriage   231

Attitudes Toward Marriage Itself   231

Marital Decline versus Marital Resilience Perspectives   233

Benefits of Marriage   234

Psychological Well-Being and Happiness   235

Physical Health   235

Economic Advantages   236

Marriage and Sex   236

Social Capital and Social Support   237

Does Marriage Benefit Everyone Equally?   237

Marital Happiness, Satisfaction, and Success   238

The Quality and Stability of the Couple's Parents' Marriages   238

Shared Values, Goals, and Characteristics   238

Age at Marriage   239

Religious Faith and Practice   240

Frequency and Satisfaction with Sexual Relationship   240

Satisfaction with Gender Relations and the Division of Labor   240

The Marriage Movement   241

Covenant Marriage   242

Communication   242

Verbal Communication   243

Nonverbal Communication   243

Listening   244

Self-Disclosure   245

Electronic Communication   246

Embracing Differences in Communication   246

■ **FAMILIES** *as Lived Experience:* Learning to Speak SAE   **249**

Conflict, Communication, and Problem Solving   250

Social Policy and Family Resilience   251

Example: The Oklahoma Marriage Initiative   251

Conclusion   252

Key Terms   252

Resources on the Internet   253

CHAPTER **9**

Becoming a Parent   **254**

Chapter Preview   255

Population and Fertility Trends Worldwide   257

■ **EYE** *on the World:* Total Fertility Rates, 2009   **258**

China's One-Child Policy   260

Japan   262

Fertility Rates in the United States   263

Historical Fluctuation   263

Delayed Parenthood   265

■ **USING** *the Sociological Imagination:* Having a Baby at 50 or 60   *266*

Deciding to Parent   267

The Rewards and Costs of Children   267

■ **FAMILIES** *as Lived Experience:* The "Costs" of Raising a Child   *269*

Remaining Childfree   270

Voluntarily Childfree   271

Adoption   272

The Social Construction of Childbirth   276

History: Towards the Medicalization of Childbirth   276

Childbirth Today   277

The Transition to Parenthood   278

Why Is the Transition So Challenging?   278

Sex Differences in the Transition to Parenthood   279

Social Policy and Family Resilience   280

Example: Maternity and Family Leaves   281

■ **SOCIAL** *Policies for Families:* The Family and Medical Leave Act   *283*

Conclusion   284

Key Terms   284

Resources on the Internet   285

CHAPTER **10**

Raising Children   286

Chapter Preview   287

Comparative Focus on Childhood and Parenting   289

■ **OUR** *Global Community:* Searching for Wages and Mothering from Afar: The Case of Honduran Transnational Families   *289*

Recent Trends   291

Socialization   292

Theoretical Approaches   292

Agents of Socialization   293

Socialization and Social Class   294

Socialization, Race, and Ethnicity   296

Socialization and Gender   297

Parenting Styles and Practices   297

"Mothering" and "Fathering"   297

■ **FAMILIES** *as Lived Experience:* We Have Love Bouncing Off the Walls at Our House   *299*

■ **FAMILIES** *as Lived Experience:* My Family: "What I Like About Being a Dad . . . and What I Don't"   *302*

Parenting Contexts   303

Teen Parents   303

Single Parents   304

Lesbian and Gay Families   307

Grandparents Raising Grandchildren   308

Social Policy and Family Resilience   310

Example: Family Allowances   310

Conclusion   312

Key Terms   312

Resources on the Internet   313

CHAPTER **11**

Families and the Work
They Do   314

Chapter Preview   315

The Changing Economy and Work   317

Trends in Child Labor   318

Recent Women's Labor Force Trends   318

The Changing Occupational Structure   320

Life in a Recession   321

Unemployment and Families   321

■ **FAMILIES** *as Lived Experience:* Unemployment Up Close and Personal   *322*

Poverty-Level Wages   323

Part-Time, Nonstandard, and Temporary Work   323

Disposable Workforce   324

Health Insurance and Reform   325

The Division of Household Labor   327

How Is Household Labor Defined and Measured?   327

Who Does What? Housework   327

Who Does What? Child Care   329

Renegotiating Family Work   330

Explanations for the Division of Labor   331

Children's Labor in the Home   331

Juggling Work and Family Life   332

Conflict, Overload, and Spillover   332

■ **OUR** *Global Community:* Why We Choose to Live in Hungary   *333*

The Time Crunch   334

Catch 22: Inflexible Full-Time Work or Part-Time Penalty   336

■ **SOCIAL** *Policies for Families:* Fixing Social INsecurity   *337*

Child Care: Who's Minding the Children?   338

Preschool-Aged Children   338

School-Aged Children   339

The Effect of Mothers' Employment on Children's Well-Being   340

Social Policy and Family Resilience   341

Example: A Comparative Look at Early Childhood Education and Child Care Policies   341

Conclusion   342

Key Terms   343

Resources on the Internet   343

CHAPTER **12**

Aging Families   **344**

Chapter Preview   345

Changing Demographics   347

Aging Around the World   347

■ **EYE** *on the World:* Comparative Aging—Percent of Population over Age 65, 2008   **348**

■ **EYE** *on the World:* Comparative Aging—Percent of Population over Age 65, 2040   **350**

Patterns of Aging in the United States   354

■ **FAMILIES** *as Lived Experience:* Celebrating My Grandmother's Birthday   **355**

Prevailing Theories of Aging   356

The Economics of Aging   357

How the Elderly Fare: Income and Assets   357

Social Security   358

The Aging Couple   359

Marital Satisfaction   360

Sexuality: Could It Be?   361

Gay and Lesbian Elders   361

Widowhood   362

Relationships with Children and Grandchildren   364

Children Leaving (and Returning) Home: "Boomerangers"   365

■ **USING** *the Sociological Imagination:* The Boomerang Generation   **366**

Grandparenthood   366

■ **FAMILIES** *as Lived Experience:* What Is It Like to Be a Grandparent?   **368**

Retirement   369

The Social Construction of Retirement: Retirement Around the World   370

Sex Differences in Retirement   371

Health   372

Declining Health Status   372

Severe Memory Loss   372

Long-Term Care   373

Social Policy and Family Resilience   375

Example: Medicare   375

Conclusion   376

Key Terms   377

Resources on the Internet   377

PART III
SOCIAL PROBLEMS AND FAMILIES

CHAPTER **13**

Violence and Abuse   **378**

Chapter Preview   379

Gender-Based Violence: An International Human Rights Issue   381

Trafficking of Women and Girls   382

■ **OUR** *Global Community:* Maya and Parvati: The End of a Dream   **383**

Intimate Partner Violence   384

How We Define and Measure Intimate Partner Violence   384

Typology of Violence   386

Stalking and Cyberstalking   386

Frequency of Intimate Partner Violence   387

Violence in Same-Sex Relationships   389

Dating Violence   390

■ **FAMILIES** *as Lived Experience:* "My Dating Violence Story"   **391**

Factors Associated with Violence   392

Consequences of Violence   393

Coping with Violence and Abuse: Reporting, Leaving, and Staying   394

■ **SOCIAL** *Policies for Families:* History of the Shelter Movement   **395**

Child Abuse   396

Types of Child Abuse   397

Factors Contributing to Child Abuse   399

Consequences of Child Abuse   400

Elder Abuse   400

Explanations for Violence and Abuse Among Intimates   401

Micro-Level Individual Causes   402

Macro-Level Societal and Cultural Causes   403

A Synthesis: Power and Control   405

Social Policy and Family Resilience   406

Example: Zero Tolerance in the Legal and Criminal Justice Systems   407

Conclusion   408

Key Terms   408

Resources on the Internet   409

CHAPTER 14

Divorce, Repartnering, and Remarriage   410

Chapter Preview   411

Measuring Divorce   413

Cross-Cultural Comparisons   413

■ **EYE** *on the World:* Comparative Divorce Rates per 1,000 People   *414*

■ **OUR** *Global Community:* Japanese Divorce, Custody, and Visitation Laws   *417*

Historical Trends in the United States   418

Factors Associated with Divorce   419

Macro-Level Factors   420

Micro-Level Factors   421

The Stations of the Divorce Experience   423

The Emotional Dimension   423

The Legal Dimension   424

The Parental Dimension   424

The Economic Dimension   425

The Community Dimension   428

The Psychic Divorce   428

Consequences of Divorce for Children   428

Short-Term Effects   429

Long-Term Effects   430

The Million-Dollar Question   431

Repartnering and Remarriage   431

■ **FAMILIES** *as Lived Experience:* Rebuilding When Your Relationship Ends   *432*

Cohabitation and Repartnering   433

Remarriage   433

Stepfamily Relationships   435

■ **FAMILIES** *as Lived Experience:* Journey to Healing   *437*

How Do Children Fare in Stepfamilies?   438

Social Policy and Family Resilience   439

Example: Initiatives to Limit Divorce   439

Conclusion   441

Key Terms   441

Resources on the Internet   441

PART IV
WHAT HAVE WE LEARNED?

CHAPTER 15

Summing It Up: Families and the Sociological Imagination   442

Chapter Preview   443

The Sociological Imagination   444

Susan, Marie, and Their Children   445

A Comparative Perspective   447

■ **OUR** *Global Community:* HIV/AIDS: Girls Are Very Vulnerable   449

■ **EYE** *on the World:* Percentage of Adults (15–49) Estimated To Be Living with HIV/AIDS, 2008   *450*

An Empirical Approach   452

Using the Sociological Imagination: Themes of the Text Revisited   453

Theme 1: Families Are Both a Public Social Institution and a Private Personal Relationship   453

Theme 2: Social Inequality Has a Powerful Influence on Family Life   454

■ **FAMILIES** *as Lived Experience:* "Tommy Johnson" and "Randall Simmons"   *455*

■ **USING** *the Sociological Imagination:* Managing the Stigma of Welfare   *457*

Theme 3: An Expanded Strengths-Based Perspective Can Improve Family Resiliency   459

Theme 4: Family Policies Reflect Historical, Cultural, Political, and Social Factors   461

Theme 5: Understanding Families in the United States Requires a Comparative Perspective   462

Future Trends: Where Are Families Heading?   463

Conclusion   465

Resources on the Internet   465

Glossary   **467**

Bibliography   **475**

Name Index   **519**

Subject Index   **527**

Credits   **534**

Preface

Family courses are popular on college campuses because families themselves are entities of keen interest. We are curious about families, and they are the center of many of our conversations, movies, television shows, songs, news stories, and cartoons. Families can offer some of the most exciting times of our lives: falling in love, getting married, or the birth or adoption of a baby. Families also can offer some of the worst times: disagreements, betrayal, violence, and divorce. What students tend to forget, however, is that families are far more than just personal relationships. Families are a powerful social institution with a set of rules, regulations, and norms (sometimes written, sometimes not) that are situated in a particular culture in a particular historical period.

I hope you find this an upbeat and high-quality text written for students in sociology, family studies programs, and social work. Many students may have taken at least an introduction to sociology course, and would therefore be familiar with general sociological concepts (e.g., culture, stratification, social structure, socialization, race, and ethnicity). I review and build upon these concepts—highlighting the "sociological imagination"—and show how they can be applied to a specific substantive area—the field of families. I want to teach students to think about families beyond their own personal experiences, and even beyond family structure in the United States. I hope to impart a passion for critical thinking as students come to see that families exist within social worlds. My overarching goal is to show that our conceptions and organizations of families are embedded within our social structure. A sociological imagination shows us that many family concerns are really *social issues* rather than merely private ones; therefore, solutions to these concerns must be social in nature as well. Embedded in each chapter are important policy considerations to illustrate what is currently being done, and perhaps even more importantly, what *can* be done to strengthen families and intimate relationships. "Social Policy and Family Resilience" identifies social policies that have made a real difference in the lives of millions in the United States and elsewhere.

Briefly, the text has several key themes: (1) families are both a public social institution and a private personal relationship; (2) social inequality has a powerful influence on family life; (3) an expanded strengths-based perspective can improve family resiliency; (4) family policies reflect historical, cultural, political, and social factors; and (5) understanding families in the United States requires a comparative perspective.

Families Are Both a Public Social Institution and a Private Personal Relationship

Families are not isolated entities, but live in larger social worlds affected by other social institutions, such as economic organizations, religious norms, and the political system. Families can best be understood by examining how they interact with (and are influenced by) other social institutions. Families cannot merely be separated as "havens" from the rest of society. Patterns of education, religious customs, economic systems, and political systems all shape family patterns, attitudes, behaviors, and the constraints and opportunities experienced by individual members. For example, specific social institutions may influence who is considered an appropriate mate; which family members work outside the home and what kind of work they do; who has the primary responsibility for housework and other domestic labor; how children are raised and disciplined; which children are to be schooled (e.g., just boys, or both boys and girls); how power and decision making among family members will be allocated; and the roles that extended family members are expected to play.

To help students realize these interconnections, this text uses numerous cross-cultural and historical examples in each chapter to clearly illustrate the interrelationship between social institutions. For example, I discuss how marriage norms are influenced by economic systems, how conceptions of gender are influenced by political systems, and how fertility is influenced by religion. I then show how the interrelationships exist in our own culture as well. It is important to recognize how our personal choices and behaviors are shaped by larger social structures. For example, how does one's level of education affect the chances of having children? And is the relationship between level of education and the likelihood of having children identical for men and women? Are children viewed as an asset in the United States, and how might views toward children be related to structural conditions, such as capitalism, urbanization, or the distribution of money and other resources?

Social Inequality Has a Powerful Influence on Family Life

Most Americans believe that the United States provides nearly equal opportunities for everyone. However, I show that American society is highly stratified on the basis of economics, power, and social status. Inequality is woven into many of our basic social structures and institutions. These patterns of social inequality filter down and shape all dimensions of family life (e.g., the neighborhood you live in, your gendered expectations, whether you are legally allowed to marry your partner, the values you are likely to hold for your children, the type of job you are likely to get, your consumption patterns, daily stressors, and your coping mechanisms). Social class, sex, race, ethnicity, and sexual orientation affect the way family members interact with one another and the way they are responded to.

Conversely, patterns of social inequality are also shaped *by* families. Americans fantasize that they can be anything they want to be, but in reality there is little substantial upward (or downward) social mobility. People usually live out their lives in generally the same social class in which they were born. Families pass on their wealth and social capital (or their lack of it) to their newest members, and this perpetuates social inequality. For example, because of U.S. inheritance laws, affluent parents can distribute their wealth to their children upon their death. Consequently, some of the richest people have only marginal employment histories. Yet others work relentlessly, often in the unglamorous but growing service sector, and find no real route to a better life. Their wages are low, they may not receive health insurance or other benefits, and they live on the margin only one paycheck away from impoverishment. My goal is to reveal to students the complexities of social inequality, and its often deleterious effects on families.

An Expanded Strengths-Based Perspective Can Improve Family Resilency

The family strengths perspective is a worldview, or perspective, based in optimism. I do not ignore family problems; in fact, I describe many problems in considerable depth—poverty, rape, racism, divorce, female genital cutting, and stalking, to name just a few. However, a strengths perspective focuses on identifying, creating, mobilizing, advocating, and respecting the resources, assets, wisdom, and knowledge that every person, and every family, has to help ameliorate problems. Rather than working from a deficit model, I want to highlight how members of our society can work together to make families more resilient. Resiliency is the capacity to rebound from adversity, misfortune, trauma, or other transitional crises and become strengthened and more resourceful. Most literature offering a strengths-based perspective focuses on micro-level factors, such as individual personality or family traits. However, I suggest that these are often not enough to help families through many challenges. Social problems require social solutions. Sometimes, we only have to look within our own communities for ideas that can improve resiliency. In other contexts, we may need to look further, perhaps to other countries, to observe their models. My goal within each chapter is to offer an example of how families can truly become more resilient, with the aid of a macro-level helping hand. Examples include maternity leave, child care, family allowance, child support, affirmative action, and universal health care.

Family Policies Reflect a Complex Set of Historical, Cultural, Political, and Social Factors

If families are public social institutions as well as private personal relationships, then we must recognize the importance of federal, state, and local involvement. The fourth theme of this text is that government regulates many conditions of families, and these policies reflect historical patterns, cultural values, social conditions, and political viewpoints. These views are represented as we enact certain policies, such as welfare reform, requiring partners to get a blood test before marrying, or passing legislation to prohibit gays and lesbians from marrying.

Conversely, historical, cultural, political, and social factors may also exercise a strong influence backhandedly by the *absence* of specific policies. For example, the U.S. government offers no systematic paid leave to women who have just given birth. This is in sharp contrast to other industrialized nations (and many nonindustrialized ones). Commonly, in other countries women will receive 6–12 months off of work with full or nearly full pay. Why does the United States offer so little to new parents? The United States is far more likely than other countries to believe that family matters are personal issues, reflecting our longstanding belief in rugged individualism. Family policies reflect values about personal responsibility versus collective good, the role of work in our lives, the expectations placed on mothers and fathers to manage the inherent conflicts between their work and family lives, and the level of concern over social inequality.

Understanding Families in the United States Requires a Comparative Perspective

The fifth theme of the text shows that one of the best ways to understand what is happening in the United States today is to examine what has happened in other times and in other places around the world. Learning how other societies structure families, how they collectively think about families, how they encourage members to interact, and how they deal with the challenges families face can provide insight into our own concerns. We cannot ignore what is happening elsewhere, because societies are becoming increasingly interconnected. New technologies, immigration, commerce across borders, and greater ease in world communication and travel have increased visibility, and the United States can no longer remain isolated. Although many problems, such as poverty or HIV/AIDS, are considerably worse in other countries, other problems loom larger in the United States than elsewhere. For example, the U.S. infant mortality rate is among the highest for developing countries, and the life expectancy rate is among the lowest. How can a society as richly endowed as the United States have such poor health statistics? Children's poverty rates are among the highest of developed countries, as are teenage pregnancy rates and the likelihood of divorce. What can we learn from other countries to better understand our own?

It is easy to ignore history and only focus on the here and now. But many of our current family issues are rooted in the traditions of the past. For example, to truly understand the high rate of divorce in the United States we should be aware of the ways in which the notion of love, which evolved in the eighteenth century, changed the entire basis on which mates were chosen, and thereby increased the likelihood of couples ending an unhappy marriage.

Chapter Overviews

Chapter 1 draws students into the study of families in an engaging manner and showcases how family scientists do their work. It introduces a sociological imagination that uses a comparative approach and empirical research to describe and explain patterns of family structure, family change, and social relationships. As a public social institution, families are not entities isolated from the rest of society. They continually change and adapt to people's needs, and to the changes found in other social institutions. This chapter introduces five specific themes that are woven into each chapter: (1) the family is a public social institution as well as a private personal relationship; (2) social inequality powerfully shapes virtually all dimensions of family life; (3) an expanded strengths-based perspective can demonstrate paths to family resiliency; (4) family policies reflect historical, cultural, political, and social factors; and (5) a comparative approach can yield insight into family structure and family dynamics.

Chapter 2 examines the functions, trends, and differences within marriage, family, and kinship patterns throughout the world. Families are found in every society because they provide functions that other social institutions cannot provide. Yet families are not monolithic or static, but continually adapt to changing circumstances. Two perspectives are presented that contrast the nature of social change upon families: modernization and world systems theory. Although the latter focuses more on the economic and political interdependence and exploitation found among nations, both agree that processes such as industrialization transform the culture and the environment, and therefore reshape the form and function of, and roles within, families.

Chapter 3 suggests that a look at history can provide us with critical insights about families today. Family historians use multiple research methods to piece together the everyday life of families in the past. Historians looking from preindustrial societies to more recent groups reveal that we have unfairly glorified families in the past. We now know that many families suffered hardship, and social problems were widespread. Yet, commonly we compare families today with the idealized version of the "normal" family of the brief period of the 1950s in which we envision that fathers earned the wages and mothers stayed at home to care for children. This chapter provides a historical overview of families. The goal is to show that our current attitudes, behaviors, and public policies relating to such family concerns as courtship, mate selection, cohabitation, marriage, sexuality, children, the elderly, and extended families are intricately connected to the past.

Chapter 4 introduces the signature concepts of sex and gender. Virtually all social institutions, whether political, religious, economic, educational, or familial, distinguish between men and women in fundamental ways that extend far beyond biological sex differences. Gender is largely a social construction; a comparative approach reveals that expected masculine and feminine behaviors differ historically and cross-culturally. Several key agents of socialization teach gendered norms, such as families, schools, toys, peer groups, and the mass media. Patriarchy is manifested around the world, as several examples show. It also persists in the United States. The ways in which sex and gender are rooted in our social structure have important implications for how families are constructed and how family members interact. Many examples will be revealed in the upcoming chapters.

Chapter 5 introduces the importance of social class to understanding families. Social stratification and social class are components of C. Wright Mills' claim that our personal experiences are in large part shaped by broad social, historical, and cultural forces. This chapter explores social stratification, social class, poverty, and family resiliency. Persons living in poverty are particularly vulnerable in terms of their health and social well-being. Strong family policies, such as the earned income tax credit or national health insurance, can go a long way in assisting families struggling to make ends meet. It is also important to recognize that social class interacts with other statuses and dimensions of stratification, such as sex, race, or ethnicity. A person is not simply rich, poor, or somewhere in the middle, but a working-class Hispanic woman, a Chinese American upper-class male, a black middle-class female, or a poor white woman; these statuses together influence our experiences. The goal of this chapter is to introduce these key concepts so that students can better understand the influence of class shown in subsequent chapters.

Chapter 6 reminds students that we all have a race and an ethnicity. Although Whites have the privilege of rarely thinking about them, it remains that skin color, physical features, country of origin, culture, and dominant language are associated with family structure and family interaction. This chapter provides an important foundation to upcoming chapters by introducing basic facts about race, ethnicity, and the changing demographic landscape of the United States. I introduce general definitions, and then look at the demographic trends and social characteristics of several racial and ethnic groups. Each race or ethnic group has a rich history and culture, and draws upon its heritage in meaningful ways to create relevant family structures. These family structures need not be denigrated simply because they differ from others. The purpose of this chapter is to introduce the idea that there is more than one model to family life, and that race and ethnicity (alone, and in conjunction with other statuses such as sex and class) provide unique opportunities and challenges, and are important statuses that frame our family lives. Race and ethnicity will be explored in depth in upcoming chapters.

Chapter 7 focuses on several key concepts surrounding the development of intimacy, including mate selection, love, sexual orientation, sexuality, and cohabitation. People become intimate, form partnerships, or marry to improve their economic conditions, for sheer survival, to increase their social standing, or to please their parents and build family alliances. Cultural traditions, the environment, social norms, and religious customs have as much to do with mate selection as love and affection, sexual convenience, or compatibility. Many cultures do not necessarily equate love with marriage, and in fact may see love as dangerous to a good marital relationship. Values also change over time. Today, in the United States, many unmarried couples engage in sexual relationships and cohabit. However, same-sex marriage continues to be steeped in controversy.

Chapter 8 examines marriage as both a social institution and a personal relationship, noting that it is recognized in some form around the world. As a social institution there are rules, rights, and responsibilities surrounding marriage because it is seen as a stabilizing force within societies. Therefore, the government sees marriage as its business. As a personal relationship, marriage is deeply meaningful to the individuals involved, although "meaningful" is conceptualized differently within social, historical, and cultural locations. Americans are highly committed to marriage. Most claim that they want to marry and consider marriage important to their personal happiness. Nonetheless, there are many changes in marriage underway. For example, people tend to marry later, and many cohabit prior to marriage or in place of marriage. Some propose to legalize same-sex marriages, and spouses are renegotiating terrain such as the division of household labor and other roles. These changes have also inspired a growing and controversial marriage movement designed to preserve, strengthen, and promote traditional marriage.

Chapter 9 focuses on the process of becoming a parent. It shows that seemingly micro-level personal issues such as whether, when, who, and how to have a baby reflect more than just biology. Values such as pronatalism shape our attitudes and behaviors. Political, religious, economic, health care, and other social institutions also shape parenthood, including fertility, pregnancy, adoption, childbirth, and transitioning to parenthood—dimensions of family life that many see as very personal. China, as the most extreme case, accepts a level of governmental policy and involvement that many other countries deem highly intrusive. Nonetheless, all countries have family policies, either explicit or implicit, that organize fertility and parenthood for their citizens. Family policies in the United States often minimize the connection between social structure (macro) and the lived experience (micro) of individual families. For example, compared to other nations, Americans are often expected to fend for themselves, as is the case with maternity and family leaves.

Chapter 10 points out that, although raising children may be universal, the act of *parenting* is highly variable. Parenting attitudes and practices depend to a large extent on the type of tasks or competencies that members of a society (or subgroup) are expected to have. "Mothering" and "fathering" include the emotional, physical, and financial work involved with caring for children, but it is important to keep in mind that these identities take place within specific historical and cultural contexts, and even in the United States today they are framed by structures of sex, race, ethnicity, and class. Parenting contexts reflect diversity, with more children being raised by single parents, gay and lesbian parents, and grandparents. Teen birthrates are in a state of flux, and it remains an important parenting environment. Many countries directly assist parents with the financial costs of raising children. The United States also does so, but leans toward annual tax credits rather than monthly assistance such as a family allowance.

Chapter 11 explores the empirical research and theoretical perspectives surrounding the topic of working families. All families do meaningful work inside or outside the home. Home and work used to be "separate spheres," largely segregated by sex. However, mothers are increasingly likely to work outside the home for pay. The changing nature of the economy has altered the context and meaning of work for many families. Jobs are becoming less secure, with nonstandardized work schedules, and fewer union protections. Many families now need two paychecks to make ends meet. No longer are work and family domains separate; instead, they interact and influence each other in many critical ways. Issues such as work–family conflicts, feelings of time deficits with children, negotiations over the division of household labor, and struggles to find suitable child care are ones that most employed families face today. Family-friendly workplace policies, such as flexible work hours, and national family policies, such as assistance with child care, can help alleviate the stress that many employed families experience.

Chapter 12   shows that the population around the world is aging rapidly. A comparative perspective helps us understand the implications of this growth in developed and developing nations. The largest increase around the world is among those aged 80 and over. The pronounced effects of these demographic changes will be felt throughout the global economy. The concerns of the elderly become all of our concerns. This chapter examines many issues among the elderly and their families—promoting social and economic well-being; supporting intimate relationships; fostering positive bonds with adult children and grandchildren; and coping with retirement, widowhood, health, and caregiving to frail elders.

Chapter 13   focuses on gender-based violence and violence among intimates. It explores sexual trafficking, definitions and measures of violence, dating aggression, spouse/partner abuse, child abuse, elder abuse, and explanations for violence. The overall goal is to show that even though violence is experienced on a deeply personal level, it is really a *social problem*. Abuse is rooted in complex and longstanding societal-level and individual-level traditions that create norms promoting violence and male privilege. However, zero-tolerance movements within our legal and criminal justice systems, along with battered women's shelters, are sprouting up throughout the country to spread awareness and help victims of violence.

Chapter 14   reminds us that homes are not always havens. The chapter introduces the intricate weaving of structural, historical, cultural, and personal factors that helps to explain attitudes toward divorce, rising and falling divorce rates, divorce policy, and how families cope with a divorce. For example, divorced women in the United States often struggle financially to support their families, given low pay structures and inadequate child support collection. To best understand divorce, I introduce both the macro and micro issues that surround it. Empirical data suggest that children are particularly vulnerable to the hardships associated with divorce, including a greater likelihood of poverty and other behavioral and social problems. Most divorced persons remarry or repartner after the divorce. A stepfamily consists of a remarried or repartnered couple in which at least one spouse has a child from a previous relationship. Stepfamilies have many unique characteristics compared to two-parent biological families. Although they offer many strengths, they also face a number of specific challenges.

Chapter 15   reviews the contributions that the sociological imagination offers to our understanding of families. The five themes that run throughout the book are reviewed and specific examples from earlier chapters are provided: (1) families are both a public social institution and a private personal relationship; (2) social inequality has a powerful influence on family life; (3) an expanded strengths-based perspective can demonstrate paths to family resiliency; (4) family policies reflect historical, cultural, political, and social factors; and (5) understanding families in the United States requires a comparative perspective. A sociological perspective shows us that families are complex entities. Despite important cultural universals that are found in families throughout the world, family structures and the relationships embedded within families reflect historical, political, and cultural contexts. They also reflect power and social inequality. The goal is to understand such issues as mate selection, marriage rituals, gendered expectations, division of household labor, fertility patterns, parent–child relationships, aging and the care of the elderly, family conflict and violence, and divorce and repartnering within these contexts. Only then can we identify trends that illuminate both the past (i.e., where we've been) and the future (i.e., where we're going) so that we may build resilient families.

Features

Each chapter begins with a **Chapter Preview** that introduces students to the chapter's main topics. A chapter-opening vignette draws students into the narrative. Most chapters conclude with a section titled "Social Policy and Family Resilience", highlighting important social policies in the United States and around the world to strengthen families. These include world family planning efforts, the Earned Income Tax Credit, family and maternity leaves, early childhood education policies, and family allowances.

Within each chapter, there are several types of features that illustrate important themes; all include critical thinking questions:

CHAPTER PREVIEW

Most of us have lived in some sort of family, so we naturally think of ourselves as "experts" on the topic. Yet our personal experiences are part of a larger picture. Although all of us experience family life as individuals, we cannot fully understand this experience without an appreciation of the environment in which it takes place. This chapter introduces the scientific study of families and shows how a sociological perspective broadens our understanding of personal relationships. However, families are more than just personal relationships; they are also an important social institution, and as such, they are socially constructed to meet human needs. Given their seemingly endless diversity, how do we study families in any systematic way? In this chapter, you will learn:

- A definition of families, showing the political reality of why definitions are important
- The importance of a sociological imagination, including the value of a comparative perspective and the use of empirical data
- The evolution of families, and the conservative, liberal, and feminist interpretations of this evolution
- The role of the state in family policy, highlighting how the U.S. approach to family policy compares with other developed nations
- The five themes of this book: (1) families are both a public institution and a private personal relationship; (2) social inequality has a powerful influence on family life; (3) an expanded strengths-based perspective can improve family resiliency; (4) family policies reflect historical, cultural, political, and social factors; and (5) understanding families in the United States requires a comparative perspective

- *What Do You Think* encourages students to think critically, analyze, and synthesize the chapter material. Questions placed strategically throughout the chapter challenge students to reflect on their own lives, take a stand, and defend their position.

WHAT DO YOU THINK?

What are the benefits of an increasingly diverse society? Can you think of any drawbacks?

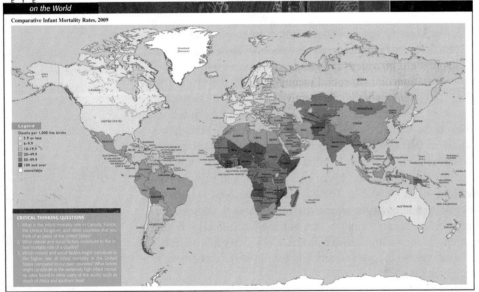

EYE on the World

Comparative Infant Mortality Rates, 2009

Legend
Deaths per 1,000 live births
- 5.9 or less
- 6–9.9
- 10–19.9
- 20–49.9
- 50–99.9
- 100 and over
- unavailable

CRITICAL THINKING QUESTIONS
1. What is the infant mortality rate in Canada, France, the United Kingdom, and other countries that you think of as peers of the United States?
2. What natural and social factors contribute to the infant mortality rate of a country?
3. Which natural and social factors might contribute to the higher rate of infant mortality in the United States compared to our peer countries? What factors might contribute to the extremely high infant mortality rates found in other parts of the world, such as much of Africa and southern Asia?

Source: Population Reference Bureau 2010c

- *Eye on the World* presents global maps that highlight international differences on relevant topics (e.g., fertility rates, income inequality, the elderly population, infant mortality, status of women) and include several critical thinking questions per map.

- *Families as Lived Experience* provides personal stories that clearly illustrate the concepts of that chapter (e.g., transracial adoption, a parent's view of pressure on young girls to wear sexy clothing, a career-oriented woman discusses what it is like to have children, rebuilding a relationship after a divorce, and celebrating a 105th birthday).

- *Social Policies for Families* highlight specific policies to support families, including their origin, implementation, and consequences (e.g., Social Security, the poverty line, health care reform, family leave policies, antimiscegenation laws).

- *Our Global Community* provides an in-depth look at family issues in another culture (e.g., trafficking of girls, Japanese divorce and custody laws, transnational families, HIV/AIDS in sub-Saharan Africa, concepts of adolescence in nonindustrialized societies, marriage and nepotism in Iraq). Learning about families elsewhere helps us better understand the world.

- *Using the Sociological Imagination* illustrates the diversity in family experiences and shows the linkages between macro-level and micro-level factors (e.g., a personal ad for polygamy, changing Hispanic views of gender, historical relationship between love and marriage, immigrant children's views of American families).

Each chapter ends with a **Conclusion**, a list of **Key Terms** with definitions and page references, and a **Resources on the Internet** section.

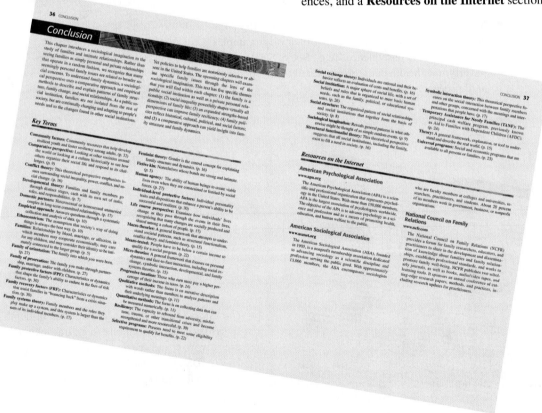

Supplements

We carefully designed a supplements package that supports the aims of *Families and Their Social Worlds* in order to provide students and instructors with a wealth of support materials to ensure success in teaching and in learning.

Instructor's Manual and Test Bank (ISBN 0205001017) Each chapter in the Instructor's Manual, authored by Margaret Walsh of Keene State College, includes the following resources: Learning Objectives, Chapter Outline, Key Terms & Concepts, Lecture Launchers, Discussion Topics, Class Activities, Suggested Readings, and Weblinks.

The Test Bank, written by text author Karen Seccombe, provides over 1,000 multiple-choice, true/false, short answer, and essay questions.

The Instructor's Manual and Test Bank supplement is available to adopters at **www.pearsonhighered.com**.

MyTest (ISBN 0205842585) This computerized software allows instructors to create their own personalized exams, to edit any or all of the existing test questions, and to add new questions. Other special features of this program include random generation of test questions, creation of alternate versions of the same test, scrambling question sequence, and test preview before printing. The MyTest is available to adopters at **www.pearsonhighered.com**.

PowerPoint Lecture Presentations (ISBN 0205001009) This complete set of chapter-by-chapter PowerPoint lecture presentations, authored by Romana Pires of San Bernardino Valley College, contains many slides per chapter specific to *Families and Their Social Worlds*. The slides provide lecture outlines, include figures and tables from the text, and reinforce the main ideas of each chapter. They offer a clean format, so professors can add their own photos or clipart.

MyFamilyKit (ISBN 0205152325) MyFamilyKit is an online supplement that offers book-specific learning objectives, chapter summaries, flashcards, and graded practice tests, as well as video clips and activities to aid student learning and comprehension. Also included in MyFamilyKit is MySearchLab, a valuable resource that includes tools for writing and conducting Internet research projects. It includes access to the EBSCO Content Select Database, MySocLibrary, as well as Social Explorer, an interactive program for analyzing Census Data from 1790 to the present.

MyFamilyKit is available with *Families and Their Social Worlds, 2e*, when a MyFamilyKit access code card is packaged with the text at no additional charge, or can be purchased separately.

Acknowledgments

A book is never a solo venture. I would like to thank all those who had a helping hand in the process of turning my ideas for a family text into reality. The encouragement you gave, the challenging questions you posed, and the personal and professional backing you offered have made this book one of which I am very proud. Thank you. The School of Community Health at Portland State University offered an ambiance conducive to writing. My good friends, especially Ali Cook and Cordie Tilghman, provided me with the extracurricular diversions that kept my project humming along at full speed. Other friends who live far away in distance but close in spirit were also invaluable, and I particularly thank Natalie Birk and

Karen Pyke, who, despite the distance, are always there for me. And I would like to offer a huge thank you to Gary Lee, Kathy Kaiser, Bill Martin, and Manley Johnson, who sparked my intellectual interest in families in the first place. They have each been wonderful mentors to me at various stages of my career, and without their attention and care, who honestly knows where I would be right now?

I extend great thanks as well to the following reviewers who offered extensive comments and ideas on this manuscript: Wendy Cook-Mucci, Southern Illinois University; Cynthia R. Hancock, University of North Carolina, Charlotte; Debra A. Henderson, Ohio University; and Karen S. Joest, State University of New York, Oneonta.

I also appreciate the tremendous help that I received from the folks at Allyn and Bacon who took my words and actually turned them into a beautiful book, including Jeff Lasser and Karen Hanson, Executive Editors; Mayda Bosco, Associate Editor; Patrick Cash-Peterson, Production Manager; Andrea Stefanowicz, Full-Service Project Manager; and Lisa Jelly Smith and Poyee Oster, Photo Researchers. Few professors want to use a book without supplements, so we all appreciate the work that Romana Pires of San Bernardino Valley College put into the beautiful PowerPoints and the creativity that Margaret Walsh of Keene State College put into the Instructor's Manual.

And, most naturally, I want to acknowledge my husband Richard, and daughters Natalie—who is now 10 years old (and in fourth grade—wow!)—and Olivia, who is a bright-eyed 8-year-old second-grader. Although many authors thank their family members for their sacrifices, I believe that writing this book actually enhanced our lives. What a unique and crazy opportunity to combine theory, methods, and application! I am appreciative of the greater Oregon Episcopal School community for continuing to take such good care of all of us.

Now, to the readers, if you have questions or comments, please send them my way. I want to hear from you: **seccombek@pdx.edu**. Someone e-mailed me recently to ask if I am a "real person." The answer is "Yes."

About the Author

Karen Seccombe is a professor in the School of Community Health at Portland State University, located in Portland, Oregon. She received her BA in sociology from California State University, Chico; her MSW in health and social welfare policy from the University of Washington; and her PhD in sociology from Washington State University. Her research focuses on poverty, welfare, access to health care, and the effects of social inequality on families. She is the author of *Exploring Marriages and Families* (Pearson)*; "So You Think I Drive a Cadillac?": Welfare Recipients' Perspectives on the System and its Reform*, 3rd edition (Allyn and Bacon); *Families in Poverty* (Allyn and Bacon); *Just Don't Get Sick: Access to Health Care in the Aftermath of Welfare Reform*, with Kim Hoffman (Rutgers University Press), and *Marriages and Families: Relationships in Social Context*, with Rebecca L. Warner (Wadsworth). She is a National Council on Family Relations fellow, and a member of the American Sociological Association and the Pacific Sociological Association, where she has held elective offices. Karen lives in Portland with her husband Richard, a health economist; her 10-year-old daughter, Natalie Rose; and her 8-year-old daughter, Olivia Lin. In her spare time she enjoys hiking and cycling near their cabin in the Oregon Cascades; walking the sandy beaches of the Oregon coast; exploring the kid-friendly playgrounds, attractions, and restaurants in Portland and surrounding areas; and traveling just about anywhere—the San Juan Islands in Washington are high on her list.

Families

AND THEIR SOCIAL WORLDS

CHAPTER 1

Families and the Sociological Imagination

CHAPTER OUTLINE

What Are Families? 5

The Sociological Imagination 8

■ **EYE** *on the World:* Comparative Infant Mortality Rates, 2009 *12*

Families and Social Change 17

The State and Family Policy 22

Themes of This Book 26

■ **USING** *the Sociological Imagination:* Ideology of "Family" Shapes Perceptions of Immigrant Children *28*

■ **FAMILIES** *as Lived Experience:* Meet Nathan Cabrera *31*

■ **OUR** *Global Community:* Adolescence Among the Maasai *35*

Conclusion 36

Key Terms 36

Resources on the Internet 37

CHAPTER PREVIEW

Most of us have lived in some sort of family, so we naturally think of ourselves as "experts" on the topic. Yet our personal experiences are part of a larger picture. Although all of us experience family life as individuals, we cannot fully understand this experience without an appreciation of the environment in which it takes place. This chapter introduces the scientific study of families and shows how a sociological perspective broadens our understanding of personal relationships. However, families are more than just personal relationships; they are also an important social institution, and as such, they are socially constructed to meet human needs. Given their seemingly endless diversity, how do we study families in any systematic way? In this chapter, you will learn:

- A definition of families, showing the political reality of why definitions are important

- The importance of a sociological imagination, including the value of a comparative perspective and the use of empirical data

- The evolution of families, and the conservative, liberal, and feminist interpretations of this evolution

- The role of the state in family policy, highlighting how the U.S. approach to family policy compares with other developed nations

- The five themes of this book: (1) families are both a public institution and a private personal relationship; (2) social inequality has a powerful influence on family life; (3) an expanded strengths-based perspective can improve family resiliency; (4) family policies reflect historical, cultural, political, and social factors; and (5) understanding families in the United States requires a comparative perspective

Family life is serious business, even in comic strips. The popularity and long lives of comic strip families make them trusted observers and reporters of the public discourse. More than 100 million people read the daily comics, and they come away with a variety of interpretations, including perceptions of ideal families, gender stereotypes, and proper roles for mothers and fathers. A research team headed by Ralph LaRossa, a sociologist at Georgia State University, systematically examined the content of 490 Father's Day and Mother's Day comic strips published from 1940 to 1999. The oldest comic in the study was *Gasoline Alley,* first published in 1919. Others such as *Blondie, Bloom County, Cathy, Dennis the Menace, The Family Circus, Garfield, Hi and Lois, Little Orphan Annie, Peanuts, Pogo,* and *Ziggy* were also included.

Focusing in particular on the roles of fathers, the researchers found that the depiction of fatherhood fluctuated significantly. In the past, fathers were often viewed as incompetent or were mocked as they performed (or tried to perform) parenting duties. Likewise, during the 40-year period from the mid-1950s to the mid-1990s, fathers were rarely shown to be supportive or nurturing. Comic strips today have a greater emphasis on fathers spending quality time with their children. "The fluctuation reflects societal shifts," says LaRossa. "When you look at the figures across six decades, they go up and down in a way understandable with what was happening in larger society."

The researchers also noted that the comics generally portrayed a homogeneous and stereotypical picture of family life. For example, virtually all characters were White. In this sample, only 5 percent of the comics featured a Black parental figure as a main character. Families also tended to be middle class, nuclear in structure, and with two parents in the home. Other family types were largely excluded (LaRossa et al. 2000).

In many ways, what could be more mundane than families—getting up, having breakfast, carpooling the kids, going to work, making dinner, doing homework, watching TV, and putting everyone to bed? At the same time, however, we are intensely curious about families; they are the center of many of our movies, television shows, songs, news stories, and cartoons. Families can offer some of the most exciting times of our lives: falling in love, getting married, or the birth or adoption of a baby. Families can also offer some of the worst times: disagreements, betrayal, violence, and divorce.

Virtually all of us grew up within some type of family, and most of us hope to recreate a new family through marriage or a partnership, and possibly with children. Although we talk about "the family" as though there is only one singular experience, we also know that there are tremendous differences. Some families do not have children, whereas others have many; some have two parents, whereas others have only one; some have biological children, whereas others include children who are adopted or who are stepchildren; some have grandparents living with them, whereas others do not. Some families celebrate Christmas, whereas others focus on different traditions during the season, such as Hanukkah or Kwanzaa. Some families are happy, whereas others are riddled with conflict.

Given the differences among families and their racial, ethnic, class, and cultural diversity, how is it possible to understand families in any systematic way? This text uses a sociological perspective to examine and interpret families. All human behavior, including family life, occurs in a social context. Together we will explore how our personal relationships are shaped by this social context.

What Are Families?

What are families? Good question. The U.S. Census Bureau defines a family as two or more people living together who are related by birth, marriage, or adoption. This definition remains the basis for many social programs and policies, including employee fringe benefits, such as health and dental insurance or family and medical leaves.

Nonetheless, this official definition does not really reflect the rich diversity of family life in society today (Allen 2004; Boss et al. 2008; Lloyd et al. 2009; Trask and Hamon 2007). Some suggest that if people *feel* that they are a family and *behave* as though they are a family, then they should be recognized as such. The focus should be on greater inclusion of family relationships. In 2001, the scholarly journal published by the National Council on Family Relations changed its name from *The Journal of Marriage and the Family* to *The Journal of Marriage and Family* (deleting the word "the") to reflect the growing recognition of multiple family forms. This change corresponds to the public's evolving attitudes toward families.

Americans, especially younger Americans, are more likely to accept divorce, cohabitation, remaining single, gays and lesbians raising children, and being childfree as legitimate lifestyles, while at the same time also espousing that marriage, children, and a strong family life are important goals toward which they strive (Pew Research Center 2010). For example, the young adult age group nicknamed the "Millennials"—those born in the 1980s and early 1990s—are more likely than older persons to believe that it is "a good thing for society or doesn't make much difference" that (1) more people are living together without getting married; (2) more mothers of young children work outside the home; (3) people of different races are marrying one another; (4) more gay and lesbian couples are raising children; and (5) more single women are deciding to have children without a male partner to help raise them (although the majority of people, regardless of age, do not think the latter is a good thing for society). This is shown in Table 1.1 (Pew Research Center 2010).

Even teenagers espouse these views, as shown in Table 1.2. Over half of high school seniors agree that having a child without being married is experimenting with a worthwhile lifestyle, and that cohabiting before marriage is a good idea (The National Marriage Project 2009).

This book uses a broader and more inclusive definition than that taken from the Census Bureau. **Families** are defined here as *relationships by blood, marriage, or affection, in which members may cooperate economically, may care for any children, and may consider their identity to be intimately connected to the larger group.*

This definition could also include **fictive kin** within its parameters. Fictive kin are nonrelatives whose bonds are strong and intimate, such as the relationships shared among unmarried homosexual or heterosexual partners, or very close friends. In fact, these bonds could be stronger than those between biological relatives. For example, one's favorite "Nana Marge" may not really be a relative at all. Fictive kin can provide important services and care for individuals, including assistance around the holiday season, or through critical life transitions, such as the birth of a child or a divorce (Muraco 2006). The term *families* as used throughout this book draws upon these relationships as well as more traditional ones.

The Political Reality: Why Definitions Are Important

Does it really matter how we define the term *family*? Yes, it matters a great deal. The definition used has important consequences with respect to informal and formal rights (Employee Benefit Research Institute 2009; Human Rights Campaign 2010). For example, neighbors, schools, and other community groups are likely to interact with family members differently

TABLE 1.1 Attitudes Toward Family Life Styles by Age Group

So-called "millennials"—those born in the 1980s and early 1990s—are more permissive than other age groups.

MORE PEOPLE LIVING TOGETHER WITHOUT GETTING MARRIED		
Age Group	**Good Thing for Society or Doesn't Make Much Difference**	**Bad Thing for Society**
18–29	77%	22%
30–45	67%	31%
46–64	54%	44%
65+	38%	58%

MORE MOTHERS OF YOUNG CHILDREN WORKING OUTSIDE THE HOME		
Age Group	**Good Thing for Society or Doesn't Make Much Difference**	**Bad Thing for Society**
18–29	73%	23%
30–45	66%	29%
46–64	56%	39%
65+	51%	38%

MORE PEOPLE OF DIFFERENT RACES MARRYING EACH OTHER		
Age Group	**Good Thing for Society or Doesn't Make Much Difference**	**Bad Thing for Society**
18–29	94%	5%
30–45	89%	10%
46–64	83%	14%
65+	67%	26%

MORE GAY AND LESBIAN COUPLES RAISING CHILDREN		
Age Group	**Good Thing for Society or Doesn't Make Much Difference**	**Bad Thing for Society**
18–29	65%	32%
30–45	59%	36%
46–64	49%	48%
65+	39%	55%

MORE SINGLE WOMEN DECIDING TO HAVE CHILDREN WITHOUT A MALE PARTNER TO HELP RAISE THEM		
Age Group	**Good Thing for Society or Doesn't Make Much Difference**	**Bad Thing for Society**
18–29	40%	59%
30–45	41%	54%
46–64	33%	65%
65+	24%	72%

Source: Pew Research Center 2010.

TABLE 1.2 Attitudes of U.S. High School Seniors Toward Marriage and Family

Attitudes of high school seniors haven't changed regarding the importance of marriage, but they also believe other lifestyles are acceptable.

PERCENTAGE OF HIGH SCHOOL SENIORS WHO . . .		
SAID HAVING A GOOD MARRIAGE AND FAMILY LIFE IS EXTREMELY IMPORTANT		
	Boys	**Girls**
1980	70%	82%
2007	71%	82%
SAID IT IS VERY LIKELY THEY WILL STAY MARRIED TO THE SAME PERSON FOR LIFE		
	Boys	**Girls**
1981–1985	56%	68%
2001–2006	57%	63%
AGREED OR MOSTLY AGREED THAT MOST PEOPLE WILL HAVE FULLER AND HAPPIER LIVES IF THEY CHOOSE LEGAL MARRIAGE RATHER THAN STAYING SINGLE OR JUST LIVING WITH SOMEONE		
	Boys	**Girls**
1981–1985	38%	36%
2001–2006	39%	32%
SAID HAVING A CHILD WITHOUT BEING MARRIED IS EXPERIMENTING WITH A WORTHWHILE LIFESTYLE OR NOT AFFECTING ANYONE ELSE		
	Boys	**Girls**
1981–1985	43%	40%
2001–2003	55%	56%
AGREED OR MOSTLY AGREED WITH THE STATEMENT: "IT IS USUALLY A GOOD IDEA FOR A COUPLE TO LIVE TOGETHER BEFORE GETTING MARRIED IN ORDER TO FIND OUT WHETHER THEY REALLY GET ALONG."		
	Boys	**Girls**
1981–1985	47%	37%
2001–2006	65%	58%

Source: The National Marriage Project 2009.

than with other nonrelated groups who live together. Families even get special membership discounts to a wide variety of organizations that roommates or friends do not get. You may find that an individual membership to a particular organization that you wish you joined is $25, but a family rate is $30, regardless of family size!

However, even more is at stake than a few dollars. The agreed-upon definition has important formal consequences that are legally recognized. For example, under most employer insurance plans only a worker's spouse and legal children can be covered by a health or dental insurance policy. **Domestic partners**, defined as adults in long-term committed relationships and responsible for each other's financial and emotional well-being, are usually excluded from coverage (Human Rights Campaign 2010). In most places around the country, domestic partners, either heterosexual or homosexual, have faced many obstacles simply because they lack the legal basis of marriage.

Employers are beginning to recognize that denying benefits to partners in committed relationships may not only be unjust, but it may also be bad for business. In 1982, the New York City weekly *The Village Voice* became the first employer to offer domestic partner benefits to its lesbian and gay employees. Since that time, over 9,300 employers have chosen to offer domestic partner benefits to an employee's unmarried partner, whether of the same or opposite sex. These employers include nearly 300 Fortune 500 companies, along with city, county, and state agencies. Documentation of proof of domestic partnership, such as financial statements or written statements by each partner, is left up to the discretion of the employer. Most employers who cover domestic partners do so regardless of sexual orientation (Employee Benefit Research Institute 2009). Despite the continued growth in the number of employers who offer domestic partner benefits, the IRS has ruled that domestic partners cannot be considered spouses for federal tax purposes.

The Sociological Imagination

Many of our personal experiences are not random. They are shaped by **social structure**, which is the organized pattern of relationships and institutions that together form the basis of society. For example, how has your sex influenced your life experience? Has being male or being female influenced your choice of a college major, your hobbies, interests, and relationships? Perhaps another way of thinking of this is: How would your life be different if you were the "opposite sex"? Likewise, how has your family structure affected you? You may have grown up with one parent, two parents, or with no parents at all. How did this structure affect your financial well-being, your social capital, and overall opportunities?

Definitions of "family" have important social, political, and economic consequences; many gays and lesbians ask that the benefits that accrue to married couples also be extended to them.

As another example, how does the U.S. health care system affect your family life? If you are one of the 17 percent of Americans without health insurance (DeNavas-Walt et al. 2010) and need health care, you may have vivid stories of its impact on you or your family and perhaps welcome health care reform.

Using a **sociological imagination** reveals general patterns in what otherwise might be thought of as simple random events (Mills 1959). C. Wright Mills stressed the importance of understanding the relationship between individuals and the society in which they lived. Family problems, such as divorce, unemployment, child abuse, limited access to health care, work-family stress, finding adequate child care, and pay inequities are more than just personal troubles experienced in isolation by a few people. They are issues that affect large numbers of people and originate in society's institutional arrangements. Individual behavior and outcomes are linked to the social structure.

Peter Berger elaborated on these ideas in his 1963 book *Invitation to Sociology*. Although we like to think of ourselves as individuals, much of our behavior (and others' behavior toward us) is actually patterned on the basis of what social categories we fall into, such as age, income, race, ethnicity, sex, and physical appearance. For example, men and women behave differently for reasons that often have nothing to do with biology. Many of these patterns are socially produced. In other words, boys and girls, men and women, are each taught and encouraged to think of themselves differently and to behave in different ways. Society lends a hand in shaping our lives. Why are over 90 percent of students in bachelor of science nursing programs female? This is obviously not the result of some biological imperative, some quirk of the occupation itself, or some random event. Rather, society even has a hand in shaping something as seemingly personal and individual as the choice of a college major (England and Li 2006).

Emile Durkheim (1897) conducted an early study on the subject of suicide, documenting how social structures affect human behavior. At first glance, what could be more private and individualized than the reasons that surround a person's decision to take his or her own life? The loss of a loving relationship, job troubles, financial worries, and low self-esteem are just a few of the many reasons that a person may have for attempting suicide. Yet looking through official records and death certificates, Durkheim noted that suicide was not a completely random event, and that there were several important patterns worthy of attention. He found that men were more likely to kill themselves than were women. He noted that Protestants were more likely to take their lives than were Catholics and Jews. He found that wealthy people were more likely to commit suicide than were the poor. Finally, it appeared that unmarried people were more likely to kill themselves than were married people. Although his study was conducted over 100 years ago, recent research indicates that these patterns persist. Suicide today is a major social problem, with more than 33,000 individuals taking their lives each year. It is the eleventh leading cause of death for all Americans, and the third for youths aged 15–24 (Centers for Disease Control and Prevention 2009i).

The sociological imagination draws attention to the fact that seemingly private issues are often public ones (Mills 1959). For example, whenever a child is orphaned because of AIDS, it is a personal tragedy. However, when the number of children orphaned because of AIDS runs over 14 million in sub-Saharan Africa alone, including 20 percent of children in Botswana, and more than 2 million children are infected themselves, AIDS is far more than a personal problem (AVERT.ORG 2010a; UNAIDS and World Health Organization 2009). It becomes a serious public issue that requires public attention to resolve.

Comparative Perspective

The sociological imagination uses a **comparative perspective** to study families. If we want to know what is happening in the United States, it is especially meaningful to compare the country to something else, such as other cultures or to other points in history. For example, an examination of the nature of dating practices or weddings in the United States becomes far more insightful when compared to the practices in other cultures, such as that of India, or at other points in time, such as in colonial America.

It is easy to sit back and assume that our society's way of doing things is always the best way. However, this **ethnocentrism** can have considerable costs. A comparative perspective allows Americans to learn how other countries and cultures organize their social life and respond to its challenges (Ember and Ember 2011). This, in turn, allows us to learn about ourselves.

Perhaps nowhere is a comparative approach more important than in the realm of family life. The structure and dynamics of families affect all of us in substantial and profound ways. Learning how other societies structure families, how they collectively think about families, and how they deal with the challenges families face can provide insight into our own questions. Many problems that we face in the United States are more serious elsewhere, such as the tremendous poverty among developing nations. Other problems loom larger here. For example, the infant mortality rate in the United States is among the worst of industrialized nations, as shown in the map on pages 12–13. The U.S. rate, at approximately 6.7 deaths per 1,000 live births, is higher than most of western Europe, Canada, Australia, New Zealand, Japan, Iceland, and Hong Kong (Population Reference Bureau 2010c). Given the vast wealth of the United States, it is alarming that the infant death rates are comparable to countries that are so much poorer, including Cuba, Croatia, and Taiwan. Why is the U.S. infant mortality rate so much higher than that of peer nations? A comparative perspective examines the organization, values, and policies of those nations and evaluates their relevance for the United States. Obviously, with respect to lowering infant mortality, they are doing something right and the United States could take note.

An Empirical Approach

The sociological imagination also values an **empirical approach**, a method that answers questions through a systematic collection and analysis of data (Neuman 2009). Uncovering patterns of family dynamics can be extremely important for building stronger families.

Most of us have commonsense ideas about intimacy, domestic violence, child rearing (or any other type of family interaction for that matter) based upon personal experience or habits, religious teachings, cultural customs, or societal laws. Because virtually all of us were raised in families, we may think we are experts on the topic. Historically, the commonsense view of violence among intimates

The infant mortality rate (deaths of children in their first year of life) is shockingly high in the United States. Other countries and regions, including Hong Kong, have significantly lower infant mortality rates than the United States.

was that it was okay for men to beat their wives—within reason. The term "rule of thumb" arises from the belief that the switch that a husband used to beat his wife should be no wider than his thumb. Common sense can change over time. Today, it is against the law in the United States for husbands to hit their wives (and vice versa). However, wife battering is not illegal in many parts of the world. There, common sense tells those societies that violence can be justified and it is the husband's prerogative to hit his wife, although again, usually within "reasonable" limits (e.g., a husband can beat, but not kill his spouse). A World Health Organization (2009) study of 24,000 women in 10 countries found that the prevalence of physical and/or sexual violence by a partner varied from 15 percent in urban Japan to 71 percent in rural Ethiopia, with most areas being in the 30–60 percent range.

If common sense is subject to historical and cultural whims, then what can we depend on to help us understand family dynamics? Sociologists and other family scientists use an empirical approach in collecting and analyzing data. The goal can be to:

- *describe some phenomenon* (e.g., how many women have been physically assaulted by someone close to them; how this compares to the number of men who are assaulted by their partners each year; how abused women and men interpret the reasons for the assault), or
- *examine the factors that predict or are associated with some phenomenon* (e.g., what factors are associated with violence among intimates; what factors predict whether a victim will report the assault to the police), or
- *explain cause-and-effect relationships or provide insight into why certain events do or do not occur* (e.g., the relationship between alcohol and violence among intimates; the relationship between attitudes of male dominance and domestic violence), or
- *understand the meanings attached to behavior or situations* (e.g., how do people interpret their roles as victims or perpetrators?).

Because of empirical research, we know that violence is a serious and pervasive social problem. About 4.8 million women and 2.9 million men are victims of intimate partner violence, according to the Centers for Disease Control and Prevention (2009g). How can a sociological perspective help people who are battered by their partners? Family scholars conduct basic and applied research to understand the phenomenon, striving to reveal information about the incidence, predictors, social factors associated with violence, and the experience of violence. Psychologists, social workers, and politicians could use this information to develop programs to prevent violence, assist victims, and treat the perpetrators. Intimate partner violence is a social problem, not simply an individual one, and the goal is to uncover the social patterns that underlie it.

Sociologists and other family scientists use different methods to collect and analyze data. A full discussion of them is beyond the scope of this text. However, Table 1.3 summarizes six primary ways of collecting data, outlining their strengths and weaknesses.

Some researchers focus on **quantitative methods** in which the focus is on data that can be measured numerically. Examples are found in surveys, experiments, or doing secondary analyses on available government statistics (such as from the U.S. Department of Justice) or another source.

Others use **qualitative methods** that focus on narrative description with words rather than numbers to analyze patterns and their underlying meanings. Examples of qualitative research methods include in-depth interviews, focus groups, observation studies, and conducting a secondary analysis using narrative documents, such as letters or diaries.

None of these methods is inherently better or worse than the others. The method used depends on the research questions that are posed. For example, if we want to better understand what family life was like in the nineteenth century, we would not want to conduct a survey. How would people who are alive today best inform us of what happened 150 years ago? Obviously, the best method would be to conduct a secondary analysis of documents that were written during that time period. Diaries, letters, or other lengthy correspondence between people, and other such qualitative data could help us understand the common everyday experiences between families. Likewise, we could analyze quantitative data from historical records to get an aggregate picture about, for example, immigration trends, age at first marriage, or the average length of time between marriage and first birth. Census records; birth, marriage, and death registers; immigration records; slave auctions and other transactions;

WHAT DO YOU THINK?

If you were conducting a study about violence, would you prefer qualitative or quantitative methods, and why?

Comparative Infant Mortality Rates, 2009

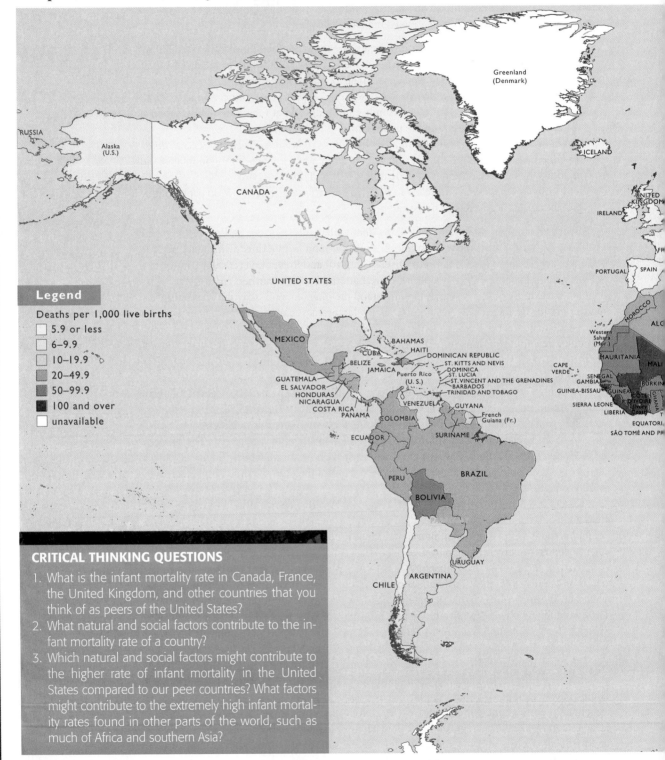

Legend

Deaths per 1,000 live births

- 5.9 or less
- 6–9.9
- 10–19.9
- 20–49.9
- 50–99.9
- 100 and over
- unavailable

CRITICAL THINKING QUESTIONS

1. What is the infant mortality rate in Canada, France, the United Kingdom, and other countries that you think of as peers of the United States?

2. What natural and social factors contribute to the infant mortality rate of a country?

3. Which natural and social factors might contribute to the higher rate of infant mortality in the United States compared to our peer countries? What factors might contribute to the extremely high infant mortality rates found in other parts of the world, such as much of Africa and southern Asia?

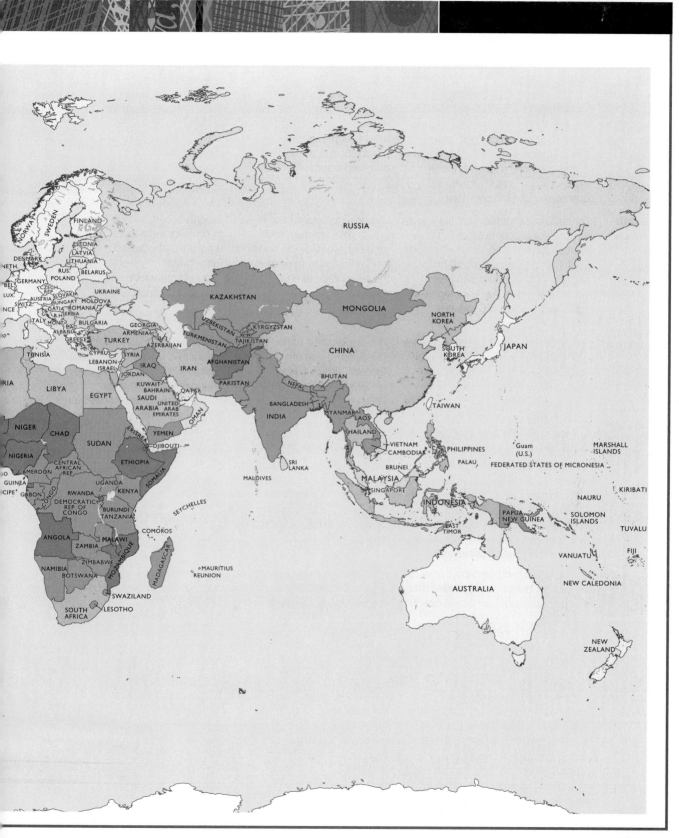

Source: Population Reference Bureau 2010c

TABLE 1.3 **Six Research Methods: A Summary**

Each research method has advantages and disadvantages. No single method is perfect. It all depends on the researcher's goals.

METHOD	APPLICATION	ADVANTAGES	LIMITATIONS
Survey	For gathering information about issues that are not directly observed, such as values, opinions, and other self-reports. Can be mail, telephone, or administered in person. Useful for descriptive or explanatory purposes; can generate quantitative or qualitative data.	Sampling methods can allow researcher to generalize findings to a larger population. Can provide open-ended questions or a fixed response.	Surveys must be carefully prepared to avoid bias. A potential for a low return or response rate. Can be expensive and time consuming. Self-reports may be biased.
In-Depth Interview	For obtaining information about issues that are not directly observed, such as values, opinions, and other self-reports. Useful for getting in-depth information about a topic. Conducted in person, conversation is usually audiotaped and later transcribed. Generates qualitative data.	Can provide detailed and high-quality data. Interviewer can probe or ask follow-up questions for clarification or to encourage the respondent to elaborate. Can establish a genuine rapport with respondent.	Expensive and time consuming to conduct and transcribe. Self-reports may be biased. Respondent may feel uncomfortable revealing personal information.
Experiment	For explanatory research that examines cause-and-effect relationship among variables. Several types: classical experimental design and quasi-experimental designs based on degree of controlling the environment. Generates quantitative data.	Provides greatest opportunity to assess cause and effect. Research design relatively easy to replicate.	The setting may have an artificial quality to it. Unless the experimental and control group are randomly assigned or matched on all relevant variables, and the environment is carefully controlled, bias may result.
Focus Groups	For obtaining information from small groups of people who are brought together to discuss a particular topic. Often exploratory in nature. Particularly useful for studying public perceptions. Facilitator may ask only a few questions; goal is to get group to interact with one another. Generates qualitative data.	Group interaction may produce more valuable insights than individual surveys or in-depth interviews. Research can obtain data quickly and inexpensively. Good at eliciting unanticipated information.	Setting is contrived. Some people may feel uncomfortable speaking in a group and others may dominate.
Observation	For exploratory and descriptive study of people in a natural setting. Researcher can be a participant or nonparticipant. Generates qualitative data.	Allows study of real behavior in a natural setting. Does not rely on self-reports. Researchers can often ask questions and take notes. Usually inexpensive.	Can be time consuming. Could be ethical issues involved in certain types of observation studies, i.e., observing without consent. Researcher must balance roles of participant and observer. Replication of research is difficult.
Secondary Analysis	For exploratory, descriptive, or explanatory research with data that were collected for some other purpose. Diverse. Can be large data sources based on national samples, e.g., U.S. Census, or can be historical documents or records. Generates quantitative or qualitative data, depending on the source of data used.	Saves the expense and time of original data collection. Can be longitudinal, with data collected at more than one point in time. Good for analyzing national attitudes or trends. Makes historical research possible.	Because data were collected for another purpose, the researcher cannot control what variables were included or excluded. Researcher has no control over sampling or other biases of the data.

church records; newspapers and magazine articles; employment ledgers; and tax records can also provide insight into the family lives of large numbers of ordinary people.

However, if we want to assess attitudes or opinions about people today, perhaps a survey or in-depth interviews would be best. If we want to ask the same questions of everyone in our sample, and offer a standard set of answers from which they can choose, such as "How many children do you personally want to have? Would you say it is zero, one, two, three, four, or five or more?", then a survey might be best. We can easily quantify the information. Or, if we are interested in broader questions about which each person in our study will elaborate in their own way, such as "How did you come to decide on the number of children that you would like to have?", we would likely use in-depth interviews, which then yield qualitative data.

Theory: Helping Us Make Sense of the World

Research is guided by **theory**, which is a general framework, explanation, or tool used to understand and describe the real world (Smith et al. 2009; White and Klein 2008). Theories are important both before and after data have been collected because they help us decide what topics to research, what questions to try to answer, how best to answer them, and how to interpret the research results. Before collecting data, theories can help frame the question. When data have been collected and patterns emerge, theories can help make sense of what was found.

Many theoretical perspectives make different assumptions about the nature of society. Figure 1.1 summarizes the most common theories applied in studying families. Some are more **macro** in nature and attempt to understand societal patterns. These include structural functionalism, conflict theory, and feminist theory. Other theories are more **micro** in nature and focus on personal dynamics and face-to-face interaction, such as social exchange, symbolic interaction,

Figure 1.1 **Summary of Family Theories**

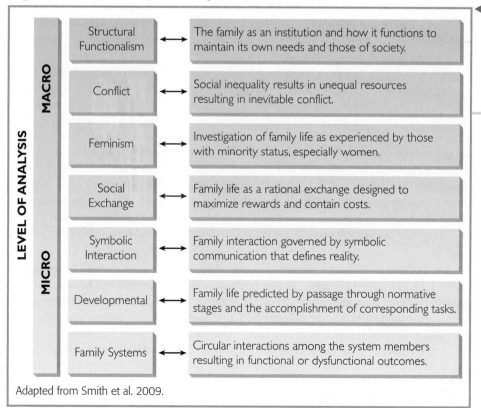

LEVEL OF ANALYSIS

MACRO

Structural Functionalism	⟷	The family as an institution and how it functions to maintain its own needs and those of society.
Conflict	⟷	Social inequality results in unequal resources resulting in inevitable conflict.
Feminism	⟷	Investigation of family life as experienced by those with minority status, especially women.

MICRO

Social Exchange	⟷	Family life as a rational exchange designed to maximize rewards and contain costs.
Symbolic Interaction	⟷	Family interaction governed by symbolic communication that defines reality.
Developmental	⟷	Family life predicted by passage through normative stages and the accomplishment of corresponding tasks.
Family Systems	⟷	Circular interactions among the system members resulting in functional or dysfunctional outcomes.

Theories range from broad macro-level theories to more individualized micro-level theories.

Adapted from Smith et al. 2009.

developmental theory, and family systems theory. We will use theory throughout this book, so let's introduce the major theories here.

Structural Functionalism **Structural functionalist theory** (often abbreviated to *functionalism*) attempts to determine the structure, systems, functions, and equilibria of social institutions, such as families. A popular theory in the 1940s and 1950s, the focus is on how families are organized, how they interact with other social systems, the functions that families serve, and how they are a stabilizing force in society (Parsons 1937, 1951). For example, Parsons and Boles (1955) focused on the division of labor in families, noting the ways in which separate spheres for men and women contributed to the stability and functionality of families. Expressive roles and tasks fell to women, whereas instrumental roles fell to men (Parsons and Boles 1955), which they argued contributed to smooth family functioning. Functionalists rarely note the tensions, conflicts, or political ideologies behind their ideas, which may explain why this trend has fallen out of fashion in recent decades.

Conflict Theory **Conflict theory** emphasizes issues surrounding social inequality, power, conflict, and social change, especially how these factors influence, or are played out, in families. Those who follow the writings of Karl Marx focus on the consequences of capitalism for families—for example, tensions and inequality generated by the gross distribution of wealth and power associated with capitalism (Marx and Engels 1867, reprinted 1971). Other conflict theorists focus on a wider set of issues surrounding conflict, inequality, or power differentials. For example, a conflict theorist might ask why virtually all elderly persons regardless of income receive government-subsidized health care (Medicare) that covers many of their health-related needs when no similar universal program exists for children. Moreover, former President George W. Bush extended prescription coverage for the elderly, again offering nothing to children. Does this difference in treatment arise because the elderly represent a large special interest group and powerful voting bloc, whereas children are virtually powerless?

Feminist Theory **Feminist theory** is related to conflict theory, but the difference is that gender is seen as the central concept for explaining family structure and family dynamics (Lloyd et al. 2009; Osmond and Thorne 1993). It focuses on the inequality and power imbalances between men and women and analyzes "women's subordination for the purpose of figuring out how to change it" (Gordon 1979). It recognizes that *gender* is a far more important organizing concept than is *sex* because it represents a powerful set of relations that are fraught with power and inequality. For example, research indicates that women do far more household labor than men even when both partners are employed full-time for pay. Feminist theorists see the gendered division of household labor as a result of power imbalances between men and women that are embedded in larger society and have virtually taken on a life of their own. It is an example of "doing gender" as West and Zimmerman (1987) say.

Social Exchange Theory **Social exchange theory** draws upon a model of human behavior used by many economists. It assumes that individuals are rational beings, and their behavior reflects decisions evaluated on the basis of costs—both direct and opportunity costs—and benefits (Becker 1981; Nye 1979). Exchange theorists would suggest that a particular type of family structure or dynamic is the result of rational decisions based upon social, economic, and emotional costs and benefits, as compared to the alternatives. For example, Becker (1981) argued that a woman often rationally chooses to exchange her household labor for the benefits of a man's income because she understands that men are more "efficient" in the labor market (they usually earn higher wages than women).

Symbolic Interaction Theory   **Symbolic interaction theory** emphasizes the symbols we use in everyday interaction—words, gestures, appearances—and how these are interpreted by others (Mead 1935). Our interactions with others are based on how we interpret these symbols. Some symbols are obvious (an engagement ring, a kiss, a smile) and show us how to interact or what roles to play. Others are less obvious and confusing to interpret, thereby causing tension or conflict in a relationship. For example, the symbol of a mother might be straightforward, and we have a general agreement, at least in U.S. culture, about her roles—but what is the role of a stepmother?

Developmental Theory   **Developmental theory** suggests that families (and individual family members) go through distinct stages over time, with each stage having its own set of tasks, roles, and responsibilities. These developmental changes include (1) married couple; (2) childbearing; (3) preschool age; (4) school age; (5) teenage; (6) launching center; (7) middle-aged parents; and (8) aging family members (Duvall and Miller 1985). Early development theorists claimed that the stages were inevitable and occurred in a relatively linear fashion, although most now recognize that there is widespread variation. For example, some families never have children. Other families have children later in life, so that parents may face tasks associated with middle age (e.g., planning for retirement) before children are launched. The developmental approach uses both micro and macro approaches to describe and explain family relationships over the various family stages (Rodgers and White 1993).

A related approach, the **life course perspective**, examines how individuals' lives change as they pass through myriad events over time, with the recognition that many changes are socially produced and shared among a cohort of people (Elder 1998; Schaie and Elder 2005). For example, sociologist Glen Elder's (1999) longitudinal study followed a cohort of children throughout the Great Depression and afterwards to see how an historical event of such large proportions affected a cohort of Americans. Another example of a cohort study would be to track men who served in combat in the Vietnam War to see how a major traumatic event such as war has shaped them.

Family Systems Theory   A system is more than the sum of its parts. Likewise, the **family systems theory** proposes that a family system—the family members and the roles they play—is larger than the sum of its individual members (Broderick and Smith 1979). Collectively it becomes a system, but it also includes subsystems within it, such as the married couple subsystem, the sibling subsystem, or the parent–child subsystem. All family systems and subsystems create boundaries between them and the environment with varying degrees of permeability. They also create *rules of transformation* so that families function smoothly and know what to expect from another member. All systems tend toward equilibrium so that families work toward a balancing point in their relationship, and they maintain this equilibrium by feedback or control. Therefore, the family systems theory is particularly useful in studying how members of the family (or subsystems within the family) communicate with one another and the rippling effects of that communication.

> ### WHAT DO YOU THINK?
>
> *Pick a family issue of interest (e.g., mate selection, the division of household labor, the consequences of divorce on children) and describe a research method you would use to study it. How would theory help guide you?*

Families and Social Change

Any cursory review of family history will show that families have undergone tremendous changes. That fact is rarely disputed. It is the *meanings* and *implications* of these changes that generate considerable debate. Today, some people are concerned that the family is in trouble (The National Marriage Project 2007, 2009), citing "the neglect of marriage," "lack of commitment by men," "loss of child centeredness," "the rise in cohabitation," and "fatherless families." Others remind us that the good old days of the past never really existed as we have fantasized about them. They argue that families have always faced challenges, including desertion, poverty, children born out of wedlock, alcoholism, unemployment, violence, and child abuse, and that change is a natural form of adaptation (Abramovitz 1996; Coontz 1997).

A Snapshot of American Families Today and How They Have Changed

Without question, a number of changes in families have taken place in recent decades. Some of the more significant changes include the following and will be discussed in greater depth in subsequent chapters:

1. *Both men and women are postponing marriage.* Because of expanding opportunities and changing norms, people are marrying at later ages than in the past. Women now marry at an average age of 26, compared to 21 in 1970. Men now marry at an average age of 28, compared to 23 in 1970.

2. *The percentage of persons who have never married has declined slightly.* About 4 percent of elderly women have never married, down from 6 percent in 1980. Among men, the decline in lifelong singlehood is less dramatic, but exists nonetheless: 4 percent of elderly men aged 65 and older have never married, down from 5 percent in 1980. In other words, people now are somewhat more likely to marry, not less likely.

3. *Family size is shrinking.* Fewer people are having three or more children today. Family size is particularly shrinking among Black and Hispanic families.

4. *The divorce rate has declined.* In the 1960s, the divorce rate began to rise rapidly, peaking at approximately 23 divorces per 1,000 married women around 1980. However, since this time the divorce rate has steadily declined to about 17 per 1,000 married women.

5. *Mothers are increasingly likely to be employed for pay outside the home.* Although single mothers usually have had to work outside the home, now more than half of married women with children even younger than two years of age are in the workplace.

6. *Single-parent households are on the rise, particularly among men.* Since 1970 there has been a 300 percent increase in single-parent households headed by mothers, although today the rate has stabilized, and a 500 percent increase in those headed by fathers. Today more than a quarter of White families, half of Black families, and a third of Hispanic families are headed by one parent.

7. *Hispanic groups are now the largest minority in the United States, comprising 16 percent of the population.* In contrast, Blacks constitute 12 percent of the population. Nearly two-thirds of Hispanics are of Mexican origin. Because birth and immigration rates are higher among Hispanics, it is estimated that their presence in the United States will continue to grow much faster than other groups.

8. *The teenage birthrate is in a state of flux.* The birthrate among teenagers rose until the early 1990s, when it began a steady and sharp decline. This decline occurred among all racial and ethnic groups, and is particularly pronounced among Blacks. However, over the past few years the rate increased slightly, and then declined again.

9. *Unmarried couples living together are becoming increasingly common.* The number of unmarried couples has increased to about 7 million. The growth has occurred in all age groups, including the elderly.

10. *The rich have gotten richer, while middle- and low-income groups have lost ground.* If we break households down into five groups based on the size of their incomes, we

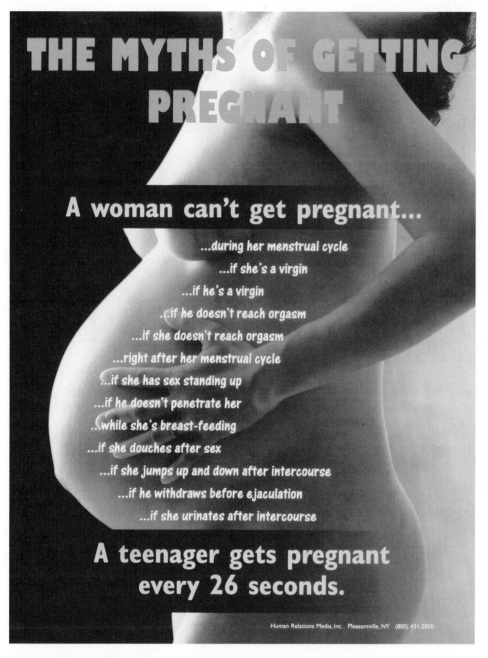

THE MYTHS OF GETTING PREGNANT

A woman can't get pregnant...

...during her menstrual cycle

...if she's a virgin

...if he's a virgin

...if he doesn't reach orgasm

...if she doesn't reach orgasm

...right after her menstrual cycle

...if she has sex standing up

...if he doesn't penetrate her

...while she's breast-feeding

...if she douches after sex

...if she jumps up and down after intercourse

...if he withdraws before ejaculation

...if she urinates after intercourse

A teenager gets pregnant every 26 seconds.

Human Relations Media, Inc. Pleasantville, NY (800) 431-2050

The teenage birthrate has declined significantly from what it was 20 years ago. This decline has occurred among all racial and ethnic groups in the United States in part due to explicit advertisements like this one that is designed to inform teenagers about sexuality and pregnancy. However, in recent years, teen birthrates have been in a state of flux, increasing slightly one year, then decreasing again the next.

would find that those with incomes in the highest fifth had an average after-tax increase four times that of the middle fifth and eight times that of the poorest fifth.

11. *The elderly population has been increasing almost four times as fast as the population as a whole.* In 1900, only a small portion of people—1 in 25—were aged 65 or older. It is likely that many younger people spent long portions of their lives rarely even seeing an elderly person. Today, we are a rapidly aging society.

Family Change as a Political Issue

Families are changing in composition, expectations, and roles. What is causing these changes? Are they good or bad? What are the consequences of family change? A debate is

Figure 1.2 **Causes and Consequences of Family Change**

What are the causes and consequences of the changing nature of families? Conservative, liberal, and feminist perspectives differ.

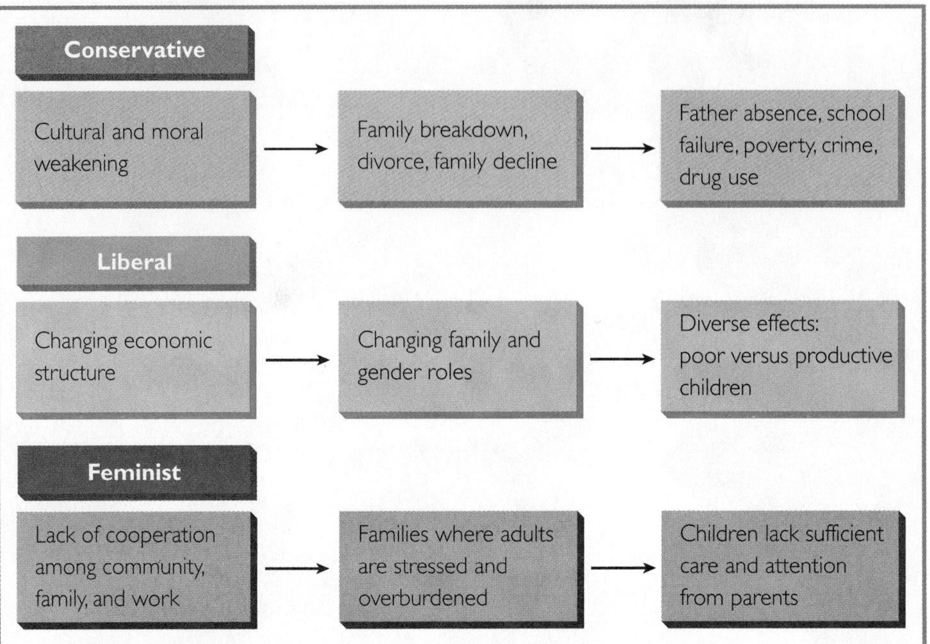

Conservative

| Cultural and moral weakening | → | Family breakdown, divorce, family decline | → | Father absence, school failure, poverty, crime, drug use |

Liberal

| Changing economic structure | → | Changing family and gender roles | → | Diverse effects: poor versus productive children |

Feminist

| Lack of cooperation among community, family, and work | → | Families where adults are stressed and overburdened | → | Children lack sufficient care and attention from parents |

Source: Giele 1996.

ongoing over the implications of these changes—a debate that is woven into the U.S. political discourse. Janet Giele (1996) summarizes three conflicting political viewpoints about the causes and consequences of changes in families, as shown in Figure 1.2.

Conservative Perspective Conservatives express grave concern that changes in family structure put children at risk (Murray 1984; The National Marriage Project 2007, 2009; Whitehead and Popenoe 2005). They suggest that many challenges families face can be linked to gross cultural and moral weakening, which in turn contributes to father absence and family disorganization through divorce or illegitimacy. This ultimately results in greater poverty, crime, drug use, and a host of other social problems that cause stress for many families. The conservative model is diagrammed in Figure 1.2 and is contrasted with the liberal and feminist perspectives that are also described here.

Conservatives argue that the weakening of the U.S. moral fabric can be traced to the modern secularization of religious practice and the decline of religious affiliation. They suggest that these trends have reshaped our cultural norms so that certain harmful practices are no longer seen as immoral, such as nonmarital sex, cohabitation, or having a child outside of marriage. When this happens, we witness the breakdown of the traditional two-parent family, which conservatives argue is the cornerstone of society. Fathers become increasingly irrelevant in the lives of women and children. Divorce rates and illegitimacy soar. Husbands divorce their wives, leaving their children "behind." They form new unions and have additional children, often without providing financially or emotionally for the children they already have. Conservatives often argue that welfare and other social programs actually serve to undermine families, rather than help them, because they encourage family breakups.

When families break up and fathers become increasingly marginalized, social problems flourish. Poverty becomes rampant, and children fail to thrive. They do worse in school, and possibly turn to alcohol, drugs, and crime to try to alleviate their suffering. Conservatives suggest that the solution to this downward spiral is to strengthen and support traditional marriage. To restore the ideal of the two-parent family, other types of families should be made less attractive. The government should minimize its support of single mothers and encourage couples to marry and rely upon one another for the care of their children.

Liberal Perspective Liberals also note that families have undergone tremendous changes in recent decades, and children face serious challenges because of these changes. However, they suggest that these challenges result from economic and structural adjustments that place new demands on families without offering additional social supports. The liberal model is also diagrammed in Figure 1.2. These changes include the loss of relatively high-paying manufacturing jobs, an erosion of the minimum wage, a decline in employer-sponsored fringe benefits such as health insurance, and a rise in the number of low-paying service sector jobs. These economic changes have several implications for families, and men and women's relationships within families. First, there is an increasing need for both husbands and wives to work and earn a two-paycheck income. Second, less time is available for pre-natal child care, and therefore a greater need for child care centers. Third, young women may be less inclined to marry men who have few good economic prospects. According to William Julius Wilson (1996), a scholar and former president of the American Sociological Association, it is partly the lack of jobs in the inner city that drives up the rate of out-of-wedlock births because the men are not considered "marriageable".

The result is the creation of an underclass. Poor children face extraordinary challenges because they do not have the social supports to weather these changes. Liberals essentially believe in a market economy, but they ask for sufficient social supports to help families in the bottom tier. Such supports include welfare benefits, job training programs, educational subsidies, expansion of programs like Head Start, and strengthening supports for working families, such as through earned income tax credits (EITCs), or high-quality child care.

Feminist Perspective The feminist perspective (also shown in Figure 1.2) blends elements of both conservative and liberal perspectives. With conservatives, they share a heightened respect for the often invisible, but very important caregiving work done in families. With liberals, they share a concern that the changes in economic conditions have had many deleterious consequences for families, particularly those that are most vulnerable. Yet, while having features in common, there are also sharp differences. The feminist perspective criticizes conservatives for exploiting female caregivers to allow men to be more active in the public realm. Meanwhile, liberals perpetuate the notion that the best families are those that are somehow self-sufficient.

Feminists attribute the difficulties children face to a lack of cooperation between the community, family, and employers to improve the quality of life. A sense of individualism permeates U.S. culture and has replaced a collective responsibility for each other's welfare. Comparative research in other countries reveals that where support is generous enough to help all families (not just the most vulnerable), poverty and its associated problems plummet, and health, education, and well-being soar. Instead, in the United States, the lack of collectivism results in families in which adults feel routinely stressed and overburdened. Although poor families may feel these stresses more acutely than the middle class, all families suffer. Children may suffer because they lack sufficient care and attention from their parents, who receive so little outside help. Instead, families are expected to fend for themselves.

Feminists critically evaluate the U.S. economic system and ask for alternative policies that place higher value on the quality of human relationships. They work for reforms that build and strengthen neighborhoods and volunteer groups, support caregiving activities, and encourage education and employment among both women and men. Family policies should be enacted

> ### WHAT DO YOU THINK?
>
> *Which perspective—conservative, liberal, or feminist—is most popular in our society, and why? Do you think it might vary across social groups, such as by age, or education, or sex? Which perspective makes the most sense to you, and why?*

to protect and nurture families, including the areas of child care, maternity benefits, health care, work guarantees, and other economic supports. In sum, feminists judge the strength of a family not by its form (dual parent versus single parent), but by the social well-being that comes from parents knowing that they have the support necessary to be family caregivers and productive workers (Giele 1996).

The State and Family Policy

Compared to many other developed nations, the United States is conspicuously lacking a national family policy, yet the importance of policy to families cannot be overstated (Bogenschneider 2006; Butterfield et al. 2010; Kamerman 2003; Strach 2007; Warner 2005). Americans are more distrustful of big government. Independence and self-reliance are seen as good virtues, and Americans are uncomfortable with offering "too much" assistance because they fear that it will decrease initiative and encourage dependence. Therefore, families are generally expected to fend for themselves with only minimal assistance. Policies and programs that are in place are usually selective in nature, and available only for a few, often as tax breaks that come once a year. Other developed countries lean more toward offering universal policies and programs that are regularly available to all citizens.

Selective versus Universal

Social policies do not exist in a vacuum; they represent a nation's history, rich cultural traditions, and values. The United States has a long history of rugged individualism and a distrust of government and its programs (Axinn and Stern 2008; Jansson 2008). Much of colonial America was populated by people trying to flee government controls or what were viewed as government intrusions into their lives. Therefore, it is not surprising that family policies in the United States reflect and promote the concepts of individualism and self-sufficiency. U.S. policies reflect our belief that people should be in charge of their own destinies. We acknowledge that some people may need a helping hand, but Americans have little tolerance for people who seem to be unwilling or unable to pull themselves up by "their bootstraps." Borrowing from early English "poor laws," U.S. policies evolved over the seventeenth and eighteenth centuries and make clear distinctions between "worthy" needy people (people who cannot support themselves through no fault of their own, such as the disabled or children) and the "unworthy" (able-bodied men and women).

Not surprisingly then, the United States has a laissez-faire approach in which families are largely left to fend for themselves (Day 2009; Gilbert and Terrell 2010; Karger and Stoesz 2010). Many programs tend to be **selective**, meaning that persons need to meet some eligibility requirement to qualify for benefits. Most often this means that persons must meet certain income thresholds; for example, people have to be below a certain income to qualify for Medicaid (a health insurance program). This is referred to as **means-tested**. Income thresholds are kept relatively low to limit the number of users of the program and thus control their costs. There is a general fear and distrust that people will take advantage of services and programs if they are made too accessible (Hancock 2004; Seccombe 2011).

However, not all programs in the United States are means-tested. Police and fire protection and public education are available to all persons, regardless of income. It is not always clear to the observer why some programs are available to everyone and others are not. For example, why is education a "right," but health insurance a "privilege," primarily available to persons with generous employers, to those who are poor enough to qualify for Medicaid (along with other criteria), or to persons over the age of 65? Is education really more important than health care? Or is it simply a result of some historical circumstance, such as early unions fighting for universal education rather than universal health insurance?

When we compare the philosophy of the United States to the philosophies of most of Europe, Canada, and other countries, we see great differences in approaches. Most developed nations have an interrelated, coordinated set of proactive and **universal programs** available to all persons that are designed to help strengthen all families. Universal programs are not means-tested; rather, they are social and economic programs available to everyone. For example, as shown in Table 1.4, in a 2008–2009 review of developed nations, the United States was the only country without universal health insurance coverage, paid maternal/parental leave at childbirth, or a family allowance/child dependency grant (Social Security Online 2010). Although Americans think of these issues in individualistic terms and expect parents largely to figure it out themselves, other countries have specific policies to ensure that all people can receive these benefits. Un-

TABLE 1.4 **Safety Net Policies in 23 Other Developed Countries Compared with the United States**

The United States is the only developed nation without universal health insurance, paid leave at childbirth, or a family allowance grant.

COUNTRY	UNIVERSAL HEALTH INSURANCE/ HEALTH CARE	PAID MATERNAL/ PARENTAL LEAVE AT CHILDBIRTH	FAMILY ALLOWANCE/ CHILD DEPENDENCY GRANT
Australia	Yes	Yes	Yes
Austria	Yes	Yes	Yes
Belgium	Yes	Yes	Yes
Canada	Yes	Yes	Yes
Czech Republic	Yes	Yes	Yes
Denmark	Yes	Yes	Yes
Finland	Yes	Yes	Yes
France	Yes	Yes	Yes
Germany	Yes	Yes	Yes
Hungary	Yes	Yes	Yes
Iceland	Yes	Yes	Yes
Italy	Yes	Yes	Yes
Japan	Yes	Yes	Yes
Luxembourg	Yes	Yes	Yes
Netherlands	Yes	Yes	Yes
New Zealand	Yes	Yes	Yes
Norway	Yes	Yes	Yes
Poland	Yes	Yes	Yes
Portugal	Yes	Yes	Yes
Spain	Yes	Yes	Yes
Sweden	Yes	Yes	Yes
Switzerland	Yes	Yes	Yes
United Kingdom	Yes	Yes	Yes
United States	**No**	**No**	**No**

Source: Social Security Online 2010.

fortunately, many parents in the United States are not able to "figure it out themselves." How does one figure out how to get health insurance when an employer does not offer it and the costs of purchasing it yourself far exceed your budget? How do you arrange for a paid maternal leave after the birth of your child when an employer tells you that you will be fired if you don't quickly return to work? How do you find a family allowance, when most people in the United States have never even heard of such a program and the government does not offer one?

In other countries, these programs are financed by **progressive taxation**—those who earn more money pay a higher percentage of their income in taxes. They have adopted these programs because their citizens tend to believe in structural explanations for poverty and inequality, and therefore look for structural solutions. Americans are much more likely to equate poverty and its consequences with individual failure, immorality, lack of thrift, or laziness. For example, when asked "why are there people in this country who live in need?" 39 percent of Americans blamed personal laziness, compared to only 16 percent of Swedes (World Values Survey 1994).

Family Policy and Family Values

Examining specific family policies (or the lack thereof) can tell a great deal about U.S. collective family values. The following example examines the sweeping welfare reform legislation passed in the late 1990s that continues to have serious consequences for poor families today. It illustrates the individualist orientation common in the United States that generally leaves families on their own to work out their problems.

Example: Welfare   Welfare has been a long standing social policy concern in the United States. Its principal cash program, **Temporary Assistance for Needy Families (TANF)**, formerly called Aid to Families with Dependent Children (AFDC), was originally designed to help protect women and their children from conditions of poverty. It was created in 1935 as Title IV of the Social Security Act, a critical piece of legislation produced during the New Deal when millions of families were suffering financial hardship. The goal was to keep single mothers out of the workforce because the general sentiment at the time was that children who only have one parent would benefit by having that parent at home.

Much has changed in 80 years. Most Americans no longer feel comfortable paying mothers to stay home and take care of their children. As the employment of mothers has become more the rule than the exception, people question the value of paying poor single mothers to stay home with their children. They ask: Is it necessary to subsidize poor and single mothers so that they do not have to work outside the home when most middle-class mothers are employed? Ignored in the discussions are the differing circumstances between the two groups. Poor single mothers must be both mothers and fathers to their children. They have no one else to rely upon to share the financial and emotional strains that accompany parenting.

Welfare programs have been accused of fostering long-term dependency, family breakups, and illegitimacy (Browning 2008). Welfare recipients are viewed by many people as lazy and unmotivated, looking for a free ride at the expense of the taxpayer (Hancock 2004; Seccombe 2011). To ensure that welfare is not too easy to get, some regions impose rigorous application procedures. For example, New York City's TANF application is among the most complex. It requires applicants to attend two eligibility interviews in two different locations, undergo fingerprinting and photographing for fraud prevention purposes, receive a home visit from an eligibility verification investigator, attend a mandatory workforce

Other developed countries have a universal approach to social programs and policies. They also have a less punitive attitude toward welfare; for example, programs to help with child care costs are universal, rather than means-tested, as they are in the United States. This ad was posted in a Canadian newspaper reminding families to apply for benefits.

Canada's
Universal Child Care plan
Choice. Support. Spaces.

For each child under six, you will receive $100 per month.

But you may need to apply.

The Government of Canada's **Universal Child Care Benefit** came into effect on July 1, 2006. It provides Canadian families with $100 per month for each child under six.

If you already receive the Canada Child Tax Benefit (CCTB), you will automatically receive the Universal Child Care Benefit. If you are one of the ten percent of families who do not receive the CCTB, you need to complete the CCTB form.

It's simple to apply
Log on to www.universalchildcare.ca and click on the application links. It's that easy. Or, visit your local Service Canada Centre to obtain the form in person. You can also call 1 800 959-2221.

You can apply anytime
The first benefit cheques have been mailed. You can apply anytime and receive payments retroactively up to 11 months from your date of application.

This initiative is part of Canada's Universal Child Care Plan which will also support the creation of thousands of real child care spaces through the **Child Care Spaces Initiative.**

For more information, visit the website at www.universalchildcare.ca

Government   Gouvernement
of Canada   du Canada

Canada

orientation, and attend daily job search classes (five days per week) for the duration of the 30-day eligibility determination period (Holcomb et al. 2003).

For decades, both Republicans and Democrats have tried to reconstruct welfare or end it entirely. In 1997, then-President Clinton implemented sweeping welfare reform legislation that set lifetime welfare payments at a maximum of five years, with the majority of adult recipients

WHAT DO YOU THINK?

Can you identify other family policies (or the lack thereof) that reflect our values? List as many as you can.

being required to work after two years. Many states have adopted significantly shorter time frames, and some make no allowances for women who have young babies. Moreover, 21 states have also adopted some form of family caps, meaning that benefits will not be increased for a child born while a mother is already receiving TANF (Rowe and Murphy 2008).

Since the passage of welfare reform, many people have left welfare, usually for low-wage work. The enforcement of time limits and work requirements, coupled with the expanding economy and low unemployment rate of the 1990s, contributed to a dramatic initial drop in the number of families receiving TANF. From March 1994 to December 2008, national caseloads fell by over 60 percent, declining from 5 million to about 1.9 million families (U.S. Department of Health and Human Services 2009).

How are these families faring? Unfortunately, many families leaving welfare for work are not better off financially (Acs and Loprest 2004; Seccombe 2011; Seccombe and Hoffman 2007). One Oregon study found that only about one-quarter of former welfare recipients were offered insurance from an employer; however, many families could not even accept these benefits because they could not afford to pay for them (Seccombe and Hoffman 2007). Very few were offered any sick leave.

Families leaving welfare struggle to make ends meet. Approximately one-third say they have had to cut the size of a meal or skip meals because they did not have enough food. Sixty percent worried at least sometimes that they would run out of food before having money to buy more. Over half reported that they had often or sometimes run out of food and were without means to buy more. Nearly half reported that they were unable to pay their mortgage, rent, or utility bills in the past year, particularly among those who left TANF most recently. Ten percent had to move in with others because of their inability to pay their bills (Acs and Loprest 2004).

Other countries have a different approach to welfare. For example, in her book *Saving Our Children from Poverty*, economist Barbara Bergmann (1996) states that only one-quarter of single mothers in France receive welfare-type benefits, compared to two-thirds of single mothers in the United States. The reason for this difference is not because France is stingy. On the contrary, France has made a successful commitment to enhancing low-tier jobs. They have improved the conditions surrounding low-tier work so that these jobs pay a living wage, and the government does not automatically eliminate an array of benefits that are vital to a family's well-being. A single mother in France who moves from welfare to work retains approximately $6,000 in government cash and housing grants. She continues to receive health insurance and pays only a small amount for child care, as do all French citizens. Therefore, France's poverty rate is considerably lower than that of the United States.

Themes of This Book

This book will introduce you to the social side of family and intimate relationships. However, you will learn more than a bunch of random facts. Five themes are woven throughout this textbook that draw from and integrate the previous discussion. Each of these themes is highlighted here.

Families Are Both a Public Social Institution and a Private Personal Relationship

Families fulfill many of our personal needs for love, warmth, and intimacy. It is within families that we raise our children and nurture their social, emotional, and physical growth. Nonetheless, we should not forget that families are also a public **social institution**. A social institution is a major sphere of social life, with a set of beliefs and rules that are organized to meet basic human needs. In addition to talking about your specific family, we talk about *the* family. Families are a social institution in much the same way our political, economic, religious, health care, and educational systems are social institutions. As we will see in Chapter 2, in early human civilizations families were the center of most activities. The earliest hunting and gathering societies were based almost exclusively on kinship. In families, we learned and practiced religion, we educated the young, and took care of the sick. This pattern was modified little until recently. With the advent of technology and the industrial revolution, other institutions developed and took on many of these functions. Today, we worship in churches, synagogues, and mosques; children are educated in schools; and we go to hospitals when we are sick.

Families continue to represent a major sphere of social life for most people—and despite their diversity, families still have a surprisingly organized set of beliefs and rules to meet certain fundamental needs. For example, in virtually every society families are considered the best place to raise children.

Families can best be understood by examining how they interact with, influence, and are influenced by other social institutions. Families cannot merely be separated out as "havens" from the rest of society. Patterns of education, religious customs, economic systems, and political systems all shape family patterns, attitudes, behaviors, and the constraints and opportunities experienced by individual members. For example, norms associated with social institutions may influence who is considered an appropriate mate, which family members work outside the home and what kind of work they do, who has the primary responsibility for housework and other domestic labor, how children are raised and disciplined, how children can be schooled, how power and decision making among family members will be allocated, and the roles that extended family members are expected to play.

However, in all likelihood, most people do not reflect very often on families as social institutions. Instead, they focus on the day-to-day experience of being in a family, either in their **family of orientation** (defined as the family they were born into) or the **family of procreation** (more broadly used to refer to the family made through partnership, marriage, and/or with children). People tend to think about their families in individualized terms, often without seeing their interconnection to larger social structures. Many aspects of family life, however, including our chances of marrying or being in a committed partnership, of bearing children, of divorcing, the kind of neighborhood we live in, the type of job we are likely to get, the sort of child care we are likely to use, our general health and well-being, and the likelihood of living to see our grandchildren, are affected by broader social structures in which we are embedded, including our sex, race, and social class.

It is important to recognize how our personal choices and behaviors are shaped by these larger social structures. For instance, how does one's level of education affect the chances of having children? Is the relationship between level of education and the likelihood of having children identical for men and women? Are children viewed as an asset, and how might views toward children be related to capitalism, urbanization, or the distribution of money and other resources?

At the same time, being mindful of these social forces does not imply that we are passive recipients of them. **Human agency** is the ability of human beings to create viable lives even when they are constrained or limited by social forces (Baca Zinn et al. 2011). Rich, poor, male, female, young, or old—we are all actively producing our lives, even in light of the structural factors that help shape our opportunities. We do have free choice, but it is important to be mindful of the ways that we are influenced by the structure of the society in which we live.

Social Inequality Has a Powerful Influence on Family Life

A second theme of this text is that social inequality is a critical organizing feature in society and has an important influence on family life. Most Americans believe that the United States provides nearly equal opportunities for everyone. However, as I will show in detail in Chapter 5, U.S. society is highly stratified on the basis of economics, power, and social status. Inequality is woven into many basic social structures and institutions. These patterns of social inequality filter down and shape all components of family life—the neighborhood in which you live, your gendered expectations, the values you are likely to hold for your children, the type of job you are likely to get, your consumption patterns, daily stressors, and your coping mechanisms. Social class, sex, race, and ethnicity affect the way family members interact with one another and the way in which they are responded to.

Conversely, patterns of social inequality are also shaped *by* families. Americans fantasize that they can be anything they want to be, but in reality there is little substantial upward (or downward) social mobility. People usually live out their lives in generally the same social class in which they were born. Families pass on their wealth and social capital (or their lack of it) to their newest members, and this perpetuates social inequality. For example, because of the U.S. inheritance laws, affluent parents are able to distribute their wealth to their children upon their death. Relatively little of the wealth is taxed and redistributed, as is the case in other countries. Consequently, some of the richest people have only marginal employment histories. They do not need to work for a living—yet others who work relentlessly, often in the unglamorous but growing service sector, find no real route to a better life. Their wages are low; they may not receive health insurance or other benefits and live on the margins only one paycheck away from impoverishment. What type of wealth or social capital do these parents have to pass on to their children?

This text examines the assumptions, values, and ideologies that are used to justify or explain social inequality and its shaping of families. We will see that the ideologies of more powerful groups are often presented as "normal" or "common sense" rather than showing their true ideological slant. The following box, "Using the Sociological Imagination: Ideology of 'Family' Shapes Perceptions of Immigrant Children," shows how U.S. culture tends to define the "normal" American family without regard to the inherent racism in such a definition.

USING the Sociological Imagination

Ideology of "Family" Shapes Perceptions of Immigrant Children

All children want to feel that they live in a typical, "normal" family. But how are definitions of "normal" constructed, and what are the consequences of living in a family that does not conform to the definition? Sociologist Karen Pyke explores these sensitive issues.

The cultural imagery of American families that we see on television and throughout the media suggests that "normal" families contain a mom, a dad, and siblings, all of whom are expected to behave toward each other in very specific ways. The problem is this cultural imagery is at odds with the reality of life for many families. The values of non-white, immigrant, and gay and lesbian families are largely excluded from this narrow imagery of "normal" families. This family ideology implicitly denigrates those families whose structure or cultural practices are different. This contributes to negative self-images and even self-derogation among members of such families, as I found in my research.

I conducted interviews with 73 grown children of Korean and Vietnamese immigrants and found that when these young adults contrasted behavior in their immigrant families with mainstream images of normalcy, they interpreted their own family life, as well as that of Asians and Asian Americans in general, as deficient. In their descriptions, they emphasized Americanized definitions of love that stress expressiveness, such as the display of affection, sentimentality, and close communication. They downplayed their parents' instrumental style of love emphasized in Asian cultures, such as their material support of children well into adulthood and—in the case of many Korean parents—their decision to immigrate in search of a better life and education for their children. However, because their parents did not conform to Americanized notions of expressive love, these children often described them as distant, unloving, uncaring, and not "normal."

Dat, 22, who left Vietnam at age 5, referred to images of normal American families he saw on television and among friends as motivating his desire for more affection and closeness with his father. "Sometimes when I had problems in school, all I wanted was my dad to listen to me, of all people," he said. "I guess that's the American way and I was raised American. . . . That's what I see on TV and in my friends' family. And I expected him to be that way too. But it didn't happen."

Similarly, Paul, a 21-year-old born in the United States to Korean immigrant parents had similar feelings. "As a child I was always watching television and watching other friends' fathers," he said. "All the relationships seemed so much different from me and my father's relationship. . . . I can remember watching *The Brady Bunch* reruns and thinking Mike Brady would be a wonderful dad to

have. He was always so supportive. . . . Basically, I used what I saw on TV as a picture of what a typical family should be like in the United States. I only wished that my family could be like that."

The widespread family ideology promotes the white middle-class, heterosexual family as the norm and the superior standard. This ideology put immense pressure on many of the children of immigrants in this study to assimilate, and encouraged some to denigrate their own ethnic family styles as deficient in comparison. They internalized a negative view of their own Asian immigrant family life, while glorifying the cultural practices associated with white families.

As Robert, 24, who emigrated from Korea at age 7, explained, "I still find myself envying white American families and wishing that my family was perfect like theirs. So basically I find myself suckered into this ideal image of the American family. And I realize, sadly, that my family is not the American family and never will be. God, you know, this really upsets me when I keep striving for this intangible thing because then I never really feel happiness or satisfaction."

Author: Karen Pyke
Sources: Pyke 2000a, 2000b.

CRITICAL THINKING QUESTIONS

1. How are definitions of the "normal American family" racist? What may be some of the consequences for young persons who feel marginalized because they don't fit the stereotype of a normal family?
2. Why does the stereotype of the "normal American family" persist? Whose interests are best served by it?

An Expanded Strengths-Based Perspective Can Improve Family Resiliency

A family-strengths perspective is a worldview based on optimism (Saleebey 2009). This text does not ignore family problems; in fact, I describe many problems in considerable depth—poverty, rape, racism, divorce, female genital cutting, and stalking, to name just a few. However, a strengths perspective focuses on identifying, creating, mobilizing, advocating, and respecting the resources, assets, wisdom, and knowledge that every person and every family has to help ameliorate problems. Rather than working from a deficit model, this text highlights how members of our society can work together to make families stronger and more resilient. Sometimes we only have to look within our own communities, but in other contexts we may need to look further, perhaps to other societies, to see the models that they use.

Resiliency is the capacity to rebound from adversity, misfortune, trauma, or other transitional crises and become strengthened and more resourceful (McCubbin et al. 1997; Ungar 2008; Walsh 2006). Let's take the example of poverty; the well-cited Kauai Longitudinal Study will show us the power of resiliency (Werner 1994, 1995; Werner and Smith 1989, 1992). Based on a sample of 698 children born in 1955 on the Hawaiian island of Kauai, researchers followed them for nearly 40 years to examine the long-term effects of growing up in high-risk environments. Approximately one-third of the children were considered high risk because of exposure to a combination of at least four individual, parental, or household risk factors, such as having a serious health problem, familial alcoholism, violence, divorce, or mental illness in the family. The children were assessed from the perinatal period to ages 1, 2, 10, 18, and 32 years. The research team found that two-thirds of high-risk two-year-olds who experienced four or more risk factors by age two developed learning or behavior problems by age 18. One-third did not have any behavior problems, and instead developed into stable, competent, confident, and productive adults. In a later follow-up, at age 40, all but two of these individuals were still successful. In fact, many of them had outperformed the children from low-risk families. Moreover, among the two-thirds of the surveyed high-risk children who had learning or behavioral problems at age 18, one-half did not exhibit these problems at age 30. As adults, they had satisfying jobs, stable marriages, and in other measures were deemed successful by the research team. Consequently, it appears that resiliency can be developed at any point in the life course. Conversely, a few individuals identified as resilient at age 18 had developed significant problems by age 30.

The evidence shows us that many adults and children reared in poverty or with other risk factors do overcome their adversities. Why is this? Most research on resilience has focused on three types of factors that promote resiliency in the face of adverse conditions: (1) individual-level protective factors, (2) family protective and recovery factors, and (3) community strengths. A young man introduced in the box on page 31, "Families as Lived Experience: Meet Nathan Cabrera," won a 2009 scholarship award from the Children's Defense Fund for his success in beating the odds against him. Can you spot any relevant individual, family, or community factors in his story that fostered resiliency?

Individual-level protective factors include individual personality traits and dispositions that enhance a person's ability to be successful. In their review of research and clinic experience, Wolin and Wolin (1993) identified seven traits of adults who survived a troubled childhood: insight (awareness of dysfunction); independence (distancing self from troubles); supportive relationships; initiative; creativity; humor (reframing the situation in a less threatening way); and morality (justice and compassion rather than revenge). For example, the resilient high-risk adolescents in the Longitudinal Kauai Study developed a sense that obstacles were not insurmountable, and they believed that they had control over their fate. They had a high degree of self-esteem and self-efficacy, and many developed a special skill or hobby that was a source of pride.

Family protective and recovery factors are central features of the resiliency literature (DeFrain 2008; Skogrand et al. 2007). **Family protective factors (FPF)** are those characteristics or dynamics that shape the family's ability to endure in the face of risk factors; **family recovery factors (FRF)** assist families in "bouncing back" from a crisis situation (McCubbin et al. 1997). Key characteristics of resilient families include warmth, affection, cohesion, commitment, clear expectations, shared goals, and emotional

FAMILIES
as Lived Experience

Meet Nathan Cabrera

Nathan Cabrera is celebrated for his ability to overcome extreme adversity to succeed in school and in life. Since 1990, the Children's Defense Fund has recognized the achievements of over 600 courageous young people who overcame incredible odds stacked against them—poverty, violence, abuse, illness—problems that would derail most young lives. Yet, with an effort and determination that are inspiring, these young men and women are thriving and becoming leaders in their communities.

Nathan Cabrera has never really had a childhood—he has had to be mature and responsible almost his entire life. Born to a 14-year-old mother who used drugs and subsequently had three more children by three different fathers, Nathan became the one responsible for taking care of the children while his mother worked afternoon and evening jobs. He could never spend time with friends because he was busy feeding and bathing his younger siblings and making sure their homework was done. With a father in prison and a teenage mother, Nathan said it was more like being raised by a peer than by a parent, and the only time he felt like a kid was when he was with his grandmother, who lives in North Carolina.

Along with juggling numerous responsibilities at home, Nathan worked hard at school, determined to show his siblings that education was the key to a normal life. But after years of watching his mother act like an irresponsible teenager, he himself eventually became rebellious and reckless. Concerned about Nathan's behavior and talk of suicide, his pastor intervened and began working with the family. Nathan's relationship with his mother improved and he helped her earn her GED. She even held down a regular job for a while but could not stop surrounding herself with the wrong crowd.

In September 2007, she was killed in retaliation for helping a friend escape from the control of a Latino gang. His father then tried to come back into

Nathan Cabrera, 2009 Children's Defense Fund "Beat the Odds" scholarship winner.

Nathan's life, but was physical and controlling and even attempted to kidnap Nathan one night. Fortunately, Pastor Frank again was there for Nathan and helped arrange a safe place for him to live. Nathan's siblings moved in with relatives of their respective fathers. Currently, in addition to maintaining his high academic standards, Nathan is running a t-shirt business with Pastor Frank, encouraging teens to avoid temptation with their t-shirts' unique designs and simple messages. He said he is looking forward to earning a business management degree and to bringing his siblings back together one day soon to all live as a family again.

Source: Children's Defense Fund 2010.

www.childrensdefense.org/newsroom/real-children-real-stories/beat-the-odds/nathan-cabrera.html

CRITICAL THINKING QUESTIONS

1. What type of factors can you identify that helped Nathan become more resilient?
2. Can you think of any formal policies or programs that would have helped him as well?

support for one another. Resilient families participate in family celebrations, share spiritual connections, have specific traditions, and predictable routines (Saleebey 2009; Walsh 2006).

There are also **community factors**, resources that help develop resilient youth and foster resiliency among adults (Walsh 2006). Blyth and Roelkepartian (1993) indicate several types of community strengths. First, opportunities for participation in community life, such as extracurricular activities in school, religious youth groups, or scouting can bond youth to their communities and teach important skills, such as teamwork, group pride, or leadership. Second, strong communities provide avenues for contributing to the welfare of others, which can foster a sense of inner strength and self-esteem. Third, involvement in the community provides opportunities to connect with role models or a confidant.

As important as individuals, families, and communities are, something is *missing*. Noticeably absent is an emphasis on *structural-level* conditions, such as national and statewide policies that can strengthen families (Seccombe 2002). As you will learn in Chapter 5, poverty contributes to poorer nutrition, lower-quality home environment, parental stress, fewer resources for learning, housing problems, and poor-quality neighborhoods, which in turn lead to further negative consequences. Can we expect families to be resilient without supportive family policies? For example, how do we best help an impoverished child who lives with his single mother? Is it enough to surround this child with a loving extended family, church, and community groups? These are important components of resiliency, but they are insufficient.

One study examined the gap in math and science achievement of third- and fourth-graders who lived with a single parent versus those who lived with two parents in 11 different countries (Pong et al. 2003). The researchers found that countries that provided the fewest policies to equalize the resources of parents, such as the United States and New Zealand, had the largest achievement gap between children in single- versus two-parent families. In contrast, those countries with family policies specifically designed to equalize resources between single- and two-parent families were far more successful in decreasing the achievement gap.

Family Policies Reflect Historical, Cultural, Political, and Social Factors

If families are public social institutions in addition to private personal relationships, then we must recognize the importance of federal, state, and local involvement (Day 2009; Gilbert and Terrell 2010; Karger and Stoesz 2010). The fourth theme of this text is that government regulates or fails to regulate many conditions of families, and these policies (or lack thereof) reflect historical patterns, cultural values, political viewpoints, and many social conditions, including the distribution of power and inequality in society. This may occur in the passing of specific policies targeting certain groups or certain aspects of family life, such as welfare reform, requiring partners to get a blood test before marrying, or passing legislation to prohibit gays and lesbians from marrying.

Conversely, historical, cultural, political, and social factors may also have great influence backhandedly by the *absence* of specific policies. For example, the U.S. government offers no systematic paid leave to women who have just given birth. This is in sharp contrast to other developed nations (and many developing ones), as you will learn in Chapter 8. Commonly in other countries, women receive six to 12 months off of work, with full or nearly full pay. A study comparing attitudes in 31 countries toward family policies reveals that the United States is far more likely to believe that family matters are personal issues than are other countries, reflecting a long-standing belief in rugged individualism. For example, an international survey asking whether women should receive paid maternity leave when they have a baby received a nearly unanimous "yes" in other countries, but in the United States, nearly a quarter of Americans said "no." Why would so many people object to women receiving paid maternity benefits?

Family policies reflect historical, cultural, political, and social factors in every society—values about personal responsibility versus collective good, the role of work in our lives, the expectations placed on mothers and fathers to manage the inherent conflicts between their work and family lives, and the level of concern over social inequality (Day 2009).

Parasuraman and Greenhaus (1997) identify three solutions that can be used when family and work conflict with one another. First, establishing policies that create more family-friendly work environments, such as paid maternity and family leaves, could alter the situation. A second approach is that employees themselves should learn specific techniques for managing their conflicts, such as choosing a one-job family pattern. A third approach would modify the meanings of the situation. It would suggest that people have family and work conflicts simply because they *want* to work more hours or *want* more money. Policies would focus on increasing personal responsibility and commitments (Bogenschneider 2006).

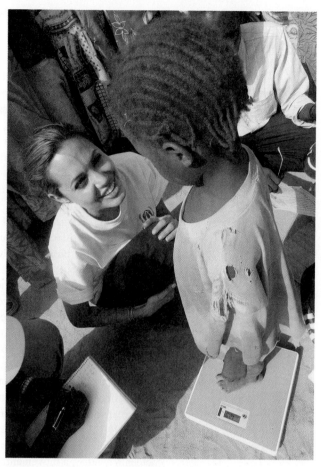

A comparative perspective is valuable because societies are increasingly interconnected with one another. Oscar-winning actress Angelina Jolie became the first recipient of the Church World Service Immigration and Refugee Program Humanitarian Award, which honored her for her work as Goodwill Ambassador for the United Nations High Commissioner for Refugees (UNHCR).

Of these three solutions, the United States most often adopts the second and third approaches. Family issues, whether they are poverty or income insecurity, work-family conflicts, or caring for dependents, are often seen as personal issues or problems. This is in contrast to many other countries that take a more structural view.

The different policy approaches between the United States and other countries will become apparent as we explore the topics of each chapter in this text. Social policies, either by their commission or omission, critically influence virtually all aspects of family life, including how families are structured or organized, and the values, attitudes, and behaviors of its members. Therefore, we will discuss relevant policy issues in each chapter, rather than relegating family policy to a concluding chapter at the end of the text.

Understanding Families in the United States Requires a Comparative Perspective

The final theme of this text focuses on the importance of learning about other cultures and other historical periods to better inform us of American families (Karraker 2008; Kelleher and Klein 2011). In the past, it was easier to ignore what was happening in the world beyond our borders, but this is no longer the case because societies are becoming increasingly interconnected. New technologies, immigration, commerce across borders, and greater ease in world travel have increased visibility and the United States can no longer remain isolated. Societies see other ways of doing things and sometimes adopt pieces of another's culture. One can now travel to many distant parts of the world and still find American fast food, such as McDonald's or Kentucky Fried Chicken. Likewise, the United States also has adopted other foods and cultural artifacts. Tacos and pizza are staples in our diets today, but once were considered exotic or regional ethnic food. How has this changed the rhythm of life in the United States?

Just as the case with culture, it is easy to ignore history and focus only on the here and now—yet many of our current family issues are rooted in the traditions of the past. For example, to better understand the current and heated debate over abortion, we should be aware that at one time, it was not opposed by religious groups, including the Catholic Church. Likewise, to truly understand the high rate of divorce in the United States, we should be aware of the ways in which the current notion of love, which evolved in the eighteenth century, changed the entire basis on which mates were chosen, and thereby increased the likelihood of couples ending an unhappy marriage (Coontz 2005).

A comparative perspective helps us understand our current situation because it informs us of alternative social arrangements and presents new ways to frame an issue or policy solution. For example, how can a comparative perspective help us understand the nature and role of adolescence in U.S. culture? This is an important concern because it is well known that adolescents commit a disproportionate number of crimes, experience higher-than-average unemployment, and face a host of other social problems, such as teen pregnancy or drug use. A comparative perspective shows us that adolescence, as we know it today, is largely a new social construction, originating in the West in the late nineteenth century as a result of newly created child labor laws and the changing nature of the labor market (Leeder 2004; Mintz 2004). Until then, children's labor was needed on farms and even young teenagers were considered mini-adults. However, with urbanization and industrialization in the late nineteenth century, a movement arose to increase the protection of young people. Social reformers known as *child savers* were particularly interested in developing social programs that were age-based and targeted toward children. Compulsory education increased the length of time children spent in school until well into their teenage years. Adolescence became a new period of transition between childhood and adulthood, but without clear-cut norms about what to expect during this period. By the twentieth century, the concept of adolescence as a separate stage of life had taken hold, and now represents a substantial component of popular culture segregated from adult-oriented culture. Unique clothing, music, and food are directly marketed toward this relatively new consumer group. Nonetheless, it is not completely clear what the developmental tasks of this age group are and how they can best serve the needs of society. Separating adolescents from adults, but giving them an unclear or unknown set of developmental tasks, has not necessarily served adolescents well. As historian Steven Mintz (2004) writes, "If there is any lesson that the history of childhood can teach us, it is the error of thinking that we can radically separate the lives of children from those of adults."

How do other cultures construct this age period? How are these social constructions related to the level of technology or wealth in society? Can we learn from other cultures, even those that are radically different from our own? The box on page 35, "Our Global Community: Adolescence Among the Maasai," describes a vivid contrast to the concept of adolescence in the West by looking at how a group living in Kenya and Tanzania sees this age period.

WHAT DO YOU THINK?

As we begin our academic journey together, what are your initial thoughts on these five themes? Do you have any personal experiences relevant to the themes?

O U R

Global Community

Adolescence Among the Maasai

The conception of adolescence and the way it is experienced are far from universal. An interesting contrast to adolescence in the West is found among the Maasai, an ethnic group living on the savannas of Kenya and Tanzania.

The Maasai are a small tribe in the mosaic of African peoples; they are tall, thin pastoralists who can be spotted miles away by their signature red clothing. Their lives are simple; they depend on their cattle and their families, living closely with the earth. Wealth is measured by the number of cattle and children a man has, and the economy is a family-based one in which all contribute to the family's well-being. The men are in charge, primarily protecting the village and caring for the animals.

For the men, the passage to adulthood is a long and rigorous process. Early on a boy is assigned to a *moran*, the group of warriors with whom he will be associated, his age mates. The moran is divided into junior and senior groups as well as the specific group with whom the boy will be circumcised. Male circumcision takes place between the ages of 13 and 17; some boys do not have younger brothers old enough to take their place caring for the animals, so they stay behind to help with the cattle until a younger brother is ready. When the circumcision takes place, the young man is not allowed to cry or yell; to do so leads to disrespect for his entire family. His parents could be beaten by members of the entire village for raising such a coward.

Once boys are circumcised, they become junior warriors and live with their age mates in a special dwelling set aside for them. The mother accompanies her son, adorning herself with elaborate beaded ear ornaments that show everyone she is the mother of a warrior. She builds a house for him while he roams about freely with his moran, having sex with women, hunting, growing his hair long, and decorating elaborate headdresses. The moran becomes so close that they even urinate together; these men are now brothers and share everything in life, even their wives when they later take them.

When the junior morans age, they become senior warriors and the life of the community is centered on them. They direct the stock, are in charge of defense and security, and occasionally deal with the local government. They are hunters and are allowed to do so by the Kenyan government, although only to a limited extent. Theirs is a most important position in that society, and the young men are now fully adults.

What about women? They build the houses, collect wood, cook, clean, milk the cows, and raise the children. Girls are circumcised by age 13, marking their availability for marriage. They, too, are adults.

From this example, one can see that adolescence as we know it at home in the United States does not exist in all cultures. Instead, being in a moran and being circumcised prepares a young man in the Maasai for his coming role in society. There is no delineation as a teen; the young man is a warrior in training and thus is fully respected and important to his society. He is responsible and his job is crucial to the survival of his society. The young woman may be married by age 13, also deemed an adult.

Source: Adapted from Leeder 2004.

CRITICAL THINKING QUESTIONS

1. What exactly is the job of an adolescent in the United States? Is it crucial to the survival of society?
2. Are there any American rituals—religious, cultural, academic—that demarcate adolescence? What rituals would you propose?
3. Is there anything in Maasai cultural traditions that could be useful to the United States?

Conclusion

This chapter introduces a sociological imagination to the study of families and intimate relationships. Rather than seeing families as simply personal and private relationships that operate in a random fashion, we recognize that many seemingly personal family issues are related to broader social concerns. To understand family dynamics, a sociological perspective uses a comparative approach and empirical methods to describe and explain patterns of family structure, family change, and social relationships. As a public social institution, families are not isolated from the rest of society, but are continually changing and adapting to people's needs and to the changes found in other social institutions.

Yet policies to help families are notoriously selective or absent in the United States. The upcoming chapters will examine specific family issues through the lens of the sociological imagination. This text has five specific themes that you will find within each chapter: (1) the family is a public social institution as well as a private personal relationship; (2) social inequality powerfully shapes virtually all dimensions of family life; (3) an expanded strengths-based perspective can improve family resiliency; (4) family policies reflect historical, cultural, political, and social factors; and (5) a comparative approach can yield insight into family structure and family dynamics.

Key Terms

Community factors: Community resources that help develop resilient youth and foster resiliency among adults. (p. 32)

Comparative perspective: Looking at other societies around the world or looking at a culture historically to see how others organize their social life and respond to its challenges. (p. 9)

Conflict theory: This theoretical perspective emphasizes issues surrounding social inequality, power, conflict, and social change. (p. 16)

Developmental theory: Families and family members go through distinct stages, each with its own set of tasks, roles, and responsibilities. (p. 7)

Domestic partners: Heterosexual or homosexual unmarried couples in long-term committed relationships. (p. 17)

Empirical approach: Answers questions through a systematic collection and analysis of data. (p. 10)

Ethnocentrism: The assumption that society's way of doing things is always the best way. (p. 10)

Families: Relationships by blood, marriage, or affection, in which members may cooperate economically, may care for any children, and may consider their identity to be intimately connected to the larger group. (p. 5)

Family of orientation: The family into which you were born. (p. 27)

Family of procreation: The family you make through partnership, marriage, and/or with children. (p. 27)

Family protective factors (FPF): Characteristics or dynamics that shape the family's ability to endure in the face of risk factors. (p. 30)

Family recovery factors (FRF): Characteristics or dynamics that assist families in "bouncing back" from a crisis situation. (p. 30)

Family systems theory: Family members and the roles they play make up a system, and this system is larger than the sum of its individual members. (p. 17)

Feminist theory: Gender is the central concept for explaining family structure and dynamics. (p. 16)

Fictive kin: Nonrelatives whose bonds are strong and intimate. (p. 5)

Human agency: The ability of human beings to create viable lives even when they are constrained or limited by social forces. (p. 27)

Individual-level protective factors: Individual personality traits and dispositions that enhance a person's ability to be successful and resilient. (p. 30)

Life course perspective: Examines how individuals' lives change as they pass through the events in their lives, recognizing that many changes are socially produced and shared among a cohort of people. (p. 17)

Macro theories: A general framework that attempts to understand societal patterns, such as structural functionalism, conflict theory, and feminist theory. (p. 15)

Means-tested: People have to be below a certain income to qualify for a social program. (p. 22)

Micro theories: A general framework that focuses on personal dynamics and face-to-face interaction, including social exchange, symbolic interaction, developmental, and family systems theories. (p. 15)

Progressive taxation: Those who earn more pay a higher percentage of their income in taxes. (p. 24)

Qualitative methods: The focus is on narrative description with words rather than numbers to analyze patterns and their underlying meanings. (p. 11)

Quantitative methods: The focus is on collecting data that can be measured numerically. (p. 11)

Resiliency: The capacity to rebound from adversity, misfortune, trauma, or other transitional crises and become strengthened and more resourceful. (p. 30)

Selective programs: Persons need to meet some eligibility requirement to qualify for benefits. (p. 22)

Social exchange theory: Individuals are rational and their behavior reflects an evaluation of costs and benefits. (p. 16)

Social institution: A major sphere of social life, with a set of beliefs and rules that is organized to meet basic human needs, such as the family, political, or educational systems. (p. 26)

Social structure: The organized pattern of social relationships and social institutions that together form the basis of society. (p. 8)

Sociological imagination: Reveals general patterns in what otherwise might be thought of as simple random events. (p. 9)

Structural functionalist theory: This theoretical perspective suggests that all social institutions, including the family, exist to fill a need in society. (p. 16)

Symbolic interaction theory: This theoretical perspective focuses on the social interaction between family members and other groups, concerned with the meanings and interpretations that people have. (p. 17)

Temporary Assistance for Needy Families (TANF): The principal cash welfare program, previously known as Aid to Families with Dependent Children (AFDC). (p. 24)

Theory: A general framework, explanation, or tool to understand and describe the real world. (p. 15)

Universal programs: Social and economic programs that are available to all persons or families. (p. 23)

Resources on the Internet

American Psychological Association

www.apa.org

The American Psychological Association (APA) is a scientific and professional organization that represents psychology in the United States. With more than 150,000 members, APA is the largest association of psychologists worldwide. The objective of the APA is to advance psychology as a science and profession and as a means of promoting health, education, and human welfare to the public.

American Sociological Association

www.asanet.org

The American Sociological Association (ASA), founded in 1905, is a nonprofit membership association dedicated to advancing sociology as a scientific discipline and profession serving the public good. With approximately 13,000 members, the ASA encompasses sociologists who are faculty members at colleges and universities, researchers, practitioners, and students. About 20 percent of its members work in government, business, or nonprofit organizations.

National Council on Family Relations

www.ncfr.com

The National Council on Family Relations (NCFR) provides a forum for family researchers, educators, and practitioners to share in the development and dissemination of knowledge about families and family relationships, establishes professional standards, and works to promote family well-being. NCFR publishes two scholarly journals, as well as books, audio/video tapes, and learning tools. It sponsors an annual conference of cutting-edge research papers, methods, and practices, including research updates for practitioners.

CHAPTER 2

Families Throughout the World: Marriage, Family, and Kinship

CHAPTER OUTLINE

Functions of the Family: Variations and Universals 40

Differences in Marriage and Family Patterns 43

■ **OUR** *Global Community:* Marriage Among the !Kung San of Southern Africa *44*

■ **EYE** *on the World:* Comparative Marital Patterns *46*

■ **FAMILIES** *as Lived Experience:* Imagination: A Personal Ad from Adolph, Mary, and Megan *50*

■ **OUR** *Global Community:* Fistulas Are a Hidden Epidemic *52*

Modernization Theory: Social Change and Families 55

World Systems Theory: Social Change and Families 57

Families Around the World: India, Japan, and Sweden 58

Conclusion 64

Key Terms 64

Resources on the Internet 64

CHAPTER PREVIEW

Every society has an institution known as family. This chapter reveals both the similarities and differences in the functions and structure of family relationships around the world. Families are universal because they perform functions that no other social institution can (or wants to) provide. However, families are also tremendously diverse because they reflect the environment, historical period, and culture in which they are found, and they continually adapt to changing circumstances. In this chapter, you will learn:

- Functions of the family, both universal features and variations

- Variations in marriage patterns, including monogamy and polygamy

- Patterns of power and authority

- Patterns of kinship, descent, and inheritance

- Patterns of residence

- Two specific theories that attempt to explain social change and families: modernization theory and world systems theory

- Differences in families around the world through comparisons of India, Japan, and Sweden

One of the traditional organizing features of the Vietnamese family has been the preference of married couples to co-reside with the husband's parents when possible. This custom, based on Confucianism, is referred to as a *patrilocal living arrangement*. When a first son marries, he is obliged to move in with his parents, at least until another brother marries and joins the family.

However, as Vietnam becomes an increasingly modernized nation, has the custom of patrilocality declined? A common theory of family change suggests that as educational and occupational opportunities expand, as adult children become more geographically mobile, and as a country becomes more urbanized, greater independence between family members is likely to emerge. The nuclear family will gradually replace extended families, and support for traditional family obligations, such as patrilocality, will decline.

Sociologists Charles Hirschman and Nguyen Huu Minh analyzed data from the Vietnam Longitudinal Study, which is based on 1,855 households in the largest province in the Red River Delta of northern Vietnam. The survey included a wide range of questions on family relationships, structure, educational and occupational history, siblings, and marriage and children.

The researchers found, somewhat unexpectedly, that the proportion of newly married couples that followed the patrilocal custom actually increased in recent decades rather than declined. Between 1956 and 1965, 72 percent of sons lived with their parents after their marriage. However, between 1986 and 1995, the percentage had increased to 83 percent. The researchers did find that the length of time sons and their wives co-resided had declined somewhat. After 5 years, fewer than 30 percent of the more recent cohorts still lived with their parents, compared to over 40 percent between 1956 and 1965.

The researchers also found that relatively few aspects of modernization contributed to a lower incidence of living with parents. Adult children who worked in nonagricultural occupations and who married later in life were somewhat less likely to co-reside with the groom's parents. Yet, overall it appears that the underlying cultural preference to live with the groom's parents immediately after marriage remains strong and grows stronger in Vietnam. Hirschman and Minh conclude that not all aspects of the traditional family structure may undergo the same tensions associated with modernization. Joint living arrangements, at least in the son's early part of marriage, may be mutually beneficial, and show no sign of declining (Hirschman and Minh 2002).

Throughout history and throughout the world, people have lived in families. As a social institution, families are at the center of all societies because they fulfill needs that few other institutions can (Ember and Ember 2011; Karraker 2008; Strathern and Stewart 2011). Yes, societies develop their own variation in how marriage, families, and kinship groups should function and what they are supposed to do, but what is surprising is the amazing similarity from one region of the world to another. This chapter explores some of these similarities and differences. Here, we will look at key concepts and theoretical issues in comparative family studies that we can draw upon as we study families throughout this text.

Functions of the Family: Variations and Universals

Why do we even have families? Drawing upon structural functionalism, the theoretical perspective introduced in Chapter 1, sociologists and family scientists often discuss families in terms of the important functions they serve for individuals and for society at large.

These functions include the regulation of sexual behavior, reproduction and the socialization of children, property and inheritance, economic cooperation, assignment of roles and status, and shared intimacy.

Marriage is the cornerstone of these functions (Bonvillain 2010; Ember and Ember 2011; Strathern and Stewart 2011). It is an arrangement that is strictly human and publicly recognizes social and intimate bonds. Cultural norms specify who is eligible to be married, to whom and to how many people an individual can marry, what the marriage ceremony will consist of, and the norms surrounding how married persons should behave. In his cross-cultural study, anthropologist William Stephens provided a broad definition of marriage. It is (1) a socially legitimate sexual union, begun with (2) a public announcement, (3) undertaken with some idea of permanence, and (4) assumed with a more or less explicit marriage contract that spells out reciprocal obligations between spouses, and between spouses and their children (Stephens 1963). The public announcement is often in the form of a wedding, which is a cultural ritual that represents a rite of passage. Wedding rituals can be quite different in terms of what the bride and groom wear, what they do, and who witnesses the event. Nonetheless, weddings are powerful rituals because they denote movement from one phase of life to another—the transition between being single and being married. Historian Lewis Henry Morgan (1962) describes the marriage and wedding arrangements of the Iroquois tribe in early North America:

> Marriage was not founded upon the affections.... When the mother considered her son of a suitable age for a marriage, she looked about her for a maiden, whom she judged would accord with him in disposition and temperament. A negotiation between the mothers ensued, and a conclusion was reached.... Not the least singular of the transaction was the entire ignorance in which the parties remained of the pending negotiation. Objection on their part was never attempted; they received each other as the gift of their parents. When the fact of marriage had been communicated to the parties, a simple ceremonial completed the transaction. On the day following the announcement, the maiden was conducted by her mother, accompanied by a few friends, to the home of her intended husband. She carried in her hand a few cakes of unleavened corn bread, which she presented on entering the house, to her mother-in-law, as an earnest of her usefulness and of her skill in the domestic arts. After receiving it, the mother of the young warrior returned a present of venison, or other fruit of the chase, to the mother of the bride, as an earnest of his ability to provide for his household. This exchange of presents ratified and concluded the contract, which bound the new pair together in the marriage relations.

Regulation of Sexual Behavior

Every culture, including ours, regulates sexual behavior. Cultural norms make it clear who can have a sexual relationship with whom and under what circumstances. One virtually universal regulation is the **incest taboo**, which forbids sexual activity (and marriage) among close family members. The definition of "close family members" differs, although it usually involves at least parents and their children, and siblings. However, sometimes the taboo is extended to one side of the family but not to the other. For example, a person may be forbidden from having a sexual relationship with cousins on the mother's side, but a partner from the father's side of the family would be permitted.

Sexual relations among close relatives increase the chance of inherited genetic abnormalities. However, it is likely that the incest taboo originated not because of biology, but because of social considerations. It is a mechanism to minimize jealousies, competition, and conflict that could undermine smooth family functioning and lead to chaos (Ellis 1963). The incest taboo is also an important mechanism for forging broader alliances by requiring marriage outside of the inner family circle.

Reproduction and Socializing Children

For a society to continue, it must produce new members to replace those who die or move away. Families have the primary responsibility for producing the newest members and for teaching them the culture in which they live. Children learn the language, values, beliefs, interpersonal skills, and general knowledge necessary to adequately function in society primarily from their families (Parsons and Boles 1955). Societies generally encourage that reproduction be done inside established families rather than randomly among unrelated partners so that parents (or some prescribed family member) will be responsible for socializing children.

Property and Inheritance

As families moved from a nomadic lifestyle as hunters and gatherers to one based on agriculture, it became possible for the first time for people to accumulate surplus property beyond what was needed for sheer survival. Friedrich Engels (1902, original 1884) tied the origin of the family to males' desire to identify heirs so that they could pass down their property to their sons. Monogamy worked in men's favor. Without it, paternity was uncertain. Therefore, men sought to strictly control women sexually, economically, and socially through marriage.

Economic Cooperation

Adults and children have physical needs for food, shelter, and clothing. Families are the first line of defense for providing these to its members. Usually there is a gendered division of labor found among societies, with certain tasks primarily performed by men and others by women. However, exactly which tasks are considered masculine or feminine varies from one society to the next.

Families are both productive and consumptive units. In the past, families produced most of their goods and services such as making soap, spinning cloth, and growing food. In industrialized societies today, family members tend to work outside the home for wages and purchase many of the items they previously produced. Therefore, these families are largely considered consumptive units.

Social Placement, Status, and Roles

All members of society relate in some way to the basic structure of that society, usually in a way that preserves order and minimizes confusion and conflict. We fit in by way of a complex web of **statuses** (positions in a group or society) and **roles** (behaviors that are associated with those positions). Through our families, we are given an identity and position in society. For example, we are born into a certain social class, ethnic or racial group, religious affiliation, or geographic region. Statuses that we are born into are called **ascribed statuses**. Ones that we obtain on our own are called **achieved statuses**; these include our level of education or the type of job we hold. Our ascribed statuses give us an identity and a way of seeing the world. Likewise, they shape how others respond to us. A Hispanic teenage girl raised by parents who are migrant farm workers has a decidedly different social placement from that of the son of a prominent white family in New York City. Social statuses influence nearly all aspects of our lives. Much of what we think of as our unique "personality" or our unique choices really arise from our initial social placement with our family.

Care, Warmth, Protection, and Intimacy

In addition to food, shelter, and clothing, research indicates that humans need warmth and affection to survive and thrive. Families are intended to provide the care, warmth, protection, and intimacy that individuals need. However, not all families give equal weight to these features. For example, in many cultures, love and intimacy are not the primary reasons for marriage and, in fact, may be completely absent. It is common in some cultures for persons to marry without having met prior to their wedding day. Their parents arranged their marriages based on factors other than love, such as economics or the wish to cultivate certain kinship ties. Nonetheless, even in these unions the protection and care of spouses, extended family members, and children are primary functions.

These are some of the functions of families. Nonetheless, how these functions are performed can differ, as can the structure of marriage and family relationships. Let's now look at some of these differences.

WHAT DO YOU THINK?

Reflecting on your own family, can you see these functions operating? Are they all of equal importance or are some more or less important than others?

Differences in Marriage and Family Patterns

How do you intend to choose your mate (or how did you choose your mate)? Would it surprise you to learn that no one really has complete "free rein" in picking a marriage partner? In some countries, the external control is obvious and deeply rooted in cultural traditions. Fathers choose their son or daughter's marriage partner with little or no input from those who will be directly affected. Marriage is viewed as an economic union between two families rather than a relationship between two individuals based on love. The prospective bride and groom are often all too happy to give such a big responsibility over to their parents (Derne 2003; Griffith 2006).

In other countries, such as the United States, young people shudder at the thought of a parent choosing their future spouse. We prefer to base marriage on romantic love and mutual attraction (Acevedo and Aron 2009; Branden 2008; Sternberg and Sternberg 2008); parental involvement appears minimal. Yet, external control over mate selection still occurs, but is more subtle. Imagine the possible reactions from family when a person marries someone outside his or her race or ethnicity, wants to marry someone of the same sex, or when the age gap between partners is particularly large with the woman being much older. The sanctions can be minor or as severe as parental rejection.

External control over mate selection, whether in the United States or a country as rigid as Pakistan, operates through norms of endogamy and exogamy. **Endogamy** refers to norms that encourage marriage between people of the same social category, such as their own racial, ethnic, religious, age, or social class background. Although marrying outside our own social category may or may not be prohibited by law, it is sanctioned to varying degrees.

In contrast, **exogamy** refers to norms that encourage marriage between people of different social categories. For example, a person is required to choose a spouse from outside his or her immediate family or must only select a partner from the other sex. The precise norms fluctuate cross-culturally. For example, in many countries it is illegal for a person to marry a first cousin, whereas in other countries, a first cousin would be seen as an ideal mate.

If marriage is not strictly a private choice, then what is it based on? Ethnographic studies by anthropologists and sociologists reveal that most marriage and family patterns reflect social, economic, and political life in a given culture (Bonvillain 2010; Ember and Ember 2011). Some cultures allow men to have more than one wife, whereas others practice strict monogamy. In some cultures, the newly married couple virtually always resides with the husband's family. They would never consider the possibility of moving to their own household, yet this is the expected practice in the United States. There are cultures that expect brothers to live together and share one wife. These marriage and family practices are not simply random. From her anthropological work, Jean Stockard (2002) suggests that they reflect the following cultural practices and conditions:

■ *The physical environment, material goods, level of technology, and subsistence, and how these have shaped the social organization.* For example, as agriculture developed, family members were needed to contribute to the labor of agriculture. In particular, non-mechanized farming economies create and sustain extended families.

■ *The significance of descent ideology and structure—the clan, lineage, and descent line.* For example, how does the matrilineal structure in historical Iroquois society (organized around female lines of descent) structure both the organization of households and marriage, shaping the meaning of marriage for bride, groom, and their kin?

■ *Social processes, especially residence practices that reproduce and sometimes modify kinship structures across the generations.* For example, how does marriage as the Chinese practice it create families in each generation that continue to focus on sons and the chain of male descendants, and not on daughters?

The following box, "Our Global Community: Marriage Among the !Kung San of Southern Africa," addresses some of these specific issues among the !Kung San of Africa.

O U R
Global Community

Marriage Among the !Kung San of Southern Africa

It is easy to fall prey to the belief that everyone in the world practices marriage patterns similar to ours: In early adulthood you meet someone, fall in love with them, and marry them. A closer look around the world reveals patterns that are in striking contrast to ours.

The !Kung San are people now inhabiting territories bordering on the Kalahari Desert, primarily in Botswana, Namibia, and Angola. They are a branch of the San peoples, an indigenous people of Africa, numbering approximately 50,000 that once occupied a vast territory in southern Africa. Given the name "Bushmen" by European colonists, they call themselves the *Ju/'hoansi*, which means "the real people." Until the 1970s, when political and economic change forced an end to their traditional way of life, they were one of the several remaining contemporary populations in the world practicing hunting and gathering. This way of life, or *subsistence adaptation*, is believed to resemble the one characterizing all human populations prior to the development of agriculture about 10,000 years ago.

Marriage among the !Kung San resembles marriage as practiced by people for most of human history. The accounts of ethnographers report that girls were typically married very young, anywhere from age 8 to 12 on average. A new bride protested marriage in general and often her parents' choice of husband in particular. The marriage ceremony itself was, from the outsider's perspective, understated and hardly noticeable. The arrangement of marriage entailed the demonstration of hunting skills by the husband, who was expected to hunt after marriage not just for his wife, but more important, for her father.

New husbands were usually at least 18–25 years old, and sometimes as old as 30, creating a disparity in the ages of bride and groom of 10 years or more. Many if not most girls married before reaching their first menstrual period, but !Kung San feel strongly that marital sexual relations must not be consummated until the young wife is sexually mature. Indeed, they do not permit a husband, older and perhaps more anxious to begin sexual relations, to force himself on his young wife, believing it would make her crazy.

Ethnographic descriptions reveal an apparent connection between a *subsistence adaptation*, in this case hunting, and the practice of marriage.

Even hunting and gathering societies have complex family structures that reinforce many of the same functions that modern families provide.

In marrying, a husband assumes an obligation called *brideservice*: He must hunt for his father-in-law for many years not only to establish but also to maintain his marriage to the man's daughter.

Marriage is a relationship involving more than just the couple. There are at least three partners to marriage, including the husband and his young wife, but most important, his father-in-law, for whom the husband must hunt. With a large stake in the outcome, the parents arrange and negotiate the marriage, a matter far too important to be left to the passions and whims of the young people.

With the establishment of a !Kung San marriage, a newly married couple assumes residence in a small house built adjacent to the house of the young bride's parents. Through the distributions of meat from a son-in-law during brideservice, the boundaries of nuclear families are regularly crossed, linking the families of the bride and groom and her parents in an important economic relationship. In addition, gifts of meat that are received by the father-in-law are shared again by him to include his daughter's family.

These patterns identify that !Kung San society has no isolated nuclear families living apart unto themselves. Each is linked in important ways to other families, as the long process of brideservice dramatically emphasizes. Meat is so greatly valued that its distribution is not based on generalized reciprocity, but is shared according to an established protocol. The husband is expected to take the best cut, giving the prime piece to his wife's parents. Following this first-order distribution, waves of further sharing follow, ending in many gifts of meat to people in the band.

The giving of meat in this society in some sense creates a kind of politics: Giving of meat creates personal prestige in receiving a good cut of meat, and redistributing shares to others also creates obligations in them. Such giving is an important part of being male.

Source: Adapted from Stockard 2002.

CRITICAL THINKING QUESTIONS

1. Do you think that the gathering done primarily by women also creates a kind of politics? Why or why not?
2. How do you think this aspect of their culture has changed since the 1970s when tremendous economic and political changes occurred?

Marriage

Marriage has real consequences for the way we experience family life. There are expectations about whom and how we marry, where we should live, who should have power, and how we inherit and trace our lineage. What are some of the specific customs and practices around marriage throughout the world?

Monogamy   Most of us see marriage as a relationship between two partners (if not for a lifetime, at least for a period of time). We call this marriage pattern **monogamy**, from Greek meaning "one union." Monogamy doesn't allow individuals to have multiple spouses. Monogamy is practiced in many parts of the world, especially in developed nations. However, we can see on the map on pages 46–47 that in many parts of the world monogamy is

Comparative Marital Patterns

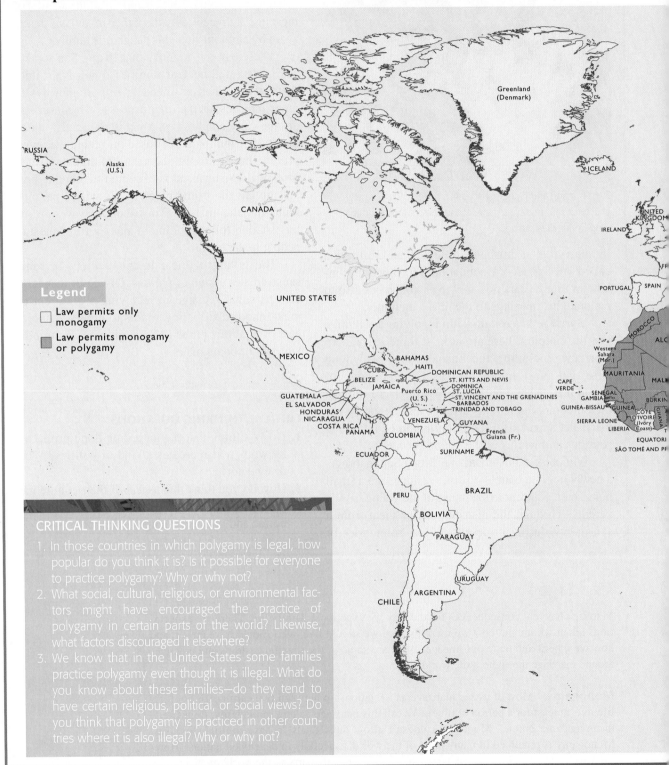

Legend

☐ Law permits only monogamy

▨ Law permits monogamy or polygamy

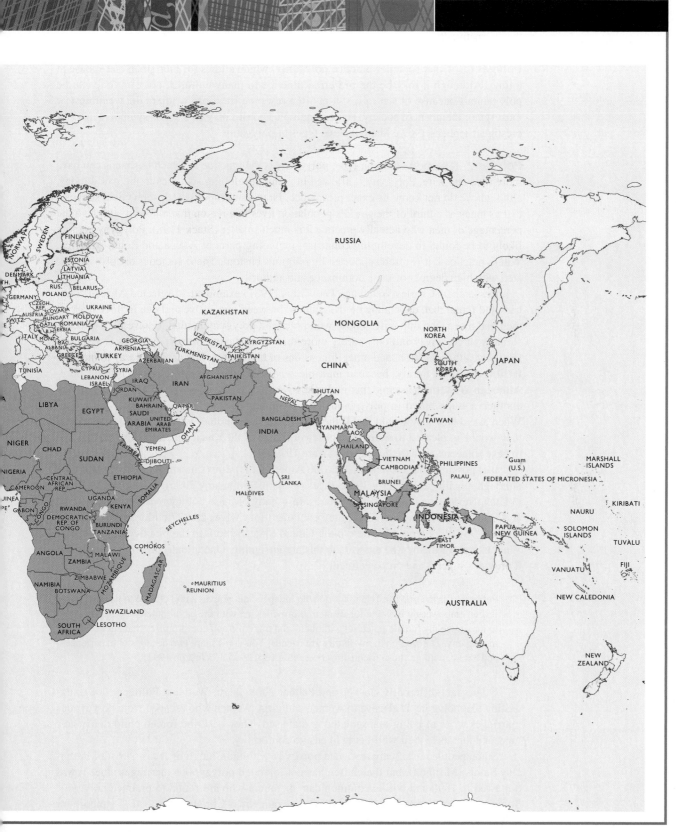

Source: Peters World Atlas 2001.

not the expected or preferred form of marriage. If monogamy is not universal, then what are the alternatives?

Polygamy   Other societies practice **polygamy**, which allows for more than one spouse at a time. Although it may be the preferred practice in many cultures, not everyone can be polygamous because of sex ratios. It is often reserved for those who are the wealthiest or most senior members of society. Having multiple spouses may be a status symbol, a mark of prestige (Stephens 1963). There are two types of polygamy.

Polygyny   The most common type, **polygyny**, is the practice in which husbands can have more than one wife. Polygyny is allowed in many developing societies in the world today, although we do not know its exact prevalence. Israeli anthropologist Joseph Ginat suggests that as many as a third of the world's population lives in a region that allows it, although the percentage of men who actually practice it is much smaller (Stack 1998). Polygyny is more likely to be found in developing countries, including parts of Africa and South America. Where practiced, it is often supported by religious custom. These societies are also associated with high degrees of male dominance and authority.

Researchers Charles Welch and Paul Glick (1981) examined 15 selected African countries and found that, depending on the country, between one in five and one in three married men had more than one wife. Those who practiced polygyny tended to have two, or occasionally three, wives and only rarely more than that. Having numerous wives is a sign of family wealth, education, and other dimensions of high status. It is used as a way to increase fertility within a family, because multiple wives increase the number of children born. Although Westerners assume that multiple wives would be jealous or competitive with one another, a study based in polygynous Nigeria indicated that the wives tend to get along. When asked how they would feel if their husbands took another wife, about 60 percent said they would be pleased to share the housework, care of their husband, and childrearing, and to have someone to share things with (Ware 1979).

It is possible that more than 100,000 American families currently practice polygyny, although it is illegal (Hagerty 2008; Tapestry against Polygamy 2006). It is primarily found in Utah, Nevada, and other western states. In a study of these polygynous families, Altman and Ginat found that, on average, they contained four wives and 27 children (Altman and Ginat 1996). Why would women in the United States submit to the practice of polygyny? What is in it for them? The answers to this are intriguing. One female supporter claims that it provides support and empowerment:

> Polygyny "is the one lifestyle that offers an independent woman a real chance to have it all . . . it is an empowering lifestyle for women. It provides me with the environment and opportunity to maximize my female potential without all the tradeoffs and compromises that attend monogamy. The women in my family are friends. You don't share two decades of experience, and a man, without those friendships becoming very special." (Joseph 1997)

Others feel differently (Jessop and Palmer 2008, 2010; Wall and Pulitzer 2008), suggesting that polygyny is abusive to women and girls. Women who escaped from polygynous marriages write of being manipulated and abused. They describe forced child marriages, rape, and threats to their well-being to ensure conformity.

Some people mistakenly associate polygyny with the Church of Jesus Christ of Latter-Day Saints (Mormon), but the church has not tolerated polygynous marriages since it was outlawed in 1890 and will excommunicate members who are found to practice polygyny. Some polygynous families are Muslims or evangelical Christians who find support for polygyny in the Quran and Bible.

Although illegal, more than 100,000 American families currently practice polygyny. One study found that, on average, polygynous families contained 4 wives and 27 children.

Despite all the media attention, many who practice polygyny lead quiet and unassuming lives, shy away from flamboyance and media attention, and in many ways are indistinguishable from other families. The box on pages 50–51, "Families as Lived Experience: Imagination: A Personal Ad from Adolph, Mary, and Megan," is an advertisement from an evangelical Christian living in Nevada looking for a third wife to join his family.

Polyandry   **Polyandry** is a marriage pattern in which several men share one wife. This type of marriage pattern is exceedingly rare and contains several unique features (Cassidy and Lee 1989; Stephens 1963). First, polyandry may occur in societies with difficult environmental conditions where poverty is widespread. It is practiced only in agricultural societies where land is severely limited and weather or other conditions are harsh. Second, the multiple husbands are usually brothers or otherwise related. They may, for example, belong to the same clan and be of the same generation. This minimizes jealousy or possessiveness. Third, the marriage often takes place because it is seen to provide economic advantages to the men involved. For example, one husband may recruit his brothers or clan to work on his land with him. Fourth, women's status is often low with a limited role in the productive economy. Girls may be seen as burdensome to families and an economic liability. Female infanticide may be practiced as a way of eliminating the need to care for girls, and therefore a shortage of women and girls for marriage may arise.

Anthropologist Jean Stockard (2002) describes the practice of polyandry among the members of the Tibetan Nyinba settlement in Nepal. The villages are established at elevations between 9,000 and 11,000 feet, and the mountainous terrain makes it difficult to support their agrarian lifestyle. Nyinba brothers are raised to cooperate both in marriage and in their labor so that the household can be sustained. Only a household with many sons will thrive in this environment, with at least one needed for agricultural work, others needed for small-scale cattle herding, and others involved in the long-distance salt trade, traveling with pack animals between Tibet and India, trading salt for grain. Marriage cannot break up the family or else they would all be impoverished. Nyinba males put cooperation above competition and jealousy. Therefore, all brothers share one wife. She marries into the family and moves into their household. As the sole woman, she does not have an elevated status; rather, she does the work that wealthier families give to slaves. She plows and weeds the fields, and performs all of the work of grain processing. She is also responsible for all domestic tasks and child care.

F A M I L I E S
as Lived Experience

Imagination: A Personal Ad from Adolph, Mary, and Megan

In truth, one does not even have to look around the world to find different marriage patterns. The following is a personal ad found on the Internet in which a family is looking for a third wife to join them. It is reprinted here, with permission from one of the wives, Mary. Although polygamy is not legal in the United States, it is practiced nonetheless in many families.

Hello, our family consists of my two wives and myself. We are all interested in our family becoming larger—if God blesses me with another wife. We are seeking a Christian lady with a kind spirit, who is levelheaded and has a positive attitude towards the Lord, their own life and towards others.

Let me tell you a little bit about us....

I am 50 years old, blond hair, blue eyes, 6 feet tall, and weigh 200 pounds. I work as a business consultant. My wives are 33 and 22 years old and they both help me in our business. We don't drink, smoke, or take drugs. We don't object to social drinking now and then. However, we do object to smoking.

We are all real home bodies. We enjoy quiet times at home alone and with friends and family. We only have a few friends and we have had them for a long time. We don't need to have a lot of neighbors or non-family around us to be happy. We value our privacy and those close to us. We find our home very enjoyable.

Mary likes to cook which is great because I like gourmet meals, especially when it is all natural and prepared at home. She also has an interest in gardening and really wants to learn to sew. Megan likes to read and discuss ideas. We all have a good sense of humor, sometimes odd, but always fun! We want a large family and plan to have children in the near future.

We are evangelical Christians. We are not legalistic nor do we believe in taboos. We study the Bible from taped classes for about an hour every night. God has given all of us instructions for life in written form, the Bible. An owner's manual for the soul. It only makes sense to learn what our Lord has to tell us. Then, of course, comes the challenging part; practicing what you know you should do. We find that taking in God's word daily and applying what we learn gives us a good basis for a strong spiritual life.

I became interested in plural marriage many years ago. My wives have learned about it since we got together. The Bible is very clear that God ordained marriage, sanctioning polygamy just as He did monogamy. There are many instances in the Bible where men practicing plural marriage were greatly blessed. God blesses people living according to His principles. I consider companionship, talking to one another, sharing thoughts and interests the most important factors in a relationship. I am affectionate, both physically and verbally. I believe mutual respect and relating honestly to others is vital to a permanent relationship.

My priorities in a relationship in order of importance are: Being loved, Companionship, Honesty, Respect, and lastly Sex. The best foundation for a good relationship is friendship. Deep friendships grow in intensity and last forever. Too much emphasis is put on sex today. You can't build a lasting relationship based only on sex. A friendship built on soul rapport is far more important and will last a lifetime. Then, sharing sexual intimacy, as an expression of genuine love, is very meaningful. We believe that marriage is a lifetime commitment. I don't believe in premarital sex and my wives are not interested in a bi-sexual relationship. We believe marriage must have a foundation built on Christian principles.

Communication is of primary importance to us. We like to discuss ideas and share personal feelings. Talking and relating to one another is so very important. We want to know how you feel, what makes you happy and what makes you sad. We don't want you to ever feel alone. We want you to know that you are supported by a family who cares, who will listen to you, who can meet your needs and a husband who cherishes you and our relationship. A good relationship is a long conversation that always seems too short. A lasting relationship depends on what each person can bring to the relationship instead of what they can take out of it. A good relationship is more than finding the right person, it is being the right person.

I am affectionate. I like to give hugs in the kitchen or cuddle during a movie. I like a woman to wrap her arms around me for no reason even when I'm busy working. I'm not a macho moron hung up on impressing dimwitted friends by neglecting you. I don't have to treat you like a slave in order to feel like a man. I am very secure in my masculinity. A woman is beautiful and designed to be feminine, responsive and loving. I enjoy a woman's companionship and affection very much.

We are looking for a woman who is positive toward the Bible and has Christian values. A woman who is a lady, gentle, loyal, faithful, and feminine. A woman who wants to wear dresses instead of Levis. A woman who wants to make a career of her husband, children, family, and home. A woman who is proud to be a wife and mother.

If you have children, they will find a home filled with lots of love, acceptance and most of all guidance. Your age is not a major issue. Friendship, honesty and respect are of utmost importance. Where you live, your past, or your economic circumstances are not at issue either. What is important is that we all get along and have the same values and principles to guide our lives and futures.

If you're interested in becoming friends, let's talk. Tell us what is important to you in life. What you like to do. What you're looking for in a relationship. What you want for your life in the future.

Source: Polygamy.com 2003. Reprinted by permission.

CRITICAL THINKING QUESTIONS

1. How do Adolph, Mary, and Megan compare to the stereotype of a polygamous family? How are they similar or different?
2. Adolph suggests that the Bible supports polygamy. Do you agree or disagree? On what basis do you agree or disagree?
3. Why do you think the United States outlaws polygamy? Do you think the United States should outlaw it?

All brothers in the household will share their wife sexually, rotating her among the men, and she is to show no favoritism. When she becomes pregnant, it is expected that she will have kept track of paternity. The Nyinba do admit that sometimes a wife will apportion paternity to a specific spouse just to make sure that all husbands have at least one offspring. As expected, sons are more highly valued than daughters, who might be denied food if it is in short supply (Stockard 2002).

Polyandry is not sanctioned by any religious groups in the United States, and in fact some that support polygyny denounce the practice of polyandry outright.

Patterns of Power and Authority

What are some ways in which power and authority are distributed in society?

Patriarchy   Women and men often receive drastically different treatment throughout the world (Brettell and Sargent 2009). The term **patriarchy**, which means rule of the father, refers to a form of social organization in which the norm is that men have a natural right to be in positions of authority over women. It is far more than an individual man controlling an individual woman. Patriarchy is manifested and upheld in a wide variety of social institutions, including legal, educational, religious, family, and economic institutions. For example, the legal system may rule that women must cover their faces or hair in public; the educational system may enforce unequal or no formal education for girls; family norms may prescribe that women only eat the leftover food after all males have finished their meal; and religious institutions may attribute male dominance to "God's will." Patriarchy is the most dominant form of authority pattern, and is particularly notable in politics, where men predominate. For example, in most of Africa, women hold less than 10 percent of parliamentary seats in government. Even in developed nations, women are grossly underrepresented. In the United States, women hold only about 20 percent of seats in the U.S. House of Representatives and Senate. Only in Rwanda and Sweden do women hold close to half of parliamentary seats (Population Reference Bureau 2010b).

Another example of patriarchy is reflected in the different literacy rates between men and women in many countries. The ability to read and write is crucial to accessing information and thereby increasing personal and political power. However, literacy rates among women aged 15–24 vary significantly, from a low of only about 40 percent in Pakistan and Bangladesh, to a high of virtually 100 percent in most developed nations (Population Reference Bureau 2010).

One final example is that of health care. Because women are so disvalued in many parts of the world, scant attention is paid to their health care needs. Yet, at the same time, their need for health care is exacerbated by patriarchy. Women and girls are more likely to suffer from malnutrition, sexual violence, and HIV/AIDS. Moreover, because many girls are married young, they also bear children when they are barely teenagers themselves, often without any prenatal care or trained personnel in attendance. This contributes to a host of reproductive health difficulties, including the epidemic of fistula—tearing of the tissue between the vagina and bladder or rectum (or both), resulting in chronic incontinence (The Fistula Foundation 2010; Wall 2006; World Health Organization 2010a). This issue, and the dramatic repercussions for women and their families are discussed in the following box "Our Global Community: Fistulas Are a Hidden Epidemic."

O U R

Global Community

Fistulas Are a Hidden Epidemic

Wubalem was a slight Ethiopian girl of 13 when she married her husband, a man she met for the very first time on her wedding day. She felt sad that she had to quit schooling in the seventh grade to marry him, but she otherwise liked her husband and felt that he was a good man. Within a year Wubalem was pregnant. When labor began, she felt it was more than she could bear, and she writhed in pain for many days. The women of the village tried to help deliver the baby, but were unsuccessful. She had no access to a nearby doctor or hospital, and finally the baby was delivered—dead. Unknown to her at the time, the obstructed labor also tore a hole in the tissue between her vagina, bladder, and rectum, and now she leaks urine and feces. Her family and community were ashamed of her and embarrassed by the smell.

Her husband wanted nothing more to do with her—she killed his baby, as he sees it—and kicked her out of their home. She went back to live with her parents, but they too felt she had shamed them, so they built a hut for her in the back of their house where she could live, alone.

A story like this is played out at least 100,000 times every year. Wubalem suffers from a fistula, a hole between her vagina and her internal organs. This hole develops over many days of obstructed labor, when the pressure of the baby's head against the mother's pelvis cuts off blood supply to delicate tissues in the region. The dead tissue falls away, and the woman is left with a hole between her vagina and her bladder, and sometimes her rectum as well. This hole results in permanent incontinence of urine and/or feces. The World Health Organization

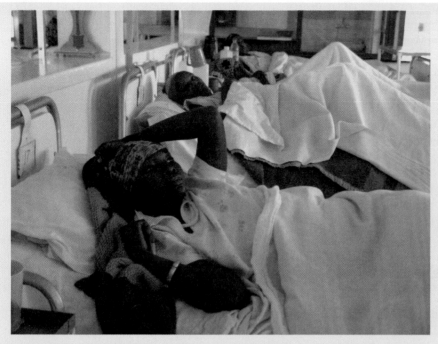

A grave public health concern is the number of women in developing countries who lack reproductive health care. One result of this is an epidemic of fistulas, a hole between the vagina and bladder and/or rectum, caused by obstructed labor.

status of girls and women. In developing nations, poverty and malnutrition stunt growth—a girl's skeleton, including her pelvis, does not fully mature. This stunted condition can contribute to obstructed labor, and therefore fistula. Couple this with very early marriage and childbearing, and we can see why fistulas are an epidemic in the developing world. Very little money is spent on women's reproductive health care—women's needs are low priority.

Yet, fistula can be treated and prevented. A fistula can be easily closed with surgery, and the patient has a good chance of returning to a normal life with full control of her bodily functions. The cost of the surgery is about U.S. $450, which includes the operation, high-quality postoperative care, and even a new dress and bus fare home. The Addis Ababa Fistula Hospital has treated more than 20,000 women over the past several decades. Their cure rate is over 90 percent. As for prevention, ready access to emergency obstetric care such as a C-section when complications arise could easily eliminate fistulas, as would delaying the age of first pregnancy. The bottom line for prevention is placing a greater value on women's lives.

Sources: Adapted from The Fistula Foundation 2010; World Health Organization 2010a.

CRITICAL THINKING QUESTIONS

1. Why do you think that so little attention has been given to this issue? Is the silence related to culture, shame, patriarchy, economics, or other factors?
2. Pretend you have unlimited resources, and are asked by the World Health Organization to develop a program to curb, treat, and/or eliminate fistulas. What would your program look like? Be sure to address the root cause.

estimates that approximately 2 million women have untreated fistula.

Fistulas are most prevalent in sub-Saharan Africa and Asia. They once were present in the United States, but were largely eliminated in the latter nineteenth century with improved obstetric care and the use of C-sections to relieve obstructed labor. Yet, nearly half of women in developing countries give birth without any trained personnel, and when complications arise no one is available to assist the woman, leading to injuries such as fistula and sometimes even death. Hospitals and personnel who can help them are often hundreds of miles away, and poor roads or a lack of transportation make travel difficult or impossible.

The majority of women who develop fistulas, like Wubalem, are abandoned by their husbands and ostracized by their communities because of their incontinence and foul smell. Most live the rest of their lives in shame, often alone. They fear going out in public because of the chronic leaking and smell.

The cause of fistulas may be obstructed labor, but the root causes are grinding poverty and the low

Matriarchy   A theoretical alternative to patriarchy is **matriarchy**, a form of social organization in which the norm or expectation is that the power and authority in society would be vested in women. I refer to this as a *theoretical alternative* because no known cases of true matriarchies have ever been recorded. It is sometimes confused with matrilineal, a kinship pattern discussed below, but in fact matriarchy is a decidedly different concept.

Egalitarian   In between these two extremes are authority patterns that could be best described as **egalitarian**. In these societies, the expectation would be that power and authority are equally vested in both men and women; for example, men and women are equally likely to be political leaders, serve in government, or influence public policy. Although the United States and many other countries are headed in this direction, it would be wrong to assume that all vestiges of patriarchy have been eliminated, as we will explore in Chapter 4.

Patterns of Kinship, Descent, and Inheritance

Where did you get your last name? How is property passed down? Who are considered to be your legal relatives? There are different ways in which a family's descent or heritage can be traced. These issues are important to sociologists and other family scientists because rules of kinship, descent, and inheritance can tell us how power is transmitted. It is common for families to pass on their wealth and assets to succeeding generations. At birth, a baby inherits two different bloodlines. We know that these are of equal importance genetically. Are these bloodlines also of equal *social* importance?

Bilateral   Developed nations most commonly use a **bilateral** pattern of descent, in which descent can be traced through both male and female sides of the family. Kin relationships are not restricted to only one parent's lineage, but recognize the lineage of both parents. For example, the United States recognizes that relatives can come from both a mother's side of the family *and* a father's side. Cousins, aunts, uncles, grandparents, and other kin can be traced to both bloodlines, which are of equal importance.

Patrilineal   A bilateral approach may seem common sense to most readers of this book; however, also common is a **patrilineal** pattern, in which lineage is traced exclusively (or at least primarily) through the man's family line. A patrilineal society would recognize a father's relatives as kin, but minimal (or at least different) connections would be established with a mother's side of the family. It is important to note that vestiges of patrilineal descent can also be seen in the United States, which practices a bilateral model. For example, most women routinely take their husband's last name when they marry. The changing of wives' names is a carryover from when, upon marriage, a woman became the legal property of her husband, and his lineage was the most important.

Matrilineal   A few societies can be characterized as having **matrilineal** descent patterns, characterized as having the lineage more closely aligned with women's families rather than men's families. This is not the exact opposite of a patrilineal pattern, however. In a matrilineal descent pattern it is not women who are in positions of power to pass on their lineage, but rather women pass it on through their family side via their brothers or other male members of the family. Even in a matrilineal society men retain the control over their lineage. A child raised in a matrilineal society could have little to do with his or her biological father, at least where lineage is concerned. The biological father may retain ties of affection, but it is the child's maternal uncles who are key male figures in the child's life, at least with respect to patterns of kinship, descent, and inheritance.

Patterns of Residence

Much can be learned about the role of marriage, family, and kinship by examining the norms surrounding the residential patterns of a newly married couple. Jean Stockard (2002) suggests that the postmarital residence pattern is a cultural practice critical to understanding broad marriage, family, and kinship dynamics: "Postmarital residence generates inequalities, which characterize relationships of the genders in societies everywhere. These inequalities are culturally constructed differently from those found in the United States.... postmarital residence... is at the heart of the analysis of marriage and gender."

Neolocal   In industrial societies like the United States, the expectation is for the couple to live separately from either set of parents. This is referred to as **neolocal**, where the newly married couple establishes its own residence and lives there independently. Sometimes a young couple will live with a parent temporarily for financial considerations (Goldscheider and Goldscheider 1994; Savage and Fronczek 1993). For example, a young couple may co-reside with either the wife or husband's parents while they go to school or save to buy a house. Nonetheless, the general expectation in the United States and most developed nations is for couples to establish their own residences immediately after marriage.

Patrilocal   However, in other parts of the world **patrilocal** residence is normative. In these countries, it is expected that the newly married couple will live with the husband's family. As shown in the chapter-opening vignette, patrilocal patterns are common in many Asian countries and other places in the world where greater emphasis is placed on extended families and patriarchy. These cultural values may then be brought to the United States as they immigrate.

Matrilocal   Far less common is a **matrilocal** pattern, in which the expectation is that the newly married couple will live with the family of the wife. Most are based on the subsistence adaptation of horticulture and use simple hoes or digging sticks, and engage in only minimal or distant warfare (Ember and Ember 2011). An example of a matrilocal culture was found among the North American Iroquois.

Modernization Theory: Social Change and Families

As societies are touched by industrialization, they undergo a process that sociologists call **modernization**. Modernization is a process of social and cultural transformation from traditional (or "third-world") societies to modern industrial societies, which touches many aspects of social life. It changes social relationships by increasing social differentiation and alters the division of labor in society. Kinship ties weaken, and nuclear families tend to predominate over extended family forms. Fertility rates decline and life expectancy increases. Some of the changes are positive, such as a higher standard of living for many people, whereas other changes are problematic, such as increased pollution.

Sociologist Peter Berger (1977) described a number of characteristics associated with the process of modernization, including:

- The decline of small cohesive communities in which social interaction occurred within primary groups of family and close friends
- The decline of traditions and expansion of personal choice
- Increasing diversity and change
- A focus on the future
- A decline in the importance of religious institutions

The Loss of Community: Gemeinschaft and Gesellschaft

German sociologist Ferdinand Tonnies (1963) suggested that modernization represents a progressive loss of **gemeinschaft** or the intimacy found in primary relationships. Prior to industrialization, families lived for generations in or near the same small community or rural village. People identified with one another, and relationships were personal and enduring. A sense of belonging to the group usually outweighed personal differences. Families were the pillars of society, family members were highly dependent on each other, divorce was rare, and patriarchy was the norm.

Tonnies argued that industrialization changed the fabric of social life. Industrialization, and the urbanization that follows, result in a society of largely impersonal secondary relationships, called **gesellschaft**. There is little sense of belonging to a cohesive group, fewer personal ties, and people are more likely to put their own needs above those of others. The role of families is more diffuse, with other secondary relationships taking over many functions normally performed within the family.

World Revolution and Family Patterns

Sociologist William J. Goode (1963, 1993) used existing data from several regions of the world including sub-Saharan Africa, India, China, Japan, and several countries in the Middle East to examine how industrialization and modernization affected family patterns, including such issues as mate selection, kinship, marital relationships, and divorce. He argued that industrialization and modernization changed families in radical ways for a number of reasons, including the geographic mobility that occurred in search of factory jobs in the cities; the resulting social mobility that occurred as people were trained into a new class of jobs as managers and supervisors; the changing emphasis from ascribed to achieved status; and the increasing specialized division of labor. Work was something increasingly performed away from the family, and men and women's roles within the family were beginning to be differentiated as never before. What changes in the family resulted from industrialization and modernization, according to Goode? These changes include a shift to the conjugal nuclear family, which entailed the following:

1. *Mate selection became freer.* Goode found that as societies developed, young adults played a greater role in selecting a spouse. Parental control waned. Young adults had greater opportunities to interact with each other without the supervision of parents and other chaperones, and romantic love became an important ingredient for marriage.
2. *A shift away from extended families.* Industrialization led to a shift from extended families, which may have been less practical with geographic mobility, to nuclear families.

Families became more isolated from their extended kin network and from the community more generally. Families also became smaller because children were increasingly viewed as an economic liability, rather than the asset they were on the farm.

3. *Kinship evolved toward bilateral.* Goode reported that when countries undergo industrialization, they tend to move toward a bilateral rule of descent, rather than remaining patrilineal or matrilineal. With industrialization, fewer people owned extensive property to be handed down to a narrowly defined set of heirs.

4. *Families became more egalitarian.* Goode found that patriarchal norms declined as countries developed. Along with the rise of romantic love as a basis for marriage, spouses emphasized the companionate nature of their relationship. However, even with the advent of industrialization, women were (and in some places still are) still denied basic rights such as voting privileges, the right to initiate divorce, or the ability to own property.

World Systems Theory: Social Change and Families

Drawing upon a conflict paradigm, some family scholars see that changes in families can be traced to changing global economic markets and political structures, a perspective called **world systems theory**. Nations, cultures, and family norms do not exist in isolation; rather, every country is inextricably tied to others in the world. Just as individuals cannot be understood without considering the cultural systems in which they live, individual nations cannot be understood without considering the world system in which they are imbedded.

Immanual Wallerstein's works *The Modern World System* (1974) and *The Modern World System II* (1980) highlight the linkages, interdependence, and exploitation among economies between nations and how these influence virtually all dimensions of social life, including family structure. The capitalist world economy is predicated on the wealth of some using the resources of others to further enhance their own wealth. The interdependence of

World systems theory highlights the economic linkages and exploitation occurring between nations, and how these influence virtually all dimensions of life, such as the child labor shown here.

nations has resulted in a modern world in which some countries remain impoverished and debt-ridden because they are exploited by other countries that have amassed great wealth at their expense. According to this perspective, the "core" countries, primarily the United States, Western Europe, and Japan, use their historical advantages to manipulate countries for their own benefit by extracting resources, profits, and cheap labor; by promoting or allowing debt; and by destroying the environment in the poorer countries. Consequently, poorer periphery and semiperiphery nations cannot industrialize or modernize and remain impoverished, in debt, with an environment that is quickly being destroyed and largely under the control of core nations often through transnational corporations.

This economic and political dependence affects family structure and family interaction in poor nations in many ways. For example, rural families in impoverished periphery nations may move from producing food crops that support traditional family structures to cash crops that are regulated by world prices. As a result, men, especially young men, must migrate to cities to find ways to support their families while women stay home and work in agriculture and raise children. This sex-based pattern of segregated migration often keeps families poor and isolated. Increasingly, mothers too are leaving children behind as they must go off to other communities (or countries) to earn a living (Goulbourne et al. 2010; Parrenas 2005).

Families Around the World: India, Japan, and Sweden

Since families are shaped by the culture in which they live, let's now look at three contrasting cultures to see how families differ—India, Japan, and Sweden.

Developing Nations, Example: India

India is one of the world's poorest nations. It is also one of the most populous at over 1.2 billion persons (Central Intelligence Agency 2010). It is the second most populous country in the world after China, but because of China's powerful one-child policy that strictly limits the number of births to one child per family (or two births in some circumstances), India could soon overtake China for the number one position.

How poor is India? The United Nations compares the purchasing power parity (PPP) of people in different countries in terms of what the money can buy in a local economy. Wealthy countries such as the United States, Canada, Japan, and Switzerland have a very high PPP, at least $29,000 per person. In a poor country like India, the PPP hovers around $3,100. This compares to at least $8,000 for most of Eastern Europe or $7,642 for China. However, much poorer countries can be found: The PPP for Ethiopia, for example, is around $900 (Central Intelligence Agency 2010). Nonetheless, India is recognized throughout the world as a poor nation, struggling to keep its people fed, clothed, and housed.

India recognized early on that its high fertility rate would impoverish its people further. Therefore, since independence in the 1950s, India has launched an aggressive campaign to reduce the number of births. This has been a difficult process, given the low education and literacy rates of many Indians, yet family planning programs have had some success. As shown in Figure 2.1, the crude birthrate has fallen from about 45 per 1,000 population in 1951 to nearly 20 children today, and is expected to fall to 17 per 1,000 by 2025

Figure 2.1 **Crude Birthrate (per 1,000 population), 1950–2025 (estimate) for India, Japan, Sweden, and the United States**

Birthrates have dropped significantly since 1950. India's still remains high, while Japan's is very low.

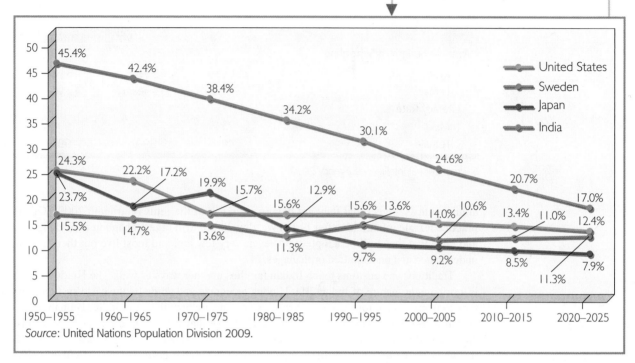

Source: United Nations Population Division 2009.

(United Nations Population Division 2009). However, given the high number of women of childbearing age, the population continues to grow rapidly.

A disturbing result of the quest to reduce the number of children is a growing sex ratio imbalance. In the natural order, slightly fewer females are born than males. Males are more likely to die in infancy (as is the case throughout the life course); therefore, the initial oversupply of males at birth contributes to a more balanced sex ratio in later life. Yet, in many parts of India the number of girls born is significantly below what would occur naturally. Overall, in India, there were 112 males for every 100 females in 2005 (Central Intelligence Agency 2010). Data from some Indian states show as many as 123 boys for every 100 girls (Premi 2002). There are more than 20 million fewer girls than boys between the ages of birth to 14. What accounts for the gross imbalance?

A clue can be found in India's practice of patriarchy (Agnes 2001; Amnesty International USA 2010). When parents have children, they have a strong preference for boys over girls because boys are viewed as economic assets, whereas girls are seen as liabilities (Patrikar et al. 2008). Spending precious family resources on girls is viewed as wasteful because it is assumed that girls will someday marry and leave the family. Often, girls are provided with less food, schooling, and medical care when these are in short supply; boys are breastfed longer than girls, and they are more likely to be fully vaccinated (Central Intelligence Agency 2010; IIPS and ORC Macro 2000). Table 2.1 compares the literacy rates and average length of schooling among males and females, and shows that females are significantly disadvantaged.

Where did all the girls go? With the push toward smaller families and with patriarchy operating so prominently, it is surmised that some parents who, through ultrasound or

TABLE 2.1 Educational Statistics: India, Japan, and Sweden

Girls have less value than boys among many parents in India and receive less education. Less than half of the women in India can read and write.

	INDIA	JAPAN	SWEDEN
Average Length of Schooling			
Male	11 years	15 years	16 years
Female	9 years	15 years	17 years
Literacy Rate			
Male	73%	99%	99%
Female	48%	99%	99%

Source: Central Intelligence Agency 2010.

amniocentesis, detect that they are having a girl, abort the fetus (Gurunath 2009). Others practice female infanticide after birth (Westley 2002). Still others abandon their daughters and hope that they will be adopted; however, very few are, and most live out their lives in underfunded and understaffed orphanages.

Traditions and customs touch Indian families in other ways as well. The Hindu religion is a prominent feature of Indian life. Hindus recognize and abide by the caste system, even though many distinctions made on the basis of caste are now illegal in India (Human Rights Watch 2009). For example, Hindus in India believe that persons in a higher caste will be "polluted" if they are in contact with someone of a lower standing. The *untouchables* or Dalits, who number nearly 40 million, may not enter the higher-caste sections of villages, may not use the same wells, wear shoes in the presence of others, or visit the same temples. Dalit children are frequently made to sit in the back of classrooms, and adults and children work in near slave-like conditions. Men often abuse Dalit women, girls are married off at young ages, and the police ignore women's complaints (International Humanist and Ethical Union 2010).

Cultures in Transition, Example: Japan

Unlike India, Japan is a highly developed nation, yet Japan has a tradition steeped in segregated and traditional gendered expectations (Mackie 2010). Women and men's roles in work,

family, and other social institutions are still highly differentiated, and somewhat unusual for a developed nation (Lee et al. 2010). For example, fewer mothers are employed full-time outside the home in Japan than in any other developed nation. Women's work is typically not on any career path, they hold few managerial or professional positions, and they do the vast majority of the housework and child care (Ishii-Kuntz 2004a, 2004b, 2006; Lee et al. 2010; National Women's Education Center, Japan 2009).

Marital and family roles are more divided in Japan than in many other developed nations, including the United States (Ishii-Kuntz 2004c). Husbands often have a workday that extends well into the evening and requires them to socialize with co-workers or clients. With husbands' extended absences from home, most childrearing and other domestic tasks fall on the shoulders of women—but it is not simply that these jobs require long absences from home. Instead, an interplay of sex and the economy operates; when women hold these jobs, they are still expected to take care of domestic responsibilities. The result is that Japanese fathers are less involved in their children's lives on a daily basis than are American fathers.

However, marriage and family life are exceedingly important in the lives of the Japanese. One example of this commitment to the family is the comparatively very low rate of divorce (United Nations Statistics Division 2010). This lower rate is likely due to several features of Japanese culture and family life: (1) Japanese culture stresses conformity and subordination of individual needs to those of the larger group; (2) the loss of income could be devastating to wives who, if employed, likely earn considerably less than husbands; and (3) closeness and co-residence with other family may buffer the effects of problematic marriages, because Japanese marriages are rarely couple-centered.

Despite the centrality of marriage and family in the heart of Japanese culture, trends show that some big changes are taking place. One such change is that fewer women are marrying, and those that do are marrying much later than ever before (Kashiwase 2002; Ministry of Internal Affairs and Communications 2009). According to national data, the median age at first marriage for women increased from 24 years in 1970 to nearly 29 years in 2008 (Ministry of Internal Affairs and Communications 2009).

Most of this change is a result of delaying rather than forgoing marriage. There are several reasons for delaying marriage, including (1) a growing gap in attitudes regarding women's roles in society; (2) increases in women's education and labor force participation; (3) an imbalance in the number of men to women; and (4) the increase in the attractiveness of single life, while at the same time a decrease in the attractiveness of traditional marriages. In the 1997 book *Japan: The Childless Society*, Muriel Jolivet outlines the pressures on women that make bearing and raising children unattractive. She suggests that the Japanese government, concerned about a birthrate that is far below replacement level, criticizes women who choose not to have children as being selfish. Only recently has the government approved birth control for widespread use, long after the rest of the world considered it safe and approved it—yet Viagra, the pill for male impotence, won approval in Japan quickly, further pointing to a double standard (Kageyama 1999).

Some women in Japan are now resisting these social pressures. Fewer women are bearing children, and those who do often have them relatively late in life, and are limiting their number. The average age for becoming a mother was 26 in 1975 and nearly 30 in 2008 (Ministry of Internal Affairs and Communications 2009). Twenty-one percent of births were to mothers age 35 and over. As Figure 2.1 shows, Japan's birthrate has declined to just 8.7 today. Japan's birthrate is expected to decline even further to 7.9 by 2025, well below replacement level. Coupled with the small number of young people and large number of elderly in Japan, as shown in Table 2.2, especially compared to India, Japan will have a low birthrate for many years to come.

TABLE 2.2 Age Structure of Population by Country

India has a high number of children; therefore, it is likely that they will continue to have a high birthrate well into the future. Japan and Sweden, in contrast, have an aging population.

	2005			**2030 (PROJECTION)**		
	0–14 years	**15–64**	**65 and over**	**0–14 years**	**15–64**	**65 and over**
India	33%	62%	5%	23%	69%	8%
Japan	14%	66%	20%	10%	59%	32%
Sweden	17%	65%	17%	17%	60%	23%

Source: Ministry of Internal Affairs and Communications 2009.

Toward Equality, Example: Sweden

Sweden is an interesting country in which to examine marriage and family patterns. It is one of the world's wealthiest nations and its people enjoy a high standard of living. The birthrate is low, but is expected to rise by 2025, as shown in Figure 2.1. Swedes are also healthy; life expectancy is at or near the world's highest. The **infant mortality rate**, defined as the number of deaths within the first year of life per 1,000 births in the population, is about 2 per 1,000. Japan's infant mortality rate is only slightly higher than Sweden, at 3 per 1,000. In contrast, the infant mortality rate in the United States is more than three times that of Sweden, whereas India's is more than 27 times higher, as shown in Figure 2.2 (Population Reference Bureau 2010b).

Swedes have sometimes been criticized as anti-family because, compared to their counterparts in the United States, they are less likely to marry and more likely to cohabitate and have children outside the confines of legal marriage. Sweden has one of the highest average ages at first marriage and one of the lowest marriage rates found anywhere in the world (Popenoe 2005). If current trends continue, only about 60 percent of Swedish women today will ever marry compared to over 85 percent of women in the United States. Instead of marrying, many Swedes prefer cohabitation.

However, these data should not necessarily be interpreted as an anti-family sentiment. Even David Popenoe (2005), a well-known advocate for traditional marriage, family, and

Figure 2.2   **2010 Infant Mortality Rate per 1,000 Births for India, Japan, Sweden, and the United States**

India has a very high infant mortality rate, whereas Japan's and Sweden's rates are very low. Note that the infant mortality rate in the United States is 2–3 times that of Japan or Sweden or other developed nations.

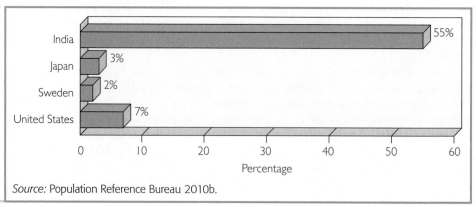

Source: Population Reference Bureau 2010b.

social relationships, says: "What most Americans don't realize is that, in a strict comparison, Scandinavia is probably preferable to the United States today as a place to raise young children."

Family life inside and outside of marriage is valued in Sweden. In fact, Swedish men are considerably *more* likely to live in a household with children, including their own biological children, than are American men (Olah et al. 2003). In other words, although fewer Swedes are married, they are not rejecting family life and committed relationships. Children born within cohabiting relationships are not stigmatized, nor are their unmarried parents.

The vast majority of mothers in Sweden are employed outside the home. A major difference between the United States and Sweden is the degree of public support provided to children and their families (Hasson 2009; Popenoe 2005; Zimmerman 2001). For example, new parents in Sweden have generous maternity and paternity leaves during which they continue to receive pay, benefits, and a job guarantee (Hasson 2009; Ministry of Health and Social Affairs 2005; Ministry of Integration and Gender Equality 2009). These benefits are also available to fathers. Nonemployed parents are eligible as well for a flat-rate benefit for the same period as the leave for employed parents.

Families also receive a **child/family allowance**, a grant from the government for each child. Families having three or more children receive an increase in benefits. The government provides these grants to help defray the costs of raising children. Generous housing allowances are also available to families with children so that citizens pay no more than 40 percent of their income in rent. Moreover, child care is subsidized by the government if a parent is in school or employed at least 20 hours per week, and parents are charged relatively modest fees based on their income. Married, cohabiting, and single parents are eligible for these benefits. These policies were enacted to (1) encourage more couples to have children, because the birthrate in Sweden was dropping sharply; (2) encourage more women to work outside the home, because Sweden had the need for additional workers; and (3) keep pace with Sweden's changing conceptions of gender and movement toward greater egalitarianism.

Gendered expectations in Sweden continue to move towards equality, and the government makes a concerted effort to push for an equal distribution of power and influence (Ministry of Integration and Gender Equality 2009). For example, for the years 2007–2010, the Swedish government increased the allocation for gender equality policy measures tenfold, and decreed, "As a result of this budget increase, gender equality policy can develop, become more vigorous and play a more active role. A gender equality perspective is to permeate all government policies" (Ministry of Integration and Gender Equality 2009).

Sweden's commitment to gender equality has paid off. As shown in Figure 2.3, women are relatively well represented in the labor force and as members of parliament (Hasson 2009). Moreover, Swedish men spend more time doing household tasks than do men in the United States, Denmark, Norway, Finland, or Hungary (Swanbrow 2002). About half of respondents in a Swedish national survey believed that the ideal family situation with children less than seven years of age is for "both parents to work, either full-time or part-time and share the responsibility for home and children equally." Almost two-thirds agreed entirely that "in order to make a marriage or a nonmarital cohabitation successful, it is important that both have jobs they like" (Olah et al. 2003). However, despite this sentiment and Sweden's public effort to equalize domestic relationships, the primary responsibility for household chores and child care continues to fall to women (Swanbrow 2002).

Figure 2.3 **Status of Women in Sweden**

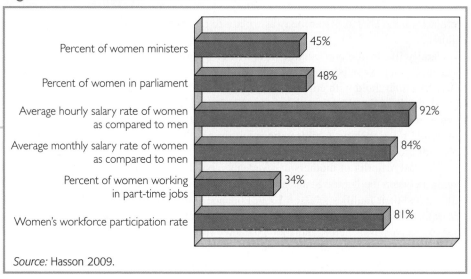

Sweden may be the most egalitarian country in the world, although they too have a way to go to achieve full equality.

Percent of women ministers 45%

Percent of women in parliament 48%

Average hourly salary rate of women as compared to men 92%

Average monthly salary rate of women as compared to men 84%

Percent of women working in part-time jobs 34%

Women's workforce participation rate 81%

Source: Hasson 2009.

Conclusion

This chapter reveals both the universal functions and variation in structure within marriage, family, and kinship patterns throughout the world. Families are found in every society because they perform functions that other social institutions cannot perform—yet families are not monolithic. As a social institution they reflect the environment, historical period, and culture in which they are found. Moreover, families are not static, but are continually adapting to changing circumstances. Two perspectives are presented that contrast the nature of social change upon families: modernization theory and world systems theory. Although the latter focuses more on the economic and political interdependence and exploitation found among nations, both agree that processes such as industrialization transform the culture and the environment, and therefore reshape the form, function, and roles within families.

Key Terms

Achieved statuses: Statuses achieved on one's own. (p. 42)

Ascribed statuses: Statuses that a person is born with, such as his or her sex, racial and ethnic background, and social class. (p. 42)

Bilateral: Descent can be traced through both male and female sides of the family. (p. 54)

Child/family allowance: A cash grant from the government for each child. (p. 63)

Egalitarian: The expectation that power and authority are equally vested in men and women. (p. 54)

Endogamy: Norms that encourage marriage between people of the same social category. (p. 43)

Exogamy: Norms that encourage marriage between people of different social categories. (p. 43)

Gemeinschaft: A type of society that emphasizes the intimacy found in primary relationships. (p. 56)

Gesellschaft: A type of society that is based on largely impersonal secondary relationships. (p. 56)

Incest taboo: A rule forbidding sexual activity (and marriage) among close family members. (p. 41)

Infant mortality rate: The number of deaths within the first year of life per 1,000 births in the population. (p. 62)

Matriarchy: A form of social organization in which the norm is that the power and authority in society would be vested in women. (p. 54)

Matrilineal: A descent pattern characterized as having the lineage more closely aligned with women's families rather than men's families. (p. 54)

Matrilocal: The married couple is expected to live with the family of the wife. (p. 55)

Modernization: A process of social and cultural transformation from traditional societies to modern societies that influences all dimensions of social life. (p. 55)

Monogamy: The law or custom that does not permit individuals to have multiple spouses. (p. 45)

Neolocal: The married couple is expected to establish its own residence and live there independently. (p. 55)

Patriarchy: A form of social organization in which the norm is that men have a natural right to be in positions of authority over women. (p. 51)

Patrilineal: A descent pattern in which lineage is traced exclusively (or at least primarily) through the man's family line. (p. 54)

Patrilocal: A married couple will live with the husband's family. (p. 55)

Polyandry: The marriage pattern that involves one woman and several husbands. (p. 49)

Polygamy: A law or custom that allows for more than one spouse at a time (gender unspecified). (p. 48)

Polygyny: The marriage pattern in which husbands can have more than one wife. (p. 48)

Roles: Behaviors associated with social positions in society. (p. 42)

Statuses: Social positions in a group or society. (p. 42)

World systems theory: A perspective that focuses on the economic and political interdependence and exploitation among nations. (p. 57)

Resources on the Internet

American Anthropology Association

www.aaanet.org

A professional organization designed to further the professional interests of anthropologists and to disseminate anthropological knowledge and its use to address human problems.

Genealogy.com

www.genealogy.com

This website will help you start your family tree, search for ancestors, and share your discoveries with family and friends.

Human Relations Area Files

www.yale.edu/hraf/

An internationally recognized organization in the field of cultural anthropology at Yale University; the mission of

Human Relations Area Files (HRAF) is to encourage and facilitate comparative studies.

National Geographic Society

www.nationalgeographic.com

This site from the National Geographic Society offers information on world cultures, the environment, kinship, maps, and magazines for children; it also provides links to related topics.

Polygamy.com

www.polygamy.com

The purpose of this site is to provide a resource for people who wish to move beyond monogamy. It promotes plural marriage by encouraging "honorable individuals" wishing to pursue polygamy as the marriage structure for their family.

CHAPTER 3

Families Throughout History

CHAPTER OUTLINE

Why Study Family History? 68

   ■ **USING** *the Sociological Imagination:* Piecing Together the History of Family Life **70**

Families in Preindustrial Societies 72

Family Life in the Preindustrial United States 73

American Families in the Nineteenth Century 79

Families in the Twentieth Century: The Rise of the "Modern" Family 82

   ▦ **SOCIAL** *Policies for Families:* The Nineteenth Amendment Is Ratified **83**

   ■ **FAMILIES** *as Lived Experience:* Coming of Age in the Depression **85**

Recent Family Issues and Their Historical Roots 86

   Conclusion 88

   Key Terms 89

   Resources on the Internet 89

CHAPTER PREVIEW

One of the best ways to understand where families are going is to understand where they have been. We often glorify families of the past, but social historians have taught us that many issues families face today are not unique and have their roots in the past. Thus, we can learn much from exploring family history. In this chapter, you will learn:

- Why we bother to explore family history, and how social historians piece together the history of family life

- How families operated in hunting-gathering, horticultural, and agrarian societies

- How family life varied in the preindustrial United States for Native Americans, European colonists, African Americans in slavery, and Mexicans

- Changes brought by industrialization, urbanization, and immigration

- The "modern" family was shaped by national events, including the two world wars, the Great Depression, and the post–World War II baby boom of the 1950s

- The 1960s and 1970s brought tremendous social changes to families and intimate relationships

- Today's relationship between families and the economy has important social roots

The following narrative describes the life of a young slave girl in nineteenth-century America who is forced to have a sexual relationship with a man she detests so that her owner can have more slave children. As heartbreaking as such an account is, what can we learn from history that has relevance today?

"Massa Hawkins am good to he niggers and not force 'em work too hard. Massa Hawkins 'lows he niggers to have reason'ble parties and go fishin', but we'uns am never tooken to church and has no books for larnin'. Dere am no education for de niggers.

Dere am one thing Massa Hawkins does to me when I can't chunt from my mind. I knows he don't do it for meanness, but I allus holds it 'gainst him. What he done am force me to live with dat nigger, Rufus, 'gainst my wants.

After I been at he place 'bout a year de massa come to me and say 'You gwine live with Rufus in dat cabin over yonder. Go fix it for livin'. 'I's 'bout sixteen year old. I took charge of de cabin after work am done and fixes supper. Now, I don't like that Rufus, 'cause he a bully.

We'uns has supper, den I goes here and der talkin' till I's ready for sleep and den I gits in de bunk. After I's in, dat nigger come and crawl in de bunk with me 'fore I knows it. I says, 'what you means, you fool nigger?' He say for me to hush de mouth. 'Dis am my bunk, too,' he say.

De nex' day I goes to de missy and tells her what Rufus wants and missy dat am de massa's wishes. She say, "yous am de portly gal and Rufus am de portly man. De massa wants you-uns fer to bring forth portly chillen.

I's thinkin' 'bout what de missy say, but say to myself, 'I's not gwine live with dat Rufus. 'Dat night when him come in de cabin, I grabs de poker and sits on de bench and says, 'Git 'way from me, nigger, 'fore I bust yous brains out and stomp on dem. He say nothin' and git out.

De nex' day de massa call me and tell me, 'Woman, I's pay big money for you and I's done date for de cause I wants yous to raise me chillens. I's put you to live with Rufus for dat purpose. Now, if you doesn't want whipping at de stake, yous do what I wants.

I thinks 'bout massa buyin me offen de block and savin' me from bein' sep'rated from my folks and 'bout bein' whipped at de stake. Dere it am. What am I's to do? So I 'cides to do as massa wish ans so I yields." (Adapted from Federal Writers Project 1936)

Why bother with history? Why not just focus on the here and now?

An historical perspective shows how social structure affects the ways families are organized and how it influences the rights, responsibilities, and roles exercised among specific family members. Many "current" family issues have their roots firmly planted in the past, and the more we know about history, the better we can understand today's families.

This chapter provides an historical overview of families. It is by necessity a brief and highly selective synopsis because the literature is extensive. The goal is to show that current attitudes, behaviors, and public policies affecting courtship, mate selection, cohabitation, marriage, sexuality, children, the elderly, and extended families are intricately interwoven with the past.

Why Study Family History?

There is widespread concern today that the family is in great trouble (The National Marriage Project 2009; Whitehead and Popenoe 2005). Family researchers David Popenoe, Barbara Dafoe Whitehead, and W. Bradford Wilcox from The National Marriage Project voice alarm about what they see as significant changes in the family, including America's relatively high divorce rate; the growth in single motherhood; the large number of people who choose not to marry or choose not to have children; the growth in children whose parents (i.e., mothers) work full-time; and the increasing numbers of people who choose to cohabit instead of marrying. They see these trends as indications that marriage is being neglected, children are no longer the center of families, and the importance of fathers is marginalized.

The popular media—television shows, newspapers, and magazines—bombard us with stories about the demise of the family. We hear that there were fewer problems in the "good old days": life was easier, family bonds were stronger, families had more authority, and people were happier. Today, abortion, divorce, teenage sex and parenthood, homosexuality, juvenile delinquency, and poverty are only some of the consequences attributed to the decline of the family and of "family values."

But is this concern about the well-being of families really new? Other family scholars tell us that the golden years of the past never really existed as we have fantasized them. Families have always faced issues of desertion, poverty, children born out of wedlock, cohabitation, alcoholism, unemployment, violence, and child abuse, and there has always been concern about them (Coontz 1997, 2000; Demos 1970, 1986; Gordon 1994, 2001; Jones 2007). In reviewing historical and cross-cultural variations in family life, we are reminded that our images of families in the "good old days" of the past—of a working dad as the sole breadwinner and mom as a full-time housewife and mother nurturing her children—are exaggerated.

With such conflicting perspectives, how do we evaluate which view is correct? Or is there truth in both views?

Having an historical perspective can reveal the answers to questions such as these. History can show the ways that families change and evolve. In fact, Popenoe, a sociologist, and Whitehead, a social historian, recently noted the possibility of a "family turnaround" beginning in the late 1990s (Whitehead and Popenoe 2003). They point to statistics that hint at this: the percentage of persons aged 35–44 who are married has increased, the divorce rate continues to decline, there is an upturn in the percentage of married persons who state that their marriages are "very happy," teen out-of-wedlock births declined and have since stabilized, and the likelihood of Black children living in a two-parent household has increased. If indeed the United States is witnessing a family turnaround, is it possible that this is simply one of many? Does history repeat itself?

For persons interested in how contemporary families work, history can provide remarkable insights (Coontz 2005). The historical literature reveals the evolution of family patterns. It shows that families are constantly changing in ways that both reflect and initiate alterations in the larger social structure. Families, as social institutions and as lived experiences, are socially constructed to meet basic human needs. Families are not isolated entities, but rather, reflect deep cultural and historical roots. History shows where we have been, how we came to where we are, and where we might be headed in the future.

Anthropologists, historians, and family scholars attempt to weave together our "social history" to tell us about daily life, customs, and lifestyles of ordinary citizens. This is a departure from the work of most historians

These two sisters remind us that there are many different kinds of families today. Families reflect changes in our social structure, including the influence of globalization. What is the likelihood that girls like these would have been sisters fifty years ago?

who focus on large-scale social events, such as wars or economic downturns. Instead, these scholars are interested in uncovering aspects of everyday family life, including power, the division of labor, relationships between parents and children, and kinship rules. Because this field is still relatively new, our knowledge about the details of the earliest families, and details about non-White or poor families in the United States, is more limited. However, attempts are being made to learn more about these groups, including African Americans, Latinos, Native Americans, Asian Americans, women, European immigrants, and the elderly. Their methods are described in the the following box, "Using the Sociological Imagination: Piecing Together the History of Family Life."

Examining families over ten of thousands of years, from the beginning of recorded human history to the present, we see that many characteristics of today's families are remarkably similar to those found in hunting and gathering societies, as shown in Table 3.1 (Yorburg 2002). Because families throughout time have largely performed the same functions as

USING
the Sociological Imagination

Piecing Together the History of Family Life

Historians, anthropologists, and family scholars draw upon many written documents, including diaries, letters, or other lengthy correspondence between people to understand the common everyday experiences of families. They analyze historical records to get an aggregate picture of, for example, immigration trends, age at first marriage, or the average length of time between marriage and first birth. Census records; birth, marriage, and death registers; immigration records; slave auctions and other transactions; church records; newspapers and magazine articles; employment ledgers; and tax records can also provide insightful clues into the family lives of large numbers of ordinary people. Researchers also analyze the remains of artwork left behind.

Preindustrial and other societies without a written language are more difficult to study. How can we possibly understand family life among hunters and gatherers? No written records are available—but all is not lost. Although imprecise, researchers may turn to the few such hunting and gathering groups that continue to exist into modern times in remote regions of the world. Anthropologists provide extensive **ethnographies**, which are detailed accounts and interpretations of some aspect of culture.

Finally, scholars may rely upon **family reconstitution**, in which attempts are made to compile all available information about significant family events and everyday life within a particular family. Any members of each generation who are still alive will be interviewed, and they will be asked to reconstruct their family history. A significant responsibility falls on the eldest members to reconstruct the generation that preceded them. Other pertinent documents will be combed as well so that family life and household patterns can be uncovered.

Historical methods are not without their limitations or their criticisms. Historical researchers work as detectives and try to obtain the widest number of sources possible as they reconstruct and interpret the past. Sometimes numerous sources are available, but unfortunately, clues are often few or sketchy. Details of family life outside of White middle classes remain somewhat limited.

CRITICAL THINKING QUESTIONS
1. How do the strengths and challenges of historical methods differ from other research methods learned in Chapter 1?
2. Do social historians use theory in their work? If so, which theories do you imagine might be most useful?

TABLE 3.1 Families in Major Types of Societies

The functions, structure, husband–wife relationships, and parent–child relationships within families have changed throughout history, but we can also see some remarkable similarities.

	HUNTING AND GATHERING	HORTICULTURAL	AGRICULTURAL	INDUSTRIAL AND POSTINDUSTRIAL
Family Functions	All-inclusive: physical care, intellectual development, emotional support	All-inclusive	Some sharing with experts, specialists	Sharing with experts, specialists in all spheres, including emotional support; emotional support becomes most important
Family Structures (forms)	Nuclear	Extended	Extended and semiextended	Nuclear and seminuclear
Premarital Sexual Activity	Unrestricted	Mixed, depending on social status; higher-status females restricted	Restricted; double standard for all females	Unrestricted, except for the deeply religious
Marital Choice	Personal preference, free choice, personal qualities	Arranged by family; social background most important	Arranged by family on basis of social status	Romantic love, personal preference, personal qualities, shared interests and values most important
Husband–Wife Relationship				
Power	Egalitarian	Varies, depending on social status	Authoritarian	Egalitarian: senior partner/ junior partner roles
Gender Roles	Work and leisure activities shared	Separate work and leisure activities	Physically and emotionally separate	Shared leisure activities, two-earner households, shared child care, less sharing of household chores
Communication	High, talking, confiding, joking	Mixed, depending on social status	Low	High, closeness, sharing, companionship, friendship most highly valued
Parent–Child Relationships	Permissive	Mixed, depending on social status	Authoritarian	Permissive/authoritative (democratic)

Source: Yorburg 2002.

outlined in Chapter 2—the regulation of sexual behavior; reproduction and socialization of children; property and inheritance; economic cooperation; social placement, status, and roles; and providing care, warmth, protection, and intimacy—it is perhaps not surprising that they organize themselves in a relatively similar fashion.

However, as societies become more complex, many family functions are shared or taken over by outsiders, such as teachers in schools, or doctors in hospitals. Max Weber (1925, reprinted 1947) suggested that as societies become more complex, the division of labor becomes more specialized for increased efficiency. This includes the job of parenthood; it is more efficient in modern developed societies to pay professionals to do many tasks that parents used to do in the past.

Let's now turn to specific times in history—preindustrial and postindustrial—to see what we have learned about families. Pay particular note to how past events shape our current understandings.

Families in Preindustrial Societies

Family Life as Hunter-Gatherers

Throughout most of human history, humans used hunting and gathering as their mode of production. They wandered in small groups of no more than 50, migrating frequently in pursuit of small animals and gathering edible plants. They made simple tools for foraging, fishing, or hunting. Possessions were few; everything the group owned had to be carried with them in their frequent moves. These societies had **subsistence economies**; families used all of what they had, and there was virtually no surplus of food or other resources. Consequently, there were few social divisions (Lenski 1984; Nolan and Lenski 1999).

Sex and age were the primary factors guiding the division of labor (Buhle et al. 2009). There was little division of labor within male or female groups; all men performed similar tasks, as did all women. There was little if any hierarchy within sex categories, and therefore labor was shared equally. However, precisely *what* was defined as men's or women's work may have differed from one group to another. Generally speaking, men's main task was to hunt for food; other tasks reserved for men varied across groups. Women's primary task was to care for any offspring. In their ethnographies, anthropologists report that mothers carried their young children with them virtually everywhere and nursed them for several years. Therefore, because women were less mobile than men, their tasks also included finding plants and hunting small animals close to home. Nonetheless, hunters and gatherers likely saw men and women as having equal importance.

Family Life in Horticultural and Agrarian Societies

About 7,000–10,000 years ago, humans discovered the advantages of staying in one place to plant and cultivate crops to supplement the food obtained by hunting and gathering (Lenski 1984; Nolan and Lenski 1999). They used crude instruments to dig holes in the ground to plant seeds. About 3,000 years ago, humans began to use animals to pull plows.

These seemingly simple advances brought widespread change. Group size increased substantially, upwards of a thousand members gathered together. Perhaps even more important, there was at times a food surplus. These two factors led to the importance of kinship group lineages. Families wanted to ensure that their surplus went only to their own members, rather than be dispersed to the group as a whole. Most lineages were patrilineal, and kinship was an important tool for survival. It was the primary form of social organization and social cohesiveness in a world without governments, schools, health care systems, or social welfare programs.

As agrarian societies became more developed and the use of more sophisticated technology in agricultural production became more widespread, social inequality increased significantly. Some kinship groups were more successful; their surpluses, land ownership, and general wealth grew disproportionately. This wealth was then passed on to their children as they became adults. Meanwhile, the children of peasants remained poor.

Children were socialized by their own kin and learned their skills by observing the adults. They rarely interacted with other families until it was time to marry. Unmarried girls and women were closely supervised. Kin groups strictly controlled mate selection because marriage was seen as an economic transition between two kinship groups. It could not be taken lightly or left to the whim of the young themselves. Most marriages included significant transfer of economic assets from one family to another via a dowry, bride wealth, or some other form of transaction (Murdock 1967). Polygyny was common.

Early European Families   Social stratification was a central feature of early European society. Among the Romans, the **patricians** as landowners were at the top of the stratification system; slaves were at the bottom. Life was segregated by sex, but women identified far more with their social class than with their sex. Patrician women were not equals with their male counterparts, but they were considerably more privileged and influential than were persons of the lower classes.

By the Middle Ages, many small farms had been lost. Instead of dividing up parcels among all sons, fathers with any wealth or property often left it only to the eldest son, a practice known as **primogeniture**. Younger sons inherited little or nothing. Over time, this resulted in fewer estates, but those that continued were of greater magnitude. The owners became extremely wealthy, which provided them with tremendous power. They became the political as well as the economic base of society. Although slavery no longer existed formally, serfs worked the land for the wealthy landowners, and were bought and sold alongside the property in a fashion not too distant from slavery.

Although the ideal type of family in horticultural and agrarian societies leaned toward the extended variety, in reality there were few extended families in early Europe, the Middle Ages, or preindustrial Europe. Mortality rates were high; most people did not live long enough to spend much time living with their adult children and grandchildren. Moreover, men and women tended to marry in their mid-twenties, or even later, and many women did not marry at all. Because only one male in a family inherited the wealth—and women wanted to marry well—there was a shortage of rich men for their female counterparts.

In one of the first major books in family history, *Centuries of Childhood*, Philippe Aries (1962) wrote of family life in the Middle Ages. He pieced together a number of historical artifacts, including art from 1,000 years ago. Perhaps one of his most important findings is that childhood as we tend to think of it today—as a separate stage of life with unique needs—did not really exist during this period. Babies and toddlers were often neglected or ignored because parents did not want to waste time, money, or affection when so many of them died. Aries reports few if any social rituals for dead children or their "grieving" parents, such as headstones to identify their graves. Those children who did survive were treated as miniature adults without child-related toys or games. Usually by age seven, children performed needed work in the fields or in the home. Poor children may have been apprenticed out, even as young as age five. However, not all scholars agree with Aries' conclusions; some believe that childhood was indeed a special time of life, although not to the extent or over the length of time we observe today (Pollock 1983, 1987).

Family Life in Preindustrial United States

Native Americans

European explorers and colonists came to the "new world" to find resources for themselves and their countries; however, they found that the land was already inhabited by people much different from themselves (Lobo et al. 2010). Referred to as "Indians" because of Christopher Columbus' erroneous belief that he had found India, the native people had existed in these lands for perhaps 30,000 years. When European settlers arrived there were nearly 18 million natives with diverse customs and speaking about 300 different languages (John 1988). Lack of understanding or empathy, racism, and ethnocentrism led to numerous conflicts and attempts to virtually obliterate Native American groups. For example, exposure to smallpox (deliberately or unwittingly), for which Native Americans had no immunity, killed millions of adults and children. By the early twentieth century, only an estimated 240,000 Native Americans remained (Wells 1982).

Most Native Americans lived in tribal societies based on lineages, and these ranged from hunting-gathering groups to larger groups using sophisticated horticultural methods. Some groups practiced polygamy, although most were monogamous. About one-quarter of the tribes were based on matrilineal descent. Among the Apache or Hopi, for example, a person traced relatives through the mother's side of the family. It was the mother's relatives, including her brothers, who played key roles in socializing children.

Historians have reported that in many native tribes women held higher status than among their White counterparts. Although the image of a second-class "squaw" has been glorified in Hollywood, in many tribes women held considerable power and were involved in political affairs, healing, and even warfare (Braund 1990; Green 2010). Puberty was generally an important life stage, and elaborate rituals were developed to celebrate it for both boys and girls (Szasz 1985). Among girls, some rituals emphasized a taboo; for example, isolating newly menstruating girls and forbidding them to eat certain foods, touch their own bodies, or interact with others. Other girls' rituals surrounding menstruation were more celebratory, with feasting, music, and dance. Young women may have married soon after reaching puberty, around age 12–15, whereas young men were several years older. The parents, along with the mother's brother in matrilineal societies, typically arranged marriage partners. Marriages forged alliances among different groups, creating useful allies during warfare. Wedding ceremonies varied, ranging from no formal ceremony to elaborate multiday affairs (Joe et al. 1999). The birth of children was extremely welcomed, but given high infant mortality rates, family sizes tended to be small. Most Native American groups were kind, loving, and permissive with their children (Buhle et al. 2009).

Although Native Americans consisted of diverse groups and conflict or wars sometimes erupted among them, nothing prepared them for the scale of massive destruction they experienced in the nineteenth century. Often under the guise of religion, "progress," or sheer economic greed, Native American groups experienced slaughter and enslavement, and were forcibly removed from their land and put onto reservations. Many traditions were difficult or impossible to maintain under these circumstances, and Native Americans suffered extreme poverty and hardship.

Colonial America: European Settlers

Family historians have given us some surprising glimpses into colonial family life. They show that the family was the cornerstone of colonial society. It was the primary social institution, helping early immigrants adapt to life in the New World. Families were perceived as an important component of the community rather than a private relationship, and therefore the community did not hesitate to get involved in family matters, including monitoring how husbands treated their wives, or how parents treated their children.

The family was, first and foremost, a "community of work" or a *business* because it was the central focus of economic production. Each household was nearly self-sufficient, and all family members—men, women, and children—worked together at productive tasks to meet their material needs. It raised the food and made most of the clothing, furniture, and household goods that the family used. Men and boys had the primary responsibility for tending the crops, although the women and girls in the family often assisted them. However, women and girls were usually exceedingly busy with household tasks. Cooking, cleaning, taking care of younger children, and making important items such as clothing, soap, or candles took up most of their day. Men and women were highly dependent on one another for survival (Degler 1983; Kulikoff 2000).

The family also served as a *school*. Formal schooling conducted away from home was extremely rare, particularly in early colonial times. Instead, it fell to parents, usually fathers, to educate their children, to teach them how to read and write, and to impart to them the vocational and technical skills needed in adult life. Formal schools began to appear toward the end of the colonial period, but they were not mandatory, and therefore many children, especially girls, non-Europeans, and poor children, did not attend them.

Moreover, families were *health and social welfare institutions*. There were no hospitals and few doctors during this period. Families, women in particular, took over the role of caring for the sick and infirm. Families also took care of the elderly, the homeless, or orphaned children. These services were not provided by outside social institutions, but by families—one's own, or someone else's (Demos 1970, 1986). Jails were rare. Instead, courts sentenced criminals and so-called "idle" people to live with more respected families in the community. Families were viewed as a natural setting in which to impose discipline, but also to encourage reform.

For both women and men, marriage and family were central events in life. Although marriages were often undertaken because of business or financial interests, love and affection between husbands and wives were expected. But how did men and women meet prospective marriage partners?

Courtship and Partnering   During the time of colonial America, casual dating was frowned upon. Parental permission was needed for a young man to see a young woman, and the couple was usually chaperoned by friends or relatives. Parents, fathers in particular, exerted considerable influence over whom a son or daughter could date. The mate selection system in the seventeenth and early eighteenth centuries is best described as one that was open to choice, but one that was also highly regulated (Farrell 1999). Although generally parents did not select their children's mates, as is the case in many parts of the world today, marriage did require parental consent. The courts could punish those who married without such consent (Wall 1990).

Despite heavy parental involvement, premarital sex and premarital pregnancy occurred with surprising frequency. According to some historians, nearly a third of women were pregnant at the time of their marriage (Demos 1970). Many became pregnant as a result of a dating practice known as **bundling**. Because a young man may have traveled a great distance to see his date or fiancée and people generally went to sleep early, he may have been allowed to stay the night at her house. Space was at a premium, so the young man and woman continued their date by spending the night in bed together, separated by a wooden board. The couple was supposedly under the watchful eye of the other family members who likely shared the bedroom, but apparently sexual relations sometimes occurred.

Household Structure   Most people in colonial America lived in nuclear families. Because people didn't live very long (average life expectancy at birth was 35–45 years in 1650) (Farrell 1999), older adults may have died before their grandchildren were born.

Families in colonial America were large by today's standards, often containing seven or eight children, as shown in Table 3.2 (Demos 1970). The age differences between children were large, and mortality rates were high. Siblings may have been 25 years apart or more in age. Therefore, some children were married and out of the house while other children were only babies.

It was common for husbands or wives to marry two or three times because of high death rates, often related to childbirth or dangers on the frontier. The surviving spouse remarried very quickly because his or her livelihood often depended upon it. Therefore, children within a household commonly had stepsiblings or half-siblings. Some households also contained servants or slaves, and these were sometimes counted as household family members in statistical records. A count of one community with 72 husbands found that 21 of them had been married before: 13 had been married twice, 3 had been married three times, 3 had been married four times, 1 had been married five times, and 1 with the number unspecified.

TABLE 3.2 Size of Families in Plymouth Colony

Many families in early colonial America had 7–9 children, although not all of them lived to adulthood.

	AVERAGE NUMBER OF CHILDREN BORN	AVERAGE NUMBER LIVING TO AGE 21	SIZE OF SAMPLE
First-Generation Families	7.8	7.2	16
Second-Generation Families	8.6	7.5	47
Third-Generation Families	9.3	7.9	33

Note: The 96 families in this sample were chosen for analysis because the evidence on their membership seemed especially complete and reliable. Also, in all these families both parents lived at least to age 50, or else, if one parent died, the other quickly remarried. Thus, in all cases, there were parents who lived up to, and past, the prime years for childbearing.
Source: Demos 1970.

Relationships Between Husbands and Wives Husbands and wives worked as a team to ensure that their family survived and thrived. A wife was considered her husband's helpmate, but not his equal; colonial America was highly patriarchal (Cott 2002; Welter 2002). The husband was the head of the family and it was his wife's duty to obey him. New England clergymen often referred to male authority as "laws" that women must accept, and in the South, husbands denounced assertive wives as "impertinent." Females were thought to be morally weaker, a belief codified by religious institutions and rationalized by the story of Eve, who was responsible for original sin by eating the forbidden fruit from the tree of knowledge. The story promotes the idea that women are a dangerous temptation to men and must therefore be controlled.

At the same time, there was a shortage of women in colonial America, and this sex imbalance tended to offset the status and position of women somewhat. Compared to their counterparts in England, women in colonial America had more rights on average, including some small measure of property rights or the right to make contracts. These rights varied from one colony to another, and sometimes from one community to another, but there is evidence that at least some women retained limited ownership of certain property after marriage.

Women's status may have also been enhanced somewhat because their economic roles inside and outside the family were recognized. As historian Carl Degler (1983) tells us:

> Over the long term of a lifetime, [their tasks] were probably more arduous and demanding than those performed by the men. One traveler in 18th century Carolina reported that "ordinary women take care of cows, hogs, and other small cattle, make butter and cheese, spin cotton, and flax, help to sow and reap corn, wind silk from the worms, gather fruit and look after the house." Looking after the house was itself a heavy task since that included not only cleaning the physical interior but the washing and mending of the family's clothes, preparing meals under the handicaps of an open fireplace and no running water, preserving various kinds of foods, making all the soap, candles, and most of the medicines used by the family, as well as all the clothes for the family. And then, as the quotation suggests, the women had to be ready at planting or harvest time to help in the fields. On top of this, of course, was the bearing and rearing of children. . . . Unlike the work of the husband-farmer, a woman's work went on after dark and at undiminished pace throughout the year.

Parenting Compared to parents today, parents in colonial America tended to be relatively strict and emotionally distant. Some of this detachment may stem from the high infant and child mortality rates during this period; parents were cautious about becoming too close with their children (Corsaro 1997).

Families tended to follow the teachings of the Bible. Parents and children read the Bible together, one of the few easily available books and sources of moral instruction. Children were thought to be born with "original sin" and needed firm discipline and severe religious training to prevent them from going to hell. Discipline was strict to break their innate rebellion and selfishness. Firm guidance was seen as necessary to ensure that children would grow up to be productive members of society. Excessive tenderness could spoil the child.

Children were treated as miniature adults in many ways (Mintz 2004); there was little concept of adolescence as there is today. As soon as children were old enough to labor on the family farm or in the household, they were put to work.

There were social class difference in childrearing patterns then, as there are now. Wealthy families tended to be more indulgent with their children than poorer families—yet, child labor of some sort was nearly universal because their labor was needed for family survival. Parents considered a boy to belong under his father's tutelage, whereas a girl's training was the domain of the mother. Daughters' education included heavy doses of domestic tasks, such as cooking, cleaning, and sewing.

Colonial America: African Americans and Slavery

The first Africans brought over to the United States were enslaved for a specified amount of time, and then were "free" and able to marry and purchase their own land. But by 1790, the slave trade was well under way with at least 750,000 Africans captured, brought to the United States against their will, and held as slaves. Hundreds of thousands more died in the long grueling ship ride to the United States where food, water, and sanitary conditions were abysmal. Slaves were used primarily in the South, where the agrarian economy relied on exploiting their cheap labor. Although not all Southern Whites owned slaves, the Southern culture supported their importation, selling, breeding, and horrendous living conditions (Faragher et al. 2009; Hine et al. 2011).

Like free Americans, most slaves lived in separate families centered on a monogamous couple, but the similarities ended there (Gutman 1976). African Americans were property and thus could be bought and sold on a master's whim. There was always the threat and the common reality of separation of family members by sale or inheritance (Scott 1982).

Masters and slaves considered slave marriages and stable families to be important. Masters encouraged marriage among slaves for multiple motives, including as a mechanism for social control. Slaves in committed relationships were considered to be better workers and less likely to run away. Married slaves were also more likely to have children, thereby making arranged "breeding" described in the opening vignette less relevant. This became more and more important by the early 1800s when the United States prohibited the importation of new slaves.

The slave trade, a dark time in U.S. history, tore families apart. Hundreds of thousands of Africans were captured and brought to the United States as slaves.

Yet in colonial America, it was not easy for a slave to find a spouse. In the North, most slaves were not allowed to associate with other slaves. They lived alone or in very small groups with their masters. In the Southern states, most slaves lived on small plantations with 10 or fewer other slaves. Nonetheless, "marriages" did occur, although not recognized legally, and true bonds were formed. A vast array of real and "fictive" kin provided slaves with a loving, supporting, and protective community, as best they could (Scott 1982).

Yet, slave marriages were fragile; one study conducted in several Southern states found that over one-third of marriages were terminated by selling off either the husband or wife to another party elsewhere (Gutman 1976). Another study reported that only 14 percent of slave couples said they lived together without some sort of disruption. The master broke up almost one-third of these, but an even higher proportion was due to an early death of one of the spouses (Blassingame 1972). However, even when slavery tore apart families, kinship bonds persisted. Children were often named after lost relatives as a way to preserve family ties.

Prior to the Civil War, there were approximately 150,000 free African Americans living in the South, and another 100,000 living in the North (Mintz and Kellogg 1989), yet even "free" African Americans were not necessarily allowed to vote, attend White schools and churches, or hold certain kinds of jobs, and they were subject to severe prejudice and discrimination. Few legal protections were available. Consequently, most free African Americans were poor, had high levels of unemployment, and were barely literate. Women had an easier time than did men in finding employment because Whites sought out women as domestic servants. Moreover, the number of free women outnumbered free men in urban areas. Together, high poverty rates and the sex imbalance of free African Americans challenged their ability to marry and raise children, and many children were reared in female-headed households. One study indicated that when property holdings, a key measure of income, were held constant, the higher incidence of one-parent families among African Americans largely disappeared (Mintz and Kellogg 1989). Poverty shapes family life.

A key concern fueling the abolition movement in the early nineteenth century involved ideas about family. Abolitionists declared an attack against slavery using passionate images of slave families being broken up on the auction block. They condemned slavery as a "system of universal concubinage," which eliminated the possibility of marriage among African American adults, destroyed families, and put women into vulnerable situations with their male masters. Harriet Beecher Stowe's *Uncle Tom's Cabin*, written in the early nineteenth century and considered a classic today, focused on how slavery destroyed opportunities for meaningful family life (Scott 1982).

In recent decades, slavery has been used to explain current African American family patterns. In an early study of marital power and decision making among families in Detroit nearly 50 years ago, researchers reported that "Negro" wives were twice as likely to be "dominant" in their families as were White wives (Blood and Wolfe 1960). However, historians have more recently revised conceptions of families under slavery. Instead of seeing slave families as inadequate, incomplete, or emasculated, historians are noting the resiliency of slave families (Sudarkasa 1999; Wilkinson 1997). The popularity of televised programs such as *Roots* in the 1970s vividly portrayed the strength of family bonds under some of the most adverse conditions possible. African American family ties were strong when they were permitted to exist. Historians note the strength of the extended family in caring for kin, and that the relationships created by "blood" were considered more important than those created by marriage (Sudarkasa 1999).

Mexicans

Mexicans had a rich history along the western and southwestern portions of what is now the U.S. border, drawn from the contributions of Native American and Spanish heritage (Acuña 2011). The Spanish elite owned large tracts of land used for grazing cattle or sheep. Others, often with a combined Spanish and Native American ancestry, were the laborers or those who had considerably smaller land holdings.

After decades of war with Mexico, the United States annexed Mexican territory in 1848. Although the Treaty of Guadalupe Hidalgo guaranteed Mexicans the retention of their property, most landowners had their land confiscated and old land grants were no longer effective. Consequently, many Mexican families who were secure and had some degree of wealth prior to annexation became laborers on land now owned by others.

Mexican laborers have been crucial to the southwestern economy for the past 160 years. Many Mexicans have been hired to do the physical labor that Whites choose not to do. During the nineteenth century, employers hired women and children as domestics, laundresses, and cooks, as well as farm laborers alongside their husbands and sons. Men were hired to work in the railroads or in mining, along with farm laboring. Their pay was little, far below what Whites typically earned, and consequently multiple family members were often employed—husband, wife, and children—so that they could feed themselves and keep a roof over their heads.

Despite economic hardships, Mexican Americans have been quite successful at preserving their traditional family structure (Buhle et al. 2009). Family relationships were paramount and took precedence over individual needs or wants, a characteristic known as **familism** (Williams 1990). Families leaned toward extended models, with several generations living together or near one another and pooling resources (Mindel 1980). Parents chose specific adults as godparents to their children, and these have come to be known as **compadres**, or co-parents. They were close family friends who adopted a co-parenting role with their godchildren. Relationships were warm and loving, and godparents provided special gifts and opportunities to their godchild. They were also authority figures expecting respect and obedience, alongside the biological parents.

Women usually worked outside the home because of economic necessity, but they defined their primary role as wives and mothers. Women were responsible for virtually all of the household labor and hands-on childrearing. When a mother was away at work, other female family members chipped in—grandmothers, aunts, cousins, and older female siblings. Mexican American families have a long tradition of **machismo**, or masculine authority, and it is demonstrated in the home, in the workplace, in sexual prowess, and in the raising of children. There is a clear double standard, with males being afforded greater leeway and sexual freedom and fathering children is a great source of pride. For example, a high premium is placed on women's virginity prior to marriage and sexual faithfulness within marriage, whereas premarital and extramarital affairs among men are expected, or at least tolerated (Del Castillo 1984; Mirande 1985). Likewise, children were socialized according to strict traditions associated with gender. Compared to boys, girls were restricted and heavily supervised in social settings.

American Families in the Nineteenth Century

Family life changed considerably in the nineteenth and early twentieth century because of two critical factors: industrialization and immigration (Divine et al. 2011; Faragher et al. 2009).

The Changing Nature of the Economy: Industrialization and Urbanization

Industrialization transformed an economy from a system based on small family-based agriculture to one of large industrial capital. Small family farms could no longer support themselves and folded or else were bought out by large commercial farming companies.

There was considerable migration to urban areas in search of jobs. During the early part of the industrial revolution, families were often separated because men moved to urban areas in search of work, leaving the rest of the family behind. More and more goods and services were produced for profit outside the home, and families purchased these with the wages they earned at outside jobs. The new industries needed large numbers of laborers, so they began to look to women and children to fill jobs alongside men. Industries could pay women and children lower wages and often considered them "better" workers because they were less demanding, more docile, and obedient. Historian Steven Mintz reveals that for many children, childhood was a time of cruelty—grim factory or farm labor, poverty, loneliness, and economic and sexual exploitation. Poor, immigrant, and Black children suffered disproportionately, working side-by-side with their mothers and fathers (Mintz 2004).

Working conditions in factories could be exceedingly dangerous, unsanitary, and inhumane. Upton Sinclair wrote of the harrowing conditions that crippled or killed many people, as he described a fictional family working in a Chicago meatpacking plant in the famous book *The Jungle*, originally published in 1906:

> Of the butchers and floorsmen, the beef-boners and trimmers, and all those who used knives, you could scarcely find a person who had the use of his thumb; time and time again the base of it had been slashed, till it was a mere lump of flesh. . . . The hands of these men would be criss-crossed with cuts, until you could no longer pretend to count them or to trace them. They would have no nails—they had worn them off pulling hides; their knuckles were swollen so that their fingers spread out like a fan. There were men who worked in the cooking rooms, in the midst of steam and sickening odors, by artificial light; in these rooms the germs of tuberculosis might live for two years, but the supply was renewed every hour. There were the beef-luggers, who carried two-hundred pound quarters into the refrigerator cars; a fearful kind of work, that began at four o'clock in the morning, and that wore out the most powerful men in a few years. There were those who worked in the chilling rooms, and whose special disease was rheumatism; the time limit that a man could work in the chilling rooms was said to be five years. There were the wool-pluckers, whose hands went to pieces even sooner than the hands of the pickle men; for the pelts of the sheep had to be painted with acid to loosen the wool, and then the pluckers had to pull out this wool with their bare hands, till the acid had eaten their fingers off. (1981, 98)

Industrialization fostered a great need for labor in new and growing industries, including factories, mills, and meat packing plants. Immigrants—men, women, and children—often filled these dirty and dangerous jobs.

Many jobs became categorized and separated by sex. Men did the heavy manual labor. Women toiled in tedious and repetitive factory jobs, and other jobs that corresponded with their domestic skills, such as seamstress. Both men and women's wages were low, and consequently children also often worked full-time, doing dirty and dangerous work.

Demographic Changes: Immigration

The large waves of **immigration** of people moving to the United States provided the labor fueling industrialization (Divine et al. 2011; Faragher et al. 2009). Millions of Irish, German, English, Scandinavian, and other northern European immigrants came to the United States in the mid-1800s, encouraged by the prospect of a better life. By the late nineteenth and early twentieth century, millions more came from southern and eastern Europe, including Greeks, Poles, Italians, Russians, and other Slavic groups. Other groups from Asia, such as the Chinese, later immigrated to work in certain industries. Between 1830 and 1930, over 30 million immigrants came to the United States.

Immigrants were an important component of the changing economy and were employed in a number of key industries. A survey of 20 major mining and manufacturing industries found that over half of the workers were foreign-born. In clothing factories, the figure was over three-quarters. In packinghouses, steel mills, textile mills, and coal mines, nearly half of the workers were immigrants to the United States (Steinberg 1981).

WHAT DO YOU THINK?

What are the similarities and differences between immigration in the nineteenth century and immigration today?

Most immigrants were poor and vulnerable. In her book *Foreign and Female: Immigrant Women in America, 1840–1930*, Weatherford (1986) describes the appalling conditions in which many immigrant families lived. Housing was crowded, substandard, and often lacked appropriate sanitation facilities. Raw sewage was strewn about, causing disease epidemics in the neighborhoods in which immigrants congregated. Upton Sinclair (1906, reprinted 1981) also describes dreadful conditions of immigrant families' neighborhoods, including the raw sewage and cesspools drawing flies and rodents where children played. Epidemics were rampant among immigrant neighborhoods. For example, a cholera epidemic killed nearly one-fifth of the residents in a crowded New York immigrant neighborhood, but the rest of the city was virtually untouched.

The strain of family life under these dreadful working and living conditions was severe and took its toll. Alcoholism, violence, crime, and other social problems stemming from demoralization plagued many families, yet immigrants continued to crowd the cities in search of work because they hoped that it would lead eventually to a better life. Many immigrants believed that if they simply worked hard enough, they would soon join the ranks of the middle and upper classes. They were ill prepared for the working conditions, living environments, and prejudice and discrimination they would face.

Class Ideology   As the poor sold their labor, a new ideology began to emerge in the middle and upper classes—one known as **separate spheres**, meaning that married women with children should stay at home, while men worked outside the home. The **cult of domesticity** glorified the domestic role and elevated it to a pinnacle achievement. A wife's primary job was to rear the children and care for the home while a husband should be the sole breadwinner (Beecher 1869; Cott 1997). The world of work was presented as a dangerous and corrupt place, unsuitable for women's delicate nature and naturally higher morals. Women should create safe havens for their husbands so that husbands may have a brief respite from the stress and corruptions of the work environment (Cott 1997). Expectations for being a good wife and mother were explicitly spelled out in self-help books.

This ideology was based on specific assumptions about the nature of men and women. Women's fundamental nature was seen as distinctly different from men's and included the virtues of piety, purity, submissiveness, and domesticity (Welter 1966). Women were supposed to be the guardian of the home and the moral values associated with it. Love was promoted as the basis for her caregiving, and love steadily became a private emotion, removed from any outside practical action to help others (Cancian 1989). Women were cut off from the outside world; they were considered too delicate to handle its harshness. They were "ladies."

These values became the dominant ideology and formed the basis of many social policies emerging during this period, such as denying women the rights to own property, to speak in many public settings, or to vote. However, this lifestyle of separate spheres was virtually unattainable for many women, including poor, working class, minority, and immigrant women (Buhle et al. 2009). Yet they too were held up to this ideal, and because they could not meet it, were considered failures. Women who had to work to support their families were looked down upon with contempt and pity, and were often viewed as less than true and virtuous women.

Not coincidentally, ideas about children began to change. Childhood and adolescence were now viewed as distinct stages in the life cycle. Children were no longer considered simply miniature adults, perhaps because middle- and upper-class families no longer had to rely upon their labor. They were seen as individuals in their own right, not simply as extensions of their parents. Children were innocent and could be molded into good or bad citizens (Degler 1980).Women, therefore, had a critical role within the family teaching children strong moral values. Childrearing books played up the importance of mothers, while making the assumption that fathers would not be around very much. Women's childrearing responsibilities were elevated in importance, and outside work was frowned upon because it would presumably take the woman away from her primary, natural, and most important work of all.

Families in the Twentieth Century: The Rise of the "Modern" Family

The early 1900s ushered in many events affecting the structure and dynamics of family life (Faragher et al. 2009). The box on page 83, "Social Policies for Families: The Nineteenth Amendment Is Ratified," chronicles the passage of the Nineteenth Amendment to the Constitution that gave women the right to vote, and reveals that the fight was neither quick nor easy. The twentieth century also contained two world wars, a depression, and the post–World War II affluence of the 1950s. Technological innovations reduced the threat of communicable diseases. They decreased the time spent on domestic labor. The automobile changed the ways families traveled and in particular, made long-distance travel much more feasible. New residential patterns—migration to the cities in search of work and the subsequent creation of suburbs and flight from the cities—increased travel and commuting time. Together, these factors decreased the time that fathers spent with their families.

These changes led to new lifestyles, family structures, and views about the family. Dating emerged as a mechanism for those in the newly defined stage of adolescence to meet one another and select mates. Schools allowed young men and women to spend time together, increasing peer influence and pressure. The movement away from parental control and an increase in discretionary income brought a change of power and roles in the couple relationship. Young men were expected to initiate and pay for dates. Women were expected to control the degree of intimacy and sexuality within the date. A 1930s study of dating conducted on the campus of Pennsylvania State University found that young men and women would readily evaluate, or rate, others in terms of their dating value. The goal was to be evaluated highly so that you could get the "best" dates. Men received top scores if they had access to an automobile, if they could dance well, and if they had more money. Young women were rated more highly if they dressed well, were good conversationalists, and were popular (Waller 1937).

Because of numerous social, technological, and demographic changes, families moved away from being a more public economic unit to a more private relationship set apart from the community and emphasizing the companionship between wives and husbands. This is what Ernest Burgess and Harvey Locke (1945) called the **companionate family**: families built upon mutual affection, sexual attraction, compatibility, and personal happiness. Young adults placed a greater emphasis on romantic love and attraction in their search for mates than did their parents and grandparents. Married partners had high expectations that the attraction should continue throughout their lives.

National Events: World Wars and the Great Depression

During the Great Depression of the 1930s, an estimated one in four workers was unemployed and searching for work (Gordon 1994). Many families were dislocated or members abandoned their families, going from town to town looking for work. Between one and two

SOCIAL

Policies for Families

The Nineteenth Amendment Is Ratified

With the end of the Civil War, the right to vote was given to Black men. Although there was widespread difficulty enforcing this right, especially in the South, women of all racial and ethnic groups were legally barred from voting until the twentieth century. What is the history behind granting the vote to women? Susan B. Anthony was a leader in this controversial movement.

The demand for the right of U.S. women to vote was first seriously organized at Seneca Falls, New York, in 1848. In that year, Lucretia Coffin Mott and Elizabeth Cady Stanton organized the Seneca Falls Convention (Flexner 1959) and drafted the "Declaration of Sentiments," which was modeled after the Declaration of Independence. The document listed various forms of discrimination against women including the denial of suffrage (the vote). Also, they wanted equal rights to attend universities, to seek all professions, and the right to share in all political offices. Furthermore, they demanded equality in marriage, freedom, and all rights that men had. They struggled to no avail.

In 1872, Susan B. Anthony was arrested along with other women who voted on November 5, in Rochester, New York. They claimed that the provisions of the Fourteenth and Fifteenth Amendments applied to all citizens, male and female, and "she [indirectly] wanted Congress to pass legislation making it possible to exercise that right." However, within two weeks after the voting incident, the women were arrested on the federal criminal charge of "having voted without the lawful right to vote."

The women were briefly imprisoned prior to the trial. Bail was at $500, and all accepted but Anthony. She preferred to stay in jail rather than pay. The judge, however, didn't want Anthony in jail, so he paid the bail himself.

The trial of the *United States of America v. Susan B. Anthony* opened on June 17, 1873. Anthony's defense was that the Fourteenth Amendment's privileges and immunities clause gave all citizens naturalized in the United States, including women, the right to vote. The judge would not allow Anthony to testify for herself—women were not allowed to address the court. After much contemplation by the judge and the contending arguments by the attorneys, the judge ruled that the Fourteenth Amendment was inapplicable and directed the all-male jury to bring in a guilty verdict. When Anthony's counsel, protesting this clearly unconstitutional procedure, requested that the jury be polled, the judge instead summarily discharged the jurors. All in all, Anthony was charged $100, but never paid it.

Susan B. Anthony was instrumental in helping women receive the constitutional right to vote.

On January 10, 1918, the U.S. House of Representatives approved the Nineteenth Amendment, which said that the right of citizens of the United States to vote shall not be denied or abridged by the United States or any other state on account of sex. Many states had already granted suffrage to women before the actual ratification of the amendment. But after a year and a half in committee, the Senate also passed the amendment. The Nineteenth Amendment became part of the U.S. Constitution on August 26, 1920, and women around the country were finally allowed to vote.

Sources: Adapted from Nemeth 2000; Dorr 1970; Flexner 1959; Gurko 1974; Kraditor 1965; Porter 1971. Text copyright 1996–1999 by David W. Koeller.

CRITICAL THINKING QUESTIONS

1. What arguments were made against letting women vote? How would those arguments stand up to scrutiny today?
2. Are these the same arguments used in other countries that forbid women from voting?

million were estimated to be homeless, sleeping in rat-infested shelters when they could afford or find them, on park benches, or under bridges (Watkins 1993). Meanwhile, persons who were fortunate enough to continue to keep their jobs often faced large declines in their wages. The box on page 85, "Families as Lived Experience: Coming of Age in the Depression," describes growing up during this turbulent period.

The stresses associated with impoverishment of this magnitude affected families in many ways. Some used destructive coping skills, such as alcohol. Children were forced to become more independent and try to supplement family wages when they could. High levels of male unemployment put pressure on women to resign from their jobs because they were seen as taking jobs away from men who had a greater "right" to them. Even the government discriminated against women: approximately half of school districts fired married female teachers, three-quarters would not hire a married woman, and in 1932 a federal order stated that only one spouse could work for the federal government (McElvaine 1993; Milkman 1976). Discrimination against minority groups also increased; their pay was drastically reduced, their unemployment reached nearly 50 percent, and some government positions held unofficial quotas (Watkins 1993).

World War II also contributed to a number of significant changes in families. As men were drafted to join the war effort, industries, factories, and other businesses needed female labor to fill in the gaps. Initially it was not easy to encourage millions of women, often married and with children, to fill the available jobs. The government, in conjunction with larger media efforts, developed a large propaganda effort promoting employment as women's patriotic duty. "Rosie the Riveter" became an important symbol of women's work as a patriotic act.

For the first time, employers provided free or low-cost childcare. Working-class jobs such as ditch digging, operating heavy machinery, or factory work were promoted to women as psychologically and emotionally fulfilling. Because of the drastic labor shortage, even racial prejudice and discrimination was less apparent: All women's labor was sorely needed and "color bars" that had previously limited the kinds of jobs minorities could hold were minimized, if only temporarily.

Another important by-product of World War II was an accelerating divorce rate. Although it had been slowly but steadily increasing for decades, during the war the divorce rate rose considerably, spiking in 1946, a year after the war ended. The war probably caused some people to marry in haste, and it also caused considerable strain when families were reunited.

Post–World War II: The Unique 1950s

As World War II ended and veterans returned from the war, women were encouraged to give up their positions for the sake of men. Some women gladly did so, whereas others resisted because they needed the pay and job experience, or enjoyed the work. Some women who refused to quit were fired. Few protective laws were in place to prohibit arbitrary firing of women or minority groups.

In the 1950s, women were encouraged to find fulfillment primarily as wives and mothers. The media no longer provided women such as Rosie the Riveter, but portrayed images of Betty Crocker instead. Movies and televisions moved away from strong women, and instead pushed softer, sexier women such as Marilyn Monroe or sweet and innocent women such as Doris Day. Popular television shows such as *Ozzie and Harriet, Leave It to Beaver,*

The post–World War II 1950s glorified domesticity, and women were encouraged to leave the workplace to find fulfillment as wives and mothers.

FAMILIES
as Lived Experience

Coming of Age in the Depression

Much of our history remains unrecorded. History books describe wars and other great events, but we know very little about the day-to-day life of Americans, including their lives during these great events. High school students in a Utah Honors English class interviewed 24 members of their community about their experiences growing up during the Great Depression. Although the Depression occurred over 70 years ago, and those interviewed were only children or young adults at the time, their memories remain vivid. Most came from farming families, a group that was particularly hard hit. Utah's gross farm income fell almost 60 percent between 1929 and 1933, and unemployment was 36 percent, the fourth highest in the nation. What was life like during the Great Depression? Below are excerpts from some of the interviews:

"The thing that I noticed most, that I remember most, was how many people needed jobs. They call them bums that came on the railroad, and they bring what they had on their backs, and come and ask for a day's work; and if you fed them, they'd work for nothing, so you'd just feed them. You could hire all kinds of men for a dollar a day. And some of them would say, "If you keep me, I'll stay for the winter." If you just give them a bed and food. And if you had a job, and you didn't take care of it, there was half a dozen waiting for your job. If you had a job you was mighty happy . . . to keep it."

—Ruth

"I remember it was awful hard times, and it was hard to get a hold of enough to buy a sack of flour and we made our own breads, cooked our vegetables, bottled our fruits, raised our gardens. We did most of our own cooking and pastry, pies,

whatever. Did it all ourselves; we hardly ever bought anything."

—Marvell

"We moved about five or six times. We would get a place to live and then on account of depression, either their son or their daughter would lose their jobs wherever they were. Then they would come back to Manti, so then we would have to move again and find a place, and that happened seven different times while we lived up there three or four years."

—Leo and Hazel

"The stock market break took so many people by surprise. My father knew that the stock market would come back up, so he put everything up on margin and that's why we lost everything. Mr. Shirley jumped from a three story window and ended his life. Several of my father's friends, bankers, committed suicide, shot themselves. It was a very traumatic time."

—Jean Anna

"We lived in a shack by the railroad tracks in Phoenix. It was so bad that they couldn't rent it to someone else, so they didn't even charge us rent. We scrounged for food, I'll tell you we scrounged for food. At about that time Roosevelt came in and started the WPA program."

—William

Source: Excerpts from New Deal Network (2003). Reprinted with permission.

CRITICAL THINKING QUESTIONS
1. What were your relatives' experiences during the Great Depression?
2. Do you think the United States could experience another depression of that magnitude? Why or why not? How would you and your family fare in a depression?

and *Father Knows Best*, provided a glimpse into the idealized American family (Coontz 2000; Pyke 2000a, 2000b).

The media blitz was successful. During the 1950s, the average age at first marriage dropped to an all-time low since records had been kept; for women it was 19 years of age. The **total fertility rate**, or the average number of children born to women, climbed upward quickly, and this period has now been labeled the "baby boom." This, in turn, contributed to the privatization of the family. The new larger families craved the spaciousness and privacy of suburbs where they could have their own yards rather than relying on community parks and play spaces for their children. In the suburbs, women cared for their children in isolation, volunteered in their children's schools and within the community, and chauffeured their children to various lessons and events. The federal government undertook massive highway construction projects that enabled long commutes from home to work by individual car rather than public transportation.

Cultural images were strong; however, this type of family was not attainable for many. Working-class and poor women, including many minority women, often worked full- or part-time because their husbands did not earn enough to support the family; even with their combined wages, they could not afford homes in the growing suburbs. Moreover, with the rising divorce rate after World War II and the growing number of out-of-wedlock births, many women needed to work because they had no husband to support them. Nonetheless, the cultural image was powerful, and many women and men ascribed to this as an ideal, even if it was unlikely to be a part of their day-to-day reality.

Social Change and the 1960s and 1970s

The 1960s marked a time of significant social change. The civil rights movement was picking up steam; the women's movement was bringing renewed attention to the prejudice and discrimination that women experience in the workplace, in the home, and in other social settings; the antiwar movement was posing serious questions about the U.S. involvement in the Vietnam War; the sexual revolution, fueled by the widespread availability of the birth control pill made us question our previous way of thinking about nonmarital sexual behavior; and the environmental movement uncovered the various threats to the environment brought on by the increasing number of automobiles, acid rain, or overpopulation. Together, these social movements changed our attitudes and changed the way we lived. For example, job ads in newspapers had long been segregated into "Jobs—Male" and "Jobs— Female" categories. The jobs for females were restricted to such jobs as bank teller, sales clerk, secretary, and nurse. This changed during the 1960s as the women's movement questioned the practice and argued persuasively that it was prejudicial and discriminatory.

What caused U.S. society to critically question so many dimensions of social life all at once? One explanation for the widespread interest in social change is the sheer number of young adults in the culture. The first wave of children born during the post–World War II baby boom was finishing high school, attending college, or being drafted to fight in the Vietnam War. Historians have suggested that high degrees of social change are correlated with a high number of young adults in society. They are old enough to be cognizant of social and economic injustice, but are too young to be preoccupied with the responsibilities associated with work and family that can detract from activism (Bidwell and Mey 2000).

> ### WHAT DO YOU THINK?
>
> *What are some images that you have of the late 1960s? What do you think are the lasting legacies of this period?*

Recent Family Issues and Their Historical Roots

As we have seen from our look at history, families are never isolated from outside events. Political actions, economic conditions, prominent religious orientations, and the development of new scientific knowledge all shape the way we view families as a social institution and influence the way we experience family life on a daily basis. Many issues we are concerned about today (e.g., teenage pregnancy, quality child care, the division of household labor, divorce) are not new issues, but have a deep and rich history. We need to know "where we've been" to know "where we are going." One example of how a sense of history shapes our understanding of current events is the way in which the economy affects the family. As we discuss the current recession, do you see any parallels to the Great Depression of the 1930s, with respect to causes, consequences, and/or solutions?

An Example: Families and the Recession

The recession that began in the late 2000s has caused hardship for many families. The civilian labor force shrunk by well over a million workers since 2008. The proportion of workers who worked full-time, year-round in 2009 was 64.8 percent, down from 68.4 percent in 2007, whereas the number of involuntary part-time workers (people whose work hours were reduced or cannot find a full-time job) rose (Bureau of Labor Statistics 2009a; 2010a).

Unemployment and Families   Although the U.S. unemployment rate averaged only 4.7 percent in late 2007, it was more than double that by September 2010 (9.6 percent) (Bureau of Labor Statistics 2010b). The unemployment rates in 2009–2010 are the highest in almost 30 years, The rate is even higher for minority groups—Black unemployment was nearly 16.1 percent in September 2010 (Bureau of Labor Statistics 2010a).

What this all means is that many breadwinners lost their jobs or had their income reduced (or worry that they will), contributing to the rise in home foreclosures, personal bankruptcies, and the number of families who cannot access the health care system because they have lost their health insurance. Let's look at some of these and related issues in more depth.

What does it feel like to look for work week after week, and turn up with nothing? When even the lowest-tier jobs have stiff competition, many people feel psychologically wounded—wanting work, but not being able to find it, let alone maintain it. Unemployment affects personal relationships. For example, high unemployment tends to lower marriage rates—people are less likely to marry if they or their potential partner cannot find a job (Edin and Kefalas 2005; Wilson 1987, 1996). Other periods of high unemployment, such as the Great Depression, led to fewer children being born. The stress associated with unemployment can also endanger relationships, contribute to domestic violence, alcohol and drug use, and harm children's social well-being (Aubry et al. 2006). For example, a study based on 4,476 school-age children in 2,569 families across the United States found that when fathers are involuntarily unemployed, children have a greater likelihood of repeating a grade or getting suspended from school (Kalil and Ziol-Guest 2007; Luo 2009).

Poverty-Level Wages   Some families earn the minimum wage or wages only slightly above it. The federal minimum wage in the United States, at $7.50 per hour in 2011, comes nowhere near to lifting even a small family out of poverty. About 2.2 million hourly workers earn the minimum wage or even less. Half of these persons are age 25 or older. These low-wage workers are distributed evenly across racial and ethnic groups (except for Asians, who are more likely to have higher wages). Women are more likely to earn minimum wage or less than are men, and it is likely that many of these women support children as well as themselves (Bureau of Labor Statistics 2009e).

Part-Time, Nonstandard, and Temporary Work   In addition to pay, another concern is that many new jobs associated with the recession are part-time, sub-contracted, temporary in nature, or occur at night. Some offer irregular work schedules. Employees working in these types of jobs with what are referred to as **nonstandard work schedules**, represent the fastest-growing category of workers in the United States (Gornick et al. 2009; Presser 2003;

WHAT DO YOU THINK?

Do you know anyone who has suffered during the recession? What happened to them? Did they lose their job or their home, have their pay reduced, or lose their health insurance? How did they cope?

Presser et al. 2008). Since 1982, temporary employment has increased several hundred percent. In other words, millions of women and men begin the workday not knowing if, and for how long, their jobs are likely to continue. There is also a growing trend towards jobs that require weekend, evening, or variable nonfixed schedules, particularly those found in the lower-paying service sector.

Some part-time and contingency workers prefer this arrangement, especially highly paid professionals who value their freedom and independence on the job or mothers with young children who would prefer to work only sporadically. But most American families prefer the assurance of a steady job with prearranged hours, and an established pay scale with fringe benefits. Families with nonstandard work schedules may find it difficult to organize childcare.

Most women do not work these schedules out of personal inclination, but because these are the required working conditions of their jobs, such as cashiers, maids, nursing aids, cooks, and waiters. Moreover, these occupations are likely to grow in the future. Working in these types of jobs has important implications for the availability and costs of formal childcare. It also affects the degree to which family, friends, and neighbors are able to provide childcare. Rhonda is one of many people who are looking for a good job with good pay (Seccombe 2011). She has a high school diploma, but has not gone to college. She is a single mother, and would like to raise her young son Bobby without relying on government assistance. She wants a permanent full-time job. Instead, however, she has been stymied by the tremendous growth in part-time, temporary positions (Seccombe 2011).

> Hopefully I can get me a job. A permanent job. My sister's trying to get me a job where she works. I put my application in last week. And it would be a permanent job. When you go through those agencies, it's just temporary work. It's just whenever they need you, and it's unfair too. Every job I've found is through this temporary agency, like Manpower, but it's only temporary. And they cut my check and my food stamps, and when my job ends, it's like you're stuck again. So I'm trying to find a permanent steady job. But it's hard around here. I've been out looking for work, and hoping that something comes through.

Rhonda may be surprised to learn that temporary agencies are booming. Manpower is one of the largest private employers in the United States, ranked 119 in the Fortune 500 list of large companies, and has revenues around $22 billion worldwide. They serve over 400,000 employer clients, and place four million workers a year in 82 countries and territories (Manpower Inc. 2009).

Conclusion

Family historians use multiple research methods to piece together the everyday life of families in the past. From these methods, we have information about family life even among the very earliest hunting and gathering societies. We also know how slavery, industrialization and urbanization, wars, and social movements have influenced family arrangements. A look at history can provide us with critical insights about families today. Many family patterns or specific concerns are rooted in the past. For example, one common concern today: Is the family in trouble? Is it deteriorating?

What seem to be simple questions are actually quite complex and can best be examined by looking at the family over time. Historians reveal that we have unfairly glorified families in the past. We now know that many families suffered hardships, many of which were not all that different from those we face today. Addressing whether recent family changes are good or bad can best be answered by taking an extended view of how families both promote and adapt to various changes in the larger society.

Key Terms

Bundling: A dating practice in colonial America in which a young man and woman may continue their date by spending the night in a bed together, separated by a wooden board. (p. 75)

Compadres: Godparents in the Mexican American community who serve as co-parents to children. (p. 79)

Companionate family: A family built upon mutual affection, sexual attraction, compatibility, and personal happiness. (p. 82)

Cult of domesticity: The glorification of women's domestic role. (p. 81)

Ethnographies: Detailed accounts and interpretations of some aspect of culture. (p. 70)

Familism: Family relationships are paramount and take precedence over individual needs or wants. (p. 79)

Family reconstitution: Attempts are made to compile all available information about significant family events and everyday life within a particular family to piece together social history. (p. 70)

Immigration: The introduction of people into a new habitat or population, such as Europeans or Mexicans moving to the United States. (p. 80)

Industrialization: Transforming an economy from a system based on small family-based agriculture to one of large industrial capital. (p. 79)

Machismo: Mexican Americans have a long tradition of masculine authority, which is exercised in the home, in the work place, in sexual prowess, and in the raising of children. (p. 79)

Nonstandard work schedules: Jobs that are part-time, subcontracted, temporary in nature, occur at night, or offer irregular work schedules. (p. 87)

Patricians: During the Roman era, these were landowners, at the top of the stratification system. (p. 72)

Primogeniture: Families during the Middle Ages leaving their wealth or property to the eldest son. (p. 73)

Separate spheres: A dominant ideology within the nineteenth-century middle and upper-middle classes that suggested that women should stay home to rear the children and take care of the home while husbands should be the sole breadwinners. (p. 81)

Subsistence economies: Economies in which families use all of what they have, with virtually no surplus of food or other resources. (p. 72)

Total fertility rate: The average number of births to women. (p. 85)

Resources on the Internet

Africans in America

www.pbs.org/wgbh/aia/

This website chronicles the history of racial slavery in the United States from the start of the Atlantic slave trade in the sixteenth century to the end of the American Civil War in 1865. It also explores the central paradox that is at the heart of the American story: a democracy that declared all men equal but enslaved and oppressed one people to provide independence and prosperity to another. A companion to *Africans in America*, a six-hour public television series.

American Historical Association

www.historians.org

A national organization for professional historians and those interested in history. Includes an annual meeting, journals, research and grant opportunities, the collection and preservation of historical documents and artifacts. The organization is designed to enhance and publicize the profession. Among its 15,000 members are faculty at secondary schools and 2- and 4-year colleges and universities, history graduate students, independent historians, and historians in museums, historical organizations, libraries and archives, government, and business.

American Indian History Resources

www.lang.osaka-u.ac.jp/~krkvls/history.html

A chronological history of events. Includes wars, writings, federal policy, oral histories, documents, maps, tribal histories, and milestones. Many links to other important websites.

CHAPTER 4

Sex, Gender, and Families

CHAPTER OUTLINE

Sex and Gender: What's the Difference? 93

■ **USING** *the Sociological Imagination:* Getting to Know Yourself **94**

■ **USING** *the Sociological Imagination:* Transgender Experience Leads Scientist to Critique Sex and Gender Differences **97**

Where Do We Learn Gender? 98

■ **FAMILIES** *as Lived Experience:* The Sexualization of Young Girls **102**

The Pitfalls of Masculinity 104

Institutional Sex Discrimination: Patriarchy 105

Does Patriarchy Exist in Western Nations? 107

■ **EYE** *on the World:* Comparative Literacy Rates—Literate Women as a Percentage of Literate Men Worldwide Between 15–24 Years, 2000–2004 *108*

Implications for Families 111

Social Policy and Family Resilience 114

Conclusion 116

Key Terms 116

Resources on the Internet 117

CHAPTER PREVIEW

Sex and gender influence virtually all aspects of families and intimate relationships. For example, they affect what is expected of us and how we behave in dating relationships, as marriage partners, and as parents. This chapter introduces the concepts of sex and gender, including both micro and macro dimensions. Subsequent chapters will examine how sex and gender influence specific family issues. In this chapter, you will learn:

- The difference between sex and gender, including biological differences and those that are socially constructed

- How we learn about gender, including through family members, toys, schools, peers, and the mass media

- Class, race, and ethnicity influences on gender

- Rigid gender expectations that can harm both males and females

- Examples of patriarchy internationally, including female genital cutting, and the power of education

- Examples of patriarchy in western nations, including the origin of last names, double sexual standards, and women's income and earnings

- How family planning policy can build family resilience throughout the world

What do you think of the statement, "If you want to increase your likelihood of staying married, you should have at least one son"? You might feel uncomfortable with such blatant favoritism of sons over daughters, yet all over the world, the presence of boys seems to hold marriages together, according to research by economists Gordon Dahl and Enrico Moretti (2003). In the United States, the parents of a girl are nearly 5 percent more likely to divorce than are the parents of a boy. The more daughters, the bigger the effect: The parents of three girls are almost 10 percent more likely to divorce than the parents of three boys. In Mexico, Colombia, and Kenya, the gap is wider. In Vietnam, it is wider still; parents of a girl are 25 percent more likely to divorce than parents of a boy.

Why do fathers apparently stick around for sons when they won't stick around for daughters? Or alternatively, why do mothers stay married if they have sons when they won't do the same for daughters? Do fathers prefer the company of sons to daughters? Do parents think a boy needs a male role model more than girls do? Do they worry that boys cannot cope with the consequences of divorce? Do they believe that a devastated daughter is less of a tragedy than a devastated son?

Dahl and Moretti suggest that explanations fall into one of two categories: Either sons improve the quality of marriage or sons exacerbate the pain of divorce. They suggest that before we decide which explanation to believe, we should look for external evidence on the demand for sons versus daughters. Do most parents prefer a son to a daughter?

In some cases, such as China with its ongoing problems of female infanticide and abandonment, the answer is obvious—but is there a preference in the United States as well? Dahl and Moretti find several clues that indicate a strong preference for sons. First, divorced women with sons are substantially more likely to remarry than divorced women with daughters. Daughters lower the probability of remarriage, and lower the probability that the remarriage will succeed. Second, parents of girls are significantly more likely to try to have another child than are parents of boys. This suggests that having at least one son appears to be more important to parents than having at least one daughter. In the United States, Colombia, and Kenya, a couple with three girls is about 4 percent more likely to try for another child than a couple with three boys; in Mexico it is about 9 percent; in Vietnam it is 18 percent; and in China, prior to the one-child policy imposed in the early 1980s, it was 90 percent. Third, Dahl and Moretti look at the marriage rates of U.S. parents who conceive out of wedlock. Among unmarried couples who are expecting a child, if an ultrasound reveals that the child is a boy, such couples are more likely to get married than if the child is a girl.

Dahl and Moretti cannot say with certainty what these data represent, or why parents seem to prefer sons to daughters. However, it seems to be a common sentiment throughout the world and leads the authors to suspect that boys preserve marriages by making marriages feel stronger, not by making divorces feel more problematic (Dahl and Moretti 2003; Landsburg 2003).

One of the first questions asked of a pregnant woman is: "Are you having a boy or a girl?" We are annoyed when a baby wears green or yellow and we receive no hints. Why are we so concerned about learning a person's sex?

Everyone knows that men and women, as well as boys and girls, are distinguished by their genitals; however, in most social situations people have their clothes on, so we look for other cues. We rely on secondary sex characteristics such as voice, facial and body hair, breasts, or height. We also rely on cultural cues. Hair length, shoes, clothing, makeup, and jewelry are cultural artifacts to more easily identify a person's sex category. Cultural norms and values tell us what males and females are "supposed" to be like. Culture accentuates secondary sex characteristics and exaggerates sex differences throughout the life course.

As early as infancy we decorate boys in blue and girls in pink, and these colors seem to matter a great deal to parents. What parents would dare dress their infant son in a pink layette?

Virtually all social institutions—whether political, religious, economic, educational, or familial—distinguish between men and women in fundamental ways. Throughout the world we are virtually obsessed with perceived sex differences, and these differences become the basis on which power is distributed. "Men are rational and therefore best suited to the world of politics; women are emotional and therefore better suited for the world of home" is a creed echoed by many people around the world. Perceptions about differences between men and women are sometimes used to deny women equal rights under the law or equal opportunities in work or education. Society seems to value the contributions of boys, girls, men, and women differently.

This chapter introduces the concepts of sex and gender and explores the ways that being male or female affects us and shapes family and intimate relationships. Subsequent chapters will examine how sex and gender influence specific topics such as developing intimacy, marriage, having and raising children, work and family, aging, domestic violence, divorce, and repartnering. Here we introduce the micro- and macro-level dimensions of sex and gender and examine how they may influence one another. It is important to have a basic understanding of these concepts before we move to subsequent chapters.

Sex and Gender: What's the Difference?

The term **sex** refers to biological differences and one's role in reproduction. Typically people think of sex based on genitalia: male and female. However, anatomical categories are not always easily identifiable, as is the case with **intersexed** individuals. The ambiguity is often the result of chromosomal or hormonal imbalances during the prenatal stage. It is difficult to get a firm number of intersexed individuals because it occurs along a continuum, and not everyone agrees on what exactly constitutes an intersexed person. The frequency of surgery needed to normalize the genital appearance runs about 1 or 2 for every 1,000 births. The genitals are usually surgically reconstructed to adhere to the child's genetic chromosomes, either XX for a female or XY for a male.

In contrast to sex, which is rooted in biology, **gender** refers to the culturally and socially constructed differences between males and females found in the meanings, beliefs, and practices associated with femininity and masculinity. These are learned attitudes and behaviors, not biological or physical qualities. Gender is **socially constructed**. We are born male or female, but we learn the culturally and socially prescribed traits associated with masculine or feminine patterns of behavior.

Gender Is Socially Constructed

In most societies throughout the world today, and certainly throughout history, men and women have been viewed as far more different than alike. We even refer to one another as "the opposite sex." For example, men are often assumed to be more aggressive, sexual, unemotional, rational, and task oriented than women, whereas women are assumed to be more nurturing, passive, and dependent. Many social roles played out in families every day reflect these presumed characteristics. For example, research shows that mothers spend far more time than do fathers on childcare, even when both work outside the home for pay, because women are thought to be more innately nurturing.

However, the suggestion that men and women are the opposite of one another is seriously flawed. Modern social science and biological researchers note that men and women are far more alike than different (Eliot 2009; Kramer 2007; Lindsey 2011). Both men and women express aggression, passivity, nurturance, rationality, instrumentality, and other gender-typed behaviors. We all possess both masculine and feminine traits although to different degrees. The box on pages 94–95, "Using the Sociological Imagination: Getting to Know Yourself,"

U S I N G
the Sociological Imagination

Getting to Know Yourself

Below is a Gender Traits Test, which is a way of judging how traditionally "male" or "female" you are in your behavior and feelings. It is adapted from the work of Dr. Sandra Bem, a psychologist who has written extensively on the subject of gender. There are no right or wrong answers, so just assess yourself on the characteristics listed, using the following scale:

1 = Never or Almost Never True
2 = Usually Not True
3 = Sometimes but Infrequently True
4 = Occasionally True
5 = Often True
6 = Usually True
7 = Always or Almost Always True

1. Adaptable	1	2	3	4	5	6	7
2. Affectionate	1	2	3	4	5	6	7
3. Aggressive	1	2	3	4	5	6	7
4. Conceited	1	2	3	4	5	6	7
5. Compassionate	1	2	3	4	5	6	7
6. Assertive	1	2	3	4	5	6	7
7. Conscientious	1	2	3	4	5	6	7
8. Eager to soothe hurt feelings	1	2	3	4	5	6	7
9. Defend own beliefs	1	2	3	4	5	6	7
10. Conventional	1	2	3	4	5	6	7
11. Gentle	1	2	3	4	5	6	7
12. Dominant	1	2	3	4	5	6	7
13. Jealous	1	2	3	4	5	6	7
14. Love children	1	2	3	4	5	6	7
15. Forceful	1	2	3	4	5	6	7
16. Moody	1	2	3	4	5	6	7
17. Sensitive to the needs of others	1	2	3	4	5	6	7
18. Have leadership abilities	1	2	3	4	5	6	7
19. Reliable	1	2	3	4	5	6	7
20. Sympathetic	1	2	3	4	5	6	7
21. Independent	1	2	3	4	5	6	7
22. Secretive	1	2	3	4	5	6	7
23. Tender	1	2	3	4	5	6	7
24. Have strong personality	1	2	3	4	5	6	7
25. Tactful	1	2	3	4	5	6	7
26. Understanding	1	2	3	4	5	6	7
27. Willing to take a stand	1	2	3	4	5	6	7
28. Truthful	1	2	3	4	5	6	7
29. Warm	1	2	3	4	5	6	7
30. Willing to take risks	1	2	3	4	5	6	7

Scoring:

Step 1: Beginning with **number one**, delete every third answer (e.g., 1, 4, 7, 10, 13, etc.)–these are "dummies" in order to keep you from skewing the test while you are taking it.

Step 2: Total up, beginning with **number two**, every third answer (e.g., 2, 5, 8, 11, 14, etc.). Let's call this "Score A."

Step 3: Total up, beginning with **number three**, every third answer (e.g., 3, 6, 9, 12, 15, etc.). Let's call this "Score B."

Step 4: Subtract Score B from Score A for the "Difference Score." For instance, if your A Score is 90 and your B Score is 70, your Difference Score is 90 − 70 = +20 (positive 20); If your A Score is 70 and your B Score is 90, your Difference Score is 70 − 90 = −20 (negative 20).

Interpreting Gender Traits Scoring:

Masculine: −20 and under

Nearly Masculine: −19 to −10
Androgynous: −9 to +9
Mostly Feminine: +9 to +19
Feminine: +20 and over

Sources: Adapted from The International Foundation for Androgynous Studies 2004; Bem 1975, 1981.

CRITICAL THINKING QUESTIONS

1. How did you score? Can you think of the micro- and macro-level factors that have influenced your score?

2. Do you think a test like this, created more than two decades ago, is still a useful inventory? Why or why not?

offers a self-test so you can assess your own personality traits. Are you more traditionally masculine, more feminine, or do you lean towards **androgyny** (having both masculine and feminine traits in near equal proportion)? Remember, there are no right or wrong answers; just take a look at yourself.

Gendered expectations are in large part socially constructed (Bonvillain 2007). They are variable across and within cultures, are historically situated, and reflect broad social patterns. Gender is not completely innate or instinctive. Rather, much of it is socially and culturally produced.

Sex Differences

Nonetheless, it is important to note that men and women are not identical; their biological differences extend beyond the ones necessary for reproduction (Helgeson 2009). Although using human subjects in this line of research presents a set of particular challenges, many studies suggest that males are generally stronger, more active, and more aggressive than females. However, in other ways males are more fragile. Males suffer from a wider variety of physical illnesses, infant mortality rates are higher among males and their life expectancy is shorter in almost all countries, including the United States (National Center for Health Statistics 2009; Population Reference Bureau 2010b). Males are afflicted with more genetic disorders and suffer from accidents at a higher rate than do females. Depression, however, is far more common among women (Cambron et al. 2009).

There is also scientific evidence that males and females may solve intellectual problems differently. Although most research points to no overall differences in levels of intelligence (measured with IQ tests), men tend to perform better at certain spatial tasks and mathematical reasoning tests. Meanwhile, women on average outperform men in terms of their precision with which they perform certain manual tasks. Women also tend to excel on tests that measure recall of words or matching items.

What is the cause of these differences? For many years, it was popular to attribute sex differences exclusively, or nearly so, to social learning. The argument was that men and women are treated differently because of gender typing, and therefore they come to behave differently and develop different skill sets. However, the accumulating evidence now suggests that some cognitive and skill differences are also present at very early ages.

These differences may result from hormones such as women's higher levels of estrogen and progesterone, and men's higher levels of androgens, including testosterone. Exposure to different hormones begins in the uterus and may have implications for the way the brain is "wired." Studies of female fetuses who have been exposed to abnormally large quantities of androgens because of a genetic defect, called *congenital adrenal hyperplasia (CAH)*, showed that the girls exposed to CAH as children were more likely to prefer playing with more typical masculine toys, such as construction or transportation toys, as compared to the other girls who preferred more typically feminine toys (Kimura 2002).

Although brain research is still in its infancy because of its complexity, there is some evidence that the size, shape, and use of the brain may differ somewhat by sex in regions involved in language, memory, emotion, vision, hearing, and navigation (Becker et al. 2008; Hines 2005). Some studies suggest that women may use more parts of their brain at once while men are more inclined to have focused responses (Onion 2005). One study conducted with mice has shown that as mammals develop in the womb, testosterone and related hormones trigger cell death in some regions of the male brain and foster cell development in other regions (Forger et al. 2004). Removing or adding testosterone to mice shortly after birth causes their brains to develop according to the presence of the hormone, regardless of their sex.

Given these intriguing studies, what is the role of nature versus nurture, and how would this play out in families? Social scientists suggest that most sex differences that we see in a given society are probably a result of both biological and social influences, with social factors powerfully shaping biological ones (Eliot 2009). This process becomes clear as we examine the wide variety of sex and gendered expectations cross-culturally. What one culture defines as distinctly feminine behavior or activities, another may see as quite masculine, as the research by the famous anthropologist George Murdock (1949, 1957) has shown. Are females more emotional—or are males? Answers to questions like this are not universal; they vary across different cultures.

Although we may all possess both masculine and feminine traits, most of us display primarily the gendered traits that are associated with our sex. Females are indeed usually more "feminine" and tend to behave in culturally prescribed feminine ways and males are more "masculine." This is likely due to the strong cultural messages received throughout our lives as well as biological forces.

Incongruence Between Sex and Gender

Most (but certainly not all) cultures have a binary view of sex and gender; you are either male and expected to behave in masculine ways or female and expected to behave in feminine ways. Exceptions to this include the Berdache in Native American culture, in which some men assume a woman's social roles in virtually every respect. They are considered a third gender and not necessarily gay or lesbian.

Transgender individuals manifest characteristics, behaviors, or self-expressions associated typically with the other gender (American Psychological Association Online 2009; Pardo 2008; PFLAG 2009). They may feel that inside, they are truly the other sex. A man may feel as relaxed, comfortable, and normal engaging in feminine traits—such as wearing certain clothing (dresses), engaging in particular grooming practices (painting nails), or having typically feminine hobbies—as he does in engaging in masculine ones, or even more so. Transgender women are not usually as obvious to us because we allow women more leeway to behave in traditionally masculine ways, such as wearing men's clothing or acting aggressively.

Transgender issues have been largely ignored, but this is beginning to change (Girschick 2008; Pfeffer 2010; Schilt 2006). Because of the long-held stigma associated with being transgender, we do not know the exact number of transgender men and women (Grossman and D'Augelli 2006). The American Psychological Association estimates that 2–3 percent of biological males may engage in cross-dressing, at least occasionally (American Psychological Association Online 2009).

Some transgender individuals harbor a deep sense of discomfort about their sex and wish to live fully as members of the other sex. Usually referred to as **transsexuals**, these individuals undergo sex reassignment surgery and hormone treatments, either male-to-female or female-to-male. Current estimates of the prevalence of transsexualism are about 1 in 10,000 for biological males and 1 in 30,000 for biological females (APA Task Force on Gender Identity and Gender Variance 2008). Surgery is expensive, costing up to $50,000 and the preparation is time-consuming and emotionally difficult. It is estimated that 100–500 sex reassignment surgeries are conducted each year in the United States, and 2–5 times this many worldwide. Perhaps 25,000 U.S. adults have undergone sex reassignment surgery (Encyclopedia of Surgery 2009). In the following box "Using the Sociological Imagination: Transgender Experience Leads Scientist to Critique Sex and Gender Differences," we meet one of these individuals, Dr. Ben Barres, formerly known as Barbara.

WHAT DO YOU THINK?

What theories introduced in Chapter 1 would you find most useful in answering the question: Are sex differences biologically or socially produced?

USING the Sociological Imagination

Transgender Experience Leads Scientist to Critique Sex and Gender Differences

Are sex and gender differences due to biology, or to the social environment? Although we may never know the exact amount that each of these factors plays, Dr. Ben Barres, an MD, PhD neurobiologist and professor at Stanford University, has a unique perspective. He has lived both as a woman and as a man. Dr. Barres, who used to be known as Barbara, underwent a sex change operation at the age of 42. He has lived happily as a man for the past 10 years.

Dr. Barres is one of many transgender men and women in the United States. What propelled him into the public light was his written response rebuking the assertion by the president of Harvard that biological differences play a major role in explaining why so few women work in the upper echelons of science, making up only 10 percent of tenured faculty. Dr. Barres firmly disagrees, and argues that women and men are treated very differently, that men have considerable privileges, and discrimination against women is rampant.

Dr. Barres explained that most men and women are unaware of the discriminatory way that women are treated because they have no basis on which to compare

that treatment. "By far, the main difference I have noticed is that people who don't know I am transgendered treat me with much more respect," compared to when he was a woman. He describes numerous incidents in his own life. For example, after giving a lecture he overheard a colleague say,

Dr. Ben Barres, a Stanford professor who underwent a sex change from female to male, has been outspoken on the issue of women's rights. He has the unique perspective of having been both sexes, and claims that women are routinely discriminated against.

(continued)

(continued)

"Ben Barres gave a great seminar today, but then his work is much better than his sister's," unknowingly referring to him prior to his sex change operation when he was named Barbara (Vendantam 2006). As an undergraduate at MIT, Barbara Barres solved a difficult math problem that stumped her mostly male classmates, and was ridiculed by her professor, "your boyfriend must have solved it for you."

Dr. Barres describes how, as a man, he is interrupted less often, is afforded greater respect for his work, and has far greater access to other physician and science colleagues. "I can even finish a whole sentence without being interrupted by a man" (Vendantam 2006).

His personal experience is bolstered by a range of studies showing bias in science. For example, when a panel of scientists evaluated grant proposals in which no names were attached, men and women scored equally well. However, when the names of the authors were included and therefore the sex revealed, women applying for research grants needed to be three times more productive than men to be considered equally competent (*Science Daily* 2006).

Critics dismiss women who complain of discrimination as being irrational and emotional, but Barres insists that it is very real. In 2004, the National Institutes of Health had 60 men (out of 64 evaluators) reviewing applications for one of its prestigious scientific awards. All nine grants were awarded to men. The next year, Dr. Barres convinced the NIH to have a more balanced set of evaluators. This time, 6 of the 13 grants went to women. His goal is to bring discrimination to light to empower women because he believes most do not even recognize that they are being treated differently.

Sources: Adapted from Science Daily 2006; Vedantam 2006.

CRITICAL THINKING QUESTIONS
1. How does the experience of Dr. Ben Barres add a unique perspective on the causes of sex and gender differences?
2. Can you devise a study that might help us further understand what sex and gender differences are biological, and which ones are socially produced by our environment?
3. Have you ever experienced sex discrimination, or received a privilege because of your sex?

Where Do We Learn Gender?

If much of gendered behavior is socially constructed and learned, where do we learn it? Through a process called **gender socialization**, we are taught the norms associated with being male or female in our particular culture (Bonvillain 2007; Eliot 2009; Helgeson 2009). Gender socialization may be a conscious effort, such as a teacher criticizing a young girl for being rowdy and "unladylike" in the classroom or scolding a young boy for displaying his emotions because "big boys don't cry." It also may occur on a less conscious level, such as parents providing different toys for their children—dress-up clothes for their daughters and war toys for their sons. The **agents of socialization**, summarized in Table 4.1, include the people, social institutions, and organizations that teach boys and girls their gendered expectations.

Family Members

Parents and other family members have the primary responsibility for introducing the gendered norms and expectations in their culture (Marks et al. 2009). They teach a child about what to wear, how to behave, what toys to play with, what the child's status is, and what the overall expectations are for the child. Consciously or not, they often treat their sons and daughters differently. They hold baby girls more gently and cuddle them more than they do

TABLE 4.1   Agents of Socialization and How They Work

We learn our gendered expectations through various agents of socialization.

Parents
- Differential treatment becomes a self-fulfilling prophecy

Toys
- Books show boys as leading characters and girls in stereotypical roles; toys are sex-typed

Schools
- Hidden curriculum encourages sex-typed behavior and teaches girls to fear academic success

Peers
- Same-sex play reinforces different interaction styles that carry over into adulthood

Mass Media
- Television, music videos, and computer games tend to focus on boys and present girls in stereotypical ways

boys. Parents of girls describe their children as more dainty and delicate than do parents of boys, and the choice of dress usually reflects this (Leaper and Friedman 2006).

Differential treatment continues throughout childhood, repeating itself over and over and creating a self-fulfilling prophecy far beyond any true existing biological differences. Parents, solely on the basis of sex, may assign rules, toys, expected behavior, chores, hobbies, and a multitude of other cultural values or artifacts differently. For example, girls may be required by their parents to do the dishes daily, whereas their brothers mow the lawn weekly; parents may allow more rough play from their sons than their daughters; teenage girls may have an earlier curfew than their brothers. When girls and boys are treated differently it is not surprising that they become more different. This then is seen by many parents as only natural, and therefore it becomes reinforced.

Fathers in particular tend to encourage their children to behave in different ways because of their sex. They emphasize achievement for their sons, while focusing more on interpersonal issues with their daughters (Gurian 1999; Maccoby and Jacklin 1974). Fathers are more involved in families that have boys, and as seen in the opening vignette, families with boys are more stable and parents may be less likely to divorce (Dahl and Moretti 2003; Landsburg 2003).

Toys

Children's toys and games are also differentiated on the basis of sex (Diekman and Murnen 2004), and girls as young as 18 months of age have shown a preference for dolls over trucks (although boys showed no preference) (Serbin et al. 2001). Toys for boys often emphasize rough-and-tumble play (e.g., sports, guns, vehicles, action figures), whereas toys for girls often focus on quiet or nurturing activities (e.g., dolls, arts and crafts, kitchens, and cooking). An analysis of virtually any children's toy store will reveal that pink aisles specialize in girl toys whereas others are reserved for toys for boys. A toy as seemingly gender-neutral as a bicycle takes on great gender significance by its color: pink for girls, blue for boys.

Although both boys and girls play with dolls, the types of dolls they play with are distinctive and reinforce traditional stereotypes. Baby dolls are popular and often come with a bottle so girls can practice feeding skills. Dolls such as Barbie reinforce stereotypes about adult women and their bodies. In contrast, dolls for boys are referred to as "action figures" and are often rugged and warlike.

Children's books give a lopsided view of the world and reinforce traditional stereotypes about males and females. A recent review of 200 top-selling children's books and a seven-year

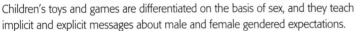

Children's toys and games are differentiated on the basis of sex, and they teach implicit and explicit messages about male and female gendered expectations.

sample of Caldecott award-winning books discovered a number of examples of gender bias. There were nearly twice as many male as female title and main characters; male characters appeared in illustrations 53 percent more than female characters; female characters nurtured more than did male main characters and they were seen in more indoor than outdoor scenes; and occupations were more gender stereotypes, with more women than men having no paid occupation (Anderson and Hamilton 2006).

Even a study of children's books evaluated as "nonsexist" by a group of independent raters still portrays housework as women's work. Although the nonsexist books were more likely than other books to show women and girls at work or playing in active and nonstereotypical ways, they also portrayed women and girls doing domestic chores, unlike the boys and men who were never portrayed doing housework (Diekman and Murnen 2004).

Schools

Daycare centers, preschools, elementary schools, secondary schools, and even college classrooms are other important arenas in which gender socialization occurs. Research a decade or two ago revealed that teachers called on boys to answer questions more often than girls, and boys were given more public praise by teachers. Teachers appeared to have lower expectations for girls than boys; teachers solved the problem or gave girls answers more quickly, whereas they expected boys to solve the problem themselves. The **hidden curriculum** informally taught girls that academic achievement could mean forfeiting popularity (Orenstein 1994). Consequently, girls tended to excel in elementary school, but by the time they reached middle and upper school, they lost confidence, and tested more poorly than boys (Kenney-Benson et al. 2006).

But something has changed (Mead 2006). Today, it appears that many girls and young women have a strong achievement ethic, are doing well in school, and are surpassing boys and young men. More girls apply to, attend, and graduate from college now than boys. Fifty-four percent of undergraduate students are women, up from only 36 percent in 1970, as are 60 percent of graduate students (Fry and Cohn 2010). Many college majors, however, remain sex-typed. Students in nursing, elementary, education, and social work are overwhelmingly

Figure 4.1 **Who Has More Education: Husbands or Wives?**

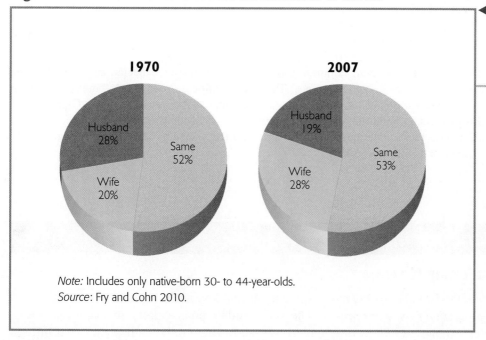

Married women now have more education than their husbands.

Note: Includes only native-born 30- to 44-year-olds.
Source: Fry and Cohn 2010.

female, whereas students in engineering and computer science are primarily male. Nonetheless, among married couples under age 45 (born in the United States), wives are now likely to have more education than their husbands, as shown in Figure 4.1 (Fry and Cohn 2010).

Peers

Young children are socialized by their same-sex peers to conform to traditional gender expectations. Martin and Fabes (2001) observed play behavior of 28 boys and 33 girls aged 3–6 over a six-month period at a university daycare facility. Although the boys and girls were not very different in most of their behaviors at the beginning of the school year, differences intensified by the spring. The more time boys spent playing with other boys, the greater the likelihood that they were observed to be rougher, more aggressive, dominance-oriented, and more active in their play the following spring. For girls, exposure to same-sex peers lowered their aggression and activity levels by the spring. The authors suggest that peers may play the role of gender "enforcers," who monitor and maintain gendered behavior by conveying the acceptable norms and the consequences if those norms are violated (Partenheimer 2001).

Psychologist Eleanor Maccoby (1998) examined children's play groups and found that children between the ages of 2 and 3 tend to prefer same-sex peer play groups when provided with the opportunity to do so. She also noted that when girls were playing with other girls, they were as active as were boys playing with other boys. However, when girls were playing with boys, they frequently stood back and let the boys dominate the toys or games. Maccoby speculated that the boys' rougher play and greater focus on competition was unattractive to girls, and girls responded by pulling back rather than by trying to exert their own play style. Maccoby suggests that these peer groups reinforce different interaction styles that carry over into adulthood: boys' groups reinforce a more competitive, dominance-oriented style of interaction, which carries over into adult male communication patterns that include greater interrupting, contradicting, or boasting. Girls' cooperative groups reinforce a style that contributes to adult female communication patterns that include expressing agreement and acknowledging the comments of others and asking questions rather than making bold pronouncements. A study in Texas found that children who engage in more same-sex play were better liked by peers and were viewed by teachers as being socially competent (Colwell and Lindsey 2005).

It is not only young children who succumb to gendered expectations. The following box "Families as Lived Experience: The Sexualization of Young Girls," indicates that the pressure for girls to conform to sexualized gendered expectations is fierce. Girls aged 13 to 17 spent $152 million on thong underwear—why? Moreover, even girls aged 7–12 are drawn to these undergarments. Peer pressure to be seen as sexual beings begins early (Levin and Kilbourne 2008).

F A M I L I E S
as Lived Experience

The Sexualization of Young Girls

Only a generation ago, childhood was thought of as a time of innocence and protection from adult preoccupations. As one father shows us, times are changing.

As the father of a ten-year old girl, I was given the task of helping her shop for back-to-school clothes. My wife, who has shopped with Jessie "since time began" (her words, of course), said that she has officially resigned from the task. It's too stressful, my wife lamented. What could possibly be so stressful about buying a few shirts, pants, socks, and underwear for a fifth-grader?

As I quickly learned after a trip to the mall, there is plenty to be stressed about. First, I was dumbfounded when I noticed that the shirts she wanted to buy were low-cut, designed to accentuate breasts that she doesn't yet have. Then, in the pants department, she picked out such tight jeans that she could barely zip them. And when she finally did get them zipped, they were so low-cut it was as though she was wearing a bikini. I tried to find some alternatives in the store, which wasn't easy given the selection, and when I found a few acceptable things she just snubbed me. Call me uncool, which Jessie most definitely did, but what's the deal with the clothes?

After the battle of the outerwear, I figured we were safe as we headed to the underwear department. I browsed elsewhere while she picked out some items and I then met her at the cash register. The socks didn't pose a problem, but when the clerk started to ring up the underwear, what little there was of it, I couldn't believe my eyes. My little ten-year-old girl, who weighs only 75 pounds, who has not yet gone through puberty, actually planned to buy red and black thong underwear!! You know what I mean - the tiny ones that ride up your crack! When I suggested an alternative, you know, the Hanes three-in-a-pack version, she glared at me and said "Dad, get real. I can't possibly be seen wearing those."

I AM real. And since when is a fifth-grader's underwear supposed to be seen, anyway? I don't get it. Am I the only dad out there who doesn't want my preteen daughter dressing like she's a college student on her way to a bar looking for a hook-up? Why are we sexualizing young girls? And why do young girls want to be sexualized? I decided to investigate these issues further.

Here's what I found. Sales marketers are now targeting a new age group called "tweens," defined as children between the ages of 7 and 12. Kids this age are no longer just children, wearing whatever Macbeth plaid skirt their mother might pick out for them. They are increasingly targeted with clothing and accessories that parallel adolescents and adults.

This marketing is related to two important issues: First, girls are on average maturing earlier and earlier. As a result of biology and exposure to endocrine-disrupting toxins flooding our environment, many girls as young as 8 or 9 have begun breast development. Second, our culture encourages girls and women of all ages to be sexual objects. Kids watch an average of 21 hours a week, and their favorite television shows and favorite pop musicians show girls and women wearing tight low-cut shirts, tight pants, short skirts, and sexualized makeup and hair—Miley Cyrus, Selena Gomez, Taylor Momsen, Britney Spears, Rihanna. Girls and women's bodies are portrayed as unnaturally thin, with unnaturally large breasts popping out of their shirts.

I also learned that chronic sexual objectification has a lasting impact because girls' image of who they are becomes grossly distorted. Girls come to see their primary self-worth as their ability to be sexual objects for male pleasure. These standards are so rigid and unattainable that girls become increasingly distressed about their bodies. A report by the American Psychological Association claimed that girls who are sexualized are more prone to eating disorders, depression, low self-esteem, impaired concentration, risky sexual behavior, and unsatisfying sexual relations when older. Think of

Marilyn Monroe, who shortly before her death admitted that she had never had an orgasm!

I also believe that chronic sexual objectification teaches boys that girls should be valued primarily for their ability to give boys sexual pleasure. Much of the pornography that is targeted to boys and young men suggests that (a) all women at all times want sex from all men; (b) women like all the sex acts that men perform or demand; and (c) any woman who does not have this initial desire can be turned on with a little force.

Armed with all this insight, I'm at a quandary. How can I protect my daughter, while at the same time honor her desire to fit in with her peers? Very tough question, indeed.

Source: American Psychological Association, Task Force on the Sexualization of Girls, 2007; Olfman, Sharma, The Sexualization of Childhood, 2009.

CRITICAL THINKING QUESTIONS
1. Why is there so much social pressure on girls to look sexy, whether they are sexually active or not? Is there equivalent pressure on boys?
2. Is marketing a reflection of consumer wants, or does marketing drive it?

The Mass Media

The mass media, including television and video games, are an increasingly important mechanism for socializing children. More than two-thirds of American households play computer or video games; 60 percent of these players are male (Entertainment Software Association 2010). In a study titled *Girls and Gaming: Gender and Video Game Marketing*, a look at 27 popular games found that many promoted "unrealistic body images and stereotypical female characteristics, such as provocative sexuality, high-pitched voices and fainting" (Media Awareness Network 2008).

Boys, especially middle-class White boys, are at the center of most television programming, playing the most roles and engaging in the most activity (Aubrey and Harrison 2004; Baker and Raney 2007). A review of recent children's television shows reveals that male characters are still more likely than female characters to answer questions, boss or order others, show ingenuity, and achieve a goal (Aubrey and Harrison 2004). A study of morning commercials showed that half of the commercials aimed at girls spoke about physical attractiveness, whereas none of the commercials aimed at boys mentioned attractiveness (National Institute on Media and the Family 2009). Incidentally, females are less likely than males to be shown eating, not an insignificant finding given the high rates of eating disorders among girls and women (National Institute of Mental Health 2009).

How Do Race, Ethnicity, and Class Shape Gender Socialization?

Let's be careful not to overgeneralize because people's experiences differ widely and because the intersections of gender, race, ethnicity, and class are complex; however, it does appear that significant class, racial, and ethnic variations exist in the gender socialization process (Hill 2002, 2005; Hirsch 2003; Wallace 2007). For example, Hill's in-depth interviews with a small sample of 35 Black parents examined the extent to which parents think gender influenced the ways in which they socialize and treat their children. All parents expressed some belief in gender equality, but middle-class Black parents expressed the strongest support.

As another example, Black women and girls are more satisfied with their body types than are their White counterparts. Blacks have a more flexible standard of attractiveness, believing that thickness and curves are more desirable than supermodel thinness. Black girls are more likely than Whites to say that they are beautiful, that they like their bodies, and that they like themselves the way they are (Bailey 2008).

Gendered expectations are rapidly changing among Hispanic groups. Older Hispanics—both men and women—tend to be more patriarchal in their attitudes and behaviors than younger Hispanics. An in-depth study with different generations of Hispanic women found that older women believe that traditional gendered expectations grant them a form of respect and protection, and they often do not understand why young women are so eager to give these up (Hirsch 2003).

The Pitfalls of Masculinity

Much of the early gender literature focused on the way that girls' and women's lives have been affected by rigid conceptions of gender. More recently, some have argued that although both boys and girls receive gender messages, perhaps boys experience even more pressure to conform to cultural stereotypes (Adams and Coltrane 2003; Kane 2006; Mead 2006; Messner 2009). Girls are allowed more leeway. They can behave in ways that have been considered masculine; for example, there is little social stigma in being a "tomboy," whereas boys are not allowed to behave in ways that are deemed feminine. To be told that "you throw like a girl" or to be labeled a "sissy" (which is the opposite of a tomboy) is tantamount to social suicide. Likewise, women have moved into many occupations traditionally held by men (such as doctor or lawyer), whereas few men find the occupations of nurse or legal secretary attractive. In the home, despite women's greater likelihood of being employed, men have not increased their time in domestic tasks at the same rate. Adams and Coltrane (2003) suggest:

> Paradoxically, masculine gender identity is also considered to be more fragile than feminine gender identity . . . and takes more psychic effort because it requires suppressing human feelings of vulnerability and denying emotional connection. . . . Boys, therefore, are given less gender latitude than girls, and fathers are more intent than mothers on making sure that their sons do not become sissies. Later, as a result, these boys turned men will be predisposed to spend considerable amounts of time and energy maintaining gender boundaries and denigrating women and gays.

The result of suppressing emotions is well noted. Problem behaviors of young boys, including use of alcohol and drugs, police detainment, fighting and other acts of aggression against their peers, school suspension, or forcing someone to have sex against her will are all associated with heightened traditional masculine ideals (Christopher and Sprecher 2000). Consequently numerous books have been published over the past decade about the "boy crisis"—how to raise emotionally healthy, well-balanced, and achievement-oriented boys (Kindlin and Thompson 2000; Biddulph and Stanish 2008).

WHAT DO YOU THINK?

Do you think it is easier in our society today to be a male or a female? Can you defend your answer?

Institutional Sex Discrimination: Patriarchy

Patriarchy, introduced in Chapter 2, is found in a wide variety of social institutions, including legal, educational, religious, and economic ones. Traditional religious texts are filled with passages demeaning women, although their interpretations may be softened in modern-day language. For instance, Christianity teaches patriarchy, as witnessed in the following passages in the New Testament (1 Tm. 2:11–15):

> Let a woman learn in silence with all submissiveness. I permit no woman to teach or to have authority over men; she is to keep silent. For Adam was formed first, then Eve; and Adam was not deceived, but the woman was deceived and became a transgressor. Yet woman will be saved through bearing children, if she continues in faith and love and holiness, with modesty.

Patriarchy is widespread and is found in virtually every society; however, it is obviously more pronounced in some societies than in others. There are many places in the world today where women cannot drive, vote, divorce, or own property in their own name. In virtually every society, women's activities and jobs carry less prestige and pay than those that are primarily held by men. Even when men and women work in identical or comparable jobs, women are paid significantly less for their effort overall. Moreover, women are underrepresented in public office and it is men who primarily make the laws that women must follow, including on issues that affect women in particular, such as abortion, birth control, or guaranteed family leave. These inequities are justified on the basis of biology ("it's human nature"), religion ("it's God's will"), or cultural customs ("that's the way we do things here").

We begin this discussion by illustrating an extreme example of patriarchy experienced in the world today. Sometimes it is easier to see how patriarchy operates by examining the most glaring example, as it is often easier to identify patriarchy elsewhere than it is within our own borders. We will then turn to gendered experiences in the United States and other developed nations: Does patriarchy operate here as well?

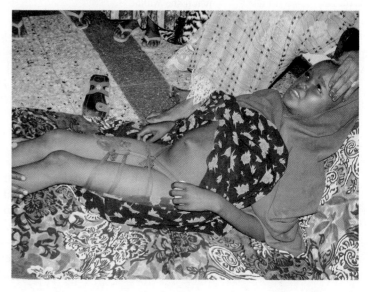

This young girl, like 100 to 140 million others, suffers as she tries to recover from the dangerous practice of "female genital cutting" or "mutilation." In an excruciatingly painful procedure, often without anesthesia, her clitoris, and possibly part of her vagina as well, is cut and removed with a knife, razor blade, or broken glass. She is then sewn up to ensure virginity.

Female Genital Cutting

I was genitally mutilated at the age of ten. I was told by my late grandmother that they were taking me down to the river to perform a certain ceremony, and afterwards I would be given a lot of food to eat. As an innocent child, I was led like a sheep to be slaughtered.

Once I entered the secret bush, I was taken to a very dark room and undressed. I was blindfolded and stripped naked. I was then carried by two strong women to the site for the operation. I was forced to lie flat on my back by four strong women, two holding tight to each leg. Another woman sat on my chest to prevent my upper body from moving. A piece of cloth was forced in my mouth to stop me screaming. I was then shaved.

When the operation began, I put up a big fight. The pain was terrible and unbearable. During this fight, I was badly cut and lost blood. All those who took part in the operation were half-drunk with alcohol. Others were dancing and singing, and worst of all, had stripped naked.

I was genitally mutilated with a blunt penknife. After the operation, no one was allowed to aid me to walk. The stuff they put on my wound stank and was painful. These were terrible times for me. Each time I wanted to urinate, I was forced to stand upright. The urine would spread over the wound and would cause fresh pain all over again. Sometimes I had to force myself not to urinate for fear of the terrible pain. I was not given any anesthetic in the operation to reduce my pain, nor any antibiotics to fight against infection. Afterwards, I hemorrhaged and became anemic. This was attributed to witchcraft. I suffered for a long time from acute vaginal infections.

This is the story of Hannah Koroma of Sierra Leone from Amnesty International (2004). This woman, like nearly 100–140 million other women and girls living in over two dozen countries in Africa and the Middle East, has experienced the painful and dangerous practice of what is described as *female genital cutting* or *mutilation* (Human Rights Watch 2010b; World Health Organization 2010b). Among countries with adequate national data, Egypt has the highest prevalence; over 90 percent of women aged 15–49 have had their genitals cut.

In one form of genital cutting, **clitoridectomy**, the clitoris is cut out of the body. In the more extreme form, **infibulation**, the vaginal lips are also cut or scraped away, and the outer portion of the vagina is stitched together, leaving only a miniscule opening for menstrual blood and urine to escape the body. The procedure is done crudely; a layperson rather than a physician usually conducts it. One study of nearly 2,000 women living in Egypt who had their genitals cut reports that only 14 percent of the cutting was performed by a doctor (Yount 2002). In an excruciatingly painful procedure, often without anesthesia, the girl is tied or held down and the instrument used may be a knife, razor blade, or broken glass. Often, the girl's body is stitched together with thorn or catgut, and her knees are bound together for several weeks for the incision to heal itself and not tear open again when she walks.

The health consequences of genital mutilation are swift, long-lasting, and severe, and include much more than a loss of sexual pleasure. Immediate consequences include possible shock, hemorrhaging, or bleeding to death. Soon afterwards, women face possible pelvic infection, dangerous scarring, and internal pain from urination and menstrual fluids that cannot properly escape the body. As they mature, they may experience infertility, a greater likelihood of miscarriage, recurrent urinary tract infections, anal incontinence, and fissures. Intercourse will be painful, childbirth will be prolonged and obstructed, it is likely that the perineal area will be lacerated, and there is a greater chance of stillborn births (World Health Organization 2010b).

In those countries where female genital cutting is practiced, it has widespread support; in fact, most women intend to continue the practice with their own daughters (Williams and Sobieszczyk 1997; Yount 2002). One national study in Sudan revealed that close to 90 percent of all women surveyed either had the procedure performed on their daughters or planned to do so. Nearly one-half of women in support of cutting favored infibulation, the most extreme form (Williams and Sobieszczyk 1997). Even better-educated women often support it. Failure to do so will make their daughters "different" or "promiscuous" and perhaps unmarriageable (Leonard 2000; Mackie 2000).

Why is this practice so popular, and why has it continued for so many years? It is deeply rooted in the patriarchal traditions (rather than religious teachings) in these societies. It has been described as "one of the most severe... means of 'educating' women about their subordinate status" (Abd el Salam 1998). Women are expected to be subject to the social and sexual control of men at all times. They are expected to be virgins at the time of marriage and must remain sexually faithful thereafter. Removing the clitoris, the source of women's sexual pleasure, ensures that they will not experience orgasm, and thus the likelihood of engaging in or enjoying sexual relationships outside of marriage is lessened. Among women whose entire external genital area has been removed, the opening that remains is so small as to forbid penetration. Husbands are virtually guaranteed that their wives are virgins.

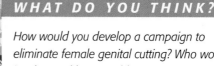

WHAT DO YOU THINK?

How would you develop a campaign to eliminate female genital cutting? Who would you involve, and how would you get your message across? How would you take into account the culture in which people live?

Female genital cutting persists, and is endorsed, perpetuated, and often conducted by other women because their status is low and their options are few. Marriage and motherhood are the primary ways in which women receive recognition. Without marriage, they bring shame to themselves and to their families. Virginity is highly valued, and this procedure helps to ensure that women's sexuality will be muted. Mothers believe that if they do not have their daughter's clitoris removed or have her infibulated, her chances of finding a husband will be reduced considerably and the daughter will bear considerable shame.

The Power of Education

One of the key determinants of women's status in society is their average level of education. In countries where women's average level of education is lower, they have little social or political power. This changes as women's average level of education begins to rise. Education offers women a new perspective on the world, the ability to read and access information, the potential to increase their economic status, improved self-esteem, and the ability to engage in public debates and bargain effectively for their rights, all of which increase their level of power in society. It also tends to lower their fertility, critical to granting women greater freedoms. Policies to improve the status of women in the world must take into consideration the importance of educating women.

Although the gender gap in primary and secondary schooling is closing somewhat, women still lag significantly behind men in many countries, especially parts of Africa and southern Asia (Ashford and Clifton 2005). Furthermore, it remains that two-thirds of the world's nearly 900 million illiterate persons are women (United Nations 2000). In virtually every country where illiteracy is high, women are less likely to be able to read and write than men. The map on pages 108–109 indicates literate women as a percentage of literate men between the ages of 15 and 24.

Does Patriarchy Exist in Western Nations?

It's easy to say, "Whew, I'm glad I live in the U.S." However, the United States has its own set of patriarchal norms and customs. Do any come to mind? How many U.S. presidents have been women? Vice presidents? Senators? How many heads of Fortune 500 companies are women? How does women's pay compare to men's? How do standards of beauty vary for men and women—some with potentially dangerous or painful repercussions (hint, think cosmetic surgery, breast implants, waxing, or even high-heeled shoes)? Over 12 million

Comparative Literacy Rates—Literate Women as a Percentage of Literate Men Worldwide Between 15–24 Years, 2000–2004

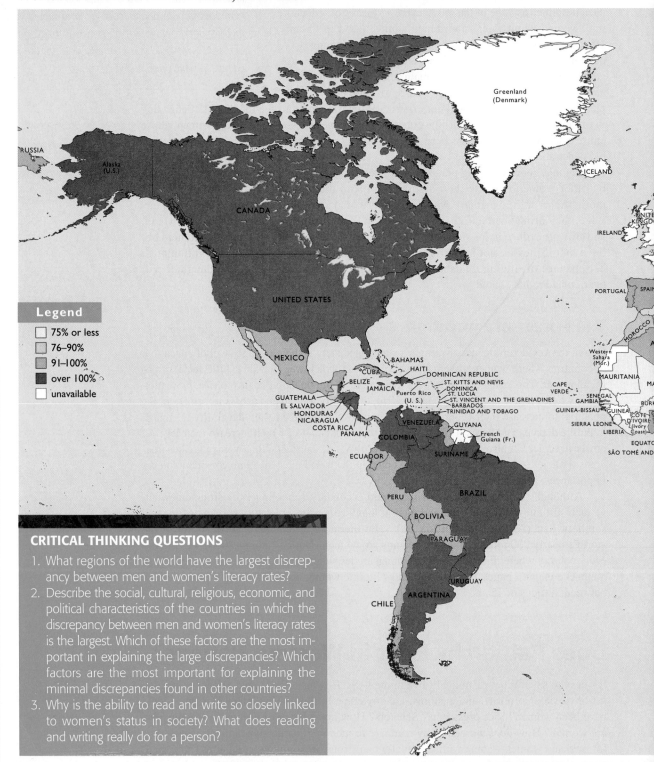

Legend
- ☐ 75% or less
- ☐ 76–90%
- ☐ 91–100%
- ☐ over 100%
- ☐ unavailable

CRITICAL THINKING QUESTIONS

1. What regions of the world have the largest discrepancy between men and women's literacy rates?
2. Describe the social, cultural, religious, economic, and political characteristics of the countries in which the discrepancy between men and women's literacy rates is the largest. Which of these factors are the most important in explaining the large discrepancies? Which factors are the most important for explaining the minimal discrepancies found in other countries?
3. Why is the ability to read and write so closely linked to women's status in society? What does reading and writing really do for a person?

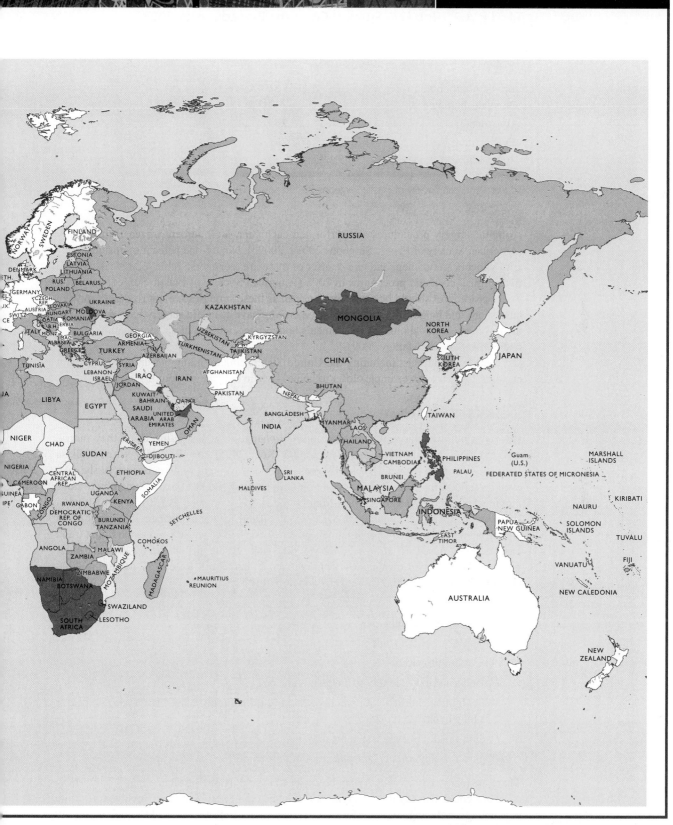

Sources: Population Reference Bureau 2010c; CIA 2010.

TABLE 4.2 Top Five Surgical Cosmetic Procedures in 2008

Standards of beauty for women are so rigid that many resort to potentially dangerous and expensive cosmetic surgery.

Breast Augmentation	307,000
Nose Reshaping	279,000
Liposuction	245,000
Eyelid Surgery	221,000
Tummy Tuck	122,000

Source: American Society of Plastic Surgeons 2009c.

cosmetic surgery procedures are performed each year, a 60 percent increase since 2000 (American Society of Plastic Surgeons 2009a, 2009b). Ninety-one percent of cosmetic surgery patients are women, and one-quarter of these are teenagers. Table 4.2 reveals the top five surgical cosmetic procedures in 2008 (American Society of Plastic Surgeons 2009c). These procedures should be cause for concern, as these surgeries are not risk free, and can have short- and long-term side effects. Women who have cosmetic surgery have internalized the media messages about "ideal" women's body image, and are dissatisfied with their own bodies (Markey and Markey 2009).

Developed nations, including the United States, contain many patriarchal norms and customs. Let's take an example closer to home—where did you get your *last name*?

What's in a Name?

Have you noticed that most women routinely change their last name when they marry, whereas men virtually never do (Jayson 2005; Keen 2005; Powell 2005)? When Melissa Smith marries John Brown, she usually goes by the new name of Melissa Brown, or she may even be called Mrs. John Brown, taking on both his first and last name. Fueled by famous movie stars such as Farrah Fawcett-Majors and sports stars such as Chris Evert-Lloyd, a small number of married women in the 1970s and 1980s began hyphenating their last name at marriage or keeping their own name (Jayson 2005). However, in recent years, that trend has reversed. Based on almost 7,000 wedding announcements in the *New York Times*, women who kept their own names declined from 23 percent in 1990 to 17 percent in 2000 (Jayson 2005). Why is this? Moreover, what does it reflect?

Some people may turn to micro-level explanations:

"I never really thought about it."

"I didn't care and he did."

"It's easier this way."

"It helps make us a family to have the same name."

"Why burden children with parents who have different last names from one another, or a long hyphenated name?"

"I didn't really like my last name anyway."

"I gave my children my last name as a middle name."

There are many reasons why it may be easier to have only one last name in a family. However, one could also say that changing a last name on all pertinent legal documents is time consuming, confusing, and interferes with one's career trajectory or makes tracking family history more difficult.

But let's look at macro-explanations as well: changing of wives' names is a carryover from older patriarchal and patrilineal customs where upon marriage a woman became the legal property of her husband. It was important to name the child after the father so that he could identify and establish "ownership" of his heirs. Surnames (last names) were created to codify inheritance rules and thereby bolster tax revenues (Stevens 1999).

WHAT DO YOU THINK?

Can you think of other examples of patriarchy in American society?

Traditions take many years to die. Until the 1970s, many state bureaucracies still prohibited women from keeping their own names after marriage and giving their children their own last names. However, the laws have since changed. So why is the tradition continued today? Historian Hendrik Hartog (2000), author of *Man and Wife in America*, suggests that much of what people do in marriage is simply done out of habit, even when the tradition has no legal or financial basis. There is a powerful pull toward reproducing tradition. Yet, these persistent traditions tell us something about women's continued roles in society.

Dr. Ben Barres, the neurobiologist and professor at Stanford University introduced in the box on pages 97–98, has something to say about male privilege. Barres has the unique experience of living as both a woman and a man. As an adult, he had a sex change operation, and has now lived for over a decade as a man. What did he learn from this experience? He is adamant that women and men are treated very differently, and that women are routinely discriminated against in ways that most are unaware of (Science Daily 2006; Vedantam 2006).

Could Dr. Barres be on to something?

Implications for Families

Gender is forged into all aspects of social life; it is particularly evident within families and close relationships. Generally, who initiates a date, pays for it, chooses the activity, and drives? Who proposes marriage? Who earns the most money in a relationship, and connected to this, who does the most housework and childrearing? Who initiates sex? Who has the most power?

The chapters throughout this text will highlight the gendered aspects of family relationships, and reveal how such macro issues as patriarchal customs and interpersonal power function to shape the microstructure of personal relationships. This text will examine seemingly everyday issues of dating and mate selection, the dynamics in marriage, childrearing, juggling work and family, and aging, as well as crises such as domestic violence, divorce, and repartnering. The following is an example that examines gender dynamics associated with labor market participation and earnings.

How Sex and Gender Matter: Income and Earnings

Most women work outside the home for pay, whether married or not, and whether they have children or not. During the 1940s through the mid-1970s, mothers tended to organize their labor force participation around childbearing and childrearing. In the 1940s and 1950s, they tried to wait until their children had grown up before returning to work; in the 1960s, mothers tried to wait until their children were in high school; and by the 1970s, it had dropped to when children were in middle school. Nonetheless, the general convention was, unless a mother had to work because of dire economic circumstances, employment was secondary to the bearing and rearing of children.

By the 1970s, a new pattern of mothers' labor force participation emerged and has continued. Today, 69 percent of married mothers, 71 percent of single mothers, and 80 percent of divorced, separated, or widowed mothers are employed for pay (Bureau of Labor Statistics 2010c). However, instead of continuing to adapt work to fit childbearing, the reverse has occurred. Childbearing and childrearing were adapted to fit the demands of work. Families delayed having children, had fewer of them, and an increasing number of women and men chose not to have children at all (Dye 2008; Mathews and Hamilton 2009). Thus, a macro-level condition of changing norms surrounding women's employment led to micro-level changes in the structure of families.

During this period, Americans also witnessed a restructuring of the U.S. economy. We moved from a family-based economy, with the household as the primary unit of economic production, to one in which we primarily rely on wages from work done outside the home. Whereas once the country was heavily dependent on raw materials and manufacturing, today the U.S. economy is heavily geared toward the provision of a wide range of services from medical care to the food and entertainment industries. Wages have declined, and families rely on two paychecks to make ends meet. Women contribute 36 percent to the family income, up from only 27 percent a generation ago (Bureau of Labor Statistics 2009e).

How do female workers fare compared to their male counterparts? The median weekly earnings of women who are full-time wage and salary workers hover around $650, or 80 percent of men's earnings, which are around $820. When comparing the median weekly earnings of persons aged 16–24, young women earned 93 percent of what young men earned (Bureau of Labor Statistics 2009a). So, things are looking up for younger women.

Table 4.3 reports women's earnings as a percentage of men's earnings between 1980 and 2008, among persons who work full-time over an entire year (Bureau of Labor Statistics 2009e). The table compares data for Whites, Blacks, Asians, and Hispanics. The data reveal that Black and Hispanic women earn incomes closest to their male counterparts, whereas the gender gap for Whites and Asians is the widest. Unfortunately, pay differences continue even among those who are most educated, as shown in Table 4.4. Women without a high school diploma earn about 76 percent of their male counterparts' salaries, whereas women with a PhD earn roughly 78 percent of men's salaries.

What accounts for the pay differentials? Realistically, differentials could be due to several factors, including **labor market segmentation**, which is that men and women often work in different types of jobs with distinct working conditions and pay. Women tend to work in less prestigious, nonunionized, and lower-paying jobs than men (Bureau of Labor Statistics 2009e). They are likely to be found working as secretaries, registered nurses, elementary and middle school teachers, and in service work, as shown in Table 4.5 (Bureau of Labor Statistics 2009e). To eliminate sex-segregated jobs in the United States, about half of male (or female) workers would have to change occupations.

The Equal Pay Act was signed in 1963, making it illegal for employers to pay unequal wages to men and women who hold the same job and do the same work. Nonetheless,

TABLE 4.3   Women's Earnings as a Percent of Men's

Black and Hispanic women earn wages closer to their male counterparts than do Whites and Asian Americans.

	TOTAL	WHITE	BLACK	ASIAN	HISPANIC
1980	64%	63%	76%	–	74%
1985	68%	67%	83%	–	78%
1990	72%	72%	85%	–	87%
1995	76%	73%	86%	–	87%
2000	77%	76%	84%	80%	88%
2005	81%	80%	89%	81%	88%
2008	80%	79%	89%	78%	90%

Source: Bureau of Labor Statistics 2009e.

TABLE 4.4   Median Weekly Earnings of Full-Time Workers by Sex and Educational Attainment

Pay differentials continue regardless of education level.

	WOMEN	MEN	WOMEN'S EARNINGS AS A PERCENT OF MEN'S
High School Diploma	$378	$497	76%
High School Graduate	$520	$709	73%
Some College/Associate's Degree	$628	$830	76%
Bachelor's Degree	$878	$1,172	75%
Master's Degree	$1,074	$1,442	74%
Professional	$1,258	$1,758	72%
Doctorate	$1,352	$1,736	78%

Source: Bureau of Labor Statistics 2009e.

TABLE 4.5   Twenty Most Prevalent Occupations for Employed Women in 2009

Occupations are still highly segregated. Women tend to work as secretaries, nurses, teachers, and cashiers—occupations with few men in them.

Secretaries and administrative assistants	3,074,000
Registered nurses	2,612,000
Elementary and middle school teachers	2,343,000
Cashiers	2,273,000
Nursing, psychiatric, and home health aides	1,770,000
Retail salespersons	1,650,000
First-line supervisors/managers of retail sales workers	1,459,000
Waiters and waitresses	1,434,000
Maids and housekeeping cleaners	1,282,000
Customer service representatives	1,263,000
Child care workers	1,228,000
Bookkeeping, accounting, and auditing clerks	1,205,000
Receptionists and information clerks	1,168,000
First-line supervisors/managers of office and administrative support workers	1,163,000
Managers, all other	1,106,000
Accountants and auditors	1,084,000
Teacher assistants	921,000
Cooks	831,000
Office clerks, general	821,000
Personal and home care aides	789,000

Source: Bureau of Labor Statistics 2009e.

employers manage to circumvent the intent of the law. Women workers make important contributions to the livelihood of their families. However, if working women earned the same as men (controlling for the same number of hours, education level, age, union status, and living in the same region of the country), their annual incomes would rise by about $4,000, and poverty rates would be cut in half. But haven't things really changed, you ask? Yes, of course, but let's not exaggerate the degree of social change. In fiscal year 2009, the U.S. Equal Employment Opportunity Commission (EEOC) received over 28,000 sex discrimination charges, an increase of over 10 percent since 2000 (U.S. Equal Employment Opportunity Commission 2010).

Social Policy and Family Resilience

We know that attitudes about sex and gender permeate all aspects of family relationships throughout the world. Can policies that pertain to sex and gender—and in particular, focus on reducing disparities—help to build stronger families? Organizations like the United Nations, the World Health Organization, and Amnesty International believe that they can. Let's take one example. The following is a discussion of how family planning programs strengthen families by delaying the age at which young girls become mothers.

Family Planning Can Make a World of Difference

Family planning efforts have a tremendous and direct impact on the quality of women's lives throughout the world. Many women and girls in developing nations are pulled out of school at very young ages to marry and give birth. It is not uncommon for girls to marry at age 12 and have a baby soon thereafter. These young children are poorly equipped physically, socially, psychologically, and economically to raise the next generation of children and, with little education, their opportunities for work, independence, and self-determination are crushed.

Postponing childbirth among young women increases their chances of receiving a good education, which is vital to their social, political, and economic empowerment. It also helps to prevent fistulas, as explained in Chapter 2. Family planning information and availability are crucial for women to improve their status in society, to receive better health care and nutrition, to fight poverty, and enable them to participate fully in their country's economic and political processes.

An estimated 215 million women in the developing world want to delay or avoid pregnancy, but are not using family planning largely because they do not have access to it, they fear side effects, or their families object

Family planning services for women around the world can dramatically increase their chance of receiving an education, reduce maternal and infant mortality, and reduce poverty, all vital to their social, political, and economic empowerment.

Figure 4.2 **Contraceptive Use Among Married Women Ages 15–49**

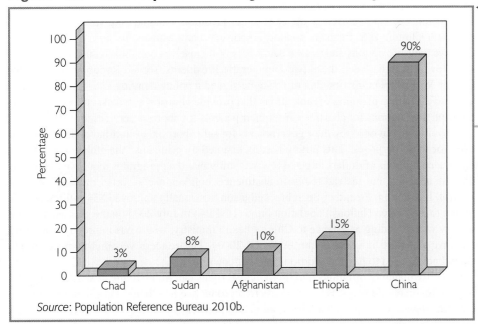

Contraceptive use is rare in many developing countries; China's one-child policy is a notable exception.

Source: Population Reference Bureau 2010b.

(Singh et al. 2009). This translates to more than half of women in low-income countries. A sample of these countries is shown in Figure 4.2 (Population Reference Bureau 2010b). Chad is a country in which only 3 percent of married women aged 15–49 use contraceptives, and 89 percent say that their desire for contraceptives is not satisfied.

Moreover, each year, more than 70,000 women die as a result of unsafe abortions (Guttmacher Institute 2009), and over 500,000 women die due to pregnancy-related causes. In fact, in Africa and South Asia, complications during pregnancy and childbirth are the leading cause of death from women of childbearing age (Singh et al. 2009). Every year, more than 1 million children are left motherless and vulnerable because of maternal death. Children without mothers are less likely to receive proper nutrition, health care, and education, which continues a cycle of poverty and poor health (United Nations Population Fund 2010a). Family planning can reduce maternal mortality significantly, possibly up to 175,000 women each year, by reducing the number of high-risk pregnancies, by allowing women to space pregnancies further apart, or by eliminating pregnancies too early in a woman's life. Family planning will also promote child survival and well-being by reducing the risks associated with childhood malnutrition and disease. Increasing birth intervals to three years could also prevent the deaths of 1.8 children under age five (United Nations Population Fund 2010b).

International family planning efforts limit the spread of HIV and AIDS. Over 33 million people lived with HIV in 2008. Young people are particularly susceptible; half of all new infections are among 15- to 24-year-olds. Worldwide, women are considerably more susceptible to the virus than men due to a combination of biological, social, and economic factors. In sub-Saharan Africa, the overall rate of infection among girls and young women was three times that of boys their age (UNAIDS 2009). The prime minister of Mozambique commented that (Abaid 2003):

> This is not because the girls are promiscuous, but because nearly three out of five are married by age 18, 40 percent of them to much older, sexually experienced men, who may expose their wives to HIV/AIDS. Abstinence is not an option for these child brides. Those who try to negotiate condom use commonly face violence or rejection.

The United States has had an on-again, off-again level of support for international family planning efforts, dependent on whether Republicans or Democrats are in political control. When "on," as is currently the case under President Obama, and was the case under President Clinton, U.S. financial support empowers many women and girls to significantly improve their life options and to take better care of themselves and their families.

However, in between these two Democratic Presidents, served Republican President George W. Bush. On his first day of office he signed a policy denying U.S. financial assistance to all family planning organizations that provide abortion services, counsel their patients on their options for abortions, refer their patients for abortion services, or educate their communities about or lobby their governments for safe abortion, even if the dollars were not used for these purposes. This policy was nicknamed by critics as "the **global gag rule**." It eliminated millions of dollars targeted toward family planning programs that have nothing to do with abortion, but instead focus on abstinence, condom use, or other methods of birth control. In addition, President Bush blocked a congressionally approved $34 million contribution to the United Nations Population Fund (UNFPA) in July 2005 on the grounds that the agency was providing assistance to China's health ministry, which has indirectly supported coercive abortions in some countries (Lobe 2003). The concern was that taxpayer funds should not be used to pay for abortions in other countries.

Family planning programs and reproductive rights can improve the quality of women's lives in innumerable ways. Having access to reproductive health and family planning services can elevate women's social, economic, and political status throughout the world. Reproductive rights are far more than a personal issue; they are intertwined with historical, cultural, economic, and political forces, and have important ramifications for these as well.

Family planning programs remain seriously underfunded. To satisfy the unmet need for contraceptives, about $1.2 billion is needed, rising to over $1.6 billion by 2015. Yet, current assistance is less than half this amount (United Nations Population Fund 2010b).

Conclusion

Virtually all social institutions, whether political, religious, economic, educational, or familial, distinguish between men and women in fundamental ways that extend far beyond biological sex differences. However, gender is largely a social construction, and a comparative approach shows us that expected masculine and feminine behaviors differ historically and cross-culturally. Several key agents of socialization are responsible for teaching gender norms, such as families, toys, schools, peer groups, and the mass media. Throughout the world people are obsessed with perceived differences between men and women, and these perceptions often become the basis for how power is distributed. Patriarchy is manifested in different forms around the world, and, despite thinking to the contrary, it persists in western nations, including the United States. The ways in which sex and gender are rooted in the U.S. social structure have critical implications for how families are constructed and how family members interact, and will be demonstrated in the upcoming chapters.

Key Terms

Agents of socialization: The people, social institutions, and organizations that teach boys and girls their gendered expectations. (p. 98)

Androgyny: Having both masculine and feminine traits in near equal proportion. (p. 95)

Clitoridectomy: A form of genital cutting or mutilation in which the clitoris is cut out of the body. (p. 106)

Gender: The culturally and socially constructed differences between males and females found in the meanings, beliefs, and practices associated with femininity and masculinity. (p. 93)

Gender socialization: Teaching the cultural norms associated with being male or female. (p. 98)

Global gag rule: Denies U.S. assistance to all organizations that provide abortion services, counsel their patients on their options for abortions, refer their patients for abortion services, or educate their communities about or lobby their governments for safe abortion with their own, non-U.S. funding. (p. 116)

Hidden curriculum: Informal school curriculum that teaches gender socialization. (p. 100)

Infibulation: The most extreme form of genital cutting or mutilation in which the clitoris and vaginal lips are cut or scraped away, and the outer portion of the vagina is stitched together. (p. 106)

Intersexed: A person whose anatomical categories are not easily identifiable. (p. 93)

Labor market segmentation: Men and women often work in different types of jobs with distinct working conditions and pay. (p. 112)

Sex: Biological differences and one's role in reproduction. (p. 93)

Socially constructed: Values or norms that are invented or "constructed" in a culture; people learn these and follow the conventional rules. (p. 93)

Transgender: Persons who feel comfortable expressing gendered traits associated with the other sex. (p. 96)

Transsexuals: Persons who undergo sex reassignment surgery and hormone treatments, either male to female, or female to male. (p. 97)

Resources on the Internet

Human Rights Watch

www.hrw.org

Human Rights Watch is an independent, nongovernmental organization, supported by contributions from private individuals and foundations worldwide. It works to prevent discrimination, to uphold political freedom, to protect people from inhumane conduct in wartime, and to bring offenders to justice. They investigate and expose human rights violations and hold abusers accountable and challenge governments and those who hold power to end abusive practices and respect international human rights law.

Institute for Women's Policy Research

www.iwpr.org

The Institute for Women's Policy Research (IWPR) is a public policy research organization dedicated to informing and stimulating the debate on issues of critical importance to women and their families. IWPR focuses on issues of poverty and welfare, employment and earnings, work and family issues, health and safety, and women's civic and political participation.

National Organization for Women

www.now.org

The National Organization for Women (NOW) is the largest organization of feminist activists in the United States. NOW has 500,000 contributing members and 550 chapters in all 50 states and the District of Columbia. Since its founding in 1966, NOW's goal has been to take action to bring about equality for all women. NOW works to eliminate discrimination and harassment in the workplace, schools, the justice system, and all other sectors of society; secure abortion, birth control, and reproductive rights for all women; end all forms of violence against women; eradicate racism, sexism, and homophobia; and promote equality and justice in our society.

Planned Parenthood Federation of America, Inc.

www.plannedparenthood.org

Planned Parenthood Federation of America, Inc., is the world's largest and most well-known voluntary reproductive health care organization. Founded by Margaret Sanger in 1916 as the first U.S. birth control clinic, Planned Parenthood believes in everyone's right to choose when or whether to have a child, that every child should be wanted and loved, and that women should be in charge of their own destinies.

CHAPTER 5

Social Stratification, Social Class, and Families

CHAPTER OUTLINE

Social Class and Family Relationships 121

What Is Social Stratification? 123

Social Class in the United States 125

■ **USING** *the Sociological Imagination:* The *Social Register*, Class or Caste? **127**

Families in Poverty 131

■ **SOCIAL** *Policies for Families:* Making Ends Meet on a Poverty Budget **135**

■ **OUR** *Global Community:* "Nalim" in Bhutan **136**

■ **EYE** *on the World:* A Comparative Look at Purchasing Power Parity, in U.S. Dollars, 2008 **138**

Social Policy and Family Resilience 146

Conclusion 147

Key Terms 147

Resources on the Internet 147

CHAPTER PREVIEW

How does your social class position shape your family and intimate relationships? This chapter introduces the concepts of social stratification and social class and explores the many ways that class is interwoven with families. How would your life be different if you had been born among the richest of families or among the poorest? In this chapter, you will learn:

■ How social class influences your family relationships

■ The difference between caste and social class, and a theoretical understanding of these systems

■ Features of the social class system in the United States, from the upper class to the underclass

■ How health and health insurance are class-related

■ How poverty is defined and measured in the United States, and how this compares to other countries

■ Differing perspectives on the causes of poverty

■ The consequences of poverty for adults and children

■ How building and improving social policy can build family resilience

■ How the earned income tax credit is an important antipoverty strategy

Is it really possible to live and survive on minimum-wage work? Many adults work in jobs that service the rest of us and earn less than $8 per hour for their efforts. Barbara Ehrenreich, with a doctorate in biology and the author of several books, decided to answer this question. She went undercover as an uneducated, inexperienced, job-seeking housewife to see if it is really possible to live on minimum-wage work. Her plan was to visit three different cities (in Florida, Maine, and Minnesota) with some money (around $1,000) plus a car to see if it would be possible to get a job and make enough money to live on. The jobs she took included waitress, house cleaner, hotel maid, and Wal-Mart clerk. In most cases, she made around the minimum wage and had no benefits. Ehrenreich takes us on an incredible journey inside a desperate world where few middle-class persons have ventured, except for perhaps a brief stint while in college. Although she maintains some advantages (she doesn't start out totally broke, she rents a car, she always has an ATM card to fall back on if she runs out of money for food or housing, she has no children, and she can walk away anytime she wants), she vividly describes the debasing and dangerous work that millions of women and men do every day. For example, while working for the Merry Maid company, she experiences firsthand the toll on the body: she learns to scrub all floors on her hands and knees and to strap vacuum cleaners on her back. Merry Maids spend their day bending, squatting, reaching, lifting, and scrubbing away grime, dirt, and feces. Nonetheless, little attention is paid to germs. The maids' focus is on mere cosmetics, and so maids may use the same wet rag on the toilet as they do on the kitchen countertops. The work is demeaning. Maids are not allowed to eat, drink, or use the bathroom for hours. When a fellow maid sprains her ankle, the boss demands, "Work through the pain!" Homeowners treat the maids no better. Ehrenreich learns to keep a steady supply of aspirin available to combat the pain and muscle fatigue.

What does her two-year journey into the lives of the working poor reveal? She itemizes the wages she made at each job, along with her living expenses. With each job, her take-home pay minus expenses left her with less than $10 per week for savings or miscellaneous spending. Housing costs consumed most of her pay. There was virtually no money left for the investment needed to "pull herself up by her bootstraps." Many people who work in these jobs must take a second low-paying and demeaning job if they have any realistic hope of improving their circumstances even slightly. Ehrenreich's main reason for carrying out the experiment was to see if her income could match her expenses "as the truly poor attempt to do each day" (Ehrenreich 2001). She demonstrates that it cannot be done and shows the economic, physical, and emotional vulnerability experienced by low-wage workers.

It is really an accident of birth that determines many things about a person's life. **Ascribed statuses** that a person is born with, such as his or her sex, race, ethnic background, and social class, are important because they lay the groundwork for a range of opportunities, privileges, and constraints.

This chapter introduces the concepts of social stratification and social class. It explores how, like gender, one's social class position is interwoven with families and touches virtually all aspects of our lives. How would your values, opportunities, and family life be different if you had been born among the richest of families? Conversely, what if you were born among the poorest—for example, to a single woman on welfare? Although the effects of social class on family structure and family dynamics are discussed in depth throughout the remainder of this book, it is important here to introduce these signature concepts and the ways in which they influence our most intimate relationships.

Social Class and Family Relationships

While social class is less visible than sex, race, or ethnicity, we are all probably aware, at least vaguely, that social class can have a big effect on our lives. We are bombarded by pictures of the rich and famous cavorting in Hollywood, and of the poor in the most desperate of situations, such as Haitians after the earthquake of 2010. In the United States, social class is often downplayed (Lareau and Conley 2008), but if you think long and hard, you know that where you come from matters. Social class is not just about money; it encompasses an entire way of seeing and experiencing the world (Eitzen and Smith 2009; Hurst 2010; Weininger and Lareau 2009). From cradle to grave, social class standing has a significant impact on our lives. Briefly, class standing influences:

- *Health status, health insurance, and access to health care.* Persons in lower social classes have higher infant mortality rates and lower life expectancy, rate their health as poorer, and suffer more mental distress than do those who are more affluent (Cohen and Martinez 2009; Heyman et al. 2009). This is due to a variety of factors, including more dangerous working conditions, more stressful living environments, poorer diet, and a lack of health insurance that limits access to health care (Coleman-Jensen and Nord 2010; Seccombe 2011).
- *Gender expectations for boys and girls, and men and women within the family.* More egalitarian roles are likely to be found in the middle- and upper-middle-class groups, whereas both upper and lower classes tend to emphasize and exaggerate the differences between males and females. Parents in lower social classes tend to have a more traditional division of household labor, and socialize their children for more traditional family and work roles (Rubin 1994).
- *The values that parents socialize in their children.* Working-class parents are more likely to value conformity and obedience to authority in their children, whereas middle- and upper-middle-class parents tend to value creativity and self-direction (Kohn 1977, 2006). Sociologist Melvin Kohn (1977) suggests that these values reflect the kinds of jobs parents hold and assume that their children will hold as well. Working-class jobs are those that tend to involve working with one's hands or machinery. They generally do not reward or expect creativity and self-direction; rather, workers are expected to follow orders and not challenge authority. In contrast, middle- and upper-class parents tend to work at jobs that focus on people or ideas (and assume that their children will as well) and, thus, creativity, problem solving, and critical thinking are more highly valued.
- *How parents interact with their children.* The **home observation of the measurement of the environment (HOME)** is a widely used tool to measure maternal warmth and learning experiences provided to the child and is associated with a variety of child outcomes. Poverty has a significant negative effect on the quality and stimulation of the home environment, even after controlling for the effects of other variables (Yeung et al. 2002). Impoverished parents are less nurturing, more authoritarian, and use more inconsistent and harsh physical discipline as a family's economic situation worsens (McLoyd 1990). Parents with low and unstable incomes experience more emotional distress and see themselves as less effective parents than do parents with higher incomes. Moreover, although child abuse can occur in any type of household, poor children have a higher probability of being abused, neglected, and injured, and are abused more severely than are their more affluent peers.
- *The likelihood of attending and graduating from college.* Persons growing up in the middle or upper class are more likely to attend college than are individuals growing up in working-class or poor families (National Center for Education Statistics 2010).

Families earning $70,000 a year or more are about three times as likely to see their child earn a bachelor's degree as are families who earn less than $25,000 per year. Although some of the difference is due simply to economics, much of it is due to dissimilar values regarding college, poorer preparation because of overcrowded and underfunded schools, and the different structural constraints associated with being able to devote yourself full-time to such pursuits. Persons from the lower classes may know few people, if any, who have gone to college, and therefore may not value a college education or see that it is worth the time and expense.

- *Dating and premarital sexual expectations and behavior.* On average, teenage girls and boys from lower social classes begin dating at earlier ages than their middle- and upper-middle-class counterparts. Moreover, they are more likely to get pregnant outside of marriage (Strayhorn and Strayhorn 2009). Once pregnant, they are more likely to have an abortion than are girls from middle- and upper-income families (Jones et al. 2010).

- *The likelihood of marriage and age at first marriage.* The relationship between class and the likelihood of marriage is complex. Although most people do marry, upper-middle-class women are less likely to marry than other groups, and when they do marry, they do so at later ages. However, a significant number of poor women also do not marry or marry late because of the limited availability of men they consider to be "good prospects" (Edin and Kefalas 2005). Poor women value marriage and have a desire to marry, but they have low marriage rates because the men they are likely to encounter are also poor and often do not have steady jobs.

- *Income and how money is spent in the family.* Consumption patterns vary by social class (Lino 2010). Poor and working-class families spend virtually all of their money on food, shelter, and basic necessities. Most of their income is spent trying to make ends meet; therefore, they have little disposable income (Hays 2003). Even holidays such as birthdays or Christmas can strain the family budget. Families in middle and upper classes have more disposable income for family outings, vacations, and holiday spending. These types of events can add spontaneity and fun to an otherwise repetitive daily routine (Seccombe 2011).

- *Hobbies and pastimes within families.* How do you spend your free time—bowling or playing golf? Should we have Sunday dinner at my brother's house or at a restaurant? Social class influences the way in which we view leisure, the time and opportunities we have to participate in leisure activities, and with whom we share time. Working-class and poor families often spend more time together than do families in higher social classes and rely on each other for material and social support (Rubin 1994; Seccombe 2011).

- *The types of stresses experienced and coping mechanisms employed.* Families in lower social classes face additional economic and social stresses because their jobs are less stable, offer less pay, and fewer benefits. Finances and budgeting are a common family stressor. Poor families worry about the most basic of needs, including an inadequate food supply (Siefert et al. 2004). Families in higher social classes have a wider range of coping strategies available to them such as travel, shopping, or working off stress physically in athletic clubs, whereas lower-income individuals may resort to coping mechanisms that provide a more immediate gratification, such as smoking or overeating.

WHAT DO YOU THINK?

What precisely causes these many social class differences? Is it money or something else?

It is important to recognize that social class interacts with other statuses and dimensions of stratification. A person is not simply rich, poor, or somewhere in the middle. Social class interacts with sex, and with race and ethnic background to shape one's experience. A person is not simply working class, but a working-class Hispanic woman; a Chinese American upper-class man; a Black middle-class boy; or a poor white girl.

What Is Social Stratification?

Social class differences can be perplexing because most Americans believe that the United States provides nearly equal opportunities for everyone. Nonetheless, it is clear that U.S. society is highly stratified and is becoming more so (Hurst 2010). Some people earn extremely high wages or have amassed great wealth, whereas other families are struggling to meet their basic needs for food, shelter, and clothing. Americans like to think of their society as a **meritocracy**, where financial and social rewards are based on their abilities, education, and skill sets, but the United States is turning its back on these ideals. For example, 30 years ago the average real annual compensation of the top 100 chief executives was $1.3 million dollars: 39 times the pay of the average worker. Today, it is $37.5 million, over 1,000 times the pay of the average worker (Economist. com 2004). Are top executives really a thousand times more able, more educated, and more skillful than the people they work with?

Money is one dimension of inequality, but so are power and occupational prestige. **Social stratification** refers to the hierarchical ranking of people within society on the basis of coveted resources. Some people have more or less of these resources than do others. Those with resources are able to pass them on to members of their family.

Caste and Class Systems in a Comparative Perspective

Generally speaking, there are two distinct types of stratification systems found throughout the world. In a **caste system**, social stratification is based on ascribed characteristics that one is born with, such as race, ethnicity, or family lineage. There is little or no opportunity for **social mobility** or movement in the stratification system based on individual effort or achievement. For example, in traditional rural Indian villages, caste members generally stay with their "own kind"; they work, marry, and socialize only with other members of their caste. Caste membership is handed down from parent to child, regardless of the child's talent, skill, beauty, or education.

The social class in which we are born has an enormous impact on our life. How do you think the privileges and opportunities bestowed on the Bush children influenced their accomplishments?

Social class, in contrast, is a system of social stratification that is based on ascribed statuses from both birth and individual achievement. Social class segments the population into groups that broadly share similar types of resources, similar lifestyles, similar values, and a generally shared perception of their collective condition.

Social class is an obscure concept because there is no universally agreed-upon division, and we cannot immediately identify which people belong to which class. Boundaries are theoretically open so that people who gain schooling, skills, or income may experience a change in their social class position. Nonetheless, we know that social classes exist in a hierarchy and are generally based on some combination of income, wealth, occupational prestige, and educational level, although some schools of thought may emphasize one resource over another.

Conceptualizations of Class: Marx and Weber For Karl Marx, a nineteenth-century German economist and philosopher, social classes are social structures formed by an historical and dynamic social process that resulted from one's relationship to the means of production. All groups in society must engage in the collective endeavor of economic production to stay alive. However, it is an endeavor fraught with conflict. The capitalist class, or the **bourgeoisie**, owns the means of production. They own the land and money needed to operate factories and businesses. Meanwhile, the **proletariat** represents those individuals who must sell their labor to the owners to earn enough money to survive. The conflict can be either open or covert, but it is always inherent in the production process, according to Marx.

Max Weber, in contrast, did not conceptualize social class as rooted in the production process. He took a multidimensional approach, emphasizing (1) **wealth**, which is the value of all of a person's or a family's economic assets, including income, real estate, stocks, bonds, and other items of economic worth, minus debt; (2) **prestige**, which is the esteem or respect a person is afforded; and (3) **power**, defined as the ability to achieve goals, wishes, and desires even in the face of opposition from others. Class is a combination of these subjective factors. In other words, noneconomic factors, such as the status that comes from educational attainment or family background, are also important causal factors in the determination of class standing.

Example: Social Class in Great Britain

A concept such as "social class" can be conceptualized differently across cultures. For example, in Great Britain social class refers to a well-known and long-established official classification scheme based on *occupation*. Beginning in 1911, and revised somewhat since then, the British government, health researchers, academics, and others routinely divide the population into broad, hierarchical groups to examine social and health issues within the population. The British system is a sanctioned social class scheme in which the government finds value in making explicit gradients in the population.

The architect of the social class system in Great Britain was T.H.C. Stevenson, a medical statistician in the country's General Register Office who was interested in mortality and fertility. Stevenson argued that occupation was more important than income or wealth in explaining the lower mortality of the wealthier classes. He suggested that one's occupation develops and reflects an approach to culture, including attitudes, behavior, lifestyles, personal choices, and values—in sum, an entire worldview.

The overall shape of the model has changed very little since Stevenson's early work. The British population, based on data from the population census, is classified according to their occupation and occupational industry into six ordinal categories, or social grades:

I	Professional (e.g., accountants, engineers, doctors, professors)
II	Managerial and Technical/Intermediate (e.g., marketing and sales managers, teachers, journalists, nurses)
IIIN	Nonmanual Skilled (e.g., clerks, shop assistants, cashiers)
IIIM	Manual Skilled (e.g., carpenters, goods van drivers, cooks)
IV	Partly Skilled (e.g., security guards, machine tool operators, farmworkers)
V	Unskilled (e.g., building and civil engineering laborers, other laborers, cleaners)

The British social class system is a strategic way that the government (and therefore Britons) conceptualizes the population. Individual Britons are generally quite clear about where they fall in the system: "I'm a two," a schoolteacher would say.

Although there have been many attempts to modify the social class scheme, the scheme has changed little because there does appear to be evidence that occupation reflects a wide range of factors that influence health and social well-being. For example, Table 5.1 shows British social class differences in mortality, coronary heart

WHAT DO YOU THINK?

The British are far more comfortable than Americans with using class as an explicit social categorization. Why is this? Would our government ever adopt the British style? Why or why not?

TABLE 5.1 Rates of Selected Health Problems, per 100,000 People, Great Britain

Great Britain uses social class categories to tabulate health statistics. Class categories are made explicit.

	SOCIAL CLASS[1]					
	I	**II**	**IIIN**	**IIIM**	**IV**	**V**
Mortality Rates	280	300	426	493	492	806
Coronary Heart Disease	81	92	136	159	156	235
Suicide and Undetermined Injury	13	14	20	21	23	47
Lung Cancer	17	24	34	54	52	82
Wheeze in the Past 12 Months, 1996	18[2]	—	20	22	23[3]	—

Notes:
[1] I Professional; II Managerial & Technical; IIIN Skilled, Nonmanual; IIIM Skilled, Manual; IV Partly Skilled; V Unskilled
[2] Classes I and II combined
[3] Classes IV and V combined
Source: Lung and Asthma Information Agency 2000.

disease, suicide and undetermined injury, lung cancer, and asthma, with persons in lower social classes having a much greater incidence of these problems than do persons in the higher social classes.

What is particularly striking about the British system of classification is how explicit and sanctioned it is. This is contrary to the way Americans view social class. Americans try to ignore class differences, although everyone knows that they exist on some level. There are pros and cons to making social class gradients explicit or keeping them implicit, but the result is the same; some people are considerably better off, and it is not always due to merit.

Social Class in the United States

Unlike Great Britain, it is unclear how many social classes exist in the United States. Politicians in the 2008 presidential and 2010 midterm elections spoke of the middle class as though it were one very large and homogeneous group.

Although it might be correct to think of class as a continuum, for practical purposes most people think of classes as ordinal categories. What makes up a class? Americans tend to think of social class as some vague combination of education, occupation, and income, and we sometimes call this **socioeconomic status (SES)**. No single measure of social class exists, nor is there agreement on how many social classes there actually are. When Americans are asked what class they belong to, most reply that they are in the "middle class." Interestingly, both poor people and rich people may claim membership in the middle class. One U.S. congressman making over $200,000 per year, told a reporter that he was in the "lower middle class." The idea that we are all middle class reflects our historical roots—many settlers from Europe were fleeing the rigid stratification systems in their home countries.

Dennis Gilbert and Joseph A. Kahl (1993) have developed one model of social class based on SES that I will draw upon here. Their model includes six categories: (1) the upper class; (2) the upper middle class; (3) the middle class; (4) the working class; (5) the working poor; and (6) the underclass. However, the U.S. government rarely, if ever, uses these categories. Unlike Great Britain, virtually the only standardized measure is the federal government's poverty line, which is discussed later in the chapter. The estimates here are drawn from data from the Congressional Budget Office, reported by the Center on Budget and Policy Priorities (Sherman 2009; Sherman and Avon-Dine 2007).

Socialite Paris Hilton exposes the excesses of the very rich. Her privileged upbringing as heiress to the $300 million Hilton hotel fortune and her frenzied partying make her seem like a perfect subject for *Lifestyles of the Rich and Famous*.

The Upper Class

This is the wealthiest and most powerful social class in the United States, and consists of only about 1 percent of the population. Although this class is small in number, its members have a tremendous influence upon the economy and the rest of society (Domhoff 2005). Their members may have very high incomes, but more importantly they own substantial wealth (Sherman 2009). They may be entrepreneurs, sit on the boards of major corporations, or may get involved in politics by either running for office or by serving in key policy positions.

The income of the upper class varies tremendously. Some have virtually no income because the money is inherited rather than earned. Others earn millions of dollars each year in salaries or stock options. However, despite the influence of the upper class, less is known about their private lives because they have been able to insulate themselves from others (Kendall 2002).

Some families have been wealthy for generations. Names like Rockefeller, Kennedy, or Hilton come to mind. These individuals and their families have been nicknamed "upper-upper class," "old money," or "bluebloods." As described in the box on page 127, "Using the Sociological Imagination: The *Social Register*, Class or Caste?," they may belong to the exclusive *Social Register*, an annual listing of elites that has been published since the late 1800s. The book advertises itself as ". . . the definitive listing of America's most prominent families, serving as an exclusive and trusted medium for learning about and communicating with their peers." Members, including recent political figures John Kerry and George Bush, have significant wealth, belong to exclusive clubs, are involved in philanthropy, and have considerable corporate, military, and political power (Domhoff 2005). Their children attend private prep schools and Ivy League colleges, where applicants are carefully screened. As sociologist G. William Domhoff (2005) writes:

From infancy through young adulthood, members of the upper class receive a distinctive education. This education begins early in life in preschools that frequently are attached to a neighborhood church of high social status. Schooling continues during the elementary years at a local private school called a day school. The adolescent years may see the student remain at day school, but there is a strong chance that at least one or two years will be spent away from home at a boarding school in a quiet rural setting. Higher education will be obtained at one of a small number of heavily endowed private universities. Harvard, Yale, Princeton, and Stanford head the list. . . . The system of formal schooling is so insulated that many upper-class students never see the inside of a public school in all their years of education. This separate educational system is important evidence for the distinctiveness of the mentality and lifestyle that exists within the upper class, for schools play a large role in transmitting the class structure to their students.

USING
the Sociological Imagination

The *Social Register*, Class or Caste?

Is the United States really an open-class system or is it more of a caste? Read the following discussion and decide.

Many middle-class people think of themselves as dominating the political and social landscape—they are, after all, the largest social class group. The middle class seems to receive the most attention at election time from politicians clamoring for votes. However, size is not to be confused with power.

The upper-upper class, the true "bluebloods," is a close-knit group that wields considerable power in society. Some even suggest that they form more of a caste than a social class because membership is based on ascription—being born into the right family—rather than achievement. As presidential candidates George W. Bush and John F. Kerry reveal, being born to families of certain means enabled them to attend the most prestigious schools that are virtually training grounds for the elite.

To illustrate their tight and cohesive bonds there is even a book listing fellow members of this privileged group. The *Social Register* has been published since 1887, and today lists about 40,000 families (*Social Register* 2003). Some may dismiss the book as nothing more than a glorified phone book—"a group of pals, really" says one entrant; others use it as an important resource to ensure that their children are socializing with others who share their economic and political interests. The *Social Register* is a powerful reminder that, for the upper class at least, ascription rather than achievement is fundamental to membership in the upper echelons of the upper class.

The *Social Register* describes families, not simply individuals. This is because most members are not known for their individual accomplishments, but are listed because of their family connections. Names include Kennedy, Roosevelt, Rockefeller, and Forbes. The families are mostly White. Listings describe the exclusive prep schools and colleges that family members have attended, the social clubs to which the family belongs, and women's maiden names so that their family lineage can be identified.

Noticeably absent are the occupations of its members. This is because individual achievements are largely irrelevant to membership. The "new rich"—people who have earned their wealth—are generally excluded. Instead, they may be listed in *Who's Who*—a book that focuses on achievement rather than ascription. The *Social Register* does not celebrate the rags-to-riches stories, but rather concentrates on those elite families who have amassed great fortunes that are passed down from generation to generation and who seem to have all the trappings of true pedigree. Old money and ancestry is what it takes to be considered for the *Social Register*.

Source: Hastings 2000.

CRITICAL THINKING QUESTIONS

1. Do you think that the upper-upper class is really a class or is it a caste?
2. How does the *Social Register* help these families insulate themselves from the rest of society?
3. Should wealth, power, and prestige come from ascription or achievement? How would you ensure that it comes from one rather than the other?

There is very little mixing with other social classes. For example, the Debutante Ball, which brings together unmarried young men and women to meet and socialize in a series of elegant parties, teas, and dances, carefully controls even dating and mate selection so that it is almost castelike.

Other members of the upper class, sometimes nicknamed the "lower upper class" or "new money," have acquired their great wealth within one generation. They often earned their money in business, entertainment, or sports. Despite their vast material possessions, which may be ostentatiously displayed, they lack the prestige of bluebloods. Microsoft founder Bill Gates, entertainer Oprah Winfrey, and homemaker extraordinaire Martha Stewart are examples of persons who have amassed great wealth within one generation, but who may not be completely accepted by those with old-time wealth. Nonetheless, most Americans look upon these persons favorably. They are seen as successfully fulfilling the American Dream and they reinforce the idea that the United States is a land of opportunity.

The Upper Middle Class

Approximately 15–20 percent of the U.S. population is categorized as upper middle class. Persons in this group are usually highly educated professionals who work as physicians, dentists, lawyers, college professors, or business executives. They see their work as a career, not simply a job, resulting from years of college and professional schooling. Careers are often central features of their lives, and distinctions between work and leisure may become blurred. Household income may be in the rough range of $100,000–$200,000, and perhaps more if both husband and wife are employed, which may be the case. Part of the reason for the increasing gap between the upper middle class and the lower social classes is the greater likelihood that both husband and wife are employed in well-paying careers. They tend to have accumulated some degree of wealth through their jobs. Individuals in the upper middle class get married later and are more likely to delay (or forgo) having children because of education, careers, or leisure pursuits. They tend to have nice homes in well-respected neighborhoods within the community and play important roles in local political affairs. Education is strongly valued for their children: The vast majority of upper-middle-class children go on to college, and many continue into graduate education or professional programs as their parents did.

The Middle Class

Despite the rhetoric of being a middle-class society, only about 40 percent of Americans fall into the middle class, with annual incomes of roughly $40,000 to even $100,000, if two adults are employed. The median annual household income in the United States was approximately $50,000 in 2009 for all households, $73,000 for married-couple households, and $33,000 for female-headed households (DeNavas-Walt et al. 2010). Members of the middle class tend to prioritize security at home and at work as very important (Taylor et al. 2008). They work in occupations that often require a college degree. Some occupations are classified as white-collar jobs such as nurses, teachers, lower- and midlevel managers, and many positions in sales or business. Some middle-class occupations include highly skilled blue-collar jobs, such as in electronics or building construction. Traditionally, middle-class jobs have been secure and provided avenues for advancement; however, with corporate downsizing, escalating housing costs, and a generally rising cost of living, many middle-class families find their lives considerably more tenuous than in the past. Thus, politicians respond to the concerns that middle-class families face. Young middle-class families may find it difficult to purchase their first home in many cities around the country, and older middle-class families find that saving for both retirement and their children's college bills stretches their budget beyond its means. However, they value home ownership and college educations for their children and hope for a secure retirement for themselves. Middle-class parents may make considerable effort and sacrifice to provide mobility resources for their children, such as limiting family size or having both parents working outside the home.

The Working Class

The title "working class" is misleading because most persons in other social classes work too. Other names for this group include blue collar, but that name is also misleading because some individuals in the working class hold white-collar jobs. Working-class families earn less than do middle-class families, earning approximately $20,000–$40,000 per year. About 20 percent of the U.S. population falls into this group. Some of these occupations may include those that require a short period of on-the-job training. Specific jobs may include salesclerks, factory workers, custodians, or semiskilled or unskilled laborers. Members of the working class report less satisfaction in their jobs than do those in higher social classes and experience less social mobility. Their jobs are often routinized and require conformity to external authority. Their work helps to form the basis for their childrearing values (Kohn 1977, 2006). They are more likely to place importance on traits such as conformity and obedience in their children rather than creativity or self-direction. Working-class individuals are often distrustful of or feel threatened by diversity. They are some of the fiercest opponents of gay and lesbian rights, affirmative action, and women's rights. Generally, working-class families are insecure (Yates 2009). They live in modest neighborhoods and have some difficulty sending their children to college, although many would like to do so. Their lives are vulnerable, and family members often live from paycheck to paycheck, with little opportunity to amass savings. Families must budget carefully to pay their monthly bills, because unexpected doctor or car repair bills can wreak havoc on the family budget.

The working class, accounting for about 20 percent of the U.S. population, struggle to pay for food, shelter, and clothing on low wages. Their earnings approximate $20,000–$40,000 per year.

The Working Poor

The working poor account for about 15 percent of the U.S. population. Their wages hover around or slightly above minimum wage and may come up to about $20,000 per year. Jobs include service workers in the fast-food, retail, or tourist industry; lower-paid factory jobs; or seasonal migrant labor. The opening vignette profiled a researcher going undercover to work in these types of jobs. Many of the working poor receive no fringe benefits such as health insurance or sick pay. Unemployment is common, and many work varying shifts, including weekends or evenings (Presser 2003; Strazdins et al. 2006). A large component of the working poor includes single mothers and their children. Some of these women intersperse work with bouts of welfare (Seccombe 2011). It is a vicious cycle: They work in a variety of low-wage jobs with hopes for a better life, but the low wages and lack of benefits leave their families exceedingly vulnerable. They then seek the safety of welfare where at least they can get their families' basic needs taken care of, such as food, shelter, and medical care. Faced with the stigma and hardship of daily living on welfare, they again obtain work, but soon find that their health and welfare benefits have been reduced or eliminated, and their families are vulnerable once more. There are many stresses in the lives of the working poor, because they live paycheck to paycheck in a constant struggle to make ends meet.

The Underclass

Gilbert and Kahl (1993) have defined this group, perhaps 3–5 percent of the population, as extremely poor and often unemployed. There are many reasons people may become destitute (Jasinski et al. 2010). They suffer from chronic poverty, homelessness, and live outside the margins of society. Some cannot work because of disability or mental illness. Others face difficult employment prospects because they lack education and job skills. Many reside in the inner cities, where job prospects are few because factories and businesses have moved across town or overseas. Their circumstances are bleak, particularly those who suffer from mental illness. Their situations may be exacerbated by racial or ethnic discrimination.

Some members of the underclass receive assistance from government welfare programs, perhaps drawing upon them for extended periods of time to live and survive. Others are ineligible for programs or do not know how to access them. Some beg for spare change during the day as people walk by and return to homeless shelters or sleep in parks at night. Children comprise 25 percent of the homeless population, and they and their parents are the fastest-growing segment of the homeless population, according to a study of homeless children in shelters in Los Angeles County. One study found that few homeless children escaped emotional, behavioral, and academic problems, and few received help for them (Honberg 2003).

Social Mobility: Fact or Fiction?

Theoretically, Americans can be anything they want to be. Most Americans believe that opportunities for social mobility exist if you simply choose to explore them. Eight in ten believe that although you may begin life poor, if you work hard you can become rich (The Economist 2006). We glorify examples of these cases. This has been labeled *The American Dream*.

However, in reality there is little substantial upward social mobility (Hurst 2010). People usually live out their lives in the same social class from which they came. Moreover, a relatively large number of people today are actually worse off than their parents. Those who do better than their parents tend to be from the highest social classes to begin with. Why do you think this is?

One reason for so little social mobility is that the tools used for upward mobility are no longer as effective as they once were. For example, although education level is an important factor in social mobility, the education system is increasingly stratified by social class, and rich children have a distinct advantage. The elite colleges hold the keys to the best jobs, but getting into these colleges depends on far more than just grades. Most elite colleges have *legacy preferences*—a program for children of alumni—that far outstrip affirmative action programs for minority or poor applicants. In the most selective eight universities in the Northeast, legacies make up between 10 and 15 percent of every class (Economist.com 2004). Meanwhile, federal Pell grants, which go to the poorest students, have been drying up. Is it any wonder that only the rich can attend expensive elite colleges? The median family income at Harvard, for example, is over $150,000, nearly three times the national average.

A second reason for so little upward mobility is that the U.S. tax structure increasingly favors rich families passing on their wealth to their heirs. This has not always been the case. Originally, one of the main purposes of taxes was to redistribute wealth so that it would not be concentrated into a few hands and passed down through the generations to erode the concept of meritocracy. Many early millionaires, such as Andrew Carnegie or the Rockefellers, donated huge portions of their wealth to projects serving the public. Now, however, over 70 percent of Americans oppose the estate tax, which would tax extremely large inheritances after the death of the estate-holder, even though only 1 household in 100 pays it (*The Economist* 2006). Repealing this tax would increase the federal deficit by over three-quarters of a trillion over its first decade (Center on Budget and Policy Priorities 2006). Although most Europeans would flatly oppose allowing the rich to transfer mass wealth to their heirs, Americans see this more favorably. "Americans want to join the rich, not soak them," reports an article in *The Economist* (2006) magazine.

Figure 5.1 **Percent Change in Real Average After-Tax Income: 1979–2006**

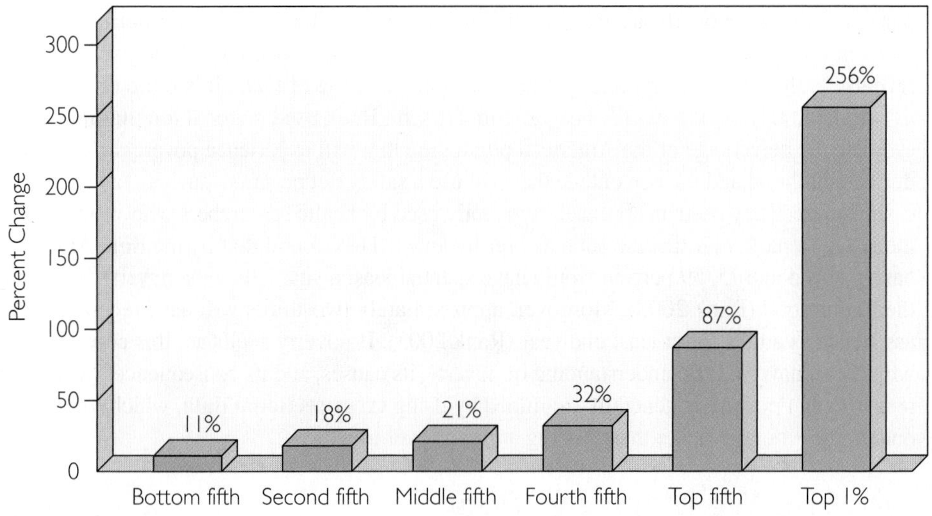

The United States is becoming more unequal; the largest after-tax gains in income are among the wealthiest.

Source: Sherman 2009.

The data are clear and unequivocal: The U.S. economy became considerably more unequal over the past several decades, with the rich receiving a far greater share of the gains than those in the middle or lower incomes (Sherman 2009). Regardless of whether one looks at wages, household income, or spending, the benefits are skewed toward the wealthiest individuals and families. As shown in Figure 5.1, those with incomes in the highest fifth had an average after-tax increase of 87 percent in their incomes between 1979 and 2006. This increase is four times that of the middle fifth and eight times that of the poorest fifth. Even more telling, those with the highest 1 percent of incomes had an increase of 256 percent.

Nonetheless, most Americans tend to blame their financial problems not on the rich, but on the poor, and increasingly on undocumented immigrants. Interestingly, despite Americans' positive attitude toward policies favoring amassed wealth, two of the world's wealthiest entrepreneurs, Bill Gates and Warren Buffett, have donated billions of dollars from their personal fortunes to fighting poverty and to large public projects, similar in spirit to Carnegie and Rockefeller.

I have introduced many ways in which social class shapes our values and opportunities. Let's now turn to those living in poverty.

Families in Poverty

Dee is a single mother who left an abusive marriage to begin anew with her 11-year-old daughter. She works the evening shift to support the two of them, while her daughter stays home alone. Kate is a middle-class woman who left her husband after his infidelity. She now lives in a small, seedy apartment, trying to support herself and her two young children on a low-paying job without child support. Robert and Maria are a happily married couple who face a crisis because Robert's serious illness caused him to lose his job, cutting off the primary source of support for them and their four children. What do these families have in common? They are all poor (Seccombe 2007).

Yet, when most people conjure up a picture of a poor person, they visualize someone who is on the fringes of society: inner-city unemployed Black men, women on welfare raising numerous children, or mentally ill homeless persons begging for change on the street. If these are the images that come to your mind, you are in for an awakening. Although inner-city Black men, women on welfare, the homeless, and other stereotypically vulnerable groups comprise a portion of those in poverty, a surprising finding is that *most Americans will experience poverty and will turn to public assistance at some point during their lives*. As sociologist Mark Rank reveals, "rather than poverty and welfare use being an issue of *them*, it is more of an issue of *us*" (Rank 2003). Along with colleague Tom Hirschl, Rank used national longitudinal data to estimate the percentage of the American population that will experience poverty at some point during adulthood and the percentage that will use a safety net program, such as food stamps or cash welfare. They used an approach frequently used by health researchers who want to assess the risk of a particular disease such as breast cancer. They found that by the time Americans have reached age 75, 59 percent would have spent at least a year below the poverty line during their adulthood (Rank 2003). Moreover, approximately two-thirds will have received public assistance as adults for at least one year (Rank 2003). If poverty spells are this common, then why do we have so little understanding of poverty, its causes, and its consequences? Part of the reason is that poverty is generally examined by using **cross-sectional data**, which look at only one moment in time rather than looking at trends over time.

What Do We Mean by "Poor"?

Terms like *poor*, *poverty*, and *impoverished* are used a great deal in everyday conversation, but exactly what do they mean? How do we define these terms?

The Social Security Administration established the official **poverty threshold** in 1964 (Orshansky 1965) as a way to measure the number of people living in poverty and to assess how it changed from year to year. Survey data in the early 1960s indicated that families spent approximately one-third of their income on food. Therefore, the poverty line was calculated from the estimated annual costs of a minimal food budget designed by the U.S. Department of Agriculture (USDA), and then multiplied by three, a method that continues today. This food budget parallels the current Thrifty Food Plan, which forms the basis of Food Stamp benefits and is the least expensive food plan developed by the USDA (USDA Center for Nutrition Policy and Promotion 2009). It is far below the amount most middle-class families spend on food. Individuals or families with annual incomes below this established threshold are counted as poor.

The poverty line varies by family size and the number of related children under age 18 living in the household. It is revised yearly based on inflationary changes in the Consumer Price Index. Thresholds are also different in Alaska and Hawaii to account for the increased cost of living. As shown in Table 5.2, the weighted average poverty threshold in 2009 was $21,954 for a family of four or $17,098 for a family of three (DeNavas-Walt et al. 2010).

TABLE 5.2 Weighted Average Poverty Thresholds in 2009 by Size of Family

The poverty line is adjusted for family size.

One Person	$10,956
Two People	$13,991
Three People	$17,098
Four People	$21,954
Five People	$25,991
Six People	$29,405
Seven People	$33,372
Eight People	$37,254
Nine or More People	$44,366

Source: DeNavas-Walt et al. 2010.

TABLE 5.3 People and Families in Poverty by Selected Characteristics, 2008

Children, Blacks, and female-headed households are particularly vulnerable to living in poverty.

Total U.S. Population		14.3%
Age	Children Under 18	20.7%
	18–64	12.9%
	Elderly 65 and Over	8.9%
Race	White (Non-Hispanic)	9.4%
	Black	25.8%
	Asian and Pacific Islander	12.5%
	Hispanic	25.3%
Family Type	Married Couple	5.8%
	Female-Headed	29.9%
	Male-Headed	16.9%

Source: DeNavas-Walt et al. 2010.

Who Is Poor?

About 14.3 percent of the U.S. population, or nearly 44 million people, lived below the poverty line in 2009, an increase of 4 million people from one year prior. Table 5.3 reports the degree of poverty in the United States by age, race, and family type. As shown, children are the age group most likely to be impoverished, at nearly 21 percent, a figure more than twice that for the elderly. About one-quarter of Blacks are poor, with Hispanics close behind. Finally, nearly 30 percent of female-headed families are impoverished, compared to about 6 percent of married-couple families.

What are the trends over time? Poverty declined significantly during the 1990s. Low-income workers benefited from a strong economy. Figures 5.2 and 5.3 show that poverty rates began increasing in 2000 among most age groups and across several racial and ethnic groups, and have risen sharply due to the recession.

What does it really mean to "live in poverty"? Can a family make ends meet on a poverty-level budget? A budgeting exercise in the box on page 135, "Social Policies for Families: Making Ends Meet on a Poverty Budget," illustrates the challenge. Perhaps you could create your own budget and see how close you are to a poverty-level budget.

Comparative Studies

Another means of addressing the scope of poverty is to compare the rates of poverty in the United States to those of other countries (Brandolini and Smeeding 2006; Garfinkel et al. 2010; Salverda et al. 2009).

The United States is one of about 40 countries considered to be high-income. Demographers and economists use a *purchasing power parity conversion* that allows us to compare not only income differences, but also the purchasing power of that income (Bade and Parkin 2011). They convert a country's average annual income to *international dollars* that can indicate the amount of goods and services a person could buy in the United States. In more developed countries, such as Norway, Canada, or Japan, it comes to $58,500, $36,220, and $35,220, respectively. People living in these countries tend to focus on **relative poverty**, which refers to the fact that some people lack basic resources relative to others in society. In contrast, **absolute poverty**, defined as the lack of resources such as food, housing, and clothing that is life-threatening, is characteristic of at least 60 low-income countries that are home to roughly half the world's people. In less developed countries (excluding China), pur-

Figure 5.2   Poverty Status by Age: 1968–2009

Poverty is rising for all age groups except the elderly.

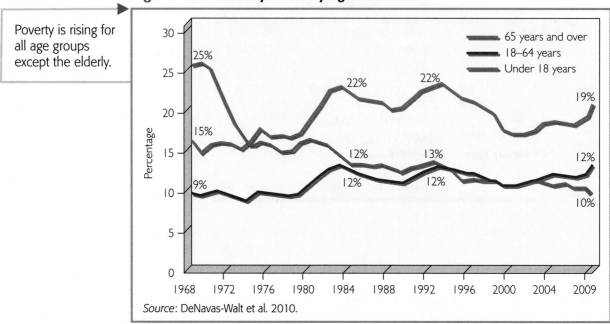

Source: DeNavas-Walt et al. 2010.

Figure 5.3   Poverty Status of People by Race and Hispanic Origin: 1966–2009

The poverty rate is rising among all racial and ethnic groups.

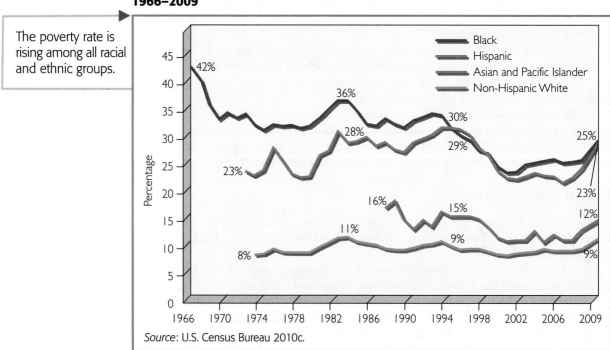

Source: U.S. Census Bureau 2010c.

Policies for Families

Making Ends Meet on a Poverty Budget

The 2009 poverty threshold for a family of three averages $17,098 per year, which comes to $1,425 per month (DeNavas-Walt et al. 2010).

Could your family of three live on a poverty budget of $17,098 per year or $1,425 per month? Let's find out by examining a sample budget. The costs in this budget are from reports by the USDA, HUD, the Center on Budget and Policy Priorities, and other consumer expenditure reports estimating the price of a "low-cost" food plan, the fair market rent for a two-bedroom apartment, and a cost estimate for childcare and other expenditures. The cost of living varies somewhat from one community to another; for example, rents may be higher (or lower) where you live than in the estimate below. You can substitute numbers from your own community if you prefer.

The question is: Is it reasonable to assume a family of three can live on $1,425 per month in the United States? Keep in mind that someone who works full-time, year-round, at approximately $8.10 per hour would earn this amount.

Sample Expenses

Rent (2 bedroom apartment and utilities):	$800
Food:	$425
Child Care	$620
Health Care	$65
Clothing	$60
Transportation	$416
Miscellaneous	$100
TOTAL	**$2,486/month or $29,832/ year before taxes**

Already, we have gone way over budget. How can we cut back?

- Find a cheaper apartment, or one in a less desirable part of town? Don't forget that children live here.

- Lower the utility bill by keeping the house colder? This is one reason why poor children are sick more often.
- Eliminate the telephone? This could be dangerous in an emergency.
- Cut back on toiletries? Toilet paper, shampoo, and tampons are basic needs.
- Eliminate car maintenance? How will the family get to work, school, or run errands? A bus system may not be available or feasible with children.

We are over budget and we haven't yet included other basic needs for this family:

School Supplies	$25
Health Insurance	$300
Entertainment	$100
Laundry	$25
NEW TOTAL	**$2,936/month or $35,232/ year before taxes**

Assumption

Even this revised budget assumes the family already has a household set up. There is no money included to buy furniture, a car, or household items like towels or dishes. In other words, even $2,936 per month is unrealistically low. As you can see, the poverty line is an inadequate measure of poverty.

CRITICAL THINKING QUESTIONS

1. What should the poverty line be based on? Should it be based on something other than the price of food? Should it remain three times the cost of a thrifty budget? What are the political implications of changing it?
2. How can a family make ends meet if a parent earns poverty-level wages?

chasing power parity averages less than $5,000 per person. This means that a person living in a country like India, Bolivia, Cambodia, or Nepal would have, on average, an income equivalent to the purchasing power of less than $5,000 if living in the United States. (It does *not* mean that persons in these countries actually have $5,000 to spend.) Given that this is an average, there are many countries with a considerably lower purchasing power, as shown in the map on pages 138–139. For instance, the purchasing power of a person living in Haiti is only $1,180 and in Sierra Leone it is only $750—meaning that he or she has the purchasing power for goods and services equivalent to someone in the United States living on only $750 per year. This clearly represents abject poverty. In stark contrast to this, the purchasing parity of a person in the United States is $46,970.

The following box, "Our Global Community: 'Nalim' in Bhutan," describes the daily life of a poor woman in Bhutan, a small country in Asia, and illustrates the toll absolute poverty can take. Yet, although poverty painfully touches all aspects of life, the poor are not necessarily unhappy. Does this seem like a contradiction to you?

The Luxembourg Income Study (LIS), initiated in the 1980s and continuing today, has standardized variables across 70 data sets to allow for some comparisons of poverty across a limited number of countries. Using several different measures of poverty across 17 developed nations, researchers are now able to make relatively valid cross-national comparisons within these countries.

O U R

Global Community

"Nalim" in Bhutan

"Nalim" is a 49-year-old farmer, wife, and mother who struggles to feed a family of 13 in her home located in a village in the Himalayas of western Bhutan. The United Nations ranks Bhutan's affluence as 146th out of 185 countries. That puts it squarely in the middle in the pack of low-income countries. It is a largely rural country with great distances between villages. Similarly to other poor nations, health problems plague the population. Infant mortality is high, and many children die from dehydration due to severe diarrhea from drinking dirty and polluted water. Life expectancy is low. Bhutan has the second-highest maternal mortality rate in the world. What is Nalim's daily life like?

Nalim shares a house with her brother, her mother, uncle, aunt, husband, her four children, a son-in-law, and three grandchildren. Her fifth child died years ago. She lives on the second story of a three-story house. The grain is stored on the top level, and the animals live on the ground floor. Although the government urges families to move animals out of the house because of disease, Nalim lacks the money for a barn. Flies and dung are everywhere. Nalim claims that she would like to move the animals outside because each of her children has suffered at least one serious illness related to their presence. Her house has no electricity or indoor plumbing. Only about 70 percent of Bhutan's population uses adequate sanitation facilities (United Nations Children's Fund 2006). There is little furniture in the house and family members sit on the floor for their meals.

Nalim's husband has a physical disability—a clubfoot—and therefore the bulk of the farming tasks fall on her and her adult daughter. "He cannot do heavy work because of his leg—he is crippled—so even before we were married he did not do that kind of work." In addition, she also is responsible for the other typical gender-based tasks of caring for children, cooking, and cleaning. "The only season when they [the men] take care of the children a lot is during the paddy time. Planting paddies is women's work, so at that time they stay home and take care of the children and cook. . . . Men never do women's things, like harvest wheat or plant paddies."

The family grows almost all of the food they consume. She worries regularly about whether the harvest will be big enough to feed her family. She confesses that she needs money too and spends about 344 ngultrum (U.S. $11.50) per month on things she cannot produce, such as salt, sugar, tea leaves, clothes, and school supplies for her children and grandchildren. To purchase her goods at the market Nalim must walk three hours each way. One pair of shoes cost 50 ngultrum (U.S. $1.70), a cost considered exorbitant, therefore only three of the children in her family own shoes.

Nalim has no formal education. "If I had gone to school, I would not be living this kind of life—where I have to be out in the fields whether it is sunny or rainy," she laments. She notes that other children her age from her village were able to go to school, but she could not because she was the only daughter at home and her labor was needed to run the household.

Poverty touches all aspects of their lives every single day. This day-to-day existence is an endless struggle to cultivate enough food to eat and keep all family members healthy and alive—yet, in the midst of all this hardship is a loving family with real warmth. Family meals are lengthy affairs with much lively conversation. The adults are keenly interested in what the children have to say, a feature sometimes missing in U.S. culture. Nalim believes that she has a very good family, "with trust and understanding among ourselves." She married her husband out of love—and her love continues today more than 20 years later. Is it possible to describe someone who lives on the brink of survival as "happy"?

Sources: D'Aluisio and Menzel 1996; United Nations Children's Fund 2006.

CRITICAL THINKING QUESTIONS
1. What factors in Bhutan and throughout the world contribute to Bhutan's high rate of poverty?
2. Do you think it is possible to describe someone who lives on the brink of survival as happy? Why or why not?

All measures of poverty show a similar pattern: The U.S. poverty rate exceeds those of 15 comparable countries with the exception of Ireland, as shown in Table 5.4. For example, using one method that defines poverty as living on less than 50 percent of the median income, 17 percent of Americans lived under half the median income, far exceeding the average for the other countries. The percentage of U.S. children who live below 50 percent of the median income is greater than any of the other countries. Among the aged, only Ireland and Australia have a higher proportion of seniors living below the median income. Comparative data such as these indicate that high rates of poverty in a wealthy developed nation such as the United States are not inevitable (Mishel et al. 2007).

Causes of Poverty

Many theories have been offered to explain the nature of poverty and account for why so many individuals are impoverished in the United States. Four major explanations are described here.

Individualism Tales of Horatio Alger–types abound—the "rags-to-riches" stories—with the moral that anyone can pull themselves up by their bootstraps with hard work, sweat, and motivation. The poor, and particularly welfare recipients, are blatant examples of those who have failed to "make it." An individualistic perspective argues that poverty is primarily a result of personal failings, and the poor generally have only themselves to blame for their predicament. This perspective suggests that the United States is still a land of meritocracy, and that hard work will reap financial and social rewards.

WHAT DO YOU THINK?

Why is the poverty rate so much lower in other peer countries than it is in the United States? What are they doing differently to combat poverty?

A Comparative Look at Purchasing Power Parity, in U.S. Dollars, 2008

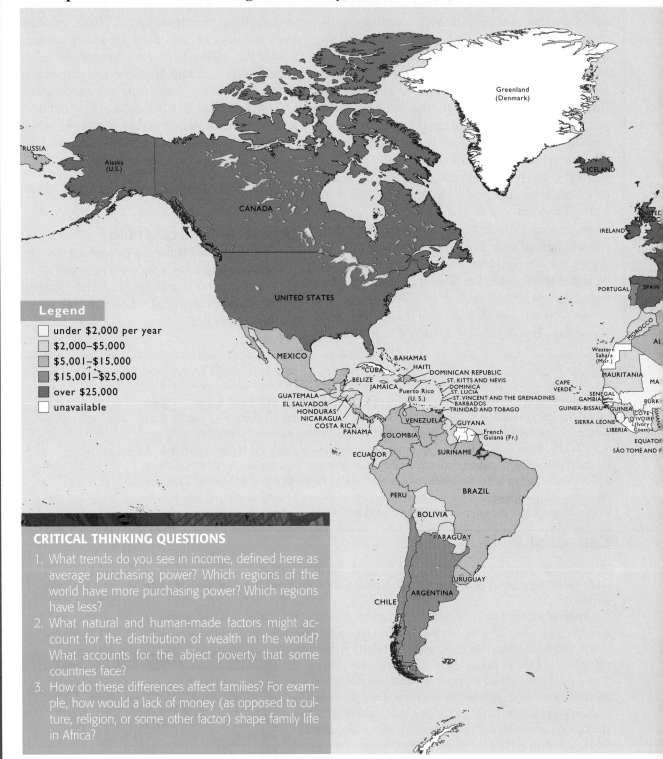

Greenland
(Denmark)

RUSSIA

ICELAND

Alaska
(U.S.)

UNITED
KINGDOM

IRELAND

CANADA

PORTUGAL   SPAIN

Legend

☐ under $2,000 per year
☐ $2,000–$5,000
☐ $5,001–$15,000
☐ $15,001–$25,000
☐ over $25,000
☐ unavailable

MEXICO

MOROCCO

Western
Sahara
(Mor.)   AL

MAURITANIA   MA

BAHAMAS

CUBA   HAITI

DOMINICAN REPUBLIC

BELIZE   ST. KITTS AND NEVIS
                          DOMINICA

JAMAICA   ST. LUCIA

CAPE
VERDE

SENEGAL

GUATEMALA   Puerto Rico   ST. VINCENT AND THE GRENADINES   GAMBIA
EL SALVADOR (U. S.)   BARBADOS   GUINEA-BISSAU   GUINEA
HONDURAS   TRINIDAD AND TOBAGO   CÔTE
NICARAGUA   SIERRA LEONE   D'IVOIRE   GHANA
        COSTA RICA   VENEZUELA   GUYANA   (Ivory
            PANAMA   LIBERIA   Coast)

BURK

COLOMBIA   French
                      Guiana (Fr.)   EQUATOR

ECUADOR   SURINAME   SÃO TOMÉ AND P

                            BRAZIL

PERU

            BOLIVIA

                PARAGUAY

                        URUGUAY

CHILE   ARGENTINA

CRITICAL THINKING QUESTIONS

1. What trends do you see in income, defined here as average purchasing power? Which regions of the world have more purchasing power? Which regions have less?

2. What natural and human-made factors might account for the distribution of wealth in the world? What accounts for the abject poverty that some countries face?

3. How do these differences affect families? For example, how would a lack of money (as opposed to culture, religion, or some other factor) shape family life in Africa?

TABLE 5.4 Extent of Poverty Across 17 Developed Countries

The United States has the highest rate of low-income children among peer countries.

PERCENT OF POPULATION BELOW 50% OF MEDIAN INCOME			
Country	**Overall**	**Children**	**Elderly**
United States	**17**	**22**	**25**
Ireland	17	17	36
Australia	14	16	30
Spain	14	16	23
Italy	13	17	14
United Kingdom	12	15	21
Canada	11	15	6
Denmark	9	9	7
Germany	8	9	10
France	8	8	10
Switzerland	8	7	18
Austria	8	8	14
Belgium	8	7	16
Netherlands	7	10	2
Sweden	7	4	8
Norway	6	3	12
Finland	5	3	9

Source: Luxembourg Income Study 2006. Cited in Mishel et al. 2007.

Over one in five children in the United States live in poverty, a significant increase over the past few years. A child is far more likely to live in poverty in the United States than in other peer nations.

Proponents of individualism argue that because everyone theoretically has an equal chance to succeed, those who fail to make it have largely themselves to blame. The popular rags-to-riches stories promote the idea that virtually anyone can pull themselves up by their bootstraps with hard work and motivation.

There is great ambivalence toward the poor (Browning 2008; Hancock 2004). Almost two-thirds of Americans believe that we can create our own fate through our own efforts (National Opinion Research Center 2009). A study of middle-class Americans across the country found that 50 percent claimed that the biggest cause of poverty is that people are not doing enough to help themselves (NPR Online 2001). Many poor persons are assumed to be lazy, unmotivated, and living off the public dole. Although most Americans rate the economy as the most important issue facing Americans today (CBS News/New York Times Poll 2009), they are relatively unconcerned about poverty and do not see it as bad for the country (60 percent). In fact, in a 2001 poll, one in five Americans thought that there were too *few* rich people (probably because they hadn't yet become rich) (Zimmerman 2001).

Persons who are more likely to espouse individualistic explanations are White, live in the southern and north-central regions of the United States, are older than 50, and have moderate levels of education. Perhaps surprisingly, welfare recipients also tend to denigrate the poor. They distance themselves from other people on welfare, despite the fact that their circumstances are not altogether different (Seccombe 2011). As "Sheri," a 27-year-old mother of three who had received welfare for seven years, said:

> I think a lot of them are on it just to be on it. Lazy. Don't want to do nothing. A lot of them are on it because a lot of them are on drugs. Keep having kids to get more money, more food stamps. Now that's abusing the system. And a lot of women are abusing the system. (Seccombe 2011)

Social Structuralism   In contrast to individualism, a social structural approach assumes that poverty is a result of economic or social imbalances within the social structure that serve to restrict opportunities for some people (Swedberg 2007). Drawing from a conflict theoretical perspective introduced in Chapter 1, the focus is on inequalities that are rooted in the social structure. For example, the U.S. economy has been changing over the last several decades, resulting in an erosion in the purchasing power of the minimum wage, a growth in low-paying service jobs, and job relocation from inner cities to the suburbs (Newman 2008; Wilson 1996). As shown in the opening vignette, Barbara Ehrenreich found that it is virtually impossible to live on a minimum or near-minimum wage, let alone support a family. Yet more than two million workers do just that, half of whom are over 25 years of age (Bureau of Labor Statistics 2009b). Although low wages may be enough to support a single person, a family trying to make ends meet would be living near or below the poverty threshold. Moreover, low-wage jobs often fail to provide families with health insurance.

These are social problems, not simply personal ones. People may find themselves vulnerable because of their social location and relationship to the social structure. A changing economy, a drive for profit inherent in capitalism, racism, patriarchal norms, and an eroding safety net have greater deleterious effects on some than on others. One woman highlights the value of this safety net as she compares what is available to families in Hungary to those in the United States. She writes in a letter to the editor of a magazine (Strong-Jekely 2006):

> . . . I live in Hungary, where the benefits for families surpass those of any other country I've heard about. Maternity leave is three years. Daycare and preschool are free. Elementary school starts at eight a.m. and runs until two p.m., with optional aftercare. Most schools also offer ballet, music lessons, computer clubs, soccer, etc., in the afternoon. We all receive a monthly family supplement grant, which increases with each child and lasts until the child turns eighteen. When the child hits school age, we get an additional lump sum at the beginning of each

school year amounting to about $100 per child to cover school supplies. All children have medical coverage through the age of eighteen—longer if they are in college—and pediatricians make house calls. If you have a child with a disability, you may stay home with the child for the rest of his/her life and receive the minimum wage. . . . There is no question that the United States needs more generous benefits for families. I am an American (my husband is Hungarian) and our choice to move to Hungary to have kids was a very conscious one. When I feel pangs of homesickness, I think of my overworked, stressed-out friends with kids back home and think: No way. I feel like I've got a balance in my life I would have a difficult time achieving in the States. I wish that all American parents had the same opportunities we've got here in Hungary to make life easier for families.

Her point is that families need programs and policies in place to remain socially and economically healthy. Families without these benefits are more likely to slip into poverty.

Culture of Poverty   The culture of poverty perspective blends features of the previous two approaches and suggests that the poor have developed a subcultural set of values, traits, and expectations as a direct result of the structural constraints associated with living in isolated pockets of poverty. The subculture is assumed to foster a weak family structure, present-time orientation, and people display a helplessness and resignation toward work (Burton 1992). The subculture is at odds with the dominant middle-class culture and downplays the importance of hard work, self-discipline, and deferring gratification. Concern is voiced about the transmission of these values from parents to their children. However, most poor adults have grown up in nonpoor, "pro-social" households (Ludwig and Mayer 2006).

Oscar Lewis (1966) first introduced this perspective as he studied poor barrios in Latin American communities. His work has sometimes been criticized as "blaming the victim," in which deviant values are seen as the causes of poverty itself. Others have suggested that his work has been misinterpreted and that Lewis's ideas are firmly grounded in a Marxist critique of capitalism. A *subculture* is a positive adaptation constructed to ease the pain associated with being part of a reserve and discarded labor force, "a process by which the poor pragmatically winnow what works from what does not, and pass it on to their children" (Harvey and Reed 1996).

Fatalism   Finally, some people believe that poverty is attributable to quirks, chance, luck, inevitable human nature, illness, low intelligence, or other forces over which people have little control, a theoretical perspective referred to here as *fatalism*. Fate does not necessarily imply destiny, but rather a form of victimization that is rooted in complex events beyond one's immediate control. Poverty is not anyone's fault *per se*, but rather is a potential consequence of unplanned, random, or natural human events or chain of events. For example, Herrnstein and Murray (1994) suggest that low intelligence is a primary cause of poverty. Arguing that intelligence is largely genetic, they claim that poor people with low intelligence quotients (IQs) give birth to another cohort with low IQs, and therefore their children are likely to remain impoverished. Seccombe and Hoffman (2007) found in their detailed in-person interviews that health problems were a primary reason why families leaving welfare for work remained poor.

> ### WHAT DO YOU THINK?
>
> *Why does poverty persist? Which explanation of poverty makes the most sense to you and why? Can you provide specific examples of these perspectives in action?*

Consequences of Poverty

Economically insecure and poor families experience more stress, disorganization, and other problems in their lives. These are difficult for all family members, but in particular, weigh heavily on children's physical, social, and emotional health (Lovell and Isaacs 2010). For this reason, let's look at the consequences of poverty on children first.

Poor children exhibit more antisocial behavior and are more likely to drop out of school or become teenage parents, are more likely to suffer from depression, and are in poorer health

(Evans et al. 2005; Federal Interagency Forum on Child and Family Statistics 2009; Linden 2009). Naturally, not all poor children suffer these outcomes. Many poor children are models of success. Nonetheless, they are more likely than other children to face a host of serious challenges. For example, Smith et al. (1997) found that children in families with incomes less than one-half of the poverty line scored between 6 and 13 points lower on various standardized tests than did children in families with incomes between 1.5 and 2.0 times the poverty line. Using three different types of assessment—IQ, verbal ability, and achievement tests—they also found that the longer the poverty spell and the more severe the poverty, the lower the score. Does this finding support the fatalistic explanation that somehow poor people are just not smart? Or might it reflect greater risk for inadequate diets, exposure to lead paint, inadequate health care, and a host of other structural factors that lead to poor school performance and lower levels of learning?

How does poverty exert its influence? Figure 5.4 summarizes the pathways through which poverty hurts children (Seccombe 2007). Poverty contributes to:

- inadequate health and nutrition
- a lower-quality home environment
- parental stress and mental health problems
- fewer resources for learning
- housing problems
- poor-quality neighborhoods

Inadequate Health and Nutrition   Research is unequivocal on the relationship between poverty and health. Poverty puts the health of children at risk in many ways, including the likelihood of having low birth weight, which in turn increases chances of serious chronic and acute illness, along with emotional and behavioral problems (Breslau et al. 2004; Federal Interagency Forum on Child and Family Statistics 2009; Gray et al. 2004). Poor children are over three times more likely to be iron deficient; 1.5 times more likely to have frequent diarrhea or colitis; twice as likely to suffer from severe asthma; 1.5 times more likely to suffer partial or complete blindness or deafness; and three times more likely to have lead levels in their bloodstream of at least 10 micrograms of lead per deciliter of blood. This is dangerous because it is at this level that harmful effects to the brain and nervous system have been noted, causing lower intelligence, reduced physical stature, impaired hearing, and behavior issues. At least 300,000 children in the United States have blood levels that are high enough to cause serious impairment (Centers for Disease Control and Prevention, Center for Environmental Health 2006).

Poor children also may receive inadequate food and nutrition. Nearly 15 percent of households experienced **food insecurity** at some point during 2008 defined by the USDA as not having enough nourishing food available on a regular basis (Nord et al. 2009). Twenty-two percent of households with children are food insecure. Children suffer the immediate pain of hunger, and the longer-term consequences of malnutrition. They run the risk of more frequent colds, ear infections and other infectious diseases, impaired brain function, and stunted growth, and are more vulnerable to lead and other environmental toxins.

Children and adults living in poverty suffer many deleterious consequences, including food insecurity and hunger, which can then exacerbate other problems such as difficulty learning. To help feed hungry families, some communities offer food pantries from which families can receive a box of staples to help their food stretch through the month.

Figure 5.4 **Pathways from Poverty to Adverse Child Outcomes**

Poverty has harmful consequences for children, which occur through six pathways.

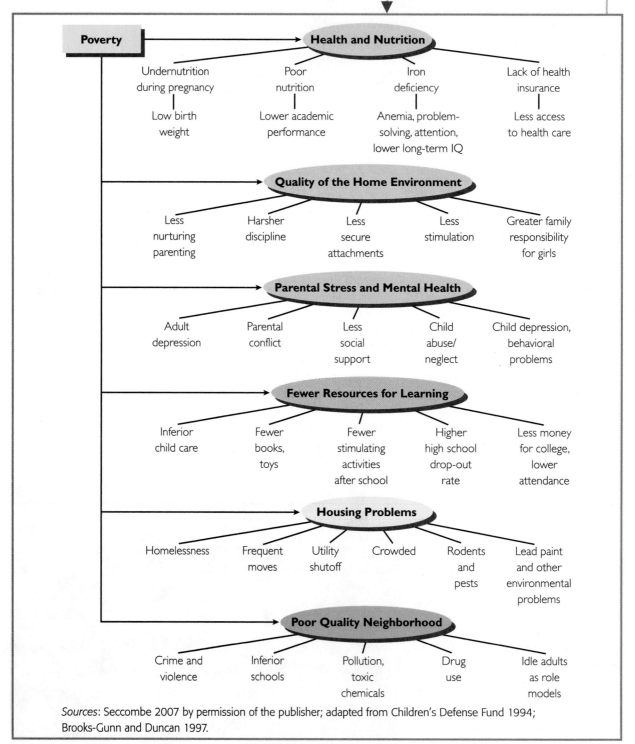

Sources: Seccombe 2007 by permission of the publisher; adapted from Children's Defense Fund 1994; Brooks-Gunn and Duncan 1997.

Quality of the Home Environment   Warm, loving relationships with parents, in conjunction with rich opportunities for learning, help children thrive. The Home Observation of the Measurement of the Environment (HOME) is a widely used interview and observation tool of parent–child interaction. It shows that poverty has a significant negative effect on the quality and stimulation of the home environment (Yeung et al. 2002). One study of the linguistic capabilities of young children found that poor children on welfare between the ages of 13 and 36 months hear only half as many words per hour as the average working-class child, and less than one-third the average of a typical child in a professional family (Children's Defense Fund 2005). Obviously, parents cannot teach their children what they themselves do not know. Moreover, poor parents are also less nurturing and more authoritarian, and they use more inconsistent and harsh physical discipline as a family's economic situation worsens.

Parental Stress and Mental Health   What else about an impoverished family environment may increase the likelihood of negative outcomes for children? One likely culprit is that parents who are living in poor conditions have a high level of stress, depression, and mental health problems related to their situation. For example, high levels of male unemployment are significantly associated with child abuse and deprivation. Although child abuse occurs in many different type of households, poor children have a higher probability of being abused, neglected, and more severely injured by abuse than do their more affluent peers (Centers for Disease Control and Prevention 2007; National Center for Health Statistics 2009).

Fewer Resources for Learning   On average, poor children have fewer resources for learning in the home, including books and educational toys. Therefore, high-quality child care and preschool programs become very important to helping them overcome the disadvantages in their home environment. Unfortunately, child care and preschool are very expensive, as you will see in Chapter 11, and far fewer subsidized spots are available than are needed. Full-time childcare can easily cost over $10,000 per year for each child (National Association of Child Care Resource & Referral Agencies 2009). Poor children also engage in fewer organized and enrichment activities (Gardner et al. 2008). Thus many poor children receive lower grades and lower scores on standardized tests; they are less likely to finish high school; and are less likely to attend or graduate from college than are other children (Federal Interagency Forum on Child and Family Statistics 2009; NICHD Early Child Care Research Network 2005).

Housing Problems   The 2010 fair market rent for a two-bedroom apartment plus utilities, according to the Department of Housing and Urban Development, would run about $1,056 in Seattle, $919 in Phoenix, $1,015 in Chicago, and $921 in Denver (U.S. Department of Housing and Urban Development 2010). Poor families cannot afford to pay this, and so they often live in crowded and disease-ridden housing that may lack proper cooking, heating, or sanitation facilities. Not surprisingly, a 2008 survey of 25 U.S. cities found that 23 of the cities reported a rise in homelessness among families (U.S. Conference of Mayors 2008).

Poor-Quality Neighborhoods   Poor children are most often isolated from the nonpoor in their communities and live in inner cities where violence, crime, truancy, loitering, and a sense of despair predominate (Gardner and Brooks-Gunn 2009; O'Hare 1995; Wilkenfeld et al. 2008). Guns kill over 3,000 children and teens each year, and homicide is the third leading cause of death among children ages 1–4, the fifth-leading cause among children ages 5–14, and the second-leading cause among teens ages 15–19. It is the leading cause of death among young Blacks ages 15–34 (Children's Defense Fund 2008).

Poverty affects the entire family, and the potentially harmful health effects of poverty on adults are also numerous. For example, poor adults have significantly higher morbidity

> ### *WHAT DO YOU THINK?*
>
> *What kinds of programs do you think are really needed to end poverty? What are you doing today to ensure that you are not poor in the future? Can you guarantee it?*

(sickness) and lower life expectancy than other adults (National Center for Health Statistics 2009). They are more likely to work in dangerous occupations and live in unsafe neighborhoods, and their homes are more likely to be located near toxic sites. As poor parents become ill, it may undermine their ability to be effective parents.

One issue with far-reaching consequences for families is that poor men and women are less likely to marry (Edin and Kefalas 2005; White and Rogers 2000). Poverty undermines economic security and makes men less attractive marriage partners. For example, Wilson suggests that a key factor in explaining the falling marriage rate among inner-city Blacks is their declining employment opportunities as jobs move to the suburbs or overseas (Wilson 1987, 1996). Poverty also undermines marital stability and leads to greater marital conflict because it increases stress or depression, which can then lead to anger, resentment, and hostility between partners, and difficulties among children (Conger and Conger 2008; Cui et al. 2007; Scaramella et al. 2008).

Social Policy and Family Resilience

Poverty is a vexing social problem affecting millions. How do we combat poverty? One example of a sound social policy that has the potential to offset poverty is the Earned Income Tax Credit. As structured, it has increased the standard of living for millions of families and pulled many out of poverty. It has been applauded as an important incentive and reward for work. However, others argue that it is not as effective as it could be.

Example: Earned Income Tax Credit

The **Earned Income Tax Credit (EITC)** is a refundable federal tax credit for low-income workers and their families. The credit can reduce the amount of taxes owed and result in a tax refund to those who claim and qualify for the credit. It has been hailed as a boon to low-income workers, in effect raising their pay by up to several dollars per hour. In essence, it is a cash subsidy for low-income workers.

To qualify for the credit, the adjusted gross income for 2009 must have been less than $45,295 for a married couple with two children, $40,463 for a married couple with one child, and $18,440 for a married couple without children (Internal Revenue Service 2010). If the credit is larger than any taxes owed, the worker will receive a cash refund from the Internal Revenue Service (IRS) after filing a tax return. In essence, the government is providing low-income workers additional money beyond what they get paid at their jobs to encourage work and to reduce poverty.

The EITC is applauded for lifting millions of adults and children out of poverty each year and is considered one of the country's largest sources of assistance for poor and low-income families. Enacted in 1975 and expanded in the 1990s, it keeps 6.5 million Americans out of poverty each year (Sherman 2009) and helps millions of other low-income families at a cost of about $54 billion (Williams and Johnson 2009). However, 15–20 percent of eligible persons fail to claim their credit, usually because they are unaware of it or need help with filling out their tax forms (Greenstein 2005).

Not surprisingly, the EITC has had a positive effect on employment because it offers a real supplement to wages for qualifying workers. The EITC makes it easier for families to transition from welfare into work by providing a critical element of security for poor families. It contributes to basic necessities, enables families to make needed purchases, and can be used as a savings cushion to offset a future job loss, illness, or other situation that can leave families vulnerable.

Yet, at the same time, it has less of an impact on poverty than it could. The EITC is a once-a-year tax credit, unlike the assistance in most other developed nations that provides monthly support. Furthermore, the EITC offsets only some of the taxes paid. It is not designed to augment wages at all.

Conclusion

This chapter has introduced the importance of social class to understanding families and close relationships, and subsequent chapters will examine specific aspects of this relationship more fully. Social stratification and social class are important components of C. Wright Mills' claim that personal experiences are in large part shaped by broad social, historical, and cultural forces. Social classes in the United States are more vague than in Great Britain. Nonetheless, one's social class position influences family lifestyle, goals, opportunities, values, choices, and constraints. Persons living in poverty are particularly vulnerable in terms of their health and social well-being. Strong family policies, such as the EITC or national health insurance, can go a long way in assisting families as they struggle to make ends meet.

Key Terms

Absolute poverty: The lack of resources such as food, housing, and clothing that is life-threatening. (p. 134)

Ascribed statuses: Statuses that a person is born with, such as his or her sex, racial and ethnic background, and social class. (p. 120)

Bourgeoisie: According to Karl Marx, the capitalist class that owns the means of production. (p. 124)

Caste system: A system of social stratification that is based on ascribed characteristics one is born with, such as race, ethnicity, or family lineage. (p. 123)

Cross-sectional data: Data collected at only one point in time rather than following trends over time. (p. 132)

Earned Income Tax Credit (EITC): A federal tax credit for low-income working families. (p. 146)

Food insecurity: Defined by the USDA as just having enough nourishing food available on a regular basis (p. 143).

Home observation of the measurement of the environment (HOME): A widely used tool that measures maternal warmth and learning experiences provided to the child; is associated with a variety of child outcomes. (p. 121)

Individualism: The belief that anyone can pull themselves up by their bootstraps and achieve success. Poverty is the result of personal failings. (p. 137)

Meritocracy: A system in which economic and social rewards, such as income, occupation, or prestige, are obtained on individual merit rather than inheritance. (p. 123)

Poverty threshold: The official U.S. government method of calculating how many people are poor and assessing how that number changes from year to year. (p. 132)

Power: The ability to achieve goals, wishes, and desires even in the face of opposition from others. (p. 124)

Prestige: The esteem or respect a person is afforded. (p. 124)

Proletariat: According to Karl Marx, individuals who must sell their labor to the owners in order to earn enough money to survive. (p. 124)

Relative poverty: The lack of basic resources relative to others in society. (p. 133)

Social class: A system of social stratification that is based both on ascribed statuses and individual achievement. (p. 123)

Social mobility: Movement in the stratification system based on individual effort or achievement. (p. 123)

Social stratification: The hierarchical ranking of people within society on the basis of specific coveted resources, such as income and wealth. (p. 123)

Socioeconomic status (SES): A vague combination of education, occupation, and income. (p. 125)

Wealth: The value of all of a person's or a family's economic assets, including income, real estate, stocks, bonds, and other items of economic worth, minus debt. (p. 124)

Resources on the Internet

Joint Center for Poverty Research

www.jcpr.org

The Northwestern University/University of Chicago Joint Center for Poverty Research (JCPR) supports academic research that examines what it means to be poor and live in the United States. JCPR concentrates on the causes and consequences of poverty in this country and the effectiveness of policies aimed at reducing poverty.

National Coalition for the Homeless

nch.ari.net

This site provides extensive information about homelessness, including the nature of homelessness in the United States. It also offers a lengthy bibliography for those seeking further information.

Urban Institute

www.urban.org

The Urban Institute is a research organization focusing on a wide spectrum of social problems and efforts to solve them. It focuses particularly on issues related to the poor and disadvantaged, including health insurance, welfare reform, poverty, and the working poor. You can access many of their working papers or full documents from their website.

United Nations

www.un.org

The United Nations website provides a wealth of information about global poverty, economic and social development, and human rights. Their website provides access to research reports and press releases.

CHAPTER 6

Race, Ethnicity, and Families

CHAPTER OUTLINE

Increasing Diversity in the United States 151

> **SOCIAL** *Policies for Families:* Arizona's Immigration Law 153

Defining Basic Concepts 155

> **FAMILIES** *as Lived Experience:* Loving Across the Color Line: A White Adoptive Mother Learns About Race 159

> **EYE** *on the World:* Comparative Ethnic and Racial Diversity 160

Hispanic Families 162

Black Families 166

Asian American Families 170

> **OUR** *Global Community:* One Child's Very Special First Fourth of July 172

American Indian and Alaska Native Families 175

Interracial and Interethnic Families 177

Social Policy and Family Resilience 179

> **Conclusion** 180

> **Key Terms** 180

> **Resources on the Internet** 181

CHAPTER PREVIEW

What is the significance of race and ethnicity to our understanding of families and intimate relationships? This chapter provides an important foundation for upcoming chapters by introducing basic facts about race, ethnicity, and the changing demographic landscape of the United States. We will explore general issues and then look at the demographic trends and social characteristics of several specific racial and ethnic groups. The goal is to lay the groundwork for exploring racial and ethnic issues in more depth in subsequent chapters. In this chapter, you will learn:

- The United States is becoming increasingly diverse

- Historical and current social issues surrounding legal and illegal immigration

- How to define basic concepts, including race, ethnicity, minority group, and racism

- Important and distinguishing characteristics of Hispanic, Black, Asian American, American Indian, and Alaska Native families, and how those characteristics affect families

- The tremendous growth in interracial and interethnic families is changing the way we think about and conceptualize racial and ethnic categories

- Affirmative action programs can have real implications for improving the economic and social well-being of families

A five-year-old-girl in Georgia is asked a series of questions in her school library as she looks at five cartoons of girls, all identical except that the color of their skin ranges from light to dark. The girl, who is White, is asked to point to the "smart" child. She points to the light-skinned doll. When asked who the "mean" doll is, she points to a dark-skinned doll. She says a White doll is "good," and the Black doll is "ugly" because "she's a lot darker."

This girl was part of a pilot study examining children's views of race, sponsored by CNN, with a renowned child psychologist from the University of Chicago serving as head of the research team. One hundred and thirty-three Black and White children from early and middle childhood were selected from eight schools in the northeastern and southeastern parts of the United States. Their average age was about seven to eight years. The purpose of this pilot study was to test the research design and survey questions, which were largely drawn from other questionnaires and inventories deemed valid and reliable. The measures assessed children's attitudes, beliefs, and social preferences about children with different skin tones.

But no one thought the results would be so telling. Do young children hold racial stereotypes? You bet they do. The five-year-old girl was not alone. White children have an overwhelmingly positive bias toward other White children and a negative bias towards Black children.

But perhaps even more startling, Black children also often evaluate Whites more positively than they do Blacks. For example, when the children were asked, "Show me the child who has skin color you don't want," 51 percent of the Black children pointed to the dolls with the two darkest skin tones (as did 86 percent of the White children). When asked to point out the "dumb" child, 50 percent of Black children chose dolls with the two darkest skin tones (as did 76 percent of the White children). When asked to identify the "nice" child, 38 percent of Black children pointed to the dolls with the lightest skin tones (along with 63 percent of the Whites). These trends were found in virtually all of the questions. They confirmed many earlier studies suggesting that minority children struggle with internalized racism. Many minority youth have come to accept Whites' negative stereotypes about Blacks.

Where do children get such attitudes? The mother of the five-year-old White girl cried and said that her daughter didn't get these views at home because they don't talk about race at all in their family. What this mother did not realize, however, is that not speaking about race is a privilege beholden to Whites. Whereas three-quarters of White families with kindergartners never or almost never talk about race, for Black parents the number is reversed, with three-quarters saying they address race with their children. Black parents begin discussing race when their children are very young because they say they have to prepare their children for a society in which skin color matters.

Sources: CNN 2010; Brown et al. 2007.

Why a separate chapter on the influence of race and ethnicity on family life? Shouldn't coverage in the subsequent chapters—marriage, children, divorce—suffice? Although every chapter in this text focuses on many different families and their experiences, family scholars are developing a greater sensitivity to the specific social meanings associated with race and ethnicity, and how these shape the structure of and interactions within families (Pew Hispanic Center 2009; Umaña-Taylor et al. 2009). For example, how does racial discrimination affect stress and psychological well-being? How do minority parents socialize children about race and racism?

This chapter introduces the importance of race and ethnicity and makes explicit the racial contexts that influence our lives. Whites have the privilege of rarely thinking about race or ethnicity; yet, the color of our skin, physical features, country of origin, culture, and dominant language also have a tremendous impact on family structure, role relationships, and family interaction. We will see many examples throughout this text, including:

- Blacks are more likely than Whites to live in *extended families*.
- American Indians have higher *infant mortality rates* than do other groups.
- Hispanics are less likely to *cohabit* than are other groups.
- Blacks are less likely than other groups to *marry*.
- Asian American families are more likely to emphasize the value of a *college education* than are other groups.
- Hispanics, particularly Mexican Americans, are less likely to have *health insurance* to cover family medical bills, resulting in a variety of negative health outcomes for their families.
- American Indian, Black, Hispanic, and Asian American grandmothers play a more significant role in the lives of their *grandchildren* than do White grandmothers.
- Asian Americans are least likely to *divorce*, whereas Blacks are most likely.
- Blacks have had the largest declines in *teenage pregnancy* compared to other groups.
- Asian Americans are most likely to be *childfree*, whereas Hispanics are least likely.
- Hispanic women and men have the lowest *median annual income* among full-time workers, and Asian American men and women have the highest.
- Whites remarry most quickly after a divorce compared to other racial or ethnic groups.

Positive attributes and specific challenges exist within each racial and ethnic group. The goal of this chapter is to better understand the ways in which race and ethnicity (alone, and in conjunction with other statuses such as sex and social class) operate in society, so that in the following chapters we can see how they specifically frame families.

Increasing Diversity in the United States

Anyone who takes a quick look at the United States cannot help but notice the nation's diversity. An assortment of ethnic restaurants is available from which to choose, within schools many languages may be spoken, and a trip to the mall reveals people dressed quite differently. The United States is quickly becoming even more diverse due to immigration patterns and birthrates among specific groups, as shown in Figure 6.1. Currently about one person in three is a member of a minority group, and in Hawaii, New Mexico, California, and Texas minorities outnumber Whites. By 2050, minority groups are likely to comprise about 54 percent of the U.S. population (Bernstein and Edwards 2008). The percentage of Blacks and American Indians will remain stable, Asian Americans will increase somewhat but remain a small group, and the largest increases will occur among Hispanics. (I use the term *Hispanic* here rather than Latino because *Hispanic* is the preferred term according to those with a preference (Suro 2006)). Although now comprising 16 percent of the population, Hispanics are expected to nearly double to 30 percent by the year 2050.

Immigration

Yue Lin Wang. Jose Gonzalez. Min Nguyen. What do these three people have in common? They have all immigrated to the United States. Their circumstances vary. Yue Lin Wang was orphaned in China because of its one-child policy and adopted by an American family when she was nine months old. Jose Gonzalez, a journalist from Cuba, came to the United States two generations ago seeking political asylum. Min Nguyen and her family escaped the

Figure 6.1 Resident Population by Race and Hispanic Origin Status—Projection: 2010–2050

The Hispanic population will increase significantly between 2010 and 2050, while the percentage of Blacks, Hispanics, and American Indians will stabilize. The percentage of Whites in the population is expected to decline sharply.

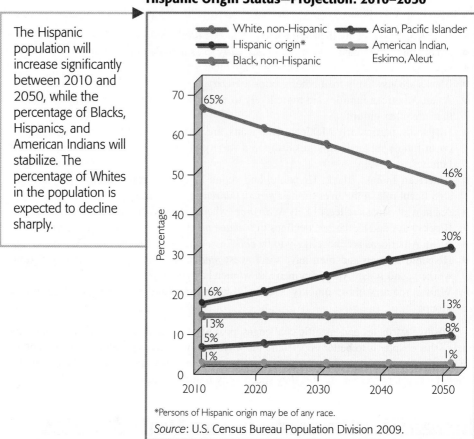

*Persons of Hispanic origin may be of any race.

Source: U.S. Census Bureau Population Division 2009.

ravages of the Vietnam War when she was only eight, after surviving for a year in a refugee camp in Laos. Over the past century, there has been a significant change in the country of origin among immigrants. In 1900, the majority of persons immigrating to the United States came from Europe. However, by 1980 four times as many Hispanics and Asians migrated to the United States as did Europeans as they fled persecution in their war-torn countries.

Today, about 38 million people, or nearly 13 percent of the U.S. population, were not born in the United States but migrated here (U.S. Department of Homeland Security 2010). The largest number of immigrants came from Mexico and South and East Asia, although immigration from Asia has slowed somewhat as political strife has abated. The percentage of Europeans immigrating to the United States is now a relatively small component of the total (Pew Hispanic Center 2010).

Characteristics of immigrants vary by their country of origin and length of time in the United States (as well as personal circumstances surrounding their immigration). For example, many Asians arriving from Cambodia and Vietnam in the 1980s came as young children. They were exposed to U.S. culture early on and are now attending college in large numbers. Their experiences in the United States may be vastly different from migrant farmworkers from Mexico. Nonetheless, some generalizations can be made: immigrants are more likely than native-born residents to be in their childbearing years; they live in larger family households; they earn less money in their jobs; they are more likely to live in poverty; and they tend to reside in central cities within a metropolitan area (Pew Hispanic Center 2010).

Illegal Immigration

Citizens of the United States are nearly equally divided over whether immigration is good for the country. However, with regard to *illegal* immigration, 85 percent of Americans in a May 2010 poll said it was a "very serious" or "somewhat serious" problem (Polling Report Inc. 2010). At the same time, most believe that illegal immigrants are taking jobs that Americans do not want, rather than taking jobs away from U.S. workers (Pew Hispanic Center 2006). Tensions have flared, and the state of Arizona passed a law in 2010 authorizing local police to check the immigration status of anyone they reasonably suspect of being in the United States illegally. More on this controversial law is found in the following box, "Social Policies for Families: Arizona's Immigration Law."

SOCIAL

Policies for Families

Arizona's Immigration Law

What should be done about illegal immigration? Arizona has taken the issue into its own hands.

About 2 million Hispanics live in Arizona, representing almost a third of the state's population. Meanwhile, there are roughly 500,000 undocumented immigrants residing in Arizona, most of whom are from Mexico. Approximately 10 percent of Arizona's workforce is undocumented. Americans in general, and Arizonans in particular, are growing weary of Mexicans sneaking over the border and plead for federal immigration reform. In the absence of national reform, in April 2010 Arizona passed a law giving police the authorization to check the immigration status of anyone they reasonably suspect of being in the United States illegally. The failure to carry identification of your legal status would be a crime.

This law has generated sharp debate: advocates say the law is needed to stop illegal immigration, and opponents say it violates civil liberties and will lead to ethnic profiling of Hispanics by the police. Most Arizona politicians support the law, as do most Arizonans and most Americans. However, President Obama voiced strong criticism.

What do Hispanics think of the law? According to studies conducted by the Pew Hispanic Center, 81 percent of Hispanics do not want local police involved with enforcing immigration laws. They prefer that it be left to federal authorities. In contrast, just 49 percent of non-Hispanics said enforcement should be mainly left to federal authorities. The difference is due to many things. First, only 45 percent

Tempers are flaring over immigration. Arizona has taken matters into their own hands and passed a law allowing local police to check the immigration status of anyone they reasonably suspect of being in the United States illegally. But will they check Whites or Asians, or just Hispanics? Critics of the legislation claim that it is ethnic profiling.

of Hispanics have confidence that police officers in their communities treat them fairly. Second, nearly 1 in 10 say that over the past year they have been stopped by police and asked about their immigration status, with native-born and foreign-born Hispanics (many of whom are here legally) equally likely to have been questioned. This law makes it even more likely that they will be stopped in the future, and many believe it is harassment and ethnic profiling. Third, a majority of Hispanics worry that they, or someone they know, will be deported. The foreign-born were more likely than native-born to say this (73 percent and 35 percent, respectively),

(continued)

(continued)

but it is clearly on many minds. And finally, one-third of Hispanics say that they, a family member, or a close friend has experienced discrimination over the past five years because of their ethnic background. Concern is that a law like this could increase hostile feelings between Whites and Hispanics.

This law will surely be challenged in the courts, but it draws attention to the deep concerns that many people have over U.S. immigration policies.

Sources: Archibold 2010; Lopez and Minushkin 2008; Pew Hispanic Center 2010.

CRITICAL THINKING QUESTIONS

1. What are your views on this legislation? What factors have influenced your opinions?
2. Do you think that attitudes toward this legislation vary by sex, social class, or among other racial or ethnic groups?

Who are these "undocumented immigrants," "illegal immigrants," or "undocumented workers"? There were an estimated 8.3 million in the United States in 2008, a significant decline from several years ago (Hoefer et al. 2010; Passel and Cohn 2009). Almost three-quarters come from Mexico or Central America where they face extreme poverty and limited job prospects in their countries. Nearly half live in couple households with children, a rate far higher than among the native-born. Often a family has mixed status, with children

TABLE 6.1 Portrait of Unauthorized Immigrants, 2008

Most unauthorized immigrants have completed high school or college, are employed, and live with children, yet their incomes are low.

	UNAUTHORIZED IMMIGRANT	LEGAL IMMIGRANT	U.S.-BORN
Educational Attainment (for ages 25–64)			
<9th grade	29%	13%	2%
9th–12th grade	18%	9%	6%
High school graduate	27%	24%	31%
Some college	10%	18%	30%
Bachelor's degree or higher	15%	35%	32%
Labor Force Participation			
Men	94%	85%	84%
Women	58%	66%	73%
Median Household Income			
<10 years in U.S.	$35,000	$41,300	$50,000*
10 years or more	$38,000	$54,100	—
Adults in Poverty	21%	13%	10%
Uninsured Adults	59%	24%	14%
Type of Household			
Couples with children	47%	35%	21%
Others with children	13%	9%	10%
Couples without children	15%	31%	31%
Single-person households	13%	17%	30%
Other	12%	8%	8%

*Median for all U.S.-born households
Source: Passel and Cohn 2009.

born in the United States to undocumented migrants (Passel and Cohn 2009). Table 6.1 compares social and demographic data between undocumented migrants, legal immigrants, and the native-born.

Nearly half of illegal immigrants entered the country with visas that allowed them to visit or reside in the United States for a limited time, but who have now overstayed. More than half entered the United States illegally, by hiding in vehicles such as cargo trucks, trekking through the desert, wading across the Rio Grande, or otherwise eluding the U.S. Border Patrol. These illegal immigrants face many horrific and dangerous situations in their trek to the United States to find work, and many do not make it. They are robbed, raped, and otherwise taken advantage of by guides, they are discovered by the border patrol, or they are killed or injured on the journey. As two men who were detected trying to come into the United States from Mexico emotionally explained in their native Spanish: "The Border Patrol treats us like animals, like dirt, like we don't matter. We know we are doing something wrong but it is not to hurt anyone but to feed our families. We have nothing to eat [at our homes]" (Arditti 2006). Those who do make it to the United States find jobs in a variety of occupations; nearly one-third work in low-paying service industries or in construction or agriculture (Passel and Cohn 2009).

Defining Basic Concepts

What are the implications of the changing composition of the United States? The answers to this question will be hotly debated in the coming years. Before addressing this issue from the perspective of families, it is appropriate to define some basic concepts. The terms *race*, *ethnicity*, and *minority group* are used frequently (Farley 2010; Schaefer 2011). Yet, do we really know what they mean?

Race

Theoretically, the term **race** refers to a category composed of people who share real or alleged physical traits that members of a society deem as socially significant, such as skin color or hair texture. Nineteenth-century biologists created a three-part classification of races: **Caucasian**, comprised of those individuals with relatively light skin; **Negroid**, comprised of people with darker skin and other characteristics such as coarse curly hair; and **Mongoloid**, representing those individuals who have characteristics such as yellow or brown skin and folds on their eyelids (Simpson and Yinger 1985).

However, this classification is considered woefully inadequate because people throughout the world display a mix of racial traits. At least 75 percent of African Americans have White ancestry, in part because many female African slaves were raped and impregnated by their White owners. It is also estimated that between 1 and 5 percent of the genes carried by American Whites are from African ancestors (Davis 1991). From a biological point of view then, Blacks and Whites comprise a continuum rather than a dichotomy. With our increase in knowledge of genetics, race has ceased to be a useful construct (Lewontin 2006). An increasing number of people are biracial, further leading social scientists to suggest that such narrow conceptions of race are not accurate or useful for understanding the diversity in society.

Ethnicity

Ethnicity is a more useful way to understand diversity because it focuses on shared cultural characteristics such as place of origin, dress, food, religion, language, and values. Ethnicity represents culture, whereas race attempts to represent biological heritage. Thus, a Black woman who recently moved to the United States, and who grew up in Jamaica, is not an

African American. Her race may be the same as that of an African American (i.e., Negroid), but her cultural heritage is likely to be very different. This distinction causes some confusion. For example, the U.S. Census Bureau classifies all Blacks according to their race—Black—not by their ethnicity. Some people, however, use the term *African American* rather than *Black* because they are interested in the uniquely African American experience. Likewise, the U.S. Census Bureau often classifies all Hispanics by race—separating White Hispanics from Black Hispanics—but generally ignores ethnicity—Mexican American, Puerto Rican, Cuban American—which masks the rich diversity found among Hispanic groups that may have little or nothing to do with skin color. After all, how much do Mexican Americans and Cubans really have in common? Other times, the U.S. Census Bureau will single out Hispanics as one ethnic group, combining Black and White Hispanics and masking the diversity within these groups.

People who share specific cultural features are referred to as members of an **ethnic group**. Many different ethnic groups exist in the United States, and hundreds throughout the world. Even Caucasians may identify themselves as members of ethnic groups such as Polish, German, or Italian, if they share interrelated cultural characteristics with others.

Minority Group

The term **minority group** refers to a category of people who have less power than the dominant group and who are subject to unequal treatment. A minority group may categorically earn less money, have less representation in politics, be disvalued, be subject to prejudice or discrimination, or be denied opportunities in society. In some cases, minority groups may actually represent the statistical majority, as is the case for Blacks in South Africa, or women in most societies around the world. Generally, a minority group has the following:

- It possesses characteristics that are popularly regarded as different from the dominant group.
- It suffers prejudice and discrimination by the dominant group.
- Membership is usually ascribed rather than achieved.
- Members feel a sense of group solidarity—a "we" feeling—that grows from shared cultural heritage and the shared experience of prejudice and discrimination.
- Marriages are typically among members of the same group (Simpson and Yinger 1985).

Racism: A Pervasive Problem that Affects Families

Let's say you are a manager for a medium-sized company and you want to hire someone for a job. You receive four interesting applications from the following people: Emily, Greg, Lakisha, and Jamal. Who are you going to call for an interview?

Researchers at the University of Chicago submitted fictitious resumes to over a thousand ads in Boston and Chicago newspapers. Resumes were randomly assigned Black- or White-sounding names, but other aspects of their resumes were similar. Those resumes with White-sounding names received 50 percent more calls for interviews. This racial gap was found across different occupations, industries, and employer size (Bertrand and Mullainathan 2004).

However, we also know that many jobs are never posted in newspaper want ads, but are advertised informally through "word of mouth" or through social networking connections. These connections, referred to as **social capital**, can be a valuable source of information about job leads. A study using a nationally representative survey found that minorities and women have much less social capital than do White men, and therefore miss many employment opportunities (McDonald et al. 2009).

Racism is the belief that race is the primary determinant of human traits and capacities and that racial differences produce an inherent superiority of one particular race (Merriam-Webster Online 2010). According to the Southern Poverty Law Center (2010), in 2009, 932 hate groups were active in the United States. All hate groups have beliefs or practices that attack or malign an entire class of people, typically for their immutable characteristics.

Racism may contain two elements: **prejudice**, defined as negative attitudes about members of a selected racial or ethnic group, and **discrimination**, which involves negative behavior towards a racial or ethnic group. Racism is alive and well as shown in the opening vignette and in Table 6.2 (New York Times/CBS News 2008).

TABLE 6.2 Black, Hispanic, White Attitudes Toward Race and Racism

Blacks, Whites, and Hispanics see race relations differently. Are Hispanics more like Whites in their beliefs and experiences, or are they more like Blacks?

WAS THERE EVER A SPECIFIC INSTANCE WHEN YOU FELT DISCRIMINATED AGAINST BECAUSE OF YOUR RACE?		
	Yes	**No**
White	26%	74%
Black	68%	32%
Hispanic	52%	47%

HAVE YOU EVER FELT YOU WERE STOPPED BY THE POLICE JUST BECAUSE OF YOUR RACE OR ETHNIC BACKGROUND?		
	Yes	**No**
White	7%	93%
Black	43%	57%
Hispanic	30%	69%

IN GENERAL, WHO DO YOU THINK HAS A BETTER CHANCE OF GETTING AHEAD IN TODAY'S SOCIETY—WHITE PEOPLE, BLACK PEOPLE, OR DO WHITE PEOPLE AND BLACK PEOPLE HAVE ABOUT AN EQUAL CHANCE OF GETTING AHEAD?			
	White People	**Black People**	**Equal**	**Don't Know/Not Applicable**
White	35%	7%	53%	5%
Black	64%	1%	30%	4%
Hispanic	41%	6%	50%	3%

DO YOU THINK RACE RELATIONS IN THE UNITED STATES ARE GENERALLY GOOD OR GENERALLY BAD?		
	Generally Good	**Generally Bad**	**Don't Know/Not Applicable**
White	55%	34%	10%
Black	29%	59%	12%
Hispanic	52%	38%	10%

IN RECENT YEARS, DO YOU THINK TOO MUCH HAS BEEN MADE OF THE PROBLEMS FACING BLACK PEOPLE, TOO LITTLE HAS BEEN MADE, OR IS IT ABOUT RIGHT?			
	Too Much	**Too Little**	**Just Right**	**Don't Know/Not Applicable**
White	27%	16%	49%	8%
Black	7%	48%	37%	8%
Hispanic	16%	29%	46%	8%

Source: New York Times/CBS News 2008.

A study of working-class men elicited racism even when no direct questions were asked about race (Lamont 2003). One White electronics technician summarized his feelings:

> I work side by side constantly with Blacks, and I have no problem with it. I am prejudiced to a point. What is a nice way to say it? I know this is a generality and it does not go for all, it goes for a portion. It is this whole unemployment and welfare gig. What you see mostly on there is Blacks. I see it from working with some of them and the conversations I hear. A lot of the Blacks on welfare have no desire to get off it. Why should they? It's free money. I cannot stand to see my hard-earned money going to pay for someone who wants to sit on his or her ass all day long and get free money. That is bull, and it may be White thinking, but hey, I feel it is true to a point. You hear it on TV all the time: "We don't have to do this because we were slaves 400 years ago. You owe it to us." I don't owe you, period. I had nothing to do with that and I am not going to pay for it. Also, I don't like the deal where a Black person can say anything about a White, and that is not considered prejudice. But let a White person say even the tiniest little thing about a Black person, and bang, get up in front of Reverend Al Sharpton and all the other schmucks. That is bull. That is a double standard all the way along the line.

Even highly educated persons exhibit racism. Physicians have described Black patients—regardless of their education and income levels—as less intelligent, less educated, more likely to abuse alcohol and drugs, less likely to follow medical advice, and less likely to participate in rehabilitation than White patients. Perhaps it is not surprising that a review of more than 100 studies by the U.S. Institute of Medicine found that discrimination itself contributes to racial disparities in health care and higher death rates among minorities from cancer, heart disease, diabetes, and HIV infection (Epel et al. 2010; Mays et al. 2007; Smedley et al. 2002; Viruell-Fuentes 2007).

Discrimination remains widespread, as noted by the Equal Employment Opportunity Commission, which had nearly 34,000 reports of racial discrimination brought to its attention in 2009 (U.S. Equal Employment Opportunity Commission 2010). A number of studies by scholar Ian Ayres found overwhelming evidence that in a variety of economic markets, Blacks and females are consistently at a disadvantage. For example, when Ayres sent agents of different races posing as potential buyers to more than 200 Chicago car dealerships, he found that dealers regularly charged Blacks and women more than they charged White men. He also found that minority male defendants were frequently required to post higher bail bonds than their White counterparts. Consequently, only 55 percent of Blacks believe that relations between Whites and Blacks are "very good" or "somewhat good," compared to 75 percent of Whites (Gallup News Service 2007).

Racism affects the physical and mental well-being of adults and children. Researchers at the University of California and the Rand Corporation, an academic and policy research organization in Southern California, surveyed over 5,000 fifth-graders and their parents from public schools in Los Angeles, Houston, and Birmingham, Alabama. Fifteen percent of children, overall, reported experiencing what they perceived as racial discrimination, and the vast majority of these encounters occurred at school. Researchers found that a greater percentage of Black children (20 percent), Hispanic children (15 percent), and children identified as "other" (15 percent) reported racial or ethnic discrimination than did White children (7 percent). They also found that children who reported feeling discrimination were more likely to have symptoms of one or more of four different mental health disorders: depression, attention-deficit hyperactivity disorder, oppositional defiant disorder, and conduct disorder (Coker et al. 2009).

Likewise, a study of immigrant and U.S.-born Hispanic college women found that those immigrants with darker skin tended to have poorer self-images. They had lower self-esteem, lower feelings of attractiveness, and a desire to change their skin color to be lighter (Telzer and Vazquez Garcia 2009).

The following box, "Families as Lived Experience: Loving Across the Color Line: A White Adoptive Mother Learns About Race," describes an episode of racism that a White mother witnesses directed toward her Black daughter.

Who Counts as "Them"?

Throughout the world, in virtually every country, some racial or ethnic groups are singled out and subjected to negative stereotyping and discrimination. The map on pages 160–161 illustrates the prevalence of minority groups in each country. Often severe tension

F A M I L I E S
as Lived Experience

Loving Across the Color Line: A White Adoptive Mother Learns About Race

What would a liberal, White, civil rights law professor have to learn about race? When Sharon Rush adopted a Black girl, she quickly learned that she had to throw out old assumptions and face deep questions about race. By living with her daughter, she learned about the harsh encounters Blacks face regularly, and describes below one example of the everyday racism levied at her daughter.

My daughter was six years old and we were on our way to New Hampshire to climb her first mountain. As we were waiting for our connecting flight, she was off exploring the waiting lounge and getting drinks of water—all within my sight, of course. A White woman sat down next to me and placed her luggage in front of her chair. She hadn't been sitting long when her connecting flight was called. As she gathered her belongings, she noticed her purse was missing. I helped her look around the immediate area for it but did not see it. We looked around perhaps ten seconds; it did not take long to see it was not there, when she loudly announced, "I bet that Black kid took it." She was pointing directly at my daughter, the only child and the only Black person in the waiting area.

If the woman had reflected for a moment before making her accusation, she would have realized how silly her conclusion was. My daughter certainly was not trying to make a getaway; she was doing ballet turns in the waiting area, oblivious to everyone around her, and clearly did not have possession of a purse. I was so stunned and offended by the woman's accusation that I could not point this out to her. Instead, I responded, "I'm sorry, but

you are talking about my daughter and I can assure you she is not a thief. Perhaps you left your purse at the ticket counter." Sure enough, she returned from the counter with her purse and flew out the door, remarking as she went, "Well, it's Friday the 13th. What do you expect?"

I was momentarily dumbstruck. I wasn't sure what I expected. Clearly, I did not expect an adult White woman to be suspicious of a six-year-old child—Black or White, girl or boy—doing ballet twirls in the waiting area of an airport. I did not expect my daughter to pose a threat to her.

My daughter did not hear the woman's accusation, but she will learn about it when she reads this book. I hope when that day comes that she will be sufficiently older and will be able to situate the racist thinking behind the accusation in the White woman and not internalize it as a message about Black inferiority. The woman's accusation was outrageous, but it was only one of many ways in which my daughter is rebuffed by White society every day.

Source: Rush 2000.

CRITICAL THINKING QUESTIONS

1. How do you think Whites, Blacks, and other minority groups would respond to this story? Do you think their responses would be similar or different? Why?
2. What special strategies do minority groups use to avoid internalizing the racism they encounter? Do these strategies work? How do Whites respond to these strategies?

Comparative Ethnic and Racial Diversity

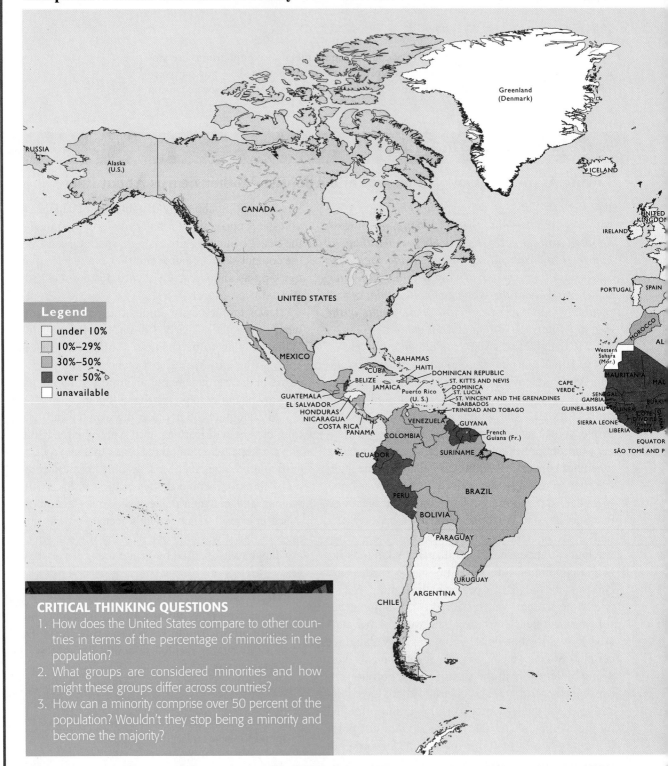

Legend
- under 10%
- 10%–29%
- 30%–50%
- over 50%
- unavailable

CRITICAL THINKING QUESTIONS

1. How does the United States compare to other countries in terms of the percentage of minorities in the population?

2. What groups are considered minorities and how might these groups differ across countries?

3. How can a minority comprise over 50 percent of the population? Wouldn't they stop being a minority and become the majority?

Source: Smith 1997.

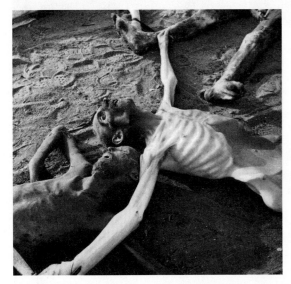

The most extreme manifestation of racism is ethnic cleansing/genocide, which is the systematic killing, torturing, or removal of persons with the intention of eliminating a specific racial or ethnic group. Can you count up the times this has occurred, over the past 75 years, including in your lifetime?

and outright conflict exist between groups, perhaps related to religious differences, disagreement over territory, or a desire to change the power imbalance among peoples. **Ethnic cleansing** or **genocide** is the systematic killing, torturing, or removal of persons with the intention of eliminating a specific racial or ethnic group. We are familiar with historical accounts of the extermination of six million Jews (and others) in the Nazi regime, but ethnic cleansing has also occurred in recent years in Rwanda and Serbia (Human Rights Watch 2010a).

Sociologists have noted that although prejudice and discrimination against minorities are widespread, their justifications may be radically different from one country to another. Sociologist Michele Lamont (2003) compared racism in the United States and France, two highly developed nations, and asked the question, "Who counts as 'them'?" Lamont interviewed 150 White working-class men living in the suburbs of Paris and New York. Instead of asking directly about racism, respondents were asked to describe the kinds of people they like and dislike, the kinds of people they feel similar to and different from, and the types of people to whom they feel inferior or superior. The Americans were much more likely than the French to mention race or skin color as a deciding factor. In particular, Blacks emerged most often as the group disdained by the White New Yorkers as "them"; yet in France, Blacks were not of concern. The French "them" were Muslim immigrants (Lamont 2003):

> Parasites . . . I hate all of them. All those people who don't have a sense of responsibility. We work so hard to support them. When you look at your pay stub and you see all that is taken away!

This brief introduction to several key elements in the study of race and ethnicity leads us to wonder how they may influence family and close relationships. Do different racial and ethnic groups have different family patterns? The answer to that question is both yes and no. On some familial issues, race and ethnicity may not have any systematic effects, but in other contexts, key differences are noted across racial and ethnic groups. These will be discussed in later chapters. Let's now describe the largest minority groups in the United States so you will have a general demographic background.

WHAT DO YOU THINK?

Have you ever witnessed or experienced prejudice or discrimination? What did it feel like? How did you respond?

Hispanic Families

A Tapestry of Cultures

The labels Hispanic (or Latino) cover groups that are so diverse that it makes almost no sense to combine them. Theoretically, Hispanic refers to persons who trace their ancestry to Latin America or Spain. In reality, it lumps together people with roots all over the world and who have wildly different cultures. A newly arrived immigrant family from Mexico has little in common with Cuban Americans who have been in the United States for two generations. Their foods, clothing, socioeconomic status, and even language are substantially different from one another. For example, affluent Cubans were welcomed in the United States during the early regime of Castro. Many were professionals in their home country. Their

Figure 6.2   Which Group Faces Discrimination? (Percent of adults saying that the group is discriminated against "a lot" in society today)

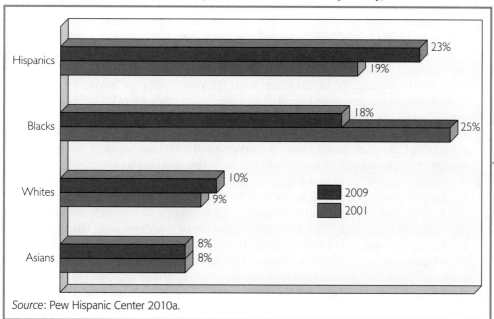

Nearly one-quarter of adults believe that Hispanics are discriminated against "a lot," which is higher than any other group.

Source: Pew Hispanic Center 2010a.

strong use of social capital has helped subsequent generations of Cuban immigrants to succeed. Today, the average income of Cuban Americans is comparable to that of Whites, and most speak English proficiently (Pew Hispanic Center 2010a). In contrast, most Mexican Americans have low incomes; some have come illegally. They work in lower-paid jobs, sometimes seasonally in agriculture. Mexicans are more likely to live in poverty and they are the group least likely to have health insurance (Passel and Cohn 2009). They do not have extensive financial resources or social capital. Despite these great differences, the U.S. Census Bureau and other research centers generally combine these groups together under the umbrella term *Hispanic*; therefore, potentially important differences in their experience cannot be assessed.

The Hispanic population in the United States is growing and changing quickly. At 16 percent of the population, Hispanics now comprise the largest minority group in the United States. Nearly two-thirds of Hispanics in the United States are Mexican Americans; Puerto Ricans constitute the second-largest group. Nearly half of Hispanics live in the western United States, and a third live in the south. Americans now see Hispanics as the racial/ethnic group most often subjected to discrimination, as shown in Figure 6.2 (Pew Hispanic Center 2010a). Nearly one-quarter of adults surveyed say that Hispanics are discriminated against "a lot" in society today, higher than any other group. This is a change from 2001 when Blacks were seen as the group most discriminated against.

Hispanic Families Today

In the past, the growth in the Hispanic population was primarily due to immigration, but today only 11 percent of Hispanic children are first-generation (i.e., born elsewhere and immigrated here [Fry and Passel 2009]). Instead, the rapid growth of the Hispanic population is fueled more by a high birthrate. Hispanic women have the highest fertility rate among all racial and ethnic groups, at around 99 births per 1,000 women compared to a national average of 69 births per 1,000 women (Hamilton et al. 2010). In other words, the Hispanic population is now expanding not solely because of immigration, but because of children born to those immigrants.

This change poses many new and intriguing questions. How will the lives of the second generation be different from the first? How much advantage comes from being raised and educated in the United States? Will the second generation retain their native language and culture?

Differences between first- and second- or third-generation Hispanics are very pronounced, and the futures of U.S.-born children of Hispanic immigrants look bright (Pew Hispanic Center 2008; 2010a). Although the second generation is still young, many are moving beyond poverty or the working-class jobs more typical of their parents, and they are twice as likely to join the ranks of the middle class. They are better educated and more likely to speak English—many see it as their primary language. Second- and third-generation Hispanics are also more likely to hold mainstream U.S. values than the more conservative and traditional values of their parents. For example, they are more likely to support a woman's right to choose an abortion, to see divorce as an acceptable solution to an unhappy marriage, and to believe that undocumented immigration hurts the economy (Pew Hispanic Center 2008, 2010a).

Second- and third-generation Hispanics are becoming increasingly assimilated and often blend in easily with Whites. However, there are so many new adult Hispanic arrivals that assimilation may not be very visible to the casual observer. Nonetheless, many of these second-generation children report personal experience with discrimination; in fact, they are more likely than their parents to believe that they have been discriminated against. Incomes are still significantly below Whites, and many do not have health insurance (DeNavas-Walt et al. 2010; Livingston et al. 2008).

These important data highlight two salient facts: (1) distinct differences remain in personal experience, values, opportunities, and constraints among Hispanic groups in the United States; and (2) differences also exist based on degree of assimilation. For example, experiences and values of the second generation are often in marked contrast to those of the first. Strong indications are that the majority of U.S.-born children of Hispanic immigrants will move beyond the working-class jobs or impoverished circumstances typical of their parents. Although the second generation is still largely young, substantial economic gains will likely accrue from the first generation to the second. They will receive more education, take jobs that demand greater skills, and be paid higher wages.

Despite their common language, the social and economic situations of Hispanic groups can be vastly different from one another; for example, Cuban Americans, as shown here, have incomes comparable to Whites, while Mexican Americans are overrepresented among the poor.

Family Focus: Bilingual Education

Most Hispanics, especially Hispanic children, speak English fluently or nearly so. Table 6.3 shows that only 17 percent of Hispanic children speak English "less than very well" (Pew Hispanic Center 2009). This is comparable to the 16 percent of Asian American children who also speak English "less than very well." Among adults, the patterns are the same—Hispanics and Asians are near equally likely to have limited English skills, yet most of the concern is about, and the "speak English" campaign is targeted at, Spanish-speaking persons,

TABLE 6.3 Language Spoken at Home and English-Speaking Ability, by Age, Race, and Ethnicity: 2008

Most Hispanics and Asians speak English very well, even if English is not spoken at home, defying stereotypes.

YOUNGER THAN 18		
	IF LANGUAGE OTHER THAN ONLY ENGLISH SPOKEN AT HOME	
Only English Spoken at Home	**English Spoken Very Well**	**English Spoken Less Than Very Well**
Hispanic	34%	49%	17%
Native born	38%	48%	14%
Foreign born	4%	56%	40%
White alone, not Hispanic	94%	5%	1%
Black alone, not Hispanic	94%	4%	1%
Asian alone, not Hispanic	36%	48%	16%
Other, not Hispanic	88%	10%	2%
All	80%	16%	5%

18 AND OLDER		
	IF LANGUAGE OTHER THAN ONLY ENGLISH SPOKEN AT HOME	
Only English Spoken at Home	**English Spoken Very Well**	**English Spoken Less Than Very Well**
Hispanic	20%	36%	44%
Native born	39%	49%	13%
Foreign born	4%	24%	72%
White alone, not Hispanic	94%	4%	2%
Black alone, not Hispanic	93%	5%	3%
Asian alone, not Hispanic	20%	39%	40%
Other, not Hispanic	80%	14%	6%
All	81%	10%	10%

Source: Pew Hispanic Center 2010a.

usually Mexican Americans. Why is there so much more concern over Hispanics who do not speak English than over Asian Americans who also do not?

I can only speculate on the answer to this question. Perhaps some of it is due to racism. As you shall see, Asian Americans have been nicknamed a "model minority" due to their economic and educational achievements, and perhaps many Americans are willing to over-look the fact that some do not know English very well. Hispanics are not given the same "pass".

Another reason may have to do with the diversity of Asian languages—Chinese, Vietnamese, Hmong, Japanese—to name just a few. It's more difficult to focus on "their" language as a roadblock when you are talking about many different languages, not just one.

A third reason may be the size of the Hispanic population in the United States; it is far larger than the size of Asian Americans. Therefore, Hispanics are seen as more

WHAT DO YOU THINK?

Can you describe important social and cultural differences between Hispanic groups that you have witnessed or are familiar with?

threatening. People are concerned about traditional American culture changing and giving way to Hispanic customs, including language.

Finally, the media play up, even exaggerate, the extent to which Hispanics speak a language other than English. Many Americans assume that virtually all Hispanics are recent immigrants (untrue), do not speak English nor do they try (untrue), and drain our education and health care system (also untrue) by needing programs such as bilingual education services. Hispanics pay taxes just like all Americans; in fact, many undocumented workers also pay taxes for services that they cannot even use.

Bilingual education is a hot topic in American public policy. It has a long history in this country, and was used to help immigrants learn English in the nineteenth century (Crawford 1999; Kloss 1998). In 1839, Ohio was the first state to pass a law requiring bilingual education if parents requested it from the schools. Many other states and communities gradually followed suit. In 1968, the U.S. Congress passed Title VII of the Elementary and Secondary Education Act, known informally as "the Bilingual Education Act," which mandated bilingual education to give immigrants access to education in their "first" language. Federal spending on bilingual education jumped from only $7.5 million in 1968 before the law was passed to $150 million by 1979 (Frum 2000).

Bilingual education was implemented in the 1970s and 1980s by teaching children primarily or even exclusively in their native language, and then transitioning at some point in elementary school to English-only instruction. Proponents argue that the more schools develop children's native-language skills, especially in reading, the higher the children score academically over the long term in English (August and Shanahan 2006; Reese et al. 2000). Proponents agree that it sounds counterintuitive, but claim that proficiency in a second language does not develop separately in the brain, but builds upon the proficiency of the native language.

Bilingual education programs still exist, but since the 1990s, the political tide has shifted, and many people now oppose these programs. They argue that they are expensive, that native language instruction interferes with or delays English development, and that they segregate students, relegating them to a second-class status (Rossell and Baker 1996). Several states, including California, Massachusetts, and Arizona, have enacted policies to greatly curb or virtually eliminate bilingual education, and federal policies now restrict the amount of time children can be taught in their native language (Slavin et al. 2010). Often, the discussion deteriorates into political attacks, with opponents arguing that bilingual education threatens our national identity, divides us along ethnic lines, and sends the message to immigrants that they can live in the United States without learning English. This was the reasoning in Arizona in 2010 that allowed their legislature to ban ethnic studies classes in high school.

Black Families

Racial and ethnic titles and categories are constantly changing. Although few people today use the term *Negro* to describe Blacks as they did in the past, what is the difference between the terms *African American* and *Black*? Often we use the terms interchangeably, but it is not technically correct to do so. Black is a broad racial category, whereas African American is an ethnic group. Most Blacks in the United States are indeed African Americans, but there are some who are not, those of Haitian descent, for example. Throughout this text, I will generally use the term *Black* to conform to Census Bureau definitions; however, the term *African American* will be used when it seems a more accurate description or when citing research by others who use that term.

Until recently, Blacks were the largest minority group in the United States and were generally considered synonymous with the term *minority*. This is no longer the case because the number and growth of Hispanic groups now exceed those of Blacks.

Overall, Black families have historically had different family patterns than White families (Hill 2005). They are less likely to be married, have more children, are more likely to have close extended family relationships, and more likely to be poor. Daniel Patrick Moynihan (1965) crystallized the discussion of these challenges in 1965 when he released the so-called *Moynihan Report* (more formally known as *The Negro Family: The Case for National Action*). In it, he suggested that the repercussions of slavery continued to be a destructive and destabilizing force to Black families, resulting in a "tangle of pathology". One of his primary concerns was the economic plight of Blacks, which caused men to leave their families, mothers to become "matriarchs," and high rates of delinquency, illegitimacy, alcoholism, and school dropout. He described these as by-products of urban structural conditions of society, failing social institutions, and racism; nonetheless, his book has sometimes been mistakenly used as criticism of Black families.

But family scholars note that Black families have many strengths (Hill 2005; Ladner 1998). Billingsley (1968) pointed out that the structure of Black families was not the cause of social problems, but was actually an adaptive response to a racist culture. He suggested that rather than considering the Black family as weak, it is showing resilience in the face of economic and social difficulties. Likewise, Hill (1972) contended that strength and stability, not weakness and instability, are characteristics of Black families. Another scholar, Charles Willie, claims that the notion of a Black matriarchy is a myth and suggests that it was really an egalitarian relationship. He believes one of the greatest gifts of Blacks to the culture of the nation has been the egalitarian family model in which neither the husband nor the wife is always in charge (Willie 1983; Willie and Reddick 2003).

Sociologist Shirley Hill (2005) suggests that the successes of the civil rights movement diversified Blacks and created new class, race, and gender divisions. Increasing numbers of Blacks are joining the middle class, and a larger number of women, in particular, are attending and completing college, as shown in Table 6.4 (Planty et al. 2009). In 1980, Black men comprised only 8 percent of college students, and Black women comprised 10 percent. Today, those figures have increased to 11 percent and 15 percent, respectively.

Therefore, to really understand Black families, scholars today are expanding their focus of racial inequality to include a broader range of intersections: How do race, sex, and social class interact to shape lived experience in families? For example, although many studies note that Black parents racially socialize their children, few look at how this socialization varies by social class. Likewise, although Black parents are less rigid in the gender socialization of their children than are Whites, rarely is this examined across social classes. Hill (2005), for example, found significant support for sex and gender equality if one looks at the educational and career aspirations parents have for their children, but beyond these overt measures, views

TABLE 6.4 Percentage of College Students Who Are Black

College attendance among Blacks is increasing, especially among Black women.

	1980	1990	2007
Male	8%	8%	11%
Female	10%	10%	15%

Source: Planty et al. 2009.

of sex and gender are sharply divided along class lines with lower-income Blacks retaining traditional ideologies.

Black Families Today

Black families tend to live in larger families and households than do Whites. For example, 18 percent of married-couple Black families contain five or more members, compared to only 12 percent of similar White families. Moreover, among female-headed households, 13 percent of Blacks live in families with five or more members, compared to less than 5 percent of Whites (U.S. Census Bureau 2006). What accounts for the difference? One factor is birthrates; Blacks average a greater number of children than do Whites. However, another important factor is the greater likelihood of Blacks who live in extended families (Cole 2003; McLoyd et al. 2000; Taylor et al. 2010).

Economic Conditions   One of the most pervasive stereotypes associated with Blacks is that they are impoverished. This is a tremendous overgeneralization. The median household income for a Black household was $32,584 in 2009. Although this is well below the average for a White household ($54,461), it is far above the poverty level (DeNavas-Walt et al. 2010). In fact, over one-third of Blacks have household incomes of at least $50,000, a 25 percent increase since 1990. Income data for married couples show particular promise; well over half of married Black couples earn at least $50,000 per year, including 30 percent who earn at least $75,000 (DeNavas-Walt et al. 2010).

This means that many Blacks are entering the world of the middle class, having worked themselves up from the working or lower classes. Most of these younger Blacks did not have parents from whom they could inherit money or receive extensive financial assistance; therefore, they have fewer assets than Whites. U.S. Census Bureau data reveal extensive differences in assets between Blacks and Whites, which have clear impacts on family consumptive patterns, family values, and family relationships. For example, only 48 percent of Black adults own their own home, compared to 73 percent of Whites. Moreover, Blacks had average wealth worth 20 cents for every dollar of assets owned by their White counterparts (Mishel et al. 2007). The discrepancy is due to three factors: (1) Whites are more likely to draw upon the assets of their parents through an inheritance or loan to be able to afford a home, car, or other high-ticket item; (2) Whites have an easier time obtaining mortgage loans from banks; and (3) homes in predominantly White neighborhoods appreciate in value more rapidly than do homes in predominantly Black neighborhoods (Oliver and Shapiro 2006).

Family Focus: Blacks and Extended Families

Nearly one in five Black children under the age of 15 lives in an extended family, more than three times the rate for Whites and nearly double the rate for Hispanics (Glick and Van Hook 2002; Saluter 1996). **Extended families** include not only parents and children, but also other family members such as grandparents, uncles, aunts, or cousins. Extended families can provide critical resources to family members, yet they have sometimes been denigrated as a characteristic of only poor families. However, Blacks (and other minority groups) are more likely than Whites to live in extended families, as shown in Figure 6.3. This is the case regardless of income level. Moreover, even among those who live in extended families, Blacks (and other minorities) are more likely to reside in families with three or more generations, unlike Whites.

Why are extended families more common among Blacks than Whites? Black families have a rich cultural heritage of drawing upon and sharing aid with other family members. One study of 487 Black parents aged 18–34, drawn from the *National Survey of Black Americans*, found that parents most often nominated their own parents as the persons they could count on for child care assistance and parental guidance (Hunter 1997).

Figure 6.3 **Percent of Population in Multi-Generational Family Household by Race/Ethnicity, 2008**

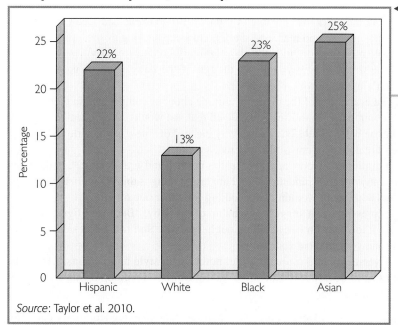

Whites are far less likely than other groups to live in extended families.

Source: Taylor et al. 2010.

This rich family and cultural heritage of Blacks is grounded in rural folkways (Wilkinson 1997). Important family rites, rituals, and ceremonies maintained the strong intergenerational ties within families. Historians have shown that extended families were highly valued during times of slavery. A review of 2,200 ex-slave narratives collected in the 1930s highlighted the important role that grandparents played in the Black community, including childrearing. Although some families were cruelly broken up by the slave trade, Blacks nonetheless keenly appreciated older relatives, real and fictive, and co-resided whenever possible (Covey and Lockman 1996). Herbert Gutman's (1976) book, *The Black Family in Slavery and Freedom*, examines plantation records and census data for a number of cities between 1880 and 1925, and documents that two-parent households prevailed during slavery and after emancipation. Even when slavery destroyed biological families, kinship networks were rewoven so that unrelated slaves could join in and be part of a family.

Researchers have found that Black families maintain a high degree of geographical closeness and a strong sense of family and familial obligation. They note that household boundaries are often more fluid than among White families, with a greater willingness to take in relatives, both children and adults, if the need arises. Black families are characterized by frequent interaction with relatives and an established system of mutual aid. Extended families can provide closeness and intimacy, help with the day-to-day routines of raising children, reduce delinquency, and transmit cultural values to children.

Grandmothers play a crucial role in Black families (Simpson and Lawrence-Webb 2009; Stevenson et al. 2007; Strom et al. 2005). They often have a central place in the rearing of their grandchildren. One study involving in-depth interviews with 19 grandmothers who were the biological mother of a teenage mother found that the grandmothers were involved in seven key functions in their roles as grandmother (Flaherty et al. 1994):

- *Managing:* Arranging of resources and activities so that they synchronize with each to meet family needs: "I didn't have nowhere to put the crib up ... and I thought it would look kind of odd sitting in the front room. So I told Terri I'd try to get her one of those little playpen cribs which could fit out here in the front room."

- *Caretaking:* Direct involvement in providing primary infant activities: ". . . in the morning after I get all the other kids out to go to school, I'll go ahead and feed Cecelia, give her a bath, brush her hair and read, and she'll go to sleep, as long as she's full . . . ."
- *Coaching:* Role modeling or guidance about primary infant care activities or maternal role: ". . . little thing—I always tell her though, if the baby's full, make sure she's burped, or don't lay her down on her back . . . ."
- *Assessing:* The evaluation of the mother's attitude about or competency in the maternal role: "She's doing better than I really expected that she would do. She really surprised me . . . giving the baby a bath. The baby's very clean. You know, some girls have babies and they don't really keep 'em . . . the way that she does it."
- *Nurturing:* Emotional support and love of the mother and grandchild: ". . . the main thing is, that's my daughter, and the second important thing is this is my first grandbaby, and I love 'em both, and I wouldn't take nothing for either one of 'em."
- *Assigning:* Expressions that suggest ownership of the baby: "Because I figure, like if I do it . . . make it too easy on her, she'll go out here again. So I told her, I said well, this is your body and your life and your baby."
- *Patrolling:* Overseeing and evaluating the mother's lifestyle and personal life goals: "I took 'em to the doctor . . . and she is going on the pill though. She's going on something."

WHAT DO YOU THINK?

Do you remember the first time you noticed that people had skin of a different color from yours? What did you think about it? If you asked your family or teachers about it, how did they respond?

Despite the many benefits that an extended family can offer to poor or rich families, the dominant ideology in the United States suggests that extended families are dysfunctional in some way. Too much interdependence is often characterized as a weakness rather than as a family strength. This is reflective of the uniquely American ideal of independence as a virtue, and that all families should be able to "go it alone" without help from family, friends, or the government. Many other cultures would disagree vehemently with this approach.

Asian American Families

Nearly 16 million U.S. residents are Asian American or Asian in combination with one or more other races, comprising about 5 percent of the total population (U.S. Census Bureau 2010b). The term *Asian* is a catchall for many different groups of people who had origins with the early peoples of the Far East, Southeast Asia, or the Indian subcontinent. Often lumped in with these diverse groups are Pacific Islanders who have origins in Hawaii, Guam, Samoa, or other Pacific Islands. Some, like Japanese and Chinese Americans, may have been in the United States for generations. Others, such as the Hmong, Laotians, Cambodians, and Vietnamese, are relative newcomers (Reeves and Bennett 2003). As is the case with Hispanics, these groups represent great diversity in culture, language, socioeconomic characteristics, and timing and reasons for migrating to the United States. Table 6.5 shows the geographic distribution of the most commonly spoken Asian languages in the United States—Korean, Chinese, Vietnamese, and Tagalog (Shin and Kominski 2010). Nonetheless, for statistical purposes most government agencies combine these groups into one large category named "Asian American," and, unfortunately, important nuances are lost. Much of what is discussed here is from government sources, and, therefore, groups are most often combined.

TABLE 6.5 Where Common Asian Languages Are Most Likely to Be Spoken

"Asian-American" is a catchall category representing a rich diversity.

Chinese

California, Maryland, Massachusetts, Nevada, New Jersey, New York, Washington

Korean

Alaska, California, Georgia, Illinois, Nevada, New Jersey, New York, Oregon, Virginia, Washington

Tagalog

Alaska, California, Nevada

Vietnamese

Alaska, California, Colorado, Georgia, Louisiana, Maryland, Massachusetts, Minnesota, Oklahoma, Oregon, Texas, Virginia, Washington

Source: Shin and Kominski 2010.

Asian American Families Today

Asian Americans tend to live in metropolitan areas in the West. California has the largest number of Asians, although Hawaii is the only state with an Asian majority. Over half were born in Asia, most commonly China, the Philippines, India, Vietnam, and Korea, and migrated to the United States at some point in their lives. Most of the others are children, grandchildren, or other descendants of immigrants who came to the United States many years ago. Chinese girls orphaned because of China's one-child policy and adopted by U.S. families are another group, although the number of new adoptions is now declining (U.S. Department of State 2010). These girls still receive widespread attention, and an essay describing one such family's adoption is provided in the box on pages 172–173, "Our Global Community: One Girl's Very Special First Fourth of July."

Asian Americans have faced considerable prejudice and discrimination in the past; for example, Japanese Americans were the only racial or ethnic group rounded up against their will during World War II and put into internment camps with their property confiscated. Some Asian Americans continue to experience prejudice today; for example, the assumption that someone named Wong doesn't speak English or isn't really an American. Nonetheless, many Asian Americans have had remarkable success; indeed, they have sometimes been nicknamed a *model minority*.

"Model Minority" As a group, Asian Americans are considered an immigration success story. Asian Americans have the highest family incomes of any group, surpassing Whites (DeNavas-Walt et al. 2010). They have the highest percentage of its workforce in white-collar positions and are more likely to graduate from college. They have the lowest rates of divorce, and their children are more likely to reside in married-couple households than are any other race or ethnic group (U.S. Census Bureau 2010b). How did diverse Asian American groups produce such successes?

Many important factors help to explain why Asian Americans are often heralded as a model minority (Farley 2010; Schaefer 2011; Zhou and Gatewood 2007). One major factor is the differences surrounding their immigration experience. People who have come from

O U R
Global Community

One Child's Very Special First Fourth of July

Many families are choosing to adopt children from other countries for infertility or humanitarian reasons. "Cloe" is a recent adoptee from the People's Republic of China. The following is a tribute by a grandmother, famous newspaper columnist Ellen Goodman, that reveals the love and pride she has in her new granddaughter.

It will be her very first parade, her very first Fourth of July. Our granddaughter will be both the newest citizen at the picnic and the newest member of our family.

Cloe, this little girl with shiny black hair and a quiet, curious stare, has come to America and to us. We have embraced her with a loyalty that is all the more tenacious for having not been preordained by biology. We have the sort of attachment that the word "adoption" cannot begin to describe.

Just six weeks ago, Cloe was halfway around the world in an orphanage in China. Six weeks before that, my stepdaughter and her husband got her photograph in the mail. It put a face—her face—on what had been a stack of papers, a mound of red tape, and of course, a hope.

Psychologists, neurologists, "ologists" of every variety may say it's impossible to bond to a photograph. But we connected to Cloe before she was named Cloe. We connected to her before she had any idea we existed or that there was a world outside the orphanage, outside the province, the country, the continent.

Before the travel papers arrived, we waited anxiously, tracking the reports of SARS, worried that Beijing would close down the border before our children became parents, before this child of China could become a child of America. But when the moment came to gather Cloe, it seemed as sudden as the wait had seemed interminable.

After all that time, she was just a plane trip away. In a single moment, a year-old child was transferred from one set of hands to another, and from one fate to another. The entire arc of her short life was transformed from being abandoned to being treasured.

Now we will take her to watch the parade of homemade flats come down the road and cheer the scramble up the greased pole. We will bring a newcomer to the American birthday party, but she has brought us to the wider world. We have made her an American and she has made us a part of the global village.

Our Cloe is one of about 20,000 international adoptions within the last year, one of the 5,000 girls from China. Over many months, we learned to spot them in the grocery store or the street. We learned to wonder what this wave of girls will make of their experience, of the great economic and political winds that changed the course of their lives.

In China, an ancient culture that still sets a higher value on the head of a boy has collided with a government policy that pressures families to have only one child. As a result, hundreds of thousands of girls are growing up in orphanages. As a very different result, thousands of girls are growing up in America, more privileged than brothers left behind.

As for Cloe, we know the joy her story brings to our family. But we can only guess at the loss to the woman who left her day-old daughter on fortune's doorstep.

My stepdaughter tells me about the final medical exam Cloe was given on the way out of China. The pediatrician carefully examined the little patient. Then looking evenly at the new parents, she said directly, "You have a very beautiful, healthy daughter. You are very lucky."

What, we still wonder, did this accomplished, modern Chinese woman make of her own country that gives away so many of its daughters? What did she feel about a culture in which this "beautiful healthy daughter" faced the options of either an orphanage or America? For that matter, what did she think of Americans? Does she think we regard the world's children as a product—made in China—to import because we can afford to?

America is continually made and remade by newcomers. But this daughter of China has reminded us how small our world is and how vast: a village you can traverse in a day and a place of stunning disconnects and differences, haves and have-nots.

Ours was already a global family, brought together with luck of the draw and the pluck of ancestors who came from places as far away as Italy and England, Russia and Germany. On this Fourth of July, we add another continent to our heritage and another child to our list of supreme good fortune. Welcome, Cloe, to America.

Source: Goodman 2003. © 2003, The Washington Post Writers Group. Reprinted with permission.

CRITICAL THINKING QUESTIONS
1. What are your views on international adoption?
2. Will children adopted from other countries—China, Guatemala, Korea, Russia—retain their own race or ethnic identity if White families raise them? What are the pros and cons of parents promoting a child's different race or ethnic identity?
3. Following up on Goodman's questions, what do you believe the female physician thinks of China? Of the one-child policy? Of the United States?

most Asian countries are generally from more privileged social classes in their countries. Many had considerable wealth to invest in their employment or educational opportunities in the United States. They also had a strong orientation to education; many were professionals with college degrees. Certainly, this is not the case for all Asian Americans; immigrants fleeing Vietnam, Cambodia, and Laos, for example, were often from rural villages and had little schooling or few employment skills.

Perhaps even more important is the long-standing emphasis on education, learning, and family that characterizes Asian culture. Individuality is de-emphasized; the well-being of the family or greater community is of primary concern. In particular, families believe that the route to success in this country is through education and hard work. Parents may undergo great sacrifice to further their children's education, which is seen as the parents' most important mission. Children take their responsibility to succeed seriously as well. A child's actions, including their successes (or failures), reflect upon the entire family. Children are not only encouraged to do well in school for themselves, but also to bestow honor on the larger family. They share the status and monetary returns with their families (Abazov 2007).

As is the case with other minority groups, Asians often pool their resources to increase their upward mobility. However, in general, Asians have been more successful than other groups in quickly moving upward. One reason for this is that the pooling of resources often extends beyond family members; some Asian groups have created self-help organizations to provide loans and other financial aid to their members for starting up new businesses. Once a family achieves success, they are expected to do more than simply repay the loan. They are also expected to help out another family if possible.

Some of these cultural values are diluted the longer a person is exposed to the U.S. values of individualism and independence (Lee and Zhou 2004; Zhou 2006). Nonetheless, the strong emphasis on family and education, coupled with the generally greater resources of Asian immigrants compared to their counterparts from other regions of the world, have allowed marked success in the United States. Despite this, or perhaps *because* of their record of achievement, Whites and other groups are sometimes prejudiced against them and resent their success.

Ignored is the fact that not all Asian Americans fit the image of the highly educated and high-earning professional. It is important to recognize that not all Asians are doing fabulously on these social indicators. Many of the more recent immigrants from Vietnam, Cambodia, and Laos lack the financial resources and social capital of other Asian American immigrants, and therefore have lower incomes and higher rates of poverty. For example, although Asians are more likely than Whites to have earned a college degree, they are also more likely to have less than a ninth-grade education (Reeves and Bennett 2003). Likewise, 12 percent of Asian Americans live in poverty (DeNavas-Walt et al. 2010; U.S. Census Bureau 2010b), a significantly higher rate than that of Whites. Immigrants from Southeast Asia—Vietnam, Cambodia, and Laos—have some of the highest rates of poverty and welfare use in the United States.

Family Focus: Generational Tension

Children born and raised in the United States by parents born elsewhere often struggle with balancing their parents' culture with that of the United States. Children who were born in another country but primarily raised in the United States are referred to as the 1.5 generation, and they face similar challenges. Together, these children may serve as linguistic and cultural brokers for their parents. They interpret for their parents American cultural norms and may be called upon to speak for their parents (who may have difficulty with English).

Immigrant children (and children of immigrants) may quickly adapt to U.S. culture, but their parents are far less likely to assimilate, preferring to retain critical elements of their own culture and language (Kibria 1993, 1997; Pyke 2000a, 2000b; Zhou and Bankston 1998). Key features of traditional Asian culture contrast sharply with U.S. culture. For example, traditionally, Asian parents are less apt to express emotion to each other or to their children; they emphasize the needs of the family over the individual; and they allow their children fewer freedoms and choices than do American parents. These cultural differences have the potential to lead to considerable tension between generations. Asian American children who were born here or who immigrated at young ages often invoke a monolithic image of U.S. family life, seeing themselves as outsiders, believing that their family does not measure up to an Americanized ideal, as discussed in Chapter 1 (Pyke 2000a, 2000b). In her study of grown children of Korean and Vietnamese immigrants, Pyke found that her respondents often viewed their parents as overly strict, emotionally distant, and deficient in comparison to what they saw as a typical American family. As one of her Korean respondents, born in the United States, said (Pyke 2000a, 2000b):

I think there is somewhat of a culture clash between myself and my parents. They are very set on rules—at least my father is. He is very strict and demanding and very much falls into that typical Asian father standard. I don't like that too much and I think it is because . . . as a child, I was always watching television and watching other friends' fathers. All the relationships seemed so much different from me and my father's relationship. . . . I guess it's pretty cheesy but I can remember watching *The Brady Bunch* reruns and thinking Mike Brady would be a wonderful dad to have. He was always so supportive. He always knew when something was wrong with one of his boys. Whenever one of his sons had a problem, they would have no problem telling their dad anything and the dad would always be nice and give them advice and stuff. Basically I used what I saw on television as a picture of what a typical family should be like in the U.S.

I only wished that my family could be like that. And friends too—I used to see how my friends in school would be in Little League Baseball and their dad would be like their coaches or go to their games to cheer their sons on and give them support. I could not picture my father to be like that kind of man I saw on TV, or like my friends' fathers.

WHAT DO YOU THINK?

How would your parents respond if you chose to marry someone of a different race or ethnic group? Would they respond more positively if the person was an Asian American as compared to other groups?

American Indian and Alaska Native Families

About 4.9 million people, or about 1.5 percent of the population, are American Indians or Alaska Natives (U.S. Census Bureau 2009b). The term *American Indian* or *Alaska Native* refers to people having origins in any of the early peoples of North, Central, and South America who maintain tribal affiliation or community attachment. Three-quarters identify themselves as belonging to a specific tribe, such as Cherokee, Navajo, Choctaw, Blackfeet, Chippewa, Muscogee, Apache, or Lumbee. Cherokee is largest, with nearly 900,000 people reporting Cherokee alone or in combination with another race, ethnicity, or tribe. Eskimo is the most populous Alaska Native tribe, with nearly 50,000 members. Nineteen percent of Alaskans are Alaska Natives or American Indians; Oklahoma (11 percent) and New Mexico (10 percent) have the second and third highest concentration of Alaska Natives or American Indians in their populations.

Most American Indians live in the community and do not live on reservations or other trust lands. About one-third live on designated American Indian Areas (AIAs), which include reservations and off-reservation land trusts; 2 percent live in Alaska Native Village Statistical Areas (ANVSAs); and nearly two-thirds live outside tribal areas (Ogunwole 2006). The largest and most populous is the Navajo Nation reservation and trust lands, which span portions of Arizona, New Mexico, and Utah. American Indians who reside off the reservation run the gamut; many return to the reservation regularly for meetings and events, and others do not return at all.

American Indian Families Today

Nearly three-quarters of American Indian and Alaska Native households are family households—significantly *higher* than for the general population. However, only 4 percent live in married-couple households, significantly *lower* than for the general population. Instead, female-headed households are nearly twice as prevalent among American Indian families as they are for the general population. Most households contain children under age 18. The average age of American Indians is only 28 years, 7 years younger than for the rest of the population, revealing larger-than-average family size and lower life expectancy.

Of the nearly 5 million American Indians or Alaska Natives, many live in substandard housing. About 10–20 percent live in homes without indoor plumbing and many do not even have kitchen facilities.

Extended families are the cornerstone of American Indian family life, with close parallels to Black and Hispanic families in many ways. Fifty-six percent of American Indians or Alaska Natives age 30 and over live with their grandchildren (U.S. Census Bureau 2009b). There is a strong cultural ethic of social, emotional, and financial support among relatives. Indeed, aunts and uncles often refer to their nieces and nephews as "daughter" or "son" (MacPhee et al. 1996).

However, the role of kinship networks extends beyond the roles found in other racial and ethnic groups. Prior to the twentieth century, kinship was

an important component of political organization and provided the primary basis for tribe governance. Although some groups were matrilineal and others were patrilineal, kinship was the basis for political power and status unknown to other U.S. racial and ethnic groups. Although this has waned considerably in recent years, kinship networks among American Indians retain considerable importance because of the ties they establish to a specific tribe.

Within families, elders are of considerable importance not only for the status and family and cultural identity that they provide, but also because of the hands-on care they offer to younger family members. Although some of the *cultural conservator* function that the elderly provide has been disvalued in recent years by younger generations as they move off the reservation and attempt to assimilate, there has been a resurgence in recognizing the importance of American Indian spirituality, language, values, and cultural traditions.

Nonetheless, American Indian families face many challenges. Infant mortality rates are high, and life expectancy is low, particularly on reservations (National Center for Health Statistics 2009; Office of Minority Health 2009). American Indians or Alaska Natives are twice as likely to have liver cancer as compared to Whites, are 2.3 times as likely to have diabetes, and are 1.6 times as likely to be obese. Furthermore, American Indian women have twice the rate of stroke of their White counterparts, and have a 40 percent higher AIDS rate (Office of Minority Health 2009).

Poverty rates are nearly triple those of other Americans and unemployment is even higher. Many American Indians live in substandard housing. For example, about 10 percent of reservation housing lacks indoor plumbing, and among some reservations the figure approaches 20 percent. Likewise, many do not have kitchen facilities. Suicide rates are far higher than the national average, especially among young men (Office of Minority Health 2008). Alcoholism is common, with up to 25 per 1,000 children born with fetal alcohol syndrome in some communities (Center for Substance Abuse Prevention 2007). Rates of accidents, violence, and domestic abuse are high, many of which involve alcohol.

Yet, despite these obstacles, tribal leaders have implemented numerous strategies to improve economic and social conditions. These include opening tribally controlled colleges, creating alcohol education programs, and strengthening core American Indian values held by youth through the rebound of traditional language programs. The Census Bureau reports that 18 percent of American Indians age 5 and over speak a language in addition to English "very well" compared to only 10 percent of the general U.S. population (Ogunwole 2006). Highly profitable (and sometimes controversial) gambling establishments fund critically needed social services, create jobs, and provide individual tribal members with cash stipends that have improved economic circumstances considerably.

Alaska Natives

Native Alaskans have been undergoing change since contact with Europeans in the mid-1700s, but the most dramatic changes have occurred in rapid succession during the past century. Many Alaska Natives live off the road system in isolated and remote communities separated from one another by vast regions of tundra or glaciers and have only recently been introduced to western ways. Cable television now broadcasts CNN 24 hours a day, The Disney Channel brings new ideas to children, and thousands of commercials fuel new desires for material goods. The result for many communities has been social and cultural upheaval.

Traditional Alaska Native cultures, like most aboriginal cultures, are tied directly to nature and the bounty it provides. The practices of hunting, fishing, and gathering constitute a direct link between the old and the new. Subsistence is quite clearly an Alaska Native cultural imperative. A recent study of Alaska Natives found that 85 percent of Natives report that subsistence is "very important" or "important" to the respondents' household, and only 7 percent said it is "unimportant" or very "unimportant" (McDowell Group 2003).

Nonetheless, most Native villages now have what researchers describe as "mixed" economies, in which small to moderate amounts of earned cash are available on a seasonal basis. This has led to a substantial cultural shift, particularly among the young, yet the jobs generally do not pull families out of poverty.

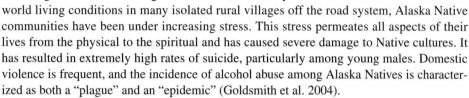

WHAT DO YOU THINK?

Compare and contrast the ways that conflict theory and structural functionalist theory would explain the plight of American Indians and Alaska Natives.

With their way of life being drastically altered, their continued fight for subsistence rights threatened, and nearly third-world living conditions in many isolated rural villages off the road system, Alaska Native communities have been under increasing stress. This stress permeates all aspects of their lives from the physical to the spiritual and has caused severe damage to Native cultures. It has resulted in extremely high rates of suicide, particularly among young males. Domestic violence is frequent, and the incidence of alcohol abuse among Alaska Natives is characterized as both a "plague" and an "epidemic" (Goldsmith et al. 2004).

These concerns have not gone unnoticed. Alaska Natives, along with federal and state governments, have attempted to improve living conditions, support people through the cultural transitions, and reduce the epidemics of violence and alcoholism, while paying tribute to the rich Native cultural heritage. With improving schools, health care, social services, and employment opportunities, culturally sensitive solutions are favored. For example, young people are increasingly taught the traditions and language of their elders; meanwhile, the importation, purchasing, and use of alcohol are banned in many rural communities.

Interracial and Interethnic Families

So far, we have discussed race and ethnicity as though they are discrete categories, but for a growing number of people, especially children, this is not the case. The number of persons of different races or ethnic background who marry is increasing, as shown in Figure 6.4 (Passel

Figure 6.4   Intermarriage Trend 1980–2008

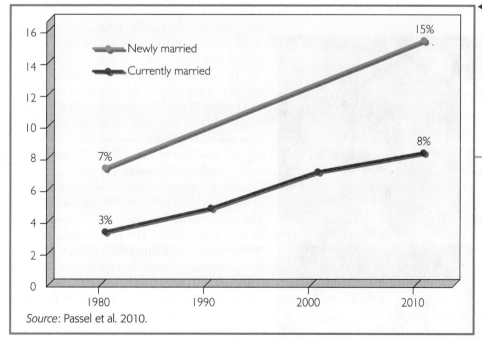

The percentage of those who married someone of a different race or ethnicity has doubled, and is highest among those who are newly married.

Source: Passel et al. 2010.

TABLE 6.6 Intermarriage Rates, by Race and Ethnicity

Asian Americans are most likely to marry outside their race/ethnicity, and Whites are least likely.

PERCENT OF NEWLYWEDS IN 2008 WHO MARRIED SOMEONE OF A DIFFERENT RACE OR ETHNICITY	
White	9%
Black	16%
Hispanic	26%
Asian	31%

Source: Passel et al. 2010.

et al. 2010) A record 15 percent of all marriages in 2008, and 8 percent of marriages overall, were between people of differing races or ethnicities. Of marriages performed in 2008, Asians were most likely to marry someone of a different race or ethnicity, whereas Whites were least likely, as shown in Table 6.6 (Passel et al. 2010).

To what extent do parents of different races identify their children as multiracial? Recent Census Bureau data help us to answer this question, because the 2000 census allowed respondents to mark more than one race for the first time. It is important because racial and ethnic identity is first established within the contexts of families. However, the 2000 census revealed that most interracial couples (66 percent) do not report their children as multiracial. Moreover, the likelihood of reporting a child as multiracial depends on the specific racial combination of the parents. For example, children of Asian-White or Black-White interracial couples are far more likely to report their child as multiracial than American Indian-White or Hispanic-White (Tafoya et al. 2004). Low levels of multiracial reporting among American Indian-White couples may be due to the fact that the American Indian population includes a large number of people with mixed ancestry and with varying degrees of American Indian identity. The low levels of multiracial reporting among Hispanic-White couples may be due to the prominence of ethnic Hispanic identity rather than racial identity. For many Latinos, the racial categories on the census forms are not particularly meaningful (Tafoya et al. 2004).

Parents of multiracial children face issues that same-race couples do not experience (Smith and Hattery 2009). For example, when both parents are White, they may know very little about how prejudice and discrimination operate, having the privilege of rarely being victims themselves. Multiracial couples do experience a great deal of prejudice and discrimination because many Americans are uncomfortable with Whites and minorities dating, marrying, and having children (Childs 2005). Therefore, although the White parent of multiracial children may not completely understand the experiences of a biracial child, they likely do have some firsthand experience of racism. They now must face new tasks of socializing and preparing their children for the racism that they are someday likely to experience. Parents report a great deal of stress

Although we often think of race and ethnicity as discrete categories, in reality an increasing number of people are multiracial or multiethnic, including President Barack Obama. His mother was White, and his father was a Black African. President Obama self-identifies as Black.

associated with trying to protect their children from prejudice and discrimination (Rockquemore and Laszloffy 2005).

In the 2006 book *Mixed: My Life in Black and White*, Angela Nissel recounts with both sadness and humor her experience growing up biracial in Philadelphia, daughter of a Black mother and White father. She describes her anxiety as she moved back and forth between Black inner-city schools and White prep schools, and her many attempts to find out where she best fit in. Her journey leads her to the discovery that being multiracial has its challenges in U.S. society, especially in terms of dating and romance. She reveals how she maintained her own sense of self, despite the racism in American society. U.S. President Barack Obama has also discussed the challenges of growing up biracial in his best-selling book, *Dreams From My Father: A Story of Race and Inheritance* (Obama 2007).

WHAT DO YOU THINK?

Do you think that the challenges associated with being biracial have lessened in recent years? Why or why not? Do you think Angela Nissel's account of growing up biracial would be different for a young person today?

Social Policy and Family Resilience

As we have seen, racism can have disturbing effects on families. In the opening vignette, even young children make assessments on the basis of race or ethnicity; yet, policies designed to increase and strengthen minority families have sometimes been met with resistance. One important and well-known policy is called *affirmative action*.

Example: Affirmative Action

Affirmative action is a set of social policies designed to increase opportunities for underrepresented groups, and one of the most misunderstood strategies of our time (Cohen and Sterba 2003; Kelley 2010; Kellough 2006; Sterba 2009). Proponents see it as proactive measures to remedy inequality, fight discrimination, and have an integrated society with equal opportunities for all members. Opponents believe it is misguided social engineering that uses quotas and preferences to replace qualified males with unqualified minorities and women. They claim it promotes reverse discrimination (Cohen and Sterba 2003).

In what ways is affirmative action a *family policy*? As a tool to promote diversity and remedy inequalities in the workplace, higher education, or government contracting, it can have real implications for enhancing the economic and social well-being of families. It has improved the lives of countless minority families by providing educational training, job opportunities, and pay on par with their White counterparts. It has done the same for women, expanding opportunities that were previously reserved for men.

Until the mid-1960s, minorities were barred from certain jobs, some universities would not admit them, and many employers would not hire them. The Civil Rights Act of 1964 made discrimination illegal in the workplace, in federally funded programs, and in privately owned facilities open to the public. The original goal of the civil rights movement had been "color blind" laws; however, many people were concerned that simply ending a longstanding policy of discrimination did not go far enough. One year later, Congress passed the Voting Rights Act, which gave the U.S. Department of Justice the power to take "affirmative" steps to eliminate discrimination. President Lyndon B. Johnson gave the U.S. Department of Labor the responsibility of enforcing affirmative action. In that role they began requiring government contractors to analyze the demographics of their workforce and to take proactive measures to remedy inequalities. Johnson stated in a 1965 speech at Howard University (Microsoft Encarta Online Encyclopedia 2004):

> You do not take a person who, for years, has been hobbled by chains and liberate him, bring him up to the starting line of a race and say, "you are free to compete with all the others," and still justly believe that you have been completely fair.

Perhaps the most controversial issue about affirmative action is whether it should use "quotas" to reach its goals. For example, if an employer knows it has a large disparity in the proportion of Hispanics in its workforce compared to the general population, it might use affirmative action to target its recruiting effort toward the Hispanic population in hopes of increasing the number of Hispanic new hires. The employer may identify a goal of how many Hispanics it wants to hire, at what levels, and in what time frame. Some argue that this is a quota system (Ethnicmajority.com 2006).

The U.S. Supreme Court has defined the scope of affirmative action policy through a series of legislative initiatives and decisions. Overall, the Court has upheld the constitutionality of affirmative action in principle, but has placed restrictions on how it is implemented. In the early case of *Regents of the University of California v. Bakke* (Oyez Project 1978), Bakke claimed that he was denied entrance to medical school while "less qualified" minorities were admitted. The Court declared that it was unconstitutional for the medical school to establish a rigid quota system by reserving a certain number of places in each class for minorities, but upheld the right of schools to consider a variety of factors when evaluating applicants, including race, ethnicity, sex, and economic status.

In a 2003 case at the University of Michigan, the Supreme Court ruled that the school's point system that gave minority applicants a better chance of acceptance was unconstitutional. The justices affirmed the law school's more individualized method of reviewing applicants, which allows race to be one of many factors in deciding whom to admit. The point system was considered by the majority of the Supreme Court justices to be too "mechanistic" and was considered tantamount to a quota system.

Despite the legislative changes, the value of affirmative action programs in schools and work settings has been established by the Supreme Court. The need is not expected to last forever: "We expect that 25 years from now, the use of racial preferences will no longer be necessary to further the interest approved today," Justice O'Connor wrote in 2003. However, as for today, affirmative action policies have been a boon to minority families in their quest to enter the middle and upper classes.

Conclusion

We all have a race and an ethnicity. Although Whites have the privilege of rarely thinking about them, it remains that skin color, physical features, country of origin, culture, and dominant language shape family structure and family interaction. Each race or ethnic group has a rich history and culture associated with it, and draws upon its heritage in meaningful ways to create relevant family structures. These family structures need not be denigrated simply because they differ from others. The purpose of this chapter is to introduce the ideas that there is more than one model of family life, and that race and ethnicity (alone, and in conjunction with other statuses such as gender and class) provide unique opportunities and challenges, and are important statuses that frame our family lives. We will see specific examples of these throughout the remainder of the book.

Key Terms

Affirmative action: A set of social policies designed to increase opportunities for minority groups and one of the most misunderstood strategies of our time. (p. 179)

Caucasian: A theoretical racial category comprised of those individuals with relatively light skin. (p. 155)

Discrimination: Negative behavior towards a racial or ethnic group. (p. 157)

Ethnic cleansing (or genocide): The systematic killing, torturing, or removal of persons with the intention of eliminating a specific racial or ethnic group. (p. 162)

Ethnic group: People who share specific cultural features. (p. 156)

Ethnicity: Representing culture, including language, place of origin, dress, food, religion, and other values. (p. 155)

Extended families: Families that include other family members such as grandparents, uncles, aunts, or cousins, in addition to parents and their children. (p. 168)

Genocide: See **Ethnic cleansing**.

Minority group: A category of people who have less power than the dominant group and who are subject to unequal treatment. (p. 156)

Mongoloid: A theoretical racial category representing those individuals who have characteristics such as yellow or brown skin and folds on their eyelids. (p. 155)

Negroid: A theoretical racial category comprised of people with darker skin and other characteristics such as coarse curly hair. (p. 155)

Prejudice: Negative attitudes about members of a selected racial or ethnic group. (p. 157)

Race: A category composed of people who share real or alleged physical traits that members of a society deem as socially significant. (p. 155)

Racism: The belief that one racial group is superior or inferior to others. (p. 156)

Social capital: connections through social networks. (p. 156)

Resources on the Internet

Anti Defamation League (ADL)

www.adl.org

The primary purpose of the ADL is to stop the defamation of the Jewish people. Their website contains newspaper articles and other national and international educational materials.

Asian-Nation

www.asian-nation.org

Asian-Nation is a one-stop information source on the historical, political, demographic, and cultural issues that make up today's diverse Asian American community. The website says, "You can almost think of Asian-Nation as an online version of 'Asian Americans 101.'"

Families with Children from China (FWCC)

www.fwcc.org

FWCC provides a network of support for families who have adopted children in China and to provide information to prospective parents. The purpose of this site is to consolidate the information that has been put together by the families of FWCC, in order to make it easier for future parents to consider adopting from China.

First Alaskans Institute

www.firstalaskans.org

The First Alaskans Institute was founded by the Alaska Federation of Natives in 1989 as the AFN Foundation, a 501(c)(3) organization. In 2000, the foundation became independent from AFN. The First Alaskans Institute helps develop the capacities of Alaska Native peoples and their communities to meet social, economic, and educational challenges, while fostering positive relationships among all segments of society. It focuses on policy, leadership, and education to improve the lives of Native Alaskans. Their motto is "Progress for the *next* ten thousand years."

National Association for the Advancement of Colored People (NAACP)

www.naacp.org

The primary focus of the NAACP is to protect and enhance the civil rights of Blacks and other minorities. The NAACP works at the national, regional, and local levels to secure civil rights. They advocate for specific legislation and initiatives.

National Congress of American Indians (NCAI)

www.ncai.org

NCAI's mission is to inform the public and the federal government on tribal self-government, treaty rights, and a broad range of federal policy issues affecting tribal governments.

National Immigration Forum

www.immigrationforum.org

The purpose of the National Immigration Forum is to embrace and uphold the U.S. tradition as a nation of immigrants. The forum advocates and builds public support for public policies that welcome immigrants and refugees and that are fair and supportive to newcomers in the United States.

Pew Hispanic Center

www.pewhispanic.org

The goal of the Pew Hispanic Center is to disseminate its research about the diverse Hispanic population in the United States to policy makers, business leaders, the media, and academic institutions. Their website contains many recent studies on all aspects of Hispanics' lives.

CHAPTER 7

Courtship, Intimacy, and Partnering

CHAPTER OUTLINE

Courtship and Mate Selection 185

■ **USING** *the Sociological Imagination:* The Historical Relationship between Love and Marriage **185**

Love 193

■ **FAMILIES** *as Lived Experience:* "Living in Mania" **195**

Sexuality 196

■ **OUR** *Global Community:* Fourteen Years of Hard Labor **200**

Heterosexual Cohabitation 207

Gay and Lesbian Intimate Relationships 212

Social Policy and Family Resilience 214

Conclusion 216

Key Terms 217

Resources on the Internet 217

CHAPTER PREVIEW

How do people become life partners? This seems like such a personal question that no amount of social research could answer it. However, personal choices are patterned and are surprisingly shaped by many intriguing social, cultural, and historical forces. This chapter explores how these forces shape courtship patterns, sexuality, and the mate selection process. Specifically, in this chapter, you will learn:

- What love has to do with courtship and mate selection

- Gender difference in the emotion of loving

- General cultural principles guiding sexuality and intimacy

- Sexual orientation and its causes

- How we learn sexual scripts as rules for sexual behavior and how scripts may differ by race, ethnicity, social class, and sex

- Sexually transmitted diseases are hidden epidemics that have enormous health and economic consequences in the United States and throughout the world

- Important issues surrounding heterosexual cohabitation, including children in cohabiting relationships

- About gay and lesbian relationships and social policy issues surrounding same-sex marriage

Trinidad

"When I was 17 years old and still in school, my father told me that he had chosen a wife for me. I realized that I did not have a choice and decided to go along with his decision. My father made all the arrangements for the wedding. We were poor, and I remember that I wore shoes for the first time on my wedding day. During the ceremony, I saw my bride's fingers were of a fair complexion, which assured me that she was a good woman. So, my love life began by seeing my wife's fingers. I saw my wife for the first time after our wedding ceremony. She was 14 years old." (Seegobin and Tarquin 2003)

Kenya

"As my sisters and I went about doing our daily chores, we choked on the dust stirred up by the herd of cattle and goats that had just arrived in our compound. I was surprised when I found out that these animals were my bride wealth, negotiated by my parents and the family of the man who had been chosen as my husband. His name is Simayia ole Mootian, and he is 27 years old. I have never met him. Because I have recently been circumcised, I am considered to be a woman. So, I am ready to marry, have children, and assume adult privileges and responsibilities. My name is Telelia ole Mariani. I am 14 years old. Here, life is difficult, and I wonder how this will change my life. I wonder whether he already has other wives. I wonder how we will live. Will we live together, or will he live away from the family to work in the city? Does he have a job? I probably will not continue in school or have a job. Instead, I will be having and taking care of children. Many people are infected with HIV/AIDS. That is changing the way children, parents, and grandparents take care of each other. I wonder whether he could have HIV/AIDS. If I become infected, who will care for our children? Will they have it? My mind is in a whirl of questions; I am excited, happy, nervous, and concerned." (Wilson et al. 2003)

Spain

"Two friends in their late 20s met at a café in downtown Madrid one morning. One of them asked the other whether he was happy with his current living arrangement or whether he desired to live by himself, independent from his parents. To this, the young man replied, 'Why should I leave my parents? I have it all where I am. My mother washes and irons my clothes, she cooks for me, and I don't have to pay rent. Plus, I don't believe that I earn enough to make it on my own. I have been trying to find a job in my field of study, and I haven't been able to find anything. Things are really hard at the moment.' To this, the other man responded, 'But what about your girlfriend? What does she think about all this?' 'She agrees with me,' the young man replied. 'I know that she would like to get married soon, but we recognize that we need to be more financially established before we can get married. For instance, we both believe that we should wait until we have enough money to buy and furnish our own apartment. And as it is, we are still able to get away and spend time together as a couple. As a matter of fact, next weekend we will be spending the weekend in Seville. So, I am content with the way things are." (Reyes 2003)

The Netherlands

"Karel and Muriel met each other at a party when they both are in their early 20s. They have seen each other at times in college classrooms but do not know each other well. A few days after the party, Karel invites Muriel for dinner at his apartment. Over the course of a year, their relationship becomes closer and they decide to move in together. Their friends approve and congratulate them on the next step in their lives. They hold a housewarming party to celebrate. After living together for several years, Karel and Muriel decide that they are ready for the next step: a home. They have their attorney draft a cohabitation contract so that they can legally organize their living arrangements. Within a few weeks, they move out of

their apartment into their newly purchased home."
(van Dulmen 2003)

These four scenarios from Trinidad, Kenya, Spain, and the Netherlands illustrate that the process by which people find partners, the ceremony or rite of passage that signifies commitment or marriage, and the expectations for partners afterwards could not be more different. People become intimate, form partnerships, or marry to improve their economic conditions, for sheer survival, to increase their social standing, or to please their parents and build family alliances.

This chapter explores the development of intimacy and mate selection, including courtship, love, sexuality, and cohabitation. Cultural traditions, the environment, social norms, and religious customs have as much to do with mate selection as love and affection, sexual convenience, or compatibility. In many cultures, they are even more important.

Courtship and Mate Selection

A lot is at stake when two people marry. They make a lifelong commitment to one another and agree to conduct themselves in a manner befitting a married couple in that culture. More is at stake in marriage than the wishes of two individuals. Families, communities, and the state have an interest in marriage as well because marriage serves political, social, and economic functions. As discussed in Chapter 1, marriage is a social institution as well as a personal relationship. Marriage is a way to consolidate wealth, transfer property, construct alliances, and organize the division of labor. These important functions are not simply left to individuals to negotiate.

What's Love Got to Do with It?

Since families, communities, and the state all have an interest in marriage, they also have a hand in controlling the mate selection process. Sociologist William J. Goode suggests that this is done by controlling or channeling **love**, which he defines as a strong emotional attachment with at least the components of sex, desire, and tenderness (Goode 1959). Goode argues that all societies try to control or channel love to some degree because as a basis for marriage, love could be disruptive to families, communities, and to the state if not controlled. The connection between love and marriage that is found in many countries is a relatively recent phenomenon, as illustrated in the following box, "Using the Sociological Imagination: The Historical Relationship between Love and Marriage"—and the connection is not without risks, according to historian Stephanie Coontz (2004).

USING
the Sociological Imagination

The Historical Relationship between Love and Marriage

As the saying goes, ". . . first comes love, then comes marriage . . . ," or does it? The following discussion by social historian Stephanie Coontz reveals that for most of history, love would have been a very poor reason to marry.

For thousands of years, marriage had little to do with love. Marriage was a way of raising capital, constructing political alliances, organizing the division of labor by age and sex, and deciding what claim, if any, children had on their parents, and what rights parents had in their children. Marriage served so many political, social, and economic functions that individual needs and desires were secondary considerations. In fact, for most people,

(continued)

(continued)

whether rich or poor, marriage was as much about getting in-laws as about finding a mate and having a child.

For the wealthy propertied classes, marriage was the main way of consolidating wealth, transferring property, and laying claim to political power. When upper-class men and women married, a dowry or bride wealth was exchanged, making the match a major economic investment by the parents and other kin of the couple. Even middle-class families had a huge economic stake in who married whom. Until the late eighteenth century, marriage was the primary method of transferring property, occupational status, personal contacts, money, tools, and possessions across generations and kin groups. For most men, the dowry that a wife brought was the biggest infusion of cash, goods, or land that they would ever acquire. For most women, finding a husband was the most important investment they could make in their economic future.

In the lower classes, marriage was also an economic and political transaction, but on a different scale. The concerns of commoners were more immediate: "Do I marry someone with fields near my fields?" "Will my prospective mate meet the approval of the neighbors and relatives on whom I depend?" And because few farms or businesses could be run by a single person, the skills, resources, and tools prospective partners brought to the marriage were at least as important as their personality or attractiveness.

For all of these reasons, love was considered a very poor reason to get married. It was nice if affection developed after marriage, and many parents allowed their children to veto a match with a partner who repelled them—but love was not the main thing that people looked for in deciding when and whom to marry. When divorce occurred, it was more often to get a better set of in-laws or because

of childlessness rather than because of a lack of love.

In the seventeenth century, a series of interrelated political, economic, and cultural changes began to erode the functions of marriage and throw into question the rights of parents, local elites, and government officials to limit individual autonomy in personal life. In the eighteenth century, the revolutionary new ideal of love triumphed in most of Western Europe and North America. Suddenly, couples were supposed to invest more of their emotional energy in each other and their children than in their natal families, their kin, their friends, and their patrons. There was a new stress on marital companionship, intimacy, and privacy. Love became the primary motivation for marriage.

However, ideas about love also destabilize personal relations between men and women. When people focused on love as the basis of marriage, they also began to demand the right to divorce. Even in stable marriages, the new values caused the couple "to be constantly taken up with each other" instead of carrying out their duties to society. In other words, the very values that we have come to think of as traditional—love—had the inherent tendency to undermine the stability of marriage as an institution even as they increased the satisfaction of marriage as a relationship.

Source: Adapted from Coontz 2004.

CRITICAL THINKING QUESTIONS
1. How is it possible that marriage as an institution has become less stable, while marriage as a personal relationship has become more satisfying?
2. Even today, some cultures do not believe that love should be a primary basis for marriage. What arguments would they make to defend their position? What grounds do you have to suggest that love should be a critical basis for marriage?

What are the various ways that families, communities, and the state try to control love?

1. *Child marriage.* One common method of controlling love is to have the child married or betrothed prior to puberty before feelings of love for another person can even develop. A child has no social or financial resources to oppose such a marriage.

2. *Kinship rules.* Some cultures clearly define the pool of eligible future spouses, such as a cousin. The major decision then is primarily *when*, rather than with *whom*, the marriage is to occur.

3. *Isolation of young people.* Socially segregating young people from one another can be a very effective means of controlling love. The goal is to eliminate opportunities for formal or informal interaction.

4. *Close supervision.* Short of isolation, some cultures watch their young people, especially young women, very carefully. A high value is placed on female chastity, and therefore, they are highly supervised whenever they are in the company of men.

5. *Formally free.* Love is encouraged and it is an expected element of mate selection. However, love remains controlled and channeled by the social contacts available to young people. Because people fall in love with those with whom they associate, love can be controlled by managing the social environment such as sending a child to particular schools, living in a certain neighborhood, involving the family in church or other civic associations, and channeling children toward a specific set of peers.

How do these rules play out across cultures? An interesting contrast in mate selection can be seen between India and the United States.

India

In other cultures, people find their mates through mechanisms that differ from those in the United States. India provides an example (Leeder 2004; Medora 2003). About 85 percent of marriages in India are arranged (Griffith 2006). Most Indians would find the U.S. belief in dating and romance as odd as we might find their idea of arranged marriage. They suggest that we are too focused on passionate love and on fun and games, to the detriment of building a solid lasting relationship.

In many parts of the world, parents choose the mate for their children, and often the children would not want it any other way. Sometimes the mate selection choice, and even the marriage itself, occurs when the children are young.

Arranged marriages in India are not necessarily forced. Young adult children are happy to hand over the task of mate selection to their parents, "Any girl I could find for myself would not be as good as the one my parents will find," says a 19-year-old college student (Derne 2003). At the same time, they often retain some degree of veto power if they don't like the person that their parents suggest.

Marriages in India are based on commitment, rather than love. Indians do not look down upon marrying someone they don't know—they believe that marriage allows a lifetime to learn to love a partner, as opposed to the American ideal of learning about a person inside and out before entering into marriage. An Indian woman described it as "Here, we get married without having feelings for the person. We base our marriage on commitment, not on feelings. As our marriage progresses, the feelings develop. In America, you base your decision to marry on feelings, but what happens when the feelings wane? You have nothing left to keep the marriage together if you get married according to feelings and then the feelings go away" (Indiamarks.com 2009).

In other words, love is not a foreign concept to Indians. They simply have a different conception of it, influenced heavily by Hinduism, the caste system, and other norms in

Indian culture. They believe that much of a person's life is predetermined by his or her karma. Marriage is something that is out of the hands of the couple, and few would attempt to change fate. Commonly, before two Indians can consider marriage, both sets of parents consult an astrologer to examine their zodiac signs to determine the couple's compatibility. The astrologer helps to determine whether this is a proper match. If it is deemed to be a good match, then families can begin to discuss issues surrounding the dowry.

Despite women's lower status in India (Gupta 2005; Pew Global Attitudes Project 2010), they are valued because of their fertility. Large families and large numbers of sons are highly desirable by most Indians. Therefore, families spend considerable time negotiating a **dowry** or the financial gift given to a woman's prospective in-laws by her parents. The woman is generally not involved in the negotiations. Parents will spend large amounts on the dowry, depending on their caste or class standing, and may be left impoverished or in substantial debt as a result.

Child marriage was outlawed in 1978 in India (Yadav 2006); however, it still is a practice in many parts of the country. Data from the Indian National Health Survey-3, based on a sample of Indian women aged 20–24, indicate that 23 percent of those who were married were wed before age 16 (Raj et al. 2009). In one province, Rajasthan, it is estimated that over half of marriages involve girls who are under the age of 15 (Yadav 2006). Child marriages free a family from the obligations of supporting a girl who the family sees as destined to leave them anyway. In the eyes of the parents it also decreases her likelihood of engaging in premarital sex or being exploited sexually, which would reduce her status and ability to marry (Bhat et al. 2005).

United States

Even in the United States, we can see the influence of culture, the economy, changing norms, historical period, and geography in shaping the ways that marriage partners are found. Although today the United States is best viewed as having a *formally free* mate selection process, in colonial America parental influence was relatively heavy. Unmarried women were highly supervised, and an unmarried couple was tightly chaperoned. Social interaction between young men and women tended to occur within their own homes or at social or church gatherings under the watchful eye of other family members.

The Origins of Dating As you have learned, the late nineteenth and early twentieth centuries brought industrialization, urbanization, and a higher standard of living and disposable income for many people. This led to new freedoms stemming from a prolonged period of adolescence, greater interaction between males and females in schools, and the availability of the private automobile. These changes created a social situation known as *dating*. As we saw in Chapter 3, the movement away from parental control and supervision brought a change of power and roles in the couple relationship. Dating was now done away from home and away from parents and family members. The young couple usually went somewhere: to a dance, a party, or dinner, or later, to a movie theater. Young men were expected to initiate and pay for dates. Men decided where the couple would go, they would make arrangements for the needed transportation, and they made the decision about what the couple would do on the date. Women largely waited to be chosen, yet frowned on last-minute invitations (saying yes indicated that no one else had chosen them). Women had little say-so in where the couple would go or what they would do. Their only realm of control was related to the degree of intimacy and sexuality within the date.

During this time, social scientists began to conduct research on dating. In 1937, Willard Waller published a study conducted at Pennsylvania State University on the dating values of college men and women. Dating was a competitive game and success was defined as having the most dates and with the right kind of person, a process nicknamed *rating and dating*. In the late 1940s, the famous anthropologist Margaret Mead was a harsh critic of the manner in which dating had evolved (Mead 1949). First, she complained that men and women defined their relationships in situational, rather than ongoing, terms; for example, you have a "date" —a formal event with an appointed time and place. This kept men and women from truly getting to know one another. Second, she argued that sexual relationships were depersonalized. Men were encouraged to "score" and the focus was on keeping tabs on who in your social circle was "going all the way" (Mead 1949).

The Changing Nature of Courtship   Margaret Mead may be pleased that today partner selection has evolved into something much less formal. Groups of young men and women often spend time together socializing, referring to the process as "getting together" or "hanging out" rather than "dating." In a group situation, young people feel more relaxed and informal. Norms have also changed so that women feel more comfortable initiating getting together. The age at first marriage has increased considerably for both men and women, which eases some pressure among young people.

Twelfth-grade students are less likely to date than they were in 1991, as shown in Figure 7.1. The percentage who claimed they *never* dated jumped from 14 percent in 1991 to 21 percent in 2000, and doubling to 28 percent in 2008 (Bachman et al. 1993, 2001, 2009). Those that claimed they date *frequently* (defined as more than once a week) declined significantly from 34 percent in 1991, to 28 percent in 2000, and down to only 23 percent in 2008. These differences could reflect the changing definition of dating itself; for instance, is "hanging out" with a group of people dating?

One study examined the evolution of dating and mate selection values over a period of nearly 60 years (Buss et al. 2001). The authors compared data from 1939, 1956, 1967, 1977,

Figure 7.1   Percentage of 12th Grade Students Who Never Date or Who Date Frequently (more than once a week), 1991, 2000, 2008

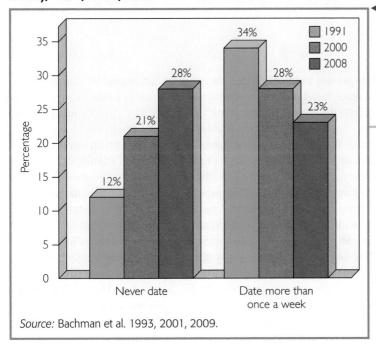

Today, high school seniors are more likely to report that they never date and less likely to report that they date frequently.

Source: Bachman et al. 1993, 2001, 2009.

TABLE 7.1 Rank Ordering of Mate Preferences Across Six Decades by Gender

The top four ranked characteristics have remained relatively stable, but the remaining characteristics have changed their rank order substantially.

Characteristic	MEN		WOMEN	
	1939	1996	1939	1996
Dependable character	1	2	2	2
Emotional stability, maturity	2	3	1	3
Pleasing disposition	3	4	4	4
Mutual attraction love	4	1*	5	1*
Good health	5	6	6	9
Desire for home, children	6	9	7	6
Refinement, neatness	7	11*	8	12*
Good cook, housekeeper	8	14*	16	16
Ambition, industriousness	9	10	3	7*
Chastity	10	16*	10	17*
Education, intelligence	11	5*	9	5*
Sociability	12	7*	11	8*
Similar religious background	13	12	14	14
Good looks	14	8*	17	13*
Similar education background	15	12*	12	10
Favorable social status	16	17	15	15
Good financial prospect	17	13*	13	11
Similar political background	18	18	18	18

Note: Asterisks highlight a preference change of at least three ranks from the first to the last assessment period.
Source: Buss et al. 2001.

1984/1985, and 1996 at several locations around the country with respect to what traits men and women value in a mate. Several changes were noted, as shown in Table 7.1, which compares 1939 to 1996. First, the largest change is the value placed on chastity in a potential mate. In 1939, chastity was the 10th most important trait out of 18 traits listed. By 1996, it was ranked 16th. Second, there has been an increased value associated with physical attractiveness in a mate cited by both men and women. For men, it jumped from 14th in 1939 to 8th in 1996. For women, it climbed from 17th to 13th during this period. A third clear trend is the increasing importance of good financial prospects in a partner, particularly cited by male respondents. Men ranked women's financial prospects as 17th in importance in 1939, jumping to 13th in the mid-1990s. Women reported a smaller change, increasing from 13th to 11th. Fourth, men are less likely today to rate domestic skills as important in a mate, dropping from 8th in 1939 to 14th in 1996. Interestingly, the trend toward more equitable sharing of housework appears to have had no impact on women's ranking of domestic skills in a marriage partner, which remains ranked 16th over the 57-year period. The final significant shift in values focuses on the importance of mutual attraction and love. Although it was ranked 4th for men and 5th for women in 1939, by 1996 it was ranked first in importance. Americans believe that attraction and love are at the center of marriage.

Why did these values shift over this sixty-year period? Changes in values accompany structural changes in society. For example, urbanization and job mobility contribute to a decline in the extended family. Likewise, changes in the economy and increased job opportunities for women result in a delay of childbirth. These structural changes may increase the importance of marriage as the primary source of intimacy (Buss et al. 2001).

Nonetheless, many traditions and values are slow to change. Research suggests that both men and women still feel comfortable with many traditionally gendered scripts. For example, as a couple contemplates marriage, they usually "get engaged." Have you noticed that only women wear engagement rings? The diamond industry claims this is a good financial investment for the couple, but it really is a holdover from the patriarchal notion of male ownership of women. It signals "hands off—she's taken." About 75 percent of all first-time brides wear engagement rings, at an average price of over $5,800 (TheKnot.com 2010).

Other longstanding social norms continue to define the field of eligible mates. These rules or customs indicate who is an appropriate mate, and include:

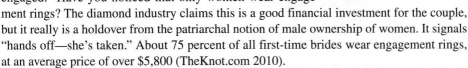

WHAT DO YOU THINK?

The study by Buss and colleagues examined the traits that men and women value in a mate in 1939, 1956, 1967, 1977, 1984/5, and 1996. How do you think the answers that men and women give today would compare to these? Has much changed since 1996? If so, what accounts for these changes?

- **Endogamy**—mate selection is expected to occur with someone inside a particular social group, such as religious group, a member of a particular social class, racial or ethnic category, or in other cultures, a member of a specific clan
- **Exogamy**—mate selection is expected to occur with someone outside of a particular social group, such as your immediate family, or your sex

Violating these social norms brings varying degrees of societal concern. For example, miscegenation laws attempted to bar interracial marriage until as late as 1967. Gay and lesbian marriage continues to be controversial today and is barred in most states around the country. Many parents would disapprove if their child married someone of a different religious faith. Not surprisingly then, most people look for **homogeneous relationships**, or partners similar to themselves. Partners tend to be about the same age and are of the same race, religion, and social class. **Heterogeneous relationships** are those in which the partners are significantly different from one another on some important characteristic, such as age or level of education.

Where Do We Meet?   As you may guess, most people meet each other at work, at school, or through friends or family, as shown in Table 7.2. A study of 3,000 Internet users found that, among people who are married or in committed relationships, over 38 percent met at work or school, and 34 percent met through family or friends. Only 3 percent met through the Internet (Madden and Lenhart 2006). In other words, most people who are married or in long-term relationships first met their partners the old-fashioned way—through face-to-face contact.

However, even if only 3 percent of married or committed persons have met their partner on the Internet, online dating services and websites have become an increasingly popular way to look for romantic partners. There are approximately 1,400 online dating sites, the largest being eHarmony with over 20 million users and Match.com with 15 million users (Scott 2009). Nearly half of adults (49 percent) know at least one person who has dated someone they met online, according to a nationwide study conducted in July 2009 (Greenberg 2009). This represents a significant increase from 2006 when only about a third said that that they knew someone who participated in online dating (Madden and Lenhart 2006).

Among those who have tried online dating, almost two-thirds believe it is a good venue for finding a mate (Madden and Lenhart 2006). Who participates? As shown in Table 7.3, they are somewhat more likely to be male, a racial or ethnic minority, urban, young, and to have lower levels of income and education, although these factors may be related to the fact

TABLE 7.2   Where Dating Partners Meet

Most people continue to meet others the old-fashioned way—at work, at school, or through family and friends.

Met at work or school	38%
Met through family or friends	34%
Met at nightclub, bar, café, social gathering	13%
Met through the Internet	3%
Met at church	2%
Met by chance, such as on the street	1%
Met because they live in same neighborhood	1%
Met at recreational facility, gym	1%
Met on a blind date or through dating service	1%
Other	6%

Source: Madden and Lenhart 2006.

TABLE 7.3   Who Uses Online Dating?

Online dating is booming. How do you think these numbers might have changed in the past five years?

All Internet Users		11%
Sex	Male	12%
	Female	9%
Race/Ethnicity	White	10%
	Black	13%
	Hispanic	14%
Geographic Location	Urban	13%
	Suburban	10%
	Rural	9%
Age	18–29	18%
	30–49	11%
	50–64	6%
	65+	3%
Household Income	Less than $30,000	14%
	$30,000–$49,999	13%
	$50,000–$74,999	10%
	$75,000+	9%
Education Level	Less Than High School	14%
	High School Graduate	10%
	Some College	11%
	College+	10%

Source: Madden and Lenhart 2006.

People are turning to Internet sites as a way to meet others, including Facebook or online dating sites like eHarmony or Match.com.

that a high proportion of Internet daters are under age 30 (Madden and Lenhart 2006). Another study of over 3,300 people ranging in age from 19–89 found that those who use online Internet dating are more sociable, despite stereotypes to the contrary (Kim et al. 2009).

What is the allure of online Internet dating? Many Internet users agree it helps people find a better match because you can get to know a larger number of people. However, online daters themselves are split as to whether it's the easiest and most efficient method of dating. Most see it as potentially dangerous and are somewhat wary of the risks, including other people misrepresenting themselves (say, by claiming they are single when they are really married) or trying to obtain personal information. Nonetheless, equal numbers of online daters report positive and negative experiences (Madden and Lenhart 2006).

Love

When we think about love, we usually see it as a private, personal relationship—full of warmth, intimacy, and passion. We care deeply about someone, and he or she in turn cares deeply about us. We *feel* love on this level, and we like it. However, our feelings do not exist in a vacuum. The way we experience love is also shaped by the social context in which we live. First, love is related to culture. In the United States, for example, the focus is on romantic love. In other cultures, this type of passion is thought to be foolish. Second, people have been socialized to see and experience love differently depending on their sex, social class, and race and ethnicity. The meanings attached to love and how we express it differ. For example, women often express their love with words, whereas men may express their love more with actions. Third, love is also related to the relationship between the people who love, including parents and children, friends, and romantic partners. These relationships are different from one another, but all contain an emotion that we call "love."

Love is a critical foundation for developing intimate relationships in the United States. How can a "feeling" be the subject of so many rules, regulations, and norms? What power does this emotion hold that parents, religions, or cultures will try to control and channel it?

Everyone wants to experience love. We want to receive love (from parents, friends, our children, and our partners) and we want to love others. In the United States today, love is a primary basis for marriage—but exactly what is love? Can we find a useful definition that would include the love between a mother and child, as well as the love shared by married or cohabiting partners? The dictionary defines love as: (1) a strong affection for one another arising out of kinship or personal ties; (2) attraction based on sexual desire; or (3) affection based on admiration, benevolence, or common interests (Merriam-Webster Online 2010). How does this differ from Goode's definition provided earlier?

Many sociologists, social psychologists, and anthropologists have studied attraction and love, attempting to describe and explain this deeply profound feeling. Anthropologist Helen Fisher studies the brain chemistry of people in love and argues that much of our romantic behavior is hardwired. Using a functional magnetic resonance imaging machine on her subjects, she suggests that our brains create dramatic surges of energy and chemicals including norepinephrine, dopamine, and seratonin that fuel such feelings as passion, obsessiveness, joy, and jealousy (Fisher 2004). Using an evolutionary perspective, Fisher views love as a drive so powerful that it can override other drives, such as hunger and thirst (Fisher 2004, 2010; Fisher and Thomson 2007).

Other researchers take a more process-oriented approach and look at the stages that love may pass through to fully develop (Kerchoff and Davis 1962; Reiss 1960), or look at the different dimensions of love and try to categorize different styles of loving (Lee 1973, 1974, 1988; Sternberg 1986). For example, Canadian sociologist John Lee (1973, 1974, 1988) reviewed thousands of works of fiction and nonfiction across the centuries dealing with love and interviewed young heterosexual men and women living in Canada and Great Britain. From his review, he developed a six-category classification scheme on various styles of love. These styles are distinct from one another, yet relationships can also be characterized by having more than one style.

- *Eros.* Eros is a love that is passionate, all-consuming, and highly sexual. This is the type of love most often presented in movies, television, and popular culture.
- *Storge.* Storge (pronounced STOR-gay) represents a love that develops slowly with the passage of time. A couple may begin as friends, and over time the relationship moves forward in its degree of commitment and intimacy. It is a comfortable love, with mutual trust, compatibility, and respect.
- *Pragma.* Pragma is a rational, down-to-earth (pragmatic) style of love based on practical considerations.
- *Ludus.* Ludus is a playful, carefree type of love. Ludus lovers are not possessive, and are more about fun and games than about commitment.
- *Agape.* Agape (pronounced ah-GAH-pay) is self-sacrificing, altruistic, kind, and patient. Partners are completely selfless, giving without any thought of getting something in return.
- *Mania.* Manic relationships are characterized by possessiveness, dependency, and jealousy. Partners are very demanding, have a high level of anxiety about their partner, and obsess over the other's whereabouts at all times, as shown in the box on page 195, "Families as Lived Experience: 'Living in Mania'."

Naturally, the types of love we experience will develop and change over a lifetime. Singles are more likely to hold manic and ludic love attitudes than married adults, whose relationships may be represented by storge. But few, if any, relationships are characterized in terms of only one type of love. The six types might be useful to help us understand how couples come together, and which couples may be most, and least, likely to have long-term relationships. For example, agape and storge are more secure types of love, whereas mania is more anxious/ambivalent, and ludus is closest to avoidant (Hendrick and Hendrick 1992).

F A M I L I E S
as Lived Experience

"Living in Mania"

Lee's work reveals that there are many different types of love. Mania is a type characterized by jealousy and obsession, as this story reveals.

The relationship began quite nicely. We were introduced by some mutual friends, and the four of us would go out partying on the weekends. Jay was so attentive to me, always calling or texting to see if I was okay, happy, and asking me questions about myself, although in retrospect I think he knew many of the answers before I told him. That should have been a clue—how did he know so much about me—but what do they say, love is blind? At first I really liked all the attention; I'm looking to have a lot of fun.

When did I realize that something wasn't right? My girlfriends made fun of him for calling and texting so often. They thought his 5–10 messages a day were crazy—"Romeo" they would call him. But I didn't really see a problem until he wanted me to quit hanging around them and to spend all my time with him. He didn't even want me to study much—I remember he got really mad and yelled at me because I didn't acknowledge his messages for 6 hours when I was at the library studying for my Calculus midterm. He seemed to be jealous of anything and everything that took my attention off of him, even for an hour. When I took off for the weekend to visit my high school buddies he cried because I wouldn't take him with me.

I began to feel really smothered and told him that I needed more space—that maybe we should see less of each other. He was just like a puppy dog, dragging around, looking weepy, and telling me he was lonely and couldn't live without me. He seemed so anxious and afraid to be alone. Then he decided that I must have met another guy, which was not the case, and he really lost it, begging me to take him back. Wow, I've never met anyone like this before. I feel badly that I hurt him, but his intensity is way too much for me.

—**Sylvia, Age 24**

CRITICAL THINKING QUESTIONS

1. What clues did you see indicating Jay has a mania style of love? What would you guess Sylvia's preferred style to be?
2. Do you think that either men or women are more likely to have a mania style of love? If so, why?

Sex Differences in Loving

It may come as no surprise to you to read that men and women, on average, experience love differently. Most people believe that women are more interested in love than are men. A cursory look at women's magazines at the supermarket checkout stand will confirm this:

"How to Make Him Fall Crazy in Love"

"The Sex Tips That Will Make Him Fall Head Over Heels"

"Don't Take No for an Answer: How to Land Your Man"

"Five New Recipes That He Is Guaranteed to Love"

"Where to Meet the Man of Your Dreams? We'll Tell You"

"Stand by Your Man Twenty-First-Century Style"

As you have learned, in the nineteenth century, love became more "feminized" and was associated with the caregiving that women do in the home; it became a private feeling, separated from the outside world of work or politics (Cancian 1987). Hence, it was often viewed as the domain of women.

WHAT DO YOU THINK?

Thinking back to what you learned in Chapters 4, 5, and 6 about sex, social class, race, and ethnicity, and the intersection of these statuses, do you think that groups experience and express love differently? For example, do lower-income Hispanic men experience and express love differently than higher-income Asian men? Do Black women experience and express love differently than White women? How do these statuses interact with one another?

However, surveys show that men in fact are more likely than women to be in or looking for committed relationships (Madden and Lenhart 2006; Madden and Rainie 2006), and they report falling in love sooner and with more people than do women (Covel 2003; Saad 2004). Men are also more preoccupied with love and relationships.

If men actually fall in love more quickly than do women and are more focused on love, why does cultural rhetoric claim the opposite is true—that women are the ones obsessed with love? There may be several reasons for this myth. In reviewing the different loving styles, one study found that, in general, men were more ludic (carefree), whereas women tended to lean towards storge (comfortable and compatible) and pragma (rational) (Hendrick and Hendrick 1992). Not surprisingly then, some women believe that men are "afraid of commitment" or "commitment phobic" (Gerson 2009; Whitehead and Popenoe 2002).

Another reason we assume that women are more loving has to do with the different ways that men and women express love and our belief that women's expressions are somehow better. This is referred to as the *feminization of love* (Cancian 1987). The problem is not that men don't express love—they do, but they often don't get credit for it because we ignore or minimize masculine-type expressions. Thus, the man who is a good provider, who takes his daughter to soccer, who folds the laundry may be showing as much love as the woman who says "I love you" regularly. He may think that "actions speak louder than words", but his partner is waiting for the words and miscommunication can result.

Men and women fall in love for many of the same reasons—similar values, emotional maturity, dependability—but men are more likely than women to fall in love for reasons related to physical attractiveness. Women are somewhat more cautious about love, taking a bit longer and using a wider variety of factors in deciding whether they are in love. These factors include physical attractiveness and similarity in values and other traits, but also ambition, industriousness, and financial prospects (Eastwick and Finkel 2008).

Reasons for falling in love appear to be associated with the ways that sex and gender are defined in our society. For most of history, women have been financially dependent on men in marriage, therefore, it made good sense to closely examine a man's economic prospects before choosing a mate. But as the context changes, so too do the reasons for choosing a mate. Since the 1970s, more married women are working outside the home for pay and their financial dependence on men in marriage has declined (U.S. Census Bureau 2010c). Therefore, with less *need* for a husband as a provider, women focus on other qualities for their intimate relationships.

As couples fall in love, they share increasing intimacy. Sexuality may be one way of expressing this intimacy.

Sexuality

Sexuality is a universal human experience. Even young children are keenly interested in their genitals and in feelings of arousal (Thigpen 2009). Among adults, sexuality is used as an expression of many different, even competing emotions. It can express love and tenderness or exploitation and revenge. Despite the universal nature of this biological phenomenon, sexual attitudes and behaviors vary remarkably by sex, across subpopulations in the United States, and across cultures throughout the world (Stombler et al. 2010). How can something as personal and private (as well as so biologically driven) as sexuality be rooted in social and

Because sex is universal, we sometimes forget that much of sexuality is socially produced. Attitudes, behaviors, and views of sexual attractiveness can differ considerably, as shown here.

cultural norms? Anderson and Taylor (2008) remind us of the following principles:

1. *Sexual attitudes and behaviors are substantially different across cultures.* For example, in many cultures it is expected that a woman will be a virgin on the wedding day. A husband, in-laws, or other kin may demand proof that this is indeed the case; they may require the woman to undergo a physical examination by a doctor who will verify her virginity, they may oversee a surgical procedure to remove the stitching that has closed off her vagina, or they may want a bloody sheet as evidence that the hymen was ruptured on the wedding night (although not all women bleed when their hymen is ruptured).

2. *Sexual attitudes and behaviors change over time.* We may have overestimated the "prim and proper" stereotype of the colonial and Victorian eras, because birth records indicate many women and men were indeed sexually active prior to marriage. However, sexuality was valued primarily in the confines of marriage and most religious and medical authorities generally did not believe that women experienced true sexual desires. Today things have changed a great deal. Sex outside of marriage is no longer taboo under many circumstances, and women are generally considered to be full sexual beings.

3. *Social institutions channel and direct sexuality.* As we learned in Chapter 2, every culture regulates sexual behavior. Cultural norms make it clear who can have a sexual relationship with whom and under what circumstances. However, even within a culture, social institutions channel and direct sexual behavior. Institutions such as the family, religion, and government dictate with whom we can have sex and under what circumstances. For example, in U.S. culture these social institutions channel adults away from sex with children or with animals. They even influence consenting adults who exchange sex for money or have a sexual relationship with someone other than their spouse.

Sexual Orientation

Another aspect of who we are concerns our **sexual orientation**, which refers to an enduring pattern of romantic, emotional, and sexual partners we choose (American Psychological Association 2009). Research now strongly suggests that sexual orientation is the result of a complex set of factors that may have a strong root in biology. A **heterosexual** orientation refers to an attraction and preference for sexual and romantic relationships with members of the other sex (e.g., a man and a woman), and a **homosexual** orientation refers to a preference for same-sex sexual and romantic relationships. The term **gay** usually refers to homosexual men, whereas **lesbian** refers to homosexual women. **Bisexual** refers to an orientation in which a person is attracted to both males and females and engages in both heterosexual and homosexual relationships. Early researcher Alfred Kinsey was instrumental in showing sexual orientation as a continuum rather than as a pair of polar opposites (Kinsey et al. 1953). He found that around one-quarter to one-third of survey respondents reportedly had at least some homosexual experience, although most still thought of themselves as heterosexual. He estimated that at least 3 percent of females were almost or exclusively homosexual as were at least 8 percent of males (Kinsey et al. 1953).

Counting the number of persons who are gay or lesbian is challenging. One reason is because having a gay or lesbian *identity* can be a very different thing from having a gay or lesbian *experience* (Ward 2010). Many people have a gay or lesbian experience, or many experiences, yet still think of themselves as heterosexual (Vrangalova and Savin-Williams, 2010).

When researchers asked in one survey, "Do you think of yourself as heterosexual, homosexual, bisexual, or something else?" about 3 percent of men and slightly less than 2 percent of women claimed either a homosexual or bisexual self-concept (Vrangalova and Savin-Williams 2010). Other studies suggest the number is a bit higher. In a national survey that draws upon a large representative sample of adults aged 18–45, 4.1 percent of respondents identified themselves as gay, lesbian, or bisexual (Gates 2006).

Yet the likelihood of having a same-sex sexual *experience* may be two or three times higher (AVERT.ORG 2010b; Erens et al. 2003). Moreover, the number of people with same-sex *interests* (whether or not they have any experience) is even higher (Vrangalova and Savin-Williams 2010). One study of young adults aged 19–26 found that 10 percent of men and 25 percent of women reported having some homosexual experience, interest, or identity (Pedersen and Kristiansen 2008). Thus, the number of persons who see themselves as homosexual or bisexual is significantly smaller than the percentage of persons who have had, or think about, a same-sex sexual experience.

What Causes Sexual Orientation?

How do we come to have a specific sexual orientation? There has been a longstanding debate regarding choice versus biology, but scientists are coming to the conclusion that a complex set of biological factors (genetics and hormones), along with possible social factors shape who we are. In other words, sexual orientation is not really a choice (American Psychological Association 2009).

One study examined different sets of siblings—identical twins, fraternal twins, and adopted siblings—one of which was known to be gay or lesbian. The purpose of the study was to determine if a homosexual orientation was more likely to occur in the other sibling in one type of sibling pair over another. The researchers found that 52 percent of the male identical twins, and 48 percent of the female identical twins (who share genetic material) were both homosexual. In contrast, in only 11 percent of the adopted siblings were both homosexual. The likelihood of fraternal twins (who share only half of their genetic material) both being homosexual was between these two groups (22 percent and 16 percent for fraternal male and female twins, respectively) (Bailey and Pillard 1991; Bailey et al. 1993).

Other research also reinforces the conclusion that biology plays an important role in sexual orientation. For example, a study published in the *Proceedings of the National Academy of Sciences* found that gay men's brains respond differently from those of heterosexual males and are more like women's brains when exposed to chemicals derived from male and female sex hormones.

Attitudes Toward Gays and Lesbians   Attitudes towards lesbians, gays, and bisexuals differ around the world. Figure 7.2 illustrates the results of a 2007 Global Attitudes research survey conducted in a number of less developed countries about their attitudes towards homosexuality. As the results show, there is significant variation across countries, with Latin America being far more supportive that "homosexuality is a way of life that should be accepted by society" than countries in Asia, Africa, or the Middle East.

For example, in Malawi and Kenya, countries in Africa, homosexuality is punishable by up to 14 years in prison, and a gay Malawi couple in 2010 received the maximum penalty, as described in the box on page 200, "Our Global Community: Fourteen Years of Hard Labor." Their sentence was later overturned because of global pressure. Meanwhile, a lawmaker with the governing party in Uganda recently proposed executing gay people (Bearak 2010b; Gettleman 2010). And the *New York Times* recently reported that police broke up a same-sex wedding in Kenya; not only were they concerned about its illegality, but they were afraid that an angry mob would stone the couple to death (Gettleman 2010).

In the United States, many people still disapprove of homosexuality, but attitudes are changing and becoming more accepting. In 2009, according to a Gallup Poll, 49 percent of

Figure 7.2   Percent of Population that Believes "Homosexuality Is a Way of Life that Should Be Accepted by Society."

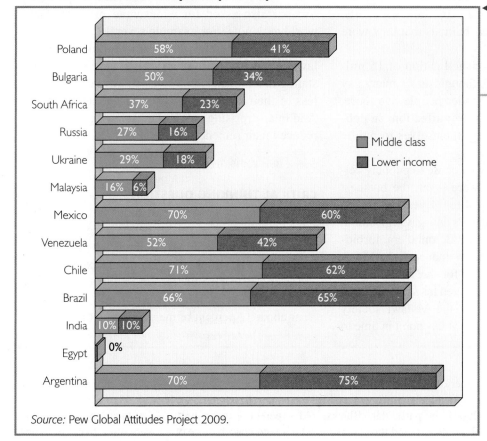

Latin America is more supportive of homosexuality than many other societies.

Source: Pew Global Attitudes Project 2009.

O U R

Global Community

Fourteen Years of Hard Labor

Malawi is one of at least 37 countries in Africa where same-sex relationships are illegal. But what is the penalty? As this feature box shows, the penalty for gays and lesbians who dare to show their love can be extremely harsh.

Steven and Tiwonge could be any gay couple in love, celebrating their engagement with a party at the hotel where Tiwonge worked. However, they are not just any gay couple. They live in Malawi, a country in Africa where homosexuality is against the law and considered detestable by most people.

Two days after a story of their engagement party hit the front page of the newspaper, they were arrested. "God calls homosexuality an abomination, which is greater than simple sin. These two must repent and ask God's forgiveness. Otherwise, they will surely go to hell," a minister said, clearly describing the sentiment of the people and the courts. Their crime was seen as so heinous that they were denied bail.

Malawi is an impoverished nation of 15 million in southern Africa. Although surely many gay men, lesbians, and transgender people live there, they dare not demonstrate their affections in public. To do so would subject themselves to public scorn, ridicule, and prison.

Steven and Tiwonge, who chose to publicly celebrate their relationship, were given the harshest penalty possible—sentenced to 14 years in prison with hard labor under Malawi's anti-gay legislation. The legislation dates from the Colonial era, forbidding "unnatural acts and gross indecency." "Maximum sentences are intended for the worst cases," said the Magistrate as he delivered his sentence. "We are sitting here to represent the Malawi society which I do not believe is ready at this point in time to

see its sons getting married to other sons or conducting engagement ceremonies." He continued, "I cannot imagine more aggravated sodomy than where the perpetrators go on to seek heroism without any remorse, in public with an [engagement] ceremony."

Crowds jeered and taunted the two men as they were driven from the courthouse to jail. People shouted, "You got what you deserve," and "Fourteen years is not enough, they should get fifty!"

But Steven and Tiwange deny that any heroics were intended; they say that they are simply in love, and were naïve about the repercussions. "I just wanted people to know that we were in love," said Tiwange. He said he considers himself a woman.

Their harsh sentence—14 years of hard labor—attracted the attention of human rights activists around the world. Activists mobilized an appeal effort but also asked for widespread protests. The world took note. For example several English lawmakers urged the Malawi government to review its laws to ensure that human rights were protected, stating that human rights apply to everyone regardless of their sexual orientation or gender identity. And in a surprising move, the Malawi government reduced their sentence.

Source: Bearak 2010; Tenthani 2010.

CRITICAL THINKING QUESTIONS

1. Where do such negative attitudes towards gays, lesbians, and transgender people originate, and do such hostile attitudes continue?
2. In what ways does silencing homosexuality and forcing it to go underground contribute to the HIV/AIDS infection of nearly 1 million people, or about 12 percent of the population of Malawi?

Americans believed homosexuality was "morally acceptable"—the first time that more people found it "morally acceptable" than "morally wrong," as shown in Figure 7.3 (Saad 2008, 2009). In particular, Blacks, older persons, those with less education, conservative Republicans, and those persons who attend church more often were more likely to believe

Figure 7.3 **Perceptions of the Morality of Homosexual Relations**

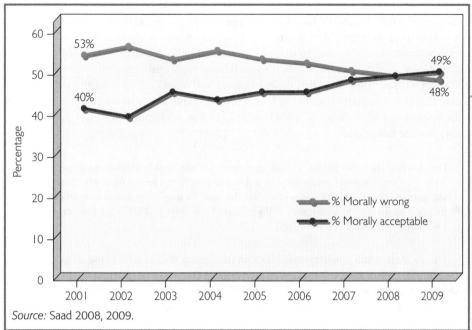

2009 was the first year in which perceptions of the morality of homosexuality shifted.

Source: Saad 2008, 2009.

that homosexuality was morally unacceptable or to hold other negative attitudes (Vincent et al. 2009).

Sexual Scripts

We assume that our sexual thoughts and behaviors are uniquely our own, but actually our sexual attitudes and behaviors are organized around **sexual scripts** that provide the norms or rules regarding sexual behavior. These scripts are socially constructed, and govern who, what, where, when, and why—*who* is an appropriate sexual partner, *what* is appropriate sexual behavior, *where* sexual activity should take place, *when* sexual behavior is appropriate, and *why* or under what conditions sexual activity should occur. For example, Americans believe that one's spouse is an appropriate sexual partner for a married person, but sex with a lover outside the marriage is not appropriate. Americans believe that sex should take place in private rather than out in the open in a public area. Americans also believe that sexual behavior is appropriate beyond simply the need to reproduce and can be enjoyed for the sake of its own pleasurable experience. Not all cultures would agree with these views.

We learn our sexual scripts from the culture in which we live, including our parents, our friends, and the mass media (Miracle et al. 2003). We combine these important messages with our personal feelings and desires and those of our partners. Together, these scripts become a blueprint and inform us what is appropriate and what is taboo (Michael et al. 1994).

Race, Ethnicity, Social Class, and Sex Sexual scripts differ by race and ethnicity, social class, and sex. For example, Whites are far more likely to engage in and receive oral sex (both cunnilingus and fellatio) than are Blacks or Hispanics. Sex, race, ethnicity, and social class interact in important ways to shape our sexual scripts. A study based on in-depth interviews with Mexican fathers who immigrated to the United States illustrates that the emphasis placed on girls' virginity is somewhat misunderstood (Gonzalez-Lopez 2004). The study found that virginity *per se* in a daughter's life was not a priority for any of the fathers born and raised in urban areas. These fathers have been exposed to less traditional values and experiences and are more likely to have attended college themselves or know someone who has. Instead of focusing on virginity for its own sake, they expressed an interest in helping their daughters postpone premarital sex so that they could finish their education without being exposed to disease, an unintended pregnancy, or exploitation by a suitor. Along with their wives, these fathers advocate more egalitarian values for a new generation of women. They hope that their daughters will attend college and go on to have careers. Therefore, virginity itself is no longer an important source of social capital, but will help them obtain other forms of social capital, such as education (Gonzalez-Lopez 2003, 2004). As one father said:

> I am worried about her having a child, that she would not be able to take care of herself and leave the family home. I would not like it. I would love her to have a formal life, that is, that she goes to school, and that she is studying. Because for me . . . my preoccupation is that she makes it all the way to a university and graduates from college. That is my preoccupation and I will always fight for it. (Gonzalez-Lopez 2004)

Unlike their urban counterparts, Mexican immigrant fathers who came from rural areas were more likely to expect their daughters to refrain from premarital sexual activity for the sake of traditional symbolism. Virginity remains highly valued, is seen as a badge of honor and integrity, and is a source of power in an exchange relationship for a potential high-status husband. As one father said:

> . . . tell me, who would not wish for his daughter to possess integrity while wearing white on her wedding day? Do you think that would not be my wish? (Gonzalez-Lopez 2004)

However, even among these fathers from rural regions in Mexico, the primary factor that shaped their views of virginity was fear—fear about pregnancy, of violence, of disease, and of a daughter's romantic involvement with men who were perceived as undesirable, such as gang members, drug dealers, or the chronically unemployed. The emphasis on virginity should not be oversimplified as elements of machismo that emphasize male dominance. Instead, these values are part of a set of social and cultural ideals that are intertwined with social class, race, ethnicity, and sex.

This intersection can also be seen vividly in Black relationships (Hill 2005). The study of intimate relationships among Blacks is often conducted in low-income communities with men and women who have been economically marginalized. Hill describes how low-income Black women "are especially vulnerable when it comes to hanging all their hopes for a better life on finding the right man" (Hill 2005, 101). She notes that the absence of the father and the lack of fatherly love in their lives, along with their own dismal economic prospects, heighten their search for a boyfriend or husband who will provide them with a home, family, and adult status. They use their sexuality to try to secure these dreams, but rarely are they successful. The low-income males in their neighborhoods see little appeal in an exclusive relationship, and in fact are rewarded by their peers for having sexual relationships with a large number of women.

Meanwhile, the pursuit of intimacy among middle-class Blacks is also shaped by class and gender dynamics, albeit different ones. The traditional norms of women "marrying up" hold little meaning in the Black community where women have made tremendous gains in education and occupational status relative to men. Significantly more Black women than men have college and graduate degrees, and more women work at jobs described as managerial/professional. In a culture where marrying "up" is valued for women, who is a bright, well-educated, professional Black woman to marry? Over half of Black women end up marrying "down," compared to only 30 percent of White women who marry men with less education and income (Hill 2005).

Components of the Male and Female Sexual Scripts   Traditionally, men have been allowed far more permissiveness in sexual behavior than have women, known as the **double standard**. Men are expected to be assertive in seeking sexual relationships, whereas women are expected to be more reticent and not appear too interested. What are some of the components of the *male* sexual script? Naturally, these components may be modified somewhat or significantly in a long-term loving relationship where a man is able to break free from cultural stereotypes and experience true intimacy. Nonetheless, here we will present the cultural images that comprise the male script—whether you personally abide by them or not, chances are they will be very familiar.

- *A man's looks are relatively unimportant, but his status is enhanced if he is with a beautiful woman.* A woman is a trophy, and the more attractive the trophy, the more of a man he is perceived as being.
- *The man always wants sex and is ready for it.* It doesn't matter much what else is going on or what his feelings are toward a potential partner. A man is like a machine and can be "turned on" immediately.
- *A man is in charge.* He is the initiator, the leader, and knows more about sex than his partner does. He would not feel comfortable asking his partner what she really likes.
- *All physical contact leads to sex.* Ideally any physical contact should lead to sexual intercourse. Touching, caressing, and kissing are not pleasurable ends in themselves.
- *A man cannot easily stop himself once he gets turned on.* Biologically, a man has great sexual needs, and he may not be able to stop once he is aroused, regardless of whether his partner asks him to stop.
- *Sex equals intercourse.* The focus of sex is on stimulating the penis. Hopefully this will be satisfactory to his partner, and if not, she is the one with a problem.
- *Sexual intercourse always leads to orgasm.* The purpose of intercourse is for the male to have an orgasm. If one does not occur, the act is incomplete or a failure. It is less important that a female has an orgasm.

What are some components of the *female* sexual script? Again, these may be modified when in an exclusive or long-term committed relationship because people can truly be themselves and move away from rigid scripts. Nonetheless, the components of the female sexual script permeate all aspects of society and illustrate critical ideas about her sexual role. We can see that it emphasizes feelings over sex.

- *Women should make themselves attractive to men to get their attention, but they should not make themselves too sexually attractive.* Women should dress "a certain way," so that they will gain the attention of men, but they also run the risk of gaining too much attention. It is up to women to sort out the appropriate type of dress, makeup, and demeanor to attract the right amount of male attention.
- *Women's genitals are mysterious.* Many girls and women know little about their bodies. They have been taught not to touch them or explore them, and many have never even used a mirror to look at them. What they do know comes from media images that tell them that their genitals have odor that must be controlled. Consequently, many women are very uncomfortable with their bodies.
- *Women should not know too much about sex or be too experienced.* Women walk a fine line today; they must not appear too uptight about sex, but they must not feel too

comfortable with it either. Women should not be too experienced because they run the risk of being labeled a slut or a whore.

- *Good girls do not plan in advance to have sex or initiate it.* To plan in advance (and take appropriate birth control precautions) may indicate that she is too experienced or likes sex too much. She cannot take the lead or she may risk her reputation.
- *Women should not talk about sex.* Many women cannot talk about sex because they are not expected to be very knowledgeable or to feel very comfortable with it. Women may feel more comfortable *having* sex than having a simple conversation about it with their partner.
- *Men should know how to please a woman.* Although he may be primarily focused on his penis and his own orgasm, a woman feels it is his job to know how to arouse her. He is supposed to know what she wants, even if she does not want to tell him (or does not know how to have an orgasm).
- *Sexual intercourse is supposed to lead to orgasm and other stimulation should be unnecessary.* Studies indicate that many women do not have an orgasm in sexual intercourse; they need additional oral or manual stimulation of the clitoris (Ross 2005; Sterk-Elifson 1994). Nonetheless, many women believe that there is something wrong with them if sexual intercourse by itself does not produce an orgasm and, therefore, even fake orgasm for their partner.

The Double Standard in Current Sexual Behavior Given the strong gendered sexual scripts in our society, it is not surprising that researchers continue to find significant differences between men and women in their sexual behavior (Fryar et al. 2007; Langer et al. 2004). Men think about sex more often than women (70 percent of men vs. 34 percent of women reported "thinking about sex every day"); are more likely to say that they enjoy sex "a great deal" (83 percent vs. 59 percent); are more likely to have visited a sex website (34 percent vs. 10 percent); and have more sexual partners. Furthermore, if there were no risks or limitations on sexual activity, men say about 13 partners would be an "ideal number," whereas women report five would be "ideal" (Fenigstein and Preston 2007).

The double standard illustrates important cultural ideas about women, men, and how they should relate to one another. It contributes to a number of problems, including a lack of knowledge about women's bodies and the mistaken idea that women have less important sexual needs. It also perpetuates the notion that male sexuality should be the normative baseline for eroticism and sexual activity.

Here's an example: Sexual intercourse is often viewed as the ultimate sexual act; indeed it is sometimes referred to as "having sex," as though other sexual activities are preliminaries or foreplay. This makes sense from a procreative standpoint since sexual intercourse is needed to make babies. However, most women need additional clitoral stimulation beyond that which is provided in sexual intercourse in order to reach orgasm (Richters et al. 2006). As shown in Table 7.4, a study based on a representative sample of over 19,000 Australians between the ages of 16 and 59 found that half of women did not have an orgasm in their most recent sexual encounter if they had vaginal intercourse only. However, if manual or oral stimulation was included, the odds of women having an orgasm increased significantly. In fact, orgasm was most likely if the sexual encounter did not contain intercourse at all!

The clitoris is, in many ways, the female counterpart of the penis. Both organs receive and transmit sexual sensations. However, in sexual intercourse, although the penis receives direct stimulation all around it, the clitoris may only receive indirect stimulation. And while the penis is directly involved in reproduction, the clitoris is unique in serving no known purpose but providing sexual pleasure. It is ironic that many cultures both past and present have viewed women as unresponsive to sexual stimulation, when it is women,

---

WHAT DO YOU THINK?

How did you learn your sexual script? Can you think of people or events that shaped your script? Have you seen any evidence of a double standard? Have you ever violated your sexual script? What were the consequences of that violation?

TABLE 7.4   Combinations of Sexual Practices Received by Women and Likelihood of Orgasm at Most Recent Heterosexual Encounter

Interestingly, sex that includes only vaginal intercourse leaves many women unsatisfied. So why do we define "sex" as sexual intercourse?

PRACTICE	PERCENT WHO HAD ORGASM
Vaginal intercourse only	50%
Intercourse + manual stimulation	71%
Intercourse + oral stimulation	73%
Intercourse + manual + oral stimulation	86%
Manual stimulation only	79%
Manual + oral stimulation	90%
Oral stimulation only	Numbers too small for reliable estimate.

Source: Adapted from Richters et al. 2006.

not men, who possess a sexual organ apparently devoted solely to providing pleasurable sensations. The double standard is powerful.

Sexually Transmitted Infections

Sexually transmitted infections (STIs) are hidden epidemics that have enormous health and economic consequences in the United States and throughout the world. STIs include chlamydia, genital human papillomavirus, herpes, trichomoniasis, gonorrhea, syphilis, pelvic inflammatory disease, and HIV/AIDS. In the United States alone, millions are infected, and an additional 19 million people become infected each year (Centers for Disease Control and Prevention 2009a). About one in four girls between the ages of 14 and 19 in the United States is infected with at least one of the most common sexually transmitted diseases.

Chlamydia is the most commonly *reported* infectious disease in the United States, with over 1.2 million diagnoses a year (Centers for Disease Control and Prevention 2010a). However, other STIs are likely far more prevalent such as genital human papillomavirus (HPV) (Centers for Disease Control and Prevention 2009j) or genital herpes (Centers for Disease Control and Prevention 2010b), but are often not reported and therefore accurate data are missing. Nonetheless, it is estimated that genital herpes is the most common STI in the United States, affecting one in five adolescents and adults.

Although people might be inclined to dismiss STIs as personal problems, they affect large numbers of people and are, indeed, *social problems*. Ideas about privacy, personal responsibility, and shame tend to exacerbate the misunderstanding of STIs, allowing them to spread at alarming rates and inhibiting effective treatment. STI rates tend to be higher among Blacks and Hispanics than among Whites. Some of this can be attributed to differences in risk behaviors (e.g., beginning sexual intercourse at an early age, multiple partners, unprotected intercourse, level of drug use). But rates also reflect social conditions like poverty, access to health care, and language barriers.

HIV and AIDS receive more media attention than any other STI because the disease is so deadly and because of the social and political implications surrounding its discovery and treatment (i.e., stigmatized as a "gay" disease). AIDS is caused by an HIV infection passed from one person to another through blood-to-blood, sexual contact, or through pregnancy, delivery, or breastfeeding. Most people with HIV will develop full-blown AIDS, although drug

Over 1 million Americans alive today have HIV or AIDS, and over half a million have died from the disease. Although HIV and AIDS are most common among men who have sex with other men, heterosexual couples are far from immune to the deadly disease, and should always practice safe sex.

treatments have allowed many people to live long and meaningful lives. HIV may not automatically be a death sentence any longer if you can get access to the expensive, but effective drug therapies that reduce the amount of virus in the body (Centers for Disease Control and Prevention 2010c).

More than 1.1 million persons are living with HIV/AIDS in the United States, about half with full-blown AIDS. Some people mistakenly believe it is no longer a problem; however, the CDC estimates there are 56,000 new cases of HIV each year (Centers for Disease Control and Prevention 2009e). Nearly three-quarters of new HIV/AIDS diagnoses were males, who are most likely to get HIV/AIDS through male-to-male sexual contact. Females, in contrast, are most likely to contract the disease through heterosexual contact, as shown in Figure 7.4.

As devastating as HIV/AIDS is in the United States, the picture here is dwarfed by that in other parts of the world, where 33.4 million people today are infected, and 25 million have already died (UNAIDS and World Health Organization 2009). Particularly hard hit is sub-Saharan Africa; with just over 10 percent of the world's population, it is home to more than 67 percent of persons with HIV (UNAIDS and World Health Organization 2009). Five percent of the adult population in sub-Saharan Africa is infected and the number is growing.

Unlike the United States, where most HIV/AIDS victims are men who have sex with other men, in sub-Saharan Africa heterosexual women and girls are most vulnerable. Power imbalances make it difficult for women to protect themselves from their husbands, who often have multiple sex partners. Moreover, young women and girls may become infected through "survival sex"—having sex with older men for a promise of food or shelter. Men seek out young girls because of the widespread myth that sex with a virgin can cure HIV. The United Nations insists that increasing the status of women and girls is a primary strategy for fighting HIV/AIDS throughout the world (UNAIDS and World Health Organization 2009).

Males in the United States are most likely to acquire HIV/AIDS through male-to-male sexual contact, whereas women most likely acquire the disease through heterosexual contact.

Figure 7.4 **Transmission Categories of Adults and Adolescents with HIV/AIDS Diagnosed During 2007**

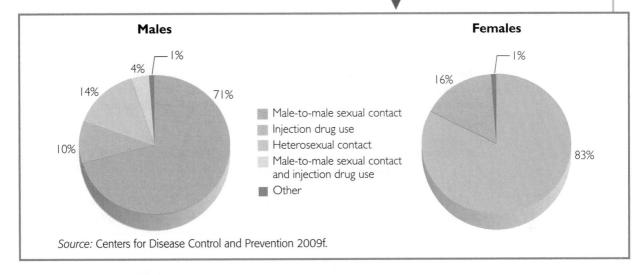

Source: Centers for Disease Control and Prevention 2009f.

Heterosexual Cohabitation

One hundred years ago we spoke little of **cohabitation**. Although some unmarrieds did live together, it was usually considered a temporary state until the couple could marry. Therefore others in the community usually treated them as a married couple (Cott 2002). Perhaps a minister was unavailable or the couple was waiting until family could arrive for the wedding.

However, as our country began to grow and urbanize, these reasons for cohabitation became much less relevant. Distances were not so vast and transportation improved. Consequently, cohabitation fell out of fashion in the early part of the twentieth century. People who lived together without being married were considered sinful, deviant, or were branded as uncouth.

This changed in the late 1960s and 1970s when people revolted against established norms and institutions (Popenoe 2008). This was a period of new freedoms for a large baby-boom youth cohort, "the sexual revolution", the availability of reliable birth control, and the "women's movement" with increasing numbers of women experiencing new freedoms in education and the workplace. People no longer felt the need to marry young, and the average age at first marriage jumped by several years. Divorce laws also changed, making it far easier for married couples to divorce because of "irreconcilable differences," further increasing the number of single adults. These macro-level changes led people to ask, why not just live together?

Today, with nearly 7 million U.S. households maintained by heterosexual cohabiting couples, virtually all of us knows someone who has, or is currently, cohabitating (U.S. Census Bureau 2009a). Unlike in the past, marriage may or may not be in the couple's future plans. Cohabitation can be an extension of dating (going "very steady") or it can be an alternative to marriage itself. However, in the United States, cohabitation lacks the formal and informal support of marriage (Sassler 2010; Seltzer 2004). People cohabit for many reasons including convenience, as a way to assess compatibility for marriage, economic considerations, or as an alternative to marriage. A primary challenge for cohabitations is that partners may have different motivations, their motivations may shift over time, or they may even disagree about whether or not they are in fact cohabiting (Seltzer 2004).

Who Cohabits?

Those who cohabit span all ages, races, and ethnic groups, and are found within all social classes. Over a third of adults say that they have cohabited, currently or in the past. Among persons aged 30–49, nearly half have cohabited (Pew Research Center 2007). In fact, today the majority of people who marry begin their union by cohabitating. Table 7.5 compares those who have cohabited to those who have not. You can see that men, Blacks, people with some college experience, and those who are not religious are more likely to have cohabited (Pew Research Center 2007).

Some people argue that cohabitation and marriage have become indistinguishable in many respects. This, however, is not quite the case (Pew Research Center 2007; Popenoe 2008). How do cohabitors differ from married couples? In comparison to married persons, cohabitors tend to be more politically liberal, have more nontraditional ideas about gender, and are more likely to share housework and breadwinning responsibilities than are married couples (Kreider and Elliott 2009; Seltzer 2004; U.S. Census Bureau 2009a). Compared to their married counterparts, cohabiting men and women:

- are considerably younger
- have less education and are significantly less likely to have graduated from college
- earn less, on average

TABLE 7.5 Characteristics of People Who Cohabit

Over one-third of adults have cohabited. Men, Blacks, those with some college experience, and those who are less religious are most likely to cohabit.

		YES, HAVE	NO, NEVER
All Adults		36%	64%
Sex	Men	39%	60%
	Female	33%	66%
Race/Ethnicity	White	34%	65%
	Black	46%	53%
	Hispanic	35%	65%
Education	College Graduate	34%	66%
	Some College	43%	56%
	High School or Less	34%	66%
Attend Church	Weekly or More	22%	77%
	Monthly or Less	45%	55%
	Seldom or Never	46%	53%
Religion	White Protestant	30%	69%
	Black Protestant	45%	55%
	Catholic	31%	69%
	Secular	56%	44%

Source: Pew Research Center 2007.

- are somewhat less likely to have children residing with them, although the differences are not large
- are nearly three times as likely to have a female who is six or more years older than the male partner, who earns more, and who is more highly educated
- are nearly twice as likely as married couples to be interracial, particularly with one Black and one White partner

Attitudes Toward Cohabitation   In a national survey, high school seniors were asked whether they agreed with the statement, "It is usually a good idea for a couple to live together before getting married in order to find out whether they really get along." Attitudes are considerably more favorable than a generation ago, with 65 percent of young men and 58 percent of young women agreeing that cohabitation is a good idea, compared to only 45 and 33 percent, respectively, in the late 1970s (The National Marriage Project 2009). Likewise, the General Social Survey, which is a large survey based on a nationally representative sample of adults, reports that 44 percent of adults agree or agree strongly with the statement, "Living together is an acceptable option."

But does "acceptable" mean that cohabitation is seen as a "good" thing? Not exactly (Pew Research Center 2007). Figure 7.5 shows the results of a study by the Pew Research Center, which conducts research studies on many political and social values. They found that overall, 10 percent of adults see cohabitation as a good thing for society, 43 percent believe that it makes no difference, and 44 percent feel that it is bad for society. Interestingly, Blacks, who are most likely to cohabit, are also more likely than other racial or ethnic groups to believe that cohabitation is a bad thing for society. As you might expect, older persons and those who attend church regularly are more likely than younger persons and those who attend church rarely to also believe that cohabitation is bad for society.

Nonetheless, cohabitation has become nearly institutionalized. It is now routine for surveys to ask about cohabitation and to include it as a separate category rather than lumping it in with "never married" or "unmarried."

Demographer Judith Seltzer (2004) notes three important demographic trends indicating that the meaning of cohabitation is changing. First, although the majority of marriages today begin by cohabitation, cohabiting unions are less likely to be a prelude to marriage now than they were in past decades. Second, cohabiting couples are more likely to be parents. One or both may have a child from a previous union or the couple may have a child together. Third, single women who become pregnant are nearly as likely to cohabit today as they are to marry the child's father.

Some people voice grave concern over these issues. They may believe that it is wrong for people to engage in sexual relationships outside of marriage, or they believe that living together is not a good way to start a healthy marriage. In particular, people voice concern that cohabitation is harmful for children (Popenoe 2008).

Are these accusations correct? The next section examines the research on cohabitation, marriage, and children.

Cohabitation and Marriage

Rachel and Adam, both just out of college and beginning their careers, have been together for over a year. While in college they each had their own apartments that they shared with roommates, but over time spent increasing number of days and nights at one another's place. Occasionally Rachel's roommate would complain, "Jeez, he's practically living here . . ." and she let Rachel know that she didn't care for a part-time third roommate, Adam, who wasn't paying rent. So, Rachel and Adam decided that once they were out of college and had more money of their own, they would get their own place. Why not, they asked? They would no longer be subject to the

Figure 7.5 Living Together Without Getting Married

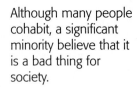

Although many people cohabit, a significant minority believe that it is a bad thing for society.

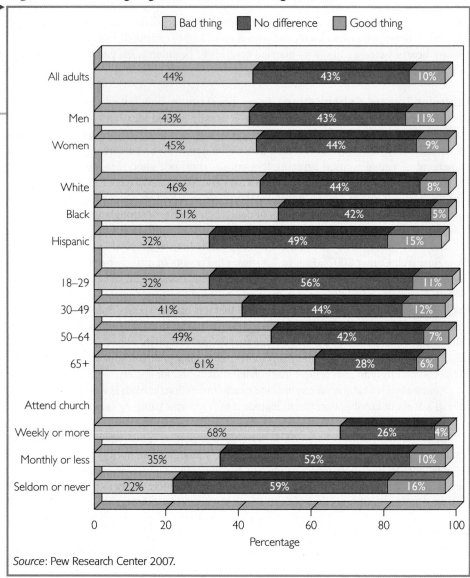

Source: Pew Research Center 2007.

complaints of other roommates, it made good financial sense, it would be easier, and it would be a good way to test if they were compatible for marriage, although they had no specific plans to marry.

Cohabitation might ease roommate problems, it might make good financial sense, and it might be easier, but is it a good test of marriage? The answer to that question is "probably not". First, cohabiting relationships generally do not last very long. About half of cohabiting relationships break up in less than a year, and less than 10 percent last 5 years or more (Seltzer 2004). However, this is highly correlated with age. Older cohabitors report significantly higher levels of relationship quality and stability than do younger cohabitors, although they are less likely to have plans to marry their partners according to a study of 966 cohabitors taken from throughout the United States (King and Scott 2005). Older cohabitors are more likely to view their relationship as an alternative to marriage, whereas younger cohabitors are more likely to view their relationship as a prelude to it.

Second, despite the logic that living together prior to marriage would give partners the opportunity to test out the relationship and therefore decrease their chances of divorce, in reality people who cohabit are actually *more* likely to have unhappy marriages and to divorce (Hohmann-Marriott 2006; Tach and Halpern-Meekin 2009). This is true for all racial groups, especially Whites, but less so among Blacks or Hispanics (Phillips and Sweeney 2005). Cohabitation after a divorce is also associated with reduced marital satisfaction in the remarriage and a higher rate of subsequent divorce (Xu et al. 2006). So why are people who cohabit with their partners prior to marriage more, not less, likely to eventually divorce?

There are two possible reasons for the positive relationship between cohabitation and divorce. The first may simply be a **selection effect**—that the type of person who cohabits may be the same type of person who would willingly end an unhappy marriage. For example, someone who values personal freedom may be both more likely to cohabit and more likely to divorce, or a person who is religious may be less likely to cohabit and less likely to divorce. It is not the case that cohabitation *causes* the divorce *per se*; rather, the relationship between cohabitation and divorce is **spurious**, meaning that both cohabitation and divorce are really caused by a third factor—in this case, the high value placed on personal freedom, or looser religious values.

The second reason may be causal in nature—perhaps there is something about the cohabitation experience that weakens relationships. For example, couples who cohabit are more likely to maintain financial independence and keep separate checking accounts (Eggebeen 2005; Landale 2002), possibly undermining a feeling of unity or creating tensions about differing contribution levels or how money is spent. It is possible that cohabiting couples are living more like singles, with less of an emphasis on permanence, and therefore are not really "testing" the relationship as if it were marriage. Consequently, when they do marry, the social expectations that come along with being a husband, wife, son-in-law, and daughter-in-law remain new and uncharted territory. Which, then, is true? Is the relationship between cohabitation and divorce only spurious, or does cohabitation really cause divorce? It is likely that both are operating to some degree, but selection effects seem to receive the most support (Tach and Halpern-Meekin 2009).

Why are there racial and ethnic differences in the relationship between cohabitation and divorce? Researchers Phillips and Sweeney (2005) speculate that it may be because Whites are more likely to characterize their relationship as a trial marriage, whereas for Blacks and Mexican Americans cohabitation is more likely to function as a substitute for marriage. They suggest, however, that more research is needed to truly understand the meanings of cohabitation across different racial and ethnic groups.

We do know that cohabiting relationships do not necessarily end easily and problem-free. For example, after dissolution, formerly cohabiting women's economic standing declines precipitously compared to men's. A substantial portion of women end up in poverty (Avellar and Smock 2005). This problem is particularly pronounced for Black and Hispanic women. This may be due to women having custody of children (33 percent of formerly cohabiting women have children living with them, compared to 3 percent of men) and women's lower earnings. Women cannot maintain the same standard of living as men after their relationship ends, and nearly one-third become impoverished (Avellar and Smock 2005).

Cohabitation and Children

About 40 percent of cohabiting couples have children under the age of 18 residing in the home, born to one or both partners (U.S. Census Bureau 2009a). Most often, the children are from one partner's previous union, but today many cohabiting couples have at least one child together. What effect does living in a cohabiting family have on children?

Whether cohabitation is good or bad for children largely depends on what alternatives exist. Possibilities include living with a single mother, living with a mother and her unmarried partner, living with a mother and her new spouse (stepfather), living with two cohabiting biological parents, or living with two married biological parents. Children can potentially benefit from living with a cohabiting partner when resources are shared with family members. For example, a study by sociologists Manning and Brown found that between 7 and 9 percent of children of cohabiting relationships faced high risk (defined as experiencing poverty, food insecurity, and housing insecurity) compared to only 2 percent of children in married biological or married stepparent families, but compared to 13 percent of children living with a single mother (Manning and Brown 2006). Likewise, Artis (2007) found that kindergarten-age children in cohabiting families average lower reading, math, and general knowledge skills than do similar children in married two-parent biological families, but many of the differences disappear when we account for differences in income, maternal depression, and parenting practices. What other differences do we see?

- Cohabiting biological fathers spend less time in activities with their children than do married fathers, although they tend to spend more time with and be more supportive of their children than do unmarried fathers who do not live with their children (even when still romantically involved with the children's mother).
- Male cohabiting partners spend less time in children's organized activities, such as school and community activities, than do married stepfathers or biological fathers.
- Children who live with their mother and her male cohabiting partner have poorer school performance and exhibit more behavioral problems than do children who live solely with a single mother, with a mother and stepfather, or with two biological parents.
- Cohabiting families spend their money differently than do married-parent families, divorced single-parent families, or never-married single-parent families. For example, compared to married families, cohabiting families spend a greater amount of money on alcohol and tobacco and a smaller amount of money on education.

Some of these differences may be due to the vagueness of the cohabiting partner's role in childrearing. For example, is a male cohabiting partner supposed to be a father-surrogate, a special adult male in the life of the child, or simply the mother's boyfriend? Few norms surround the role of a cohabiting partner, and families are largely left on their own to negotiate this social terrain.

It seems that, in general, children receive the most support and do the best when they are reared in households with two married biological parents (Amato 2005; DeLeire and Kalil 2005; Osborne et al. 2007). However, this is not the case for all families; some married-couple households are fraught with conflict. Moreover, not all families can be constructed with two married parents anyway. Rather than embrace only one type of family structure as "best" and others as "less than," let's examine the possible strengths and challenges of a variety of family forms. This information can then be used to create policies and programs support those in need.

WHAT DO YOU THINK?

Would you cohabit (or have you cohabited)? Why or why not? Do you think cohabitation is a good thing for society, makes no difference, or is bad for society? Can you trace the influences that shaped your attitudes (religion, peers, parents, etc.)?

Gay and Lesbian Intimate Relationships

A look at other countries reveals varied opinions and policies surrounding gay and lesbian intimate relationships. For example, in 2001 a law went into effect in the Netherlands that gave gays and lesbians the right to marry and adopt children. Dutch civil servants wed nearly 2,000 couples in the first 6 months after same-sex marriage was legalized. Even Cuba's Fidel Castro said that homosexuality was "a natural human tendency that simply must be respected" (Data Lounge 2004). The United States has been slower to warm up to same-sex relationships.

Gay and Lesbian Commitment and Cohabitation

Despite popular stereotypes that homosexuals, particularly gay men, have frequent sex with multiple partners, in reality many gays and lesbians lead quiet and unassuming lives in committed monogamous relationships and cohabit (Biblarz and Savci 2010; Peplau and Beals 2004; Weston 1991). Estimating the number of gay and lesbian couples is difficult; many fear identification because of discrimination or abuse (Kaiser Family Foundation 2001). With this caveat in mind, the American Psychological Association (2009) suggests that between 40 and 60 percent of gay men and between 45 and 80 percent of lesbians are currently involved in a committed relationship. In addition, between 18 and 28 percent of gay couples and 8 and 21 percent of lesbian couples have lived together 10 years or more (Kurdek 2004).

Many gay men, such as the couple here, live together happily in supportive and loving monogamous partnerships, despite the public image of swinging single bars and bathhouses.

Differences Between Homosexual and Heterosexual Couples

Do gay and lesbian couples differ significantly from heterosexual couples? To answer this question, the late family scholar Lawrence Kurdek (2006, 2007, 2009) collected data over time from gay, lesbian, and heterosexual married couples and compared many aspects of their relationships. He looked at such things as relationship quality, level of commitment, level of satisfaction with the relationship, social support from family and friends, conflict and its resolution, and equality. He controlled for important sociodemographic variables (e.g., age, months living together, or whether the couple had children) so that any findings could be attributed to sexual orientation rather than to other factors.

Kurdek found that there were very few differences between gay and lesbian couples and heterosexual couples, and most differences he did find were very small. For example, his research found that both gay and lesbian couples were more comfortable with closeness compared to their married counterparts, were more open with their partner, and were more autonomous in the relationship. Lesbians, in particular, reported greater levels of equality in their relationship and higher satisfaction. Gays and lesbians also reported receiving less support from family members than did the married couples, although lesbians reported greater support from friends. Overall, on three-quarters of the indicators there were no significant differences between gays and lesbians and heterosexual married couples. It would seem that heterosexual and homosexual couples are more alike than they are different.

Differences Between Gay and Lesbian Couples

Kurdek (2003) then assessed how gay and lesbian couples differ from one another. He found even fewer differences between gay and lesbian couples than he did when he compared them to married couples. There were virtually no differences between the two groups in the predictors of relationship quality, social support, and the likelihood of dissolution. The most significant results emerged in the relationship-related attitudinal questions, where there were differences in three of the eight variables: lesbian couples reported stronger liking,

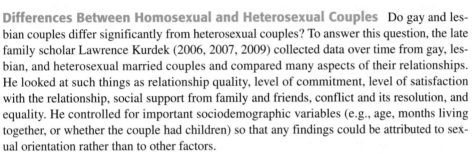

> ### WHAT DO YOU THINK?
>
> *In what ways do prejudice and discrimination against same-sex couples affect their relationships?*

trust, and equality than did gay couples. Again, it appears that differences among committed couples are generally minimal, whether same-sex or married heterosexual.

Social Policy and Family Resilience

One of the most compelling family policies on the table today is whether to allow same-sex couples to marry. Why do gays and lesbians want to be able to marry and what specific benefits would they receive under marriage that they do not otherwise have? What are the concerns surrounding same-sex marriage, and how might allowing same-sex couples to wed strengthen or weaken marriage overall? This next section will explore the policy controversy surrounding same-sex marriage.

Example: Civil Unions versus Same-Sex Marriage

Ask just about anyone, and they will tell you that marital status matters. There are at least 1,400 documented legal rights associated with marriage that are not granted to cohabiting couples. These vary from joint parenting and adoption, to immigration and residency for spouses, to veterans' discounts, to crime victims' recovery benefits. Some of these rights are given to members of **civil unions**, a public policy designed to extend some benefits to partners who are not legally married. But as shown in Table 7.6, civil unions do not provide the same degree of protection as marriage. For example, partners in civil unions cannot file joint federal tax returns.

Spousal privilege is common in U.S. legal, economic, and social institutions. As one heterosexual woman put it (Cruz 2004):

> Marriage supports families, and it also supports married people. It is not always easy being married, but on life's hardest days—if you're in the hospital, if you are in a funeral home, if you are in court—being married matters. It's even truer on some of the best days in life: the birth or adoption of a child, the purchase of your first home, the celebration of your vows. On good days and on bad days, I'm glad I'm wearing a wedding ring.

The Canadian Parliament voted to allow same-sex marriage legislation throughout the country by a vote of 155–138 in June 2005. Canada became the third country after Belgium and the Netherlands to allow gays and lesbians to marry.

The battle to give gays and lesbians the right to wed is far more controversial in the United States. Former President George W. Bush supported a constitutional amendment prohibiting same-sex marriage. To date (late 2010), there are only five states that allow same-sex couples to marry: Massachusetts, New Jersey, Connecticut, Iowa, and Vermont (National Conference of State Legislatures 2010). The United States is in a state of flux over this important social policy and human rights issue. Attitudes are shifting, and more people are agreeing that gays and lesbians should be granted the right to marry. Overall, more than half of U.S. adults now support civil unions, and 39 percent support same-sex marriage. As you can see in Table 7.7, women, Hispanics, young adults, and college graduates express the most support (Pew Research Center for the People and the Press 2009).

What is the history behind civil unions and same-sex marriage? Vermont led the country with the adoption of a civil union bill in 2000. By a vote of 79–68, Vermont moved the national debate to a new phase. Afterwards, the civil union law was challenged, but in 2002 the Vermont Supreme Court refused to repeal the law.

Advocates see same-sex marriage as a civil rights issue: Gays and lesbians should not be discriminated against and forbidding them to legally wed is an overt form of discrimination.

TABLE 7.6 Benefits of Marriage versus Civil Unions

Civil unions provide some benefits and support to couples, but they remain a far cry from marriage.

	MARRIED COUPLES	UNMARRIED COUPLES	CIVIL UNIONS
Portability of Rights	Union automatically recognized in all 50 states.	Can register as domestic partners in some states.	Usually only recognized in the state that approves them. But recently in New York, a civil union from Vermont was recognized in a wrongful-death suit.
Gifts and Property Transfers	May make unlimited transfers and gifts to each other.	Any gift or transfer worth more than $10,000 in a year requires filing a federal gift tax return.	Same as unmarried couples, larger gifts and transfers are subject to federal tax.
Income Tax Status	"Married filing jointly" generally works to the advantage of couples when one earns much more than the other, but creates a penalty when their incomes are similar.	Unmarried couples cannot file jointly, although an adult with custody of a child can file as "head of household."	A couple can file only state tax returns jointly, federal returns are filed individually.
Child or Spousal Support	Criminal penalties are imposed on spouses who abandon a child or a spouse.	Unmarried partners have no legal obligation to support their partners or partner's children.	In state where the union is granted, the courts can impose penalties on a partner who abandons a child or a spouse.
Medical Decisions	A spouse or family member may make decisions for an incompetent or disabled person unless contrary written instructions exist.	A health-care proxy, prepared before a problem occurs, can designate anyone, including a partner, to make decisions.	Partners in the state where the union was granted can make health decisions, but in other states that authority may not be recognized.
Immigration	U.S. citizens and legal permanent residents can sponsor their spouses and other immediate family members for immigration purposes.	Not allowed to sponsor a partner or other immediate family members.	Not allowed to sponsor a partner or other immediate family members.

Source: Graff 2004.

Because they generally do not see homosexuality as a choice, they equate restrictions on same-sex marriage with the restrictions on interracial marriage that were strictly enforced in some states and repealed only a generation ago. Advocates believe that allowing same-sex couples to marry does not harm or diminish heterosexual marriage or hurt society in any way. Pointing to the few countries that do allow gays and lesbians to wed, they note no ill effects. Love and public commitment should be encouraged, rather than squelched. Others proponents suggest that this is an issue that should be left up to individual states to decide.

Opponents' views vary, but some invoke religion, suggesting that same-sex marriage is immoral and is in violation of God's teaching. For example, the Catholic Church decries homosexual acts because they do not lead to procreation. Early American antisodomy laws discouraged all forms of nonprocreative sex (including heterosexual oral and anal sex).

TABLE 7.7 Percent Who Favor Same-Sex Marriage

	FAVOR
Total	39%
Men	34%
Women	43%
White	39%
Black	26%
Hispanic	45%
18–29	58%
30–49	38%
50–64	35%
65+	22%
College graduate+	49%
Some college	42%
High school or less	32%
Attend services. . .	
Weekly or more	22%
Monthly/yearly	47%
Seldom/never	54%

Source: Pew Research Center for the People and the Press 2009.

Islam has a similar view. Others simply suggest that marriage has *always* been defined as between a man and a woman and see no need to change it. In particular, concern is voiced that allowing gays and lesbians to wed elevates the status of their relationship to that of a heterosexual couple and legitimizes their right to have and raise children. Some opponents support civil unions or domestic partnerships for gays and lesbians, but draw the line at legal marriage.

The issue of whether to allow same-sex couples to legally marry is controversial. There are many opinions on the subject, steeped in deeply held values. Perhaps the most vexing question is: How would allowing same-sex couples who are in loving and devoted relationships to wed weaken the social institutions of marriage and family? The answer to that question has never been fully answered.

Conclusion

This chapter introduces several key concepts surrounding the development of intimacy, including mate selection, love, sexual orientation and sexuality, and cohabitation. People become intimate, form partnerships, or marry to improve their economic conditions, for sheer survival, to increase their social standing, or to please their parents and build family alliances. Many cultures do not necessarily equate love with marriage, and in fact may see love as dangerous to a good marital relationship. However, in the United States, love and intimacy are increasingly valued and are intertwined with marriage. Yet, changes are taking place in dating and mate selection in the United States. Today, dating is more informal, and unmarried couples engage in sexual relationships and often cohabit. However, same-sex marriage continues to be steeped in controversy, with wider support for civil unions.

Key Terms

Bisexual: An attraction to both males and females. One who engages in both heterosexual and homosexual relationships. (p. 197)

Civil unions: Public recognition of a relationship that is more restrictive than marriage and offers fewer rights and privileges. (p. 214)

Cohabitation: Unmarried partners living together. (p. 207)

Double standard: Men have been allowed far more permissiveness in sexual behavior than have women. (p. 203)

Dowry: The financial gift given to a woman's prospective in-laws by her parents. (p. 188)

Endogamy: Norms that encourage marriage between people of the same social category. (p. 191)

Exogamy: Norms that encourage marriage between people of different social categories. (p. 191)

Gay: Usually refers to homosexual men. (p. 198)

Heterogeneous relationships: Those in which the partners are significantly different from one another on some important characteristic. (p. 191)

Heterosexual: An attraction and preference for sexual relationships with members of the other sex (e.g., a man and a woman). (p. 198)

Homogeneous relationships: Those in which partners are similar to one another. (p. 191)

Homosexual: Refers to a preference for same-sex sexual and romantic relationships. (p. 198)

Lesbian: Homosexual woman. (p. 198)

Love: An enduring bond based on affection and emotion, including a sense of obligation toward one another. (p. 185)

Selection effect: People who engage in some behavior (e.g., cohabitation) are different from those who do not. (p. 211)

Sexual orientation: The sex that one is attracted to. (p. 197)

Sexual scripts: A social construction that provides the norms or rules regarding sexual behavior. (p. 201)

Spurious: An apparent relationship between two variables that is really caused by a third factor. (p. 211)

Resources on the Internet

Alternative to Marriage Project

www.unmarried.org

The Alternatives to Marriage Project (ATMP) is a national nonprofit organization advocating for equality and fairness for unmarried people, including people who choose not to marry, cannot marry, or live together without marriage. They provide support and information, fight discrimination on the basis of marital status, and educate the public and policymakers about relevant social and economic issues.

American Social Health Association

www.ashaSTD.org

The American Social Health Association (ASHA) is a nongovernmental agency recognized by the public, patients, providers, and policymakers for developing and delivering accurate, medically reliable information about STIs. It provides educational pamphlets, referrals, help groups and shares access to in-depth information about sexually transmitted diseases.

Division of STD Prevention

www.cdc.gov/STD

The Division of STD Prevention, at the Centers for Disease Control and Prevention, provides national leadership through research, policy development, and support of effective services to prevent sexually transmitted diseases (including HIV infection) and their complications such as enhanced HIV transmission, infertility, adverse outcomes of pregnancy, and reproductive tract cancer.

National Gay and Lesbian Task Force (NGLTF)

www.ngltf.org

The NGLTF is the national progressive organization working for the civil rights of gay, lesbian, bisexual, and transgender people, with the vision and commitment to building a powerful political movement. They work in advocacy, grassroots training, informing policy, organizing, and partnering with other organizations. One of their current issues of interest is same-sex marriage.

Marriage: A Personal Relationship and Social Institution

CHAPTER 8

CHAPTER OUTLINE

The Universality of Marriage 220

  ■ **EYE** *on the World:* Percentage of Women Aged 20–24 that Were Married/in Union Before the Age of 18 *222*

  ▨ **OUR** *Global Community:* Iraqi Marriages: "It's Safer to Marry a Cousin Than a Stranger" *224*

The Changing Nature of Marriage 226

  ▨ **SOCIAL** *Policies for Families:* Antimiscegenation Laws *229*

Benefits of Marriage 234

Marital Happiness, Satisfaction, and Success 238

The Marriage Movement 241

Communication 242

  ▨ **FAMILIES** *as Lived Experience:* Learning to Speak SAE *249*

Social Policy and Family Resilience 251

  Conclusion *252*

  Key Terms *252*

  Resources on the Internet *253*

CHAPTER PREVIEW

Marriage is something that is found around the world—from Greenland in the north to the southern reaches of Chile. It is both a deep personal relationship and a social institution. This chapter reveals similarities and contrasts in conceptions of marriage, explores the consequences of marriage for health and well-being, and describes current controversies and social policies surrounding marriage. In this chapter, you will learn:

■ Marriage is universal and the importance of such rituals as the wedding ceremony

■ Despite being universal, the structure of marriage and its expectations can be substantially different from one culture to another

■ Marriage is changing rapidly in both structure and meaning, including declining marriage rates, delayed marriage, racial and ethnic intermarriage, and same-sex marriage

■ Current attitudes and expectations about marriage, including nonmarital sex, dual jobs and dual career marriages, division of household labor, and nonmarital childbearing

■ The debate over whether marriage as an institution is declining or resilient

■ The benefits of marriage according to research, including physical and mental health, economic advantages, sexuality, social capital, and social support

■ The pros and cons of the effort to strengthen traditional marriage, including the marriage movement, covenant marriage, and statewide marriage initiatives

Does marriage matter? Sociologists and demographers Mary Elizabeth Hughes and Linda J. Waite tracked the marital history and health of nearly 9,000 women and men in their fifties and sixties using data from the longitudinal Health and Retirement Study. They examined four dimensions of health at mid-life: chronic conditions such as heart disease and diabetes, mobility limitations, self-rated health, and depressive symptoms. They found that when married people became single again—either by divorce or because of the death of a spouse—they suffered a decline in physical health from which they never fully recover. Divorced or widowed persons had worse health on all four dimensions, including 20 percent more chronic health conditions. One of their most striking findings concerned those who had never married. For decades scientists have speculated that those who have never married have poorer health than married people because of having fewer resources, lower incomes, and less emotional support. However, Hughes and Waite found that people who divorced or widowed actually had worse health problems than those who had been single their entire lives. In these formerly married individuals, it's as though the benefits of marriage never existed. But does marrying again improve their health? Their study shows that it seems to help only a little. Dimensions of health that develop slowly, such as chronic conditions and mobility limitations, continued to be a problem even among the remarried. People in second marriages had 12 percent more chronic health problems and 19 percent more mobility problems than those who were continuously married. In contrast, remarriage did seem to heal depression. But we know not all marriages are created equal. Some marriages offer love and social support, while others are fraught with tension and stress. Is it marriage itself, or a happy marriage, that has such positive effects? Social scientists and epidemiologists show that poor marital quality may erase many of the health advantages of marriage. For example, unhappily married couples are at higher risk for heart attacks or other cardiovascular problems. Why? Marital stress is associated with unhealthy behaviors (e.g., alcohol abuse), depression, hostility, and nonadherence to medical regimens, all risk factors for negative health events later on.

(Hughes and Waite 2009; Parker-Pope 2010; Partenheimer 2003).

What is it about marriage that can apparently keep people well—or make them sick? Why is marriage considered to be so important around the world? This chapter will explore some central tenets about marriage as both a social institution and a personal relationship. It will examine similarities and differences in marriage across cultures, show how marriage is changing, explore the consequences of marriage for the health and well-being of each partner, and describe the controversy surrounding the growing movement toward preserving and strengthening traditional marriage.

The Universality of Marriage

Marriage is recognized in some form worldwide. As a social institution there are rules, rights, and responsibilities surrounding marriage with significant state involvement. Only certain people qualify for marriage. For example, in the United States, same-sex couples cannot legally marry in most states. Children also cannot marry, and in many parts of the country, first cousins are prohibited from marrying as well. Governments often set a minimum legal age for marriage; in Yemen it is only 15 years, and nearly one-third of young women are married before turning 18 (Roudi-Fahimi 2010). The map on pages 222–223 compares the frequency of child marriages throughout the world.

Why is the government so concerned about something as seemingly private as marriage that it would establish laws to regulate it? Shouldn't you be able to marry who you want, when you want? The government is involved because as a social institution, marriage is seen as a stabilizing force (for example, by serving as the mechanism through which to socialize children) and the government sees this as its business. Yet, the rules, rights, and responsibilities surrounding marriage differ across social, historical, and cultural contexts. For example, interracial marriage was illegal in some states as recently as a few decades ago and it remains illegal in certain parts of the world today. Given these universals and distinctions, I define **marriage** here as a legally and socially recognized relationship that includes sexual, economic, and social rights and responsibilities between partners.

As a personal relationship, marriage is deeply meaningful to the individuals involved, although "meaningful" is conceptualized differently within social, historical, and cultural contexts. Feelings of love and sexual intensity may be the core experience in one culture, but these feelings may be totally irrelevant to marriage elsewhere. For example, about 85 percent of marriages in India are arranged (Griffith 2006). "I would never want to make such an important decision all by myself," reports a college-educated young woman, eager for her parents to choose her mate. Many Indians think Americans do not take marriage seriously enough. They believe that the U.S. concepts of dating and romance are irresponsible because when the fun ends, a divorce begin (Leeder 2004). In China, most parents no longer arrange their children's marriages; however, they continue to play a central role in marital relations. Marital quality is strongly influenced by the quality of the relationship with the extended family (Leeder 2004). Iraqi marriages may seem highly unusual to Americans, as shown in the box on pages 224–225, "Our Global Community: Iraqi Marriages: It's Safer to Marry a Cousin Than a Stranger." In a world that is dichotomized into kin and strangers, it is not surprising to hear an Iraqi woman say, "It is safer to marry a cousin than a stranger." A look at Iraq reveals that the norms surrounding marriage have a ripple effect on other aspects of the social structure.

What do Americans want from marriage? They want love, which they see as a relationship full of passion, romance, sexual energy, and tenderness. They want a spouse who is a best friend, who is compassionate, understanding, and nurturing. They expect marriage to ward off loneliness and to be an oasis from the hustle and stress of their daily lives. Couples who have children seek a connection to the past and a bridge to the future. Americans want a complex set of relationships and emotions from marriage, and they want it for their entire lives (Acevedo and Aron 2009; Branden 2008; Knobloch-Fedders and Knudson 2009; Sternberg and Sternberg 2008).

Yes, marriage may differ from place to place, but one universal feature of marriage is that its beginning is marked in some way by a ceremony. Yet, even the ceremonial procedures differ in important ways. In some cultures they are festive; in others they are somber. Many have a party or reception with food and drink. Some parties include both sexes; others are segregated. For example, an Islamic marriage ceremony is a private affair, and the lavish reception afterwards is strictly segregated by sex. Women dance with one another in their finest attire and celebrate the happy occasion together, whereas men are likewise celebrating in another room down the hall.

Wedding Ceremony

Think about the last wedding you attended. What color was the bride's dress? Without knowing anything about the specific couple or about the wedding itself, most people would venture a guess that the bride's dress was white. Other features about the wedding itself are probably also relatively routine. It most likely occurred in a church, there were people in attendance watching and afterwards there was a celebration of some sort with cake being served. If marriage is such a personal experience, why is the ceremony to mark it so routine?

Percentage of Women Aged 20–24 that Were Married/in Union Before the Age of 18

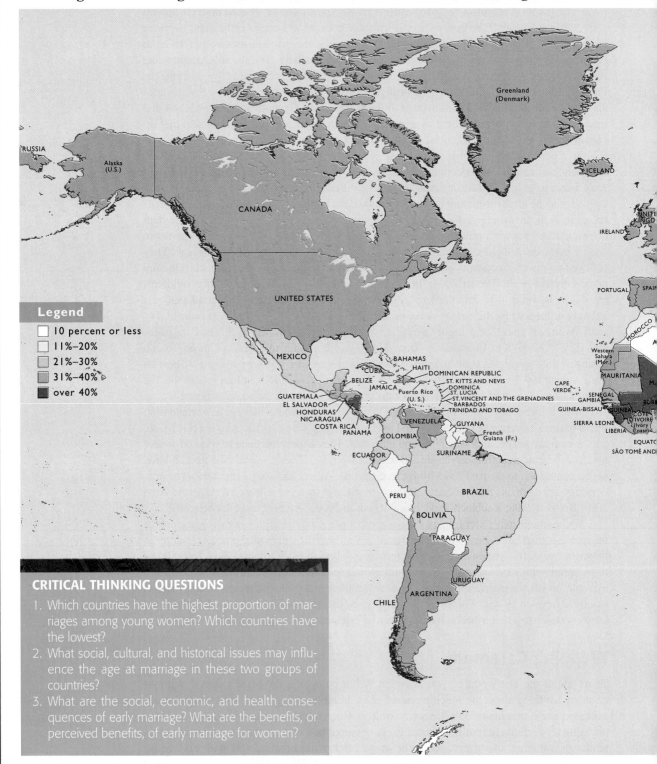

Legend

- ☐ 10 percent or less
- ☐ 11%–20%
- ☐ 21%–30%
- ☐ 31%–40%
- ■ over 40%

CRITICAL THINKING QUESTIONS

1. Which countries have the highest proportion of marriages among young women? Which countries have the lowest?

2. What social, cultural, and historical issues may influence the age at marriage in these two groups of countries?

3. What are the social, economic, and health consequences of early marriage? What are the benefits, or perceived benefits, of early marriage for women?

Source: United Nations Children's Fund 2009.

O U R
Global Community

Iraqi Marriages: "It's Safer to Marry a Cousin Than a Stranger"

Americans would shudder at the thought of an arranged marriage; not so in many parts of the world. An understanding of different mate selection processes can teach Americans a lot about a culture, as shown in the following Iraqi example.

Iqbal Muhammad does not recall her first glimpse of her future husband because they were both newborns at the time, but she remembers precisely when she knew he was the one. It was the afternoon her uncle walked over from his house next door and proposed that she marry his son Muhammad. "I was a little surprised, but I knew right away it was a wise choice," she said, recalling that afternoon nine years ago, when she and Muhammad were both 22. "It is safer to marry a cousin than a stranger."

Her reaction was typical in a country where nearly half of marriages are between first or second cousins, a statistic that is one of the most important and least understood differences between Iraq and the United States. The extraordinarily strong family bonds complicate virtually everything Americans have done and are trying to do in Iraq, from capturing Saddam Hussein to changing women's status to creating a liberal democracy.

"Americans just don't understand what a different world Iraq is because of these highly unusual cousin marriages," said anthropologist Robin Fox of Rutgers University. "Their world is divided into two groups: kin and strangers."

Iraqis frequently describe nepotism not as a civic problem but as a moral duty. Iqbal's uncle and father-in-law, Sheik Yousif Sayel, the patriarch in charge of the clan's farm explained, "In this country, whoever is in power will bring his relatives in from the village and give them important positions." He continued, while sitting in the garden surrounded by some of his 21 children and 83 grandchildren. "That is what Saddam did. . . ."

Saddam married a first cousin who grew up in the same house as he did, and he ordered most of his children to marry their cousins. Yousif said he never forced any of his children to marry anyone, but more than half of the ones to marry have wed cousins. The patriarch was often the one who first suggested the match, as he did with his son Muhammad nine years ago. "My father said that I was old enough to get married, and I agreed," Muhammad recalled. "He and my mother recommended Iqbal. I respected their wishes. It was my desire, too. We knew each other. It was much simpler to marry within the family."

A month later, after the wedding, Iqbal moved next door to the home of Yousif. Moving in with the in-laws might be an American bride's nightmare, but Iqbal said her toughest adjustment occurred five years later, when Yousif decided that she and Muhammad were ready to live by themselves in a new home he provided just behind his own. "I felt a little lonely at first when we moved into the house by ourselves," Iqbal said. Muhammad said he too felt lonely in the new house, and he expressed pity for American parents and children living thousands of miles from each other. "Families are supposed to be together," he said. "It's cruel to keep children and parents apart."

Yousif, who is 82, said he could not imagine how the elderly in the United States cope in their homes alone. "I could not bear to go a week without seeing my children," he said. Some of his daughters have married outsiders and moved into other patriarchal clans, but the rest of the children are never far away.

Muhammad and three other sons live on the farm with him. The other six sons have moved 15 miles away to Baghdad, but they come back often for meals. During the war, almost the whole clan took refuge at the farm, returning to the only place they had been able to trust through the worst of Saddam's rule.

Cousin marriage was once the norm throughout the world, but it became taboo in Europe after a long campaign by the Roman Catholic Church. The practice became rare in the West, especially after evidence emerged of genetic risks to offspring. However, it has persisted in some places, notably the Middle East, which is exceptional because of both the high prevalence and the restrictive form it takes. In other societies, a woman typically weds a cousin outside her social group, like a maternal cousin living in a clan led by a different patriarch. However, in Iraq, the ideal is for the woman to remain within the clan by marrying the son of her father's brother, as Iqbal did.

Source: Tierney 2003.

CRITICAL THINKING QUESTIONS

1. Why does Iraq prefer that the woman remain in the clan by marrying the son of her father's brother, rather than marrying a cousin in a different clan? In other words, is the purpose of cousin marriage simply to ensure that children find a suitable spouse or is there more involved in the choice than that?
2. How do American ideals of romance and love fit in with the Iraqi scheme? What would they think of our ideals?

What is the true meaning or purpose of the wedding ceremony?

Elaborate weddings have become an important symbol of achievement on the part of the couple and a statement to guests that the couple has "made it" (Otnes and Pleck 2003). Weddings are

big business, and families spend an average of $20,398 on this single event (The Wedding Report, Inc. 2010). Even families of modest means will spend large sums on an elaborate wedding with traditional rituals. Ingraham (1999) suggests that "the wedding industrial complex" is not unlike the "military industrial complex"—a huge multibillion dollar entity that is dominated by many intertwined social institutions. The cultural rituals associated with weddings involve exploitive practices: "Retailers are aware that the public regards the wedding gown as a sacred item and have sought to combine profit making with the redesign of the bridal store as a quasi-sacred space" (Otnes and Pleck 2003).

Although marriage has different social expectations historically and cross-culturally today, one universal feature of marriage is that its beginning is marked in some way by a publicly recorded ceremony.

The romantic aura of weddings leads us to believe that it is simply a party to celebrate a new marriage. However, weddings serve a much greater purpose than what is seen on the surface. Weddings codify dominant social arrangements including patriarchal norms. The custom of fathers walking their daughters down the aisle and "giving them away" says something about women's status, as does the custom of the bride throwing her garter to a pack of eager men or tossing her bouquet to see who the next "lucky" bride will be. These examples of patriarchy are so entrenched that we rarely notice them, but critical thinking requires that we examine the issues we take for granted to see what hidden values are represented.

Many nonwestern countries are amending their wedding ceremonies so that they will look more like those found in the West (Leeder 2004). Women may now wear white wedding dressing instead of their traditional clothing. Families, even poor ones, may feel obligated to spend a handsome sum on the party. As sociologist Elaine Leeder (2004) witnessed on her trip to Zambia:

> The brides were in fantastic white wedding dresses. They had long trains, flowers, tiaras, the
> whole works. Near them were the future husbands, some of them in suits, tuxedos, or the

WHAT DO YOU THINK?

Why do some women in nonwestern countries want to adopt Western traditions, such as wearing a white wedding dress? In what ways is this shift beneficial or problematic?

traditional African garb of their ethnic group. . ... I spoke with some people who were waiting and learned that this was the first of at least two ceremonies that each couple would have. This was the state-sanctioned event, which looked more western, with white gowns and government officials. Later the couple would return to their village, and another ceremony would take place, one that followed the traditions of the couple's ancestors. Sometimes, among those families that were more urbanized and educated—the "white weddings" would include some element of the traditional, tribal weddings. But for the most part, the state and the tribal ceremonies were very different events.

The Changing Nature of Marriage

We hear a lot that the importance of marriage is declining, or marriage is no longer as important as it once was (The National Marriage Project 2009). In what ways is marriage in the United States changing?

Marriage Rates

In the United States, most people want to marry and eventually do so. Although the practical necessity of marriage has declined as more women have become self-supporting and men have become more comfortable in the domestic arena, the symbolic importance of marriage has remained high. Marriage is now a sign of prestige rather than conformity, because it often comes *after* a certain level of attainment (after a job, a career, savings, or children) rather than before.

Among the roughly 240 million Americans aged 15 and over, 52 percent are currently married (U.S. Census Bureau 2010a). This represents a significant decline in recent years. As shown in Figure 8.1, Whites, Hispanics, and Asians have the highest percentages of married persons, whereas Blacks have the lowest; in 2009 only 33 percent of Blacks aged 15 and over were married.

Sometimes, these findings are misinterpreted to mean that Blacks do not value marriage; however, research shows us that this is not the case (Edin and Kefalas 2005; Seccombe 2011). Blacks have a strong desire to marry, but many do not marry because they have set high

Figure 8.1   Percent Married, 15 and Over, by Race/Ethnicity, 2009

Asian Americans are most likely to be married, and Blacks are least likely. Yet, this does not mean that Blacks value marriage less.

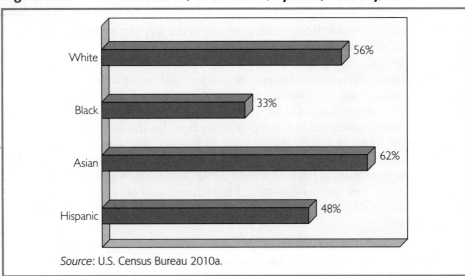

White 56%

Black 33%

Asian 62%

Hispanic 48%

Source: U.S. Census Bureau 2010a.

standards for marriage and they cannot meet the criteria they have established. They want stable employment, a secure home, and an expensive wedding. As one young man revealed: "I'd like to do things right [when it comes to marriage], instead of cutting corners and doing everything half-assed. I'd rather get engaged for two years, save money, get a house, and make sure the baby's got a bedroom [than get married right now]". His girlfriend added, "and I get a yard with grass, plus, I want a nice wedding" (Edin and Kefalas 2005). Given unstable employment and minimum-wage jobs, many of these goals are unattainable. In other words, macro-level factors such as economic conditions can shape our micro-level choices including whether we choose to marry.

A second macro-level reason for lower marriage rates among Blacks is a skewed sex ratio in some Black communities, which makes it difficult to find partners. For example, the rate of incarceration among Blacks is six times that of Whites (Sabol et al. 2009). Even though the number of Blacks in prison has declined by nearly 18,500 since 2000, Black men are 30 times more likely to be jailed than Black women, skewing the sex ratio for available mates.

A third reason for lower rates of marriage among Blacks is the higher school dropout rate among Black men (National Center for Education Statistics 2009). Black women are more likely than Black men to graduate from high school, go to college, graduate from college, and go on to graduate or professional school. This makes it more difficult for educated Black women to find peers to marry. Given all these reasons, perhaps it is not surprising that Black teenagers are significantly less likely to assume that they will marry than are Whites (Crissey 2005).

Figure 8.2 compares the marital status of men and women aged 15 and older between 1970 and 2009 (U.S. Census Bureau 2010a). The figure reveals that the percentage of both

Figure 8.2 **Marital Status of the U.S. Population 15 Years and Over by Sex: 1970 and 2009**

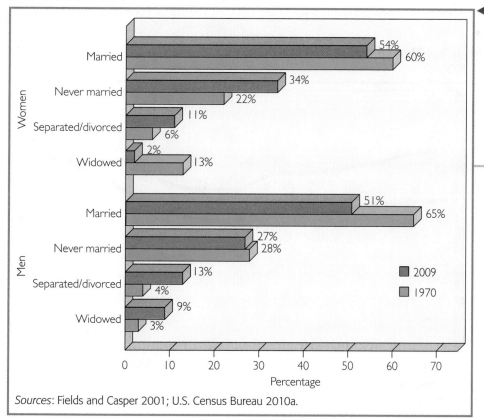

A snapshot in time reveals that fewer people today are married than in 1970. However, most of the never married and divorced will eventually marry (again).

Sources: Fields and Casper 2001; U.S. Census Bureau 2010a.

men and women who were currently married has declined, and the percentage that were separated or divorced has more than doubled. However, it is likely that most of these divorced and separated men and women will marry again. Americans are infatuated with marriage. Compared with many other developed nations Americans marry sooner, and if they divorce, remarry more quickly. The figure also shows us that the percentage of persons aged 15 and over who were widowed has changed very little since 1970. The small rise in the percentage of never-marrieds in the population, especially among men, is primarily due to postponing the age at which marriage occurs, rather than foregoing marriage altogether.

Delaying Marriage

Ask your grandparents at what age they married, and don't be surprised if it was by age 19 or 20. Men and women are now older when they marry. One psychiatrist wrote in 1953 that "a girl who hasn't a man in sight by the time she is 20 is not altogether wrong in feeling that she may never get married," and therefore young women set their sights on finding a husband early (Coontz 2007). Today, the average age for marriage has risen to 26 and 28 years for women and men respectively, increasing by several years in just a generation, as shown in Figure 8.3 (U.S. Census Bureau 2009c). The delay of marriage is occurring among all racial and ethnic groups. This is likely due to greater educational and economic opportunities, especially for women. As increasing numbers of women go to college, graduate school, or begin careers, they are more likely to postpone getting married and having children. It's not necessarily that marriage is less appealing; it's just more appealing to wait.

Racial and Ethnic Intermarriage

People have a tendency to partner with others who are like themselves, a concept described in Chapter 7 as homogeneous relationships. Racial and ethnic boundaries have been a key

Figure 8.3 **Median Age at First Marriage, Age 15 and Over, by Sex, 1890–2009**

The age at which both men and women marry hit an all-time low in 1950 since records have been kept.

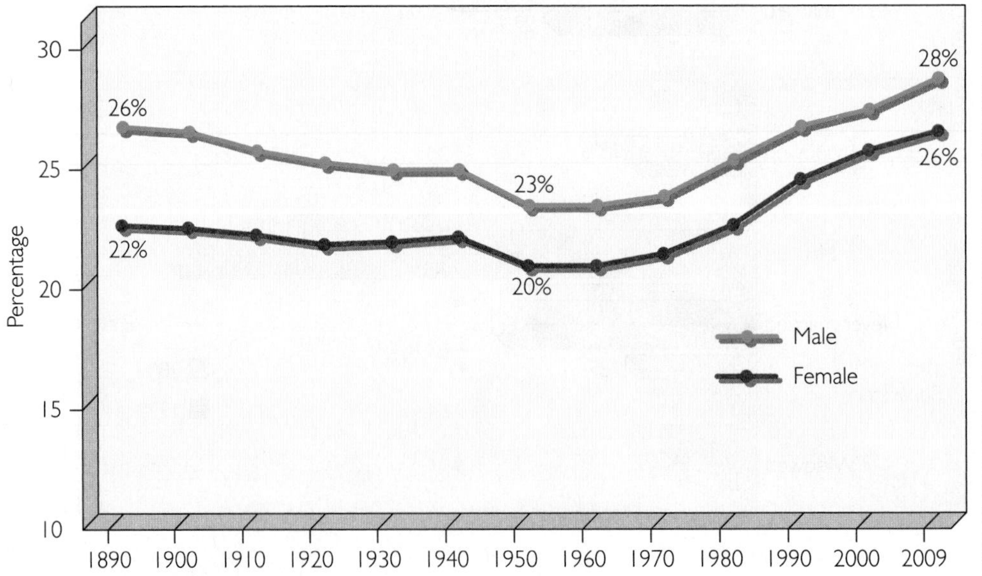

Source: U.S. Census Bureau 2009c.

element of homogeny because race and ethnicity are master statuses that bestow a wide variety of privileges and constraints upon groups of people. As we learned in Chapter 6, most social scientists believe that racial and ethnic groups represent social constructions, yet racial and ethnic categories have become the basis for stratification and inequality. Norms governing marriage can influence this stratification and inequality by either maintaining boundaries between groups (thereby perpetuating privileges and constraints) or by breaking down the boundaries and encouraging assimilation between groups.

Interracial marriage may have always been part of the U.S. landscape; however, it was considered a dark and sinister feature for much of history. As early as colonial America, children were born of unions between American Indians, Europeans, and Blacks; the early U.S. censuses included a category called *mulatto* to describe persons of multiple races. Nonetheless, laws banning marriage between Whites and other races, referred to as **antimiscegenation laws**, were common well into the twentieth century, as shown in the following box, "Social Policies for Families: Antimiscegenation Laws". The U.S. Supreme Court struck down such laws in 1967; however, Alabama was the last state to formally repeal its antimiscegenation law through a state constitutional amendment as late as 2000.

S O C I A L

Policies for Families

Antimiscegenation Laws

In the United States, states define laws governing marriage. Today marriages can be freely contracted between people of different races in all states, but laws banning marriage between Whites and other races—or antimiscegenation laws—were common from Colonial times into the twentieth century.

The first antimiscegenation law was passed in Maryland in 1661 and prohibited marriage between Blacks and Whites. By the end of the nineteenth century, most states had similar laws. In 1880, California prohibited the issuance of licenses for marriage between Whites and Negroes, mulattos, and Mongolians (a term mainly applied to Chinese at that time). In 1909, California added Japanese to its list of races forbidden from marrying Whites, and in 1945 the California gover-

Laws banned marriage between Whites and other races, referred to as antimiscegenation laws. The U.S. Supreme Court struck down these laws in 1967 in the case of Loving v. Virginia. Richard Loving and his wife, Mildred Jeter, are shown here. However, Alabama was the last state to formally repeal its antimiscegenation laws in 2000.

nor signed an expanded bill that prohibited marriage between Whites and Negroes, mulattos, Mongolians (which included Chinese and Japanese), and Malays.

The end of World War II led to a gradual erosion of antimiscegenation laws. Between 1946 and 1957, large numbers of foreign-born wives and children of U.S. military personnel were permitted to enter the United States under the GI Fiancees Act or War Brides Act of 1946. Although most of those admitted were from Europe, some foreign-born Japanese and Korean wives and children were also admitted after the occupation of Japan following World War II and the Korean War. The War Brides Act required extensive background checks and the prohibition of marriages with women who had worked as prostitutes or

(continued)

(continued)

bar hostesses. The rigorous requirements and checks were not relaxed until 1957.

Meanwhile, antimiscegenation laws were being challenged in the courts. In 1948 the California Supreme Court ruled the state's antimiscegenation law unconstitutional, Oregon repealed its law in 1951, and 13 other states followed suit over the next 16 years.

The most well-known and celebrated victory in the struggle against antimiscegenation laws was the 1967 U.S. Supreme Court ruling in the case of *Loving v. Virginia*. Richard Loving, a White man, married Mildred Jeter, a Black woman, in Washington, D.C. When the couple returned home to Virginia, they were arrested and convicted of violating Virginia's antimiscegenation law. The couple was sentenced to a year's imprisonment or a 25-year exile from Virginia. Rather than risk imprisonment, the couple moved to Washington, D.C., and sued the state of Virginia in 1963. The Virginia Supreme Court of Appeals upheld the law in 1966. The case was then appealed to the U.S. Supreme Court, which declared in 1967 that Virginia's antimiscegenation law and similar laws in 15 other states were unconstitutional. However, several states had bans on interracial marriage in their constitutions for many years, even though the laws were not enforceable. Alabama was the last state to repeal its antimiscegenation law through a state constitutional amendment in 2000.

The main purpose of the antimiscegenation laws was to prevent marriage between Whites and individuals considered non-White. Marriages between different non-White races generally were not prohibited. Thus, these laws were clearly meant to maintain the power and privilege of Whites and to uphold widely held beliefs in those days about racial separation, difference, and purity.

Sources: Adapted from Lee and Edmonston 2005; Sickels 1972.

CRITICAL THINKING QUESTIONS

1. How do you feel about interracial dating and marriage? Do you distinguish between groups (e.g., it is okay between some groups but not others)? How were your attitudes formed?
2. How would antimiscegenation laws maintain the power and privilege of Whites? Can you provide some examples?

Today, many people continue to oppose people of different racial or ethnic backgrounds marrying, as the book, *Navigating Interracial Borders: Black-White Couples and Their Social Worlds* by Erica Chito Childs reveals. Drawing on personal accounts, in-depth interviews, and focus group responses, Childs provides compelling evidence that sizable opposition still exists toward Black–White unions. Her analysis of media sources shows that popular films, Internet images, and pornography also continue to reinforce the idea that sexual relations between Blacks and Whites are deviant (Childs 2005).

Nonetheless, attitudes toward interracial and interethnic relationships have become more favorable in the past 30–40 years (Rosenfeld 2008). Seventy-nine percent of adults approve of Black–White marriages, up from only 48 percent in 1994, and 29 percent in 1972 (Carroll 2007; Gallup News Service 2007). Childs questions these data, however, because she frequently found that people who attest in surveys that they approve of interracial dating will also list various reasons why they and their families would not, should not, and could not marry someone of another race. Even many college students, who are heralded as more racially tolerant and open-minded, do not view interracial couples as acceptable when those partnerships move beyond the point of casual dating (Childs 2005).

As shown in Chapter 6, interracial marriage is increasing, but is still relatively rare. **Interethnic marriage** (with partners coming from different countries or different cultural, religious, or ethnic backgrounds) is more common than interracial marriage; however, it also challenges homogamy norms. These marriages require that partners be sensitive to cultural differences and the social and political forces that have created or perpetuated these differences. A study about intermarriages between Western women and Palestinian men found that patriarchy and east-west power relations affect the women. They face marginalization as women and as "foreigners" (Roer-Strier and Ben Ezra 2006). One man described the pressure he felt from his mother and sisters about his American wife, "My mother and sister told me, 'Poor you, you will eat only fast food . . . foreigners want to be the same as men . . . with an Arab you might be happier.' You know, it's like brainwashing. If you are not convinced in your ideas and you don't have confidence in your thinking it is very difficult" (Roer-Strier and Ben Ezra 2006).

Same-Sex Marriage

Another way that marriage is changing is the increased focus on same-sex marriage. As described in Chapter 7, this issue remains very controversial. Attitudes are in a state of flux on this important social policy and human rights issue. As of this writing (late 2010), same-sex marriage is legal in Massachusetts, New Jersey, Connecticut, Iowa, and Vermont (National Conference of State Legislatures 2010).

Attitudes Toward Marriage Itself

Most Americans, regardless of race, ethnicity, or income have very positive views toward marriage and rate a good marriage as one of the most important aspects of life (The National Marriage Project 2009; Taylor et al. 2007b). These views have not weakened over the past several decades. For example, the percentage of high school seniors who believe that "having a good marriage and family life is extremely important" has remained stable over the past 25 years, with 82 percent of girls and 70 percent of boys agreeing with this statement (The National Marriage Project 2009). This is shown in Figure 8.4. However, what constitutes a "good" marriage? Looking at historical patterns, personal definitions of a good marriage have evolved to keep up with social, economic, and technological changes.

During colonial America, marriage was largely an instrumental relationship, as shown in Chapter 3. Marriage was critical for personal and community survival. As such, the community played an important role in regulating marriage as an institution and regulating roles within the relationship. During the late nineteenth and early twentieth centuries, marriage

Figure 8.4   Percent of High School Seniors Who Said Having a Good Marriage and Family Life Is "Extremely Important," by Period, United States

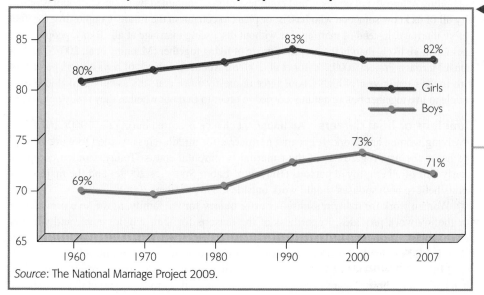

Girls are more likely than boys to place high value on a good marriage and family life. Their views have been relatively stable since 1960.

Source: The National Marriage Project 2009.

began to evolve into a more companionship model, where love and affection were expected dimensions of the relationship. The couple's privacy was highly valued, and the community's influence took a backseat (Burgess and Locke 1945). The Industrial Revolution moved work away from the home, and many middle-class men and women found themselves in separate spheres, doing different but complementary tasks for the family. The segregated roles deemed appropriate for men and women were a strong cultural norm, despite the fact that most poor and immigrant families needed the labor of both husband and wife to make ends meet.

The technological changes, world wars, and social problems of the early twentieth century contributed to increased privacy and a movement away from community involvement in marriage. New residential patterns included the growth of secluded suburbs, private automobiles made commutes more isolating, and the movement of women out of the labor market following the world wars and the Great Depression detached women from others in their communities.

Veroff, Douvan, and Kulka (1981) noted that beginning in the 1960s, people began to question the institution of marriage, raising concerns that it was too restrictive. Nonetheless, during this period people continued to marry, and there were only modest increases in the number of young people wanting to remain single (The National Marriage Project 2009; Thornton and Young-DeMarco 2001). It appears that people did not really want to discard marriage, but rather they wanted to mold it to the changing nature of the times so that it could be of better benefit. What are some of the changes occurring in U.S. culture since the 1960s? How have these changes affected marriage?

Nonmarital Sex   One way in which marriage is changing is that most people now believe that sexual relations between unmarried adults is not wrong. Marriage is no longer seen as the sole way to fulfill sexual needs. Sexual relations among unmarried persons had been strongly frowned upon in the past (although occurring with surprising frequency). Attitudes began to shift in the 1960s, ushering in major changes in the sexual freedoms given to unmarried persons. In 1970, half of survey respondents believed that premarital sex was always or almost always wrong, a figure that had dropped to only 38 percent by 2007 (Taylor et al. 2007b). Therefore, people no longer need to turn exclusively to marriage to fulfill their sexual needs. However, there are large differences in opinion by age. Persons in their twenties are more than twice as likely to approve of nonmarital sexual relations as people in their fifties (Carter 2006).

Attitudes About Cohabitation   With nearly 7 million U.S. households maintained by cohabiting heterosexual couples, and countless more maintained by same-sex couples, virtually all of us know someone who has, is, or plans to cohabit in the future. Couples live together before marriage, instead of marriage, or without discussing marriage at all. Today, people of all ages are more likely than in the past to approve of living together (Manning et al. 2007; The National Marriage Project 2009; Taylor et al. 2007b). About two-thirds of boys and 58 percent of girls in their senior year of high school agree or mostly agree that "it's usually a good idea for a couple to live together before getting married in order to find out whether they really get along."

Dual Jobs or Dual Careers   An important change occurred during the 1960s and 1970s involving women and work. It became normative for middle-class women to work outside the home for pay, regardless of their marital or parental status. Today, women comprise nearly half of all employed persons (Bureau of Labor Statistics 2009e) and the majority of adults believe both spouses should work outside the home (Paul 2006).

Women work for many reasons—as extra money for the family, as the sole provider, or for the joy work provides. Regardless of the reasons for their employment, and whether wives think of their employment as a "job" or a "career," their work has deeply shaped marriage, including the distribution of power, decision making, and household labor (Bianchi and Milkie 2010). Blacks and Mexican Americans are more supportive of working wives than are Whites; however, ironically, they are also more likely to suggest that the man should be the main breadwinner (Blee and Tickamyer 1995; Kamo and Cohen 1998).

Division of Household Labor   Today, more people are thinking about and questioning the division of household labor. Studies using several different methods to collect data show that the average married woman does two to three times more housework than the average married man (Bianchi and Milkie 2010; Bureau of Labor Statistics 2008). Even when both work full-time outside the home, wives' contributions to housework generally far exceed their husbands'. The term *second shift* refers to the idea that after women return home from work, they in essence have a second shift of work consisting of household labor and child care (Hochschild 1989). This is a carryover from earlier times in which housework was defined normatively as "women's work." Attitudes toward the division of household labor are in a state of flux, and changing norms require that behaviors be negotiated (and renegotiated) within the context of the relationship.

Nonmarital Childbearing   About 20 years ago, Murphy Brown, a television character who epitomized the single professional woman of the time, shocked viewers by choosing to have, and raise, a baby outside marriage. Then-U.S. Vice President Dan Quayle condemned the controversial television show, saying Murphy Brown was mocking the role of fathers and glorifying single motherhood. What do today's Americans think about single women having children?

Overall, most people do not think it is such a great idea, as shown in Figure 8.5. Although people are somewhat more tolerant of having children outside of marriage than they were a generation ago, 44 percent of adults still believe that it is always or almost always wrong (Taylor et al. 2007b). Interestingly, there is little variation in attitudes except by age, with older adults being far more opposed to having children outside of marriage than are younger people.

It appears that attitudes about marriage—its purpose, its structure, and what makes a marriage "good"—have changed significantly over the past several decades. People are more accepting of nonmarital sex and nonmarital childbearing. They are increasingly likely to cohabit with a partner. Couples hold high expectations that the relationship should meet their needs for companionship and intimacy. Traditional gender expectations regarding employment and household labor are being redefined and are subject to negotiation. Views about marriage are less rigid than in the past, and people are marrying at later ages, but overall the literature shows that Americans remain enthusiastic about marriage.

Marital Decline versus Marital Resilience Perspectives

Given all of these changes, is marriage in the United States in a state of decline or is it strong and viable? We all seem to debate the state of marriage today. According to the **marital decline perspective**, the institution of marriage is increasingly being threatened by hedonistic pursuits of personal happiness at the expense of a long-term commitment. People are no longer willing to remain married through "better or worse" because the U.S. culture has become increasingly individualistic. Proponents of this perspective argue that the decline in marriage rates causes a host of other social problems from poverty to the erosion of neighborhoods. Their goal is to create a culture that is more supportive of marriage and discourages threats to marriage, such as cohabitation and divorce (The National Marriage Project 2009).

In contrast, others reject the idea that U.S. culture has become more individualistic, resulting in a decline of marriage and a host of other social ills. The **marital resilience perspective** notes that many marriages in the past were also highly troubled or unfulfilling, but were held together because of stigma, economics, or fear. Today, women and men can more easily end a poor marriage. Those supporting this perspective say divorce is not necessarily cause for alarm because it gives adults another

> ### WHAT DO YOU THINK?
>
> *Think back to your parents' generation, or better yet, your grandparents' generation. What were some of the norms or expectations surrounding their marriage? How have these changed with respect to your own ideas about marriage? Can you identify why your ideals are different from those in previous generations? What structural factors or conditions may account for these differences?*

Figure 8.5 **Attitudes Toward Unwed Women Having Children**

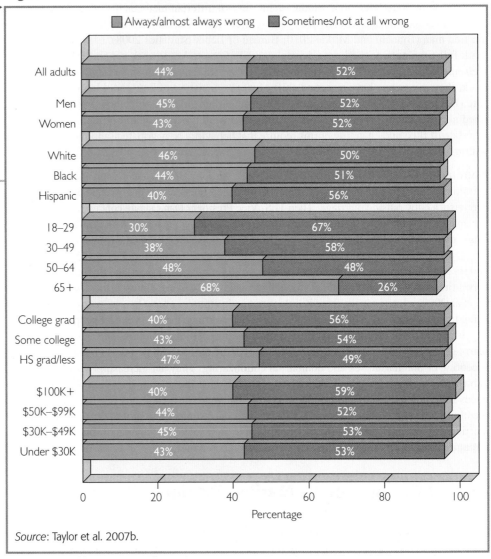

Although many attitudes towards marriage have become more permissive, many people still have a dim view of having children outside of marriage.

Source: Taylor et al. 2007b.

chance at happiness and provides the opportunity to end a dysfunctional home life for children. They suggest that the real threats to marriage and families are social problems such as poverty, poor schools, discrimination, or a lack of social services that families need to remain strong and healthy. They conclude that family disorganization is a result of these types of problems, not necessarily the cause of them (Fincham and Beach 2010).

Benefits of Marriage

Regardless of your perspective—marital decline or marital resilience—Americans are ardent believers in marriage. Most Americans marry—less than 4 percent of persons aged 75 and over have never married, a figure that has remained relatively constant over time (U.S. Census Bureau 2010a). If marriage ends in divorce, most remarry again (sometimes several times). Why do we find marriage so intriguing?

Researchers talk about a **marriage premium**, meaning that married people are happier, healthier, and financially better off than those who are not married, including cohabitors (DeNavas-Walt et al. 2010; Fagan 2009; Manzoli et al. 2007; Waite and Gallagher 2000). But does marriage *cause* people to be happier, healthier, and wealthier? Or are people who are happier, healthier, and wealthier more likely to marry in the first place, known as a selection effect? In truth, marriage is both a cause and a consequence of these advantages.

Psychological Well-Being and Happiness

Married people are happier than those who are single, cohabiting, separated, or divorced (Bierman et al. 2006; Taylor et al. 2006). One study found that 43 percent of married persons reported that they were "very happy" with life in general, compared to only 24 percent of unmarried persons who felt that way (Taylor et al. 2006). This has been a consistent research finding over many years, for men as well as women, for young and old, although the gap in happiness is not quite as great among the elderly. At the other end of the spectrum, married people are least likely to say they are unhappy with their lives. Stack and Eshleman (1998) examined the relationship between personal happiness and marital status in 17 developed nations that had "diverse social and institutional frameworks." They concluded:

> Married persons have a significantly higher level of happiness than persons who are not married. This effect was independent of financial and health-oriented protections offered by marriage and was also independent of other control variables including ones for sociodemographic conditions and national character.

Married persons score higher on other measures of psychological well-being, are less likely to be depressed, have higher self-esteem, and feel more in control of their lives (Fagan 2009; Frech and Williams 2007), although differences may be minimal among the married and long-term cohabitors (Willetts 2006). The relationship between marriage and psychological well-being seems to be particularly strong for men (Waite and Gallagher 2000). As Whitehead and Popenoe (2004) explain:

> One key reason is wives. Married women provide emotional support and physical care to their spouses. They monitor their husband's health habits, encourage them to seek medical treatment, when necessary, and often find a doctor or health professional to provide such treatment. In addition to TLC, wives commonly provide SDRs (stable domestic routines). Along with better health practices, stable routines help to reduce job absenteeism, quit rates and sick days and thus to strengthen men's workforce attachment. Moreover, since the majority of married women today work outside the home, including over half of wives with young children, men gain financial advantages from their wives' workforce participation. Wage-earning wives reduce pressure on husbands to be the sole breadwinner while, at the same time, increasing family income and assets, the traditional measure of a husband's contribution to the family. (p. 8)

While some of the difference in happiness between married and unmarried persons may be due to a selection effect—happy people are more likely to marry in the first place—researchers are quick to point out that marriage offers a number of protections, such as social support and companionship, that can significantly boost psychological well-being.

Physical Health

On average, married persons are healthier than unmarried persons, as shown in the opening vignette (Hughes and Waite 2009; National Center for Health Statistics 2009; Schoenborn and Adams 2010). Married persons live longer and are less likely to die from the leading causes of death, including heart disease, many types of cancers, or stroke. Married persons also engage in less risky behaviors, resulting in fewer car accidents, and lower murder and suicide rates. They drink less alcohol and are therefore less likely to suffer alcohol-related complications, such as cirrhosis of the liver. Married persons have better health habits than their unmarried counterparts, they are more likely to have health insurance, and they receive more regular health care.

However, as the opening vignette also illustrated, it is important to distinguish between types of marriages when examining health (and possibly other) data. It is not simply marriage that improves health outcomes, but rather, a *good* marriage that entails love, support, and personal fulfillment (Parker-Pope 2010).

We have shown that marriage is correlated with better health for both men and women. However, is marriage the *cause* of better health? Possibly, yet there is a competing explanation as well; it could simply be that healthy people are more likely to marry, another selection effect. Perhaps healthy people are more likely to come into contact with prospective marriage partners, have more stable employment, or have higher self-esteem—all considerable pluses when attracting a spouse. Which explanation makes the most sense? The answer is, again, that both are likely operating: Although healthy people are more likely to marry, there is also something about marriage itself that directly contributes to health and well-being. The health advantages associated with marriage are clear; and, again, husbands seem to derive greater benefit than wives do. Mortality rates for unmarried men are twice those for married men, whereas the difference between married and unmarried women is considerably smaller.

Economic Advantages

People who are married earn more money and accumulate greater assets than those who are single or divorced, regardless of race or ethnic background (DeNavas-Walt et al. 2010; Thomas and Sawhill 2002). One study found that among elders on the verge of retirement, those who were not continuously married had 63 percent less wealth than those who had remained married (Wilmoth and Koso 2002). Another study reported that even after controlling for age, education, job characteristics, work experience, and other background factors, married men averaged over 12 percent more per hour than single men. Married men whose wives stay at home earn over 30 percent more than their single counterparts (Chun and Lee 2001).

Women receive financial gains from marriage as well (DeNavas-Walt et al. 2010; Lerman 2002). Although married women do not earn more than their single counterparts, they benefit indirectly because of their husband's income and greater earning power. Married women are able to pool their resources with a spouse; they have greater household income and assets; they have increased access to health insurance and retirement benefits; and are more likely to receive financial assistance (e.g., gifts or loans) from extended family members.

Once again, we must closely examine the meaning behind the correlation between marital status and economic well-being. Is it fair to say that marriage is the *cause* of the higher income and assets among the married? Or is it possible that those with higher income-earning potential are more likely to marry in the first place? After all, researchers have found that men with poor economic prospects are often not deemed to be good marriage partners (Edin and Kafalas 2005; Wilson 1987, 1996). Again, it is likely that the relationship is reciprocal and runs in both directions, as is the case with health and psychological well-being. Stronger economic conditions are both a cause and a consequence of marriage.

Marriage and Sex

Despite stereotypes that suggest that married sex is an oxymoron, married people are sexually active and report enjoying sex more than their cohabiting counterparts, according to a comprehensive study of adults (Waite and Joyner 2001). In one study of men and women aged 45–49 who have a regular sex partner (presumably a spouse, but possibly not), 65 percent of men and 61 percent of women reported that their sex lives were extremely or very physically pleasurable and 69 percent of men and 62 percent of women reported that their sex lives were extremely or very emotionally satisfying, with little variation across racial or ethnic groups (AARP 2005). Even many older adults—those in their sixties, seventies, and beyond—enjoy relatively active sexual lives (DeLamater and Sill 2010; Lindau et al. 2007).

Social Capital and Social Support

Social capital refers to the goods and services that are by-products of social relationships among people. It includes the connections, the social support, the information, and other benefits that are produced through relationships among people. Marriage is an important source of social capital because it creates obligations and social bonds that can provide support in times of need between spouses; between parents and children; between the married couple and their extended families; and between the couple and the community (Whitehead 2004). These obligations are a part of the social norm of "being married." Consequently, marriage generates higher levels of help, support, and care than other kinds of personal relationships. For example, although single parents receive significant family support, they generally do not receive sustained help and support from the absent biological parent's side of the family. Close to 17 percent of married parents reported support from the father's kin, whereas just 2 percent of single mothers and no unwed mothers received financial support from relatives of the father (Hao 1996).

With all these benefits, it could lead us to believe that all marriages must be happy and successful. Unfortunately, this is not always the case.

Does Marriage Benefit Everyone Equally?

In her classic study of marriage, Jessie Bernard (1972) claimed that there were two versions of marriage: "his" and "hers." She argued that men and women experience marriage differently, and men accrue greater benefits than do women. But she wrote 40 years ago—hasn't a lot changed since then?

Not really. People still write about "his" and "her" marriages (Waller and McLanahan 2005) because men continue to benefit from women in some interesting ways. For example, married men are happier, suffer from less depression, and experience less distress than do married women. Moreover, there is a growing gap in married men's and women's happiness. In the 1970s, women reported being happier than men, but today this has reversed (Leonhardt 2007; Parker 2009; Stevenson and Wolfers 2007).

What might account for this change? The most likely explanation is that women now have a much longer "to-do" list than they once did, and they often feel rushed and stressed (Parker 2009). Women are expected to take care of the children, pick them up after school, and be actively involved in the P.T.A., all the while managing an exciting career. As one woman explained it, her mother's goals in life "were to have a beautiful garden, a well-kept house, and well-adjusted children who did well in school. I sort of want all those things too, but I also want to have a great career and have an impact on the broader world" (Leonhardt 2007). Although most women are pleased to have a wide variety of options before them, many find that juggling all these competing demands actually detracts from, rather than enhances, their happiness (Parker 2009).

Likewise, the benefits associated with marriage can also be quite different across social classes and racial and ethnic

WHAT DO YOU THINK?

Which best explains each of the specific benefits of marriage: the marriage premium or the selection effect? Can you think of any examples where marriage premiums or selection effects might operate differently among racial and ethnic groups? Do they operate differently across social classes?

groups. For example, the economic benefits that married couples accrue are largely dependent on wages paid, and most minority groups earn significantly less than Whites. For example, in 2009, the median income of White (non-Hispanic) households was about $56,000 and $66,000 for Asians. This is much higher than the median household income of $34,000 for Blacks and $38,000 for Hispanics (DeNavas-Walt et al. 2010).

Marital Happiness, Satisfaction, and Success

Researchers have attempted to study marital quality since the pioneering work of Burgess and colleagues in the mid-1940s. The undertaking is difficult because there are a multitude of ways to define happiness, satisfaction, and success, and little agreement on the best way to do so. For example, does the absence of divorce imply marital success? Can a single-item question such as "How satisfied with your marriage are you?" really measure something as complex as marital quality or satisfaction with marriage? Do "happy," "satisfying," and "successful" marriages always occur together or, for example, can a marriage be unhappy, but successful—meaning the couple did not divorce? Moreover, can a cross-sectional study, which collects data at only one point in time, really measure the deep and profound feelings associated with the concepts of marital happiness, satisfaction, and success? Longitudinal studies that follow couples over time are much preferred over cross-sectional ones. Nonetheless, despite these real caveats with measurement or data collection, researchers note that about 64 percent of men and 60 percent of women report that they are "very happy" with their marriage (Popenoe 2007). Several variables are associated with happier, more satisfying, and successful marriages.

The Quality and Stability of the Couple's Parents' Marriages

Individuals whose parents have happy and stable marriages are more likely to have happier and long-lasting marriages themselves (Teachman 2002, 2004). Adult children model their own parents' behavior, both positive and negative. Parents who have strong communication skills or who value commitment in their relationship model these types of behaviors for their own children. Conversely, parents who have a conflict-ridden relationship or who divorce place their children at greater risk for an unhappy marriage in the future.

Shared Values, Goals, and Characteristics

Do "opposites attract" or do "birds of a feather flock together"? In other words, do people tend to marry others who are very different from—or similar—to themselves?

Couples with very different backgrounds face more challenging odds of achieving a happy marriage. These relationships may violate social norms and carry a degree of stigma in some circles. The couple may be perpetually identified as "that old man who married a trophy wife" or "the welfare mom who snagged that rich guy" or "that White lady who married a Black guy." Heterogamous relationships also are less likely to have a shared set of values, history, or culture corresponding to their social backgrounds and characteristics. The White woman who married a Black man probably has little real conception of the ways that race and racism have touched her husband's life, and despite her love and good intentions, will always remain somewhat of an outsider. Many heterogamous marriages overcome these challenges, but overall, couples with more similar backgrounds and characteristics have a greater chance of success. Nonetheless, heterogamous marriages are becoming more common,

Figure 8.6   Brides, Grooms Often Have Different Faiths

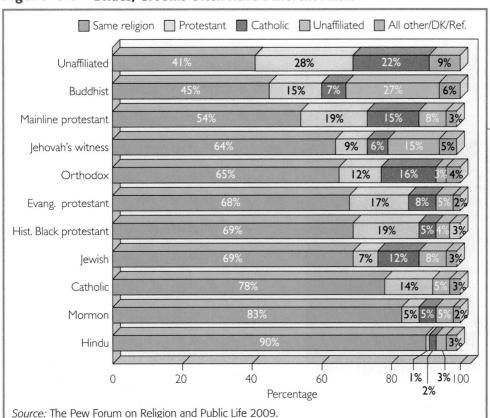

Certain religious groups, including Catholic, Mormon, and Hindu, rarely marry outside their faith.

Legend: Same religion | Protestant | Catholic | Unaffiliated | All other/DK/Ref.

Group	Same religion	Protestant	Catholic	Unaffiliated	All other/DK/Ref.
Unaffiliated	41%	28%	22%	9%	
Buddhist	45%	15%	7%	27%	6%
Mainline protestant	54%	19%	15%	8%	3%
Jehovah's witness	64%	9%	6%	15%	5%
Orthodox	65%	12%	16%	3%	4%
Evang. protestant	68%	17%	8%	5%	2%
Hist. Black protestant	69%	19%	5%	4%	3%
Jewish	69%	7%	12%	8%	3%
Catholic	78%	14%	5%	3%	
Mormon	83%	5%	5%	5%	2%
Hindu	90%		1%	2%	3%

Percentage

Source: The Pew Forum on Religion and Public Life 2009.

including people of different religious faiths. Buddhists and the religiously unaffiliated are the most likely to have a spouse or partner with a different religious background, while Mormons and Hindus are the least likely to marry or live with a partner outside their faith, as shown in Figure 8.6 (The Pew Forum on Religion and Public Life 2009).

Similar personality traits are important as well (Partenheimer 2005). One study found people are attracted to mates with similar values. But once in a committed relationship and dealing with the challenges of daily life, personality factors, such as the degree to which a person is an extrovert or an introvert, become at least as or even more important (Shanhong and Klohnen 2005).

Age at Marriage

Generally, couples who wait until they are older to marry have more happy, satisfying, and successful marriages (Heaton 2002). The reasoning is that older couples are more prepared for marriage and its responsibilities, they have greater financial resources, and may have their jobs or careers under way. One government study found that 59 percent of marriages for women under age 18 ended in divorce or separation within 15 years, compared with 36 percent of those married at age 20 or older (National Center for Health Statistics 2002). Early marriages are often associated with an unplanned pregnancy. Therefore, couples may stop their education, which puts them at a greater risk of poverty and other stresses. It appears that people who marry young are more likely to divorce, but among those who beat the

One of the factors associated with successful, happy marriages is religion. People who are more religious and attend church more frequently report higher levels of commitment to their partners, higher levels of marital satisfaction, fewer negative interactions, and less thinking and talking about divorce.

odds and remain married, their marriages may be as satisfying as couples that marry later.

Religious Faith and Practice

Religion is important to many people. Seventy-one percent of U.S. adults are "absolutely certain" there is a God, and 56 percent claim that their religion is very important to their lives (Pew Research Center 2008). A study of over 2,000 adults in Oklahoma suggests that religious faith and practice are strongly associated with marital quality (Johnson et al. 2002). In this survey, respondents were first asked about their general religiousness: "All things considered, how religious would you say that you are?" Then they were asked about their involvement in religious services: "How often do you attend religious services?" The data revealed that people who were more religious, regardless of their age, sex, the age at which they married, or income, reported higher levels of commitment to their partners, higher levels of marital satisfaction, less thinking and talking about divorce, and lower levels of negative interactions. The connection between shared religiosity and marital quality has declined somewhat, especially among the younger generation; however, it still remains that those who share a religious faith with a spouse report higher marital satisfaction than those who do not (Myers 2006).

Frequency and Satisfaction with Sexual Relationship

For most married couples, sex remains a vital part of their lives. Couples who report having regular or frequent sex, and who report enjoying their sex life, are also more likely to evaluate their marriages favorably (Goodwin 2009; Holmberg et al. 2010). The quality and quantity of sex are associated with feelings of love. For example, a study of women in both heterosexual and lesbian long-term relationships found that sexual satisfaction was linked to stronger relationships and mental well-being for both types of couples (Holmberg et al. 2010).

Satisfaction with Gender Relations and the Division of Labor

WHAT DO YOU THINK?

I raised this issue in the opening of this section, but now let me ask you: Do "happy," "satisfying," and "successful" marriages always occur together, or can you have one or two of these traits but not all three?

Couples who have more egalitarian attitudes about sex and gender, especially men, tend to have higher levels of marital happiness (Helms et al. 2006; Kaufman and Taniguchi 2006). Marital satisfaction is higher among couples who share the housework. In particular, when women perceive that the division of household labor is unfair (i.e., that they are doing the bulk of the work and do not want to), marital conflict increases, depression increases, and satisfaction with their marriage plummets (Frisco and Williams 2003; Weigel et al. 2006).

The Marriage Movement

Some Americans are uncomfortable with changes witnessed in families over the past few decades and yearn for a more traditional marital structure and set of social roles. Armed with information showing the benefits of marriage, groups of family scholars, therapists, and civic leaders have come together in what is called the **marriage movement** in hopes of influencing public policy to promote and strengthen traditional two-parent marriages. A report called *The Marriage Movement: A Statement of Principles, 2000* (Institute for American Values 2000) outlines a broad political agenda in the following areas:

- reduce unmarried pregnancy
- increase the likelihood that unmarried couples expecting a baby will marry before the child's birth
- reduce divorce
- reduce or prevent excessive conflict in married couples
- encourage married couples to have children if they want them
- protect the boundaries of marriage by distinguishing it from other family and friendship units including cohabiting ones
- treat the married couple as a social, legal, and financial unit
- transmit and reinforce shared norms of responsible marital behavior, such as encouraging permanence, fidelity, financial responsibility, and mutual support
- communicate the preference for marriage as the ideal family form, particularly to young people of reproductive age (The Marriage Movement 2004)

Drawing upon the "family decline" perspective outlined previously, the marriage movement suggests that the decline of traditional marriage is responsible for a host of social problems, at considerable expense to the taxpayer (Marriage Movement 2004):

> Divorce and unwed childbearing create substantial public costs paid by taxpayers. Higher rates of crime, drug use, education failure, chronic illness, child abuse, domestic violence and poverty among both adults and children bring with them higher taxpayer costs in diverse forms: more welfare expenditure; increased remedial and special education expenses; higher day-care subsidies; additional child-support collections.... While no study has yet attempted precisely to measure these sweeping and diverse taxpayer costs stemming from the decline of marriage, current research suggests that these costs are likely to be quite extensive. (p. 11)

The marriage movement was further advanced by former President George W. Bush, who pledged $1.5 billion to a "Healthy Marriage Initiative" during his presidency to impart the attitudes, values, and skills to encourage unmarried couples to enter marriage and married couples to maintain their vows. Much of that money was taken from cash welfare programs for low-income single parents and shifted to marriage education programs.

What are some criticisms of the marriage movement? The marriage movement has been criticized as ill-conceived, ineffectual, anti-gay, and a means for using public money to empower and fund religious organizations (Furstenberg 2007). They argue that social problems are not caused by a decline in traditional marriage *per se*, but from a lack of support for all types of families—traditional and nontraditional alike (Coontz 2006; Furstenberg 2007).

Critics of the marriage movement suggest that, unfortunately, some marriages are not good matches, do not benefit children and spouses, cannot be fixed, and that the decline of marriage is not the primary cause of poverty, delinquency, abuse, illness, or drug use (Amato 2004; Huston and Melz 2004). They claim that problems facing families are complex and have roots stemming from changes in social structure, rather than simply as a result of declining rates of marriage (Mintz 2003).

WHAT DO YOU THINK?

Given the benefits of marriage, do you think the government should be involved in promoting marriage? Why or why not?

One problem that affects the strength and viability of all families is economic instability (Edin and Kissane 2010; Seccombe 2011). Stable employment at a livable wage is a prerequisite for establishing secure, lifelong relationships. Yet, many poor women have difficulty finding partners who hold steady, fairly well-paid jobs. The poor are less likely to marry and more likely to divorce than the more affluent, yet the marriage movement minimizes structural concerns, and instead views poverty as a result, rather than a cause of family disorganization.

Structural changes in the economy mean that many families need two earners to support a middle-class standard of living. A result is severe stress as families attempt to balance work and family needs, such as housework, child care, and quality time together for the married couple. This stress can contribute to many negative family outcomes, including marital conflict, parent-child alienation, child abuse and neglect, and other tensions that adversely affect children's functioning and well-being. Moreover, with weakened extended family networks that offer social support and assistance, many families, regardless of their type, face difficult obstacles (Mintz 2003). Thus, many social problems are the result of economic instability and the lack of support for struggling families.

Covenant Marriage

In the quest to elevate the status of marriage and restrict access to divorce, there is a small but passionate movement toward developing **covenant marriage** (Brown 2008; Covenant Marriage Movement 2008). Couples can sign a document in which they pledge to follow certain rules, including (1) some marriage preparation; (2) full disclosure of all information that could reasonably affect the decision to marry; (3) an oath of lifelong commitment to marriage; (4) acceptance of limited grounds for divorce (e.g., abuse, adultery, addiction, felony imprisonment, separation for two years); and (5) marital counseling if problems threaten the marriage (Hawkins et al. 2002).

Covenant marriage options now exist in three states—Arizona, Arkansas, and Louisiana—although only a small fraction of persons in those states choose it (Nock et al. 1999; Spaht 2002). Court clerks who issue marriage licenses are supposed to tell couples about the option of covenant marriage, but sometimes they fail to do so. Those couples who have chosen covenant marriage are more religious and more politically conservative than average couples.

Communication

At one time or another, we have probably all said:

"That's not what I said!"

"You're not listening to me!"

"That's not what I mean!"

"I don't know what you're talking about!"

"You don't understand!"

We have been communicating since we were born, and using words to make our needs and wants known since we were toddlers. Why then is communicating sometimes so tricky? Why do we have difficulty expressing what we mean? Why do other people have such trouble receiving our messages?

Communication is an interactive process, using symbols like words and gestures, that includes both sending and receiving messages. Each person brings to the process his or her own life history, assumptions, and interpretations. We communicate verbally and nonverbally (Tubbs and Moss 2008), and these forms do not always send the same messages; for instance, we may smile while criticizing. Turner and West summarize the general concepts of communication this way:

- *Communication is a transaction:* all human behavior is a continuous exchange, and partners are simultaneously senders and receivers of messages.
- *Communication is a process:* it is dynamic and always changing, and culture, race and ethnicity, and sex are critical.
- *Communication includes co-construction of meanings:* each partner speaks a language and interprets meaning in a way acquired from his or her family of orientation.
- *Communication uses symbols:* in order to construct meanings or definitions, we rely on symbols that can be verbal like words or nonverbal like gestures.

It's no wonder expressing yourself, being understood, and understanding others can be challenging at times! Yet good communication is particularly important for marriage and intimate relationships (Galvin et al. 2008; Smith and Wilson 2009).

Verbal Communication

Verbal communication is the spoken exchange of thoughts, feelings, or other messages (DeVito 2011; Dunn and Goodnight 2011). It includes the content of the words themselves, and the tone and the expression used. Were the words said in a playful bantering tone, in a heated exchange, or an aggressive stance? One study compared three groups—happily married couples, couples seeking marriage therapy, and couples in the process of divorce—and found happily married couples showed more effective verbal communication skills in their typical daily lives than did the other two groups (Smith et al. 2008).

Words are symbols that represent something else. The word *dog*, for example, triggers an image of a four-legged animal. However, drawing upon symbolic interaction theory introduced in Chapter 1, we know that people attach meaning through their experiences and interactions with others. The word *dog* may conjure in your mind a furry friend curled up on your bed, or a growling creature with giant fangs. The word *single* may conjure in your mind an image of a happy bachelor enjoying his freedom, or a lonely person who longs for a loving relationship. We cannot be in charge of the meanings that people derive from our messages; therefore, we want to communicate as clearly as possible.

Nonverbal Communication

An awkward silence; a smile; eye contact; holding hands; a grimace; our posture; a squint; aggressive hand gestures; rolling the eyes—these are all forms of **nonverbal communication** (Seiler and Beall 2011). We use nonverbal messages all the time to convey attitudes and express emotions, from love and affection to contempt and disdain. In fact, we may use nonverbal messages more often than verbal messages when we want to discuss the state of our feelings within the relationship (Koerner and Fitzpatrick 2002). For example, if a partner feels jealous of the attention given to another person, he or she is likely to communicate nonverbally—rolling the eyes, being silent, or pulling away from touch—rather than saying, "You know, I feel insecure when you talk with Pat at parties because I worry that you're rejecting me."

Figure 8.7   Hand Gestures

OK sign

France: you're a zero; **Japan:** please give me coins; **Brazil:** an obscene gesture; **Mediterranean countries:** an obscene gesture

Thumbs up

Australia: up yours; **Germany:** the number one; **Japan:** the number five; **Saudi Arabia:** I'm winning; **Ghana:** an insult; **Malaysia:** the thumb is used to point rather than the index finger

Thumb and forefinger

Most countries: money; **France:** something is perfect; **Mediterranean:** a vulgar gesture

Open palm

Greece: an insult dating to ancient times; **West Africa:** "You have five fathers," an insult akin to calling someone a bastard

A problem with nonverbal messages is that they are easily misunderstood. Does the furrowing brow mean you are deep in thought, or expressing disapproval? Does that smile represent happiness or nervousness? Are you yawning from boredom or sleepiness? The potential for misinterpretation is made even greater by cultural differences. Figure 8.7 shows how specific hand gestures have significantly different meanings from one country to another. What can be a sign of support or friendliness in one place can be a crude or vulgar gesture elsewhere.

For example, Hispanics in casual conversation stand or sit much closer to each other than two Whites (Kaleidoscope 2003). Therefore, in a conversation between a White and a Hispanic, we may find the Hispanic person moving closer to talk, while the White person backs away because the closeness feels awkward. Eye contact is another example. In the United States, eye contact is considered polite and shows interest in another person and his or her conversation. However, in other cultures, such as in many Hispanic cultures, eye contact between men and women is a clear sign of sexual suggestiveness and invitation.

Listening

Many students have taken a speech class while in college, but how many have had a class on listening? Yet, learning how to listen—truly listen—is an acquired skill, and one that is very important for effective communication (Lane 2010). **Listening** involves giving thoughtful consideration to what we hear. It is a complex process involving selecting, attending to, constructing an understanding from, remembering, and responding to verbal and nonverbal messages (Beebe et al. 2011).

At the heart of just about any communication problem is poor listening—not poor hearing—but the act of not really listening and understanding what the person is saying. For example, if a friend talks to you about their frustration with a partner, a poor listener may interrupt, change the subject, or share their own views about that person: "Oh, I agree that Sally doesn't seem to get it. Do you know what she said to me? You won't believe it. . . ." They might even wander off the topic to talk about their own partner, "Oh yeah, you know what my girlfriend does? It drives me crazy. . . ." This person is not really listening to his friend. A good listener focuses on what the person is saying and is not distracted or thinking of their own response. He or she listens to both the content and the feelings that are associated with that content (Kelly 2008).

One type of listening is referred to as **active listening** (Perkins and Fogarty 2005). This is when you are extremely attentive, with good eye contact and body language, and encourage the person to continue talking. You may paraphrase what the person is saying, or ask for clarification or further details so that they will be encouraged to continue talking. Some examples of active listening include:

"You seem to be frustrated about that. Is that because . . . ?"

"Tell me what happened next?"

"How did that make you feel?

"What do you think we should do?"

Active listening involves asking good questions, listening non-judgmentally, empathizing, and paraphrasing (Perkins and Fogarty 2005). As summed up by Beebe, Beebe, and Redmond (Beebe et al. 2011), a good listener: (1) stops; (2) looks; (3) listens; (4) asks questions; and (5) reflects by paraphrasing.

Self-Disclosure

One of the primary ways we can use communication to help create satisfying marriages is through **self-disclosure**, or telling your spouse something private about yourself that he or she would not otherwise know (Galvin et al. 2008; Lane 2010). A useful way of viewing self-disclosure is the "Johari window," shown in Table 8.1. The table distinguishes how much information you know about yourself, how much others know about you, and how much you are willing to disclose.

The *Open Window Pane* includes information that is clearly visible or known, such as your physical appearance or where you live. The *Blind Pane* includes information others can see in you, but you cannot see in yourself. You might think you are a talented manager, yet others think you exhibit weak leadership skills. The *Hidden Pane* contains information you wish to keep private, such as your fantasies. The *Unknown Pane* includes everything neither you nor others know about you. For example, you may have hidden artistic talent you have not explored. Through self-disclosure, we open and close the window panes so we may become more intimate with others (Luft 1969).

TABLE 8.1 Windows on Myself

What do we know about ourselves, and what are we willing to disclose to others?

	KNOWN TO SELF	UNKNOWN TO SELF
KNOWN TO OTHERS	**Open Window Pane** known to self and others	**Blind Window Pane** blind to self, seen by others
UNKNOWN TO OTHERS	**Hidden Window Pane** open to self, hidden from others	**Unknown Window Pane** unknown to self and others

Sources: Luft 1969; Luft and Ingram 1955.

Communication takes many forms, including verbal and nonverbal, listening and disclosing. What type of communication do you see here? Are there sex differences in their communication styles?

However, for self-disclosure to benefit a relationship, there must be reciprocity and support (Galvin et al. 2008), a tenet of the social exchange perspective introduced in Chapter 1. That is, both partners should feel free to be honest with each other and supportive of the feelings being shared. Disclosing feelings can be risky, for not all feelings are positive. Yet, if spouses support each other in sharing both the good and the bad, trust can develop. Lack of support, or a negative response to self-disclosure, can be detrimental to the quality of a relationship.

Electronic Communication

Increasingly, people "talk" to each other electronically; in other words, they really don't talk at all, they write. Unlike the days when we relied on the postal service to send a message from here to there, electronic messaging is instantaneous, which has changed the way we communicate. As of 2009, 125 million people were on MySpace or Facebook (DeWolfe and Anderson 2009). A study conducted at the University of Texas reports that over four-fifths of students and staff have Facebook accounts (Baron 2008). Some people use these so often that about one-third of students reported that they either agreed or strongly agreed to the statement, "I feel addicted to Facebook" (Vanden Boogart 2006). Likewise, college students are required to have e-mail accounts, so electronic messages are simply a part of life.

Electronic communication is now how many of us communicate daily (Ramirez and Broneck 2009). How has our increased reliance on the electronic written word changed the face of communication? Linguist Naomi Baron suggests many changes have, or will, occur, such as greater informality; new words (i.e., "cookie" or "spam"); increased ability to screen messages; more relationships, but with less depth to them; and the ability to share information instantaneously (Baron 2008).

Embracing Differences in Communication

In this textbook, I have discussed a few of the fundamental ways that people differ from one another, and the ways in which these differences manifest themselves in families and intimate relationships. Our sex, social class, race, and ethnicity, for example, contribute to an overall perspective that influences how we relate to others as friends, as partners, as spouses, and as parents. This includes how we communicate with one another.

Sex Differences: Are You from Mars or Venus?   Do men and women communicate differently? Popular self-help books such as *Men Are from Mars, Women Are from Venus* (Gray 1992) have widespread appeal because people are concerned about communication and genuinely want to understand one another better.

> While driving to visit friends in another part of the city, Marcus and Renée got lost. Feeling they may be late, Renée suggests they stop and ask for directions, but Marcus refuses. He is uncomfortable asking for help and believes there's no guarantee a stranger will give accurate information anyway. He's sure he can find the way himself and would rather just drive around until he does so. This doesn't make sense at all to Renée, who is getting angry. She isn't embarrassed about asking for directions and believes anyone who doesn't know where he or she is should admit being lost and ask for help.

TABLE 8.2 Conclusions Drawn from Research on Sex Differences in Communication

It's not your imagination—there ARE many sex differences in communication.

Quantity of Talk: Who Talks the Most

- In task-oriented cross-sex groups, men talk more than women.
- In friendly same-sex pairs, women prefer to spend time talking; men prefer to share activities like sports or hobbies.

Topics of Talk: What Do Men and Women Talk About?

- Women talk more about private matters, such as family, relationship problems, other women or men, clothing, and feelings.
- Men talk more about public matters, such as sports, money, and news, and they tell more jokes.

Vocabulary: Do Men and Women Use Different Words?

- Women more often use weak expletives ("oh dear" or "oh my"), whereas men more often use stronger expletives, including obscenities.
- Women use more color detail terms than men (mauve, teal).

Grammatical Constructions: Do Men's and Women's Syntax Differ?

- Women use more qualifiers ("somewhat," "kind of," "I guess").
- Women use more disclaimers ("I'm no expert, but...," "Don't get mad but...").
- Women are more likely to use polite forms of conversation, such as, "May I please have..." "I'm sorry about that..."

Taking Turns: Who Controls Interaction?

- In cross-sex pairs, men interrupt women more than women interrupt men.
- Women ask more questions and men make more statements during conversation.
- Men successfully initiate topics more often than do women.

Sources: Trenholm 2008; Arliss 1991.

Linguists have noted a number of sex differences, as shown in Table 8.2 (Ivy and Backlund 2008; Trenholm 2008; Wood 2009). One sex difference in communication is in the way we self-disclose. Women tend to be more verbal in disclosing their feelings about the relationship; men, in contrast, tend toward more physical displays. Yet wives may complain they want more than just the presence of men in their lives; they want more regular verbal displays of affection. "Tell me you love me," she says. "I'm here, aren't I?" he responds.

This disparity leads to a kind of misunderstanding between husbands and wives. Both are self-disclosing, but they do not always get credit for it, given their different styles. It may be the *perception* of disclosure that makes the difference in the quality of marriages (Uebelacker et al. 2003). Women do not see as much communication disclosure from their husbands as they want, which helps explain why women show lower rates of satisfaction in marriage than do men.

What causes these differences? Linguist Deborah Tannen (1994), who has studied sex and gender differences in communication extensively, believes they stem from the fact that men and women grow up in different "cultures". Women's culture, she believes, stresses intimacy and connection with others. Men's culture values autonomy and individual achievement. These different perspectives influence men's and women's topics of conversation, their communication styles, and their interpretations of one another's messages. Throughout their lives men and women learn how to use behavior in sync with their gender identities.

Men learn that being competitive and strong is a way of expressing masculinity. Women learn that stressing connection and feelings is feminine. This explains why many men don't seem to mind driving around rather than asking for directions (which might reveal weakness) (Trenholm 2008).

Race, Ethnicity, and Communication   Given that we are more likely to interact with people who are like ourselves, it is not terribly surprising that members of a particular social class or race or ethnic group develop their own ways of communicating through words, gestures, or expressions (Allen 2004). For example, linguists have documented substantial differences between Standard American English (SAE), variants of which are spoken by Whites and some Blacks in the United States, and African American English (AAE), variants of which are spoken by many Blacks. These linguistic differences include actual words, syntax, acoustics, and rules for subject-verb agreement (Clopper and Pisoni 2004). Listeners can identify a speaker's race from his or her speech, even if only hearing short snippets of speech (Grogger 2009), and this identification has been used to discriminate against Blacks. For example, a study that asked Black- and White-sounding telephone callers to inquire about an advertised apartment for rent found that Black-sounding callers were more likely than White-sounding callers to be told the apartment was already rented (Massey and Lundy 2001).

Social Class and Communication   Basil Bernstein's and William Labov's pioneering work on social class and linguistics also showed substantial differences in how language is used by different groups (Bernstein 1960, 1973; Labov 1966, 1972). For example, members of the working class tend to speak less SAE, use more words of simple coordination such as "like" or "but," and use fewer pronouns compared to the middle and upper-middle classes (Bernstein 1973; Wardhaugh 2010). The box on page 249, "Families as Lived Experience: Learning to Speak SAE," describes a working-class young woman's realization that she spoke differently from her peers. Although some sociolinguists question the utility of traditional conceptualizations of social class (Mallinson and Dodsworth 2009), it is widely recognized that people with different levels of income, education, and occupational prestige communicate in diverse ways. Yet, at the same time, groups sometimes "break code"—they know what SAE is and can weave in and out of it when it suits their interests (Bernstein 1973). Even President Obama has been seen giving speeches with two different linguistic styles: one for a largely upper-middle-class White audience in which he closely followed SAE, and one for an audience comprised of the Black working-class "brothers," in which his accent, word choice, and tone differed.

Cultural Differences in Communication   Culture is another macro-level factor that shapes our communication. In the early part of the twentieth century, anthropologist Edward Sapir (1949) and his student Benjamin Whorf noticed that language shapes our culture, and at the same time, our culture shapes our language. The pattern runs both ways. This is known as the **Sapir-Whorf hypothesis**. They studied the language patterns of several different cultural groups and found, for example, that among the Hopi Native Americans one word is used for every creature that flies, except for birds. That may seem odd to modern-day English speakers, but for the Hopi, flying creatures occupied a single category.

Likewise, Native Alaskan groups have many different words for snow. Given that their culture revolves around snow, this makes good sense. After all, snow can be soft, crunchy, wet, melting, or powdery, to name just a few descriptors, and how Alaska Native groups are able to use this snow depends on what type it is. In comparison, however, residents of Miami, Florida, probably have few words in their repertoire for snow because it is not a meaningful part of their everyday lives.

FAMILIES
as Lived Experience

Learning to Speak SAE

Standard American English (SAE) is the so-called "gold standard" of speech. Yet many families, in particular minority and lower-income families, have learned other speech patterns. These can be disadvantageous when they become assimilated with other groups, such as in college or on the job.

"Okay, here's the deal: I'm a working-class girl done good.

Please allow me to rephrase that.

I would like to share that I am a highly successful woman who has roots in the working class.

Do you see the difference in these two ways of speaking? My words, syntax, tones, even gestures change depending on the group I'm with. It hasn't always been that way.

I was raised in a working-class family with notoriously bad grammar. Around them parts we said 'ain't', as in "I ain't hungry no more," and fixin', as in "Hey Janey, you fixin' to get to the store soon?" We all spoke this way in my family, as did many people within my community, so I really wasn't aware that my grammar was incorrect. I don't even remember my teachers calling me on it.

Things changed drastically when I went to college. Because I did well in high school, I had the fortunate opportunity to attend a prestigious college in the Northeast. I would like to say that I loved the experience, but the culture shock was so overwhelming that I might as well have landed on Mars. In particular, I noticed that people did not speak the same way I did. They didn't have my accent, they used different words, and they used those words in a different pattern. I immediately felt inadequate. One incident stands out in particular: In one of my math classes I wanted to ask the professor to expand upon his explanation, so I simply asked "How come?" He stared at me. "How come?" he repeated. Then he said it again more loudly than the first, "HOW COME?" The class snickered. At first I didn't catch what they were laughing about. But then it came to me, "I mean, why?" I gulped. Later that day I withdrew from the class.

That same day I also went to the English department and asked the secretary if the department offered any English tutors "for, you know, people who talk differently." She was a sweet lady, "Oh, you mean for people who have English as a second language? Sure honey, let me get you a list." I didn't dare tell her that I was looking for a tutor for me. But I contacted the first name on the list, Darcy, and I am forever grateful. She taught me to speak "Standard American English," as she called it. We met weekly for an entire year, and I practiced almost daily. The drills included verbal and nonverbal communication, as well as the written word.

I can now easily pass as an upper-middle-class student at my college. I know how to "talk the talk." However, when I go back home to see my mama and pa, I'm just one of the working-class girls done good.

By the way, I think I'll stop by to see my old math professor just to say 'hey.' "

—**Janey Age 20**

CRITICAL THINKING QUESTIONS
1. What is it about social class that contributes to different speech patterns? Can you think of specific issues that would cause these differences?
2. Why is an upper-middle-class speech pattern, SAE, more valued than other speech patterns?

Think about the Sapir-Whorf hypothesis in your world today. Today's technology-driven culture has given way to many new words—chances are, words like *cell phone*, *texting*, *"friending,"* and even *PC* were not a part of your parents' vocabulary at your age. And, our language also shapes our culture. New words like *Attention Deficit Disorder* or *gifted* have created new dimensions of our culture, with special educational programming and even medicine to go along with these labels. At one time we just called people disruptive or smart, but now we have words that help to shape our culture's collective worldview (Beebe et al. 2011).

Understanding how language influences and is influenced by culture is critical in our global world (Asante et al. 2007; Lustig and Koester 2010). Success at interpersonal relationships on the job and in our social life depends on our ability to communicate with persons who may have a different cultural orientation than our own. We need to understand how cultures differ and how these differences influence our forms and styles of communication.

Conflict, Communication, and Problem Solving

The potential for conflict is inherent in any relationship (Lane 2010). **Conflict** occurs when members of the group disagree over two or more options to make a decision, solve a problem, or achieve a goal (Beebe and Masterson 2006). It can result from differences between group members in personality, perception, information, tolerance for risk, culture, and power or influence.

Research on marital communication has focused primarily on its ability to help reduce conflict and improve problem solving. The way couples communicate about their differences has real implications for marital happiness and stability. Conflict in any marriage or personal relationship is normal and to be expected. The key is *how* we communicate and deal with conflict.

In his extensive body of work, including his book *Why Marriages Succeed or Fail*, John Gottman (1994) takes an in-depth look at how couples communicate and resolve their differences. He distinguished between **regulating couples**, who generally use communication to promote closeness and intimacy and who tend to use constructive rather than negative comments even during arguments, and **nonregulated couples**, who have far more negative exchanges. Nonregulated couples may use the following techniques:

- *Contempt:* This is an attitude of superiority to one's spouse. One way spouses exhibit contempt is by rolling their eyes while their partner is talking.
- *Defensiveness:* This is an effort to defend yourself and your position in an argument when you feel attacked.
- *Criticism:* This includes making negative evaluations of the other person's behavior or feelings.
- *Stonewalling:* This is a type of withdrawal technique through which some partners show they are refusing to listen to their spouse.
- *Belligerence:* This challenging behavior is meant to establish power in the relationship.

Gottman's research suggests there may be a pattern to conflict. He and his colleagues observed 130 couples at the beginning of their marriage, and then followed them for six years (Gottman et al. 1998). At the end of six years there had been 17 divorces, and the communication pattern of those who divorced appeared different from that of the others. In particular, there seemed to be an initiation of verbal conflict by the wife, perhaps as a result of something in the relationship she did not like or feel was fair. This was followed by the husband's refusal to accept input from his wife. The wife then reciprocated with negativity, and the husband made little or no effort to de-escalate it. The couples who ended the study in happy, stable marriages had more positive exchanges, including humor, affection, and interest.

These findings should not be taken to mean wives start all the arguments in marriage. Rather, women are more likely to verbalize their feelings—one study of nearly 4,000 men and women found that 32 percent of men compared to 23 percent of women say they bottle up their feelings in a spat (Parker-Pope 2007).

Instead, Gottman's work suggests both husbands and wives can work on their communication styles to reduce the amount of negativity and hence reduce the likelihood of unhappiness and divorce. Wives may think of better ways to communicate that soften the beginning of conflict, and husbands can learn to accept influence from their wives and reduce their own negative comments.

WHAT DO YOU THINK?

Can you think of any macro-level factors that might affect the degree or type of conflict and communication?

Social Policy and Family Resilience

The marriage movement has brought the institution of marriage into the national spotlight (Fincham and Beach 2010). Although research notes many positive effects of marriage on couples and children, it is also a highly contested political issue: Can, and should, government be involved in promoting traditional marriage at the exclusion of other types of relationships? Oklahoma has begun a large experiment designed to promote marriage and reduce divorce, and it has received widespread support from residents of that state.

Example: The Oklahoma Marriage Initiative

The University of Oklahoma and Oklahoma State University economists conducted a study on what Oklahomans needed to do to become a more prosperous state. They concluded that factors such as the high divorce rate, high rates of child deaths due to abuse, and high rates of nonmarital childbirths were contributing to Oklahoma's weak economy. The study prompted the development of a series of programs and policies now known as the *Oklahoma Marriage Initiative* (2010). The primary goal of the initiative is to support marriage and reduce the divorce rate. Other related goals include increasing the number of children who live in "healthy two-parent households" (Oklahoma Marriage Initiative 2005). These goals are to be achieved by collaboration between the department of human services and many social service programs to provide couples with the skills and tools needed to form and sustain healthy marriages.

Although then-governor Keating recognized that the program could be controversial, a baseline study conducted in Oklahoma indicated significant support for the initiative. Eighty-five percent of adults in a representative sample indicated that they felt "very good" or "good" about "a statewide initiative to promote marriage and reduce divorce." Sixty-six percent of those who were married or romantically involved indicated that they would consider attending relationship education courses. Support was found across racial and ethnic groups, with Blacks offering the highest degree of support (Johnson and Stanley 2001). The program continues today and is funded with $10 million that was originally targeted for the cash welfare program, Temporary Assistance for Needy Families (TANF). Because one of the goals of TANF is to strengthen marriage, funds could be diverted from TANF to the marriage initiative that serves all income groups as long as some of the services remained targeted to the poor.

The initiative includes free skill-based marriage and relationship courses to couples and individuals across the state. Courses are led by pastors and lay leaders in the faith community, social service providers, business leaders, community volunteers, tribal groups, mental health groups, and minority group specialists. They are not designed to be marriage counseling, but to provide some skills to help navigate the problems that are inevitable in relationships and marriages. Skills-based marriage education includes practical information to help partners connect, communicate actively, and process anger effectively. Other programs are designed to inspire and motivate rather than teach specific skills. Regardless of the type of program, the overall theme of the workshops and related media efforts is to encourage, strengthen, and preserve traditional two-parent marriage. Other types of family constellations are seen as inferior.

Opponents are outraged that money intended to help poor women and children on welfare is being diverted to promote a traditional marriage program. They believe the money would be better spent on providing meaningful job training or educational opportunities for the poor. They also question whether it is the state's role to push traditional marriage, which, by definition, denigrates other family forms.

Conclusion

Marriage is both a social institution and a personal relationship and is recognized in some form around the world. As a social institution, rules, rights, and responsibilities surround marriage because it is seen as a stabilizing force within societies, and therefore the government sees marriage as its business. Cross-cultural research shows that feelings of love and sexual intensity can be the core experience of marriage or these feelings may be totally irrelevant to it. Americans are highly committed to marriage. Most claim that they want to marry and consider marriage important to their personal happiness. Nonetheless, many changes in marriage are underway. People tend to marry later, and many cohabit prior to marriage or in the place of marriage. Some propose to legalize same-sex marriages, and spouses are renegotiating terrain such as the division of household labor and other roles. These changes have also inspired a growing marriage movement designed to preserve, strengthen, and promote traditional marriage. Despite the changes in marriage, it remains as popular as ever and is associated with many benefits. Effective communication is an important ingredient of successful relationships, and it is important to understand and embrace differences in communication styles.

Key Terms

Active listening: A form of communication in which the listener is extremely attentive, with good eye contact and body language, and encourages the person to continue talking. (p. 245)

Antimiscegenation laws: The banning of marriage between Whites and other races. (p. 229)

Communication: An interactive process, using symbols like words and gestures, that includes both sending and receiving messages. (p. 243)

Conflict: Members of the group disagree over two or more options to make a decision, solve a problem, or achieve a goal. (p. 250)

Covenant marriage: A type of marriage that restricts access to divorce, requires premarital counseling, and includes other rules and regulations. (p. 242)

Interethnic marriage: Partners coming from different countries or having different cultural, religious, or ethnic backgrounds. (p. 230)

Listening: The process of giving thoughtful attention to what we hear. (p. 244)

Marital decline perspective: Suggests the institution of marriage is being threatened by hedonistic pursuits of personal happiness at the expense of a long-term commitment. (p. 233)

Marital resilience perspective: Suggests ending an unhappy marriage is not necessarily cause for alarm because it gives adults another chance at happiness and provides the opportunity to end a child's dysfunctional home life. (p. 233)

Marriage: A legally and socially recognized relationship that includes sexual, economic, and social rights and responsibilities between partners. (p. 221)

Marriage movement: A group of family scholars, therapists, and civic leaders who have come together in hopes of influencing public policy to promote and strengthen traditional marriage. (p. 241)

Marriage premium: People who are married are happier, healthier, and financially better off than those who are not married, including cohabitors. (p. 235)

Nonregulated couples: Couples who have many negative communication exchanges, such as criticism or defensiveness. (p. 250)

Nonverbal communication: Communicating without words, and which includes gestures, expressions, and body language. (p. 243)

Regulating couples: Couples who generally use communication to promote closeness and intimacy and tend to use constructive rather than negative comments even during arguments. (p. 250)

Sapir-Whorf hypothesis: The idea that language shapes our culture, and at the same time, our culture shapes our language. (p. 248)

Self-disclosure: Telling a person something private about yourself that he or she would not otherwise know. (p. 245)

Social capital: The connections, social support, information, and other benefits that are produced through relationships among people. (p. 237)

Verbal communication: The spoken exchange of thoughts, feelings, or other messages. (p. 243)

Resources on the Internet

Marriage Builders

www.marriagebuilders.com

An online learning community for solving marriage problems, improving relationship skills, celebrating marriage, and achieving happiness with a partner. The goal is to promote success in marriage and other committed relationships by offering practical, how-to articles, and skills-training programs.

National Marriage Project

www.virginia.edu/marriageproject/

The mission of the National Marriage Project is to strengthen the institution of marriage by providing research and analysis that inform public policy, educate the American public, and focus attention on the consequences of marriage decline for millions of American children. They publish an annual report, *The State of Our Unions: The Social Health of Marriage in America.*

WeddingChannel.com

www.weddingchannel.com

This website is devoted to showing you "everything you need to plan the perfect wedding." Illustrates the big business associated with traditional weddings, including "30,000 photos to find the perfect wedding dress, hairstyle, cake, bouquet and more."

Becoming a Parent

CHAPTER 9

CHAPTER OUTLINE

Population and Fertility Trends Worldwide 257

■ **EYE** *on the World:* Total Fertility Rates, 2009 *258*

Fertility Rates in the United States 263

■ **USING** *the Sociological Imagination:* Having a Baby at 50 or 60 *266*

Deciding to Parent 267

■ **FAMILIES** *as Lived Experience:* The "Costs" of Raising a Child *269*

The Social Construction of Childbirth 276

The Transition to Parenthood 278

Social Policy and Family Resilience 280

■ **SOCIAL** *Policies for Families:* The Family and Medical Leave Act *283*

Conclusion 284

Key Terms 284

Resources on the Internet 285

CHAPTER PREVIEW

Most, but not all, adults become parents. How does the process of deciding if, when, and how we will be parents unfold? What types of changes does parenting bring? This chapter focuses on the process of becoming a parent. The transition to parenthood can be surprisingly challenging, yet tremendously rewarding. In this chapter, you will learn:

■ Population and fertility trends worldwide, and the ways in which some countries, such as China, try to limit their population growth, whereas other countries, such as Japan, try to increase theirs

■ Fertility rates in the United States are changing, with more families delaying or forgoing parenthood

■ The rewards and costs associated with children

■ Large numbers of couples are remaining childfree, often by choice, but sometimes because of infertility problems

■ There are many types of adoptions—including open, closed, transracial, and international—and many nontraditional families are adopting, including single parents, and same-sex couples

■ The natural process of childbirth has been vastly medicalized in the United States

■ The transitions to parenthood can be challenging and men and women often face differences in these transitions

■ Other developed nations offer extensive paid maternity and family leaves to help new parents

A growing number of adults are having children with more than one partner. Because of higher rates of cohabitation and divorce, men and women might have children with two, three, or even more partners. This is known as "multiple partner fertility." At least 8 percent of men aged 15–44 report multiple partner fertility, and the likelihood increases with age. Many people assume that this is probably a bad thing for children, but an empirical approach can shed far more light on this issue than can personal opinion.

Researchers from Child Trends decided to explore the questions of whether and how parenting with multiple partners is associated with the well-being of young children. They examined the influence of fathers' multiple partner fertility on two aspects of children's well-being in the preschool years: (1) externalizing behaviors, such as whether the child is defiant, cannot concentrate or sit still, is disobedient, has angry moods, gets in fights, destroys his or her own things or those of other children, has a hot temper, and hurts animals or people; and (2) physical health. They looked at a variety of issues that might mediate the relationship between multiple partner fertility and children's externalizing behaviors or physical health, such as paternal depressive symptoms, paternal stress, and the degree to which fathers are engaged with their children.

The analyses were based on the Fragile Families and Child Well-Being study, which collected data on over 4,000 unmarried parents in 20 large cities across the United States. Of fathers included in the sample, a third—about 1,000—reported multiple partner fertility. Using sophisticated statistical techniques, the data revealed several important points: (1) fathers' experience of multiple partner fertility was associated with children's negative externalizing behaviors, but was not significantly associated with children's health; (2) parental depression, but neither parental stress nor engagement with children, was a significant mediator of externalizing behaviors—that is, multiple partner fertility was associated with higher levels of depressive symptoms, which in turn were associated with higher levels of child externalizing behaviors; and (3) fathers' involvement was a significant mediator of health. This study provides evidence that men's multiple partner fertility is important for understanding children's well-being. The authors write, "Multiple partner fertility is often the result of an unplanned pregnancy or relationship turbulence . . . consequently, programs that address male fertility should educate men, as well as women, starting at a young age, about the potential negative ramifications of unplanned pregnancies and union instability as a means of avoiding multiple partner fertility" (Bronte-Tinkew et al. 2009).

Parenting occurs in many different contexts today. The two-parent-two-sex family structure certainly predominates, but we also see single parents, gays and lesbians raising children, and as the opening vignette describes, multiple partner fertility. This chapter focuses on issues surrounding fertility and parenthood. The likelihood of having children has declined alongside family size; however, most adults do become parents through either birth or adoption. **Pronatalism** is the value of promoting children as a normal, natural part of a happy life, and suggests those who voluntarily remain childfree are selfish, immature, and lonely. Pronatalism is supported by social institutions. For example, religious institutions often encourage large families by discouraging the use of birth control. We can see pronatalism in government policy. The Japanese government took only six months to approve the impotence-treatment drug Viagra, but birth control pills designed to prevent pregnancy were studied for years and have only recently been approved. Even in the United States many insurance companies cover the costs of Viagra but do not cover the costs of birth control (Keenan 2008; NARAL Pro-Choice America Foundation 2010).

Population and Fertility Trends Worldwide

There is reason to believe that fundamental changes are occurring in the values associated with having children in many parts of the world today. As educational and economic opportunities for young women continue to expand in both developed and less developed nations, a wider range of lifestyle options becomes available. Coupled with the increasing availability of relatively effective birth control (and a growing acceptance of singlehood, cohabitation, and divorce), many women are having far fewer children than ever before. Nonetheless, the world's population continues to expand.

The world's population is currently growing at a rapid rate, but this has not always been the case. The population did not reach 1 billion people until about the year 1800. Then, it increased to 1.6 billion only 100 years later. Today, after another century, the world's population is about 7 billion in 2011, and depending on the projection used, could reach over 8 billion by 2025 (Bremner et al. 2009). If the concept of a billion is difficult to comprehend, consider the following:

- If you were a billion seconds old, you would be 31.7 years of age.
- The circumference of the earth is 25,000 miles. If you circled the earth 40,000 times, you would have traveled 1 billion miles.

Population growth occurs unevenly. Less developed countries contain about 81 percent of the world's population. In some countries, such as Niger, the median age of the population is only 15 years; therefore, the population is likely to grow rapidly because so many people are of childbearing age. In contrast, Japan has the oldest median age—44 years old—and the country is concerned about population decline. Why such a difference? Population change is linked to many important issues for families, including health threats, infant mortality, life expectancy, the status of women, and overall quality of life.

The median age of a population reflects two important trends that occur at opposite ends of the lifespan. First, it represents **fertility rates**. There are several different ways to report fertility: (1) average number of children born to a woman during her lifetime; (2) number of children born per 1,000 women aged 15–49 (many countries use age 49 as the cutoff; however, the United States normally uses age 44); and (3) number of children born per 1,000 population.

The map on pages 258–259 shows fertility rates throughout the world in 2009. Using the method calculating the average number of children born to a woman during her lifetime, we can see that South Korea, China, Taiwan, and much of Western and Eastern Europe have fertility rates below 1.5, well below replacement level. Countries with fertility rates this low must rely on immigration to maintain their population (Population Reference Bureau 2010b).

Generally speaking, the fertility rate in developing nations far exceeds the rate in developed nations. In Niger, for example, an average woman bears 7.4 children, whereas in Taiwan she has only 1.0 (Bremner et al. 2009). This is because in many developing nations less than half of married women aged 15–49 use some sort of contraceptive, as shown in Table 9.1 (Haub and Kent 2009). Part of this is due to obstacles such as inadequate funds for supplies and the lack of comprehensive programs to educate couples on their options. Moreover, large families are often valued as a means of social security. With few government aid programs, large numbers of children are important social, economic, and political resources that can help maintain and provide for families. In reality, having many children will likely keep families impoverished, but as William Ogburn's (1964) cultural lag theory notes, nonmaterial culture (e.g., norms, values) changes more slowly than material culture.

In addition to fertility rates, the median age also reflects a country's **mortality** (death) **rates**. You would think that countries with a high mortality rate (i.e., a greater number of people dying) would grow their populations slowly. However, fertility and mortality rates are often positively related to one another; that is, those countries that have the most births

Total Fertility Rates, 2009

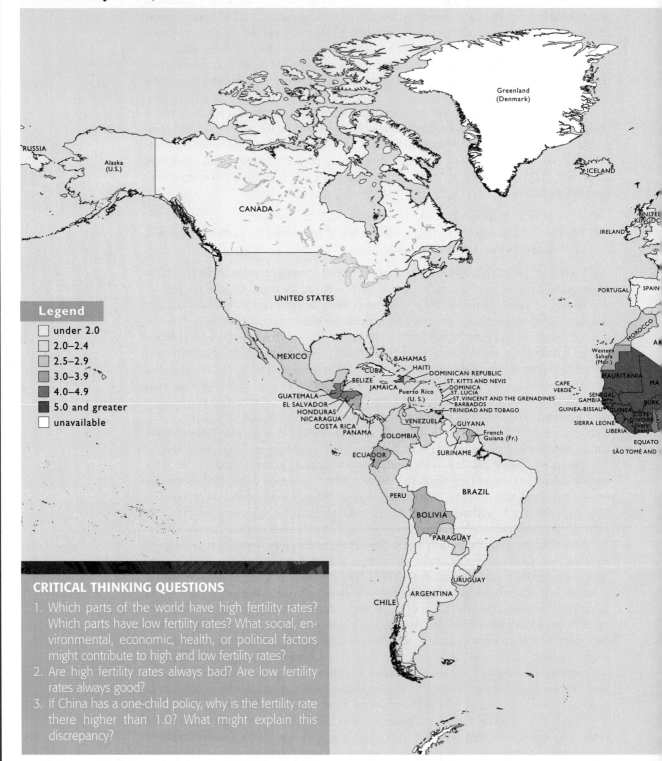

Greenland
(Denmark)

RUSSIA

Alaska
(U.S.)

ICELAND

CANADA

UNITED
KINGDO

IRELAND

UNITED STATES

PORTUGAL   SPAIN

Legend

	under 2.0
	2.0–2.4
	2.5–2.9
	3.0–3.9
	4.0–4.9
	5.0 and greater
	unavailable

MEXICO

BAHAMAS

CUBA   HAITI

BELIZE   DOMINICAN REPUBLIC

JAMAICA   ST. KITTS AND NEVIS

GUATEMALA   Puerto Rico   DOMINICA

EL SALVADOR   (U. S.)   ST. LUCIA

HONDURAS   ST. VINCENT AND THE GRENADINES

NICARAGUA   BARBADOS

COSTA RICA   TRINIDAD AND TOBAGO

PANAMA   VENEZUELA   GUYANA

COLOMBIA   French
Guiana (Fr.)

ECUADOR   SURINAME

MOROCCO

Western
Sahara
(Mor.)

MAURITANIA   MA

CAPE   SENEGAL   BURK

VERDE   GAMBIA

GUINEA-BISSAU   GUINEA

SIERRA LEONE   CÔTE
D'IVOIRE   GHANA
(Ivory
Coast)

LIBERIA

EQUATO

SÃO TOMÉ AND

PERU   BRAZIL

BOLIVIA

PARAGUAY

URUGUAY

CHILE   ARGENTINA

CRITICAL THINKING QUESTIONS

1. Which parts of the world have high fertility rates? Which parts have low fertility rates? What social, environmental, economic, health, or political factors might contribute to high and low fertility rates?

2. Are high fertility rates always bad? Are low fertility rates always good?

3. If China has a one-child policy, why is the fertility rate there higher than 1.0? What might explain this discrepancy?

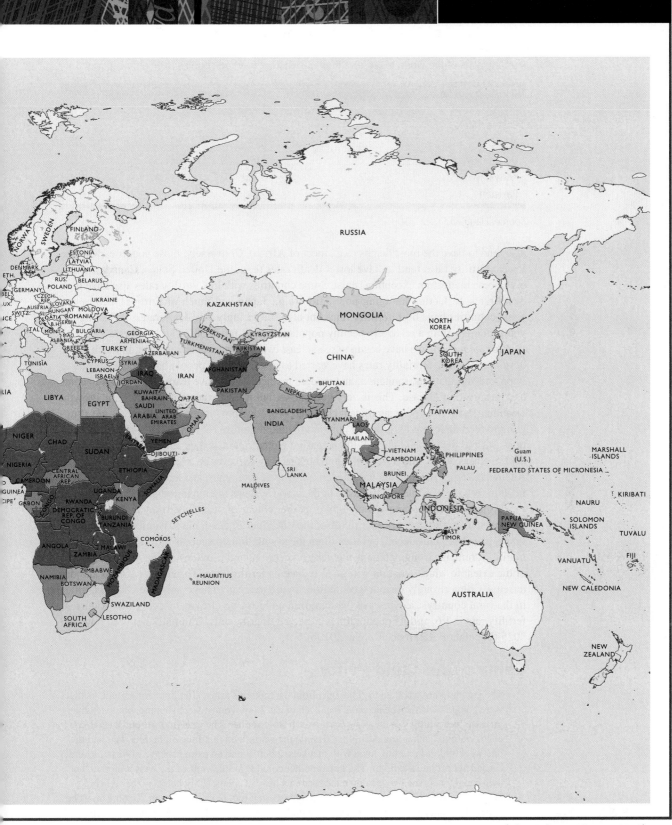

Source: Population Reference Bureau 2010b.

TABLE 9.1 Use of Modern Contraceptives Among Married Women of Childbearing Age Remains Low in Some Countries

In many parts of the world today, less than one-third of married couples use contraceptives.

Contraceptive Use (%)	
World	55%
United States	68%
Mexico	67%
Bangladesh	48%
Kenya	32%
Pakistan	22%

Source: Haub and Kent 2009.

also tend to have the most deaths (e.g., most of Africa). Conversely, those countries with the lowest fertility rates tend to have lower death rates (e.g., the United States, Canada). However, some interesting exceptions exist. Some countries with low fertility rates also have high death rates, reflecting an aging population (e.g., Japan and much of Europe). Moreover, some countries have high fertility rates but also surprisingly low death rates, reflecting the youthfulness within a relatively healthy population (e.g., much of Central America).

In recent years, we have begun to see at least two important changes. First, in much of the developing world, mortality rates have started to decline. More people have been exposed to improved vaccinations, sanitation, and modern medicines and have learned new ways to combat the spread of disease. This is very good news, but it also exacerbates population growth. Declining death rates pose significant challenges for food production. Many nations are struggling to feed their rapidly growing population, and therefore rely on the aid of wealthier nations, such as the United States. With increasing globalization, some countries are in enormous debt to other nations, and it is highly unlikely that they will ever be able to repay what is owed. Attempts to repay the debt are virtually crippling their economies and making it even more difficult to feed their people, a basic tenet of the world systems theory, introduced in Chapter 2.

As an outsider looking at the plight of poorer countries, it is easy to say that they should reduce their fertility rates further to offset their declines in death rates. Family-planning programs have been introduced, but they often meet with limited success in rural regions where traditions remain strong. China is a notable exception, and provides an interesting example of the extent to which a nation will go to reduce its fertility rate. Through incentives and deterrents, China strongly encourages families in urban areas to have only one child. Families in the rural countryside can have two children under some circumstances. China's current fertility rate is 1.6, and its population is expected to grow only minimally between now and 2025 (Population Reference Bureau 2010b).

China's One-Child Policy

The grandmother wrestled the baby girl from the mother's arms, after hours of arguments that were going nowhere. The decision had been made. Both women were sobbing, but the baby girl slept peacefully, not knowing what was in store for her. The grandmother put several layers of clothing on her granddaughter, despite the warmth on this June night. She then laid the one-week-old girl in a box lined with blankets, a bottle, and an extra package of formula, and carried her off into the night. The grandmother could hear the wails of the baby's mother, her own daughter, as she headed down the road to a nearby village. "My baby, my baby, bring back my baby . . . ," the mother cried, although she felt too, deep in her heart, that this must be done. The grandmother quickly scurried with her bundle toward the park, which was eerily deserted in the late night. In the light of the moon she kissed her granddaughter for the very last time, propped up the bottle next to the sleeping baby, and set the baby and her makeshift bed on a bench located in a popular area of the park. The grandmother looked up above with tears in her eyes and prayed to her god that the child be found safely and quickly in the early dawn light. With that, she disappeared alone into the night, never to see or hear of her granddaughter again.

This is a story that has occurred tens, if not hundreds, of thousands of times in China. What would prompt a grandmother to take her granddaughter away from her parents and abandon her in a public place? The answer lies in a complex interweaving of government policy and cultural traditions.

China, like many countries, had a population that was rapidly rising, and the government worried about its people—would there be enough resources to feed and house everyone sufficiently? To combat tremendous population growth, in the late 1970s, the Chinese government implemented what is known as the **one-child policy**. It consists of three main points: (1) delayed marriage and delayed childbearing; (2) fewer and healthier births; and (3) one child per couple (with a few exceptions, such as if the first child is disabled). The policy has since been modified somewhat. In rural areas a family may be allowed to have a second child if the first one is a girl, although certain rules surrounding the second birth are in effect (Hays 2010).

Families who follow the one-child policy can be rewarded with extra salary, larger houses, or better jobs. The official sanction for violating the one-child policy is a stiff fine. Second or subsequent children may not be eligible for social, educational, and health care benefits. The government actively promotes the one-child policy through massive media efforts that include newspapers, radio, television, theater, music, local performances, and schools; by a thorough set of laws and policies that govern marriage and fertility; and by strategically placing compliance officers in workplaces and in neighborhoods. For example, each city, county, and township has a family-planning station focused on publicity and education. Most Chinese willingly comply with the policy and see it as good for the country.

The one-child policy has been both praised and condemned around the world (Fitzpatrick 2009; Hays 2010). It has been applauded as an effective tool for ensuring that China will be able to support and feed its people, increase their standard of living, and combat widespread poverty. In this regard, it has been highly successful. China's population has been reduced by 300 million people (which is about the number of people who live in the entire United States), relieving some of the obvious stresses of overpopulation. Families are more able to concentrate their limited resources on one child, thereby leading to higher standards of living, higher levels of education, and increased income. Women are able to work outside the home instead of raising multiple children (Rosenberg 2009).

However, China's one-child policy has also been criticized as an abuse of human rights because of the disappearance of girls, both before and after birth. The sex ratio is becoming highly imbalanced, with the recent Chinese census finding 32 million more boys than girls under age 20 (LaFraniere 2009). What has happened to all of these girls is a matter of speculation (Hesketh et al. 2005). Some girls are

To combat population growth, the Chinese government implemented what is known as "the one-child policy"; however, the cultural preference for boys has resulted in a severe sex-ratio imbalance.

not recorded in the birth statistics and are therefore uncounted in the census. They are "noncitizens" and ineligible for any government benefits. Others are abandoned, such as the little girl in the story, because there is no formal mechanism to put a child up for adoption. Still, others are killed in utero or quickly after birth, although the number of these is likely declining (Hesketh et al. 2005). Chinese officials have banned elective amniocentesis and have attempted to restrict the use of ultrasound scanners that would determine the sex of the fetus so as to stop the selective abortion of female fetuses. Yet, the number of female births continues to be less than what would be expected given the number of male births in the population.

Why is it that girls, rather than boys, have disappeared? In China, where generally only one child is allowed, girls are viewed as an economic liability and parents see boys as a better investment. Sons are expected to carry on the family lineage and take care of their aging parents. When a woman marries, she turns her focus to her husband's family. Customs like these reinforce the preference for sons—daughters are seen as expensive, wasting precious resources and providing little or no security for parents in old age. Although the Chinese government has expanded women's opportunities, rights, and obligations in recent decades, longstanding patriarchal attitudes change slowly.

Japan

In contrast to China, which is trying to limit births, the Japanese government is trying to increase the country's birthrate. Nearly one-quarter of Japan's population is 65 or older. The rapidly aging population, coupled with a birthrate of only about 1.26 births per woman—far below replacement level—shows a declining population. Projections are that the population of Japan will decline from 127 million today to 90 million by 2055 (Haub 2010; Ministry of Internal Affairs and Communications 2009). One of the reasons that women in Japan have so few children is because they have the near exclusive responsibility for taking care of them rather than sharing the workload with their partners (Lee et al. 2010). Japanese fathers, especially those who work on salary, spend very little time with their children. This is due in part to the demands made on employed men, but also due to the cultural ideas that child care is women's work (Demetriou 2010).

However, hoping to encourage more births, the government instituted the "Angel Plan" in 1994 to help couples raise children. The government reasoned that if they can encourage fathers to become more involved in the lives of their children, families might choose to have more births. Their campaign profiled a well-known Japanese celebrity playing with his son, with a slogan claiming "A man who doesn't raise his children can't be called a father" (Ishii-Kuntz 2003; Ishii-Kuntz et al. 2004).

Because fertility rates remained low, in 2009 Japan introduced a much broader version of the Angel Plan. The government recognized the difficulty that people feel in having to choose between work and marriage/parenthood. In Japanese surveys, over 90 percent of couples said that they did want to marry and would like to have at least two children (Haub 2010). Therefore, the new program intends to remove aspects of Japanese society that encourage people to become "workaholics." The goal is to make society more conducive to sharing childrearing and household chores, allowing men to spend more time at home, and allowing mothers with young children to work outside the home. Specifically, the revised Angel Plan's goals include (Haub 2010):

- encouraging workers to use 100 percent of their paid annual leave (as opposed to the current 47 percent)
- reducing by half the number of employees who work 60 hours or more per week, currently at 11 percent
- increasing the amount of time husbands spend on child care and housework from the current 1 hour per day to 2.5 hours per day

WHAT DO YOU THINK?

Which country's fertility campaign do you think is most likely to obtain its goals—China or Japan? Can you defend your answer? What advice can you offer to India, which shares China's burgeoning population, or Germany, which shares Japan's low fertility rate?

- increasing the proportion of persons aged 60–64 who are working from 53 percent currently to 60 percent
- reducing the number of so-called "freeters," or youths who skip from one part-time job to another, from the current 1.9 million to 1.5 million or less by helping them find permanent employment

Will the Angel Plan succeed in encouraging more births, and will the Japanese be able to support their large number of elderly? Japan's demographic future is uncertain.

Fertility Rates in the United States

Historical Fluctuation

Now, let's turn to the United States, where some interesting fertility patterns emerge. One of these is its degree of fluctuation, as shown in Figure 9.1 (Hamilton et al. 2010; Martin et al. 2005). The birthrate shows remarkable highs and lows, often occurring in quick succession. In 1920, a period of relative affluence and limited birth control, the U.S. fertility rate (defined here as the number of live births per 1,000 women aged 15–44) hovered around 118 per 1,000 women. Yet, only 15 years later, the fertility rate plummeted, bottoming out in 1935 to 77 per 1,000 women. Why would such a steep decline occur in such a short amount of time? Birth control measures were still fairly limited in the 1930s, so that could not be the primary factor.

A sharp decline such as this tells us that fertility rates are far more than simply biological phenomena. Personal choices (i.e., whether to have a baby) are influenced by macro-level structural conditions and social trends. During the 1930s, the United States fell into a deep economic depression. Because of the dire consequences of the "Great Depression", fewer people were marrying, others were marrying later, and many families split up to pursue employment wherever they could find it. Not surprisingly, the birthrate declined accordingly.

Figure 9.1 Total Fertility Rate per 1,000 Women Aged 15–44, 1920–2008

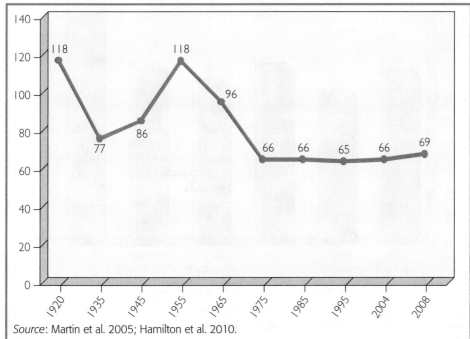

The U.S. fertility rate fluctuates according to macro-level factors: economic conditions, population trends, wars, and social change.

Source: Martin et al. 2005; Hamilton et al. 2010.

However, a decade later, as the depression was ending and the United States moved into and out of World War II, the birthrate rose to a level not seen for decades. By 1950, the fertility rate rose to 106 per 1,000 women aged 15–44, a period that has since been described as the "baby boom." The United States experienced a degree of affluence after the war, couples married younger, and the number of employed married women working outside the home declined. Women were encouraged to find fulfillment as wives, mothers, and homemakers, as articles and advertisements in "women's magazines" indicated (Friedan 1963). Family, particularly motherhood, became a primary cultural goal.

Yet, by the early 1960s the fertility rate began to drop again. This period, and through the 1970s, is sometimes referred to as the **baby bust**, and rates continued on a downward trend to about 69 births per 1,000 married women today (Hamilton et al. 2010). What happened during this period? There are a number of micro-level reasons for the rapid decline in fertility rates. One demographic explanation is that the sheer number of women of childbearing age was lower in the 1970s, which translates into fewer children being born. Also, birth control pills became readily available. Other reasons for the decline in fertility rates are more social in origin and represent changing attitudes about women's social and family roles. More women began going to college, including graduate and professional schools, and gained employment in new fields. Women saw that additional options were available to them, so many chose to delay childbearing, or not to have children at all.

Another interesting pattern is that U.S. fertility rates are higher than virtually any other developed nation (Population Reference Bureau 2010b). The United States is one of the few developed nations whose birthrate approaches replacement level. Other countries must rely on immigration to maintain their population size.

Fertility rates vary across racial and ethnic groups in the United States. Some are likely to have more children than others, as shown in Figure 9.2. Data from the

Figure 9.2 **Fertility Rate by Race and Ethnicity per 1,000 Women Aged 15–44, 2008**

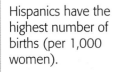

Hispanics have the highest number of births (per 1,000 women).

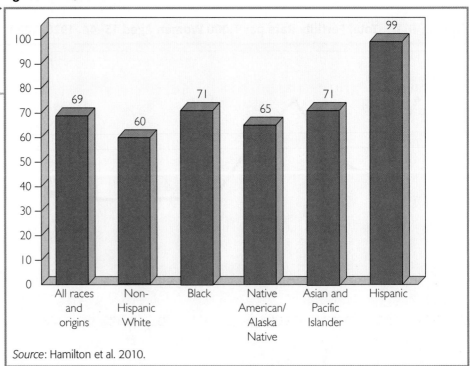

Source: Hamilton et al. 2010.

U.S. Census Bureau indicate that non-Hispanic Whites and American Indians/Alaska Natives have the fewest children on average (60 and 65 births per 1,000 women aged 15–44, respectively). Hispanics have the highest fertility rate at 99 births per 1,000 women (Hamilton et al. 2010).

Delayed Parenthood

I didn't plan to have my first baby at 41. It just sort of happened that way. I married my first husband when I was in my late twenties. We thought we would have at least two children, maybe even three, well before my fortieth birthday. But, well, it wasn't a very strong marriage. I was 34 years old when we divorced. I hoped to remarry and even joined a few singles-type clubs to speed the process along. It took me almost four years to find the right man. We married nearly one year after our first date. That's pretty quick, I guess, but I knew it was the right thing to do. Less than two years later, Jack was born. He's beautiful! He's wonderful! I couldn't be happier. The best thing about waiting is that I don't have to struggle so much between my career and my family. I'm not trying to build them both simultaneously. I also feel a bit more settled down. I have a rock-solid relationship with my husband—I wouldn't have had that in my first marriage. But there have been some challenges. Throughout the pregnancy I worried about birth defects. Jack is fine but you just never know. I guess another downside is that I would like a sibling for him. If you start your family later, you can run out of time to have another child. We might start looking at the opportunities to adopt. (Alexis, age 42)

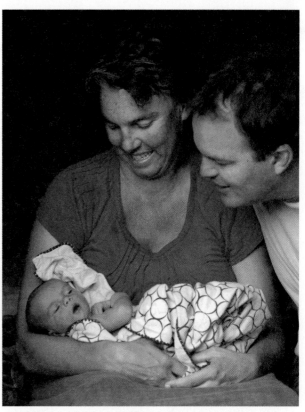

Many women and men are delaying the age at which they have their first child because of educational or career opportunities. Modern technology can assist older couples in getting pregnant.

Another interesting new pattern is the delay in having children. In 1970, the average age at which women had their first birth was around 21.4 years, but today, it is around age 25 (Mathews and Hamilton 2009). Another way of seeing the change is this: about 27 percent of women aged 30–34 do not have children today, compared with only 16 percent of women in that age group in 1970 (U.S. Census Bureau 2008b). It is likely that many of these women will eventually have one or more children; they are simply postponing the age at which they have them. (Note: The Census Bureau does not keep equivalent data on men.)

Delayed parenthood is more than simply a biological phenomenon. The reasons for later parenthood are often social in nature (e.g., women wanting to pursue education or careers; the delayed age at first marriage; the rise in the number of second marriages). The response to persons having a child in their 40s, 50s, or even 60s takes on an interesting twist depending on the sex of the parent, as shown in the box on pages 266–267, "Using the Sociological Imagination: Having a Baby at 50 or 60." Although most people hardly bat an eye if a man becomes a father at age 50, attitudes are quite different if a woman becomes a mother at 50.

Now that we've covered the big picture, let's look specifically at the micro-level decisions people make about whether or not to become parents.

WHAT DO YOU THINK?

What do you predict will be the fertility trends over the next 20 years in the United States? Will fertility increase, decrease, or stay the same? What is the evidence for your answer?

USING
the Sociological Imagination

Having a Baby at 50 or 60

There is a lot of public concern about teenagers being too young to have a baby, but when is a person too old to have a baby? In the past, biology answered that question, at least for women. However, modern technology has changed this, and with the help of donor eggs women can now have children considerably later in life.

At first glance, Judith Cates's life seems the picture of ordinary as she brushes the hair of her five-year-old twins, picks up their toys, and takes them to pizza parties. However, a closer look at their family reveals something highly unusual. Judith is 63 years old and gave birth to her girls when she was 57. "They keep us laughing with everything they do and say," said Cates. "If I wasn't so old, we'd try for two more."

Marilyn Nolen also came to parenting a little later in life than she expected. She became the proud mother of twin boys when she was 55 years old, and now, at 65, is raising her two rambunctious 10-year-olds. Judith and Marilyn are leaders in a growing trend. Although birthrates have dropped among women in their teens, 20s, and 30s, the 40-and-beyond group has had an increase in birth rates (Hamilton et al. 2010). The Centers for Disease Control and Prevention reports 7,349 first-time mothers between ages 45 and 54 in 2007, a 5 percent increase in one year (Hamilton et al. 2009).

What is happening here? Assisted reproductive technology (ART) seems to be the answer. Women over 40 have only a 10 percent chance of getting pregnant without it, and the odds of a woman getting pregnant naturally in her 50s or even 60s is virtually zero. However, all of these women can get pregnant with relative ease using eggs from younger women, and they can expect reasonably normal pregnancies and healthy babies. It is older women's eggs, not their uteruses that decline at menopause, leading to age-related fertility problems.

Researchers tracked the fates of 77 post-menopausal women aged 50–63 who underwent in-vitro fertilization with donor eggs at the University of Southern California over a 10-year period. Each woman had to pass a thorough medical exam, including a cardiac stress test and a uterine lining biopsy to ensure that the womb could still respond to the hormones that would be given to support the pregnancy. The women had, on average, three to four embryos transferred. All told, 42 of the 77 women had live births—including three who each had two consecutive births—for a total of 45 births producing 61 babies (31 single children, 12 sets of twins, and 2 sets of triplets), all of them healthy. Some complications such as pregnancy-related high blood pressure do increase with age, but there was no definitive medical reason for excluding these older women from becoming pregnant on the basis of age alone.

Still, helping women in their 50s and 60s become pregnant is controversial. The ethics committee of the American Society of Reproductive Medicine concluded that the practice is not unethical but should be discouraged. Others echoed that view, warning against widely promoting the practice. "Just because you can do something doesn't mean you should," said Robert Stillman, medical director of the Shady Grove Fertility Reproductive Science Center in Rockville, Maryland. The center refused to treat women older than 50, the average age of menopause. However, there are no restrictions on men's ages for fertility treatment.

Yet, researchers have found that older adults often make excellent parents. A study of 30,000 households showed that people who had children in their 40s were better off financially, spent more time with their children, and had a closer connection to their children's friends than younger parents, according to Brian Powell, a sociology professor at Indiana University. His research can be summarized: The older the parent, the better off the child. He could not analyze the results of parents who had children in their 50s and 60s because statistically there are so few of them, but the presumption is that the findings would be consistent.

The medical, psychological, and social effects of late motherhood deserve careful consideration. However, for women who want to go down that path, the odds of success are remarkably good when they use donor eggs from women in their 20s and 30s.

Source: Hamilton et al. 2009, 2010; Hefling 2004; Hutchison 2010.

CRITICAL THINKING QUESTIONS

1. What arguments can you make for and against helping a 50- to 60-year-old woman to have a successful pregnancy by allowing her to use donor eggs?

2. Some people claim it is unethical or inappropriate to help women in their 50s or 60s have babies. Do you think these people would make the same argument against men who are in their 50s or 60s fathering babies? Why or why not?

3. A number of older men in recent years have fathered children while in their 50s and 60s, including Paul McCartney, Michael Douglas, and Larry King. Have they (or their younger wives) experienced stigma because of it? What if the reverse occurred—a 55-year-old woman had a baby with her 35-year-old husband? Is there a double standard?

Deciding to Parent

In the past, adults became parents without much forethought. It was just something that happened. Today, as pronatalism is on the decline, having children may be an explicit (or implicit) decision. What are some issues surrounding the decision of whether or not to become a parent?

The Rewards and Costs of Children

There are two contrasting pictures of how children affect adults' lives. One is bright and rosy, emphasizing the emotional rewards. The other is dark and gloomy, emphasizing the emotional or financial costs. For many people, the realities are somewhere in between. First, let's look at the costs:

The Costs of Parenting No doubt about it, children are costly. I don't just mean dollars and cents. Parents experience more stress, have lower psychological well-being, and face greater declines in intimacy with their partner, compared to those without children (Doss et al. 2009; Gorchoff et al. 2008; Knoester and Eggebeen 2006; Simon 2008). And *then* there's the money.

Economists often talk about **direct financial costs** (out-of-pocket expenses for things such as food, clothing, housing, and education) and **opportunity costs** (lost opportunities for income by working only part-time or not at all because of children). In many developing nations, children are a valuable source of labor, and their economic benefits to the family may exceed their financial and opportunity costs. However, in developed nations like the United States, the cost of children is the primary explanation for the decline in fertility rates. The U.S. Department of Agriculture estimates that a typical two-parent, middle-class family spends about $222,360 (pretax) raising a child to the age of 18 (Lino 2010). Expenses include housing, food, transportation, clothing, health care, education/child care, and other miscellaneous expenses (personal care items, recreation expenses, etc.), and are based on the Consumer Expenditure Survey. And remember, this is only *one* child. It does not include the

Figure 9.3 **Expenditure Shares on a Child from Birth Through Age 17 as a Percentage of Total Child-Rearing Expenditures, 2008**

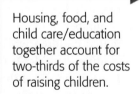

Housing, food, and child care/education together account for two-thirds of the costs of raising children.

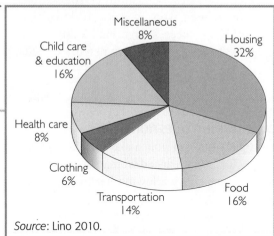

Source: Lino 2010.

cost of college tuition, which averaged $7,020 at a public university during the 2009–2010 academic year, and is rising over 6 percent annually (College Board 2009).

What costs so much money? Figure 9.3 shows average expenses for a typical American two-parent family with two children. These cost estimates are for the youngest child. As you can see, housing is the most expensive item.

With a financial picture such as this, one might wonder why anyone would want children at all. What are the rewards of being a parent?

Rewards of Parenting Perhaps one reason that studies bleakly focus on the financial or emotional costs of parenthood is that the rewards are more difficult to measure. The emotional feelings of love and devotion are harder to quantify. However, children can bring tremendous joy and purpose into people's lives, as shown in the box on page 269 "Families as Lived Experience: The 'Costs' of Raising a Child" (Hansen 2002). A nationwide Gallup poll asked parents about the things they gained most from having children. Common responses included "children bring love and affection"; "it is a pleasure to watch them grow"; "they bring joy, happiness, and fun"; "they create a sense of family"; and "they bring fulfillment and a sense of satisfaction" (Gallup Poll 2001). Parents experience great satisfaction and take considerable pride in seeing their children's accomplishments—excelling in the school spelling bee, singing in the church choir, giving her first violin recital, making the winning goal in the soccer game—and parents take some of measure of credit for their child's success. Another study by the Pew Charitable Trust asked people where they find the most fulfillment in their lives. Eighty-five percent of parents said the relationship with their minor children was most fulfilling, whereas only 23 percent with jobs or careers evaluated those as most fulfilling (Taylor et al. 2007a).

Another reward of parenting is that it tends to provide the parents with more opportunities to interact with relatives, neighbors, and friends (Gallagher and Gerstel 2001; Nomaguchi and Milkie 2003). Children provide links for parents with social institutions such as churches or schools, thereby providing further opportunities to develop relationships.

Having children is also a symbol that a person has reached adulthood. Parents are assumed to be more stable than childfree adults. This works to men's advantage in the workforce, where they are seen as more reliable and dedicated to the job, as the term *family man* implies (Seccombe 1991).

FAMILIES
as Lived Experience

The "Costs" of Raising a Child

Without a doubt, raising children is expensive! So, what do you get for your money?

The government calculated the cost of raising a child from birth to age 18 and came up with $222,360 [numbers updated by author] for a middle-income family. Talk about sticker shock! That doesn't touch college tuition. For those with children, that figure leads to wild fantasies about all the money we could have banked if not for _____ (insert your child's name here). For others, that number might confirm the decision to remain childfree. However, $222,360 isn't so bad if you break it down: It translates into $12,353 a year, $1,029 a month, or $238 a week. That's a mere $34 a day—almost a dollar and a half an hour. Still, you might think the best financial advice says don't have children if you want to be "rich." What do you get for your $222,360?

1. Naming rights; first, middle, and last.
2. Glimpses of God every day.
3. Giggles under the covers every night.
4. More love than your heart can hold.
5. Butterfly kisses and Velcro hugs.
6. Endless wonder over rocks, ants, clouds, and warm cookies.
7. A hand to hold, usually covered with jam.
8. A partner for blowing bubbles, flying kites, building sandcastles, and skipping down the sidewalk in the pouring rain.
9. Someone to laugh yourself silly with no matter what the boss said or how your stocks performed that day.
10. You never have to grow up.
11. You get to finger-paint, carve pumpkins, play hide-and-seek, catch lightning bugs, and never stop believing in Santa Claus.
12. You have an excuse to keep reading the *Adventures of Piglet and Pooh*, watching Saturday morning cartoons, going to Disney movies, and wishing on stars.
13. You get to frame rainbows, hearts, and flowers under refrigerator magnets and collect spray-painted noodle wreaths for Christmas, handprints set in clay for Mother's Day, and cards with backward letters for Father's Day.
14. There is no greater bang for your buck.
15. You get to be a hero just for retrieving a Frisbee off the garage roof, taking the training wheels off the bike, removing a splinter, filling the wading pool, coaxing a wad of gum out of bangs, and coaching a baseball team that never wins but always gets treated to ice cream regardless.
16. You get a front row seat to history to witness the first step, first word, first bra, first date, and first time behind the wheel.
17. You get to be immortal.
18. You get another branch added to your family tree, and if you're lucky, a long list of limbs in your obituary called grandchildren.
19. You get an education in psychology, nursing, criminal justice, communications, and human sexuality that no college can match.
20. In the eyes of a child, you rank right up there with God, Santa Claus, the Easter Bunny, and the Tooth Fairy.
21. You have all the power to heal a boo-boo, scare away the monsters under the bed, patch a broken heart, police a slumber party, ground them forever, and love them without limits, so one day they will, like you, love without counting the cost.

Source: Hansen 2002.

CRITICAL THINKING QUESTIONS

1. If it costs middle-income families approximately $222,360 to raise a child to age 18, but wealthy families pay more and lower-income families less, what additional or fewer items are these other children receiving? Are the items extras? Are they necessities?
2. What do you see as the emotional rewards of parenting? How do you evaluate these against the financial costs, particularly if you want more than one child? Is it possible, or fair, to compare emotional and financial issues?

WHAT DO YOU THINK?

Do you want to have children? What do you see as the rewards and costs for you personally?

Remaining Childfree

About one in five women between the ages of 40 and 44 do not have children, double the number just a generation ago (Dye 2008). It is possible that a small number of these women may still have children, but most will not. At first, this seems like a radical departure from the past, but a look through history reveals other time periods with similar or even higher rates of childlessness. For example, during the Great Depression of the 1930s, about 25 percent of women in their childbearing years did not have children (Graybill et al. 1958).

Who is most likely to be childfree today? Women aged 40–44 who do not have children are a diverse group; however, overall, they tend to have completed college or graduate school, are native born, and live in central cities and metropolitan areas. Blacks and Whites are most likely to be childfree and Hispanics are least likely (Dye 2008).

People have different reasons for remaining childfree (Koropeckyj-Cox 2002). Some are childfree because of longstanding infertility; others postponed childbearing until age-related infertility prohibited it; and others chose to remain childfree voluntarily.

Infertility   Not all individuals without children are childfree by choice. **Infertility** is the inability to get pregnant after one year of trying (Centers for Disease Control and Prevention 2009c). It is a medical problem affecting about 12 percent of adults of childbearing age in the United States, and cuts across all income groups and racial and ethnic categories. Infertility affects men and women equally; 30 percent of infertility is due to a female factor, 30 percent to a male factor, and in the remaining cases, it results from problems in both partners or from indeterminate causes (Resolve: The National Infertility Association 2010).

Medical technology offers treatment options to women and men trying to conceive a child, including hormone treatments, intrauterine insemination, and more advanced technologies like in vitro fertilization (IVF) with or without egg or sperm donation, and surrogacy. **Assisted reproductive technology (ART)** includes all fertility treatments in which both egg and sperm are handled. For example, during IVF, a woman will use ovulation-stimulating drugs to produce an excess number of eggs. These eggs are then surgically

TABLE 9.2   **2007 Pregnancy Success Rates**

ART success rates vary by the woman's age. Women under 35 are three times more likely to have a successful ART treatment than women aged 41–42.

TYPE OF CYCLE	AGE OF WOMEN			
	35	**35–37**	**38–40**	**41–42**
Fresh Embryos from Nondonor Eggs				
Number of cycles	42,119	23,503	20,608	9,535
% of cycles resulting in pregnancies	46%	37%	28%	18%
% of cycles resulting in live births	40%	31%	21%	12%
Average number of embryos transferred	2.2	2.5	2.8	3.1
% of pregnancies with twins	33%	28%	22%	14%
% of pregnancies with triplets or more	3.5%	4.5%	4.0%	2.5%
Frozen Embryos from Nondonor Eggs				
Number of transfers	10,515	5,386	3,518	1,125
% of transfers resulting in live births	34%	30%	25%	21%
Average number of embryos transferred	2.2	2.2	2.4	2.5

Source: Centers for Disease Control and Prevention 2009c.

removed and fertilized in a dish with sperm. If fertilization takes place, the physician implants the embryo(s) into the woman's uterus.

About 120,000 ART cycles were conducted in 2007 that used the women's own eggs, and another 16,000 that used eggs from a donor. About one-third of these resulted in a birth. In other words, it averages about three attempts (at over $12,000 each) to have a successful birth (Centers for Disease Control and Prevention 2009c). Success rates, however, differ by a woman's age, as shown in Table 9.2. Some insurance companies will cover part of the costs, whereas other insurers will not cover ART at all (American Society for Reproductive Medicine 2009).

Many issues surrounding ART are controversial. For example, how many embryos can be implanted at one time? No U.S. laws address this, but the American Society for Reproductive Medicine recommends implanting no more than two because of risk to the mother and fetuses. However, some physicians ignore these recommendations, as shown by Jon and Kate (Plus Eight) Gosselin of reality TV fame, and Nadya Suleman, nicknamed the Octomom, who bore eight children (after already having six older ones).

Another issue is what happens to unused embryos. Should they be destroyed, sold, saved indefinitely, or used for research? These are questions that society is only beginning to grapple with.

One controversy surrounding ART is how many embryos should be implanted at one time? The American Society for Reproductive Medicine recommends implanting no more than two but some physicians and their patients ignore these recommendations, as shown by Nadya Suleman, the so-called "Octomom," after giving birth to eight children (while also having six older ones).

Because of the high rate of ART failure, and because some women have repeated miscarriages and cannot carry a fetus to term, some people are turning to surrogacy instead. **Surrogacy** involves a relationship in which one woman gives birth for another person (or couple) who then adopts or takes legal custody of the child.

Surrogacy can be accomplished in different ways. Most often, the husband's sperm is implanted in the surrogate by artificial insemination. In this case, the surrogate mother is both the genetic mother and the gestational mother of the child. At other times, when the intended mother can produce fertile eggs, but cannot carry a child to term, her egg is removed, combined with her partner's sperm in IVF, and then implanted in the surrogate mother.

Surrogacy, too, is not without ethical considerations (Hall et al. 2008). States have conflicting laws surrounding surrogacy; for example, some require at least one parent to have a genetic link to the child (Saul 2009). Surrogacy also raises concerns about "renting out bodies" and the potential for exploiting low-income women or those in developing nations. In some countries, such as India, surrogate motherhood for wealthy Americans is becoming a big business (Gentleman 2008).

Voluntarily Childfree

As a child I usually preferred the company of adults, or at least older children. As a teen I never wanted to babysit—boring! Today, I am much more interested in my career, travel, and hanging out with my husband. Don't get me wrong—I'm a caring person. I volunteer for Meals on Wheels twice a month, and I am involved in a number of social issues in my community. It's just that, well, I don't want to have kids (Janine, age 33).

Increasing numbers of men and women are voting no on parenthood (Kelly 2009). Having children is now considered in most circles an option rather than a mandate for a happy marriage. For example, in 2007, only 41 percent of surveyed adults reported that "children are

Figure 9.4 Linking Children and a Successful Marriage (percent)

Most adults think that children are "very" or "rather important" for a successful marriage.

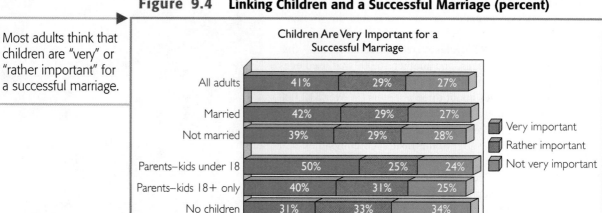

Children Are Very Important for a Successful Marriage

	Very important	Rather important	Not very important
All adults	41%	29%	27%
Married	42%	29%	27%
Not married	39%	29%	28%
Parents–kids under 18	50%	25%	24%
Parents–kids 18+ only	40%	31%	25%
No children	31%	33%	34%

Source: Taylor et al. 2007a.

very important for a successful marriage", down from 65 percent in 1990. As shown in Figure 9.4 (Taylor et al. 2007a), there is very little difference in attitudes between those who are married or not married, while differences remain between parents and the childfree. However, even among parents, one-quarter believe that children are not very important for a successful marriage.

The decision to forgo children is usually not made once, but many times because people undergo a *process* of deciding about children. They might think about whether or not to have children while in their 20s then revisit the issue in their 30s, like Janine, and again in their 40s.

Women usually have firmer opinions than men about forgoing parenthood (Koropeckyj-Cox and Pendell 2007a, 2007b; Koropeckyj-Cox et al. 2007). It is men, not women, who are more likely to report that "it is better for a person to have a child than to go through life childless" (Seccombe 1991).

A common concern that childfree people express is "Will I regret my decision? Will I be lonely in my old age?" However, elderly persons without children do not seem to be disadvantaged. For example, older childfree adults have similar or lower rates of depression compared to other older adults (Bures et al. 2009).

Adoption

Adoption touches the lives of many people. It provides parents to infants who are given away at birth, and for older children whose parents have died or had their parental rights revoked. It offers individuals and couples a way to add children to their families when they cannot conceive or carry a pregnancy to term. It provides an avenue for humanitarian assistance by offering a home to a child without one. And, it can provide a legal relationship between an adult and a nonbiological child for whom the adult is already caring, such as a stepchild, or the child of a gay or lesbian partner.

Although only about 4 percent of Americans are adopted, one survey based on a representative nationwide sample of 1,416 adults found that 64 percent reported a direct personal experience with adoption; they, a family member, or a close friend was adopted, had adopted a child, or had relinquished a child for adoption (National Adoption Information Clearinghouse 2002).

Despite its prevalence, little attention is paid to adoption in current college textbooks that focus on family issues. A content analysis of 21 family textbooks and 16 undergraduate readers reveals that 4 of the 21 texts reviewed (19 percent) and 3 of the 16 readers reviewed (19 percent) offered no coverage of adoption at all (Fisher 2003). Among those books that did

TABLE 9.3   Number of Positive and Negative Points Made About Adoption, by Type of Book

Why do negative points about adoption far outweigh the positive?

TYPE OF BOOK	POSITIVE POINTS	NEGATIVE POINTS
Texts (21)	38	57
Readers (16)	10	37
All books (37)	48	94

Source: Fisher 2003.

discuss adoption, coverage was very brief. Moreover, as shown in Table 9.3, the negative points made about adoption far outnumbered the positive points. Books tended to comment on potential problems, such as the behavioral and psychological problems among adoptees; the unavailability of healthy children; the high costs of adoption; legal problems; the stigma surrounding adoption; ideological or ethical problems associated with adoption; long waits; or the unknowns about the child's genetic background or physical or emotional treatment. They failed to mention that most adoptions work out well and are beneficial for both parents and children.

Once stigmatized and often kept secret, adoption is now more open and socially supported than ever (Small 2007). Adoptions can occur through licensed public agencies that specialize in placing children in adoptive families, known as **public adoptions**. Adoptions can also be arranged directly between adoptive parents and the biological birth mother, usually through the assistance of an attorney. These are referred to as **private adoptions**. In these adoptions, the attorney may contact social workers, other attorneys, doctors, or place a notice in a newspaper looking for a woman who intends to relinquish her child. Although baby "selling" is prohibited, the adopting couple likely will pay the birth mother's medical fees and often her living expenses and other miscellaneous expenses. Private adoptions tend to be more expensive than public adoptions, although they are more common because they are likely to result in the adoptive family obtaining an infant. The children in public adoptions are often older or have special needs.

Whether public or private, most adoptions in the past were conducted under a cloak of secrecy. Unless the adoption was occurring among kin, chances are it was a **closed adoption**, with all identifying information sealed and unavailable to all parties. Adopted children knew nothing about their birth parents or their genetic makeup. Much has changed in the past two decades. Adoptions are far more likely to be **semi-open adoptions**, in which biological and adoptive families exchange personal information through a social worker or attorney, but have no direct contact, or **open adoptions**, which involve direct contact between the biological and adoptive families. The contact can run the gamut from a one-time meeting to a lifelong relationship. Semi-open and open adoptions can have many advantages for the child, birth mother, and adoptive parents (Miall and March 2005).

We know that women who put their children up for adoption are often young, with limited education and financial means. But who adopts children? Most adoptive parents are married, highly educated, and have higher-than-average incomes. Compared to other mothers, adoptive mothers are less likely to work full-time outside the home.

Transracial Adoptions   Most adoptive parents are White, yet 40 percent of children in the United States available for adoption are Black. This raises a controversial issue: Is it appropriate to place minority children with White families (Simon and Roorda 2009)? In the 1970s, the Association of Black Social Workers and Native American activists strongly objected to placing Black and American Indian children with White families, suggesting that transracial adoptions amounted to cultural genocide. Afterward, the number of transracial adoptions declined sharply. However, a longitudinal study conducted over 20 years found that minority children placed in White homes generally develop positive racial and ethnic identities and are knowledgeable of their history and culture (Simon and Alstein 2000). Today, there is less stigma surrounding transracial adoptions, and they are more common.

Single-Parent Adoptions A generation ago, if a single woman presented herself to an adoption agency to apply for a child, she probably would have been turned away. Much has changed in 30 years. Today, single women are actively involved in adoption, particularly with children who are older, are racial or ethnic minorities, or are from other countries. Seventeen percent of adoptions are conducted by single women (Jones 2008). However, single men still experience bias. Despite growing recognition of men as nurturers, there is still suspicion that "a single man could not be sensitive to a child's needs" or "I wonder what kind of man wants to raise a child alone" (Marindin 1987).

Adoption by Gays and Lesbians Lesbians and gays have always adopted, though in the past they usually hid their sexual orientation. Today, just as gays and lesbians are becoming more visible in other aspects of American society, they are being considered more seriously as potential adoptive parents. As of 2010, states no longer ban adoption by gays and lesbians. Yet only 10 states allow for openly gay and lesbian couples to jointly adopt: California, Connecticut, Illinois, Indiana, Maine, Massachusetts, New Jersey, New York, Oregon, and Vermont, as well as Washington, D.C. (Human Rights Campaign 2009). In other states, the only real recourse is for one partner to adopt and then for the other partner to apply as the second parent or co-parent.

There are many concerns surrounding same-sex couples adopting children, many of which are based on stereotypes or myths about sexual orientation or homosexuality. What are these concerns, and what do research findings suggest (Biblarz and Savci 2010; Biblarz and Stacey 2010; Stacey and Biblarz 2001)?

- *Homosexual parents will molest their children.* No scientific research finds a significant link between homosexuality and pedophilia.
- *Children raised in homosexual households will become gay.* Research findings suggest that children raised by gay and lesbian parents are no more likely to become homosexual than children raised by heterosexuals.
- *Children raised in gay or lesbian households will have mental health problems.* Children of same-sex parents show either no difference from those of heterosexual parents, or show a reduction in levels of anxiety, depression, behavioral problems, and traditional gender stereotypes. They also score as high or higher on self-esteem and secure attachments.
- *Children will be teased and harassed.* Children of gay and lesbian parents may be vulnerable to teasing and harassment, particularly as they approach adolescence. However, gay and lesbian parents go to great lengths to prepare and support their children.

The leading medical society of pediatricians, the 65,000-member American Academy of Pediatrics, endorses the legal rights of homosexuals to adopt a partner's child, saying "children deserve to know their relationships with both parents are stable and legally recognized" (Hall 2002).

WHAT DO YOU THINK?

If so many people are touched directly or indirectly by adoption, why do you think there is so little discussion of adoption in college-level family textbooks? Do you think that adoption carries a stigma?

International Adoption The number of Americans adopting children from other countries has declined sharply over the past few years. American parents adopted almost 13,000 foreign-born children in 2009, down from 23,000 in 2005 (U.S. Department of State 2010a). New standards have made adoption more difficult. Figure 9.5 reports how many children have been adopted over the past decade from China, Guatemala, and Russia, the top three countries in terms of international adoptions over the past decade.

Figure 9.5 Trends in International Adoption 1995–2009—Number of Children Adopted from China, Russia, and Guatemala

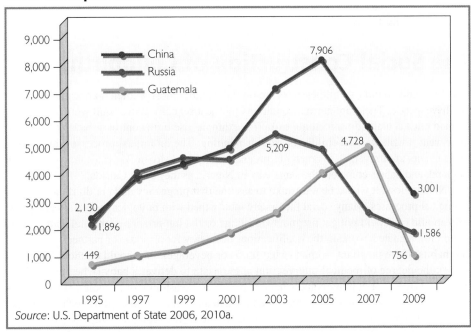

Source: U.S. Department of State 2006, 2010a.

The number of children adopted from other countries peaked in the mid-2000s, but has fallen sharply since then.

Political decisions or social problems often produce orphans who need families. For example, adoptions from China are in response to the strict one-child policy enforced by the Chinese government and adoptions in Russia are in response to the extreme poverty following the transition to a market economy. New on the list of popular countries for adoption is Ethiopia—many Americans are concerned about the large number of AIDS orphans. There were 2,277 U.S. adoptions of Ethiopian children in 2009, up from only 442 in 2005 (U.S. Department of State 2010a). Although only 330 children were adopted from Haiti in 2009, there is a surge of interest because of the 2010 earthquake that left thousands of children orphaned.

People look to international adoptions because of the declining availability of U.S.-born babies available for adoption. This is due to (1) a declining teenage pregnancy rate; (2) increasing use of contraceptives; (3) declining numbers of women placing their children up for adoption; (4) the availability of legal abortion; and (5) the declining stigma of unwed motherhood. Prospective parents are also looking internationally because adopting within the United States is slow, costly, and often has stricter guidelines such as age restrictions. Moreover, there is usually a more clear-cut termination of birth parents' rights in international adoptions that appeals to many people. Finally, some people adopt internationally for humanitarian reasons or because they have a personal interest or stake in that part of the world.

Children adopted from other countries are generally not available for adoption until they are at least six months to one year old, and in the case of Eastern Europe, sometimes considerably older. Most have spent all or much of their infancy in orphanages, and depending on the country, may have been exposed to certain risks, including parasites, or deficits in cognitive, social, physical, and medical attention. However, most children do well when placed with an adoptive family, and within a year, few children display atypical

Families in the United States adopted 13,000 children in 2009 who were born in other countries. Most children thrive when placed with a loving family.

behavior or socioemotional problems, especially if adopted young (Beverly et al. 2008; Johnson 2009; LeMare et al. 2007). Organizations for adoptive families, such as Families with Children from China (FCC), offer education, support, play groups, and celebration of the children's birth heritage.

The Social Construction of Childbirth

Infertility and voluntary childlessness are on the rise, but most women do become pregnant and have a child. These are normal conditions for most sexually active adult women; that is, a woman must actually do something extra (for example, use birth control or have an abortion) to prevent pregnancy and childbirth from happening. The biological processes involved in these events are universal. Women get pregnant the same way in Bangladesh as they do in England, and babies come out the same way in Nigeria as they do in Canada.

Nonetheless, it would be a mistake to assume that pregnancy and childbirth are simply biological processes. Many social factors are intertwined with biological processes that guide who should or should not get pregnant (ideal age or the importance of marital status); who should impregnate a woman (the qualifications necessary for a spouse or partner); conditions and habits of the pregnant woman (what foods or beverages she should or should not consume); the degree of medical intervention appropriate to deliver a baby (whether a baby is born in a hospital or at home); and what a baby is fed (breast milk or formula). How we conceive children, give birth to them, and care for them are highly influenced by social contexts.

Children are born every minute in all parts of the world. However, what may be considered normal, healthy, and appropriate childbirth practices in one time or place may be viewed as dangerous or barbaric in another. Even something as routine as the position a woman gives birth in—laying down on her back or squatting—reflects the relationship between social norms and social structure.

History: Towards the Medicalization of Childbirth

Until the nineteenth century, childbirth was considered largely "women's business," attended to by mothers, sisters, friends, and **midwives** who are attendants trained to help with childbirth (Cassidy 2007). Doctors were generally absent because childbirth was not considered a medical event. Midwives believe that for most women childbirth is a normal part of life and their job is to help women do what they already know innately how to do.

By the middle of the nineteenth century, obstetricians seeking to develop the medical specialization of obstetrics worked to eliminate midwives (Dawley 2003; Marland and Rafferty 2005). To achieve their professional dominance, physicians began claiming that childbirth was inherently dangerous, required medical assistance, and that midwives were inadequately trained to deal with the complex nature of delivering babies. Their desire to eliminate midwives had little to do with the safety of birth itself, but was due to professional turf battles. Social class and race were drawn into the debate—one's choice in birth attendant was an element of social prestige. Having a white upper-class male attendant was considered far more prestigious than being attended to by a minority or working-class female attendant.

As providers shifted, so did the role of women in childbirth (Wagner 2008). Instead of being largely in control, women surrendered to the power and authority of doctors, lured by the promise of new technology and painkillers. Childbirth began to be viewed as a medical event in need of drugs and technological intervention, which is referred to as the **medicalization of childbirth**. In the early 1900s, the German method of "twilight sleep" was introduced in the United States; a combination of morphine for pain relief and scopolamine and amnesiac that caused women to have no memories of giving birth (Cassidy 2007). Since it was difficult to apply technology to childbirth in the home, births were moved to a hospital. In 1900, about half of births in the United States occurred in the hospital, largely by social class and across racial and ethnic lines (Dawley

2003; Rooks 1997). By 1970, virtually all births occurred in hospitals. With this change of venue, birth shifted from being a normal, home-based event to a hospital-based and sickness-oriented experience (McCool and Simeone 2002; Wagner 2008). As sociologist Barbara Katz Rothman (1991) reminds us:

> The first thing to remember is that obstetrics is a surgical specialty. The management of childbirth within hospitals is essentially the same as the management of any other surgical event. . . . In surgery, the ideology of technology is dominant. Perhaps more clearly than anywhere else in medicine, the body is a machine, the doctor a mechanic.

In hospitals throughout most of the twentieth century, women routinely had their pubic areas shaved, were strapped down to cold metal labor and delivery tables with their legs up in stirrups (the most painful and unnatural position for childbirth), were given drugs that fogged the mind of mother and baby, were given enemas to empty the bowels (which usually empty on their own anyway in the early stages of labor), were hooked up to IVs and external fetal heart monitors that limit a laboring woman's mobility (and increase her pain), and were given episiotomies that cut through the perineum toward the anus to enlarge the vaginal opening (which often contributes to tearing). Husbands and partners were barred from the birth. This was the dominant birth paradigm until the 1980s when large numbers of women stepped up and asked for alternatives.

Most women have babies in a hospital, but those who opt for home births with a skilled birth attendant are pleased with the more personal approach, less invasive procedures, and the impressive safety record.

Childbirth Today

By the 1980s, books circulated advocating more natural birthing methods, arguing that although medical technology can save lives, it is overused, and causes emotional, financial, and physical problems. Birth settings responded as families demanded that hospital policies and environments focus on a mother's needs. Hospitals made their birth rooms more personal and cozy; a woman could write her own birth plan, possibly labor in water, and could use alternative positions for birth. However, hospitals still largely treat childbirth as a medical event and use technology that many claim is invasive without producing better results (Block 2008; Wagner 2008).

Some women choose to give birth outside of hospitals. **Birth centers** are freestanding facilities, usually with close access to, but not affiliated with, a hospital. They are usually staffed by midwives, offer home-like amenities, and provide families with the autonomy to choose their own birthing experience. However, insurance companies are less likely to cover births within a birthing center.

A small number of women are opting for home births attended by trained midwives. One study found that 91 percent of women who had their last baby at home would prefer to have their next baby at home. Among those who had experienced both a home birth and a hospital birth, 76 percent preferred the home birth, citing factors as safety, avoiding medical interventions common in hospital births, previously negative hospital experiences, more control, and a familiar home environment (Boucher et al. 2009). With skilled attendants present, women with low-risk pregnancies have outcomes as safe at home as in hospitals (de Jonge et al. 2009; NHS Knowledge Service 2009).

One study, which matched 1,046 hospital births with 1,046 home births, found that women giving birth in a hospital were five times more likely to have high blood pressure in labor, nine times more likely to have a severe perineal tear, three times more likely to have a postpartum hemorrhage, and three times more likely to have had a Cesarean section (C-section). Serious repercussions arose for the babies as well. Babies born in a hospital were six times more likely to have had fetal distress before birth, four times more likely to have needed assistance to start breathing, and four times more likely to have developed an infection. There were no birth injuries at home, but 30 infants in the hospital suffered injuries from their birth (England and Horowitz 1998).

At the same time, elements of the medicalization of childbirth may be as fierce as ever (Block 2008). About one-third of babies are now delivered by C-section. (Hamilton et al. 2010). This is the highest rate ever recorded anywhere in the world. C-sections are the most frequent operations performed in the United States, and many hospitals require a C-section for subsequent births if the first one was delivered by C-section. Hospitals worry about uterine rupture, even though the risk may be only 1 percent (Cohen 2009). The World Health Organization (WHO) argues that many C-sections performed in the United States are medically unnecessary, potentially dangerous, and do not improve our infant or maternal mortality statistics, which are among the worst in the developed world (Population Reference Bureau 2010b). In fact, a growing number of C-sections are actually "elective" surgeries arranged for the convenience of the mother or the physician (Korn 2010).

The Transition to Parenthood

The birth or adoption of a child is one of the most significant life events. People plan in anticipation, yet the transition to parenthood can be surprisingly difficult (Kluwer 2010). In the past, when extended families were more common, grandparents, aunts, and uncles all could help teach new parents how to parent a child. For example, female relatives could help a woman learn to breastfeed, which many women have trouble with. They could offer sage advice about dealing with a colicky baby, they could teach a parent how to hold or swaddle his or her child, how to get the baby to sleep through the night, or even how to change a diaper correctly. These things are not innate; they must be learned. How do new parents learn how to take care of a baby when extended family are not around? Many new and expecting parents turn to advice books such as the best-selling books *What to Expect When You're Expecting* (Murkoff and Mazel 2008) or *What to Expect the First Year* (Murkoff et al. 2003), the series of advice books by Dr. Sears that emphasize attachment parenting (Sears and Sears 2001), or the book by La Leche League International (2010) advocating breastfeeding, *The Womanly Art of Breastfeeding*. These books have helped calm the nerves of many new parents, but the books are not without their critics. Some believe that they do more harm than good by promoting their own opinions as a gold standard; in other words, a woman *must* breastfeed, a baby *must* co-sleep with parents, babies *must* not be allowed to cry or else the child will grow up emotionally disadvantaged in some critical way. The more likely truth is that there are multiple ways of raising healthy, happy, and well-adjusted children.

Why Is the Transition So Challenging?

New parents are often shocked with the amount of "work" involved in taking care of an infant (Cockrell et al. 2008). When a baby arrives, everything changes. Parents are no longer free to do as they please, but must quickly adapt to the 24/7 care of a new life. This is difficult, and made even more challenging by the fact that new parents are sleep-deprived. Newborns have no sense of day or night; their cycles of crying, feeding, wetting, crying again, sleeping, and then crying again go on around the clock. As a result, 40–70 percent of couples experience stress, conflict, and a decline in marital satisfaction during this time (Gottman and Gottman 2008). As one new father said, "I mean, if I'm watching him during the day—she's at work—forget about doing anything. It's constant attention. You can't read, you can't study, you can't paint, you can't do anything. You really got to sit there and watch him" (Walzer 1998).

The "pop" literature is full of survival "how-to" books. Sociologist Alice Rossi (1968) suggested why the transition to parenthood can be so challenging, comparing the parent role to other acquired adult roles, such as becoming a spouse. She explains:

- *Pronatalist sentiment may pressure people to become parents* even though they may not really want to or be ready to parent. However, once a baby is born, there is little or no chance to change one's mind about parenthood.
- *Most parents have little or no previous experience in child care.* They must quickly learn how to care for a completely dependent human being.
- *Becoming a parent is abrupt, unlike other adult roles.* Expecting a baby is not the same thing as having one. New parents are suddenly on duty 24 hours a day, 7 days a week.
- *The transition to parenthood necessitates complex changes in the couple's relationship.* Activities become more instrumental, and the division of labor becomes more sex-based. The brunt of the workload and lifestyle changes falls on the woman.

However, several factors mediate the challenges faced by new parents including the child's temperament, the parents' expectations about their child, the assistance they would receive from kin, their marital adjustment and communication skills, the father's parenting behavior, whether the baby was planned, and the sex of the child (Bouchard et al. 2006; Knoester and Eggebeen 2006; Mulsow et al. 2002). For example, a quiet couple who have an active, fussy, colicky baby needing little sleep, and who have no family around to help will probably have a more challenging transition to parenthood than the couple who has a so-called "easy" baby who cries or fusses little, and has family around to help out on weekends. The good news is that, after the initial disruption, satisfaction and happiness resume, and couples generally do well (Demo and Cox 2000).

Sex Differences in the Transition to Parenthood

We know far more about how women are changed by becoming parents than we know about men. That's because in most families, babies spend considerably more time with their mothers, as shown in Table 9.4 (Drago 2009). As will be discussed in Chapter 11, women have more child care responsibilities. With half of mothers with children under the age of one in the labor force, work-family stress is a serious problem for many families, women in particular (Bianchi and Milkie 2010).

TABLE 9.4 Time Spent in the Parenting of Infants Under Age 1 (hours and minutes)

Mothers spend far more time with children than fathers do, particularly in solo child care.

	PARTNERED MOTHERS	PARTNERED FATHERS
Total Child-Care Weekdays	11:05	5:01
Solo Child Care	8:08	2:06
Primary Child Care (other parent helped)	3:15	1:25
Total Child-Care Weekends	11:58	9:31
Solo Child Care	5:50	3:11
Primary Child Care (other parent helped)	3:19	1:52

Source: Drago 2009.

However, as sociologist Susan Walzer (1998) explains, the transition to parenthood is far more than just a matter of the logistics of juggling work and family. Her study with 25 couples who recently had a baby revealed that the images of what it takes to be a "good" mother or "good" father are socially constructed and inextricably linked with views about sex and gender. Parenthood is a vivid example of "doing gender." She writes:

"Mother" and "father" are social categories that existed before the individuals I interviewed became parents—or were born. These social categories have particular meanings attached to them—meanings that are socializing influences on new parents and that are institutionalized in cultural imagery associated with motherhood and fatherhood.... New parents are channeled toward differentiation by social arrangements, and especially by cultural imagery that constructs what it means to be a "good" mother or father, wife or husband, woman or man. (p. 7)

These images set up a difficult situation for women because the image of a *good mother* is one who is always there and available for her child, yet the image of a *good woman* is to work and have a career. How do women do both? These two cultural images are at odds with each other.

Men, in contrast, do not face this contradiction in roles. Being a *good father* generally means that he supports his family. A father who does minimal caregiving tasks may still be perceived as a devoted, involved, and good father.

Walzer suggests that mothers and fathers think about babies in different ways, and they analyze their thoughts so that they fit the culturally appropriate image of "good" mothers and fathers. Mothers are expected to expend considerably more mental energy on their babies than are men. For examples, mothers worry more about their babies (and they worry about the way they are perceived by others), they buy and read the self-help books, they process the information and then translate it to instruct their husbands or partners, and they manage and orchestrate child care and the division of household labor.

Social Policy and Family Resilience

The transition to parenthood is a challenge for most families, and the challenge is exacerbated by family policies that seemingly fail to recognize the structural pressures associated with a new baby. One of these pressures involves time, including the ability to take time off from work when having a baby.

Author Judith Warner (2005), in her book *Perfect Madness: Motherhood in the Age of Anxiety* describes the assistance available to her as a new mother living in France:

I was living in France, a country that has an astounding array of benefits for families—and for mothers in particular. When my children were born, I stayed in the hospital for five comfortable days. I found a nanny through a free, community-based referral service, then employed her, legally and full-time, for a cost to me of about $10,500 a year, after tax breaks. My elder daughter, from the time she was eighteen months, attended excellent part-time preschools, where she painted and played with modeling clay and ate cookies and napped for about $150 per month—the top end of the fee scale. She could have started public school at age three, and could have opted to stay until 5 P.M. daily. My friends who were covered by the French social security system (which I did not pay into), had even greater benefits: at least four months of paid maternity leave, the right to stop working for up to three years and have jobs held for them, cash grants, after their second children were born, starting at about $105 per month.

And that was just the beginning. There was more: a culture. An atmosphere. A set of deeply held attitudes toward motherhood—toward adult womanhood—that had the effect of allowing me to have two children, work in an office, work out in a gym, and go out to dinner at night and away for a short vacation with my husband without ever hearing, without ever thinking, the word "guilt." (pp. 9–10)

She later presents a jolting contrast after she returns to the United States:

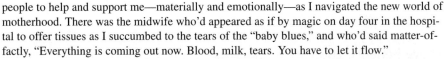

Do you think that people without children should pay (through higher taxes) to help those who do have children? Why or why not?

I knew what had worked for me in France. It wasn't just that I had access to a slew of government-run or subsidized support services; it was also that I'd had a whole unofficial network of people to help and support me—materially and emotionally—as I navigated the new world of motherhood. There was the midwife who'd appeared as if by magic on day four in the hospital to offer tissues as I succumbed to the tears of the "baby blues," and who'd said matter-of-factly, "Everything is coming out now. Blood, milk, tears. You have to let it flow."

There was my local pharmacist who, unasked, filled my shopping bag with breast pads. The pediatrician who answered his own phone. The network of on-call doctors who made house calls at any time of the day or night. The public elementary school principal who gave us a personal tour of her school and encouraged us to call her if we had any questions. In short, an extended community of people who'd guaranteed that I was never, from the moment I became a mother onward, left to fend for myself alone. (pp. 30–31)

What is the impact of this collectivist orientation? The French receive a great deal of government assistance when they have a baby. This assistance begins early in the child's life, made possible by the existence of three kinds of parent leaves: 16 weeks of paid maternity leave for the mother; 11 days of paid paternity leave for the father; up to three years of unpaid leave for either parent with their job guaranteed (provided they have been on the job for at least one year) (United Nations Statistics Division 2010).

Example: Maternity and Family Leaves

In Detroit, Michigan, Rhea, a first- time mother, is trying to get used to the thought of putting her six-week-old son in day care so she can get back to work. "It's hard to imagine leaving him for nine hours a day with a stranger, but I need the money" she laments. Across the border in Toronto, Canada, Kim is back at work after 14 months of paid maternity leave. "It was terrific," she says. "I was still making enough money to get by while I was at home with Ethan." Across the ocean, in Sweden, Nils is looking forward to splitting 16 months of parental leave at 80 percent pay with his girlfriend, whose baby will be born any day, "It's great that we both have the time to bond with him."

The United States has by far the least generous maternity and family leave policy of any developed nation (United Nations Statistics Division 2010). Other countries have long recognized that working families need to tend to their children and other family members. Rather than seeing work-family as a source of conflict, their policies promote their integration. Strong families are viewed as an important social, cultural, and economic resource. As Canada's former Prime Minister Jean Chretien said (Center for Families, Work, and Well-Being 2001):

There is now overwhelming scientific evidence that success in a child's early years is the key to long-term healthy development. Nothing is more important than for parents to be able to spend the maximum amount of time with newborn children in the critical early months of a child's life. Therefore, I am proud to announce today that the government will introduce legislation in this parliament to extend employment insurance maternity and parental benefits from the current maximum of six months to one full year.

The prime minister is referring to a growing body of research on the benefits that family leaves have for children, their parents, and their parents' employers (Bergemann and Riphahn 2009; Galtry and Callister 2005; Yang 2009). Long leaves are associated with better maternal physical and mental health, and lower rates of infant mortality. Moreover, women are likely to breastfeed for longer periods if they have extended leave benefits.

Employers also benefit from longer parental leaves. Women are more likely to return to work after childbirth in those countries that have more lengthy leaves. It is more cost-effective to develop a well-planned parental leave policy than it is to rehire and retrain new employees.

Consequently, virtually all developed nations except for one offer paid maternity leaves, as shown in Table 9.5 (United Nations Statistics Division 2010). For example:

- Japan offers 14 weeks of paid leave at 67 percent of a worker's salary.
- Denmark offers 52 weeks of paid maternity leave at 100 percent of a worker's salary.
- Spain offers 16 weeks of leave at 100 percent of a worker's salary.
- Canada offers 15 weeks at 55 percent of salary.

TABLE 9.5 Maternity Leave Benefits, 2009

Compare the United States with both developed and developing nations—we come up far short.

	LENGTH OF MATERNITY LEAVE	PERCENTAGE OF WAGES PAID IN COVERED PERIOD	SOURCE
Developing Nations			
Bangladesh	12 weeks	100	Employer
Bulgaria	135 days	90	Social Security
Bolivia	60 days	100 of min wages + 70 of wages	Social Security
China	90 days	100	Employer
Cuba	18 weeks	100	Social Security
Egypt	50 days	100	Employer
India	12 weeks	100	Social Security/Employer
Iran	90 days	67	Social Security
Iraq	62 days	100	Social Security
Mexico	12 weeks	100	Social Security
Morocco	14 weeks	100	Social Security
Nigeria	12 weeks	50	Employer
Vietnam	4–6 months	100	Social Security
Developed Nations			
Canada	17–18 weeks	55 for 15 weeks	Employment Ins
Denmark	18 weeks	90	State
Finland	105 days	70	Social Security
France	16 weeks	100 up to a ceiling	Social Security
Ireland	14 weeks	70 or fixed rate	Social Security
Italy	5 months	80	Social Security
Japan	14 weeks	60	Health Ins/Social Security
Netherlands	16 weeks	100	Unemployment Fund
New Zealand	14 weeks	100 up to a ceiling	State
Spain	16 weeks	100	Social Security
Sweden	14 weeks	390 days—80; 90 days—flat rate	Social Security
Switzerland	8 weeks	80	Social Security
United Kingdom	14–18 weeks	6 weeks—90; flat rate after	Employer
United States	**12 weeks**[a]	**0**	**—**

[a] Applies only to workers in companies with 50 or more workers.
Source: United Nations Statistics Division 2010.

S O C I A L

Policies for Families

The Family and Medical Leave Act

The Family and Medical Leave Act is the closest thing the United States has to the extensive family leave policies found in other industrialized nations.

1. *What is the Family and Medical Leave Act?* The Family and Medical Leave Act (FMLA) is a federal law that provides unpaid, job-protected leave to eligible employees, both male and female, to care for their families or themselves for specified family and medical conditions. FMLA provides eligible employees with up to 12 workweeks of unpaid leave over a year for the birth, adoption, or foster care placement of a child; care of a spouse, son, daughter, or parent with a serious health condition; or their own serious health condition that causes an inability to work.

2. *Which employers are covered by FMLA?* FMLA covers private-sector employers with 50 or more employees. Public employers are covered regardless of the number of workers they employ.

3. *Which employees are eligible for FMLA?* To be eligible, an employee must have worked for the employer at least 12 months and at least 1,250 hours within a 12-month period before the leave begins.

4. *What is a "serious health condition" under FMLA?* A "serious health condition" includes illness, injury, impairment, or physical or mental condition that involves inpatient care (defined as an overnight stay in a medical facility) and any related incapacity, and continuing treatment.

5. *How does an employer confirm a serious health condition?* An employer may require a medical certification that gives medical facts confirming the type of serious health condition. If the certification is for the employee's own serious health condition, it may require information on the employee's inability to perform essential job functions. An employer may require additional medical opinions at the employer's expense.

6. *How much leave can be taken at one time?* FMLA leave can be taken all at once (12 workweeks); 1 week; or 1 day at a time; on an intermittent basis in small blocks of time for a single qualifying condition; or on a reduced schedule of usual hours. Intermittent and reduced schedule leave can be used for the birth, adoption, or foster care placement of a child only if the employer agrees to it.

7. *What benefits does an employee receive during FMLA leave?* Benefits such as group health insurance coverage must be maintained during FMLA leave under the same terms and conditions as if the employer was working. A worker has a right to all benefits as provided during other forms of paid or unpaid leave and to benefit changes.

8. *What are an employee's rights upon returning from FMLA leave?* An employee must be returned to the same job or an equivalent job held before leave began with the same pay, benefits, and other terms and conditions of employment.

Source: ChicagoLegalNet.com 2003.

CRITICAL THINKING QUESTIONS

1. It took the United States until 1993 to pass FMLA, which provides only unpaid leave to certain qualified workers. Why did it take this long? Why is FMLA less generous than the leave available in other countries? Who would oppose FMLA—and why? Who would support it? Why?

2. Why did working families have difficulty mobilizing for an expanded or more generous leave policy?

What type of family leave policy exists in the United States? The U.S. Congress has been relatively slow to act, finally passing the **Family Medical Leave Act (FMLA)** in 1993. It requires employers with over 50 employees working for them (within a 75-mile radius) to provide 12 weeks of *unpaid* leave to eligible employees (both men and women) to care for themselves or their immediate families with specified medical conditions. Conditions include childbirth or adoption; care of child, spouse, or parent with a serious health condition; or their own serious condition that renders them unable to work. Employees must have worked for the employer at least one year or 1,250 hours to be eligible for FMLA. Employers in small firms are not required to offer leaves at all. Low-income workers are disproportionately ineligible for FMLA, despite needing it the most (Ray et al. 2009). Details about FMLA are outlined in the box on page 283, "Social Policies for Families: The Family and Medical Leave Act."

However, in reality, few people can afford to take unpaid leave. Therefore many come back to work shortly after their short-term disability, vacation, or sick pay has been exhausted. In a survey about the use and impact of family and medical leave, 34 percent of workers said they needed, but did not take leave (Commission on Family and Medical Leave 1996). Lower-educated and minority women are least likely to take leave after giving birth, probably because they cannot afford to (U.S. Census Bureau 2006).

Families may have vacation or sick pay that they can take, and if lucky, they have paid for short-term disability insurance that may cover six weeks of leave after a vaginal birth and eight weeks of leave following a birth by C-section. However, because the leave is "disability" related, it would not provide any leave time for men or for parents of children who are adopted, and is only available to those who paid for this special insurance coverage in advance.

California is an example of a state taking matters into their own hands because of federal inaction (California Work and Family Coalition 2010). Families can have up to six weeks of paid leave at 55 percent of a worker's pay—up to $987 a week in 2010—while they care for family needs. Since the program was created, about 740,000 Californians have received claims (The Paid Family Leave Collaborative 2009). This is fewer than expected, perhaps because many lower-income families are unaware of the program, and few people can really live on only 55 percent of their pay.

Conclusion

This chapter introduced issues surrounding fertility in the United States and throughout the world. It also revealed that seemingly personal issues such as whether, when, who, and how to have a baby represent a complex intertwining of biological and social forces. Values, such as pronatalism, shape attitudes and behaviors. Political, religious, economic, health care, and other social institutions also shape family life, including fertility, pregnancy, adoption, childbirth, and transitioning to parenthood—dimensions of family life that many see as exceedingly personal. China, as the most extreme case, accepts a level of governmental policy that many around the world deem highly intrusive. Nonetheless, all countries have family policies, and those in the United States often minimize the connection between social structure (macro) and the lived experience (micro) of individual families. Compared to other nations, Americans are often expected to fend for themselves, as is the case with maternity and family leaves.

Key Terms

Assisted reproductive technology (ART): All fertility treatments in which both egg and sperm are handled. (p. 270)

Baby bust: Period from the early 1960s through the 1970s when U.S. fertility rates dropped significantly. (p. 264)

Birth centers: Freestanding facilities, usually with close access to, but not affiliated with a hospital; childbirth is approached as a normal, healthy process. (p. 277)

China's one-child policy: Most families in China are allowed by law to have only one child. (p. 261)

Closed adoption: All identifying information is sealed and unavailable to all parties. (p. 273)

Direct financial costs: Out-of-pocket expenses for things such as food, clothing, housing, and education. (p. 267)

Family Medical Leave Act (FMLA): Governmental act that requires employers with over 50 employees working for them (within a 75-mile radius) to provide 12 weeks of unpaid leave to eligible employees (both men and women) to care for themselves or their immediate families with specified medical conditions. (p. 283)

Fertility rates: Average number of children born to a woman during her lifetime (total); number of children born per 1,000 women aged 15–49 (refined); or number of children born per 1,000 population (crude). (p. 257)

Infertility: The inability to conceive a child. (p. 270)

Medicalization of childbirth: Childbirth viewed as a medical event in need of drugs and technological intervention. (p. 276)

Midwives: Attendants trained to help women give birth and who believe that childbirth is a normal part of life. (p. 276)

Mortality rates: Measures of the number of deaths for a given population. (p. 257)

Open adoptions: Involves direct contact between the biological and adoptive parents. (p. 273)

Opportunity costs: Lost opportunities for income by working only part-time or not at all because of children. (p. 267)

Private adoptions: Arranged directly between adoptive parents and the biological birth mother, usually through the assistance of an attorney. (p. 273)

Pronatalism: A cultural value that encourages childbearing. (p. 256)

Public adoptions: Occur through licensed public agencies. (p. 273)

Semi-open adoptions: Biological and adoptive families exchange personal information through a social worker or attorney, but have no direct contact. (p. 273)

Surrogacy: One woman gives birth for another person (or couple) who then adopts or takes legal custody of the child. (p. 271)

Resources on the Internet

Alan Guttmacher Institute

www.guttmacher.org

This website offers information on reproductive issues, family planning, teenage pregnancy, and other issues in fertility. The Alan Guttmacher Institute publishes a bimonthly periodical called *Family Planning Perspectives*, a scholarly review of research and policy.

National Adoption Information Clearinghouse

www.calib.com/naic/index.cfm

Congress established the National Adoption Information Clearinghouse in 1987 to provide free information on all aspects of adoption. The mission of the clearinghouse is to connect professionals and concerned citizens to timely and well-balanced information on programs, research, legislation, and statistics regarding the safety, permanency, and well-being of children and families.

Resolve: The National Infertility Association

www.resolve.org

Resolve is an organization dedicated to providing information and support to people who are experiencing infertility, and general public education and advocacy. It provides information about medical treatment, adoption, and childfree living.

Population Reference Bureau

www.prb.org

The Population Reference Bureau offers timely information about world population statistics and trends. Topics include education, employment, fertility, family planning, health, income, marriage and family, youth, and aging.

CHAPTER 10

Raising Children

CHAPTER OUTLINE

Comparative Focus on Childhood and Parenting 289

■ **OUR** *Global Community:* Searching for Wages and Mothering from Afar: The Case of Honduran Transnational Families *289*

Socialization 292

Parenting Styles and Practices 297

■ **FAMILIES** *as Lived Experience:* We Have Love Bouncing Off the Walls at Our House *299*

■ **FAMILIES** *as Lived Experience:* My Family: "What I Like About Being a Dad . . . and What I Don't" *302*

Parenting Contexts 303

Social Policy and Family Resilience 310

Conclusion 312

Key Terms 312

Resources on the Internet 313

CHAPTER PREVIEW

What does it mean to be a mother, a father, a parent? How are these roles different from one another? This chapter explains that mothering and fathering encompass the emotional, physical, and financial work involved with caring for children; however, these identities and the roles associated with mothering and fathering are in large part socially constructed. In this chapter, you will learn:

- Differences and similarities across cultures with regard to parenting

- Three theoretical approaches regarding the socialization of children

- The importance of several agents of socialization

- How socialization is affected by social class, race, ethnicity, and gender

- "Mothering" and "fathering" concepts, roles, and expectations differ

- The unique characteristics of specific parenting contexts, including teenage parents, single parents, cohabiting parents, gay and lesbian parents, and grandparents raising grandchildren

- Parents in the United States receive less financial help from the government than is the case for parents in many other developed countries—for example, have you ever heard of a "family allowance"?

I met Sarah several years ago when I was interviewing families for a research project about the health of low-income families, and whether they were about to get the health insurance and health care they need. I will always remember her. She was one of more 500 people interviewed in Oregon by telephone and one of more than 80 people who had also agreed to participate in in-person interviews. I went to her home, but before undertaking the "business" of the interview, it was clearly important to Sarah that I meet her son Jake, who has severe cerebral palsy and developmental disabilities. She carefully and lovingly presented Jake, an 8-year-old, who was lying on a blanket on the floor of her cramped living room, wearing nothing but a diaper. His skin was pale, as though he had never been exposed to sunlight. Although he was the size of a typical third grader, in all other respects, Jake was like an infant.

Sarah described for me what parenting Jake has been like. "He's eight years old and he doesn't talk. He makes sounds, more or less to indicate what he needs. He's in a wheelchair because he doesn't walk. So it's basically like having a three-month-old child that cries whenever it needs anything, and as a mom you do the same thing that any mother would. You go down a checklist: you've just eaten; you've just had your diaper changed so it's a matter of a guessing game of what he needs or wants. His favorite sound is "uh", which sometimes means he wants a drink of water. But "uh" also means he can't reach his toy, or "uh" means you're watching TV and not feeding me."

She continued, "My child is eight years old and the plain fact is, he's eight years old and he can't do anything for himself except play with his toys and his newspaper. If I set him here on the floor he stays in this vicinity—he falls over on his side, he rolls on his tummy, he turns himself around a little, but he's subject to this part of the house because that's where I put him. Other than crying, I could leave him here all day long if I so desired and that would just have to work because there is nothing he could do about it. Not that I would, and let me tell you, that boy's got a great set of lungs."

Sarah went on to tell me of the difficulties raising Jake. She can take nothing for granted, "You can't have somebody come over and babysit at your house for five dollars. You're not talking about a kid who can say, 'I'm tired, I want to go to bed,' or 'Can we watch a movie?' or 'I'm hungry now.' I fear having any other sort of daycare take care of him because of the fact that he doesn't complain about things. Does that mean he's going to sit in the corner for an hour and a half? There's no way of knowing, and in this day and age, God knows, he can't tell me if someone is doing anything unmentionable to him. I just pray to God every time he leaves the house that the person I'm sending him to school with is dependable and not some weirdo." (Seccombe and Hoffman 2007)

Parenthood may be universal, but the act of *parenting* varies considerably. Parenting depends on micro-level characteristics specific to the parent or to the child, as shown by Jake's needs. But parenting is also influenced by macro-level social, cultural, and historic trends. As discussed in Chapter 3, prior to the eighteenth century, little attention was given to children's needs as we think of them today. Parenting was adult-centered; if a child did not contribute to the parents' welfare, then he or she could simply be abandoned.

Today, parents spend a great deal of time reflecting on what is in the best interest of their child and are concerned about ways to enhance their child's social and emotional well-being. Many parents worry about the "right" type of child care, the "right" type of discipline, the "right" type of food. "Right" is now defined as not only what works for the parent, but also what is best for the child. Yet even today, parenting values and parenting tasks differ by race, ethnicity, and social class.

This chapter examines the empirical research and theoretical perspectives surrounding raising children. We will see that child rearing values and behaviors are embedded in larger macro-level social structures.

Comparative Focus on Childhood and Parenting

Like historical events, culture has important effects on parenting attitudes and practices (Creighton et al. 2009; Umaña-Taylor et al. 2009; White et al. 2009). What may be seen as good parenting in one culture may be looked upon with disdain elsewhere. Should parents and children sleep together? Should parents send daughters to school? Is it okay to whip a child who disobeys? Should children work to help support the family? LeVine (1977, 1988) suggests that there are three universal parenting goals:

- ensuring physical health and survival
- developing behavioral capacities for economic maintenance
- instilling behavioral capacities for maximizing cultural values, such as morality, prestige, and achievement

However, the emphasis placed on these three goals, and how they are implemented, may differ cross-culturally. This may be due to divergent cultural values, but also to structural forces operating in society, such as poverty or racism. The following box "Our Global Community: Searching for Wages and Mothering from Afar: The Case of Honduran Transnational Families" introduces a **transnational family**—defined as a family divided between two nations—who straddles the United States and Honduras because of the abject poverty in their home country (Schmalzbauer 2004). The need for survival wages forces many parents to live away from their children, with repercussions for both children and adults. Other women, such as grandmothers, aunts, sisters, or oldest daughters, must step in and care for the children while the parents live thousands of miles away. *Other-mothering* is central in the history of poor communities throughout the world (Aranda 2003; Schmalzbauer 2004).

O U R

Global Community

Searching for Wages and Mothering from Afar: The Case of Honduran Transnational Families

Millions of mothers and fathers have made a dangerous trek to the United States in search of work, often forced to leave their own children behind in their home country. This is a story of Rosalia, a mother of five, and her struggle to keep her family "together" as they live thousands of miles apart.

Rosalia is a Honduran mother of five. She has been in the United States for six years and came to the United States on a tourist visa as part of a religious delegation. Her family's situation in Honduras was dire. She was working part-time managing the upkeep of a local church while her husband Ernesto worked as a bus driver. However, even with both of them working, they were barely scraping by, and the opportunities for mobility, especially for their children, appeared severely limited. They had talked for years about making the risky trip to the north to the United States to seek a better future. Rosalia's church trip proved the perfect opportunity. When the religious delegation was over, she slipped away to the house of a Honduran friend in Boston, with whom she stayed while working a patchwork of jobs to save money to bring her husband and children across the border.

(continued)

(continued)

Now, after three years of hard work, Rosalia has paid for her husband Ernesto and three youngest children's illegal journey to the United States. Her two oldest children, Magda and Franklin, remain in Honduras. They make do without their mother and father, for the most part understanding their parents' need to go north and the logic of bringing only the youngest children who could still benefit from a U.S. education. Franklin drives a taxi. He harbors some anger toward his parents for leaving, but remains committed to their family. On his slim income alone, Magda and Franklin would not be able to meet even their most basic needs, yet with the financial help they receive from their parents, they are able to get by. They have paid off the family's debts and they recently bought a refrigerator for the kitchen and a television, which, when they can get it to work, allows them to bond with their parents and siblings by watching the same *telenovelas*. Rosalia and Ernesto's family has not been together for six years, but they try to maintain closeness via weekly phone calls and a shared understanding that being apart is the only way for them to make ends meet.

The family of Rosalia is typical of many families who, because of severe financial hardship and limited opportunities, have transnationalized, negotiating the economic opportunities of two nations to sustain themselves and to pursue their hopes for a better future. Although divided by thousands of miles and by politics and culture, many transnational families maintain close ties across the distance. However, emotional struggle is a daily part of life. Parents express the greatest distress about trying to maintain connections with children who were very young when they left. Young children have difficulty understanding why their parent(s) had to leave, and they often do not remember the parent well. Going home to visit is a dangerous proposition, and visits can be confusing for children and painful for everyone upon departure.

Thousands of miles and a heavily guarded border prevent parents from taking care of their children, while the politics and legal mandates of immigration make it impossible for most families to know if their reunification will be possible. However, without transnationalizing, poor families often cannot secure their survival. Millions of families represent a new family form born out of the inequality in the global economy and reproduced by means of dependence on a transnational division of labor.

Source: Schmalzbauer 2004.

CRITICAL THINKING QUESTIONS

1. What kinds of jobs do you think Rosalia was able to get when she came to the United States? How much did she earn? Do you think the jobs provided fringe benefits such as health insurance?
2. What should be the response of the United States to illegal immigrants? If they are doing labor that helps the United States or U.S. citizens, should they be allowed to stay? Should they be allowed to bring their families? Should they receive publicly funded services, such as education or health care?
3. How would world systems theory explain the structural circumstances surrounding the rise in transnational families? What additional insights would feminist theory have to add?

Parenting attitudes and practices largely depend on the type of tasks or competencies that members of society are expected to have (Garcia-Coll 1990). For example, if a culture expects adults to be economically self-supporting, parenting attitudes and tasks will likely involve fostering individual achievement in their children through school or sport; involve teaching children about handling money through an allowance or some similar means; and may encourage children to learn about the world of work through part-time jobs or in other ways contributing to the family economy. Other cultures that stress economic cooperation would approach parenting differently. Why would parents try to foster individual achievement in their children if a culture does not particularly value that trait or see it as important to success?

In some cultures, parents (particularly mothers) and their children sleep together on a regular basis for many years. An American woman visiting the Yoruba of West Africa describes her surprise at cultural differences in family sleep patterns (Kurchinka 1998):

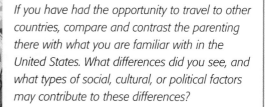

WHAT DO YOU THINK?

If you have had the opportunity to travel to other countries, compare and contrast the parenting there with what you are familiar with in the United States. What differences did you see, and what types of social, cultural, or political factors may contribute to these differences?

I quickly discovered there weren't any cribs in this compound. In fact, there weren't any cradles, bassinets, infant seats, or walkers. Babies (any child under three) were either being carried on their mother's back, playing at her feet, or sleeping with her on a mat. My questions concerning bedtime and night feedings were met with confusion. Babies slept when they were tired and rolled from their mother's back to her breast when they were hungry. Mothers hardly stirred in their sleep while babies fed. There weren't any issues about bedtime and night feeding. They were amazed when I explained that in our country babies were placed in cribs or cradles to sleep. When I clarified that the apparatus was frequently set in another room, away from the mother, they were horrified. They couldn't imagine banishing a baby to another room, away from its mother.... My life with the Yoruba taught me that many of our most firm child-rearing rules are based on cultural preferences rather than fact. Who is to say whether babies should sleep alone in cribs or on mats with their mothers?

What do the U.S. preferences and beliefs in this example tell us about our culture? Our babies sleep in separate beds called cribs, they sleep in separate rooms away from their parents, and many are fed from bottles rather than from their mother's breast (Centers for Disease Control and Prevention 2009d). The United States values the separation of children and parents to a larger degree than in other cultures; for instance, most young children spend significant time with paid caregivers; adolescent children's reference group is peer-oriented rather than family-oriented; young adult children choose their own mates; and adult children prefer to live separately from their aging parents. Other cultures value greater levels of interdependence throughout the life cycle, beginning in infancy (Han et al. 2009; Karraker 2008; Waldfogel 2006).

Parenting attitudes and practices reflect cultural expectations about the types of tasks or competences that members of society are expected to have. Some cultures emphasize interdependence of family members much more than does the United States. Therefore, mothers and babies may be inseparable for years.

Recent Trends

These cultural differences make us wonder where we stand today. Is parenting so different everywhere that we can find no common themes? No, not really. Cross-cultural research identifies at least three trends with respect to child rearing that exist in both developed and developing countries (Adams 2004; Adams and Trost 2004).

1. *Although parents are central to child rearing, other people and social institutions are also involved in raising children, including grandparents and other relatives, day care settings, governmental agencies, schools, and factories.* Related to this is the rising tide of women's employment outside the home. Even in historically poor and patriarchal countries such as Bangladesh, increases in women's employment are changing the nature of families, the distribution of spousal power, and the care of children in important ways (Ahmed and Bould 2004).
2. *Parents around the world increasingly expect parental permissiveness and child independence.* There is a decline in the value placed on obedience to parental authority, and more

emphasis placed on independence and personal responsibility. Certainly not all cultures meet these changes with unabashed enthusiasm, but growing trends are apparent.

3. *A higher value is placed on boys than on girls in most societies around the world.* The traditional preference for sons is based on family inheritance and the desire for sons to care for aging parents. These values persist in several countries, such as China, Kenya, and India, but in many places the reasons for male preferences are more vague and are simply based on tradition rather than "rational" economics.

Socialization

Socialization refers to the lifelong process through which we acquire the cultural values and skills needed to function as human beings and participate in society. Socialization is unique to human beings because children are helpless at birth and have few instincts compared to other animals. Although the debate about how much of human nature is biological and how much is socially produced is not yet answered definitely and perhaps never will be, we do know that socialization is a powerfully complex process that imparts the qualities and cultural traits we think of as human.

Theoretical Approaches

Social psychologists have elaborated on many theories to explain child development and the process of socialization. Three of the more prominent ones are discussed here.

Sigmund Freud and the Psychoanalytic Perspective

Sigmund Freud (1856–1939) lived in an era when biological explanations of human behavior were prevalent, as were male dominance and sexual repression. All of these historical and cultural factors influenced his proposition that human behavior and personality originate from unconscious forces within individuals. Freud suggested that human development occurs in three states that reflect different components of the personality. The **id** is the part of the personality that includes biological drives and needs for immediate gratification. The id is present at birth and readily visible in young children; however, this aspect of personality continues throughout our lives. The **ego** is the rational component of personality that attempts to balance the need for immediate gratification with the demands of society. It arises as we become aware that we cannot have all that we desire and that our needs must be balanced with the demands of society. The **superego** is our conscience, which draws upon cultural values and norms to help us understand why we cannot have everything we want.

Jean Piaget and Cognitive Development

Jean Piaget (1896–1980) was a Swiss psychologist whose research focused on how people think and understand. He was particularly interested in how children come to understand the world and make meaning of their experiences. He identified four stages of cognitive development that are rooted in biology and based upon age. The first stage occurs in the first two years of life, and is called the **sensorimotor intelligence**. The infant and toddler understand the world primarily through touch, sucking, listening, and looking. Children begin to organize and exercise some control over their lives. The second stage, **preoperational thought**, occurs between ages 2 and 7 as children learn language, symbolic play, and symbolic drawing. They do not grasp abstract concepts and their knowledge is tied to their own perceptions. The third stage, **concrete operational thought**, occurs between the ages of 7 and 12. During this period, children begin to see the causal connections in their surroundings and can manipulate categories, classification systems, and hierarchies in groups. The final stage of cognitive development is **formal operational thought**, which begins in adolescence and continues through adulthood.

During this stage, children develop capacities for abstract thought and can conceptualize more complex issues or rules that can be used for problem solving.

Charles Horton Cooley and George Herbert Mead: The Self   Charles Horton Cooley (1864–1929) and George Herbert Mead (1863–1931) turned attention to a sociological perspective by arguing that a person cannot form a self-concept without social contact with others. A self-concept is not present at birth, but arises from social experience with others. Cooley and Mead minimize Freud's claim of biological drives or Piaget's assertion that humans develop chronologically as they age. Instead, they claim that human behavior and self-identity are shaped by interactions with others and the meanings attached to those interactions. Cooley suggested that we come to see ourselves as others perceive and respond to us, a process he described as the **looking-glass self**. For example, we will see ourselves as thin or heavy, intelligent or less intelligent, as attractive or unattractive, as trustworthy or irresponsible, based on the way that other people perceive and respond to us. Mead extended Cooley's insight in several ways, including the view that social experience includes **symbolic interaction**; we interact not just with words, but also with important symbols and meanings, such as eye contact or a wave of the hand. Mead also elaborated on Cooley's work by focusing on **role taking**, which is the process of mentally assuming the role of another person to understand the world from his or her point of view and to anticipate his or her response to us. This helps us to become self-reflective. Mead suggests that the self is divided into two components: the "I" and the "me." The "I" is the subjective element of the self and represents spontaneity and interaction that we initiate. The "me" is the objective element of self, reflecting the internalized perceptions of others toward us. Both the "I" and the "me" are needed to form the social self. In other words, the feedback loop is critical—we initiate behavior that is ultimately guided by the ways that others see us.

Agents of Socialization

Chapter 4 introduced the various ways persons, groups, or institutions collectively referred to as agents of socialization teach children about the norms and values of their particular culture (Rohall et al. 2011). These will be briefly recapped here:

- *Family members, particularly parents,* have the greatest impact on socializing children because they provide the first exposure to a particular culture. Parents provide children with a place to live, food to eat, clothes to wear, vocabulary to learn, medical care when sick, and they introduce the child to values and customs (Bee and Boyd 2007). They also pass on to the child his or her socioeconomic status and social position in terms of race, ethnicity, and religion.
- *Schools and child care* enlarge children's worlds by introducing them to people and settings different from their immediate family. Schools organize and teach children a wide range of knowledge, skills, and customs, including the political ideology of the society. Schools also provide important lessons more covertly, which is sometimes referred to as a *hidden curriculum*. For example, children learn about the value of competition through spelling bees and games at recess (Rouse and Barrow 2006).
- *Peer group relationships* take on increasing importance as children enter adolescence. Peers usually reward conformity rather than deviations, so children learn to look, dress, talk, and act like others in their group. For example, young people learn which specific clothing styles are popular and which are not. Peers are a powerful agent of socialization and have tremendous influence, particularly during adolescence as young people begin to distance themselves from their parents (Cobb 2007; Garrod et al. 2008).
- *Toys and games* also reflect culture and teach children important messages about what it means to be a member of society. As discussed in Chapter 4, this is vividly seen in the

TABLE 10.1   Technology Ownership by Household Type

Media and technology play important roles, especially in families with children.

	ALL ADULTS	MARRIED WITH CHILD(REN)
	n = 2,252	n = 482
Cell phone(s) in household	84%	95%
Computer(s) in household	77%	93%
Internet household	77%	94%
2+ televisions	83%	88%
2+ home computers	39%	58%

Source: Kennedy et al. 2008.

ways in which toys and games inform children about what it means to be a boy, girl, man, or woman in U.S. culture. Play tends to be sex-typed, with toys, games, and peer group play styles differentiated on the basis of sex (Bee and Boyd 2007).

- *The mass media,* especially television, is an increasingly important mechanism for socializing children (Brooks-Gunn and Donahue 2008; Calvert 2008). Ninety-eight percent of households have at least one television set, and over 80 percent have two or more. Over three-quarters of households—and 93 percent of married-couple households with children—have at least one computer in the home, as shown in Table 10.1 (Bureau of Labor Statistics 2010c; Kennedy et al. 2008).

In other words, socialization teaches children about the culture in which they live. However, the socialization process is not completely uniform. It varies by sex, as we saw in Chapter 4. It also varies by social class, race, and ethnicity.

Socialization and Social Class

Your social class position has a large effect on the ways you have been socialized (Crompton 2006). First, social class affects how much money parents have to spend on their children, influencing where they live; the quality of schools they will attend; the type of neighbors and friends they will have; the type of clothing they will wear; and the type and amount of toys, hobbies, and enrichment activities they are likely to have, such as piano lessons or being on a sports team. Participation in these programs costs money, requires parental involvement, and may necessitate significant preparation time, all of which low-income children may not have (or have little of) (Weininger and Lareau 2009). Yet, these activities can boost academic and social achievement and social development (Gardner et al. 2008; Granger 2008; Society for Research in Child Development 2008).

But social class affects more than just material goods. It also affects the values, norms, and expectations that parents have for their children. For example:

Children imitate those around them, including family, peers, and who they see in the mass media.

- When parents are asked to choose from a list of childhood traits those they consider most desirable for their children, lower-income parents tend to choose traits such as obedience, conforming, staying out of trouble, and keeping neat and clean. In contrast, higher-income parents tend to choose traits such as creativity, ambition, independence, curiosity, and good judgment (Kohn 1977, 2006).

- Lower-income parents tend to be more controlling, authoritarian, and arbitrary in their discipline and are more apt to use physical punishments, whereas higher-income parents tend to be more democratic and are more receptive to their children's opinions (Berlin et al. 2009).

- Higher-income parents tend to show more warmth and affection toward their children, talk to them more, and use more complex language than do parents from lower-income families (Berns 2001; Kohn et al. 1990).

Sociologist Melvin Kohn suggested that parents value traits in their children that reflect the parents' world, particularly their world of work (Kohn 1977). Lower-income parents tend to emphasize conformity and related traits because these are characteristics that will be useful in the working-class jobs that their children are likely to hold in the future. For example, success on an assembly line requires obedience and conformity, not creativity, ambition, or curiosity. Those traits could actually sabotage good job performance. In contrast, upper-income parents are likely to have jobs that entail working with people or ideas and involve self-direction and creativity. Upper-income parents value these characteristics and socialize their children to have them.

Therefore, class differences in socialization reflect not only simple economic resources, but also the core values that parents hold as they try to prepare their children for the roles in society that they will likely have. We learn these values in our family of orientation, and we then reproduce these values in our families of procreation (Crompton 2006).

To illustrate the power of social class, let's examine the work of sociologist Annette Lareau, who spent considerable time with 88 families of school-age children (Lareau 2003; Weininger and Lareau 2009). She spent time with families during meals, on trips to school and extra-curricular events, and on errands and appointments, visiting them about 20 different times over the course of her research study. She, too, found strong social class differences in the ways parents interacted with their children. For example, middle-class parents enrolled their children in organized activities that they believe transmit important life skills. They disciplined their children by talking with them. They valued creativity and independent thought. As one middle-class father told her, "One of the things I think is important is just exposure. The more I can expose children to, with a watchful eye and supervision, the more creative they can be in their own thinking. The more options they will be able to see for themselves, the more they get a sense of improved self-esteem, self-worth, and self-confidence. I think it is something they will carry over into adulthood" (Weininger and Lareau 2009).

In contrast, children from working-class and low-income families engaged in fewer organized activities and were far more likely to spend their free time with their family and neighborhood friends. Working-class parents were more likely to see themselves as authority figures, and to issue directives rather than to try negotiating with their children. One mother spoke for many when she explained to her daughter why she must do something, "Because I said so and I'm your mother" (Weininger and Lareau 2009). Lareau also found that working-class parents were more likely to discipline their children with physical punishment and spanking.

Despite differences, let's be careful not to overgeneralize. Weininger and Lareau also found that middle-class parents routinely exercised subtle forms of control while attempting to instill self-direction in their children, whereas working-class and low-income parents tended to give children considerable autonomy in certain parts of daily life (Weininger and Lareau 2009). For example, because working-class parents generally do not view life as a series of "teachable moments" they are less likely to try to manipulate or hover over their children.

WHAT DO YOU THINK?

What would a conflict theorist have to say about social class differences in child rearing?

For example, one young girl, Katie, typically comes home after school, fixes a snack, and then decides by herself what to do. Sometimes, she rides her bike, other times she watches television or plays with her younger brother or cousin. She has long stretches of unstructured leisure time and the choice to fill it spontaneously however she chooses. In contrast, her middle-class peers are given a structured menu of activities from which to choose.

Socialization, Race, and Ethnicity

As shown in Chapter 6, the United States is becoming more ethnically and racially diverse, creating a need for sensitivity and understanding that values and customs may differ among groups. The following story illustrates the importance of recognizing differences in cultural values (Berns 2001):

> One day, a fifth-grade teacher noticed that Juanita, normally a tidy youngster, had a brown smear of dirt on one arm. That day and the next, the teacher said nothing. However, when Juanita came to class with the mark on her arm the third day, the teacher told her to go wash her dirty arm. When Juanita said it was not dirty, the teacher told her not to argue and to do as she was told. Juanita complied. Several days later, her parents took Juanita out of school to attend the funeral of her sister. Two weeks had passed and Juanita had still not returned to school, so the principal went to her home to find out why. Juanita's mother told the principal that when someone is ill, each family member places a spot of oil and soil somewhere on the body. "We are one with nature. When someone is ill, that person is out of balance with nature. We use the oil and soil of our Mother, the earth, to show her we wish our sick one to be back in balance with nature. When Juanita's teacher made her wash her arm, our oneness with nature was broken. That is why her sister died. The teacher caused her death; Juanita can never return to her class." (p. 276)

Racial and ethnic families may differ from the majority culture in terms of how they practice religion or medicine, their degree of family ties and sense of family obligation, their gendered patterns of behavior, and how strict or permissive parents should be with their children. Racial and ethnic families may differ on the importance placed on group cooperation or individual achievement. For example, the Japanese value conformity and loyalty to the group more than do Euro-Americans. Reflecting these values, Japanese parents encourage their children to be interdependent with others from early infancy.

One important difference between the socialization practices of white and minority parents is that minority parents must teach their children about their cultural heritage, prejudice, and discrimination, while providing their children with the coping skills necessary to develop and maintain a strong and healthy self-image (Barr and Neville 2008; Bentley et al. 2009; Tamis-LeMonda et al. 2008). Referred to as **racial (or ethnic) socialization**, parents' communication is important in shaping children's attitudes, beliefs, and their own self-efficacy in dealing with racial and ethnic experiences. Racial or ethnic socialization can instill a sense of identity, pride, and enculturation. Parents teach their children about religious traditions, cook specific types of food, celebrate cultural holidays, speak a particular language or dialect, and impart a set of values associated with their group identity (Umaña-Taylor et al. 2009). Parents who have a higher level of education, who are married, and who have warmer relationships with their children are more likely to have frequent discussions about their racial or ethnic heritage (Brown et al. 2007).

Racial and ethnic socialization also includes teaching the hard truths about racial oppression in society. When parents see instances of unfair treatment toward their children, they become even more protective, and step up their cautions and warnings to children about racial and ethnic issues and relationships (Hughes and Johnson 2001). This supportive parenting has been shown to reduce the harmful effects of racism, including anger, hostility, and aggressive behavior. For example, a study of over 300 Black adolescent males found that those young Black males who had supportive parents were less likely to respond with anger or hostility to perceived discrimination, and when angered, were less likely to behave aggressively (Simons et al. 2006).

Socialization and Gender

Chapter 4 identified many ways in which gender is constructed by families, social institutions (e.g., schools), and cultural artifacts (e.g., toys). Although there is no definitive answer about precisely how much of our gendered selves is related to biology, most scientists suggest that gender differences probably are a result of biology and social environment (Sax 2006). They maintain that social and cultural factors are very powerful and shape biological factors. Children learn about what it means to be a girl or a boy in a particular culture in a particular historical period first by the images, words, play, and rituals of their parents. Statements such as "big boys don't cry," "you throw like a girl," "let's play dress-up," "you're my little tomboy," "help your mother with the dishes," and "help your dad take the trash out" teach us about how masculinity and femininity are defined across time, culture, and social location.

Parents are a major force in shaping the gendered attitudes of their children, as we learned in Chapter 4. One such gendered attitude is that boys have higher confidence in their academic abilities. A recent study based on nearly 500 11th and 12th graders found no differences in verbal, numerical, figural, and reasoning intelligence, yet the boys and their parents rated their intelligence higher than girls and their parents rated theirs.

Parents also shape the gendered views of their children by their own behaviors. For instance, a longitudinal study that followed children for 30 years found that sons who grew up in households in which their mothers stayed home while their fathers worked outside the home held more traditional gendered views as adults than did sons with dual-working parents (Cunningham-Burley 2001).

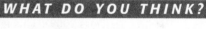

WHAT DO YOU THINK?

Can you identify specific ways that social class, race, ethnicity, or your sex influenced the way in which you were socialized? Which status has the largest effect? How do these statuses interact with each other?

Parenting Styles and Practices

Over 40 years ago, researchers studied parenting practices and developed a typology that is still used today. Baumrind noted that children who seemed the most competent and contented, who had the fewest behavioral problems, and who had the most academic successes were reared by parents who were demanding and maintained high levels of control over their children, but were also warm and receptive to their children (Baumrind 1966, 1968; Baumrind and Black 1967). She referred to this as an **authoritative parenting style**. Parents of withdrawn, fearful, or distrustful children often had an **authoritarian parenting style** that was strict, punitive, and less warm. Parents who adopted a **permissive parenting style** put few controls or demands on their children, and often raised children who were aggressive and impulsive. Can you guess which type of parenting style yields the best results? In sum, developmental psychologists believe that an authoritative parenting style produces the traits in children thought to be most desirable (Cheah et al. 2009; Dumas et al. 2009).

"Mothering" and "Fathering"

"Mother" and "father" are nouns. They refer to biological lineage, but they also indicate legal and social ties, which are not always the same as biological lineage. An adopted child may think of someone as "dad" even though she has no biological connection to him. And she may have no real connection at all to the person who biologically fathered her. We can see that the seemingly simple nouns "mother" and "father" are not always so simple. They are both biological and social statuses. So what do we mean when we say "mothering" or "fathering"? These terms are even more complex because they represent both an identity and a specific set of tasks.

"Mothering" as an Identity   What is "mothering"? Most people will think of the emotional and physical work involved with caring for children, but it is important to keep in mind that mothering takes place within specific contexts and is framed by sex, race, ethnicity, and class (Arendell 2000; Hays 1996; Roxburgh 2005; Warner 2005). The expectations associated with mothering are socially constructed—they are created by society and are never static, but forever changing. What is seen as "good" or "appropriate" mothering in one place and time may be perceived quite differently elsewhere. Anthropological literature provides many examples of the variability in mothering, suggesting that it is primarily Western societies in which women (and their partners) raise children in isolation. Anthropologists illustrate other models that draw upon an extended circle of family, including older siblings, grandmothers and grandfathers, aunts, uncles, and cousins.

In the United States, motherhood is a powerful identity, more powerful than either marital status or occupation. Women with children report experiencing greater meaning in their lives than do childfree women (Ross and Van Willigen 1996). Ironically, however, they also report greater distress and depression than do childfree women (Ali 2008; Doss 2009). This is because of the stresses associated with the extensive and ongoing emotional work; the increased household labor; the reduction in income (e.g., a mother quitting work or working only part-time); the increased financial needs that accompany children; and the lack of social support and government assistance they receive for their mothering tasks.

Compared to other developed nations, mothering in the United States is more intense and fraught with anxiety (Warner 2005). In her book *Perfect Madness: Motherhood in the Age of Anxiety*, author Judith Warner describes how American mothers fret about the pros and cons of combining work with employment or debate whether young children benefit from child care or should stay at home. In contrast, women in other countries are more able to relax and feel confidence in their abilities as mothers. Much of this confidence comes from knowing that they are not mothering alone, but that they have a cadre of social and health professionals ready to help them and their children—midwives, physicians, nannies, and professional child care providers, as described in Chapter 9.

"Mothering" as an Activity   Mothering can bring tremendous personal satisfaction, personal growth, and sheer love: "We have love bouncing off the walls at my house," one mother describes in the box on pages 299–300, "Families as Lived Experience: We Have Love Bouncing Off the Walls at Our House". Most women want to become mothers; however, mothering, especially in the United States, is not without personal and financial costs.

Mothers are more involved with their children than are fathers. Mothers do the majority of socialization, hands-on care, emotional work, discipline, transporting, and management (e.g., making the twice-yearly dental appointment) (Craig 2006; Jacobs and Kelley 2006; Poortman and van der Lippe 2009). Mothers spend over twice the amount of time per day caring for children under the age of six as do fathers, including about three times the amount of time per day spent on actual physical care. Among children of all ages, mothers are far more involved than fathers, even when both work full-time outside the home (Lee and Waite 2005).

How does employment affect the time a woman has to spend mothering? Employed mothers spend about 27 hours per week engaged with or accessible to their children as compared to 32 hours a week for mothers who do not work outside the home (Sandberg and Hofferth 2001). They engage in virtually the same activities with their children as do mothers who do not work.

FAMILIES
as Lived Experience

We Have Love Bouncing Off the Walls at Our House

The following story reveals the process of one woman's decision to become a mother. It reveals some of the satisfaction, personal growth, and love that she experienced, but these are not without some personal and professional costs. With paltry maternity leaves, high child care costs, and minimal other supports, women often pay a price for having children.

I never thought I would have any children. I've often reflected on that decision, including the causes and consequences of it, and I now delightfully muse on the recent radical departure from that decision. I have an 18-month-old daughter who is the light of my life, and I am very happily pregnant again. This time, it looks like I'm having a son.

I was committed to never having children because I was extremely focused on my career. I am an attorney working in a well-respected firm in a city on the west coast and have been climbing the ladder toward becoming a partner. I worked long hours at a demanding job that I thoroughly enjoy and loved to spend whatever little free time I have camping and hiking with my husband, Chris, and our dog, Max. I just didn't see how a child would fit into this scenario.

But to be honest, I knew I didn't want children long before I established my career and hectic life. I was committed to never having children because I didn't have a very happy childhood. I joyfully left home for college at 17.

After four years of college, three years of law school, and a couple of internship/clerking-type stints, I landed a dream job and have been here ever since. I met my husband while grocery shopping one day after work, believe it or not. We later met for lunch, and really hit it off, and married about a year later. We were both 28 years old.

Life was humming along nicely, when suddenly I had a few life-altering events occur all at once. First, my mother was diagnosed with breast cancer. It was a complete shock to me—although

we are not particularly close, I always imagined that she would *be there*. Soon afterwards, my friend's husband was seriously injured in a car accident. Watching her grieve and helping her through it was an extremely emotional experience for me. About 6 months later, another friend got divorced. As is often the case, she didn't even really reveal that she was having serious marital problems until she could keep it a secret no longer.

These three events occurred within a year's time and I spent a lot of time thinking about the meaning of life. One important thing I learned is that I wanted to be a part of something larger than just Chris and me. I recognized that a sense of family, which I really never had much of, was actually very important. Motherhood began to intrigue me. "So, do you want to have a child?" I asked Chris. He gasped. Then he smiled. I knew that meant yes.

However, by this time I was 35 years old, and I read up on how fertility declines with age. I thought I might have missed the opportunity to be a mother—but, alas, I was pregnant within six months. Wow. Now what, Chris?

Little Katie was born in the early morning hours after nine months of a relatively easy pregnancy. She is the light of our lives. However, after the initial euphoria diminished, we were faced with the daunting task of how to take care of her; more specifically, how do we combine our challenging work with the needs of family? My parents and I still don't get along well, and Chris's parents live a thousand miles away.

I took a 4-month maternity leave, but the latter half was unpaid because I had used up all my vacation pay. Things got a little tight financially. I went back to work, but finding child care for an infant proved to be a challenge. After what seemed like 50 telephone calls or visits to home-run day cares and day care centers, I finally found a good one that had an opening. Full-time care for Katie cost us about $1,100 per month.

(continued)

(continued)

During this time, I began a transformation. In the quest to balance work and family, I found that I preferred to have the scale tipped toward family rather than toward work. How could this be? I've always loved my job and didn't mind putting in 50- to 60-hour weeks—but no more. I tried to limit it to 40, then down to 30 hours. Fortunately my law firm was willing to let me go down to part-time, although they made it clear that there would be career costs involved.

I met a group of stay-at-home moms at a library function. We get together regularly and I enjoy their camaraderie, yet I feel like I have a foot in two very different camps. On Monday, Wednesday, and Friday, I don the dress-for-success outfit and play attorney. At work we rarely talk about children—even though most of my male colleagues have them. We are all business; I'm not even sure they know my daughter's name. Then on Tuesday and Thursday I don the mothering outfit—complete with food stains from my baby—and talk with other women about nothing but mothering. I'm not even sure these friends know what type of law I practice. They never ask, and to be honest, I don't ask them many questions about their "other" lives—but are mothers really *not* supposed to have any other life? I feel disjointed. Which hat am I wearing today?

Combining work and family is difficult psychologically and financially, yet this is also a very exciting time. As it turns out, we have love bouncing off the walls at our house.

—**Alexis, age 36**

Source: Seccombe 2006.

CRITICAL THINKING QUESTIONS

1. How do childhood experiences shape our adult desires to have children? Do you think this woman's circumstances are unusual or typical? How have your experiences shaped your desires?
2. Why is combining work and family so difficult psychologically? Do you think it was equally difficult for her husband? Why or why not? Will it be (or is it) difficult for you?

Nonetheless, many employed mothers feel guilty about the time they spend away from home. There is a cultural contradiction: Even though most mothers work outside the home, they must deal with critical judgments for doing so. Yet if a mother stays at home, she pays the price of being treated as an outsider by the larger world. There does not seem to be any way to get it right. As one woman laments (Hays 2001):

> I felt really torn between what I wanted to do. Like a gut-wrenching decision. Like, what's more important? Of course your kids are important, but you know, there's so many outside pressures for women to work. Every ad you see in magazines or on television shows this working woman who's coming home with a briefcase and their kids are all dressed and clean. It's such a lie. I don't know of anybody who lives like that. (p. 317)

"Fathering" as an Identity   Despite the stereotype of fathers as only "breadwinners," fathers have played other social roles throughout history, including moral overseer, nurturer, and a gender model for their sons (Coltrane 1996; LaRossa 1997; Marsiglio and Pleck 2005; Marsiglio et al. 2005). However, specific details about the hands-on role they have played with their children are sketchier. Sociologist Jessie Bernard (1973) traces the historical development and the changes in male roles in families in the United States. She observes that the Industrial Revolution in the mid-nineteenth century transformed men's roles into that of the "good provider," in which the focus shifted primarily to his breadwinning capabilities. Instead of participating in the more nurturing and caretaking aspects of family life as they had done in the past, fathers were removed physically and emotionally from the work done at home. Being a good provider became the dominant concept of male identity. Moreover, having an employed wife was indicative of his failure to provide for his family and threatened to undermine his position as "head of the household."

Most people want to have children; however, "mothering" and "fathering" are really quite different roles and activities. Mothers spend far more time than fathers do on their children's physical care, while a greater portion of fathers' time is spent in play.

This model continued until the 1970s and 1980s, when the women's movement and other social movements changed views about men's and women's positions and activities within the family. As more married women with children sought employment, families began to restructure themselves. Men are becoming more involved in domestic life, and many are relieved that they no longer have the economic burden of being the sole breadwinner.

During the past 20–30 years, there has been an explosion in research on fathering: What do fathers do with their children; what are the outcomes; and what are the meanings associated with being a father? We now believe a father should be engaged with his children, and many programs exist to promote this relationship (Cowan et al. 2009; Hawkins et al. 2008). Male-only social movements, such as the Million Man March on Washington, D.C., illustrate that men in U.S. culture are wrestling with their role as fathers, and many hope to increase public awareness about the meaning and importance of fathers in their children's lives (King et al. 2004).

"Fathering" as an Activity   How involved are fathers in their children's lives? Mothers perform the vast majority of parenting tasks; however, paternal involvement appears to be increasing (Smith 2004). A generation ago fathers spent only about 2.5 hours per week in direct child care, whereas today that figure has nearly tripled. Meet one of these "new" dads, Cade, in the box on page 302, "Families as Lived Experience: My Family: 'What I Like About Being a Dad ... and What I Don't'"

Involved fathers take pride and pleasure in their participation, although they may try to justify why their participation is less than their wives', as these two men do (Gerson 2001):

I guess we both have to do some sacrificing; that's basically what it is to be a parent. It's probably not going to be fifty-fifty.... I think the mother would have a tendency to do a little more. But even sixty-forty is pretty good compared to the average.

I wish I did more, but our time reference is quite different. I'll say, "Okay, I'll do that, but let me do this first." But she will frequently get frustrated and just not be able to stand the thought that it's not done, and then go ahead and do it. (p. 335)

FAMILIES
as Lived Experience

My Family: "What I Like About Being a Dad … and What I Don't"

What is it like to be a "father"? Cade offers you his perspective.

I've always assumed I would have a few kids. While I've never been obsessed about it, I just figured that when I met the right person, we would get married and have two or three kids soon thereafter. I had to confront that image head-on when I was in a serious relationship after college. Amari was clear—she didn't want children. Not now, not ever. I didn't understand her decision at first—she spoke of how they would limit her career options, she would have to do most of the work, and she didn't really enjoy the company of children. Now, I'm a pretty enlightened guy, so I thought I could convince her that her number one and two concerns just really weren't issues. But my rational reasoning fell on deaf ears. So, I then considered forgoing kids for her sake. But that didn't last. We finally had to acknowledge that there is really is no way to compromise on the issue, and so we ended our relationship.

Several years later, I met Elyssa; several years after that, we married; and voila, today, we have two fabulous kids. Nathan is now six, and Liza is five. What do I like about being a dad?

I feel like I now have a greater purpose in life than just focusing on myself. I know that these two are going to make the world a better place, and I am here to show them how to do it. Also, they are fun. I get a kick out of their silly antics. We love to work on model airplanes in the living room, eat ice cream for breakfast on Saturdays, and play on the swings at the park. They make me feel like I'm a kid again. I took Nathan canoeing last month, and I'm really looking forward to him getting a little older so we can do more things like that together. Elyssa and I also have a strong bond as parents, and I feel confident that it will never be broken.

Now that I've said all this, let me tell you that being a dad can also be a real drag. Okay, while I'm glad to focus on someone other than just myself, it would be nice to focus on me once in a while! Remember sleeping in late on Saturdays? Forget it. Liza is up every day at 6:00, and Nathan is up soon after. Elyssa usually gets up with them, but sometimes she's just so darn tired that I do it. And the house is usually a mess, with toys everywhere, dirty laundry piled up, and dishes in the sink. Speaking of which, the amount of housework that needs to be done is just ridiculous. I feel like I'm always cooking, cleaning, and soothing somebody, but to be honest, Elyssa is far more involved in it than I am. One more thing, and this is a big one—our sex life has taken a turn for the worse. We're both so busy with work and kids that we almost have to pencil it in on the calendar—well, that's her excuse anyway. And, I never thought I'd be doing "date-night"—an evening planned way in advance—there just isn't any spontaneity when you have to line up a teenage babysitter.

So, while I'm really glad I'm a dad, it is not all a party, believe me. It's hard work. But would I have it any other way? Not on your life.

—Cade, Age 34

CRITICAL THINKING QUESTIONS

1. Although you only hear from Cade, can you describe his family relationships? Look for clues throughout his story. What type of marriage do you think he has? Is he an involved parent? Does he seem to favor one child over another?
2. What macro-level factors affect Cade's experiences? Can you see macro-level influences with both Amari and Elyssa?

How does involvement on the part of fathers affect their children's well-being? Father involvement can enhance children's social, emotional, and cognitive well-being (Bronte-Tinkew et al. 2008; Sarkadi et al. 2008). In an analysis of nearly 100 studies on parent–child relationships, father love (measured by children's perceptions of paternal acceptance/rejection, affection/indifference) was as important as mother love in predicting the social, emotional, and cognitive development and functioning of children and young adults (Horn and Sylvester 2006; Rohner and Veneziano 2001).

Many children do not live with their fathers because of death, divorce, separation, or because their parents never married (Grall 2009). Nearly half of U.S. children will experience living without a biological father for some period of their childhood. Some of these children see their fathers regularly, while others see their fathers sporadically or infrequently. Boys generally have more frequent contact with their nonresident biological father than do girls (King et al. 2004; Mitchell et al. 2009). Racial and ethnic differences exist as well in specific activities (staying overnight, playing sports, going to religious services, talking about dating) however, no one racial or ethnic group stands out as being significantly higher or lower on father involvement (King et al. 2004).

> ### WHAT DO YOU THINK?
>
> *Thinking back on the ways you were raised, can you identify patterns of mothering and fathering? Were these patterns different from others that you knew well, such as among friends or cousins?*

Parenting Contexts

The traditional family has given way to a variety of different family arrangements. Growing numbers of singles, gays and lesbians, grandparents, stepparents, cohabiting couples, and extended families have altered the social context of parenting and have fueled new legal debates over parental rights and responsibilities (Bianchi et al. 2006). We will explore several of these contexts here.

Teen Parents

More than 400,000 teenagers had babies last year, which comes to about 42 births for every 1,000 women under the age of 20 (Hamilton et al. 2010). After declining significantly since the mid-1990s, the birthrate among teens rose for the first time in the mid-2000s, but is now declining again. The declines have been large among all racial and ethnic groups, as shown in Figure 10.1. Social demographers will be watching future trends closely.

The negative biological, social, and economic consequences of early parenting in the United States have been well documented (Advocates for Youth 2009; The Annie E. Casey Foundation 2009; Hoffman 2006): Teen mothers are 2.5 times as likely to die in childbirth as are older mothers, their infants are twice as likely to be of low birth weight, and the babies are nearly three times more likely to die within the first month of life. Are teenagers poorly equipped biologically to be mothers? Not necessarily. Many of these biological problems have social roots; teen mothers are more likely to be poor and lack proper nutrition and prenatal care.

Other repercussions are more social and economic in nature. Teen mothers are more likely to drop out of school than are other teens, are considerably poorer, and more likely to receive welfare. Adolescent mothers are also less knowledgeable about child development than are other mothers, are less prepared for childrearing, and are more likely to be depressed. Children born to teen mothers have lower math and reading skills and increased behavioral problems, although many of these differences may be related to the background of the mother rather than her teen pregnancy *per se* (Levine et al. 2007). It is therefore not surprising that social workers, health professionals, educators, researchers, and parents are alarmed at the relatively large number of teens—both young women and men—involved in adolescent pregnancies. It has been estimated that teen childbearing costs taxpayers at least $9.1 billion for health care, child welfare, and in lost revenues (Hoffman 2006).

Figure 10.1 **Teenage Fertility Rates per 1,000 Women Aged 15–19 by Race and/or Ethnicity for 1991 and 2008**

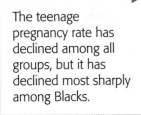

The teenage pregnancy rate has declined among all groups, but it has declined most sharply among Blacks.

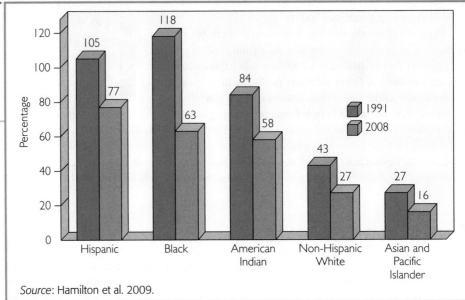

Source: Hamilton et al. 2009.

Why is the teenage birthrate now in a state of flux after more than a decade of decline? There is no single explanation. A large study of high school youth sponsored by the Centers for Disease Control and Prevention revealed that the likelihood of teens having sex has not really changed. What has changed is that those who are sexually active are slightly less likely to use birth control than they were a decade ago, condoms in particular (Santelli et al. 2009). Researchers point to several key factors, including a trend toward early puberty for girls, earlier and more frequent sexual activity, (The Annie E. Casey Foundation 2009; Centers for Disease Control and Prevention 2008b). Other factors may include the decreased stigma associated with births outside of marriage and the highly publicized pregnancies of several celebrity teens, changing economic conditions that diminish educational or job opportunities, and complacency that followed the decade of progress in reducing teen pregnancy (Holcombe et al. 2009; National Campaign to Prevent Teen and Unplanned Pregnancy 2009).

Single Parents

Single-parent families are often seen as problematic and have been referred to as *broken homes*. Today, many people take exception to that term.

The vast majority of single-parent families are single-mother families, and the terms are often used interchangeably—if you say "single parent" people typically think of a single mother. These kinds of families have been maligned for causing juvenile delinquency, poverty, and a host of social problems. The concern with such a sweeping generalization is that (1) there are different kinds of single-parent families with different kinds of circumstances (a teenager vs. a 40-year-old executive); (2) there are different paths to becoming a single parent (never marrying, divorce, or widowhood); (3) the cause-and-effect relationship is unclear (e.g., Does poverty cause single parenthood or does single parenthood cause poverty?); and (4) single parenthood is less problematic in other developed nations because of a wide number of social supports they provide that are notably

Figure 10.2 Family Households with Children Under 18 by Type: 1950 and 2009

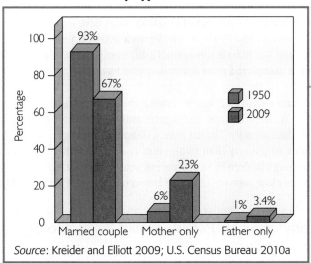

Households are increasingly headed by single parents.

1950
2009

Source: Kreider and Elliott 2009; U.S. Census Bureau 2010a

lacking in the United States (e.g., a higher minimum wage, child care assistance, and nationalized health care).

Nonetheless, the number of single parents is on the rise, and the likelihood of children living within a single-parent household for some or all of their childhood is increasing. Figure 10.2 shows the percentage of children living in single-mother and single-father households, and how these numbers have increased. In 1950, only 6 percent of households with children were maintained by a single mother; now it is 23 percent. Only 1 percent of households in 1950 were maintained by single fathers, but it has grown to 3.4 percent (Kreider and Elliott 2009; U.S. Census Bureau 2010a). Table 10.2 also shows that about one-third of children now live with only one parent, and the likelihood of living with a single parent is highest among Black children (65 percent) and lowest among Asian and Pacific Islander children (16 percent) (The Annie E. Casey Foundation 2009).

The route to single parenthood can take many different paths. Some women have babies outside of marriage. Others become single parents because of divorce or widowhood. Some are teenagers and others are older adults. We can make some generalizations about single parents—they are more likely to be impoverished and on food stamps, they are less likely to own a home, and they have lower levels of education (DeNavas-Walt et al. 2010; Kreider and

TABLE 10.2 Percent of Children Living in Single-Parent Families by Race, 2008

Nearly two-thirds of Black children live in single-parent families, twice the national average.

Non-Hispanic White	23%
Black or African American	65%
American Indian	50%
Asian and Pacific Islander	16%
Hispanic or Latino	38%
Total	32%

Source: The Annie E. Casey Foundation 2009.

Elliott 2009; Mather 2010). Yet, we should guard against sweeping generalizations because the different routes to single parenthood do produce different results.

Much of the concern surrounding single parents is targeted toward young women having babies outside of marriage. However, 15 percent of single mothers have a bachelor's degree or higher. Seventeen percent are at least 30 years old (Ventura 2009). If you think about it, unmarried women in their 30s and 40s offer a substantially different portrait of single parenthood—they are likely to have completed their education and have jobs, perhaps even well-paying careers.

Table 10.3 compares the poverty rate in 22 countries among children in single-parent versus other family types. Most of Western Europe has significantly lower rates of poverty among single-parent households than does the United States, although single parents appear to be universally more vulnerable to poverty than two-parent families. Of the 22 selected countries, the rates of poverty among children in single-parent households are highest in the United States, although Canada is a close second (UNICEF Innocenti Research Centre 2000).

TABLE 10.3 Child Poverty* in Single-Parent Families Relative to Other Family Types

Over half of American children living in single-parent families are poor, but this is not the case in other developed nations.

	POVERTY RATE OF CHILDREN IN	
	Single-Parent Families	Other Families
Australia	36%	9%
Belgium	14%	4%
Canada	52%	10%
Czech Republic	31%	4%
Denmark	14%	4%
Finland	7%	4%
France	26%	6%
Germany	51%	6%
Greece	25%	12%
Hungary	10%	10%
Ireland	46%	14%
Italy	22%	20%
Luxembourg	30%	3%
Mexico	28%	26%
Netherlands	24%	7%
Norway	13%	2%
Poland	20%	15%
Spain	32%	12%
Sweden	7%	2%
Turkey	29%	20%
United Kingdom	46%	13%
United States	**55%**	**16%**

*Poverty defined as 50% of median national income.
Source: UNICEF Innocenti Research Centre 2000.

Why is poverty so much less likely in other countries? Most developed countries offer universal family or child cash allowances and an assortment of other cash programs and social policies such as child care and health insurance specifically designed to help families with children. These programs and policies lift the income of families so that they are not impoverished.

Cohabiting Families   In some cases, what might first be viewed as a "single-parent" household is not really a single household at all (Kreider and Elliott 2009; Mather 2010). The single parent may be cohabiting with another adult. As cohabitation has increased, perhaps between 40 and 50 percent of nonmarital births are to mothers living with their child's father (Osborne 2005). Of children living with a single mother, about 11 percent actually lived in a household with their mother and her unmarried partner. White children are more likely to live with their cohabiting mother and her partner than are Blacks, Asians, or Hispanic children (Fields 2004).

Of children living with a single father, a third of them were actually living with their single father and his partner. Hispanic children were more likely to live with their cohabiting father and his partner than were White, Black, or Asian children. The parents' partner in these families plays varying roles. Some have close, near parent-like relationships with the children, and others are more distant.

Lesbian and Gay Families

Lesbians and gay men are still fighting for a basic human right: to be recognized and accepted as families. Because they cannot yet marry in most states, their relationships are often ignored or trivialized. The small amount of research on same-sex families tends to focus on lesbian families rather than families formed by gay males, furthering the stereotype that gay men are not interested in committed relationships with partners and nurturing relationships with children (Biblarz and Stacey 2010). However, these stereotypes are untrue (Kurdek 2008; Spock 2004). Many gays and lesbians are partnered, and about one in three lesbian couples and one in five gay couples are raising children (Pawelski et al. 2006).

There are many pathways for same-sex couples to become parents, including adoption, artificial insemination, or using a surrogate. However, most same-sex families are formed as stepfamilies, in which the children were conceived in an earlier heterosexual relationship by one of the partners (Allen 1997).

For the most part, same-sex parents have a great deal in common with heterosexual parents (Kurdek 2005; Patterson and Hastings 2007): they struggle to get their children to school on time, take their children to soccer practice after school, and they get involved in the local PTA. Their children grow up as well-adjusted and happy as do those in heterosexual families (American Psychological Association 2010; Biblarz and Stacey 2010). Yet, although most aspects of raising children are similar, a few differences do arise (Biblarz and Stacey 2010; Erera 2002; Spock 2004; Stacey and Biblarz 2001):

About 7 million gays and lesbians are parents, perhaps through adoption, artificial insemination, surrogacy, or as stepparents to a partner's children. Same-sex families have a great deal in common with other families, but also face some unique challenges given the prejudice and discrimination surrounding same-sex relationships.

■ *The decision to parent is generally a deliberate choice that reflects a strong commitment to raising children.* Studies tend to show either no difference among homosexuals and heterosexuals in their fitness to parent, or same-sex couples having a slight advantage.

For example, lesbian mothers exhibit more parenting skills and awareness of child development than heterosexual couples, and there is greater similarity between partners' parenting skills (Flaks et al. 1995). Likewise, compared to heterosexual fathers, gay fathers go to greater lengths to promote their children's cognitive skills, are more responsive to their children's needs, and are more involved in activities with children.

- *Lesbian and gay families are more likely to be affected by loss.* Lacking institutional constraints and support such as legalized marriage, lesbian and gay relationships are somewhat more likely to dissolve than are heterosexual ones. However, because lesbians and gay men cannot legally marry, their trauma may not be publicly recognized or as easily supported. U.S. society acknowledges the tremendous disruption caused by a divorce; however, a "breakup" may be trivialized. Lesbian and gay families may experience other losses as well. Lesbian and gay stepfamilies are created following a divorce (as are heterosexual stepfamilies), and children experience a loss of family members.

- *Lesbian and gay families must cope with homophobia and discrimination.* Same-sex relationships are stigmatized, and living openly as a family leaves them vulnerable to ridicule or discrimination. Although attitudes are shifting, many people still condemn same-sex relationships as unnatural or immoral. Violence against gays and lesbians is a possibility (Shepard 2009). Just as racial and ethnic minorities must teach their children about racism, gay and lesbian parents must teach their children about prejudice and discrimination against them as well.

- *Lesbians and gay men often have a close network of friends whom they regard as "fictive kin" who provide emotional and social support.* Social support is crucial from family and friends as a way to ward off oppression and to create a safe and supportive environment for lesbians, gay men, and their children. They often have developed a close network of friends whom they regard as a sort of extended family. They are there to celebrate birthdays; participate in commitment ceremonies; babysit when needed; and in countless ways, offer the love and support that are needed to keep a household and a family running smoothly.

Grandparents Raising Grandchildren

My granddaughter, Ruby, came to live with me when she was eight years old. I really didn't know what to do, but there was no other choice. My daughter, her mother, was just up to no good. She'd leave Ruby home alone when she went out partying. Sometimes she didn't even come home at night. I think she's using drugs. And Ruby's dad, who knows where he is. So, I just told my daughter, Ruby's gotta live with me. And my daughter didn't even put up a fuss. (Bonnie, age 58)

Some children live with and are under the custodial care of their grandparents. The U.S. Census Bureau estimates that about 7 million children live with their grandparents (Kreider and Elliott 2009). Sometimes the child's parent(s) also live with the grandparent. But the greatest growth has occurred among grandchildren living with grandparents on their own without a parent present. Now, about 3 million children live only with their grandparents, like Ruby.

Where are these children's parents? Mothers and fathers are absent for many reasons, including death, desertion, incarceration, substance abuse, physical or mental illness, employment problems, HIV/AIDS, and child abuse. Among Whites, alcohol and drug abuse were major reasons, whereas among Hispanics and Blacks, financial need was commonly cited (Goodman and Silverstein 2006). One study of 129 grandparents raising their grandchildren examined the situations that precipitated this relationship (Sands and Goldberg-Glen 2000). There were multiple problems in the homes of the grandchildren's parents that led the grandparents to take over their grandchildren's care. The most commonly reported problem was substance abuse, but the parent's inability to care for the child, neglect, and psychological and financial problems were also cited as factors. Many of these problems are long-term issues for families. When the grandparents in this study first began to care for their grandchildren, only one-third expected to be the caregiver until the grandchild grew up, but by the time of the interview, over 75 percent of grandparents assumed that they would care for their grandchild until adulthood.

What are some of the characteristics of these intergenerational families that are maintained by the grandparents (Fields 2003; Kreider and Elliott 2009; U.S. Census Bureau 2006)?

- Coresident grandmothers outnumber coresident grandfathers five to three. One reason is that women live longer, and therefore are more likely to reach an age where they have grandchildren. Another reason is that women are more likely than men to assume a caregiving role; grandmothers may feel more obliged to take in grandchildren. Grand-mothers are also more likely to be widowed and have lower incomes and may therefore want to live with their children or grandchildren for companionship or support.
- The majority of grandparents raising their grandchildren are younger than age 65. One-third are younger than age 50, and nearly half are between the ages of 50 and 64. Only 1 in 5 is aged 65 or older.
- Grandchildren in grandparent-maintained families are more likely to be Black, younger, and living in the south, compared with grandchildren who live in intergenerational households maintained by their parents.
- Grandchildren living in grandparent-maintained families are more likely to be poor than other grandchildren, as shown in Figure 10.3. They are also less likely to receive health insurance and more likely to receive public assistance.

Grandparents raising grandchildren have a unique set of both challenges and strengths. Children separated from their parents have likely experienced trauma, but living with a

Figure 10.3 Percentage of Grandchildren in Poverty, Receiving Welfare, and Not Covered by Health Insurance, by Living Arrangement

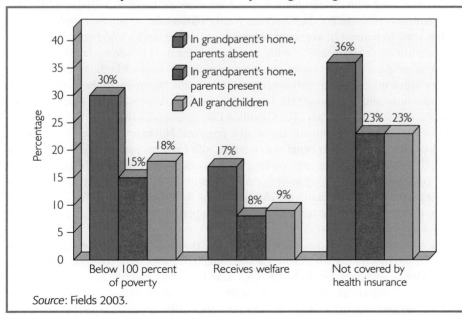

Source: Fields 2003.

Children who are being raised by grandparents are among the most vulnerable. They are more likely to live in poverty, receive welfare, and be without health insurance.

grandparent—rather than with a nonrelative or in an institution—can minimize that trauma by providing a sense of continuity and family support. Furthermore, many grandparents find meaning and satisfaction in caring for their grandchild.

Nonetheless, many of these families face considerable challenges (Goyer 2006; USA.gov 2010; U.S. Census Bureau 2008a). First, grandparents talk about the physical exhaustion they feel trying to keep up with their grandchildren. Second, some grandparents have physical or mental health problems that make caring for a child more difficult. Third, many grandparents have low incomes, and have difficulty paying housing bills and purchasing enough food for a healthy diet. And finally, many grandparents feel poorly equipped to help their grandchild through the trauma he or she experienced. One study with 42 grandparents who were primary caregivers to their grandchildren found that they were in high agreement that their grandchildren would benefit from a specially designed support group geared to address the child's feelings of anger, guilt, and depression, adjusting to the loss of a parent, and helping them to understand the parent's substance abuse or other problems (Smith et al. 2002).

Social Policy and Family Resilience

As April 15 approaches and American families with children fill out their tax returns, they will find some relief in the form of the expanded child tax credits ($1,000 per child in 2010). Yet, we cannot ignore the fact that Americans still receive considerably less support with regard to the costs of rearing children than families in many other countries.

Example: Family Allowances

The United States is one of the few developed nations that do not provide **family allowances**. These are cash benefits given to families with children by the government with the amount dependent upon the number or age of children (Centre des Liaisons Europeennes et Internationales de Securite Sociale 2006). The purpose of this cash grant is to help offset some of the costs associated with raising children. These are universal benefits, available to all families, regardless of income. For the most part, family allowances are modest benefits worth a little less than 10 percent of average household income for *each child*, but they can comprise a significant component of family income to large or low-income families. Family allowances are paid by government, business, or a combination of both. Many European countries began offering family allowances as early as the beginning of the twentieth century (Kamerman and Gatenio 2002). In Canada, family allowances were considered the first real social welfare program (The Canadian Encyclopedia 2010).

Does the United States provide any similar program? Not exactly; however, the United States does provide several tax benefits to families with children, particularly to low-income families. For example, low-income working families could apply for the refundable earned income tax credit (EITC) as long as their income was under $40,545 in tax year 2010 (married, filing jointly, with one qualifying child) (Internal Revenue Service 2009). The EITC is designed to offset some of the taxes that low-income persons would otherwise pay, thereby serving as an inducement to work.

The United States provides other benefits. For instance the government helps offset child care costs by offering a tax credit for some qualifying expenses; however, unlike most other developed countries, family benefits for Americans with children are usually not universal, but are means-tested. Applying for these tax benefits can be confusing; a family must be aggressive and savvy enough to understand the tax system, what programs are available, and be familiar with eligibility requirements and ceilings. The net effect is that those U.S. families who most need assistance are often the least likely to apply or be aware of the benefits. For example, 25 percent of those eligible for the EITC do not receive it (Internal Revenue Service 2009). Even when persons do receive assistance, it likely comes just once a year rather than on a monthly basis. These tax concessions are critical to low-income families; yet, they do not make up for the lack of family allowances and other special cash benefits targeted to children in many other countries.

Currently 88 countries worldwide provide family allowances (Kamerman and Gatenio 2002). In some countries, family allowances may be supplemented by many other cash programs or tax credits, including birth grants, school grants, child rearing or child care allowances, adoption benefits, special supplements for single parents, guaranteed minimum child support benefits, and allowances for adult dependents and disabled children. By providing these cash benefits, governments are directly helping families with the costs associated with raising children and indirectly helping to lower the rate of child poverty (Institute for Family Policies 2008).

Typically, family allowances have one or more of the following objectives (Kamerman and Gatenio 2002):

- *Horizontal equity*—The redistribution of income from childless households to families with children, in recognition of the heavier financial burden incurred by child rearing.
- *Vertical equity or redistribution*—Supplementing the incomes of poor and modest income families with children as a means of reducing or preventing poverty.
- *Strengthening labor force attachments*—In some countries, benefits are only available to families with children who have at least one parent in the workforce, or higher benefit levels are offered to families attached to the labor force.
- *Social inclusion/exclusion*—Particularly as the European Union moves toward greater unity among its member states, family allowances are viewed as an instrument that can foster societal cohesion and progress.

Family allowance benefit levels are structured in different ways. Several countries provide a uniform rate per child, regardless of the number of children in the family (Australia, Spain, Norway, and Sweden), whereas in other countries benefits increase with each additional child or are larger for the third, fourth, or fifth child (Italy, Belgium, France, Germany, and Luxembourg). In still others, such as the United Kingdom, the benefit is higher for the first child, whereas in France a family is only eligible for the allowance after the second child is born. Many countries provide higher benefits for older children (Austria, Belgium, France, Luxembourg, and the Netherlands). Some countries provide a higher or special benefit for families with very young children (Austria, France, Germany, and Portugal) to make it possible for a parent to remain at home during a child's early years (until the child is age 3; age 1 in Portugal).

Benefit levels may also be reduced as income rises or by including the benefit in taxable income, as in Spain and Greece. In some countries, benefit levels vary by geographic region. Austria, Germany, and Spain offer national benefits that vary by region, due to differences in the cost of living. Norway also supplements the family allowances of families in the Arctic region. Despite these differences, an important similarity is that there is no stigma attached to receiving benefits. Receipt is considered a right of citizenship, and countries actively encourage their residents to apply for benefits.

Coverage is generally extended to children from the time of birth to the age of majority or completion of formal education, provided other eligibility criteria are met. In almost all developed countries, the universal family allowance is awarded to the mother or to the person caring for the child. The income-related cash benefit is more likely to go to the wage-earning parent (or to either parent if both are employed).

Given that poverty rates are significantly higher in the United States than elsewhere, it might be worth taking a look at family allowances to determine how they could offset poverty for millions of Americans (Kamerman and Gatenio 2002).

Conclusion

This chapter has explored several dimensions of parenting. It suggests that although raising children may be universal, the act of *parenting* varies widely. Parenting attitudes and practices depend to a large extent on the type of tasks or competencies that members of a society (or subgroup) are expected to have. Mothering and fathering bring to mind the emotional, physical, and financial work involved with caring for children, but it is important to recognize that these identities take place within specific social, historical, and cultural contexts, and are framed by structures of sex, race, ethnicity, and class. Families are becoming increasingly diverse with more children being raised by single parents, gays and lesbians, and grandparents. These contexts raise new challenges and are of critical policy concern, yet a strength-based perspective asks that we also acknowledge what these families have to offer. Often the challenges can be mitigated through sound family policies. For example, many countries directly assist parents with the financial costs associated with raising children. The United States also does so, but leans toward annual tax credits rather than monthly assistance from a family allowance.

Key Terms

Authoritarian parenting style: Strict, punitive, and not very warm. (p. 297)

Authoritative parenting style: Demand and maintain high levels of control over their children, but also warm and receptive to their children. (p. 297)

Concrete operational thought: Piaget's third stage of cognitive development; occurs between the ages of 7 and 11 or 12 when children begin to see the causal connections in their surroundings and can manipulate categories, classification systems, and hierarchies in groups. (p. 292)

Ego: According to Sigmund Freud, the rational component of personality that attempts to balance the need for immediate gratification with the demands of society. (p. 292)

Family allowances: Cash benefits given to families by the government. (p. 310)

Formal operational thought: Piaget's fourth stage of cognitive development; children develop capacities for abstract thought and can conceptualize more complex issues or rules that can be used for problem solving. (p. 292)

Id: According to Sigmund Freud, the part of the personality that includes biological drives and needs for immediate gratification. (p. 292)

Looking-glass self: According to Cooley, we come to see ourselves as others perceive and respond to us. (p. 293)

Permissive parenting style: Having few controls or demands on the child. (p. 297)

Preoperational thought: Piaget's second stage of cognitive development; occurs through ages 6 or 7 as the child learns language, symbolic play and symbolic drawing, but does not grasp abstract concepts. (p. 292)

Racial (or ethnic) socialization: Teaching minority children about prejudice and discrimination; the coping skills necessary to develop and maintain a strong and healthy self-image. (p. 296)

Role taking: According to Mead, it is the process of mentally assuming the role of another person to understand the world from his or her point of view and to anticipate his or her response to us. (p. 293)

Sensorimotor intelligence: Piaget's first stage of cognitive development; infants and toddlers understand the world primarily through touch, sucking, listening, and looking. (p. 292)

Socialization: The lifelong process through which we acquire the cultural values and skills needed to function as human beings and participate in society. (p. 292)

Superego: According to Freud, it is our conscience, which draws upon our cultural values and norms to help us understand why we cannot have everything we want. (p. 292)

Symbolic interaction: Humans interact not just with words, but also with symbols and meanings. (p. 293)

Transnational family: A family living between two nations, often in search of work that pays a survivable wage. (p. 289)

Resources on the Internet

Administration for Children and Families (ACF)

www.acf.hhs.gov

This federal agency funds a variety of family assistance programs at the community level. They provide data on many issues relevant to children and parenthood. Particularly helpful are their fact sheets about important issues and programs (child abuse, the Head Start program, and child support enforcement).

Children's Defense Fund

www.childrensdefense.org

The mission of the Children's Defense Fund is to Leave No Child Behind and to ensure every child a good start in life and successful passage to adulthood with the help of caring families and communities. They provide useful data on the education, health, income, and well-being of vulnerable families and children.

ChildStats.gov

www.childstats.gov

This website offers access to federal and state statistics and reports on children and their families, including population and family characteristics, economic security, health, behavior and social environment, and education. Reports of the Federal Interagency Forum on Child and Family Statistics include *America's Children: Key National Indicators of Well-Being*, the annual federal monitoring report on the status of the nation's children.

The Clearinghouse on International Developments in Child, Youth, and Family Policies

www.childpolicyintl.org

The Clearinghouse provides cross-national, comparative information about the policies, programs, benefits, and services available in the advanced industrialized countries to address child, youth, and family needs. Coverage focuses on 23 advanced industrialized countries. Expansion to other countries and other parts of the world is planned.

UNICEF

www.unicef.org

UNICEF, the United Nations Children's Fund, is part of the Global Movement for Children—a broad coalition dedicated to improving the life of every child. UNICEF's staff works in 157 countries around the world to assure equality for those who are discriminated against, girls and women in particular. The UNICEF website offers current information about the state of children's lives throughout the world.

CHAPTER 11

Families and the Work They Do

CHAPTER OUTLINE

The Changing Economy and Work   317

Life in a Recession   321

■ **FAMILIES** *as Lived Experience:*
Unemployment Up Close and Personal   *322*

The Division of Household Labor   327

Juggling Work and Family Life   332

■ **OUR** *Global Community:* Why We Choose
to Live in Hungary   *333*

■ **SOCIAL** *Policies for Families:* Fixing Social
Insecurity   *337*

**Child Care: Who's Minding
the Children?**   338

Social Policy and Family Resilience   341

Conclusion   342

Key Terms   343

Resources on the Internet   343

CHAPTER PREVIEW

This chapter examines the work that families do inside and outside the home. It may have been true in the past that one's place of employment and one's home were two different domains with little overlap, but this is no longer true. Issues such as work-family conflicts, feelings of time deficits with children, negotiations over the division of household labor, and struggles to find suitable child care are well known to most families today. In this chapter, you will learn:

- Ways in which the economy and work have changed for families, including changes in child labor and women's labor force trends

- Changes in the occupational structure, such as the rise in part-time, nonstandard, and temporary work

- Juggling work and family life is stressful for many families, although certain policies can help reduce the stress and time crunch these families feel

- How household labor is defined and measured and discover who does the bulk of the work in the home

- Who is taking care of children as most mothers and fathers now work outside the home for pay

- What the United States could learn from other countries about early childhood education and child care policies

It's 7:40 A.M. when Cassie Bell, 4, arrives at the Spotted Deer Child Care Center, her hair half-combed, a blanket in one hand, a fudge bar in the other. "I'm late," her mother, Gwen, a sturdy young woman whose short-cropped hair frames a pleasant face, explains to the child care workers in charge. "Cassie wanted the fudge bar so bad, I gave it to her," she adds apologetically.

"Please, can't you take me with you?" Cassie pleads. "You know I can't take you to work," Gwen replies in a tone that suggests that she has been expecting this request. Cassie's shoulders droop. However, she has struck a hard bargain—the morning fudge bar—aware of her mother's anxiety about the long day that lies ahead at the center. As Gwen explains later, she continually feels that she owes Cassie more time than she gives her.

Arriving at her office just before 8:00, Gwen finds on her desk a cup of coffee in her personal mug, milk no sugar (exactly as she likes it), prepared by a co-worker who managed to get in ahead of her. As the assistant to the head of public relations at a company called Amerco, Gwen handles responses to reports that may appear about the company in the press—a challenging job, but one that gives her satisfaction. As she prepares for her first meeting of the day, she misses her daughter, but she also feels relief. There is a lot to get done at Amerco.

Gwen used to work a straight eight-hour day. However, over the past three years, her workday has gradually stretched to 8.5 or nine hours, not counting the e-mail messages and faxes she answers from home. She complains about her long hours to her co-workers and listens to their complaints—but she still loves her job. Gwen picks up Cassie at 5:45 and gives her a long, affectionate hug.

At home, Gwen's husband John, a computer programmer, plays with their daughter while Gwen prepares dinner. To protect the dinner "hour"—8:00 to 8:30—Gwen checks that the phone machine is on. After Cassie's bath, Gwen and Cassie have "quality time" or "Q.T." as John affectionately calls it. Half an hour later, at 9:30, Gwen tucks Cassie into bed.

There are, in a sense, two Bell households: the rushed family they actually are and the relaxed family they imagine they might be if only they had time. Gwen and John complain that they are in a time bind. What they say they want seems so modest—time to throw a ball, to read to Cassie, to witness the small milestones of her development, not to speak of having a little fun and romance themselves—yet even these modest wishes seem strangely out of reach. Before going to bed, Gwen has to e-mail messages to her colleagues in preparation for the next day's meeting. John goes to bed early, exhausted—he's out the door by seven every morning.

This is an excerpt from the best-selling book, *The Time Bind* (Hochschild 1997). Sociologist Arlie Hochschild reports that for many people, working hours have increased, and work has replaced home as the place of friendship, meaning, and even relaxation. Based on in-depth interviews with working families, she writes of a cultural reversal—as work has encroached on family time, the rewards of work have increased relative to those of family life. Home is where increasing numbers of people feel stressed by the demands of children and spouses, by household labor, and feelings of lack of control, and work is now where people obtain personal satisfaction.

Sociologist K. Jill Kiecolt reexamined these ideas using data from the General Social Surveys. Has there been a cultural reversal? Her conclusions say no, at least not for women. She found that over a 20-year period, the percentage of women for whom work was more satisfying than family life actually shrank, while men's percentage remained the same (Kiecolt 2003). She also found that respondents with preschool-aged children were more likely to find a home a haven, which belies the idea in *The Time Bind* that individuals are less psychologically invested in their families than in the past. According to Kiecolt, a cultural reversal has not occurred; work has not become more satisfying than home despite the stresses people face as they try to juggle work and family roles.

Since the Industrial Revolution, we have considered "work" as an activity that was done outside the home. Home and work were separate spheres, generally unrelated to one another, and largely segregated by sex. Today we recognize that work and family are not separate domains, but are highly interrelated. First, a majority of mothers work outside the home whether married or not, including mothers with preschool-aged children. Dual-worker or dual-career families are seen as normal rather than the exception.

Second, the organization of work done inside the home has an influence on the work done outside the home. Issues such as how child care, housework, or emotional labor is divided up between partners influence worker productivity, absenteeism, and retention. For example, how do parents negotiate who leaves work early to pick up a sick child from school? Single working parents juggle this alone, whereas two-parent families are negotiating family labor.

Third, specific work policies have the ability to reduce work-family tensions and conflicts that parents experience through flex-time, part-time work options, health insurance, sick pay, parental leaves, and other important family-friendly fringe benefits (Kelly et al. 2010; Whitehead 2008).

Today's families feel more pressure than ever. Work encroaches on family as the number of single-parent households and dual-earner households continues to rise, hours on the job increase, and job benefits erode. Employment has not kept pace with the changing nature of the workforce by offering a family-friendly environment. Nonetheless, despite a work "speed-up," most adults want to have children; they are not willing to sacrifice children for the sake of work. They hope to find and maintain some semblance of balance in their lives. This chapter examines key issues and challenges in the work that families do both inside and outside the home.

The Changing Economy and Work

The context of work and family life has undergone some big changes in the past several hundred years. In early colonial America, most families worked closely with the land, as we learned in Chapter 3. The labor of men, women, and children was considered invaluable to the success of the family enterprise. Men and women usually had different tasks; however, during planting and harvesting all family labor was needed in the fields. In other words, although sex may have been a central construct in dividing up labor, the line between men's and women's work was sometimes blurred.

In the nineteenth century, the U.S. economy was evolving from agriculture toward industrialization. Work transformed into something that was done away from home, and people were paid wages for their labor. People moved to urban areas in search of jobs, and many small family farms could not support themselves and folded. An urban middle class emerged, with men going off to work outside the home, and women doing the unpaid work inside it. More and more goods and services were produced for profit outside the home, and families purchased these with money from the wages they earned at outside jobs.

Meanwhile, an ideology emerged suggesting that a woman's proper role was in the home, serving as nurturer to her husband and family. Women and men increasingly inhabited "separate spheres." Yet, the new industries needed large numbers of laborers so, in addition to recruiting men, they increasingly looked to young, poor, minority, and immigrant women and children. In 1890, 17 percent of women were in the labor force. Most of these women were unmarried and without children (Coontz 2000). Much of the work was dangerous and dirty, because minimal occupational safety standards existed compared to today. Thus, women's roles became increasingly intertwined with class and race; poor or minority women *had* to work, whereas white middle-class women could bask in the glory of true womanhood far away from the world of work.

Trends in Child Labor

Child labor is common throughout the world. Parents rely on children to help tend the herds, work in agriculture, carry water from its source to the home, take care of younger siblings, and work in factories.

American children, too, have contributed significant labor to families, with few protections until recently. As industrialization took hold and families moved from farms into urban areas in search of work, poor children often toiled beside their parents in dangerous factories, textile mills, canneries, and mines (Child Labor Public Education Project 2010). Poor families needed the labor of all members to earn enough for even minimal food, shelter, and clothing. In fact, children were often preferred as laborers because they were seen as less expensive, less likely to strike, and more docile. Thousands of children were employed in dismal working conditions doing hard labor for only a fraction of the wages paid to men or women.

Opposition to child labor began to grow in the northern states, seen in the first state child labor law in Massachusetts in 1836 that required children under 15 working in factories to attend school at least three months per year, or the 1892 Democratic Party platform that proposed a ban on factory employment for children under 15. Many factories moved south to avoid the growing protections of young workers. By the early decades of the twentieth century, the number of child laborers in the United States peaked and then began to decline as the labor and reform movements grew more outspoken about the horrendous plight of many young children. New protective laws were passed during this era, and by 1938, for the first time a minimum age of employment and maximum hours of work for children were regulated by federal law (Child Labor Public Education Project 2010).

Children conduct a large proportion of the world's labor. They work in manufacturing, agriculture, child care, and even in war. Their labor often cuts short their education.

Recent Women's Labor Force Trends

You can really see how women's opportunities have changed by looking at my family. My grandmother, who never worked outside the home, is pretty adamant that mothers should not be working. She talks about that a lot, and is worried about the state of families today. Meanwhile, my mom thinks it's okay for mothers to work as long as their children are in school. That's what she did—she waited until my brother and I were in first and third grade. Today, I feel differently. I'm planning to go to medical school, and I just assume that I'll be working when I have my children. I think women can have a fulfilling career and have children at the same time.

—Abby, Age 22

Until recently, most American married women with children did not work outside the home for pay. Figure 11.1 shows how trends have changed in recent years. Even in 1970, only a little more than a generation ago, just 40 percent of married mothers worked. However, by 1980, we saw the largest increase in any 10-year period: The majority of mothers, whether married, single, or divorced, were now employed outside the home for pay. This shift reflects increasing job and educational opportunities for women, the idea of the women's movement becoming commonplace, and changes in the economy. Mothers in the 1980s worked for a variety of reasons, as do mothers today, including for sheer economic need or personal fulfillment. Today, 69 percent of married mothers,

Figure 11.1 Employment Status of Mothers by Marital Status: 1970–2009

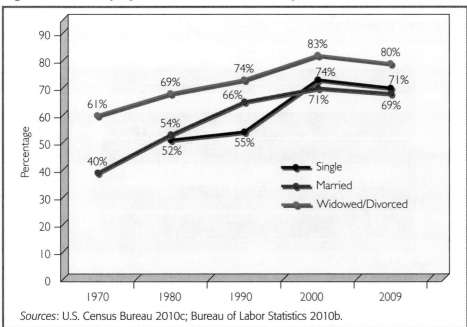

Today, the majority of mothers work outside the home for pay regardless of marital status.

Sources: U.S. Census Bureau 2010c; Bureau of Labor Statistics 2010b.

71 percent of single mothers, and 80 percent of divorced, separated, or widowed mothers are employed for pay (Bureau of Labor Statistics 2010b). The likelihood of mothers working dipped a little in the early 2000s, but has started to slowly rise again.

Mothers with older children are more likely to work than are mothers with younger children, regardless of marital status, race, or ethnicity (Bureau of Labor Statistics 2009e). Figure 11.2 shows the percentage of mothers who are employed, by the age of their youngest

Figure 11.2 Mothers' Employment by Age of Youngest Child and Race/Ethnicity, 2008

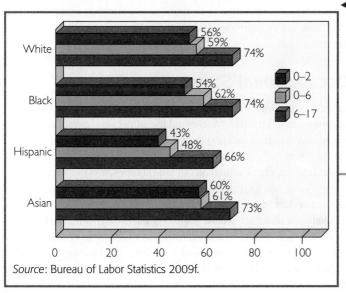

Most mothers with even the youngest children (age 0–2) work outside the home for pay. Asian American mothers are most likely to be employed; Hispanics are least likely.

Source: Bureau of Labor Statistics 2009f.

Figure 11.3 Is the Increase in Working Mothers with Young Children Generally a Good Thing for Society, a Bad Thing for Society, or Doesn't It Make Much Difference?

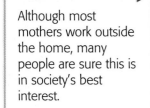

Although most mothers work outside the home, many people are sure this is in society's best interest.

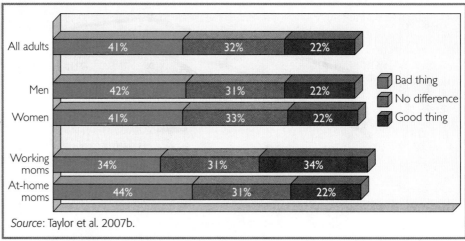

	Bad thing	No difference	Good thing
All adults	41%	32%	22%
Men	42%	31%	22%
Women	41%	33%	22%
Working moms	34%	31%	34%
At-home moms	44%	31%	22%

Source: Taylor et al. 2007b.

child, by race and ethnicity. It shows that Asian American mothers are most likely to be employed when their children are young. Hispanic mothers are least likely to be employed at all ages of their children. Among families with children ages 6–17, the employment rates of White, Black, and Asian American mothers are comparable.

Yet, despite the fact that most families have an employed mother, *attitudes* toward working mothers are less positive than one might imagine. A national survey based on a representative sample of adults asked, "Is the increase in working mothers with young children generally a good thing for society, a bad thing for society, or doesn't it make much difference?" Only 22 percent said that the increase in working mothers was a good thing for society, and 41 percent said it was a bad thing. There were no real differences between men and women, but there were stark differences between the opinions of mothers who work outside the home and those who do not, as shown in Figure 11.3. Younger adults are also more likely than older adults to view working mothers in a positive light (Morin and Taylor 2008; Taylor et al. 2007a).

Next, let's take a look at how both technology and globalization are changing the nature of the occupational structure.

The Changing Occupational Structure

U.S. industries have undergone rapid restructuring in the past few decades in response to technological changes and global competition. First, the widespread use of personal computers (virtually unheard of 30 years ago, believe it or not), cell phones, fax machines, and pagers has changed the way we do business and the way we conduct our personal life. We buy e-tickets for our flights, order groceries over the Internet, check e-mail on our Blackberries, text our friends to see what's on the agenda for the weekend, and Skype our mom when we're on vacation. Many companies use these technologies to conduct business 24 hours a day, 7 days a week. More and more people can do their "work" from just about anywhere, including the dining room table as their children romp in the living room. Work enters home. Likewise, our home life enters the work arena. Thus, for many people the boundaries between work and family are blurring. Sometimes this works out well (e.g., maybe you can reduce your child care costs if you can do some of your work at home). However, for others the burst of technology has actually increased stress levels.

Second, many jobs are being outsourced to other countries as companies search for cheaper labor costs and fewer government regulations (Galinsky et al. 2009; Whoriskey 2009). Manufacturing jobs, sales, and service are being shipped overseas. Is your computer on the blink? When you telephone a call center for help, it is quite likely that someone in India will answer the phone. Consumers appreciate the 24/7 economy and we benefit from the lower cost of goods and services, but outsourcing jobs contributes to widespread job losses in this country. The number of manufacturing jobs has also declined considerably—jobs that tended to pay livable wages because of union protections have now gone overseas.

Coupled with technology and globalization, today's families also face a severe economic recession. Let's examine the current economic climate so that we can better understand the relationship between work and family (Holzer et al. 2011).

WHAT DO YOU THINK?

How does world systems theory, presented in Chapter 2, inform our understanding of the changing occupational structure?

Life in a Recession

The recession that began in the late 2000s caused hardship for many families. The civilian labor force shrunk by nearly 1 million workers between 2008 and 2010 (Bureau of Labor Statistics 2010b).

Unemployment and Families

The unemployment rate in late 2010 was 9.6 percent, almost double the rate of late 2007, as shown in Table 11.1 (Bureau of Labor Statistics 2010a). The unemployment rates during this recession are the highest since late 1982. But this overall rate masks the fact that unemployment is far higher for minority groups. For example, Black unemployment was nearly double that of Whites in late 2010 (Bureau of Labor Statistics 2010a). This means that many breadwinners lost their jobs or had their income reduced, contributing to the rise in home foreclosures and personal bankruptcies.

What does it feel like to look for work week after week and turn up with nothing? When even low-paying jobs have stiff competition, many people feel psychologically wounded (Elder et al. 1992). Unemployment affects personal relationships as shown in the box on page 322, "Family as Lived Experience: Unemployment Up Close and Personal."

A study done during the Great Depression of the 1930s found that unemployed men experienced considerable distress, and they often took out their frustration and depression on their wives and families (Elder 1999). More recent work shows that the high unemployment

TABLE 11.1 Unemployment Rates, November, Odd Years

The unemployment rate is double what it was just a few years ago.

1999	4.1%
2001	5.5%
2003	5.8%
2005	5.0%
2007	4.7%
2009	10.0%
September 2010	9.6%

Sources: Bureau of Labor Statistics 2009d, 2010e.

F A M I L I E S
as Lived Experience

Unemployment Up Close and Personal

We hear about the recession and unemployment a lot in the news, but what does unemployment really feel like? As systems theory explained, family members are interdependent. When one family member loses his job, this loss touches others in the family as well.

I grew up in a typical middle-class family, if there is such a thing as a "typical" middle-class family. My dad worked as a manager for a small company, and my mom was a teacher's aide. We had the basic trappings, you know, a three-bedroom house in the suburbs, two cars, and a vacation to the beach every summer. Our lifestyle wasn't fancy, but I never had to worry about whether we had enough money to buy some new school clothes every fall, or whether we would get enough to eat. My parents always stressed that my brother and I will go to college, and they saved a little money towards that goal to help with tuition. In other words, life was secure.

All that changed when I was in high school and my dad lost his job. They gave him a few months of severance pay, but that was it. I remember the frightened look on his face when he came home from work one day, and asked my brother and I to leave the room so he could talk to my mom alone. I could hear them talking softly, and then I heard my mother cry. I was dying to know what was wrong.

About 20 minutes later they called my brother and me back into the room, and told us that, after this week, my dad would no longer be working at his company. I didn't really understand what that meant financially. I even thought, "Cool, he'll be home more. Maybe he can go to more of my soccer games." I didn't understand what it meant to be unemployed.

I learned quickly, however. To save money, my parents immediately cut our cable television, Internet access, and most after-school activities and summer camps. They let me continue the soccer season, since it was already paid for, but the rest had to go. My brother was really upset about giving up his art lessons because art has always been important to him, and he's really pretty good.

There were also no more allowance, dinners out, or 10 dollars here and there when I wanted to go to the movies. I heard, "no, we can't afford it" daily, and it got old real quickly. By the third month, my parents began to sell some of our possessions—mostly things stored out in the garage that we didn't use, but still, it felt weird to be selling stuff off.

But even more unsettling than the financial issues were the changes I saw in my parents. My father spent the first few months of his unemployment actively seeking work, not finding any, and then it was like he just gave up. He would just sit around the house watching TV and sometimes not even shave or get dressed. He didn't really come to my soccer games either, "Sorry son, I just don't feel like it today," he would say. My mom would get upset because when she would come home from her job the house would be kind of a mess. My brother and I had chores of course, but we didn't think it was our job to clean the whole house! My dad wouldn't even fix dinner most nights. Obviously, this made my mom even more upset and they began to argue a lot. I remember her calling him a "pig" once, and it really broke me up because they never used to talk like that to each other. I'm sure he was depressed, but no one knew what to do about it.

After about 8 months, my father did finally get another job. But things weren't automatically rosy then either. I don't know all the details, but I sense that his bout with unemployment caused them to go into considerable debt. You know, credit cards, home equity loans, and that sort of thing. And our college savings account? That disappeared too. I think their marriage is getting back on track though. Whew, things were rough for awhile.

—Luke, Age 18

CRITICAL THINKING QUESTIONS
1. Can you use the family systems theory, introduced in Chapter 1, to better understand the unemployment situation in Luke's family?
2. How might the changing occupational structure—technology and globalization—affect job loss and the job search?

experienced by inner-city Blacks affects marriage rates. Black women are hesitant to marry a man without prospects for stable employment (Edin and Kefalas 2005; Wilson 1987, 1996). The stress associated with unemployment can also endanger relationships, contribute to domestic violence, and harm children's social well-being (Aubry et al. 2006). For example, a study based on 4,476 school-age children in 2,569 families across the United States found that when fathers were involuntarily employed, children had a greater likelihood of repeating a grade or getting suspended from school (Kalil and Ziol-Guest 2008; Luo 2009). It is clear that macro issues, such as unemployment, affect our personal relationships.

Poverty-Level Wages

Some families earn the minimum wage or wages only slightly above it. The federal minimum wage in the United States, at $7.50 per hour in 2011, comes nowhere near to lifting even a small family out of poverty. At $7.50 per hour, working 40 hours per week yields less than $300 per week before taxes (yes, people working at minimum wage still pay taxes). Working 52 weeks a year, a full-time employee would average around $15,600 per year. How does a person or a family pay for rent, utilities, food, clothing, and other incidentals on minimum wage? Because this rate is so low, 14 states have adopted state minimum wages that are higher than the federal wage. Washington and Oregon have the highest state minimum wages in the nation at $8.55 and $8.40 per hour, respectively (Wage and Hour Division, U.S. Department of Labor 2010).

About 2.2 million hourly workers earn the minimum wage or even less. Half of these persons are age 25 or older. These low-wage workers are evenly distributed across racial and ethnic groups, with the exception of Asians who are more likely to have higher wages. Women are more likely to earn minimum wage than are men, and many are supporting children as well as themselves (Bureau of Labor Statistics 2009b).

Recognizing that the minimum wage is far too low to support a family, the concept of paying a **living wage** is taking hold. A living wage ordinance requires employers to pay wages that are above federal or state minimum wage levels, usually ranging from 100 to 130 percent of the poverty line. Only a specific set of workers is covered by living wage ordinances, usually those employed by businesses that have a contract with a city or county government or those that receive economic development subsidies from the locality.

Part-Time, Nonstandard, and Temporary Work

In addition to pay, another concern is that many jobs are now part-time, subcontracted, or temporary. Some offer only irregular work schedules. Employees working in these types of jobs, called **nonstandard work schedules**, represent the fastest-growing category of workers in the United States (Gornick et al. 2009; Presser et al. 2008). Since 1982, temporary employment has increased several hundred percent. In other words, millions of women and men begin the workday not knowing if, or for how long, their jobs are likely to continue. Women are overrepresented in these arrangements, particularly in those characterized by lower wages and fewer benefits (Prokos et al. 2009).

Some part-time and contingency workers prefer this arrangement, especially highly paid professionals who value their freedom and independence on the job or mothers with young children who would prefer to work only sporadically. Most American families, however, prefer the assurance of a steady job with prearranged hours, and an established pay scale with fringe benefits. Families with nonstandard work schedules may find it difficult to organize child care, because most child care centers are only open between 7 A.M. and 6 P.M. Furthermore, child care centers usually require a paid commitment to a particular schedule, such as a Monday through Friday schedule or a Monday, Wednesday, Friday schedule. When a parent works full-time one week, three days the next week, and four half days the next, it wreaks havoc on child

Women contribute over one-third of a family's income, but many work in the low-paying service sector with nonstandardized work schedules.

care arrangements, school schedules, and parenting tasks, creating stress (Davis et al. 2008; Joshi and Bogen 2007; Perry-Jenkins et al. 2007). Most women do not work these schedules out of personal inclination, but because these are the required working conditions of their jobs as cashiers, maids, nursing aides, cooks, and waiters.

Rhonda is one of many people looking for a stable job with good pay (Seccombe 2011). She has a high school diploma, but has not gone to college. She is a single mother, and would like to raise her young son Bobby without relying on government assistance. She wants a permanent full-time job. Instead, she has been stymied by the growth in part-time, temporary positions (Seccombe 2011):

Hopefully I can get me a job. A permanent job. My sister's trying to get me a job where she works. I put my application in last week. And it would be a permanent job. When you go through those agencies, it's just temporary work. It's just whenever they need you, and it's unfair too. Every job I've found is through this temporary agency, like Manpower, but it's only temporary. And they cut my check and my food stamps, and when my job ends, it's like you're stuck again. So I'm trying to find a permanent steady job. But it's hard around here. I've been out looking for work, and hoping that something comes through (p. 177).

Rhonda may be surprised to learn that temporary agencies are booming. Manpower is one of the largest private employers in the United States, ranking 119 in the *Fortune* 500 list of large companies, with revenues around $22 billion worldwide. They serve over 400,000 employer clients, and place 4 million workers per year in 82 countries and territories (Manpower Inc. 2009).

Disposable Workforce

Turnover rates in many low-income jobs are high. Sometimes, people quit work in hopes of finding something better. However, these workers are also likely to be laid off; they are the expendable workforce. They work in the service industry performing routine tasks. To management, people in these largely unskilled or semi-skilled jobs are interchangeable. A high turnover rate is not seen as problematic, and in fact, may even be considered desirable to avoid providing health insurance and other benefits. These disposable workers earn less than those on the regular payroll and must live with the uncertainty that their jobs may permanently end today when they clock out at 5:00 P.M. Their anxiety is high, and for many, unemployment insurance is not an option.

Eliza, a single mother of four children, epitomizes the plight of many people who are looking for work, but find that they are at the mercy of employers who do not provide stable employment. Eager to work, Eliza was delighted to find a job in a fast-food restaurant. She told them up front that she was looking for 30–40 hours of employment per week. Knowing this, they hired her, but instead of meeting her needs, her boss routinely asked her to leave work early, unpaid, during the slow periods. She was hired to fill an organizational need and was released as soon as the need for her labor abated. Because Eliza's income was so much less than she anticipated and did not cover her bills, she quit (Seccombe 2011):

That's something I need is a job. I've been looking. I just can't find the right one. I used to work at <fast food industry>, but I wasn't making much money. By the time I caught the city bus, went out there, by the time I got to my kids, I spent all the money that they gave me. I liked the job, but it was just that I had to pay 75 cents to get to work, and paid 75 cents to get back. If I missed the bus I had to give somebody $3.00 or $4.00 to take me. And they wouldn't give me enough hours. I told them when they gave me this job that I needed at least 30–40 hours a week. I just can't afford to work less. But I was wasting my time going out there. I had to be at work by 11 o'clock, but they would send me home by 2 o'clock. I didn't even get 20 hours a week. You hear what I'm saying? Ten or 12, maybe. I think what they was doing was hiring you for the busy hour, and once the busy hour passed, you was sent out of there. I had to quit because it was costing me too much to go way over there (p. 206).

Health Insurance and Reform

In 2010, Congress passed, and President Obama enacted, sweeping reforms to our health care system. Many of these reforms will be eased in through 2014. In brief, the health care legislation will do the following (Kaiser Family Foundation 2010):

- Most individuals will be required to have health insurance by 2014.
- Individuals who do not have access to affordable employer coverage will be able to purchase coverage through a health insurance exchange with "credits" available to make coverage more affordable to some people. Small businesses will be able to purchase coverage through a separate exchange.
- Employers will be required to pay penalties for employees who receive credits.
- New regulations will be imposed on health plans that will prevent health insurers from denying coverage to people for any reason, or for charging higher premiums based on health status or sex.
- Medicaid will be expanded to 133 percent of the federal poverty level ($14,404 for an individual and $29,327 for a family of 4 in 2009 for all individuals under age 65).

This legislation was hotly contested by many groups, vehemently supported by others, and criticized by some who said it did not go far enough. Why all the fuss?

Many Americans have trouble getting the health care they need when they are ill because they are without health insurance. Unfortunately, in 2009, 51 million Americans had no health insurance, a number that was rising quickly and was estimated to continue to rise if the system was not reformed substantially, as shown in Table 11.2 (Commonwealth Fund Commission on a High Performance Health System 2009; DeNavas-Walt et al. 2010). How can so many people be uninsured in a country as wealthy as the United States?

The short answer to this question is that the United States has traditionally had a **fee-for-service health care system**; in other words, if you get sick or injured, you must *pay* for medical care. Other countries roll the price of health care into their taxes so that there is little or no additional cost when you are sick or injured.

During World War II, when wage freezes were in effect, some large companies decided to offer health insurance as a fringe benefit of the job. Why not? Insurance was cheap to

TABLE 11.2 How Many Uninsured in the United States, 2000–2009

The number of people without health insurance has been steadily rising, prompting President Obama and Congress to enact health care reform.

2000	40 million
2004	43 million
2008	46 million
2009	51 million

Sources: Kaiser Family Foundation 2009; Commonwealth Fund Commission on a High Performance Health System 2009; DeNavas-Walt et al. 2010.

purchase because health care costs were relatively inexpensive and few drugs were available. To compete for labor, medium-sized and small businesses decided to get into the act as well (Blumenthal 2006).

By the 1950s and 1960s, Americans began to equate health insurance with employment—you get a job and you get insurance. We forgot that this connection began through a simple historical accident (e.g., wage freezes), and we also forgot that no other developed nation tied health insurance to employment. In all developed nations (and many less developed ones), access to health care is a guaranteed right of citizenship, much like education or access to police protection.

However, by the 1970s and 1980s, health care costs began to rise substantially. Small businesses were the first to say, "Hey, we cannot afford this." Today, companies of all sizes are dropping health insurance coverage completely or asking workers to pay more of the costs of the insurance plan (Kaiser Family Foundation and Health Research & Educational Trust 2010). Less than 60 percent of Americans now receive health insurance from an employer, either as an employee or as a dependent (spouse or child) (DeNavas-Walt et al. 2010). Among low-income workers, only about one-third receives employer-sponsored insurance. Clearly, the connection between health insurance and employment is eroding.

Well, then, why not just purchase insurance yourself if you cannot get it from an employer? Many cannot afford it, as the average price of family coverage is nearly $14,000 per year (Kaiser Family Foundation and Health Research & Educational Trust 2010). Also, just because a person applies for insurance doesn't mean that he or she will be granted coverage; many people have been turned down by insurance companies because of a preexisting condition. Moreover, most Americans do not qualify for **Medicaid**, the federal-state health care program for certain categories of poor people.

The consequences of being without insurance can be devastating (Hadley 2007; Kaiser Commission on Medicaid and the Uninsured 2010; Schwartz 2007). Compared to those with insurance, people without health insurance:

- Are twice as likely to postpone seeking health care, are over four times as likely to forgo needed care, and are more than twice as likely to have a needed prescription go unfilled.
- Pay large sums of their own money for their limited care, thereby reducing the amount of money for food, heat, and other necessities. One-third of uninsured patients and half of low-income uninsured patients say that doctors make them pay upfront before any health care is rendered. Medical bills are a major financial hardship, and contribute to debt and bankruptcy.
- After an accidental injury, are less likely to receive any care, are twice as likely to receive no recommended follow-up care, and are more likely to report not fully recovering.

I have discussed how the changing economy and our current recession directly touch the lives of families every day. However, these factors *indirectly* influence families as well, for example, by encouraging women to join the labor force. Women work for many reasons, including job satisfaction and a sense of fulfillment, as well as money. Unlike a generation or two ago, however, many more women now feel that they *need* to work to make ends meet. Alone or together with their partners, they provide an important financial resource to the family.

Given that most parents—fathers and mothers—work outside the home, we must ask ourselves how this has changed the nature of the work done *inside* the home. How has the context of housework and child care changed? Who is doing what? What new challenges, opportunities, and stressors does this bring?

WHAT DO YOU THINK?

Can you identify four or five ways in which the recession has negatively affected families? Can you identify any positive repercussions of the recession? Do you think these effects differ by social class, race, ethnicity, or sex?

The Division of Household Labor

The work at home that feeds, clothes, shelters, and cares for us is just as important as the work that occurs in the labor market. Yet, unfortunately, household labor was considered "women's work," and not deemed worthy of scientific study until roughly 30 years ago. Since then, a tremendous amount of research has been done to examine who does what in the home, under what circumstances, and why and how housework is embedded in complex processes relating to the social construction of sex and gender.

How Is Household Labor Defined and Measured?

How is **household labor** defined? Generally, it refers to unpaid work that is done to maintain family members and/or a home (Knodel et al. 2004). It usually excludes child care and other types of emotional labor and caregiving. According to national surveys, the five most time-consuming major household tasks are (1) meal preparation or cooking; (2) housecleaning; (3) shopping for groceries and household goods; (4) washing dishes and cleaning up after meals; and (5) laundry, including washing, ironing, and mending clothes. Coltrane (2000) refers to these as **routine household labor**, because they are repetitive and less able to be postponed than are other tasks. Although some people enjoy some or all of these activities (Poortman and van der Lippe 2009), most people say that they do not enjoy routine household work (Kroska 2003), referring to it as boring, onerous, and mundane. Other tasks, which are called **occasional labor**, occur less frequently and have more flexibility in timing, such as gardening, paying bills, household repairs, or servicing the car.

Some people may wonder how something as private as housework can actually be a researchable topic. Household labor is studied in many different ways, including surveys based on self-reports made by one partner (usually the woman) or both partners, or by time diaries that are kept over a specific period. As you might guess, there is often a discrepancy between partners when assessing how much time each spends on housework (Lee and Waite 2005; Schiebinger and Gilmartin 2010). Men and women both report spending a greater number of hours on tasks than their partners say they do. Men are also more likely than women to claim that housework is shared equally. One study with over 350 couples found that 40 percent of men claimed that housework such as cooking, cleaning, and laundry was shared equally, compared to 31 percent of the women who made that claim. Moreover, only 15 percent of men reported that the wife always does these tasks; however, 25 percent of women said that this was indeed the case (Davis and Greenstein 2004).

Who Does What? Housework

Regardless of the way that housework is defined or measured, the research indicates that women do significantly more housework than men. The size of men's and women's contributions vary across studies, but most find that women spend two to three times the amount of time on various household tasks that men do (Bureau of Labor Statistics 2008; Hook 2006; Lee and Waite 2005; Schiebinger and Gilmartin 2010). Table 11.3 estimates the number of hours spent on housework per week, showing the difference between surveys and diary methods. The results indicate that (1) women do significantly more housework than men; (2) the amount of time supposedly spent on housework varies a lot by how it is measured; and (3) the proportion of housework done by husbands ranges from 33 to 42 percent, on average.

Women of all income groups tend to do the routine housework. A study of 1,222 college professors in the natural sciences found that they too have a traditional division of labor, as shown in Figure 11.4. Women scientists' share of core household tasks, such as cook-

Figure 11.4 Division of Household Labor in Scientists' Homes: Who Does What and Time Spent

Even among well-educated college professors, women tend to do the routine labor.

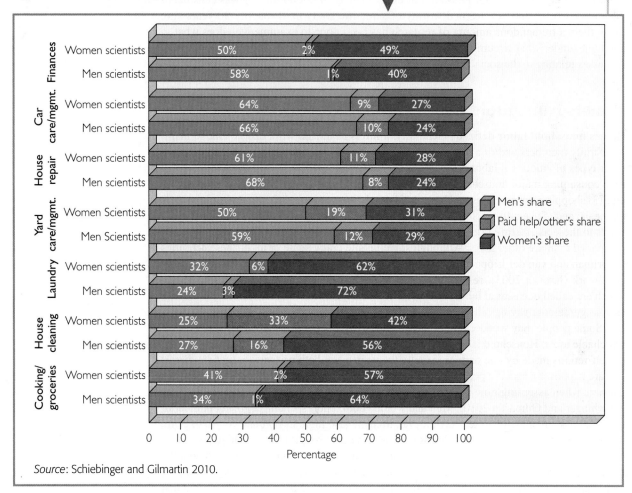

Source: Schiebinger and Gilmartin 2010.

ing, grocery shopping, laundry, and housecleaning, was almost double that of men scientists (Schiebinger and Gilmartin 2010). Men contribute more to yard and car care, house repair, and finance, but this occasional labor is periodic and averages less than five hours per week.

The typical pattern in dual-earner families is presented in the book *The Second Shift* by sociologist Arlie Hochschild (1989). In her sample of 50 dual-earner couples, 20 percent shared the housework equally. In 70 percent of families, men did somewhere between one-third and one-half of the housework, and in 10 percent of families, men did less than one-third. She found that at the end of a long workday, women returned to do their "second shift"—their second job of housework and child care, which included arranging, supervising, and planning, in addition to accomplishing actual tasks. For the most part, men returned home to "help." She found that women, on average, work an extra 15 hours per week, compared to men.

The gender imbalance in the division of household labor is found throughout the world, although the extent of the imbalance varies, as shown in Table 11.3 (Davis and Greenstein 2004). Again, although men and women give somewhat different reports, Russia is the only country in which the majority of men and women say that housework is shared equally. This likely represents both the greater number of Russian women employed outside the home as

TABLE 11.3 Husbands' and Wives' Responses to Housework Questions

Of the countries listed, the Japanese are least likely to share housework and Russians are most likely.

		WHO DOES THE HOUSEWORK?				
		Always Wife	**Usually Wife**	**About Equal**	**Usually Husband**	**Always Husband**
Bulgaria	Husband	20%	49%	26%	2%	2%
	Wife	38%	33%	28%	1%	0%
Czech Republic	Husband	20%	48%	31%	1%	1%
	Wife	22%	39%	37%	2%	0%
Estonia	Husband	8%	43%	44%	4%	0%
	Wife	22%	41%	35%	2%	1%
West Germany	Husband	22%	52%	22%	1%	4%
	Wife	51%	37%	11%	1%	1%
East Germany	Husband	12%	52%	31%	2%	2%
	Wife	38%	38%	24%	1%	0%
Hungary	Husband	26%	38%	31%	2%	3%
	Wife	40%	31%	27%	2%	1%
Japan	Husband	63%	30%	5%	0%	2%
	Wife	79%	19%	2%	0%	0%
Netherlands	Husband	22%	51%	25%	1%	0%
	Wife	40%	42%	18%	1%	0%
Poland	Husband	33%	43%	19%	2%	3%
	Wife	52%	30%	14%	3%	1%
Russia	Husband	4%	27%	67%	3%	0%
	Wife	9%	29%	60%	1%	0%
Slovenia	Husband	29%	47%	18%	3%	3%
	Wife	46%	36%	18%	0%	0%
United Kingdom	Husband	22%	43%	30%	4%	2%
	Wife	41%	35%	22%	1%	1%
United States	**Husband**	**15%**	**42%**	**40%**	**2%**	**1%**
	Wife	**25%**	**42%**	**31%**	**2%**	**1%**
All Nations	Husband	22%	44%	30%	2%	2%
	Wife	38%	35%	26%	1%	0%

Note: Total working sample N = 10,153.
Source: Davis and Greenstein 2004.

well as cultural norms about men and women's roles in the family. In contrast to Russia, only 5 percent of Japanese men and 2 percent of Japanese women report that the cooking, cleaning, and laundry are equally shared. Instead, housework is highly segregated by sex in Japan, with most husbands and wives reporting that the wife always does the housework.

Who Does What? Child Care

The answer to who does what with respect to child care is not much different than who does the housework (Bureau of Labor Statistics 2008; Craig 2006). Mothers spend more time with their children than do fathers, regardless of employment status. One study of over 1,800 couples who completed time diaries revealed that when both partners are employed, 76 percent of

Men's share of housework is on the rise, but remains far short of that of their wives and partners. Housework remains highly gendered, with men performing the "occasional" labor, such as taking out the garbage or working in the yard, which have greater flexibility on when they can be done.

the time spent on child care is performed by the mother. When mothers are not employed and fathers are, they perform 83 percent of the parental labor. Even if the father is not employed, and the mother is, she still performs the majority of the child care, accounting for 53 percent (Pailhe and Solaz 2008).

What specifically are mothers doing? One study compared the time that mothers and fathers spend on various child-rearing tasks: spiritual, emotional, social, moral, and physical guidance; helping with homework; providing companionship, advice, and mentoring; sharing leisure and activities; fostering independence, intelligence, and responsibility; and providing caregiving, protection, discipline, and income. The researchers found that mothers are more involved than fathers in all domains studied, with the exception of providing income. Mothers were rated as "often" or "always" involved in each domain, whereas fathers were rated as "sometimes involved" in each domain, except for providing income. Seven of the nine lowest-rated domains for fathers were in the expressive domain (Finley et al. 2008).

An interesting side note is that fathers are willing to spend more time with their sons than their daughters, and fathers are even willing to reduce their own private leisure to spend time with their sons (Mammen 2009). Boys get more of their father's time than do their sisters, or do girls in all-girl families.

Renegotiating Family Work

Many families are renegotiating how labor is performed, as shown in Table 11.4. Men's time spent in housework is on the rise, increasing by possibly 30–50 percent over the past generation (Galinsky et al. 2009; Sullivan and Coltrane 2008). Nonetheless, despite these very real changes, family work is still not shared equally. Mothers have less time for leisure, regardless if they work full-time, part-time, or not at all (Bureau of Labor Statistics 2008). Even when both mother and father work full-time, fathers have nearly an hour more of leisure each workday than do mothers.

With the lack of leisure and the high demands of children, home, and work, mothers experience more stress and burnout than do their husbands (Parker 2009; Schor 2002). In particular, when women value equality in the home but end up doing the majority of household labor themselves, their sense of fairness is violated and happiness with their marriage declines (Claffey and Mickelson 2009; Lavee and Katz 2002). Men may compare themselves to what their fathers did, and therefore believe "Wow, I am doing a lot," whereas many women compare their partners to what they are doing and say, "This isn't fair."

TABLE 11.4 Percent of Husbands Who Report Taking the Most Responsibility or Share Equally

Husbands report doing more housework and child care than did husbands of the past.

	1992	2008
Cooking	34%	54%
Housecleaning	40%	53%
Child Care	41%	49%

Source: Aumann and Galinsky 2009.

Explanations for the Division of Labor

Several theories have been used to analyze the relationship between sex and the division of household labor, including (1) the time availability perspective; (2) the relative resources perspective; and (3) the gender perspective ("doing gender").

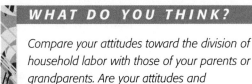

WHAT DO YOU THINK?

Compare your attitudes toward the division of household labor with those of your parents or grandparents. Are your attitudes and expectations different? If so, what accounts for this change?

Time Availability Perspective suggests that the division of labor is largely determined by (1) the need for household labor, such as the number of children in the home and (2) each partner's availability to perform household tasks, such as the number of hours spent in paid work (Shelton 1992). Both husband and wife are expected to perform domestic work to the extent that other demands on their lives allow them; simply put, the partner who has the most time available because of fewer other commitments will spend more time on housework. However, it is unclear whether women do the majority of the housework because they spend fewer hours in paid labor or whether they spend fewer hours in paid labor because they have to do most of the housework (Evertsson and Nermo 2004).

Relative Resources Perspective is grounded in the premise of exchange theory (Becker 1981; Blood and Wolfe 1960). It posits that the greater the relative amount or value of resources contributed by a partner, the greater is his or her power within the relationship. This power can then be translated into bargaining to avoid tasks such as housework that offer no pay and minimal social prestige (Bittman et al. 2003). However, working-class partners frequently provide relatively similar resources to the family, yet their roles are often highly segregated (Rubin 1976). Resources are usually defined as monetary ones, but they can take other forms as well, such as occupational prestige, education level, or even good looks or an exceptionally charismatic personality.

Doing Gender suggests that gender itself is the ultimate explanatory variable, not how much time a partner has available or how many resources he or she brings to the relationship. "**Doing gender**" suggests that housework is so ingrained as women's work that it functions as an area in which gender is symbolically created and reproduced (Fenstermaker Berk 1985; West and Zimmerman 1987). Wives do most of the housework because it is expected of them as women and they have heard these messages since childhood. Likewise, men do less because housework is not a part of their gendered identity. This is likely why many men and women feel that the division of household labor is fair even when it is not split equally between partners. Gendered norms exert a powerful influence on what we see as normative. When we remember the household tasks we may have done as children, most women will report that they were involved in "inside" domestic labor, such as helping with cooking, cleaning, or taking care of siblings, and men will remember that they were more involved in "outside" labor, such as mowing the lawn. In other words, even girls do more routine labor, whereas boys do occasional labor. Moreover, which is more highly valued? Typically, we pay a lot more for someone to mow our lawn than babysit our children. These gendered values are so ingrained that we rarely question this logic.

Children's Labor in the Home

There are other people in the household too, so it is wise to look beyond husbands and wives. How much, and under what conditions, do sons and daughters provide housework or child care? What impact does their labor have on themselves and their families? There are many reasons that children perform household labor. Some parents are attempting to socialize their children to future adult or parental roles by teaching a child how to use the vacuum or washing machine. Other parents simply need the extra assistance to keep up with housework and child care demands, thereby needing a child to babysit a younger sibling after school (Blair 2000; Dodson and Dickert 2004).

Young children's housework is less gendered than adults or teens and may include things such as picking up toys or making one's bed. By the teenage years, girls do about twice the amount of housework as boys. The work performed by girls tends to be routine chores performed inside the home, such as cleaning, cooking, or caring for siblings, whereas boys do occasional outside chores, such as yard work. A longitudinal study that followed a group of boys through young adulthood found that boys who did more household chores as a child did more of the routine housework as an adult (Anderson and Robson 2006).

Children in two-parent, dual-earner families and children of highly educated families tend to do less housework and child care than do children in other family types. Lower-income families and single-parent families rely on children, especially daughters, to a considerable extent to help with numerous household tasks and to take care of younger siblings (Dodson and Dickert 2004).

Juggling Work and Family Life

We often hear that we can "have it all ..." but in all honesty, combining work and family is not very easy. If you or someone you know well is combining work and family, you have probably seen them struggle to meet the very different needs associated with children, a job, and a spouse or partner. Compare these struggles with Lara's situation, an American mother living in Hungary, described in the box on page 333, "Our Global Community: Why We Choose to Live in Hungary." As the example shows, balancing work and family doesn't really have to be as challenging as it is in the United States.

Conflict, Overload, and Spillover

Researchers have been studying the ways that work and family influence each other (Bass et al. 2009; Goodman et al. 2009; Voydanoff 2008; Whitehead 2008). Out of this research have come several important concepts that help us begin to understand the reciprocal relationship between work and family life.

One such concept is **work–family conflict**, which is the tension people feel when the pressures from paid work and family roles are incompatible in some way (Nomaguchi 2009). The conflict can go both ways: Work is made more difficult by virtue of participation in the family role (e.g., it is difficult to work the expected overtime at your job because of needing to pick up your children from day care), and participation in family roles is made more difficult by work (e.g., it is difficult to get to your son's baseball practice every Wednesday afternoon because of the department meeting scheduled at 4:00). Work–family conflict has increased for both men and women in recent decades (Nomaguchi 2009; Winslow 2005).

People feel greater work–family conflict when (Voydanoff 2004):

- *The demands of paid work and family responsibilities are higher* (e.g., the boss expects you to work overtime regularly)
- *Resources that help them manage those demands are fewer* (e.g., little money to hire an adult babysitter who could drive your son to soccer practice)

OUR
Global Community

Why We Choose to Live in Hungary

How do family policies in the United States compare to other countries? We are aware that wealthy developed nations, such as France or Sweden, have generous policies and programs for families, but how about less wealthy developing nations?

I live in Hungary [a country in Eastern Europe], where the benefits for families surpass those of any other country I've heard about. Maternity leave is three years. Daycare and preschool are free. Elementary school starts at 8 a.m. and runs until 2 p.m. with optional aftercare. Most schools also offer ballet, music lessons, computer clubs, and soccer in the afternoons.

We all receive a monthly family supplement grant, which increases with each child and lasts until the child turns 18. When the child hits school age, we get an additional lump sum at the beginning of each school year amounting to about $100 per child to cover school supplies.

All children have medical coverage through the age of 18—longer if they are in college—and pediatricians make house calls. If you have a child with a disability, you may stay home with the child for the rest of his or her life and receive the minimum wage.

There is no question that the United States needs more generous benefits for families. I am an American (my husband is Hungarian) and our choice to move to Hungary to have kids was a very conscious one. When I feel pangs of homesickness, I think of my overworked, stressed out friends with kids back home and think: No way. I feel like I've got a balance in my life I would have a difficult time achieving in the States. I wish that all American parents had the same opportunities we've got here in Hungary to make life easier for families.

—**Lara**

Source: Strong-Jekely 2006.

CRITICAL THINKING QUESTIONS
1. Is Hungary a rich nation? Where does Hungary get the money to spend on these types of services? Why doesn't the United States have the money to spend this way, or does it?
2. Would you prefer the system of helping families in Hungary or the system in the United States? Defend your choice. What arguments would those people who feel differently make? How would you refute those arguments?

■ *Perceptions of demands that they feel they must fulfill are higher* (e.g., trying to be the "perfect" parent)

Another concept, **role overload**, is the feeling of being overwhelmed by many different commitments and not having enough time to meet each commitment effectively (Duxbury et al. 2008; Pearson 2008). Role overload can lead to stress and depression. A recent study of over 700 mothers randomly selected to participate found that those who felt the most overload between their work, parent, and spouse roles had lower levels of mental well-being than did other women who perceived less role overload. *Perception* of overload is key. Simply working more hours did not necessarily lead to more feelings of overload; in fact, women who worked less than 30 hours per week or *more than* 35 hours per week had fewest feelings of role overload. What appears to make the difference in role overload is not how many hours you have worked, but how much support you have. Mothers with higher incomes (who can, presumably, hire more help), higher marital quality, and higher-quality jobs were least likely to feel role overload (Glynn et al. 2009).

Another related concept, **spillover**, refers to the negative (or sometimes positive) moods, experiences, and demands involved in one sphere that carry over or "spill over" into the other sphere (Davis et al. 2008). How do you purge the rushed and hectic mood at work when you now have to grocery shop with your toddler? How do you play with your children after work, when your boss is still sending you e-mails in the evening? With the creation of computers, Blackberries, cell phones, and other important technology, work increasingly encroaches on family time (Conley 2009). Other people may be required to travel for their jobs. These demands mean that families have trouble finding "quality time."

Likewise, family demands can spill over into employment. Who takes care of the children on teachers' workdays at school? How do you go to work ready to face the day's challenges when you know your child has a fever of 101 degrees? Even if you can arrange child care when your child is ill, the stress at home affects your work performance.

I mentioned that spillover could also be positive (Poelmans et al. 2008). One study measured positive family-to-work spillover by asking 156 couples to respond to statements such as "My family gives me ideas that can be used at work," or "My family helps me face challenges at work." The researchers found that in families with higher cohesion, such as feelings of togetherness and support of one another, both mothers and fathers expressed more positive family-to-work spillover. In particular, women who were satisfied with housework arrangements perceived more positive spillover, whereas satisfaction with their marital relationship increased men's positive spillover (Stevens et al. 2007).

The relationship between work and family is gendered (Galinsky et al. 2009). Men receive pressure from their employers to fulfill work obligations and to ignore or minimize family obligations (Coltrane 1997; Hertz and Marshall 2001). The idea is to let someone else, presumably the wife, take off from work when a child is sick or has to go to the dentist. Women get more pressure from home to fulfill home obligations at the cost of work obligations. Consequently, although men may miss out on more family functions (e.g., missing their child's violin recital or school play), they are not necessarily "penalized" at work for having children in the same way that women are penalized (Stone 2008).

Most research on the interface of work and family has been conducted in Western countries; however, a recent study using data from the IBM Corporation in 48 countries reveals that significant work–family conflicts are experienced throughout much of the world (Hill et al. 2004). In particular, the concern is usually on how the conflict affects family life, not necessarily how it affects work. In other words, work was thought to be more detrimental to family than family was thought to be detrimental to work. The research found that having a spouse or intimate partner contributed to a reduced conflict for women in the East and West, but not for women in developing countries. They also found that responsibility for children contributed more than twice as much to conflict for women as it did for men, likely due to the fact that women carry a larger load of child care responsibilities than do men.

What are the consequences of work–family conflict, role overload, and spillover? Stress is certainly one. Eighty-six percent of working moms say that they sometimes or frequently experience stress in their lives, as compared to 44 percent of working dads (Parker 2009). Poor health is another consequence. In fact, only 28 percent of employees in 2008 said their health was excellent, compared to 34 percent in 2002 (Aumann and Galinsky 2009). But much of this stress occurs because families do not feel that there is enough time to do it all, and do it well. In this next section, let's look at the time crunch that many families feel.

The Time Crunch

What are the largest challenges parents report facing today? Feeling rushed and not spending enough time for themselves and their children seems to top the list. For example, a sample of parents were given a list of challenges they might face and asked to rate them. Forty

TABLE 11.5 Who Feels the Time Crunch the Most?

Women feel crunched for time. They especially feel that they do not have enough time for themselves.

Parents Who Say . . .	Not Enough Time for Self	Not Enough Time for Kids
All Parents	56%	32%
Working Full-Time		
Women	79%	48%
Men	53%	36%

Source: Rankin 2002.

percent of full-time workers reported that balancing work and family is the biggest challenge they face as a parent (Rankin 2002). Another study that used two different national samples found that nearly 50 percent of parents residing with their children feel that they spend too little time with them (Milkie et al. 2004).

Women are more likely to experience a time crunch as shown in Table 11.5. They are short on time for themselves and their children. Another recent study from the Pew Research Center, which conducts surveys on social and demographic trends, found that 40 percent of working moms (versus 25 percent of working dads and 26 percent of stay-at-home moms) say they "always feel rushed" (Parker 2009). Finally, a qualitative study found that nearly half of parents feel they spend too little time with their children (Milkie et al. 2004).

Yet, ironically, parents actually spend *as much time or even more* time with children than they did in the past (Bianchi et al. 2006; Kendig and Bianchi 2008; Sandberg and Hofferth 2001). Researchers have looked at how time is spent, and several trends are noted:

- The amount of time both mothers and fathers spend with children is on the rise, regardless of employment status.
- Mothers continue to spend significantly more time with their children than do fathers.
- Unemployed mothers spend more time with their children than do employed mothers.

If parents spend more time with their children than they used to, why do parents report that they aren't involved enough? One reason is that *expectations* for parenting have changed. Parents, especially mothers, are expected to be far more involved in their children's lives than they were in the past—a trend that some think is actually detrimental to children (Cline and Fay 1990; Honore 2008). Parents hover over their children, paying extremely close attention to their children's experiences and trying to ward off any problems before they emerge. This constant vigilance has given rise to a new nickname—"helicopter parents." Parents cart their children from playdate to playdate; orchestrate their children's after-school activities; confront and blame teachers when "Johnny" doesn't do well on his spelling test; and e-mail, text, or call their children daily when they are away at college. The availability of technology is often to blame for the explosion in helicopter parenting—cell phones have been called the world's longest umbilical cord (Briggs 2006).

Perhaps another reason why parents feel that they aren't spending enough time with their children is their inability to respond spontaneously to their children because of encroaching employer demands (Daly 2001). As parents work more hours per week and as work conditions and hours become less standardized, parents may find it increasingly difficult to meet their children's needs. They apparently continue to spend time with their children, but it may be at greater personal cost, such as lack of leisure activities, exercise, or sleep (Nomaguchi and Bianchi 2004; Pelham 2010).

TABLE 11.6 From 1997–2007, Full-Time Work Grows Less Attractive to Moms

Working mothers increasingly like the idea of only working part-time, whereas stay-at-home mothers are increasingly satisfied with their choice.

CONSIDERING EVERYTHING, WHAT WOULD BE THE IDEAL SITUATION FOR YOU—WORKING FULL-TIME, PART-TIME, OR NOT AT ALL OUTSIDE THE HOME?				
	Working Mothers		**At-Home Mothers**	
	1997	**2007**	**1997**	**2007**
Full-Time Work	32%	21%	24%	16%
Part-Time Work	48%	60%	37%	33%
Not Working	20%	19%	39%	48%
Don't Know	0%	0%	0%	3%

Note: Based on mothers with children under age 18.
Source: Taylor et al. 2007b.

Consequently, a growing majority of mothers report that they would prefer to work part-time or not at all, as shown in Table 11.6 (Taylor et al. 2007b). Among working mothers with minor children (age 17 and under), just one in five say full-time work is the ideal situation for them, down from a third who felt this way in 1997. Fully three in five (up from almost half in 1997) of today's working mothers say part-time work would be their ideal, and another one in five would prefer not working at all outside the home.

If mothers would prefer to stay at home, then why do they work? There are many reasons; some are financial, others might be related to the fear they would be unable to enter the job market later or would reenter with a large disadvantage compared to other workers. The box on pages 337–338, "Social Policies for Families: Fixing Social INsecurity," addresses some of these concerns, and offers a proposal to help families have a parent at home if they prefer to do so. It is an innovative idea that would allow people to draw Social Security for a three-year period while raising children.

Catch 22: Inflexible Full-Time Work or Part-Time Penalty

Part of parents' tension over balancing work and family is due to an increasing workweek with little control over working conditions—when they work, how long of a day they work, or whether they can take time off (Bunting 2005; Kornbluh et al. 2004; Morrissey 2008). Meanwhile, work is demanding more time of its employees: the average American worked 48 more hours per year—six extra days per year—than did Americans just a generation ago (Morrissey 2008).

As noted, some parents opt to reduce their work hours to part-time, or wish that they could (Parker 2009; Taylor et al. 2007b). However, they generally pay a steep price for this added flexibility. Workers who go part-time or to a nonstandard (temporary, contract) route earn nearly $4.00 per hour less than regular full-time workers. They are also less likely to receive a pension, health insurance, or other benefits.

These drawbacks to part-time work have been eliminated in many other countries. For example, in 1997, the European Union drafted a directive "to eliminate discrimination against part-time workers and improve the quality of part-time work" (Official Journal of the European Communities 1998). The directive prohibits employers from treating part-time

S O C I A L

Policies for Families

Fixing Social INsecurity

Most people want to be parents, yet must work to provide for their children. Studies show that the majority of mothers would prefer to stay home while the children are young. The following is an intriguing idea—allow new families to draw upon Social Security.

Ask parents, and many of them will tell you that they would like to be able to take some time out from their jobs to devote more attention and energy to their young children. Parents, especially mothers, would like to work part-time, or stay home altogether. What is stopping them? One factor is the well-founded anxiety about the career setbacks that such an arrangement would cause. They want the continued rewards of work, but with scaled-down hours. For many families, though, the biggest barrier is practical: they simply can't afford to reduce their work hours.

Here's a proposal to help families. Why not allow working parents to draw Social Security benefits for up to three years during their prime child-rearing years? This would give moms and dads a real choice about how much time to spend working and how much time to spend with their kids. Those who elected to "borrow on their Social Security" would repay the system when they returned to work. For example, government could increase the employee's share of the payroll taxes

they pay when parents return to work, parents could defer their age of retirement with full Social Security benefits on a year-for-year basis, or parents could accept a reduced monthly benefit, as those who opt for early retirement do now.

How much of a difference would this make for parents trying to make ends meet? Plenty, it turns out. Taxes and child care costs take such a big bite out of parents' incomes that even modest Social Security benefits could replace the income from an average job. For example, a parent earning a second salary of $30,000 (assuming the spouse or partner also makes $30,000) would only net about $10,065 after taxes, child care, and work expenses (see table).

Mothers or fathers who elect to access Social Security early would probably stay home during their children's earliest years. But children's needs don't magically disappear at age three. A fifth grader struggling in school or a troubled teenager can also demand parental attention. This policy would let parents decide what makes sense for them and their families.

One issue that would need to be addressed is overcoming barriers to reentering the workforce. Although long leaves are common in other countries, it is probably unrealistic to ask employers to guarantee someone's job after a leave of a year or more. Continuation of health insurance would also

Net Income After Taxes, Child Care, and Work Expenses Example: A two-earner couple, where each parent makes $30,000

The second salary:	$30,000
Subtract:	
Social Security and Medicare taxes	2,295
Additional state and local taxes	1,500
Estimated additional federal income tax	6,180
Additional child care (estimated at $120/week)	6,240
Commuting cost ($25/week times 50)	1,250
Cost of work clothing and dry cleaning	870
Cost of restaurant meals on work days ($25/week times 50)	1,250
Other (nonreimbursed expenses, paid help, meals out, etc.)	350
Net Income	**$10,065**

(continued)

(continued)

need to be addressed. More fundamentally, we need to change the national mind-set, so that nurturing children is seen as a respectable and worthwhile accomplishment, and as something that strengthens the worker's attachment to employment, not as something that interferes with it.

The proposal offered here—allowing parents to actually draw Social Security at two points in their lives—could offer real relief from the time crunch to the millions of Americans struggling to meet the dual demands of work and family every single day. In the past century, we focused on meeting the needs of the elderly. Today, we recognize that compelling needs emerge earlier in our lives as we are raising our families. Yet our policies have not adequately changed to compensate for the massive entry of women into paid employment. Our Social Security system has long

been thought of as providing a measure of financial security in return for a lifetime of work. What could be a more vital contribution to the future of our country than having the time to raise children well?

Sources: Official Journal of the European Communities 1998; Parker 2009; Rankin 2002.

CRITICAL THINKING QUESTIONS
1. Do you think a program like this that would allow parents to draw upon Social Security as they raise their children would be popular among Americans? Why or why not? Would it be stigmatized as welfare?
2. What do you think might be some logistic barriers to adopting this type of program? Do you think the barriers (if any) are surmountable?

workers less favorably than comparable full-time workers (unless they can demonstrate that the differential treatment is justified). It addresses issues of pay equity, Social Security, job benefits, training and promotion opportunities, and collective bargaining rights. How does this directive actually work? Germany grants the right to work part-time in firms that have more than 15 workers; Belgium grants employees the right to work at 80 percent of full-time for five years; the United Kingdom allows employees the right to request flexible and part-time work to care for a child under age six or a disabled child under age 18, and Sweden allows parents to work six hours a day until their children turn eight (Gornick et al. 2007). All parents in these nations, rich or poor, have these legal rights.

Child Care: Who's Minding the Children?

With increasing numbers of mothers turning to employment over the past several decades, many children are spending substantial amounts of time in the care of someone other than their parents. Let's look at this issue, and one question to keep in mind is: Are the availability, quality, and cost of child care private matters or public concerns?

Preschool-Aged Children

More than 11 million children under age five are in some type of child care arrangement (National Child Care Information and Technical Assistance Center 2010). Some dual-earner families may arrange working different shifts so that one parent can always be home with the children, and a few turn to other relatives, but most families use formal child care arrangements. These include **day care centers**, where care is provided in nonresidential facilities, **family child care providers**, where care is provided in a private home other than the child's home, or **nannies/babysitters**, where the child is cared for in the home by a nonrelative. In fact, many parents have multiple arrangements (e.g., with grandmother on Tuesday and Thursday and day care center on Monday, Wednesday, Friday), to ensure that

Figure 11.5 **Primary Child Care Arrangements for Children Under Age 5**

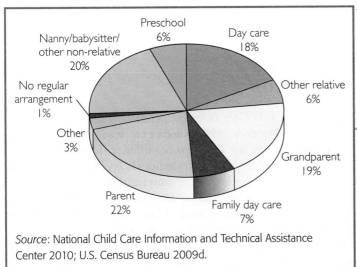

Many different types of child care arrangements are available, and parents often use multiple methods.

Source: National Child Care Information and Technical Assistance Center 2010; U.S. Census Bureau 2009d.

their children are well cared for and to minimize costs. Figure 11.5 shows the primary child care arrangements of young children.

The type of child care that parents use varies by race, ethnicity, and income. For instance, Hispanics are less likely to use day care centers than are other racial groups and are more likely to use care by a relative. Wealthier families are more likely to use center-based care, whereas relative care is more common among lower-income families (Capizzano and Adams 2004; Laughlin and Rukus 2009).

These differences reflect both culture and the costs of child care. Relative care and care provided by other families are usually the least expensive child care options. Full-day child care costs in a center-based facility can easily cost over $10,000 per year per child (National Association of Child Care Resource & Referral Agencies 2009), which is higher than the costs of college tuition at a state university! Nannies and babysitters may cost even more; a perusal of the want ads in a newspaper and several nanny agencies in my hometown of Portland, Oregon suggested that most adult nannies/babysitters charge $12–$18 per hour. However, more than one in four families with young children earns less than $25,000 per year (Children's Defense Fund 2005); therefore, most forms of formal child care remain out of their reach without some sort of public subsidy.

School-Aged Children

As children begin school, the costs of child care are reduced, but working parents must look for child care arrangements to supplement the school day. Most school-aged children (6–12 years old) with employed parents are supervised before and after school by family, nanny/babysitters, and before- and after-school programs. However, largely because of cost, some school-aged children are left unsupervised, called **self-care**. Almost one in 11 elementary-school children aged 5–11, and one in three middle-school children aged 12–14 take care of themselves after school on a regular basis (Johnson 2005; Laughlin and Rukus 2009).

Although self-care is certainly not always harmful (it may make a child more independent), there are also potential problems with unsupervised children. Yet, most states do not have legal age limits on when it is appropriate to leave a child alone (U.S. Department of

Health and Human Services, Administration for Children and Families 2006). Some states may have guidelines that are distributed to child protective services and enforced at the county level. They often suggest that a child should be at least 12 before being left alone and at least 15 before caring for younger siblings, but we all recognize that children's maturity levels differ.

The Effect of Mothers' Employment on Children's Well-Being

One headline reads: "*Study Finds Child Care Does Impact Mother-Child Interaction*" (NICHD Early Child Care Research Network 1999). Another one reads: "*New Longitudinal Study Finds Having a Working Mother Does No Significant Harm to Children*" (ScienceBlog.com 1999). Which one is correct? Both studies report findings from studies using large, longitudinal, nationally representative samples. The first one uses data from the National Institute of Child Health and Human Development (NICHD) Study of Early Child Care, a longitudinal study of approximately 1,300 children. The second one uses data from the National Longitudinal Survey of Youth (NLSY), a survey of approximately 12,600 individuals. How can two good data sources yield opposite conclusions?

Determining the effects of mothers' employment and child care on children's well-being is a challenging task. It is made more difficult by the use of different measures of well-being, different types of child care settings and their varying quality, different types of relationships that mothers and children have (regardless of employment or child care), the role of the father and other family members in child care, the mother's physical and emotional health, the child's temperament, the age of the child, the mother's hours of work and other working conditions, and many other factors that may not yet even be identified. Because of all the confounding variables, it is not surprising that some studies report a negative association between mother's employment and cognitive and social outcomes such as less attachment or a child's greater level of aggression (Belsky et al. 2001), whereas others find positive outcomes such as children's higher language and other academic skills, especially among poor children (Loeb et al. 2007).

A study that caught tremendous media attention was led by Jay Belsky, a family scientist at Penn State University. His research team found that children who were in child care for more than 30 hours per week during the first four years of life were somewhat more likely to behave aggressively as compared to those who had been in child care for less than 10 hours per week (Belsky et al. 2001). These findings attracted widespread attention because few other issues are as fraught with worry as the choice of child care as shown in the opening vignette. However, both groups of children in the child care setting exhibited levels of aggression that were well within the normal range. And, a follow-up study tracked the same children through early elementary school and found that, by third grade, children who spent longer time in child care had higher math and reading skills. But it also found that children with longer time spent in child care had poorer work habits and social skills, although the effects were very small and within the normal range (Lewin 2005).

Also using a large and nationally representative sample, Hickman (2006) compared the effects of day care centers of children's math and reading skills after they entered school. Using a cross-sectional research design—which is a snapshot in time—she found that kindergartners who attended day care the year before did exhibit higher skills. However, when she used a longitudinal design—following children over several years—she found the difference did not persist, and that some social skills deteriorated.

WHAT DO YOU THINK?

Could you design a study that would, once and for all, answer the question about the effects of mothers' employment on children's well-being? Use your imagination, and the knowledge you have gained throughout this book.

In the United States, working parents are primarily on their own to pay for the costs of child care. However, in many other developed nations, access to high-quality child care is considered a public good, and, therefore, the government subsidizes the cost.

It appears that the relationship between mother's employment and child well-being is somewhat mixed and contradictory because the results are relatively minor and dependent on many confounding variables. Perhaps the most important factor is the quality of care that the child experiences (Perry-Jenkins et al. 2000). Children in poor-quality child care have been found to be delayed in language and reading skills, display more aggression, demonstrate lower mathematical ability, have poorer attention skills, and have more behavioral problems than children in higher-quality child care.

Social Policy and Family Resilience

Child care is a necessity for most families, but it remains largely a private matter in the United States. Families are left on their own to find the highest-quality care that they can afford. However, quality controls are limited and vary by state. For example, first aid requirements differ and are nonexistent in some states. Pay for child care workers is low—those working in a center average less than $10 an hour (Bureau of Labor Statistics 2009b; Center for the Child Care Workforce 2010; National Association of Child Care Resource & Referral Agencies 2009). Few receive fringe benefits such as health insurance, sick pay, or vacation time, and turnover is high.

In contrast, not all developed countries think of child care as a private matter. Some see it as a public concern, as a social good that can ultimately benefit everyone. What can other countries teach the United States about how to structure quality child care and early education to the benefit of everyone?

Example: A Comparative Look at Early Childhood Education and Child Care Policies

Early childhood education and care (ECEC) has become an important issue in many parts of the world because of the rise in labor force participation of mothers, the push for single mothers to work rather than receive public aid, and a growing interest in ensuring that all children begin elementary school with basic skills and ready to learn (Organisation for Economic Co-operation and Development 2007). ECEC programs enhance and support children's cognitive, social, and emotional development.

A three-year study of 12 developed nations compared the availability and structure of ECEC programs. Several interesting points were noted. To begin with, access to ECEC is a statutory right in all countries except the United States. Although compulsory school begins at ages 6 or 7, ECEC availability begins at one year in Denmark, Finland, and Sweden (after generous maternity and family leave benefits are exhausted); at two and a half years in Belgium; at three years in Italy and Germany; and at four years in Britain. Most countries have full coverage of 3- to 6-year-olds.

In contrast, in the United States there is no statutory entitlement until age 5–7, depending on the state. Access to publicly funded ECEC programs is generally restricted to at-risk children (usually defined as poor or near-poor—such as the Head Start Program). Furthermore, the demand for these programs among vulnerable groups far outstrips their availability. Only New York and Georgia have developed universal prekindergarten programs for all four-year-olds regardless of family income (The Clearinghouse on International Developments in Child, Youth, and Family Practices 2001, 2005, 2009).

In most of the 12 countries reviewed, governments pay the largest share of the costs, with parents covering only 25–30 percent. Countries may also make arrangements for sliding-scale payments for low-income families to help make programs affordable. Most countries require staff to complete at least three years of training at universities or other institutes of higher education. Their earnings reflect their levels of education.

In contrast, U.S. parents pay an average of 60–80 percent of ECEC costs. Some of these costs can be recouped through tax benefits, but many low-income families find the tax system confusing and therefore end up using informal or unregulated child care. In the United States, there is also no agreed-upon set of qualifications for staff. Their status and pay are low and turnover is high. Other countries make a clear investment in their ECEC. Denmark devotes 2 percent of its gross domestic product (GDP), with Sweden and Norway close behind. In contrast, the United States devotes less than half of 1 percent of its GDP to early childhood services (Organisation for Economic Co-operation and Development 2007). Ironically, the United States is a leader in research on child development, but has not developed the programs that research suggests are needed and which are increasingly available in other developed nations.

Conclusion

This chapter examines the empirical research surrounding the topic of working families. All families do meaningful work inside or outside the home, but the overall trend has been an increase in mothers working outside the home for pay. The changing nature of the economy has altered the context and meaning of work, which also influences family life. Employment is becoming increasingly temporary, with nonstandardized work schedules and fewer union protections, such as job-related fringe benefits. This has tremendous implications for how families combine work and family. Many families now need two paychecks to make ends meet. No longer are work and family domains separate; instead, they interact and influence each other in many ways. Issues such as work–family conflicts, feelings of time deficits with children, negotiations over the division of household labor, and struggles to find suitable child care are issues that most employed families face today. Family-friendly workplace policies, such as flexible work hours, and national family policies, such as assistance with child care, can help alleviate the stress that many employed families experience.

Key Terms

Day care centers: Child care provided in nonresidential facilities. (p. 338)

Doing gender: Housework is so ingrained as women's work that it functions as an area in which gender is symbolically created and reproduced. (p. 331)

Early childhood education and care (ECEC): An international term for day care, preschool, and other programs to ensure that all children begin elementary school with basic skills and ready to learn. (p. 341)

Family child care providers: Child care provided in a private home other than the child's home. (p. 338)

Fee-for-service health care system: When you are sick or injured, you must pay for medical care. (p. 325)

Household labor: Generally refers to the unpaid work done to maintain family members and/or a home. (p. 327)

Living wage: Ordinances that require employers to pay wages that are above federal or state minimum wage levels, usually ranging from 100 to 130 percent of the poverty line. (p. 323)

Medicaid: The federal-state health care program for the eligible poor. (p. 326)

Nannies/babysitters: Child care provided in the home by a nonrelative. (p. 338)

Nonstandard work schedules: Jobs that are part-time, subcontracted, temporary in nature, occur at night, or offer irregular work schedules. (p. 323)

Occasional labor: Household tasks that are more time-flexible and more discretionary, such as household repairs, yard care, or paying bills. (p. 327)

Relative resources perspective: The greater the relative amount or value of resources contributed by a partner, the greater is his or her power within the relationship; can then be translated into bargaining to avoid tasks such as housework that offer no pay and minimal social prestige. (p. 331)

Role overload: Feeling overwhelmed by many different commitments and not having enough time to meet each commitment effectively. (p. 333)

Routine household labor: Nondiscretionary, routine tasks that are less able to be postponed, such as cooking, washing dishes, or cleaning. (p. 327)

Self-care: School-age children who are unsupervised and taking care of themselves. (p. 339)

Spillover: The negative (or sometimes positive) moods, experiences, and demands involved in one sphere that carry over or "spill over" into the other sphere. (p. 333)

Time availability perspective: Suggests that the division of labor is largely determined by (1) the need for household labor, such as the number of children in the home; and (2) each partner's availability to perform household tasks, such as the number of hours spent in paid work. (p. 331)

Work–family conflict: Inter-role conflict in which the role pressures from the work and family domains are mutually incompatible in some respect. (p. 332)

Resources on the Internet

Bureau of Labor Statistics

www.bls.gov

A component of the U.S. Department of Labor, this website provides detailed data on all aspects of employment, including occupational classifications, wages, benefits, health, and safety. Information is provided on women and minority workers.

Economic Policy Institute

www.epi.org

The mission of the Economic Policy Institute is to provide research and education in order to promote a prosperous, fair, and sustainable economy. The Institute stresses real-world analysis and a concern for the living standards of working people, and it makes its findings accessible to the general public, the media, and policy makers.

Families and Work Institute

www.familiesandwork.org

Families and Work Institute (FWI) is a nonprofit center for research that provides data to inform decision making on

the changing workforce, changing family, and changing community. They also offer a speaker's series and lectures.

Institute for Women's Policy Research (IWPR)

www.iwpr.org/index.cfm

The IWPR conducts research and disseminates its findings to address the needs of women, promote public dialogue, and strengthen families, communities, and societies. IWPR focuses on issues of poverty and welfare, employment and earnings, work and family issues, health and safety, and women's civic and political participation.

Mothers and More

www.mothersandmore.org

Mothers and More is a nonprofit organization dedicated to improving the lives of mothers through support, education, and advocacy. They have chapters throughout the United States. They see themselves as a part of an extended community of individuals and organizations talking about and working on the issues that impact mothers' lives.

Aging Families

CHAPTER 12

CHAPTER OUTLINE

Changing Demographics 347

■ **EYE** *on the World:* Comparative Aging—
Percent of Population Over Age 65, 2008 *348*

■ **EYE** *on the World:* Comparative Aging—
Percent of Population Over Age 65, 2040 *350*

■ **FAMILIES** *as Lived Experience:* Celebrating
My Grandmother's Birthday *355*

Prevailing Theories of Aging 356

The Economics of Aging 357

The Aging Couple 359

**Relationships with Children and
Grandchildren** 364

■ **USING** *the Sociological Imagination:* The
Boomerang Generation *366*

■ **FAMILIES** *as Lived Experience:* What Is
It Like to Be a Grandparent? *368*

Retirement 369

Health 372

Social Policy and Family Resilience 375

Conclusion 376

Key Terms 377

Resources on the Internet 377

CHAPTER PREVIEW

The United States, along with many other countries, has a radically shifting population. Instead of a focus on children, as has been the case for most of history, we are increasingly becoming nations of older people. This chapter discusses what it means to have increasing numbers of older persons in the population and examines issues such as retirement, Social Security, widowhood, and health, which are quickly becoming concerns for all of society. In this chapter, you will learn:

- Patterns of changing demographics in the United States and around the world

- The prevailing theories of aging

- Economic issues, including income, assets, and poverty

- The history and social philosophy of Social Security

- How aging couples fare, including aspects of marital satisfaction, division of household labor, sexuality, and widowhood

- Relationships with adult children and grandchildren

- Retirement as a socially constructed status that is increasingly important to men and women in the United States

- The health status of elders declines with age, and the United States faces many critical policy issues surrounding Medicare and long-term care for frail elders

For older adults, it really is better to give than to receive, a University of Michigan study suggests. The study finds that older people who are helpful to others reduce their risk of dying by nearly 60 percent compared to peers who provide neither practical help nor emotional support to relatives, neighbors, or friends. "Making a contribution to the lives of other people may help to extend our own lives," said the paper's lead author, Stephanie Brown, a psychologist at the University of Michigan Institute for Social Research (ISR).

For the study, funded in part by the National Institutes of Health, Brown analyzed data on 423 older couples, part of the ISR Changing Lives of Older Couples Study. This study was a random community-based sample of people who were followed for five years to see how they coped with the inevitable changes in later life.

During the first set of interviews, the husbands and wives were asked a series of questions about whether they provided any practical support to friends, neighbors, or relatives, including help with housework, child care, errands, or transportation. They were also asked how much they could count on help from friends or family members if they needed it. Finally, they were asked about giving and receiving emotional support to or from their spouse, including being willing to listen if their spouse needed to talk.

Over the five-year period of the study, 134 people died. In her analysis of the link between giving and receiving help and mortality, Brown controlled for a variety of factors, including age, sex, and physical and emotional health. "I wanted to rule out the possibilities that older people give less and are more likely to die, that females give more and are less likely to die, and that people who are depressed or in poor health are both less likely to be able to help others and more likely to die," said Brown.

She found that people who reported providing no help to others were more than twice as likely to die as people who did give some help to others. Overall, Brown found that 75 percent of men and 72 percent of women reported providing some help without pay to friends, relatives, or neighbors in the year before they were surveyed.

Receiving help from others was not linked to a reduced risk of mortality, however. "If giving, rather than receiving, promotes longevity, then interventions that are designed to help people feel supported may need to be redesigned so the emphasis is on what people can do to help others," said Brown. "In other words, these findings suggest that it isn't what we get from relationships that makes contact with others so beneficial; it's what we give."

(University of Michigan News Service 2002)

One hundred years ago, our understanding of the physical and social aspects of aging was negligible. The elderly were a small proportion of the population and their absolute numbers were also small. We assumed that old age meant deterioration. Few people worried about dementia or Alzheimer's disease; instead the person was simply called "old," as though senility and old age were synonymous. Today, we know far more about aging than we did in the past, and yet we also recognize that we still have far to go. The demographics of the United States and worldwide are rapidly changing, and the proportion of elderly within the population is increasing faster than any other age group. They are a force to be reckoned with, as political clout often accompanies size. Yet, in many ways, aging is a social construction, not simply a biological phenomenon. Yes, we all grow older, but how aging is defined, how it is perceived by other members of the culture, and the policy implications that come from these definitions and perceptions can vary quite a lot.

This chapter examines the demographic changes underway and explores what it means to have increasing numbers of older persons in the population. The issues that aging families face and how we choose to address these issues—retirement, Social Security, widowhood, health, and family caregiving—are bound to become concerns for all members of society.

Changing Demographics

The world is in the midst of a powerful revolution—a *demographic* revolution. The changes that an aging population brings will be felt by all of us, from the richest nations to the poorest ones.

Aging Around the World

The world population is aging at an unprecedented rate. Between now and 2015, the world's **elderly** population, defined as age 65 and over, will grow by over 870,000 people each *month*, from 506 million in 2008 to 1.3 billion in 2040 (Kinsella and He 2009). The number of older persons will soon outnumber the number of children under age 5 for the first time in history.

Many people think that this growth occurs only in developed nations like the United States, but that is incorrect. Yes, it is true that most developed nations have a high and growing proportion of elderly. Japan is the "oldest" country, with almost 22 percent of the population age 65 or older; Italy and Germany are close behind (Kinsella and He 2009).

Between now and 2015, the world's elderly population will grow by over 870,000 people each month. Most will be in poorer developing nations that have few provisions for taking care of elders.

However, the absolute numbers of elderly in poor, less developed nations are very large, and their numbers are increasing at a staggering rate that far exceeds the rate in developed nations. Sixty-two percent of the world's elderly population live in developing nations, and will increase to 76 percent in 2040. The maps on pages 348 through 351 show us that the changes will be explosive in many parts of the world. In many countries, the elderly population is expected to double or even triple, including Singapore, Colombia, Brazil, Costa Rica, the Philippines, Indonesia, Mexico, South Korea, Egypt, Bangladesh, China, and Peru (Kinsella and He 2009). These countries tend to be poorer and often are without economic or health care provisions for their elderly. The question of how to take care of these elders will become one of the most vexing policy issues in the coming decades. The effects will be felt far beyond the borders of individual nations; they will spread throughout the global economy.

To complicate these issues even further, the largest increase around the world is in the **oldest-old cohort**—those aged 85 and over. The oldest-old currently constitute about 19 percent of all elders, but will grow quickly, given the large number of births in the 1940s and 1950s and people living longer lives due to better nutrition, sanitation, and health care developments. These benefits have been more readily available in developed countries; therefore, the oldest-old groups are heavily concentrated there, but increases in this cohort will be found throughout the world as shown in Figure 12.1. In the Ukraine, those persons 80 and older comprise only 19 percent of all elderly, but by 2040, they will jump to 31 percent (U.S. Census Bureau 2010d).

As more people live to the oldest ages, we will see more chronic conditions such as arthritis, osteoporosis, and dementia (Centers for Disease Control and Prevention and the Merck Company Foundation 2007). These types of conditions require more medical care and more personal help with cooking, cleaning, bathing, and home repair. Who will provide this care to an increasing number of elderly? Most countries have few government agencies or even private nursing homes. The vast majority of elderly around the world will be cared for by their adult children, often in their 60s or 70s themselves.

Reasons for the Rapid Growth   Why is the world's population aging so quickly? There are two reasons: (1) people are living longer and (2) fewer babies are being born.

Comparative Aging—Percent of Population over Age 65, 2008

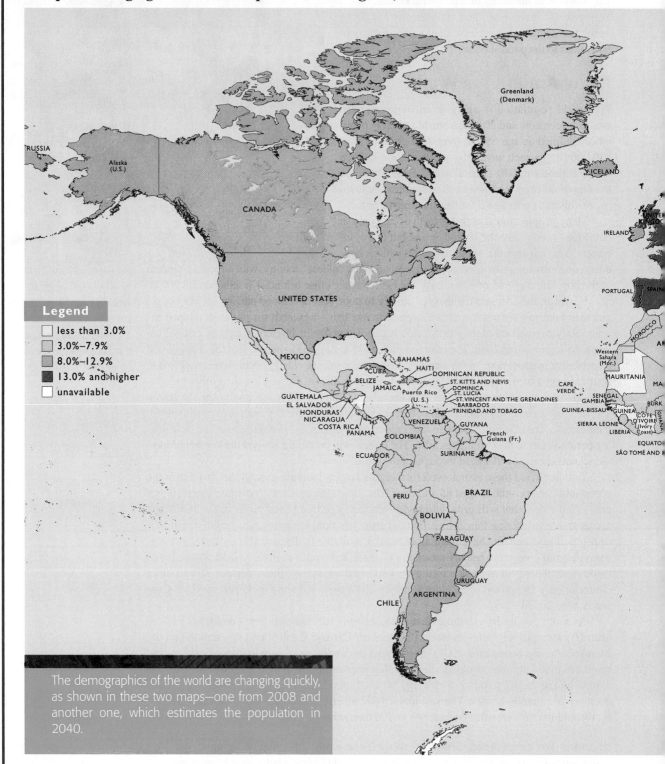

Legend
- less than 3.0%
- 3.0%–7.9%
- 8.0%–12.9%
- 13.0% and higher
- unavailable

The demographics of the world are changing quickly, as shown in these two maps—one from 2008 and another one, which estimates the population in 2040.

RUSSIA

FINLAND
DENMARK
ESTONIA
LATVIA
LITHUANIA
RUS.
BELARUS
POLAND
GERMANY
SLOVAKIA
UKRAINE
MOLDOVA
AUSTRIA
HUNGARY
ROMANIA
SWITZ.
CRO.
B. HERZ.
BULGARIA
ITALY
MONT.
MAC.
ALBANIA
GREECE
TURKEY
TUNISIA
CYPRUS
SYRIA
LEBANON
ISRAEL
IRAQ
IRAN
JORDAN

KAZAKHSTAN

MONGOLIA

NORTH
KOREA

GEORGIA
ARMENIA
AZERBAIJAN
UZBEKISTAN
KYRGYZSTAN
TURKMENISTAN
TAJIKISTAN
AFGHANISTAN
CHINA
SOUTH
KOREA
JAPAN

LIBYA
EGYPT
KUWAIT
BAHRAIN
QATAR
SAUDI
ARABIA
UNITED
ARAB
EMIRATES
OMAN
PAKISTAN
NEPAL
BHUTAN
TAIWAN

NIGER
CHAD
SUDAN
ERITREA
YEMEN
DJIBOUTI
BANGLADESH
INDIA
MYANMAR
LAOS
THAILAND
VIETNAM
CAMBODIA
PHILIPPINES
Guam
(U.S.)
MARSHALL
ISLANDS

NIGERIA
CENTRAL
AFRICAN
REP.
ETHIOPIA
SOMALIA
SRI
LANKA
BRUNEI
PALAU
FEDERATED STATES OF MICRONESIA

CAMEROON
GUINEA
GABON
CONGO
UGANDA
KENYA
MALDIVES
MALAYSIA
SINGAPORE
KIRIBATI

DEMOCRATIC
REP. OF
CONGO
RWANDA
BURUNDI
TANZANIA
SEYCHELLES
INDONESIA
NAURU
SOLOMON
ISLANDS

ANGOLA
MALAWI
COMOROS
PAPUA
NEW GUINEA
TUVALU

ZAMBIA
ZIMBABWE
MOZAMBIQUE
MADAGASCAR
EAST
TIMOR
VANUATU
FIJI

NAMIBIA
BOTSWANA
MAURITIUS
REUNION
NEW CALEDONIA

SWAZILAND
SOUTH
AFRICA
LESOTHO
AUSTRALIA

NEW
ZEALAND

Comparative Aging—Percent of Population over Age 65, 2040

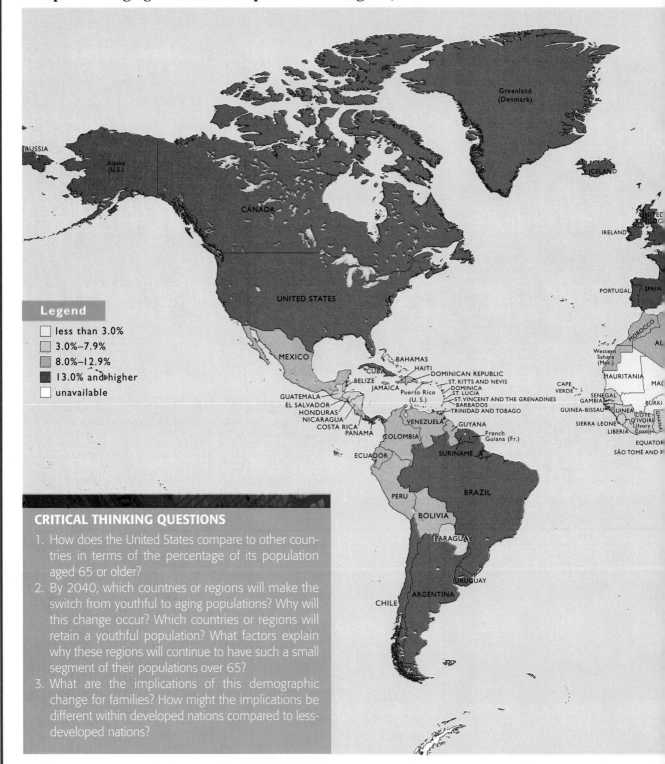

Legend
- [ ] less than 3.0%
- [ ] 3.0%–7.9%
- [ ] 8.0%–12.9%
- [ ] 13.0% and higher
- [ ] unavailable

CRITICAL THINKING QUESTIONS

1. How does the United States compare to other countries in terms of the percentage of its population aged 65 or older?

2. By 2040, which countries or regions will make the switch from youthful to aging populations? Why will this change occur? Which countries or regions will retain a youthful population? What factors explain why these regions will continue to have such a small segment of their populations over 65?

3. What are the implications of this demographic change for families? How might the implications be different within developed nations compared to less-developed nations?

Source: Kinsella and Velkoff 2001.

351

Figure 12.1 **Oldest-Old as a Percentage of All Older People: 2008 and 2040**

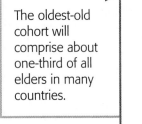

The oldest-old cohort will comprise about one-third of all elders in many countries.

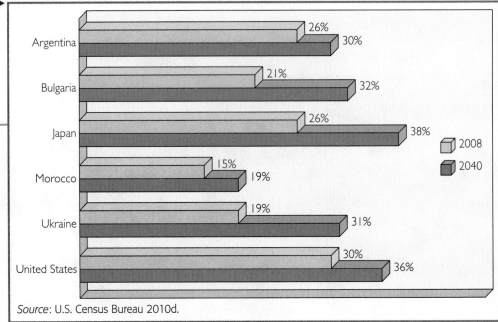

Source: U.S. Census Bureau 2010d.

Obviously, the first reason for a rapid growth in the elderly population is that more people are living longer. **Life expectancy** (how long a person can expect to live) can be calculated at any age. However, usually data representing life expectancy *at birth* are reported; for a girl or boy born today, how long on average can she or he be expected to live? Extraordinary strides have been made in extending life expectancy in much of the world. In 1900, U.S. life expectancy was 48 years for males and 51 years for females. Today, it has increased to 75 for males and 80 for females (Heron et al. 2009; Xu et al. 2010). Other countries have made even larger advances because of improved nutrition, sanitation, health care, and other scientific discoveries. Infectious diseases such as influenza, smallpox, or measles that killed many people in the past have been controlled in many parts of the world.

However, a few countries have experienced no substantial gains in life expectancy, and others have actually experienced a decline (Economic and Social Council 2010). Why is this? The HIV/AIDS epidemic has had a horrific impact on life expectancy, particularly in parts of Africa. In Botswana, female life expectancy is 28 years lower than it would be in a world without HIV/AIDS (Velkoff and Kowal 2007).

A second reason for the tremendous growth in the elderly population around the world is a decline in fertility rates; fewer babies are being born. Countries with low fertility rates such as Japan and Western Europe tend to have high proportions of the elderly. With fewer births over an extended period of time, cohorts of older persons make up an increasing proportion of the population. Demographers use the term **demographic transition** to refer to the process in which a society moves from a situation of high fertility rates and low life expectancy, to one of low fertility rates and high life expectancy.

Figure 12.2 on page 351 shows three population pyramids from 1950, 1990, and the projections for 2030. Each pyramid shows the population by age, sex, and how they differ among developed and developing countries. In 1950, birthrates were high,

WHAT DO YOU THINK?

How will developing countries deal with their increasing numbers of older persons who require care? Do you think their approach will be different than the approach in developing countries, such as the United States? How do the approaches reflect money, culture, religion, and other macro-level factors?

Figure 12.2 Population Age–Sex Structure in Less Developed and More Developed Countries, 1950, 1990, and 2030

The structure of the population is changing. Younger people make up a smaller portion of the population, whereas, the elderly are rapidly increasing in size. This is especially true in more developed countries.

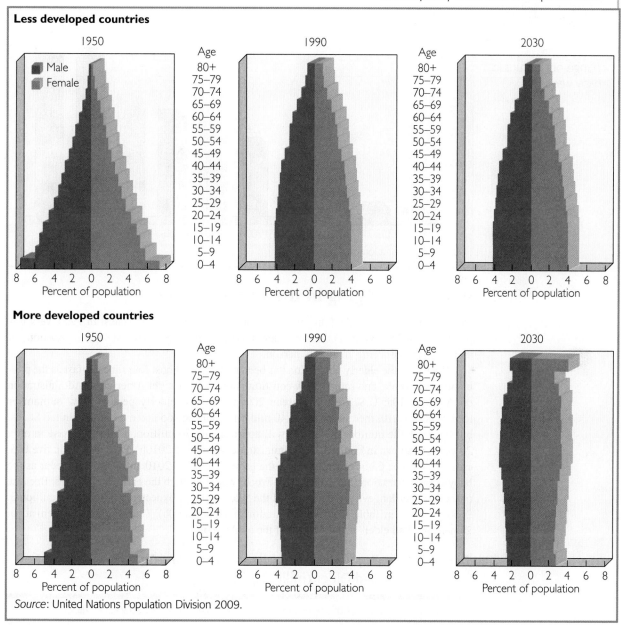

Source: United Nations Population Division 2009.

life expectancy was low, and the number and proportion of elderly in the population were small, particularly in developing nations. However, by 1990, the population in developed nations had changed. Birthrates were lower in 1990; therefore, there was a noticeably large "bulge" in the pyramid among those aged 25–45. This age group is known as the post–World War II **baby-boom generation**. By 2030, patterns are expected to shift in both developed and developing nations, as birthrates continue to decline and life expectancy increases (Kinsella and He 2009; Kinsella and Phillips 2005). The "pyramids" are no longer pyramids.

Figure 12.3 **Millions of Persons 65+ in United States, 1900–2030**

The baby boomers, born after World War II through the early 1960s, will soon be elderly. Their sheer numbers are likely to change our culture in many ways.

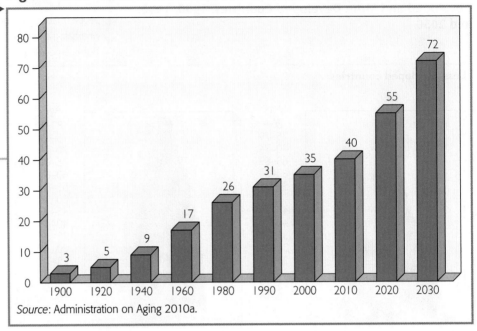

Source: Administration on Aging 2010a.

Patterns of Aging in the United States

Only a century ago people didn't live very long even in the United States. In 1900, very few people—1 in 25—were aged 65 or older. Younger people probably spent long portions of their lives rarely seeing an elderly person.

But today, the elderly population has been increasing almost four times as fast as the population as a whole, and seniors now constitute one of every eight Americans (Administration on Aging 2010a; U.S. Census Bureau 2009a). In fact, elderly persons now outnumber teenagers. In 2010, there were about 40 million people age 65 and over in the United States, but by 2030, the number of seniors will approximate 70 million, a huge increase in only 20 years, as shown in Figure 12.3 (Administration on Aging 2010b). By then, one in five U.S. citizens could be 65 or older. Much of the growth between 2010 and 2030 will occur as the baby-boom generation (those born after World War II through the early 1960s) ages. Because of their greater longevity, the number of the "oldest-old" is expected to jump to 19 million in 2050, as shown in Table 12.1 (Administration on Aging 2010b). That would make them about 25 percent of all elders and 6 percent of the total population.

TABLE 12.1 **Population Projections for Persons Age 85 and Older (millions)**

The number of elderly in our population will be quite high between 2030 and 2050.

2000	4.3
2010	5.8
2020	6.6
2030	8.7
2040	14.2
2050	19.0

Source: Administration on Aging 2010b.

Moreover, the number of persons living to be at least 100 years old—**centenarians**—is also rapidly increasing. Even as recently as a generation ago, we rarely met anyone who was 100 or 105 years old. In 1990, there were only about 36,000 centenarians in the entire country. Yet, the number of centenarians by 2050 may exceed one million (Administration on Aging 2009).

Who are these centenarians, and what are their lives like? I'd like to introduce you to one—my grandmother. She lived to the ripe old age of 108 and a half, and sadly, passed away as this book was going to press. You can take a glimpse into her life in the following box "Families as Lived Experience: Celebrating My Grandmother's Birthday."

FAMILIES
as Lived Experience

Celebrating My Grandmother's Birthday

As more adults are living past 100, many families now are celebrating birthdays that would have been unheard of a generation or two ago. The essay below asks you to ponder what such a birthday could mean.

My extended family gathered in Montana for my grandmother's birthday—she had just turned 105. Yes, you read that correctly—105! We celebrated the marvelous and very long life of this amazing woman. But wait, that was three and a half years ago. She is now over 108! She was born in 1901, and just imagine the changes she has witnessed:

■ William McKinley was president of the United States when she was born.

■ Henry Ford showcased the first model T for $950 when she was 7 years old.

■ World War I began when she was 13.

■ Women did not receive the right to vote until she was 19.

■ The Roaring Twenties occurred when she was in her 20s.

■ World War II, the deadliest war in history, began when she was 38.

■ The case of Brown v. Board of Education, which decided that separate schools for Black children were inherently unequal, was not settled until she was in her 50s.

■ Medicare, the health insurance program for the elderly, was created when she was 64—just in time!

■ Personal computers were not readily available until she was in her 80s.

■ Cell phones were not commonplace until she was well into her 90s.

Happy 105th birthday, Grandma!

■ Her youngest great-grandchild, Olivia, was born when she was 102; her youngest great-great-grandchild (to date), Crosby, was born when she was 107.

Here's to you, Grandma!
Love,
Karen

Note: My grandmother Blanche Coy Seccombe died peacefully at the age of 108 and a half as this book was in press.

CRITICAL THINKING QUESTIONS

1. If you live to be my grandmother's age, what type of social and political changes do you think could occur during your lifetime?

2. What social and health programs are needed in our society to help care for the growing number of centenarians?

Not all groups are equally likely to reach old age. Minorities are underrepresented in the aging population, given their size in the population overall. About 17 percent of elderly are minorities: 8 percent Black, 6 percent Hispanic, 2 percent Asian, and less than 1 percent American Indian or Alaska Native. However, by 2030, minorities will comprise about 28 percent of all elders, an increase, but a smaller one than would be expected given their size in the overall population, as you learned in Chapter 6. This is due in part to their lower life expectancy. For example, a White girl born today can anticipate living an average of 81 years, 4 years longer than a Black girl.

Changing demographics bring with them a growth in the study of aging. The field of **gerontology** has evolved since the 1940s into an interdisciplinary science of aging that draws upon biology, medicine, and the social sciences, including sociology, psychology, and family studies. Let's turn now to some of the theories gerontologists use in their work.

Prevailing Theories of Aging

Gerontologists study both micro- and macro-level issues with respect to aging. What is the aging experience like? How is society structured to meet the needs of the elderly? Some theories focus on micro-level issues, emphasizing the individual and his or her adaptation to aging; others focus on macro issues, looking at the structure of society and cultural values and how these facilitate or inhibit successful aging. The following are some of the more common theories found in the gerontological literature (Estes 2001).

- *Disengagement theory* explores the process by which elders and society simultaneously disengage from one another. This process of mutual separation is seen as a natural and universal part of the aging process and has laid the foundation for retirement policies and separate housing for seniors. It is a theory that was particularly popular in the 1950s and 1960s in the heyday of the broader functionalist paradigm. The withdrawal from society was viewed as beneficial or functional because it allowed an orderly transition from one generation to the next.

- *Activity theory* is interested in discovering the ways that the elderly continue the roles and activities they have developed over the life course or develop new ones to substitute for other losses. It is also a theory developed and popularized in the 1950s. A primary assumption behind this perspective is that aging is more successful and people are happiest when they remain active and stay involved in hobbies, interests, or social roles. Older people have the same social and psychological needs as do younger people and generally do not withdraw unless confined by poor health or a physical limitation.

- *Continuity theory* was developed to explain a common research finding: Aging does not bring a radical departure from earlier years. Although there may be important changes in health and social circumstances, a large proportion of older adults show considerable consistency over time in their patterns of thinking, activity profiles, living arrangements, and social relationships. The continuity theory suggests that most people learn continuously from their life experiences and draw upon these experiences as they continue to grow and evolve.

- While these earlier theories focused on micro issues, the *life course perspective* broadens this to view the aging process as one phase of an entire lifetime. This perspective bridges micro- and macro-level perspectives. Age cohorts have been shaped by important historical, economic, and social factors that may have arisen at any time in the life course, such as the Depression, World War II, or the civil and women's rights movements of the 1960s. The life course perspective reveals how these events shape the attitudes and behaviors of age cohorts.

- *Critical theory* notes that many theories about aging reinforce ageist attitudes about the elderly and legitimize policies that reinforce dependency at the expense of empowerment.

Aging is a social process, not simply a biological one, and many experiences of the elderly are shaped by the inequalities they have encountered throughout the life course, such as racism, sex discrimination, or economic inequality. We must critically evaluate societal arrangements and examine how they foster or inhibit successful aging. These arrangements include social institutions, statuses, roles, and the distribution of power that runs across them.

- *The political economy perspective* is a component of critical theory. In particular, it describes the role of capitalism and the state in contributing to systems of power, domination, and marginalization of the elderly. It examines the role of the economic system, government, the military, the criminal justice system, business, labor, social welfare institutions, and other social structures in shaping, legitimizing, and reproducing power (Estes 2001).

- *Feminist theory* is an analysis of women's experience, the identification of gender oppression, and is emancipatory in nature. It suggests that women's experiences may be different from men's, and these differences are often ignored or disvalued in the knowledge base. It acknowledges that women come from different cultures, places, historical times, racial and ethnic groups, and social classes, which further shape their gendered experiences. However, as a class of people, women are routinely disvalued, ignored, or oppressed around the globe.

The Economics of Aging

Two contrasting images emerge in discussions of the economic conditions and well-being of the elderly. One projects an image of retired tycoons with expensive second homes in Palm Springs, California, or on the Florida coast, and driving large well-outfitted motor homes. The other image is in stark contrast. The elderly are portrayed as poor, alone, living in ramshackle housing, and eating dog food to stay alive. Although there are elderly who fit each of these stereotypes, the reality is that most elderly are somewhere in the middle of these extremes.

How the Elderly Fare: Income and Assets

The median household income of a person age 65 or older in the United States is about $31,000, according to data from the Census Bureau (DeNavas-Walt et al. 2010). This income comes from a number of sources, as shown in Figure 12.4 (Employee Benefit Research Institute 2010). The largest segment, 40 percent, comes from Social Security. Earnings comprise 26 percent of the average income of elders, and pensions account for 20 percent. Assets such as stocks, bonds, or income from rented real estate, and other unknown sources make up the remainder. These figures represent overall averages; however, there are some critical differences, such as the income differences between men and women, between Whites and racial or ethnic minorities, or between different age groups. Likewise, income, pensions, and annuities are a much larger component of the portfolios of White males, whereas elderly women and minorities derive a greater share of their income from Social Security.

Figure 12.4 Distribution of the Elderly's Income, 2008

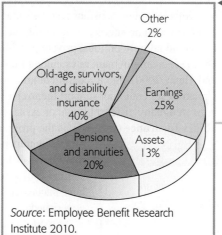

Source: Employee Benefit Research Institute 2010.

> The largest proportion of income for the elderly comes from Social Security. This is an important source of financial assistance.

TABLE 12.2 Poverty Rates by Age, 2009

AGE	POVERTY RATE
Under 18	20.7%
18–64	12.9%
65 and older	8.9%

Source: DeNavas-Walt et al. 2010.

Poverty and the Triple Jeopardy: Aging, Sex, and Race   Overall, the elderly are less likely than any other age group to live in poverty, as shown in Table 12.2, largely because of income programs like Social Security (DeNavas-Walt et al. 2010; Employee Benefit Research Institute 2010). Nonetheless, certain segments of the U.S. elderly population are vulnerable to becoming impoverished, including the oldest-old, women, and minorities. For example, only about 8 percent of elderly non-Hispanic Whites are impoverished compared to 24 percent of Blacks, 20 percent of Hispanics, and 14 percent of Asian/Pacific Islander elders. When age, sex, and minority statuses are combined—say an 85-year-old Hispanic woman—this is called a **triple jeopardy**, and her chances of being impoverished increase to over 50 percent (He et al. 2005). This is because of the cumulative disadvantages minorities and women have experienced throughout their lives. Structural barriers to employment during adulthood result in their greater economic vulnerability in old age. In addition, an older woman is more likely to be widowed and to live alone, increasing her likelihood of poverty.

Social Security

The United States is one of over 150 countries that have some sort of financial program for elders. Each program operates somewhat differently, but provides at least some financial benefit to help the elderly make ends meet.

In the United States during the late nineteenth and early twentieth centuries, few companies had private pensions for seniors, and the government did not provide public pensions. Consequently, elderly persons who could still work usually continued to do so. In 1900, two-thirds of men over 65 were employed, compared to only about 17 percent today (Taylor et al. 2009). Many other industrialized nations introduced publicly funded pension programs for the elderly, including Germany in 1889, Great Britain in 1908, Sweden in 1913, Canada in 1927, and France in 1930 (Cockerham 1997).

Bills for public pensions were introduced many times in the U.S. Congress between 1900 and 1935 with no success. But during the Great Depression, it became obvious that the elderly could not rely on jobs, private pensions, savings, or their families for financial support. By 1935, unemployment rates among those 65 and older were well above 50 percent (Hardy and Shuey 2000), and a federal commission determined that nearly half of all seniors in the United States could not support themselves. The Social Security Act was passed in 1935, and it created many different kinds of assistance programs. One, **Old Age, Survivor, and Disability Insurance (OASDI)**, is the program we have come to know as "Social Security". It offered seniors public pensions as a response to the austere poverty that many of them endured. It is now seen as an earned right for seniors, not a form of welfare. Payments from Social Security have successfully reduced the percentage of seniors who are impoverished.

OASDI retirement benefits are financed by a tax on earnings up to a certain level that is set by Congress. For the year 2010, that

> **WHAT DO YOU THINK?**
>
> *What kinds of changes to Social Security are you willing to support, and which ones do you oppose?*

Figure 12.5 Retiree Confidence that Social Security Will Continue to Provide Benefits of at Least Equal Value to Benefits Received by Retirees Today

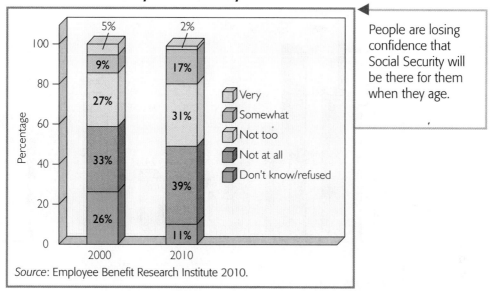

Source: Employee Benefit Research Institute 2010.

People are losing confidence that Social Security will be there for them when they age.

earnings level was $106,800. Any earnings over that amount are not taxed. The tax is paid by both the employee and the employer, at a rate of 6.2 percent each (Social Security Online 2010). The Social Security tax has been called regressive because it essentially taxes low earners at a higher rate than high earners. Let me provide an example: let's say "Bob" earned $106,800 in 2010; he, therefore, paid 6.2 percent of his income or $6,408 in Social Security taxes. Meanwhile, "Jose" earned twice that amount, or $213,600, but paid 6.2 percent only on the first $106,800 he earned, so he also paid $6,408. The rest of Jose's income is tax-free. In reality, Bob paid 6.2 percent of his total income in Social Security tax while Jose only paid 3.1 percent. Therefore, as a higher wage earner, Jose is in effect taxed at a lower rate.

The Social Security program is facing an impending challenge that causes many people to wonder if it will be around to help them in old age, as shown in Figure 12.5. Only 11 percent of retirees in 2010 were very confident that Social Security will continue to provide benefits of at least equal value, down from 26 percent who felt that way in 2000. The difficulty lies in the fact that we have an increasing number of people living longer (drawing upon Social Security) and have fewer people in the cohort behind them to pay into the system. Thus, in 10–20 years, as the baby boomers retire, how can Social Security remain solvent? There are a number of options. First, the retirement age for benefits has been raised for younger cohorts to 66 or 67 years. Other sacrifices may be needed to keep the program solvent, such as increasing the tax rate above the current 6.2 percent, eliminating the regressive cap so that all income is taxed instead of just the first $106,800, raising the retirement age even further, or changing Social Security to a means-tested rather than universal program.

The Aging Couple

Most married older couples have a relationship that has endured many years. Newspapers are full of stories of couples celebrating their fiftieth or sixtieth wedding anniversaries. Together, the couple has faced life and its transitions: the birth of a child, job opportunities,

Figure 12.6 **Percentage of Older Men and Women Who Are Married or Widowed (2009)**

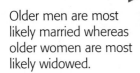

Older men are most likely married whereas older women are most likely widowed.

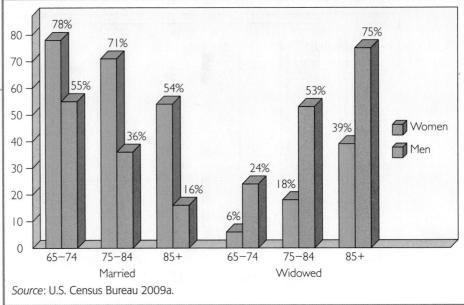

Source: U.S. Census Bureau 2009a.

disappointments, the effort to balance work and family, the departure of children from home, and their becoming a couple once again.

Most men and women are married as they enter late adulthood. For example, over three-quarters of men age 65–74 are married, as are more than half of women. However, as we age, the likelihood of being married begins to decline, particularly for women (U.S. Census Bureau 2009a). Among those age 85 and over, over half of men remain married, compared to only 16 percent of women, as shown in Figure 12.6.

This next section examines several important dimensions of the couple relationship: marital satisfaction, sexuality, gay and lesbian elders, and widowhood.

Marital Satisfaction

We assume that marriage is an important buffer against loneliness and isolation in old age. Most older adults report being happy in their marriages, but about 20–25 percent exhibit strong or moderate social and emotional loneliness (Gierveld et al. 2008). Those who are most lonely tend to have a spouse with health problems, do not communicate frequently with their spouse, often disagree with their spouse, or evaluate their sex life as unpleasant.

How does the degree to which couples are satisfied with their spouses and their relationship change over the life course? One early study of 400 couples married in the 1930s looked at their marital satisfaction over 20 years. Each member of the couple evaluated the relationship soon after marriage, and then again 20 years later. Using a number of different measures, the study found that marital satisfaction had diminished over time (Pineo 1961).

More recent studies have usually been cross-sectional—that is, they look at one moment, like a snapshot in time—because it is very difficult to track couples for 20, 30, or 40 years. Cross-sectional studies generally report that the marital satisfaction of couples may instead be curvilinear, or "U-shaped." This means a marriage starts with a high level of satisfaction, begins to drop as couples have children, and then rises again when the children leave home (Morgan and Kunkel 1998).

However, sociologist Norval Glenn examined several cohorts of families over a 10-year period, including couples who had married from the 1930s through the 1980s, and his work casts doubt on whether marital satisfaction actually rises after the children leave home (Glenn 1998). Glenn found no evidence of the upturn; he suggested instead that variation in marital quality may simply be due to cohort differences—that is, people of different cohorts, or ages, have different expectations about marriage.

Sexuality: Could It Be?

My husband and I probably enjoy sex more today than we did when we were younger. All of our children are now grown up and out of the house, which I'm sure helps our sense of privacy and stress. I don't have to worry about getting pregnant anymore because I'm way past that stage. Also, our sex seems more affectionate now, if that's possible—what I mean is that the goal isn't just on having your own orgasm, but really relaxing and pleasing the other person. Our sense of love and commitment after all these years really shines through. Seriously, I think sex is better now. (Diane, aged 62)

Most people retain their interest in sex well into old age. Elders who are married or partnered are usually sexually active.

A common misperception about the elderly is that they are no longer sexually active. In the classroom, any discussion of elders' sexuality is largely met with snickers or looks of disbelief. In response to that, I ask students, "Well, at what age do you plan to give up sex?" Then, I hear gasps.

Sexuality remains an essential element of the lives of the elderly (DeLamater and Sill 2010; Kontula and Haavio-Mannila 2009). A large majority of elders have a positive view of sexual relationships, and if married or partnered, it is quite likely that they are still sexually active (AARP 2005). AARP conducted a large survey about sexuality in midlife and beyond, based on a sample of over 1,600 older adults. Three-quarters of men aged 60–69 who have a regular sexual partner report engaging in sexual touching or caressing at least once per week over the previous 6 months, and nearly half reportedly engaged in sexual intercourse at least weekly. Among men aged 70 and older, about one-third report having sexual intercourse weekly or more. Many also engage in oral sex.

Another study based on a random sample of over 3,000 adults aged 57–85 reported similar conclusions. Although the likelihood of sexual activity does decline with age, 39 percent of men aged 75–85 are still sexually active, as are 17 percent of women (Lindau et al. 2007). A primary reason that the figures are not higher than this is simply that no partner is available: rates of widowhood are high.

It appears that it is time to debunk the myth that the elderly are asexual. The continuity theory can help us understand that the elderly were young once, and just as young adults today do not plan to give up their sexual lives as they age, neither do today's elderly.

Gay and Lesbian Elders

When most people think of a gay or lesbian person, chances are they do not think of a senior citizen. Nonetheless, somewhere between 1.4 and 3.8 million elderly are lesbian, gay, transgender, or bisexual (LGTB), a population that may number 7 million by 2030 (Grant 2009). Most of these people are women. Although they face many of the same issues that other elders face, such as health problems or the need for reliable transportation or housing assistance, they also have many unique concerns. Most federal programs and laws treat same-sex couples differently from married heterosexual couples (Cahill et al. 2000; Grant 2009; Solarz 2008):

- Social Security pays survivor benefits to widows and widowers, but not to the surviving same-sex life partner of someone who dies. This may cost LGTB elders $124 million per year in lost benefits.
- Married couples are eligible for Social Security spousal benefits, which can allow them to earn half their spouse's Social Security benefit if it is larger than their own. Unmarried partners in lifelong relationships are not eligible for spousal benefits.
- Medicaid regulations protect the assets and homes of married spouses when the other spouse enters a nursing home or long-term care facility; no such protections are offered to same-sex partners.
- Tax laws and other regulations of 401ks and pensions discriminate against same-sex partners, costing the surviving partner in a same-sex relationship tens of thousands of dollars a year, and possibly more than $1 million over a lifetime. For example, if a person with a 401k pension plan dies, the money rolls over to a *legal spouse* without any tax penalty. However, since gays and lesbians cannot legally marry in most states, the surviving partner would have to pay a 20 percent federal tax.

The effect of this unequal treatment is striking. Assume Deborah dies at age 50 with $100,000 in her 401k account, which she leaves to her life partner, Lonnie, also age 50. Lonnie will receive the sum less taxes (at least $20,000), for a total of no more than $80,000. Lonnie cannot roll the sum over into a tax-free IRA. If Lonnie were a man—let's call him Larry—as Deborah's widower, Larry would receive the full $100,000 and could shield it from taxes until age 70 1/2. The survivor of the legally married couple has a nest egg to invest that is roughly 20 percent larger than that of the surviving spouse in the same-sex couple. The nest egg can grow in a tax-deferred account until the maximum age of disbursement for the surviving spouse in a legally married couple. The surviving spouse of the same-sex couple, however, cannot roll the initial disbursement into an IRA (Cahill et al. 2000).

Even basic rights such as hospital visitation or the right to die in the same nursing home as one's partner are regularly denied to same-sex couples. U.S. government policies on the aging population assume heterosexuality, close relationships with children, and extended families to provide basic needs as we age.

These policies have social, economic, and health consequences for gay and lesbian elders (Grant 2009; Hu 2005). They may hide their sexual orientation from their health care and social service providers out of fear, further compromising their ability to get needed care and assistance. Several studies document widespread homophobia among those entrusted with the care of U.S. seniors. Therefore, many gay and lesbian seniors remain hidden, reinforcing isolation and forgoing services they may truly need.

Widowhood

The death of a spouse or partner stands as one of life's most stressful events (Holmes and Rahe 1967). It means the loss of a companion and friend, perhaps the loss of income, and the ending of a familiar way of life. Widowhood can occur at any point in the life cycle, but because it is most likely to occur among the elderly, research tends to focus on that population.

Over 14 million persons are classified as widowed in the United States; about 85 percent of them are women (U.S. Census Bureau 2010a). The number of persons who have *experienced* widowhood, however, is much larger than that because some have remarried.

Women are more likely to be widowed than are men for three primary reasons. First, mortality rates among females are lower than for males; therefore, they live to older ages. The life expectancy of females at age 65 exceeds that of males by nearly 7 years. Second, wives are typically 2–3 years younger than their husbands and consequently have a greater chance of outliving them. Third, widowed women are less likely to remarry than are widowed men. There is a lack of eligible men because cultural norms encourage older men to date and marry younger women, but not the reverse (Berardo and Berardo 2000; He et al. 2005).

We have all heard statements suggesting that an elderly person often dies soon after his or her spouse dies. "He just gave up...."; "She died of sadness...."; "He saw no reason to go on after Rose died....". But is there any truth to this so-called "widow effect"; that is, is there really an increased probability of death among new widows and widowers? Two Harvard sociology professors decided to answer this question by following nearly 4,500 U.S. couples age 67 and older for 5 years (Elwert and Christakis 2006). They found that there does seem to be truth to the widow effect; the likelihood of death does increase after a spouse dies. The "widow effect," however, does not occur equally among racial and ethnic groups. White men were 18 percent more likely to die shortly after their spouses' deaths, as were 16 percent of White women. But among Blacks, a spouse's death had no effect on the mortality of the survivor.

Why would widowhood contribute to an early death for Whites, but not for Blacks? Upon marrying, Blacks and Whites appear to receive many of the same health, financial, and socioemotional benefits, such as emotional support, caretaking when ill, and enhanced social support, so what could account for the "widow effect"? We do know that Blacks are almost twice as likely to live with other relatives (Pew Research Center 2010), are more active in religious groups, and when married are less likely to adhere to a traditional gendered division of labor, which may reduce dependence on a spouse. It seems that Blacks may somehow manage to extend the benefits of marriage into widowhood and are, therefore, less likely than Whites to die soon after their spouse passes on (Elwert and Christakis 2006).

The Process of Grief and Bereavement   People handle their grief over the death of a loved one in a variety of ways. Some try to remain stoic; others cry out in despair. Some people fear death, whereas others, perhaps because of a strong religious faith, see it as part of a larger "master plan."

One of the more popular perspectives on death and dying is based on the work of Elizabeth Kubler-Ross (1969). Her work with 200 primarily middle-aged cancer patients suggested five somewhat distinct stages that dying people and their loved ones experience. Although some critics say that not everyone experiences these stages, or in this order, Kubler-Ross's work is useful nonetheless. The five stages are:

- *Denial:* Many people first refuse to believe that they or a loved one is dying. They may ask for additional medical tests, desire a second or third opinion, or in other ways deny that death is near.
- *Anger:* When coming to grips with the truth, some people become angry. They may project this anger toward friends, family, people who are well, or medical personnel.
- *Bargaining:* The dying person or loved one may try to forestall death by striking a bargain with God.
- *Depression:* Depression may set in when the dying person or their loved ones realize they cannot win the fight against the illness or disease. They may be depressed over the symptoms of their condition (chronic pain) or effects of their treatment (hair loss). As they see and plan for their future, the loss they face can feel overwhelming.
- *Acceptance:* Eventually, a patient and/or loved one may come to accept the approaching death. In this stage, they may reflect on their lives together.

These five stages are highly individualized. No two people pass through them at exactly the same pace, and many people may go back and forth between stages before finally reaching acceptance.

Is Widowhood More Difficult for Men or Women?   Who do you think has a more difficult time adjusting to widowhood—men or women? The preponderance of research points to men's greater difficulty coping with widowhood (Carr 2004; Lee and DeMaris 2007; Lee et al. 1998). Men are generally more dependent on their spouse for social and emotional support. They are less likely to have close relationships with same-sex widowed friends (Felmlee and Muraco 2009), are more likely to be older, may have poor health themselves, have fewer family ties, and are less proficient at domestic tasks.

On the other hand, older women have largely been financially dependent on their husbands and when widowed may face substantial difficulties. First, their incomes and assets are significantly less than men's (DeNavas-Walt et al. 2010). Two-fifths of widows fall into poverty at some time during the five years after their husband's death, a higher proportion than widowed men or divorced women. The loss of income and assets is far greater for Black and Hispanic widows than for Whites (Angel et al. 2007). We do know that widows who have worked tend to report less depression than those who have not worked (Pai and Barrett 2007).

Second, widows may face the daunting practical problems of maintaining a house alone. A study of 201 widows drawn from public death records in a Midwestern metropolitan area found that financial problems were not a primary cause of stress for widows (although they were a major cause of stress for women getting divorced). The researchers found that the lack of practical support, such as help with home repairs, significantly increased widows' stress (Miller et al. 1998).

A study of 200 older individuals found that widowed men are more likely than their female counterparts to want to find another romantic partner. Carr found that 6 months after a spouse had died, 15 percent of men, compared to less than 1 percent of women, were dating, and 30 percent of men, compared to 16 percent of women, claimed that they wanted to remarry (Carr 2004). Men's higher likelihood of remarriage can be attributed to at least two factors: (1) they have a greater pool of eligibles and (2) they may be more motivated to find someone to take care of them and share their lives (Carr 2004).

Relationships with Children and Grandchildren

Over time, most families undergo a number of important transitions, such as the birth or adoption of children, raising and launching those children into adulthood, and becoming grandparents. Developmental theory, introduced in Chapter 1, recognizes that families, like individuals, change over time and go through a number of critical developmental stages.

Overall, older parents and their adult children remain emotionally linked as children leave home, cohabit, marry, and are employed (Greenfield and Marks 2004; Umberson et al. 2010; Umberson 2006). Both generations report strong feelings of connection to each other, although parents often have stronger feelings of attachment to their children than their children have to them. Generally, adult children and their parents want to get along, and therefore try to avoid those topics that cause tension in the relationship. However, relationships are complex, and they may contain elements of intimacy and conflict at the same time.

As adult children become partnered, cohabit, or marry, they are likely to see their parents less frequently than before (Bucx et al. 2008). However, as young adults have children of their own, they tend to see their parents more frequently again. Yet, because of the recession, we are witnessing a growing number of young adults who move out of their parents' home, then move back in again for financial reasons.

Children Leaving (and Returning) Home: "Boomerangers"

In the past, women's primary reason for leaving home was marriage, for men it was marriage or the military. Few adults moved back into their parents' home.

But today, economic difficulties are causing many people to rethink their living arrangements (Taylor et al. 2010; Wang and Morin 2009). A 2009 Pew Research Center survey found that among 22- to 29-year-olds, one in eight say that, because of the recession, they have "boomeranged" back to live with their parents after being on their own (Pew Research Center 2010). Many adult children return to their parents' home, move out, return, and move out once again. Sound familiar? These adult children have been nicknamed the Boomerang Generation, or "Boomerangers" (Fredrix 2008; Sukel 2008; Wang and Morin 2009). The box on page 366, "Using the Sociological Imagination: The Boomerang Generation," gives us a glimpse of this common family scenario.

Children who return home face both advantages and disadvantages, as do their parents (Ward and Spitze 2007). Young adults may experience greater emotional and economic security living with their parents. If they have children of their own, they may benefit from having a grandparent participate in child care. Likewise, older adults may benefit by having their children near them to provide assistance with various tasks of daily living, such as yard work, cooking, or cleaning. Older adults may also appreciate having their grandchildren with them.

Co-residence has some marked disadvantages, however. Older parents and adult children may return to the roles they played when the children were teenagers. Parents may try to establish a curfew or establish rules governing their adult child's behavior or clothing. If the adult child has lived alone for a period of time, he or she is likely to resent these rules and see them as intrusions.

Having adult children back in the home can alter the parents' lives considerably. They may not be able to retire as early as they wish; they may have to postpone plans to travel; they may need to reorganize their own finances to offer assistance to their children; they may need to rearrange furniture and space within the house; and they may find themselves doing extra cooking and cleaning. Children often return home when they have special needs and little or no money, and parents may feel obligated to help them out regardless of their own personal and financial situation. Yet, many older adults also face financial hardship because of the recession, and they may have had to reduce their spending, cope with unemployment, and face a loss of savings and assets (Brown 2009; Mossaad 2010; Soto 2009).

Even if they do not live together, most elderly help out their adult children financially, emotionally, and with tasks such as child care assistance. Social exchange theory, introduced in Chapter 1, is a useful tool for thinking about the exchanges made between adult children and their aging parents. It focuses on the costs and benefits for different types of family interactions, including the exchange of aid, financial and otherwise. Until parents are very old and frail, they give out far more assistance to their children than they receive from them. They may lend money to their adult children for a down payment on a new car or new house, they may set up a fund for their grandchildren's college costs, or they may be an important safety net in times of illness, divorce, or other family crisis. A nationwide study of 10,000 older adults between the ages of 48 and 70 asked about the degree to which they help their adult children (Fleck 2009):

- 70 percent gave cash for day-to-day expenses
- 40 percent helped with mortgage or rent payments
- 24 percent provided money for health care
- 23 percent helped pay for day care costs
- 21 percent provided funds for education

USING
the Sociological Imagination

The Boomerang Generation

The current recession has caused high unemployment and home foreclosures, and has reduced the incomes of many. One way of coping is to take in a roommate or to move back in with parents. Many are turning to the latter—returning home to Mom and Dad.

Children who move away to college often return to their parents' home afterwards while they look for a job. However, a growing number of older adults are moving home after job losses, accumulation of credit card debt, divorce, or the need to save for a down payment on a home. About 49 million people live in a household with two adult generations, up from only 42 million doing so in 2000.

Anna, age 27, lived on her own for several years until she lost her job and was unable to find another one. With mounting bills, she did what many other young adults are doing today, but what was rare a generation or two ago—she moved back in with mom and dad. By her own estimation, her parents spend about $1,000 per month helping her with her car payment and insurance, health insurance, and costs associated with going back to school, not to mention food and shelter. Her father is retired, her mother is nearly so, and they may not be able to support Anna much longer. "It's kind of hitting me finally that I need to get out there and find a job," she said, "even if it's just part-time just to help out however I can."

People like Anna have been nicknamed the Boomerang Generation, or "Boomerangers." They move out, return home, then move out again, sometimes many times. They find it difficult to maintain jobs, health insurance, and their lifestyles, and come back home to mom and dad for help. Financial planners receive many calls from elderly parents asking for advice. As one financial planner reports, parents "jeopardize their financial freedom by continuing to subsidize their children. We have a hard time saying no as a culture to our children, and they keep asking for more." Some parents delay or scale back their plans for retirement to help their adult children weather a financial or emotional crisis.

Not all parents are unhappy having their children come home again. Shirley, 80, is pleased to help out her boomerang daughter Jo Ann, a 52-year-old single parent who lost her job as an events planner at an upscale resort. Jo Ann struggled financially with several lower-paying jobs until Shirley invited her to move back home. "I've got three kids and any of them can come home if they want," she said. Meanwhile, Jo Ann is saving for a down payment on a house. While she loves her parents, she does feel a bit embarrassed by her living arrangement, "but you take humble steps in order to move forward."

Source: Fredrix 2008; Taylor et al. 2010.

CRITICAL THINKING QUESTIONS
1. How do the economic issues discussed in Chapter 11, such as globalization and the recession, relate to the experiences of the boomerangers?
2. Do you think parents' receptivity to their adult children moving back home might vary by the sex of the adult child? By race or ethnicity? By social class? Why or why not?

Do your parents ever help you out? It's likely they will at some point. Adult children are almost four times more likely to receive financial assistance from their aging parents as they are to provide it to them, and almost twice as likely to receive practical and emotional help as they are to give it (Dykstra and Komter 2006).

Grandparenthood

Most parents eventually become grandparents. On average, first grandchildren are born to adults who are in their late 40s or early 50s although the age is increasing as young couples wait longer to have children. Some people may not become grandparents until they are in their 70s. Children today are more likely to have all four grandparents alive when they are born, and most will continue to have at least two grandparents alive when they reach adulthood (Szinovacz 1998; Uhlenberg and Kirby 1998).

Grandparent roles are relatively new in society. Increasing longevity and fewer children have meant that the grandparent generation is no longer still raising their own younger children when their oldest marries and has children. Until the twentieth century, grandparents did not generally have the time or resources to be intimately involved in the lives of their grandchildren.

Grandparenting Today   The role of a grandparent has changed over the past century. First, being a grandparent has become a role distinct from parenting itself because grandparents are now unlikely to have their own children still living in the home. Second, it has changed because the elderly are healthier, better educated, and have greater economic security than in the past. Third, grandparents, grandfathers in particular, are now more likely to recognize the importance of having direct emotional involvement with young children. Grandfathers have opportunities to participate in nurturing children that seemed unavailable to them as fathers or to grandfathers in the past. Finally, families can more easily travel long distances and communicate by telephone or computer.

Most grandparents report that their relationships with their grandchildren are meaningful and pleasurable (AARP 2007; Reitzes and Mutran 2004). In their national study of grandparents, Cherlin and Furstenberg (1986) found that 55 percent of grandparents reported having a *companionate* relationship with their grandchildren. This means that they enjoy recreational activities, occasional overnight stays, and even babysitting. The relationship is intimate, fun, and friendly. About 30 percent had *remote*, or emotionally distant, relationships with their grandchildren, often because they lived far away. Another 15 percent of grandparents were more *involved*, with more frequent interaction or possibly even living together. For one man's personal essay on what grandparenthood means to him, see the box on the pages 368 and 369, "Families as Lived Experience: What Is It Like to Be a Grandparent?".

Most grandparents report that their relationships with their grandchildren are meaningful and fun. Grandfathers are now more likely to recognize the importance of having close emotional involvement with young children and have opportunities to participate in ways that seemed unavailable to them as fathers.

Sex Differences in Grandparenting Styles   Grandmothers and grandfathers often have different styles of interaction with their grandchildren (Barnett et al. 2010). Grandmothers are more likely to be involved in planning and orchestrating family activities, nurturing their grandchildren, and assuming caregiving responsibilities (Walker et al. 2001). This is consistent with their role as family **kinkeeper**, or having the primary responsibility for maintaining family relationships (Fingerman 2004). For example, it is usually the women in the family who are responsible for sending greeting cards on holidays and birthdays. In contrast, grandfathers are more likely to focus on practical issues and spend more time together exchanging help and services, particularly with their grandsons. One consequence of this difference in style is that family members generally feel more obligation toward and are closer to their grandmothers than to their grandfathers (Dubas 2001; Monserud 2008).

Racial and Ethnic Differences in Grandparenting Styles   In racial and ethnic minority families, grandmothers

---

WHAT DO YOU THINK?

What type of relationship did you have with your grandparents when you were younger—companionate or something else? Did your relationship with your grandmother differ from your relationship with your grandfather? If so, how did this difference reflect gender in your family?

FAMILIES
as Lived Experience

What Is It Like to Be a Grandparent?

Most students reading this book have experience as a grandchild, but what is it like to be a grandparent? Although grandparenthood can mean different things to different people, the following story reveals the joy and happiness grandparenthood can bring.

A seven-year-old girl said about her grandmother: "She's old on the outside, but she acts like she's young on the inside." She hit the nail on the head! Living longer means that more of us now lead three lives: first as children, second as adults with careers and most likely as parents, and third as retirees from careers—and for most of us as grandparents. During each of these lives, we continually discover and learn new things. We find sides of ourselves that we did not know existed. Our third life is a time for discovering new talents and creative possibilities in our inner worlds. It is a time for applying the wisdom of the ages to ourselves.

Being a grandparent means different things. Although grandparenting is not the dominant aspect of most of our lives, it is an aspect that is more important than most of us realize. For some of us who are actively raising our grandchildren, it is the most important part of our lives. Some of us are estranged from our children and from our grandchildren because of strife in our families. But most of us live at some distance from our grandchildren and manage to maintain an active role in their lives through the mail, the telephone, and visits.

As grandparents, we have important symbolic and practical functions in our cultures. We are important simply for what we mean as the oldest living representatives of our families. We can be a matriarch or a patriarch for our families. Our roles as family historians, mentors, and role models can confer status and respect on us.

Without grandparents, there is no tangible family line. Children who have had no contact with grandparents miss knowledge of their ancestry. They may not be able to muster a confident sense of the future as concretely represented by the fact that older people have seen their futures become the present and the past. As grandparents we are the links to the past in our families. We are the repositories of information about our genealogies. That information often becomes useful material for themes that our grandchildren write in school, and sometimes it flowers into full-fledged writing about our family trees.

As grandparents, we can provide advice to our children that is hopefully appreciated. We can bring our families together and foster and maintain communication between them. We can play healing roles in assuaging the challenges, hurts, and disappointments in our families. We are the conveyors of traditions in our families and in our cultures.

We have much to offer our families and our communities. We are the people who have been there. Whatever wisdom is should lie in us. We can see through the posturing of our everyday world. We can identify with the life stream and the cycles of human existence. We know that disappointments, heartaches, and pain are natural parts of life. We know that life goes on without us. We have had enough dreams and life experiences to know that the mystical may be more real than the rational.

We also have the luxury of living our lives more or less as we wish. We have more control over our schedules because of the relinquishing of the responsibilities of the workplace. We have time to reflect and to enjoy the simple things in life. We can take time to appreciate the pleasures of simply being alive. We can enjoy the clouds, the trees, the flowers, and the smell of the air. We also can devote our time and energies to helping those who are less fortunate. Most importantly, we can relive and resolve the past in our memories.

We gain profound meaning in life from the love and respect of our juniors. The attachment between grandparent and grandchild is second in emotional power only to the bond between parent and child. The arrival of a grandchild usually triggers a dormant instinct to nurture in us. This is accompanied by joy in the birth or adoption of our grandchild; by recalling our own experiences as a parent and as a grandchild; and by thoughts about continuity of our own lives in the next generation.

Our grandchildren have as much to offer us as we have to offer them. We can enjoy our pleasures with them without the responsibility of rearing them. The love and attention we give them builds their self-esteem. Their interest in our company and in our stories reminds us of our importance to our families. We offer each other the sense of belonging not only to our families but also to the human family.

As grandparents and as senior citizens, we are gaining an increasing amount of power in our society not only in the political arena but also in the moral leadership of our society. We really do have much to offer even though there is a tendency to disparage the elderly. We can advocate for the interests of the elderly, not only of our own but also of those of us who are subjected to elder ageism and abuse. But most importantly, we are aware of the interests and needs of future generations. We are in a position to be powerful advocates for children and parents.

As grandparents, we are crucial resources for our families. But the art of grandparenting requires commitment, understanding, practice, and perseverance. We can offer approval, loving delight of our grandchildren, and reliable support for our own offspring. We are the link between the past and the present and even the future! It is through our grandchildren that we and humanity itself flow in the stream of life.

Source: Westman 1998.

CRITICAL THINKING QUESTIONS
1. How do the esteem, power, and importance of grandparents differ cross-culturally?
2. What macro-level factors influence our personal experiences of grandparenting?

frequently have important and influential roles in child rearing, often mimicking parent-like behavior (Dilworth-Anderson 2001; Pew Research Center 2010). As discussed in Chapter 6, a study by psychologist Andrea Hunter examined Black mothers' and fathers' reliance on grandmothers for parenting support. She used a sample of 487 parents aged 18–34 years old from the National Survey of Black Americans and examined their responses to the following questions: (a) "Do you have anyone who gives you advice about child rearing or helps you with problems having to do with children? If yes, what is this advisor's relationship to you?" and (b) "Do you have someone to count on to take care of the children? If yes, what is this person's relationship to you?" She found that 57 percent of the mothers and 56 percent of the fathers reported that they relied on grandmothers for parenting support, relying on them more frequently than anyone else. Most said that they receive both advice and child care from the grandparent.

Three theories are often used to explain why racial and ethnic minority families are more likely than White families to use grandparents (and other kin) as caregivers for their grandchildren (Uttal 1999). The *cultural* explanation suggests that these practices are the product of different cultural experiences and adaptations. The *structural* explanation conceives of child care arrangements as an adaptation to structural constraints, such as racism or poverty. The *integrative* explanation combines these and suggests that these arrangements are due to the intersection of cultural values with structural constraints, operating alongside gendered expectations. In interviews with seven Black mothers, seven Mexican American mothers, and 17 Anglo American mothers, Uttal found that the major difference among the groups was how the mothers *felt* about using kin for care. White Anglos tended to feel that relying on grandparents and other kin was inappropriate or problematic, whereas Black and Mexican American mothers willingly accepted this help because they felt that it was appropriate and acceptable.

Retirement

Work provides us with more than an income. It also is an important part of our identity. We say, "I *am* a nurse …" "I *am* a middle-school teacher …" "I *am* a firefighter …" as though we *are* the occupation. Consequently, retirement is an important event because it alters a major identity as well as reduces our income.

TABLE 12.3 Labor Force Participation Rates Among the Elderly, 2000–2009

By age 65, most adults have retired, although more of them are still working now because of the recession.

	2000	2009
Age 55–64	59%	65%
Age 65+	13%	17%

Source: Pew Research Center 2009.

Still, many people eagerly await this change and see retirement as a legitimate, earned privilege. The median age at retirement fell from 69 years in 1950 to 64 years in 2008, during a time when life expectancy increased substantially (Social Security Administration 2009). However, with the current recession, many people are working longer, as shown in Table 12.3. In 2000, only 59 percent of persons aged 55–64 were employed, as compared to 65 percent in 2009. Likewise, only 13 percent of persons aged 65 and over were employed, as compared to 17 percent in 2009.

The Social Construction of Retirement: Retirement Around the World

Historically speaking, retirement is an anomaly. Throughout most of history, families needed all of its members to work to support themselves. This is the case in many countries today, as seen in Figure 12.7. Unlike in more developed nations, elders in less developed countries often remained employed well into old age. For example, in Bangladesh, over 70 percent of men aged 65 and over are in the labor market, as are 27 percent of the women (Kinsella and Velkoff 2001). It is important to remember that life expectancy in less developed countries is significantly lower as well; therefore, it is likely that many individuals work their entire life. There is no such thing as retirement at any age.

For significant numbers of elderly to be able to withdraw from the labor force, four conditions must exist in a society (Morgan and Kunkel 1998):

- a society must produce an economic surplus that is large enough to support its nonemployed members.
- there must be a mechanism in place to divert some of that surplus to the nonemployed members, such as through a pension or government transfer program.
- nonemployed members should be viewed positively by the rest of society, and their activities or leisure must be seen as legitimate.
- the nonemployed members must have accumulated an acceptable number of years of productivity to warrant support by the other members of society.

These conditions materialized in the United States after industrialization during the nineteenth and twentieth centuries. However, today, these four conditions are under threat. The cost of caring for the elderly—Social Security, health care programs, and private retirement plans—are consuming a greater share of our country's gross domestic product (Schieber 2008). Furthermore, they compete with funding for other groups. Programs for children, for example, have received a declining proportion of federal spending (Uhlenberg 2009).

Figure 12.7 Labor Force Participation Rates in Less Developed Countries for Men and Women Aged 65+

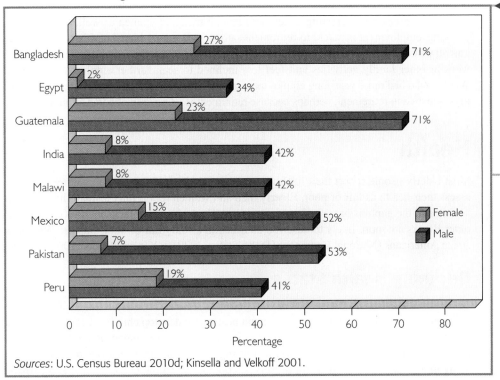

In less developed countries, men often continue working until they are no longer physically able. There is no such thing as "retirement."

Sources: U.S. Census Bureau 2010d; Kinsella and Velkoff 2001.

Sex Differences in Retirement

People often associate retirement with men, but as more women enter the labor force, retirement is relevant for them as well. Today, with almost half of the workforce comprised of women, and with the majority of workers married to other workers, couples are forging new retirement paths. Couples face not only two retirements, but they must also coordinate their retirements and address whether to take up other paid work after they retire.

Researchers at Cornell University conducted a five-year study of retirement with 762 men and women between the ages of 50 and 72 who were selected from six large employers in New York. They found that men in the sample began to plan for retirement earlier than did the women (ages 49 and 54, respectively), although they retired at similar ages (Han and Moen 1999). Newly retired men and women both reported more conflict in their relationship, compared to couples who had not retired or those who had already retired. Conflicts arise in these families more often when one spouse, particularly the wife, is still employed while the other spouse begins to retire. This escalated conflict may be due to their difference in role status and power, with men in this cohort being happier when their wives conform to more traditional gender norms (Moen et al. 2001; Szinovacz and Harpster 1993).

Given the differences in men and women's employment experiences over the life course in terms of continuity, occupations, pay, and expectations, it is possible that they would have different experiences associated with retirement as well. Overall, men are more satisfied with retirement than are women; 71 percent of

WHAT DO YOU THINK?

Do you think there is any correlation between the status of the elderly in society and their labor force participation rates? Why or why not?

men and 56 percent of women report that they are better off in their retirement than the five years just before retirement (Quick and Moen 1998). Although good health and a comfortable postretirement income are some of the most important predictors of happiness during retirement, there are some interesting differences among men and women as well. For example, part-time employment is linked to retirement satisfaction among men, but this is not the case among women. Researchers speculate that women are more likely to be busy with volunteer work or other family activities and feel less inclined to seek further employment for pay. Women who had more year-long employment gaps during their working years are more likely to be satisfied in retirement, perhaps because retirement is a less dramatic transition for them.

Health

Most elderly people report their health as good or excellent. Only about a quarter of elders assess their health as fair or poor. Elderly men and women report only a small difference in health, and the gap has narrowed in recent years (Cummings and Jackson 2008). However, older Blacks are more likely to describe their health as only fair or poor than are Whites or Asian Americans (National Center for Health Statistics 2010; Yao and Robert 2008).

Declining Health Status

There is no denying, however, that as we age our health declines in a number of ways. We are more likely to lose some of our vision and hearing; to develop chronic conditions such as arthritis, heart disease, or diabetes; and to suffer severe memory impairment (National Center for Health Statistics 2010). We are increasingly likely to need someone to help us with many things that we used to do for ourselves: cooking, cleaning, home repairs, and perhaps even personal care. The health status of older adults is a result of a complex set of factors, including individual factors, such as diet, exercise, and heredity, and structural factors, such as socioeconomic status, racism, and access to health care.

Researchers have measured the degree of physical impairment by using a common set of **activities of daily living (ADLs)**, such as bathing, dressing, eating, getting into and out of bed, walking indoors, and using the toilet. **Instrumental activities of daily living (IADLs)** include meal preparation, shopping, managing money, and taking medication. By using a common set of measures, gerontologists can track elders' degree of impairment and can make some comparisons across different samples. Millions of elderly persons cannot perform these tasks. As people age, they likely become more disabled (Wolff and Kasper 2006). Gerontologists estimate that the number of older persons needing significant and long-term care will increase over the next 50 years as the oldest-old cohort expands: 14 million elders may need significant care by 2020 and 24 million by 2060.

Severe Memory Loss

Perhaps one of the most difficult disabilities facing elders, and those who care for them, is severe memory loss, known as **dementia**. Dementia includes a decline in memory and in at least one of the following cognitive abilities, a decline severe enough to interfere with daily life (Alzheimer's Association 2010):

- Ability to generate coherent speech and understand spoken or written language;
- Ability to recognize or identify objects, assuming intact sensory function;
- Ability to execute motor activities, assuming intact motor abilities, sensory function and comprehension of the required task; and
- Ability to think abstractly, make sound judgments and plan and carry out complex tasks.

Alzheimer's disease is by far the most common form of dementia, affecting about 5.3 million persons, and is the seventh leading cause of death for people of all ages, and the fifth leading cause of death among persons aged 65 and over (Alzheimer's Association 2010). The disease starts subtly—a person may have difficulty remembering names or recent events. It progresses over the course of years, and later symptoms include impaired judgment; disorientation; confusion; behavior changes; lack of recognition of loved ones; and eventually the inability to walk, speak, and even swallow. Alzheimer's is ultimately fatal. Given the changing demographics of our country, and the growing size of the oldest-old cohort, we will see a large increase in people with Alzheimer's—10 million baby boomers are expected to eventually develop it.

Unfortunately, no treatment is yet available to fully stop the deterioration of brain cells in Alzheimer's disease. The U.S. Food and Drug Administration has approved five drugs that temporarily slow the worsening of symptoms for about 6–12 months, on average, for about half the individuals who take them. Given that the direct and indirect costs of Alzheimer's and other dementias are estimated at $148 billion each year, not to mention the cost in terms of families' heartache and despair, it is no wonder researchers are vigorously pursuing an agenda of prevention, treatment, and cure (Alzheimer's Association 2010).

Long-Term Care

It is clear that many elders need **long-term care**, which is care for their chronic physical or mental conditions that will likely never go away. How do we care for the growing numbers of elderly who can no longer care for themselves?

Formal Care Some elderly persons in the United States rely on **formal care** provided by social service agencies on a paid or volunteer basis. This could include a variety of types of care: paid visiting nurses, meals or housecleaning programs, a paid personal attendant, assisted living, or nursing home care.

Assisted-living facilities are a booming business, with about 33,000 operating in 2009 (Helpguide.org 2010). They vary in scope: some assisted-living facilities are little more than apartments for seniors with optional food, housekeeping, and entertainment services, and others provide more skilled nursing care. The price varies by what is included, but averages somewhere around $30,000–$40,000 per year (Assisted Senior Living 2009; MetLife Mature Market Institute 2009).

Nursing homes provide the most intensive level of care, at an average cost of almost $75,000 per year (Assisted Senior Living 2009; MetLife Mature Market Institute 2009). They are available for those who cannot be cared for at home and have likely moved beyond what most assisted living centers can provide.

Informal Care In contrast to formal care, most elders in the United States rely primarily on **informal care**, which is unpaid care by someone close to the care recipient, such as

WHAT DO YOU THINK?

How would you react if you realized at around age 60 that you were becoming forgetful and were losing your memory? How would you cope with this realization?

As the number of elderly continues to spiral upward, a pressing public policy question is who will care for them. A spouse is generally the first person in line to provide care, and if he or she is unavailable, an adult daughter or daughter-in-law usually helps. However, as more women are employed, it is difficult for them to provide the long-term care that many elders need.

How Iraq Happened • Gadget Gift Guide
U.S. NEWS & WORLD REPORT
Taking Care of Mom & Dad
A BOOMER'S GUIDE
• How to plan ahead
• New payment strategies
Plus: Getting the most from Medicare
www.usnews.com

a spouse, daughter, or son (National Alliance for Caregiving and AARP 2009). They provide a wide variety of hands-on care.

A spouse is usually the first person in line to provide care if she or he is able, usually the wife, given males' shorter life expectancy. When a spouse is unavailable or is unable to provide this level of care, adult children, usually daughters, step in. Some of these adult daughters also have their own children under age 18 to care for, and are, therefore, referred to as the **sandwich generation**.

Caregiving patterns differ across racial and ethnic lines. Studies overall report that minorities tend to provide more care and hold stronger beliefs about filial obligation (Pinquart and Sorenson 2005). Minority caregivers were more likely than their White counterparts to be adult children (rather than spouses), and they tended to be younger.

A study of 341 lesbian, gay, bisexual, or transgender adults aged 50 and over living in New York reported that 46 percent of the respondents were providing or had provided caregiving assistance to a family member, partner, or close friend within the past five years (Cantor et al. 2004). Nearly half of these provided care for a member of their family of origin, usually a parent, and two-thirds reported that they were the sole or primary caregiver. One-third believed that more was expected of them than from other family members; it was assumed that they had fewer obligations or other personal responsibilities because they were unmarried. The others who reported having provided care within the past five years were caring for a partner who was ill, disabled, or suffering from an age-related disability (e.g., Alzheimer's disease) or HIV/AIDS.

There are also cross-cultural differences in caregiving. One study, which used data from 12,166 adult children from 2,527 Taiwanese families, found that sons generally carry the major responsibility for taking care of their older parents (Lin et al. 2003). Daughters fulfill the son's roles primarily when a son is not available, reflecting the patriarchal customs of Taiwanese society in which sons bear the primary responsibility for the continuation of the family line.

The Strain of Caregiving   Caring for elderly parents or a spouse can be a labor of love, but it is also time-intensive, potentially expensive, and often stressful, as shown in Table 12.4 (National Alliance for Caregiving and AARP 2009; National Family Caregivers Association 2008). Most caregivers provide assistance seven days a week, with little help from formal services. A recent national survey of more than 1,200 caregivers found that more than a third of caregivers provided all the help to the person they cared for during the past 12 months and received no help from anyone else. Among caregivers who did receive some assistance, one-third said they provided most of the unpaid care (National Alliance for Caregiving and AARP 2009). Because most female caregivers are employed, they have to make sacrifices at work to accommodate caregiving, including going in late or leaving early, working fewer hours, taking a leave of absence, turning down a promotion, choosing early retirement, or giving up work completely—sacrifices that cost an average of $240,000 in lost wages over a lifetime (Houser 2007; National Alliance for Caregiving and AARP 2009). Caregivers often spend their own money to provide medicines, groceries, or other supplies to the person they are caring for. Over one-third of Blacks and one-quarter of Whites reported in a national survey that they spend between $101 and $500 of their own money every month to provide care. Not surprisingly, Blacks are more likely than Whites to say that caregiving creates a financial hardship for them (National Alliance for Caregiving and AARP 2009).

As society continues to age, the United States could benefit from an explicit plan for caring for frail elders. If caregiving is indeed a personal responsibility to be provided by family members, then families can be strengthened by a variety of financial and policy benefits, such as tax credits, paid family leave, free or low-cost senior day care, or respite care. Moreover, although the Family Medical Leave Act allows for 12 weeks of unpaid leave from

TABLE 12.4 Strain and Stress of Caregiving

Three-quarters of caregivers say that caregiving is somewhat or very stressful, and half say that it has caused some or a great deal of financial hardship.

Caregiver's Health	
Excellent or very good	57%
Average	26%
Fair or poor	17%
Impact of Caregiving on Caregiver's Health	
Made it better	8%
No impact	74%
Made it worse	17%
Emotional Stress for Caregiver	
Very stressful	31%
Somewhat stressful	44%
Not at all stressful	25%
Financial Hardship for Caregiver	
Great deal	15%
Some hardship	34%
No hardship	51%

Source: National Alliance for Caregiving and AARP 2009.

employment to allow a person to care for a sick or disabled relative (in qualifying workplaces), same-sex partners do not have these same privileges.

Social Policy and Family Resilience

Health care is a rapidly growing segment of the U.S. economy, and the elderly use a significant portion of health care services. How do they pay for their health care costs? Although some elders have private insurance, most elders draw primarily or exclusively upon a federal program known as Medicare.

Example: Medicare

Created in 1965, **Medicare** is a federal health insurance program for people age 65 and older (and younger people receiving Social Security Disability Insurance payments or suffering from a few specified conditions).

Medicare has kept millions of elderly from impoverishing themselves to pay for their health care costs by making health insurance far more affordable and available to them. Because it is a universal rather than means-tested program, it has no stigma attached to it. Virtually all elderly qualify, so administrative costs are significantly lower than other programs that have stringent income requirements.

Medicare, however, is not without its critics. First of all, Medicare does not provide elders with "free" health care. Given high deductibles, copayments, and payments for things not covered under Medicare, elderly persons can spend thousands of their own dollars each year on medical care. Consequently, almost 90 percent of elders have some form of additional insurance, a "medigap" policy, which they often pay for themselves. Only the poorest elderly, about 15 percent, may qualify for **Medicaid**, the federal–state health care program that is designed to serve poor persons, regardless of age, and which also covers long-term care for the poor (Kaiser Family Foundation 2009).

Second, health care providers who see patients with Medicare are reimbursed by the government at a lower rate than by private insurance companies. Therefore, many providers refuse to accept Medicare patients. They are not required by law to accept Medicare, and they complain that reimbursement is too low and cumbersome. Consequently, of those Medicare patients who reported looking for a new primary care physician, 28 percent reported a problem finding one who would see them (MedPAC 2009).

Third, the changing U.S. demographic structure has some potentially distressing repercussions for the Medicare program (Kaiser Family Foundation 2009). Medicare is primarily funded through Social Security taxes; working people pay taxes today for programs used by the elderly today. In the future, as the U.S. population ages, there will be fewer working adults paying taxes relative to the number of elderly persons needing Medicare services. There were about 5 workers for each beneficiary in 1960, and 3 in 2000, but there will be only 1.9 by 2040 (De Lew et al. 1992). Couple this with rising health care costs, and the country will be facing a serious challenge. Without changes, Medicare will consume 6.4 percent of our Gross Domestic Product in 2030, up from 3.5 percent today (Federal Hospital Insurance and Federal Supplementary Medical Insurance Trust 2009). To deal with this problem, Congress could modify the program in several ways, such as increasing the amount that elders pay out of their own pockets by raising deductibles and copayments, covering fewer services, or even raising the age at which people are eligible for Medicare services, as has been done with Social Security. The goal is to keep Medicare solvent well into the future because our society recognizes that the health of seniors is a social concern, not merely an individual problem.

However, this goal raises interesting concerns about other age groups. Why do elders have a health care program on their behalf and children do not? This question is legitimate and has caused some tension among advocates of different generations. Without detracting from the serious needs many elders face and the lives that Medicare has saved or improved, extending coverage to one vulnerable age group while withholding coverage from another is a uniquely American inconsistency found in no other developed nation. Instead, all developed nations (and many developing ones) have some sort of national health insurance program designed for all citizens, regardless of age. Health care reform passed in 2010 will offer some measures to close the gap, but the fact that such an inconsistency could materialize in the first place illustrates the lack of coherent family policy in the United States.

Conclusion

The population around the world is aging rapidly, with immense implications for families and other social institutions. A comparative perspective is important for understanding these implications because the most rapid growth in the aging population is occurring in developing nations, which are often poor, and, therefore, less equipped to handle the strain on economic and health care resources that this growth will bring. To complicate these issues further, the most striking increase around the world is among those aged 80 and over. The pronounced effects of these demographic changes will be felt throughout the global economy. In the United States, the elderly have achieved great success in actively promoting the concerns of an aging population. Given their size, their concerns become the concerns of everyone. This chapter examined ways of promoting social and economic well-being; supporting intimate relationships; fostering positive bonds with adult children and grandchildren; assessing concerns around retirement, widowhood, and caregiving; and looking at ways to improve health, access to health care, and health policy.

Key Terms

Activities of daily living (ADL): A common set of measures that gerontologists use to track elders' degree of impairment, such as bathing, dressing, eating, getting into and out of bed, walking indoors, and using the toilet. (p. 372)

Baby-boom generation: Persons born after World War II through the early to mid-1960s. (p. 352)

Centenarians: Persons who are age 100 and older. (p. 355)

Dementia: Severe memory loss, the most common form of which is Alzheimer's Disease. (p. 372)

Demographic transition: The process in which a society moves from a situation of high fertility rates and low life expectancy, to one of low fertility rates and high life expectancy. (p. 352)

Elderly: Persons who are age 65 and over. (p. 347)

Formal care: Care for the elderly that is provided by social service agencies on a paid or volunteer basis. (p. 373)

Gerontology: An interdisciplinary science of aging that draws upon biology, medicine, and the social sciences, including sociology, psychology, and family studies. (p. 356)

Informal care: Care for the elderly that is unpaid, usually done by someone close to the elder. (p. 373)

Instrumental activities of daily living (IADL): Includes activities such as preparing meals, shopping, managing money, using the telephone, doing housework, and taking medications. (p. 372)

Kinkeeper: The person who has the primary responsibility for maintaining family relationships. (p. 367)

Life expectancy: How long a person can expect to live, usually calculated from birth. (p. 352)

Long-term care: Assistance for chronic physical or mental conditions that are long-term, and in the case of the elderly, may never go away. (p. 373)

Medicaid: A federal/state health care program designed to serve poor persons, regardless of age, and also covering long-term care for the poor. (p. 376)

Medicare: A federal health insurance program primarily for people age 65 and older. (p. 375)

Old Age, Survivor, and Disability Insurance (OASDI): A cash pension program for seniors that is known as "Social Security." (p. 358)

Oldest-old cohort: Usually defined as those persons aged 80 and over. (p. 347)

Sandwich generation: Adult children, usually daughters, who are caring for both their parents and their own children. (p. 374)

Triple jeopardy: People who face multiple disadvantages in society (e.g., old, female, and minority). (p. 358)

Resources on the Internet

AARP

www.aarp.org

Formerly known as the American Association of Retired Persons, this organization now represents over 34 million members aged 50 and over, whether they have retired or not. The goal is to increase the quality of life for older Americans, and AARP does this through advocacy, education, volunteer, and social opportunities.

Association for Gerontology in Higher Education (AGHE)

www.aghe.org

This national organization is devoted primarily to gerontological education. The purpose of AGHE is to foster the commitment of higher education to the field of aging through education, research, and public service. The website contains information about careers in gerontology.

Foster Grandparent Program

www.seniorcorps.gov/about/programs/fg.asp

The Foster Grandparent Program offers seniors age 60 and older opportunities to serve as mentors, tutors, and loving caregivers for children and youth with special needs. They serve in community organizations such as schools, hospitals, Head Start, and youth centers.

Gerontological Society of America

www.geron.org

The Gerontological Society of America (GSA) is a nonprofit professional organization with more than 5,000 members in the field of aging. GSA provides researchers, educators, practitioners, and policy makers with opportunities to understand, advance, integrate, and use basic and applied research on aging to improve the quality of life as one ages.

National Institute on Aging

www.nia.nih.gov

This government agency provides extensive data on its website on the aging population in the United States. There are also many links to other relevant sites.

CHAPTER 13

Violence and Abuse

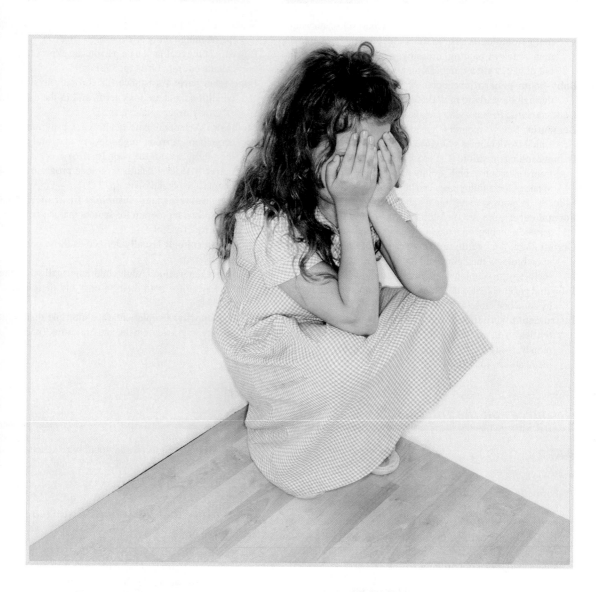

CHAPTER OUTLINE

Gender-Based Violence: An International Human Rights Issue   381

■ **OUR** *Global Community:* Maya and Parvati: The End of a Dream   *383*

Intimate Partner Violence   384

■ **FAMILIES** *as Lived Experience:* "My Dating Violence Story"   *391*

■ **SOCIAL** *Policies for Families:* History of the Shelter Movement   *395*

Child Abuse   396

Elder Abuse   400

Explanations for Violence and Abuse Among Intimates   401

Social Policy and Family Resilience   406

   Conclusion   408

   Key Terms   408

   Resources on the Internet   409

CHAPTER PREVIEW

Many family problems are really *social problems*. Violence is one of these. It is rooted in complex and longstanding traditions promoting violence and male privilege. In this chapter, you will learn:

- Gender-based violence as a national human rights issue

- How violence is defined and measured

- About dating violence, sexual aggression, and rape

- Features of spouse/partner abuse, including its frequency, the factors associated with abuse, and how victims cope

- The types of child abuse, factors that contribute to child abuse, and the consequences of abuse

- Who are the perpetrators and the victims of elder abuse

- Theoretical explanations for violence and abuse among intimates

- Ways in which legal and criminal justice systems are speaking out in favor of zero tolerance

Perhaps the most controversial form of family violence is spanking. Does it even qualify as violence? Some say no, others say it depends, and still others say yes, most definitely. Family violence research pioneer Murray Straus (Straus 1979, 1990, 2003; Straus and Donnelly 2001; Straus et al. 1980) sees it as an insidious form of violence, one that most of us ignore, but one that causes great harm for the individual hit and the society at large that condones this type of violence. His more recent research has unearthed a startling new discovery: children who are spanked have lower intelligence quotients (IQs) than those who are not. Moreover, the difference is large enough to lower national IQ scores in countries where corporal punishment of children is routine.

This landmark study first examined the relationship between spanking and IQ in the United States, and then turned to see what the relationship looks like on an international basis. First, Dr. Straus and his colleague, Dr. Mallie Paschall, studied a nationally representative sample of 806 children in the United States aged 2–4 years, and a second representative sample of 704 children aged 5–9 years. Both groups were tested once, and then retested four years later, in a longitudinal research design. They found that the IQs of children aged 2–4 who were not spanked were five points higher four years later than the IQs of those children who were spanked. Likewise, the IQs of children aged 5–9 who were not spanked were nearly three points higher four years later than other children their age who were spanked. They also found that the more a child was spanked, the more his or her IQ was affected. "How often parents spanked made a difference. The more spanking, the slower is the development of the child's mental ability. But even small amounts of spanking made a difference," Dr. Straus said.

Next, the researchers examined secondary data obtained from the International Dating Violence Study, which involved 17,404 college students at 68 universities in 32 countries. The study included two items about spanking, and respondents could "strongly disagree," "disagree," "agree," or "strongly agree" with each one:

- I was spanked or hit a lot by my parents before age 12
- When I was a teenager, I was hit a lot by my mother or father

The researchers used the percentage of students who "agreed" or "strongly agreed" to estimate the corporal punishment rate in each country. They then compared those rates to the national average IQ, while controlling for many important variables such as mother's education level or socioeconomic status. This statistical technique allows researchers to make sure that any differences are likely to be due to IQ rather than the fact that some countries are poorer than others, or that mothers in some countries may have lower educational levels than others.

The analysis showed that the countries with higher corporal punishment rates also had students with lower average IQs. The strongest association between spanking and IQ was found among those students whose parents continued to spank them into their teenage years. Why is this? Straus and Paschall speculate that, first, corporal punishment is extremely stressful, even exhibiting similarities to posttraumatic stress symptoms, and these symptoms are associated with lower IQ. Second, a higher national level of economic development underlies both fewer parents using corporal punishment and a higher national IQ.

The researchers are glad to see a movement away from corporal punishment throughout the world, and hope that it may signal future gains in IQ scores. Twenty-four countries have banned corporal punishment, and attitudes are changing even in nations that have not implemented the ban.

However, some researchers question the causal link that Straus and Paschall suggest. For example, perhaps the relationship is spurious, meaning that there is another issue going on that may affect both corporal punishment and IQ. For example, average education levels are rising, and better-educated parents use less corporal punishment and are more likely to engage in activities to increase children's IQ, such as reading to them regularly. At this point, the answers are not all in. (Straus and Paschall 2009)

What do former talk show host Oprah Winfrey, singer Rihanna, and actress Pamela Anderson have in common? In addition to being celebrities, they all have had the frightening experience of being abused within their families or close relationships. Rihanna and Pamela Anderson were victims of violence by their intimate partners. Oprah Winfrey revealed that several members of her extended family sexually abused her as a child. We find violence in families to be particularly abhorrent because we like to idealize families as safe havens, but they often are not.

This chapter will explore the issue of family violence and abuse, often called **violence among intimates**, describing how these are related to the social context in which a person lives. Although violence among intimates is experienced on a personal level, it is a *social problem* interwoven with cultural values, norms, social institutions, and gendered expectations. Why do I call it a social problem? First, it affects large numbers of people. Second, violence isn't completely random—we can detect particular patterns and risk factors among both victims and perpetrators. Third, the causes, consequences, and solutions must address macro-level factors, such as social, cultural, and economic environments.

I begin this chapter with an international perspective on violence and abuse. We then turn to the United States and examine intimate partner violence, including how Americans define and measure violence among intimates. We will then address child abuse and the abuse of the elderly. Many so-called "personal problems"—whether they be violence, poverty, substance abuse, unemployment, or poor health—are really problems deeply rooted in the broader social structure. Let's begin by focusing on violence in a broad context—gender-based violence.

Gender-Based Violence: An International Human Rights Issue

Violence is a widespread problem around the world, and women and girls are overwhelmingly its victims. Because violence against women and girls is so common, it is often referred to as **gender-based violence**, defined by the U.N. General Assembly as (Senanayake 1999):

> Any act of gender violence that results in or is likely to result in physical, sexual or psychological harm and suffering to women, including threats of such acts, coercion, or arbitrary deprivations of liberty, whether occurring in public or private life.

This would include, among other things:

- Intimate partner violence
- Sexual abuse
- Forced prostitution
- Female genital mutilation
- Rape
- Honor killings
- Selective malnourishing of female children

Gender-based violence is an epidemic, and occurs in both developed and developing nations (Kristof and WuDunn 2009; United Nations Population Fund 2007). It causes more death and disability in women between the ages of 15 and 44 years than cancer, malaria, traffic accidents, and war *combined* (Senanayake 1999). Human Rights Watch and the United Nations, both international organizations dedicated to protecting the human rights of people around the world, report that many countries have horrendous records on addressing violence against women and girls. For example, in Uganda, many women are infected with HIV and will eventually die because the government has failed in any meaningful way to condemn, criminalize, or prosecute violence against women in the home. In Pakistan, officials at all levels of the criminal justice system do not believe domestic violence is a matter for criminal courts. Moreover, women who have been sexually assaulted and attempt to file charges face police harassment and disbelief and may themselves face arrest and prosecution for engaging in extramarital sex. In South Africa, the police and courts treat complaints by battered women as less serious than other assault complaints, and there are persistent problems with the provision of medical expertise to courts when women have been abused. In Jordan, "honor killings" occur when families deem women's behavior improper, and despite some legislative reforms, the perpetrators receive lenient sentences from the courts. In Russia and Uzbekistan, police scoff at reports of domestic violence and harass women who report such violence to stop them from filing complaints (Human Rights Watch 2001, 2010a).

Abuse of women and girls is often tolerated by the legal system. Discriminatory attitudes of law enforcement officials, prosecutors, and judges, who often consider domestic violence a private matter beyond the reach of the law, reinforce the batterer's attempts to demean and control his victim. Women's low social status and a long-established pattern of active suppression of women's rights by successive governments have contributed to the escalation in violence. Government often fails to acknowledge the scale and severity of the problem, much less take action to end the violence against women. As a result of such dismissive official attitudes, crimes of violence against women continue to be perpetrated with virtual impunity.

Trafficking of Women and Girls

> Rania, a poor Moroccan young woman wanted a better life. She signed a contract that she couldn't read and set off to work as a cleaner in Cyprus. But when she arrived, a man told her that she was going to work in a cabaret, drink with the customers, and have sex with them when they wanted it. She refused, and begged to be sent home, but she was told that she must repay her travel expenses. Rania was raped. However, she feared that if she found a way to return home, her strict Muslim brother would kill her for "having sex before marriage" and damaging her family's reputation. When she finally was able to flee, social workers took her to a government shelter for victims of sexual exploitation. While police investigated her case, she stayed in Cyprus and finally got her job as a cleaner (U.S. Department of State 2009).

Trafficking in persons (the illegal and highly profitable business of recruitment, transport, or sale of human beings into all forms of forced labor and servitude) is a tragic human rights issue affecting over 12 million people throughout the world (U.S. Department of State 2010b). Some are forced into manual, military, or domestic labor (Bales and Soodalter 2009; Beah 2007), but many become sexual slaves (Kristof and WuDunn 2009). The U.S. State Department estimates that 1.4 million persons, mostly women and girls, are trafficked across international borders annually for use as involuntary sex workers (U.S. Department of State 2010b). Many are coerced, kidnapped, sold, deceived, or otherwise trafficked into sexual encounters, as illustrated in the story of Maya and Parvati in the box on pages 383–384, "Our Global Community: Maya and Parvati: The End of a Dream." Increasingly around the world, girls are sought out in the mistaken belief that they are less likely to be HIV-positive. In reality, they are most vulnerable to HIV infections because their bodies are physically unready for sex and may tear more easily.

Sexual trafficking results from a broad range of factors, including poverty, inequality, and economic crises. Globalization has triggered an influx of money and goods, further aggravating disparities between rich and poor, and promoting new levels of consumerism. Coupled with patriarchal norms in which women and girls are disvalued, some families sell their

O U R

Global Community

Maya and Parvati: The End of a Dream

The sale of women and girls for sexual purposes—trafficking—is, unfortunately, big business in many parts of the world. This moving account describes what happened to two teenage girls leaving Nepal for what they hoped would be a better life in India.

For millions of people in India, Bombay is a city of dreams. Among these people were Maya and Parvati, for whom the city seemed a Promised Land of prosperity, a heavenly escape from their hard work at home. But these dreams were not to be.

Maya and Parvati were two teenage mountain girls from a small village about 105 kilometers northwest of the capital, Kathmandu. Life was intolerable in their mountainous village where utter poverty and lack of opportunity have made hardship, starvation, and scarcity the villager's daily way of life. The girls wanted to escape. Finally, one spring day, the two girls left their village along with a group of other young girls and two men. Their journey brought them to Boudhanath, one of the largest market centers for hand-made woolen carpets. Maya and Parvati were employed by one of these factories, and joined the huge number of carpet weavers, most of whom had come from the mountain regions to start a new life.

After about six months, an old woman originally from their home village but who now lived in Bombay offered to take them there. For the girls, it was as if their dreams had come true—Bombay was to them the ultimate city of joy. The silk sarees and golden ornaments of the women returning from Bombay, and most of all their prestige, had made a deep impression on the minds of these deprived girls.

So they eagerly agreed to go with the woman on the trip. During the trip, they were sold to an infamous brothel in Sonagachhi, Calcutta. Their trafficker disappeared with the Rs. 25,000 that she made from the sale. Maya and Parvati were not taken to Bombay, but were imprisoned, beaten, raped, and tortured. They were forced to become sex slaves in one

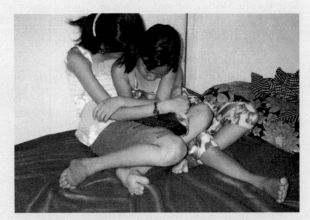

About 1.4 million people are trafficked across borders to be used as sex slaves. They are beaten, tortured, raped, or killed by brothel owners if they fail to comply.

of the largest red-light areas in the world, where dozens of young girls are brought every day to start a life of hell. The majority of the 40,000-plus prostitutes in Sonagachhi are from Nepal.

After two cruel years, a seemingly magical change happened in the lives of Maya and Parvati. Two of their regular customers from Bengal rescued and married them in Bow Bazar, Calcutta. Unfortunately, this was not the end of their suffering; their husbands began bringing "customers" home, filling their own pockets by selling the flesh of their wives.

One day, Maya's husband took her to Bombay. This trip to Bombay meant big changes in her life; it separated her from her best friend, Parvati, and gave her another terrible shock: Maya's husband sold her in Kamathipura, otherwise known as Falkland Road of Bombay, another large red-light area in Asia, harboring around 200,000 prostitutes. It is believed that the Kamathipura red-light area is the oldest prostitution ring, and which was started by the British Army with the abduction of women from Germany at the time of the East India Company rule. Maya learned later that she had been sold for Rs. 15,000 and her

(continued)

(continued)

husband disappeared, just like the old village woman in Sonagachhi, Calcutta. Although she was deeply shocked by her abandonment, Maya was not new to the trade now. Maya met several other Nepali women in the brothel where she lived, and learned that all of them had a more or less similar story to tell.

She spent about 28 months in a dark room of this Kamathipura brothel receiving, on the average, four or five customers daily. Maya was forced to entertain all types of customers, from school boys and sick old men to men with venereal diseases and sexual perverts. She had to accept the mistreatment by the customers and the cruelty of the brothel owner as a part of her everyday life. For her services, she received nothing but two meals a day, and occasionally, small tips given to her by kind customers. She stayed inside her dark room waiting for customers so that her Gharwali (brothel owner) would make money; she was never allowed to go out. Bombay,

once her land of dreams, was now nothing more than the dark room and filth of the brothel area.

She became infected with several sexually transmitted diseases, and was admitted to a hospital where she was treated for more than three months. A sympathetic doctor in the hospital released her from the brothel. Three years after leaving her village, Maya returned, where many of her relatives and neighbors sympathized with her and her tragic situation. She died soon after. As for Parvati, who knows what happened to her.

Source: ABC/Nepal 2003.

CRITICAL THINKING QUESTIONS

1. Why didn't Maya and Parvati simply leave the brothel in Calcutta if they were unhappy there? What would you have done differently, if anything?
2. What can be done to eliminate human trafficking?

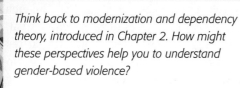

WHAT DO YOU THINK?

Think back to modernization and dependency theory, introduced in Chapter 2. How might these perspectives help you to understand gender-based violence?

daughters to traffickers or put them in vulnerable positions as domestic workers in far-off urban locations. Husbands, who have virtually complete control over their wives, may sell or "rent" them out for money.

Women and children who are trafficked into prostitution face many dangers (Farr 2005; Territo and Kirkham 2010; U.S. Department of State 2009). In addition to injuries and disease associated with multiple sexual encounters, they become dangerously attached to pimps and brothel operators and become financially indebted to them. Moreover, they may become addicted to drugs that have been given to subdue them. If women and children do manage to escape and return to their families, they may be rejected because of the stigma associated with prostitution.

Intimate Partner Violence

Intimate partner violence refers to violence between those who are emotionally or sexually intimate, such as spouses, partners, or those who are dating. The violence can encompass physical, economic, sexual, or psychological abuse, and many abusive situations involve more than one type.

How We Define and Measure Intimate Partner Violence

The "dark side" of families, including spouse and partner abuse, was not widely discussed among family scientists or researched systematically until the 1970s. What we did know about abuse before then was obtained from small, nonrepresentative samples in isolated case files of social workers, psychologists, or the police. These data had the potential to be very biased because only certain types of abuse, and certain types of abusers, come to the attention of professionals.

However, since the 1970s, with the help of the women's movement and a spotlight on women's issues, family and social scientists have been trying to piece together a more accurate depiction of spouse and partner. Researchers have been trying, with some success, to amass large and representative samples to understand how often spouse and partner violence occurs, who is likely to be a victim, and its causes and consequences.

Sociologist Murray Straus and his colleagues conducted some of the earliest nationwide studies of family violence in the United States beginning in the mid-1970s. They conducted interviews with over 2,000 married or cohabiting adults with children between the ages of 3 and 17, and from these interviews they developed an important conflict assessment tool known as the **Conflict Tactics Scale (CTS)** that is commonly used today (Straus et al. 1980). In the CTS, people are asked about how they deal with disagreements in relationships. The following list is used in part or in its entirety in a variety of studies:

- *Nonaggressive Responses:*

  Discussed an issue calmly

  Got information to back up your side of things

  Brought in or tried to bring in someone to help settle things

  Cried

- *Psychologically Aggressive Responses:*

  Insulted him/her or swore at him/her

  Sulked or refused to talk about the issue

  Stomped out of the room or house

  Did or said something to spite him/her

- *Physically Aggressive Responses:*

  Threatened to hit him/her or throw something at him/her

  Threw or smashed or hit or kicked something

  Threw something at him/her

  Pushed, grabbed, or shoved him/her

  Slapped him/her

  Kicked, bit, or hit him/her with a fist

  Hit or tried to hit him/her with something

  Beat him/her up

  Choked him/her

  Threatened him/her with a knife

  Used a knife

Is There a Twist?   Who do you think is more likely to be a victim of violence, males or females? Some studies using the CTS have found that *men* are more likely to be victims of physical aggression than are women. This twist may seem surprising. Is it true that men are more likely to be victims?

Not really. These counterintuitive findings have been questioned on several grounds (Fulfer et al. 2007; Kishor 2005). For one thing, men are less likely than women to remember their own acts of violence, and they may not perceive their acts as abusive. A second problem is that CTS respondents are asked to tell the researcher how they responded to a situation of conflict or disagreement. Yet, violence and abuse can take place without a preceding disagreement, and therefore the CTS may again underreport some violence by men. A third problem is that women are more likely to experience the most extreme forms of violence, some of which the CTS doesn't list, including severe beatings and even murder. Finally, the CTS does not include acts of sexual violence or aggression, which are far more likely to be perpetrated by men.

Consequently, more recent studies show that women are more likely to be victims of intimate partner violence than are men. However, this does *not* mean that intimate partner violence against men is rare or inconsequential. Almost one-quarter of intimate partner homicides are committed against men, nearly 350 a year (U.S. Department of Justice, Bureau of Justice Statistics 2007).

Typology of Violence

Relationship violence can take many forms. Family researcher Michael Johnson draws attention to the importance of making critical distinctions among types of violence, motives of perpetrators, the status of both partners, and the cultural context in which violence occurs. He has identified four patterns of violence (Johnson 2000, 2008, 2009):

- **Common couple violence (CCV)** (or situational couple violence) arises out of a specific argument in which at least one partner lashes out physically. It is less likely to escalate or involve severe injury; yet, it is this type of violence that is usually captured in research studies.
- **Intimate terrorism (IT)** is motivated by a desire to control the other partner. It is more likely than CCV to escalate over time and to cause serious injury, although some cases of IT involve relatively little injury. The primary feature of this type of abuse is the general desire for control.
- **Violent resistance (VR)** is the nonlegal term associated with self-defense. Research on VR is scarce, and it is conducted almost entirely by women. Engaging in violent resistance may be an indicator that a person will soon leave the abusive partner.
- **Mutual violent control (MVC)** refers to a pattern of behavior in which both partners are controlling and violent; they are battling for control. Again, this is an understudied phenomenon.

Johnson suggests that if we want to understand the true nature of domestic violence, we must distinguish between these different types. For example, victims of intimate terrorism are more likely to be injured, to experience posttraumatic stress syndrome, to use painkillers, and to miss work than are other types (Johnson and Leone 2005). Moreover, common couple/situational violence dominates the general surveys, whereas intimate terrorism and violent resistance dominate agency caseloads, which may lead to different conclusions (Johnson 2008).

Stalking and Cyberstalking

Stalking is receiving greater attention since California passed the first anti-stalking law in 1990. **Stalking** consists of obsessive contact or tracking of another person—attention that is unwanted and causes a reasonable person to be fearful. It touches the lives of 3.4 million adults annually (Baum et al. 2009). It is a combination of many unwanted acts that, by themselves, are not abusive—such as sending flowers or gifts, calling on the telephone, or sending an e-mail—but when taken together, may constitute a form of mental abuse. Stalking exists on a continuum. It may be so subtle that the victim may not even be aware it is happening—it's just "business as usual," or, in contrast, the perpetrator may purposefully try to instill terror in the victim (Logan and Walker 2009).

Given the importance of computers, the Internet, and e-mail in our lives, some stalkers harass or threaten their victims electronically, a phenomenon known as **cyberstalking**. Repeated unwanted attention could come in the form of e-mail, faxes, bulletin boards, texts, chat rooms, or other types of media (Stalking Resource Center 2009). One factor that distinguishes cyberstalking from other forms of stalking is ease; one can repeatedly threaten and harass a person by simply clicking a button. In fact, programs can be set up that send messages at random times when the sender is not even physically present at the computer, or private information or rumors can be posted for others to see. Although the contact may be indirect, it can be threatening nonetheless.

Frequency of Intimate Partner Violence

The results from the early surveys by Straus, Gelles, and Steinmetz (1980) show an alarming rate of spouse and partner abuse in the United States. These results have been confirmed in more recent studies. About 4.8 million women and 2.9 million men are victims of intimate partner violence, according to the Centers for Disease Control and Prevention (2009g). This conforms to the National Violence Against Women survey conducted by the U.S. Department of Justice—about 25 percent of women and 8 percent of men have been victims of intimate partner violence (Tjaden and Thoennes 2000, 2006). Among women who reported being victims of rape or physical assault, the perpetrator in 76 percent of the cases was an intimate partner (defined as current or former spouses, opposite and same-sex cohabiting partners, dates, boyfriends, and girlfriends) (National Institute of Justice and Centers for Disease Control and Prevention 1998).

Figure 13.1 reports gender differences in the types of physical assaults that women and men endure by intimate partners. The most common types of violence experienced by women are being pushed, grabbed, or shoved (18 percent) and being slapped or hit (16 percent). Nearly 1 percent of women have had a gun or knife used on them. Women were two to three times more likely than men to report that an intimate partner threw something at them, pushed, grabbed, or shoved them. However, in looking at the more dangerous assaults, women were 7–14 times more likely to report that they had been beaten up, choked, tied down, threatened with a gun, or had a gun used on them (National Institute of Justice and Centers for Disease Control and Prevention 1998).

Women are particularly vulnerable when pregnant (Campbell et al. 2007; Samandari and Martin 2010). It is estimated that between 4 and 8 percent of women experience domestic violence during their pregnancy (Gazamarian 2000; Saltzman et al. 2003). The effects of this violence can be devastating to the mother and her unborn child. Women face a variety of potential pregnancy complications, including anemia, infections, bleeding, and low weight gain. Pregnant women who suffer abuse are more likely to experience depression and attempt suicide. They are also more likely to use tobacco, alcohol, and illegal drugs during pregnancy, possibly harming the fetus (Datner et al. 2007).

Racial and Ethnic Differences   Black, Hispanic, and Native American women are more likely than Whites to experience violence (Few and Bell-Scott 2002; Few and Rosen 2005; Johnson and Ferraro 2000; West 2003). This may be due to socioeconomic constraints and their lack of resources, racism, cultural values, or immigration status. One study of 2,400 low-income Blacks, Whites, and Hispanic women found that 30 percent of low-income Blacks experienced spouse or partner violence, as did 24 percent of Hispanic women and 19 percent of Whites (Frias and Angel 2005). Importantly, they discovered that the difference across Hispanic groups was quite large, as shown in Table 13.1; 29 percent of Hispanics of Mexican descent had experienced moderate or severe violence, compared to only 21 percent of Puerto Ricans and 13 percent of Dominicans. Likewise, Hispanics who were born in the United States, and those who were proficient in English were all more likely to have experienced violence than their Hispanic counterparts born elsewhere. Although this is a sample

Figure 13.1 Percentage of Persons Physically Assaulted by an Intimate Partner in a Lifetime by Type of Assault and Sex of Victim

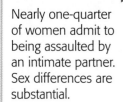

Nearly one-quarter of women admit to being assaulted by an intimate partner. Sex differences are substantial.

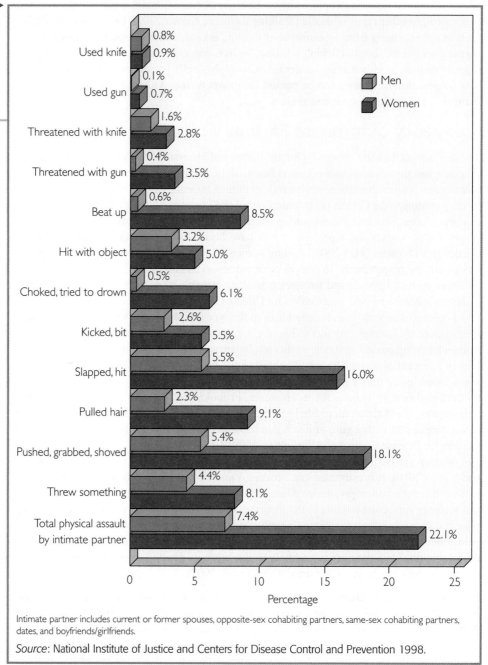

Intimate partner includes current or former spouses, opposite-sex cohabiting partners, same-sex cohabiting partners, dates, and boyfriends/girlfriends.

Source: National Institute of Justice and Centers for Disease Control and Prevention 1998.

of low-income groups only, these differences highlight the importance of distinguishing between different Hispanic groups and their experiences, rather than lumping Hispanics into one homogeneous group (Frias and Angel 2005).

Furthermore, minority women may be less likely to report the abuse because of their distrust of the criminal justice system born by their experiences with prejudice and discrimination. For example, Black women are more likely to turn to friends or family for help in an abusive

TABLE 13.1   Race and Ethnic Differences in Intimate Partner Violence Among a Low-Income Sample of Women

Intimate partner violence occurs across all income groups, although it may be highest among Blacks and Mexican Americans.

	MODERATE VIOLENCE N = 370	SEVERE VIOLENCE N = 223	NO VIOLENCE N = 1,703
Race or Ethnicity			
White	11%	8%	81%
Black	20%	10%	70%
Hispanic	14%	10%	76%
Mexican	17%	12%	71%
Puerto Rican	13%	8%	79%
Dominican	7%	6%	87%
Other	14%	8%	78%
Hispanic Characteristics			
Born in the U.S. mainland	17%	14%	69%
Less than 15 years old when migrated to U.S.	17%	8%	74%
More than 15 years old when migrated to U.S.	8%	4%	88%
U.S. Citizenship			
Yes	15%	12%	73%
No	11%	5%	84%
English Proficiency	10%	11%	9%

Source: Frias and Angel 2005.

situation, rather than rely on law enforcement or shelters for assistance (Few and Bell-Scott 2002). Others may be less likely to report their abuse because of their undocumented status.

Violence in Same-Sex Relationships

Until recently, we knew very little about intimate partner violence among gays and lesbians, probably for the same reason that we knew very little about their relationships in general—the focus of study tends to be on majority groups (e.g., heterosexuals) (Kaschak 2002; Ristock 2009). A book about intimate partner violence published as recently as 2001, *Couples in Conflict* (Booth et al. 2001), includes 17 chapters on recognizing and responding to domestic violence, but does not include any chapters on violence in gay and lesbian couples. Despite this glaring omission, the rate of abuse in gay and lesbian relationships is similar to or even higher than that in heterosexual relationships, around 25–30 percent (Aardvarc.org 2008; Burke et al. 2002). Like heterosexual couples, violence is usually not a single event, but represents a pattern in the relationship. Gay and lesbian couples are not immune to violence, abuse, jealousy, and struggles over power and control.

Some people may dismiss intimate partner violence among gay men or lesbians as less serious—"Come on, shouldn't men be able to defend themselves from one another?" "How much harm can two women do?" "Why doesn't he just leave—what's stopping him?" (Cruz 2003; Ristock 2009). However, the violence that same-sex couples inflict can be substantial and no less serious than the violence inflicted by abusive heterosexual men or women on their partners. One study found 79 percent of gay male victims had suffered some physical injury, with 60 percent reporting bruises, 23 percent reporting head injuries and concussions, 13 percent reporting forced sex with the intention to infect the victim with HIV, 12 percent reporting broken bones, and 10 percent reporting burns (Merrill and Wolfe 2000). Thus, the issue of intimate partner violence deserves the same attention in gay and lesbian relationships as it does in heterosexual ones.

Dating Violence

> I didn't want to tell anybody what happened to me because I was too ashamed and embarrassed that I let it happen. I figured my friends would say, "We told you so," because they didn't like my boyfriend. But I loved Shane, and I never expected him to hit me. I don't say I was a victim, because I want to think on some level that he did love me as much as I loved him.

> I started dating Devan when I was 15; he would regularly slap and punch me. One time when I reached for a piece of cake, he called me "a fat ugly pig." No one knew about it. But once, he beat me so bad that I ended up in the hospital with a black eye, a broken rib, and bruises all over my body.

Violence against women is typically cast as a problem facing adults, but many girls or young women also endure sexual violence or battering, as described in the box on pages 391–392, "Families as Lived Experience: 'My Dating Violence Story.'" Young women between the ages of 16 and 24 experience the highest rates of violence by a current or former boyfriend (Manganello 2008). Likewise, 30–40 percent of teenage girls aged 14–17 know a peer who has been hit or beaten by a boyfriend. Yet, violence against girls and young women is often not given the attention needed to address the problem and make them safe. The results of this silence are severe. A Harvard School of Public Health (2001) study found that female teenagers who experienced dating violence are significantly more likely to engage in substance abuse, risky sexual behaviors, and suicide.

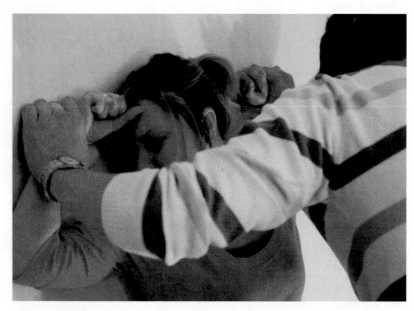

Girls and young women often do not report the abuse and suffer in silence. They fear parents' and friends' reactions, are embarrassed, worry of retaliation, or are afraid that they may never meet anyone better. "I think near the end, one of the reasons I was scared to let go was: 'Oh, my God, I'm 27.' I was worried that I was going to be like some lonely old maid. . . ." (Few and Rosen 2005). Sexual violence, in particular, is underreported.

Violence against young women is a hidden epidemic. About 13 percent of teenage girls who have been in a relationship report being physically hurt or hit, and 30–40 percent of teenage girls aged 14–17 know a peer who has been hit or beaten by a boyfriend.

Sexual Aggression and Rape   College students are particularly vulnerable to rape and sexual assault. A recent study by the U.S. Department of Justice reveals that 3 percent of college women are raped in a given nine-month academic year. Although that might not sound like a lot of women when you first read the number, ponder it more slowly. For a campus with 10,000 women, it means 350 rapes over the 9-month period. Over a typical 5-year college career, that's about 2,000 rapes for those 10,000 women—and that doesn't even include the risk in the other three months of summer (Fisher et al. 2000). Another way of putting it: between 20 and 25 percent of college women have been raped at least once while at college (Centers for Disease Control and Prevention 2008a). Other studies come to similar conclusions; for example, a study of nearly 200 college students found that 23 percent reported that they had been raped at least once (Flack et al. 2007).

Who is being raped, and who is doing the raping? Among college students, about 80 percent of victims and perpetrators know each other; they are intimate partners, "friends," roommates, acquaintances, and classmates. Women are raped by their study partner on the way to the library, by the guy they just met at the party in the dorm, by their roommate's brother, or by the partner they are involved with.

Most women who are raped or beaten know their attackers, often intimately.

FAMILIES
as Lived Experience

"My Dating Violence Story"

In the following story, "Alicia" describes the pressure she felt to have a sexual relationship before she was ready. You'll note that the ending could go a number of different ways.

We met in chemistry fourth period. He was one of the cutest boys in school and a star on our soccer team. Although he seemed pretty shy to our classmates, he would talk hours on end to me. He made me feel special and I began to feel very strongly towards him. One night, we were in my parents' basement watching his favorite television show. We started French kissing and I felt so pretty and wanted. He leaned me back on the couch and put his hand up my skirt. I wasn't too sure I wanted to go further since we had only been dating for two weeks. I told him I wasn't ready and he got up and stormed out.

I was concerned I had done something wrong so I called him on his cell phone a few moments later. He didn't pick up. Later that night, my phone rang and I rushed to it, hoping it was him. It was. He said that I act like a baby and that real women have sex. He called me a tease and told me that if I wanted to be his girl that I would have to have sex with him. My eyes started to fill with tears. I knew

I wasn't ready. When I first started high school, I made a vow to myself that I'd wait until I was in a long-term committed monogamous relationship with someone whom I loved before I started having sex. But now I'm starting to question myself, and it makes me feel confused. I tell him that I'm scared and he calls me a "slut" for having him in my house when my parents weren't home. He says, "I probably have all kinds of guys down there just to tease them and kick them out." But I didn't kick him out, he just left! I'm starting to get really confused because just yesterday he was telling me how pretty and special I was. Now he's calling me names. What did I do to deserve this?

Maybe I should have just had sex with him. Maybe he is right. I tell him I have to go and I'll see him in school tomorrow. He asks me if he can come over again tomorrow and I say...

The story described above can end in many different ways depending on whether or not this young woman knows she has a right to say and do what she wants.

He asks me if he can come over tomorrow and I say, "You said very nasty and untrue things about

(continued)

(continued)

me because you were upset that I told you I wasn't ready. I do not want to be mistreated by someone I like and if you don't have enough respect for me to understand my decision to not have sex then I would rather we just be 'friends'." He hung up the phone and we never spoke again. But I was ok with that. Four months later, I met a boy at summer camp who is supportive and willing to wait until I am ready. I am glad I decided to do better for myself.

Source: Advocates for Youth 2009.

CRITICAL THINKING QUESTIONS

1. Have you, or someone you know well, been in a similar situation? Did that story end differently or in a similar fashion? How do you think most of these stories end?

2. Have the pressures put on women to be sexual changed over the last few generations? Do you think women in your parents' generation felt these same pressures? Why or why not?

WHAT DO YOU THINK?

What is it about a college environment that makes rape and sexual assault so prevalent? What do you think is happening at your college? What can or should be done about it? How can feminist or conflict theory guide you?

The work of Mary Koss and her colleagues (Koss and Cook 1993; Koss et al. 1987) sheds some interesting light on college-age perpetrators. In a survey of 32 college campuses, she found that although fully 12 percent of men had committed acts that would fit the legal definition of rape or attempted rape, only 1 percent thought their actions were criminal. Many made a distinction between "forcing a girl to have sex" and "rape," as though they are different. The law, of course, makes no such distinction.

"Date Rape" Drugs   Alcohol or drugs are often involved in a sexual assault (Roudsan et al. 2009). **Date rape drugs** such as Gamma hydroxybutyrate (GHB), Rohypnol (popularly known as "roofies" or "roofenol") or ketamine hydrochloride (Ketamine) can immobilize a person to facilitate an assault (U.S. Department of Health & Human Services, Office of Women's Health 2008). The effects of these drugs cause people to be physically helpless, lose muscle control, feel very drunk, or lose consciousness, and they often cannot remember what happened. The drugs usually have no color, smell, or taste and can be easily added to flavored drinks without the victim's knowledge. How can you protect yourself? Do not accept drinks from other people; open containers yourself; keep your drink with you at all times, even when you go to the bathroom; do not share drinks; do not drink from punch bowls or other large, common, open containers because they may already have drugs in them; do not drink anything that tastes or smells strange (sometimes GHB tastes salty); and have a designated nondrinking friend with you to make sure you stay safe.

Factors Associated with Violence

Although most women who are assaulted are done so by intimate partners rather than by strangers, it is important to recognize that most men do not abuse their partners. What specific factors are associated with intimate partner violence? Several characteristics increase the odds (Delsol et al. 2003; DeMaris et al. 2003; National Coalition Against Domestic Violence 2009), although violence occurs in all types of relationships:

- *Youth.* In most violent relationships, the partners are under the age of 30.
- *Low levels of education.* Often, the husband/male partner has a high school diploma or less.

- *Low income or employment problems.* Family income may be below or near the poverty line, or the man may be unemployed. They may live in an economically disadvantaged neighborhood.
- *Drug or alcohol use.* Often, one or both partners use drugs or alcohol frequently and may use it as an excuse for conflict and violence.
- *Abuse in family of orientation.* One or both partners may have witnessed or experienced abuse as children.
- *Specific personal traits.* These may include extreme jealousy, possessiveness, a bad temper, low self-esteem, unpredictability, verbal abuse, aggressive tendencies such as fighting with others, and cruelty toward animals.

Researchers have rarely studied the relationship between occupations and violence, other than to use broad categories, such as between white-collar and blue-collar jobs. Sociologist Scott Melzer (2002) looked carefully at the relationship between a man's job and his likelihood of committing violence. He wondered whether people in violent jobs were more likely to be violent toward their partners. Melzer used data from the National Survey of Families and Households, a large and nationally representative sample of adults, to answer these questions. The key violent occupational categories are (1) supervisors of police and detectives; (2) supervisors of guards; (3) police and detectives (public service); (4) sheriffs and bailiffs; (5) correctional institution officers; (6) guards and police (excluding public service); (7) protective service occupations; and (8) current members of the armed forces. Persons in these violent occupations were compared with those holding managerial jobs to see if they were more likely to commit violence. Other important variables were controlled statistically so that the specific independent effects of occupation on violence could be seen. These variables included the man's age, education, children in the home, whether he had an alcohol or drug problem, unemployment, and the proportion of the couple's income earned by the woman. The study found that men who work in physically violent occupations were 1.43 times more likely to commit violence against a spouse or intimate partner than were those in managerial jobs (Melzer 2002). These, however, were not the only occupational categories significantly more likely to commit violence. Those men in clerical jobs (a traditionally female occupation) and those in professional positions were also far more likely to be violent compared to those holding managerial jobs. Men who were unemployed or who earned less than a third of the couple's income were also at a greater likelihood of committing violence. Age was also noted as a strong predictor of male violence; an 18-year-old man is twice as likely as a 38-year-old man to be violent. However, the single strongest predictor of violence is a man having an alcohol or drug problem. These men are 4.6 times as likely to commit violence as are men without such a problem (Melzer 2002).

Consequences of Violence

Intimate partner violence can have tragic results. In general, victims of repeated violence over time experience more serious consequences than victims of one-time incidents (Johnson and Leone 2005). Minor forms of bruises, scratches, and welts are most common, but broken bones, severe bruising, or back pain are other consequences of violence.

Some consequences are not as visible, but just as real. Intimate partner violence, and the chronic stress that accompanies it, can wreak havoc on the immune and endocrine systems, inducing fibromyalgia, gynecological disorders, irritable bowel syndrome, or gastrointestinal problems (Centers for Disease Control and Prevention 2009g; Leserman and Drossman 2007). Because physical violence is also typically accompanied by emotional or psychological abuse, many victims are depressed, have anxiety and sleep disturbances, have low self-esteem, are socially isolated, and have thoughts of suicide (Afifi et al. 2009; Centers for Disease Control and Prevention 2009g). Victims of intimate partner violence are more likely to behave in unhealthy ways, such as engaging in high-risk sexual behavior (e.g., having unprotected sex or trading sex for food or money); using harmful substances (e.g., smoking cigarettes or using illicit drugs); or having unhealthy diet-related behaviors (e.g., binging and purging food).

Despite the clear need for mental health care, many women, minority women in particular, often experience barriers to getting care. These barriers may include cultural issues, language differences, or lack of services and providers in poor or ethnic communities (Bryant-Davis et al. 2009; Rodriguez et al. 2009; Weaver 2009).

In addition to the consequences to the individual, there are also societal consequences. In other words, you and I are affected by intimate partner violence even if we don't know anyone who is a victim or perpetrator (which, I must say, is highly unlikely). Victims lose nearly 8 million days of paid work a year, the equivalent of more than 32,000 full-time jobs. Costs exceed 8 billion dollars, most of which goes to medical and mental health care (Centers for Disease Control and Prevention 2003; Max et al. 2004).

Coping with Violence and Abuse: Reporting, Leaving, and Staying

One of the primary ways of coping with intimate partner violence is to report it to authorities. Nonetheless, about three-quarters of violent acts go unreported to law enforcement. Women are less likely to report violence if they know the offender, if they are of the same sex, or if they are sexually assaulted. The reasons for not reporting the violence are many—believing that the violence was "too minor," having feelings of embarrassment, having a fear of reprisal, feeling that the police could not do anything, or the victim's worry that she would not be believed. In particular, if the offender were a spouse or partner, victims were likely to fear reprisal and to think that the police could not do anything to help (Felson and Pare 2005).

A common question is why women stay in an abusive situation. The truth is, however, that most do not stay. A longitudinal study revealed that by 2.5 years, three-quarters of battered women had either left the relationship or the abuse had ended (Campbell et al. 1998).

Leaving, however, is often a *process* rather than a single event (Kim and Gray 2008). It may be difficult for some women to garner the courage or coordinate the logistics to leave immediately. This is where the typology discussed by Johnson (2008, 2009) comes into play. The diverse types of intimate partner violence have repercussions for one's ability to leave the situation. For example, men engaged in IT use on their victims a wide range of control tactics that can cripple a victim's sense of command over her own life. What are some of these control tactics that may make it difficult for victims to leave an abusive and violent relationship?

- *Blaming the victim:* "If you weren't so stupid, I wouldn't have to hit you." After hearing blaming comments often enough, some women believe them. Their self-esteem is eroded, and they begin to believe that they must deserve the abuse and be unworthy of a positive, loving relationship.
- *Shame:* Feelings of embarrassment and shame are common among abused women because they know that many other women are not abused. They worry that other people will look down on them for either provoking the abuse or for tolerating it. Or they may be embarrassed at how their spouse/partner will be perceived by others. They may try to hide their bruises under makeup or clothing.
- *Financial dependency:* Some women are particularly vulnerable because they are financially dependent on men. They may lack job skills or recent employment experience. Some perpetrators foster this economic dependence by not letting their wives/partners

establish credit in their own name, and refusing to put their wives' or partners' names on financial accounts.

- *Isolation:* The abuser may initiate isolation as a control tactic, or the woman may initiate it out of shame. In either case, abused women are often cut off from family and friends. They may cease going to church, to work, or to school. They have little social support and no one to turn to for a "reality check."

- *Fear of retaliation:* Fear is an important reason why some women linger in abusive relationships. The perpetrator may have threatened the woman, her children, or her pets. Because he has been abusive before, the threats are real and many victims live in fear.

- *Love and hope:* Many abused women harbor fantasies that their abuser will somehow miraculously change. They do not want the relationship to end; they just want the abuse to stop. They believe that if they just work harder in the relationship the abuse will somehow cease.

- *Commitment to the relationship:* When we marry, we agree to take our partner "for better or worse, until death do we part." Although we take these vows seriously, most people would probably leave an out for particularly harsh circumstances, including domestic violence. However, some people believe that they must endure their marriage regardless of the costs.

- *Fear of being alone:* Some women are unsure whether they can live alone and take care of themselves. Women have been socialized to derive a great deal of their social status through their affiliations with men. When this is coupled with possible financial dependence, we can see why some women may be hesitant to leave an abusive situation.

Other difficulties may exist as well, including having no place to go, no access to checking or savings accounts, or limited support from the legal system. Despite a restraining order, it is possible for an abuser to repeat the assault. Some women flee to the safety of a shelter, sometimes referred to as battered women's shelters or domestic violence shelters. The following box, "Social Policies for Families: History of the Shelter Movement," describes the development of battered women's shelters as safe havens. They have helped thousands of women on the road to a safe and more secure life.

WHAT DO YOU THINK?

Think of a specific incidence of intimate partner violence that you may be familiar with—a parent, a friend, yourself, or even a case you read about or watched on television. Use the information in this section to understand it further (e.g., where does it fit into Johnson's typology, what factors were associated with the violence, did any control tactics make it difficult for the victim to leave?).

SOCIAL

Policies for Families

History of the Shelter Movement

Shelters designed exclusively for women and their children fleeing violence are a relatively new phenomenon. The following essay reveals how the issue of domestic violence became defined as a social problem, and how shelters—originally marginalized—began to take root in many communities.

Violence among intimates may have existed since the beginning of time, but for most of human history it has not been viewed as a social problem. In fact, it was not recognized as a pervasive social problem in the United States until the mid-1970s, when research was published revealing its high frequency. Soon after, a grassroots battered women's movement gained momentum. The movement was inspired by the feminist analysis of rape as a social and political issue. Battered women began to speak out about the

(continued)

(continued)

physical abuse they were suffering in their marriages and intimate relationships.

At first, battered women helped one another individually by setting up informal safe homes and apartments where they could hide from their abusers and have a brief respite while they reorganized their lives. In an environment free from intimidation of their abusers, battered women began to speak openly and soon discovered the commonality of their experience. Their bond with other women and their children lay in their sense of isolation and their need for safety. Moreover, the women realized that society was largely indifferent to their plight, and they found support lacking from social and judicial systems. As these issues began to be publicized, women of all races, cultures, ages, abilities, and walks of life began to expose the violence they suffered. It quickly became clear that battering was a pervasive problem, and a nationwide movement started to take shape.

Initially, the movement focused on the acute need for safe shelter for themselves and their children. Unless a woman was safe, she could not effectively evaluate her situation and make clear decisions about her future. Operating on extremely low budgets bolstered by volunteers, shelters began to open up around the country. Although only a handful of such programs existed in the mid-1970s, today, there are more than 1,600 shelters, hotlines, and safe-home networks nationwide. The growth in the number of battered women's programs and their level of funding has been remarkable; nonetheless, many of the 3,000 counties in the United States still do not have services available to battered women. Moreover, among those counties that do have shelters, most remain inadequately funded and must turn away as many women as they accept. Most continue to rely heavily on donations and volunteers.

Shelter programs may differ somewhat in size, scope of services, and sources and level of funding; however, all share the premise that no one deserves to be beaten, and that battered women and their children need special resources to end the violence in their lives. The most critical functions include crisis intervention and safety provision for battered women and their children, and operation of a 24-hour hotline. Women and their children may stay at the shelter only one night, or they may stay for several weeks or even months, depending on the demand for and supply of space. Typical shelter services include legal, economic, housing, and medical advocacy; court accompaniment; employment and job training assistance; support groups for residents and nonresidents; and child care and counseling programs for children. This array of programs is designed to help women muster the confidence to leave an abusive situation, and to provide the initial resources to make it happen.

Sources: Florida Coalition Against Domestic Violence 2003, National Center on Domestic and Sexual Violence 2010.

CRITICAL THINKING QUESTIONS

1. If violence among intimates is an age-old problem, why was it not recognized as a pervasive social problem in the United States until the mid-1970s?
2. If the need is so great, why are battered women's shelters dependent on volunteer time and donations rather than funded at adequate levels by state or local governments?

Child Abuse

He never listens to me. I try to tell him things, and he just doesn't seem to hear me unless I give him a good wallop.

A mother hits her child. Is this child abuse? Does it matter if the mother uses an open hand or a *fist*? How about if she uses an *object* to hit her child? Does it matter if her hitting leaves a *welt*? Does the *reason* for hitting the child make a difference? How about the *age* of the child? Does it matter *where* the child was hit? Does it matter how *often* the child is hit? Let's amend the story a bit.

My 15-year-old son never listens to me. I try to tell him things, and he just doesn't seem to hear me, unless I give him a good wallop across his bare back with my belt.

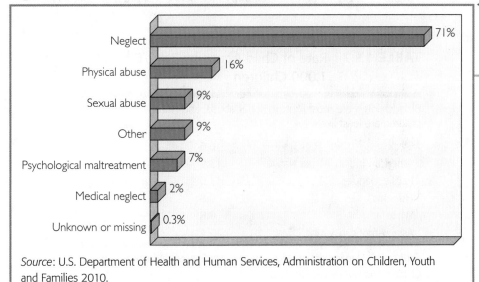

Child abuse is an attack on a child that results in an injury and violates social norms. Sometimes these norms are ambiguous, as in the case above. Most parents believe it is appropriate to spank children, and surveys generally find that about half to two-thirds of parents report having slapped or spanked a child. Meanwhile, others suggest that this is child abuse because spanked children are more likely to be depressed, to abuse animals, and eventually assault their own partners (Busby et al. 2008; Christie-Mizell et al. 2008). Even Dr. Phil, the famous sex and family advisor, opposes spanking (Dr. Phil.com 2009).

But often, the abuse is so egregious that there is little doubt, and government agencies become involved to protect the child. According to the U.S. government, 772,000 children were estimated to be victims of abuse in 2008 (U.S. Department of Health & Human Services, Administration on Children, Youth, and Families 2010). The good news, if there is any, is that the number of substantiated abuse cases has declined by nearly 20 percent since 2004.

When does discipline become child abuse? Is spanking abuse? Is name calling? There is a wide range of opinion about what constitutes child abuse, and definitions vary across time and place. Nonetheless, some physical or emotional acts are clearly reprehensible— over 1,700 children die every year in the United States from abuse.

Types of Child Abuse

There are several different types of child abuse, as shown in Figure 13.2 (U.S. Department of Health & Human Services, Administration on Children, Youth, and Families 2010):

- **Neglect** is the most common form of abuse and involves the failure to provide for the child's basic needs, such as failing to provide adequate food, clothing, shelter, a safe environment, supervision, or medical care to a dependent child.

Figure 13.2 **The Most Common Types of Child Abuse**

Type	Percentage
Neglect	71%
Physical abuse	16%
Sexual abuse	9%
Other	9%
Psychological maltreatment	7%
Medical neglect	2%
Unknown or missing	0.3%

Neglect is the most common form of child abuse.

Source: U.S. Department of Health and Human Services, Administration on Children, Youth and Families 2010.

- **Physical abuse** involves inflicting physical injury and harm upon a child. This may include hitting, shaking, burning, kicking, or in other ways physically harming a child. Among substantiated child abuse cases, nearly one in six involved physical abuse. The most extreme cases may result in the death of a child. The most common forms of death were skull fracture and internal bleeding.
- **Sexual abuse** involves inappropriate sexual behavior with a child for sexual gratification. It occurs in about 9 percent of substantiated child abuse cases. It could include fondling a child's genitals, making the child fondle the perpetrator's genitals, and progressing to more intrusive sexual acts such as oral sex and vaginal or anal penetration. Sexual abuse also includes acts such as exhibition or in other ways exploiting the child for sexual purposes.
- **Psychological maltreatment** involves about 7 percent of substantiated cases of child abuse and includes verbal, mental, or psychological maltreatment that destroys a child's self-esteem. Abuse of this nature often includes threatening, degrading, or humiliating the child, and extreme or bizarre forms of punishment, such as confinement to a dark room or being tied to a chair for long periods of time. It is likely that emotional abuse occurs far more frequently than what can be substantiated.
- **Medical neglect** represents a small (2 percent) but important type of abuse, and involves delaying or forgoing a child's needed medical, dental, or prescription care.
- *Other abuse* is a general definition that includes abuse that does not easily fit into the above categories, such as abandonment, threats of harm, or congenital drug addiction.

Over 1,700 children died in 2008 as a result of abuse and neglect; 60 percent were 1 year of age or younger, and 80 percent were under age 4 (U.S. Department of Health & Human Services, Administration on Children, Youth, and Families 2010). Annually, more children under the age of 4 die from abuse and neglect than from falls, choking, drowning, fires, or motor vehicle accidents.

Abuse occurs in all income, racial, religious, and ethnic groups, and in all types of communities. Female victims outnumber male victims, especially in cases of sexual abuse. Black children have the highest rates of victimization, American Indians/Alaska Natives the second highest, followed by Pacific Islanders, Whites, Hispanics, and Asians as shown in Table 13.2.

Most people who abuse children are not strangers, but are biological family members, as shown in Table 13.3. Eighty percent are family members (most often the mother).

TABLE 13.2 **Rate of Child Abuse by Race/Ethnicity per 1,000 Children**

Black children are most likely to suffer abuse, and Asian American children are least likely.

Black	16.6
American Indian/Alaska Native	13.9
Pacific Islander	11.6
Hispanic	9.8
White	8.6
Asian American	2.4

Source: U.S. Department of Health and Human Services, Administration for Children and Families 2010.

TABLE 13.3 Perpetrator's Relationship to the Victim

Who is most likely to abuse children? Their parents.

Parent	81%
Other Relative	4%
Unmarried Partner	2%
Other	4%
Unknown/Missing	9%
Daycare Provider	1%

Source: U.S. Department of Health and Human Services, Administration on Children, Youth and Families 2010.

Factors Contributing to Child Abuse

Complex combinations of social, cultural, and personal factors explain child abuse, but perhaps surprisingly, fewer than 10 percent of abusers are considered mentally ill.

The following are potential risk factors.

- *Stress.* Parents that experience a great deal of stress are more likely to abuse their children. The stress could be brought on by many factors, including illness, unemployment, marital conflict, financial problems, or even the specific traits of the child. For example, premature infants who require special care and who may cry harder and more frequently have an increased risk of abuse. Likewise, children with physical or developmental difficulties are more likely to be abused. Alcohol and drug use are key risk factors for abuse. They can aggravate stress, decrease coping skills, and impair judgment.
- *Social Isolation.* Parents (and other caretakers) who abuse children tend to be socially isolated. They may have little contact with other family members, have few friends, and belong to few community organizations. Sometimes this isolation predates the abuse (they abuse because they are so isolated) and in other families the abuse may predate the isolation (they isolate themselves to hide the abuse from others). Regardless, these families lack social support to help them with their stress, anger, and the challenges of raising children.
- *Learned Behavior.* A parent is more likely to abuse his or her child if the parent was abused as a child. It has been estimated that about 30 percent of abused children become abusive parents themselves, 10 times the rate of all parents (Kaufman and Zigler 1987). Parents who are able to break the cycle of abuse realize, perhaps through therapy or a supportive partner, that the abuse was wrong, and they learn other ways to deal with their frustrations.
- *Unrealistic Parental Expectations.* Some adults have unrealistic expectations about parenthood. Very little in life prepares us for the challenges associated with being a parent. Although we require a test to verify fitness to drive an automobile, virtually anyone can become a parent. There is no required course or formal certificate to verify that we have mastered a certain level of knowledge and skills. Therefore, some people become parents with little information regarding child development, and little sense of the self-sacrifice required to be a parent. This ignorance can translate into lashing out in undesirable and destructive ways.
- *Demographic Characteristics.* Several demographic characteristics of the parents have been identified as risk factors, including age, marital status, and socioeconomic status. Young parents, especially teens, are more likely to engage in abusive behaviors

WHAT DO YOU THINK?

What kinds of programs, policies, or services are needed to eliminate (or at least greatly reduce) child abuse? Are these programs feasible for the United States to offer? Why or why not? If they are feasible, then why do we not offer them?

because they have little knowledge about child development, have unrealistic expectations about parenthood, and are unprepared for its demands. Single parents are twice as likely as married parents to abuse their children. Low socioeconomic status is another risk factor. Parents who earned less than $15,000 or $20,000 per year were 12–16 times more likely to physically abuse their children, 18 times more likely to sexually abuse them, and 44 times more likely to neglect them (Sedlack and Broadhurst 1998). The most common explanation for this difference is that low-income parents are under a great deal of stress, have lower levels of education, have inadequate support systems, and higher rates of substance abuse. They are also more likely to be young and unmarried—other factors associated with child abuse.

Consequences of Child Abuse

Child abuse has numerous physical, cognitive, and emotional consequences for children. Abuse leaves approximately 18,000 children permanently disabled each year. Negative health consequences continue into adulthood for many victims, including increased rates of gynecological problems, migraine headaches, digestive problems, asthma, and a host of other disorders (Child Welfare Information Gateway 2006; Goldman et al. 2003).

Perhaps even more insidious are the emotional scars left behind (Maas et al. 2008; Walsh et al. 2010). Abuse is trauma. Physically abused children tend to be more aggressive and more likely to get involved in delinquent activities, have difficulty in school, and be involved in early sexual activity, which can result in teen pregnancy. This does not mean, however, that all physically abused children have these outcomes. One study reviewed the findings of 21 published reports on child abuse to note any trends in children's behavior. They found that the number of abused children having difficulty in educational, behavioral, or emotional domains varied greatly, and a child may do poorly in one domain, but excel in another. About one in five abused children had difficulty and functioned poorly in all domains (Walsh et al. 2010). The emotional trauma can be longlasting. Even as adults, children who have been abused are more likely to suffer nightmares, depression, panic disorders, and have suicidal thoughts (Hyman 2000). It can also affect their relationship with their own children, increasing the likelihood of poor attachment, neglect, and abuse (Briere and Jordan 2009). The costs of child abuse are far too great to ignore.

Elder Abuse

Rosemary, 85 years old, has arthritis and heart disease. When she lost her husband last year, she moved in with her 50-year-old daughter, Rhonda. The situation is difficult for all of them. Sometimes, Rhonda feels at the end of her rope, caring for her mother, worrying about her college-age son, and fearing for her husband who may lose his job in this recession. Money is tight, and Rhonda doesn't have much energy to deal with her mother's endless needs. Recently, Rhonda lost her temper and slapped her mother. She is also considering using her mother's Social Security checks to pay for her son's college bills.

WHAT DO YOU THINK?

Is it wrong of Rhonda to use her mother's money to help pay for her son's college bills? Why or why not?

Elder abuse is a term referring to any knowing, intentional, or negligent act by a caregiver or any other person that causes harm or a serious risk of harm to a vulnerable adult. The specificity of laws varies from state to state, but broadly defined, abuse may be (National Center on Elder Abuse 2010):

- *Physical Abuse.* Inflicting, or threatening to inflict, physical pain or injury on a vulnerable elder, or depriving them of a basic need.
- *Emotional Abuse.* Inflicting mental pain, anguish, or distress on an elder person through verbal or nonverbal acts.
- *Sexual Abuse.* Nonconsensual sexual contact of any kind.
- *Exploitation.* Illegal taking, misuse, or concealment of funds, property, or assets of a vulnerable elder.
- *Neglect.* Refusal or failure by those responsible to provide food, shelter, health care, or protection for a vulnerable elder.
- *Abandonment.* The desertion of a vulnerable elder by anyone who has assumed the responsibility for care or custody of that person.

Exact data are hard to come by, but the Survey of State Adult Protective Services (APS), which is the most rigorous national study of state-level APS data, found 565,000 reported and substantiated cases of abuse among persons aged 60 and over (National Center on Elder Abuse 2006). Ninety percent of these cases occurred in a domestic setting, not in an institution such as a nursing home or hospital. Reports of elder abuse to adult protective services are on the rise, increasing 20 percent over recent years. Because only about one-quarter of abuse cases are reported and substantiated by adult protective service agencies, it is likely that the true extent of elders who are abused each year may even exceed 2 million (American Psychological Association 2010).

Abusers are most often relatives, caregivers, or others close to the elderly victim. Many of these elders, like Rosemary, are frail and vulnerable, and are dependent on others to meet their basic or financial needs (Centers for Disease Control and Prevention 2009g). They face unique barriers to reporting violence, including mobility limitations, fear of being institutionalized, and fear of not being believed. Like other forms of violence among intimates, elder abuse often goes unreported because the elderly are reluctant or unable to talk about it to others.

Caring for frail older people can be difficult and stress-provoking (see Chapter 12). This is particularly true when older people are mentally or physically impaired, when the caregiver is ill-prepared for the task, or when the needed resources are lacking. Under these circumstances, the increased stress and frustration of a caregiver may lead to abuse or willful neglect. Researchers have found that abusers of the elderly (typically adult children) tend to have more personal problems than do nonabusers. Adult children who abuse their parents frequently suffer from such problems as mental and emotional disorders, alcoholism, drug addiction, and financial difficulty.

Explanations for Violence and Abuse Among Intimates

A quick survey of your classmates would probably show that virtually everyone abhors violence in families and intimate relationships. Why then is it so widespread? Two perspectives help us to explain violence among intimates. One focuses on micro-level individual causes, while the other examines macro-level societal and cultural factors that contribute to violence. In reality, both factors come into play.

Micro-Level Individual Causes

Focusing on the individual level, two explanations are often cited: (1) the intergenerational transmission of violence and (2) the stress explanation.

Intergenerational Transmission of Violence   Drawing upon Bandura's (1977) social learning theory, the **intergenerational transmission of violence** perspective (sometimes called the *cycle of violence*) suggests that we learn norms and behaviors by observing others, including violence. Families of orientation are the primary source of early learning. Therefore, it is likely that many adults who abuse their spouses, partners, or children are modeling the behavior they witnessed growing up. Perhaps they witnessed abusive or violent behavior between their own parents, or perhaps they were abused as young children. When we observe people to whom we are close engage in certain types of behavior, we learn scripts for our futures. In this case, the script includes an acceptance of aggressive behavior between family members or intimate partners.

Research has found a tendency towards intergenerational transmission—children, particularly boys, who witness or experience abuse are more likely to be in abusive relationships as an adult than are other children (Briere and Jordan 2009; Busby et al. 2008; Walker et al. 2009). For example, a study based on 45,000 responses to a Web-based survey, the "Relationship Evaluation Questionnaire" (RELATE), found that 10 percent of couples without any reported violence in their family of orientation were violent in their current relationship, as compared to 32 percent of couples who reported that they had either witnessed or experienced violence in their home as children (Busby et al. 2008). Granted, although the sample is large, it is not based on a representative sample because people who completed RELATE may have been part of a class, workshop, or found the questionnaire on their own search of the Web. Nonetheless, it provides some degree of evidence of the intergenerational transmission of violence perspective.

It is also true that most people who witness or experience abuse as children do *not* abuse others. An early 1980 study by Straus, Gelles, and Steinmetz reported a startling statistic: sons of the most violent parents were 1,000 times more likely to abuse their partners than the sons of nonviolent parents, but still, this only translates into a rate of 20 percent. That means that 80 percent of those sons witnessing the most extreme forms of violence do *not* abuse their own partners. Likewise, the RELATE study found that more than two-thirds of people who witnessed or experienced violence as children were not in an abusive relationship (Busby et al. 2008). Therefore, it is very important to note that the intergenerational transmission of violence refers to a greater *likelihood* of engaging in violence; it is not referring to determinism. Many persons who witnessed or experienced abuse as children grow up to be caring, supportive partners and parents without a hint of perpetuating violence and abuse.

Stress   Violent relationships often contain inordinate amounts of stress, such as chronic under- or unemployment, economic issues, or other job or family difficulties (Straus 1980). Many stressors are highly correlated with income. For example, lower-income groups are more likely to face unemployment or underemployment, are less likely to be insured, and are more likely to have health problems in their families. Moreover, lower-income families have fewer coping mechanisms available to help them ward off the impact of the stressors. They have fewer savings and other assets to tide them over during a period of unemployment or underemployment, they do not have the resources to purchase health insurance privately, and they are more likely to engage in unhealthy coping mechanisms that jeopardize their health, such as smoking or eating poorly nutritious foods (rather than taking a trip to Hawaii to ward off stress). Not surprisingly then, violence is more likely to occur in lower-income households, although it does occur at all income levels.

Families are expected to learn how to manage and effectively deal with the stressors on their own. Few families seek outside support, such as counseling or working with community agencies in dealing with the problems they face. If a family cannot cope adequately with the stress or crisis that occurs, the tension created can push them toward violence (Child Welfare Information Gateway 2006; Goldman et al. 2003).

Macro-Level Societal and Cultural Causes

These two theories—the intergenerational transmission of violence and stress explanations—help us understand why some people are violent, but they do not place individual actions in their social context. Some would argue that stress by itself doesn't necessarily lead to violence, but rather, we should look at social and cultural attitudes that perpetuate violence as a response to stressors (Straus 1980). Straus found that men who assaulted their partners were not just stressed, but were likely to believe that physical punishment of children and slapping a spouse were appropriate behaviors (Straus 1980). Where do these attitudes come from? At least three well-cited macro-level explanations are proposed for violence and abuse: (1) patriarchy; (2) cultural norms that support violence more generally; and (3) norms of family privacy.

Patriarchy   In many cultures, violence against women is not only tolerated, but holds a wide degree of support. Using demographic and health surveys from seven countries—Armenia, Bangladesh, Cambodia, India, Kazakhstan, Nepal, and Turkey—one study estimated that the acceptance of "wife beating" ranged from a low of 29 percent in Nepal to a high of 57 percent in India (women only) and 56 percent in Turkey (men only) (Rani and Banu 2009). In most of these countries, persons with lower incomes and education levels were more accepting of violence; however, so were younger persons.

Because women are socialized in the same patriarchical culture as men, they often support (and even perpetuate) the patriarchy that can lead to violence. One study interviewed 450 women living in three cities in the West Bank to assess their attitudes toward "wife beating." Overall, the women perceived violence against wives to be justified if a wife insults her husband (59 percent), if she disobeys her husband (49 percent), if she neglects her children (37 percent), if she goes out without telling her husband (25 percent), if she argues with her husband (11 percent), and if she burns the food (5 percent). Sixty-five percent of the women agreed with at least one reason for wife beating, and those with less education, who have more than one child, make few household decisions, and have been married less than 10 years were most agreeable (Dhaher et al. 2010). Another large study of over 2,500 married women conducted in Minya, Egypt, found that 27 percent had experienced at least one beating since adulthood, and 4 percent had been beaten so severely that a doctor was needed. Only 27 percent of the surveyed women believed that a husband is "never justified" in beating his wife, whereas 52 percent believe that a husband is "seldom or sometimes justified," and 21 percent believe that a husband is "often justified" in beating her. The authors found that the more dependent a woman was on her husband because of having little education or living with his kin, and the more socially isolated she was, the more likely she was to be abused and support that abuse (Yount 2005).

Japan, a modern, developed nation, is also among the most patriarchal, and not surprisingly, also has high levels of violence against women (Nagae and Dancy 2010). In-depth qualitative interviews with an admittedly small sample (11 women) indicate that physical, emotional, and even sexual abuse are systematic problems. Communication between spouses tended to be unilateral, with husbands dominating the conversation. The women identified the patriarchal society as a major contributor to violence (Nagae and Dancy 2010).

Why is abuse against women so prevalent? One theory is patriarchy. When women are not valued, viewed as sexual property, or have little social or economic status, violence against them may be woven into the fabric of society. This woman proudly signs autographs, oblivious to the fact that she is a victim of patriarchy, yet also perpetuating it by becoming a willing sexual object.

But what about patriarchy in the United States? After all, not every American believes in equal rights, or that men and women should share power and authority (Flood and Pease 2009). Men establish their dominance by eschewing any semblance of femininity and often take more aggressive posturing. "You throw like a girl," "you're a sissy," and "quit acting like a woman" all show contempt for the feminine. Men are taught that toughness, competitiveness, and controlling behavior are masculine attributes, and many adopt these attributes with a vengeance.

Cultural Norms Support Violence   A second macro-level explanation focuses on the fact that some cultures are more tolerant of violence in general than others. Violence is very public, readily seen on television screens or at the theaters. In the United States, many types of violence are condoned, including in sporting events. Football, hockey, rugby, wrestling, and race car driving are notoriously violent sports, and the millions of fans who watch these events expect nothing less, all in the name of fun. Yet at other times, this same pushing, shoving, or fast driving is completely inappropriate. Your professor cannot tackle you because you failed to read the assigned material. The difficulty lies in the fact that sometimes these lines get blurred. When is it okay to hit, and when is it not okay? Or, when does hitting turn into abuse?

For example, many adults hit their children. However, are we talking about slapping, shoving, hitting, or beating? Is the child 4 or 14 years old? If corporal punishment is allowed under some circumstances, it is not surprising that in the heat of passion the boundaries of when it is and is not appropriate are sometimes blurred. To avoid the distinction between acceptable and nonacceptable family violence, 22 countries fully prohibit hitting children, including countries as diverse as Sweden and Romania (Project NoSpank 2007). The United Nations Committee on the Rights of Children has recommended that all countries prohibit spanking in the family and other institutions (Vandivere et al. 2003).

Norms of Family Privacy   What goes on in U.S. families is generally a private matter (Berardo 1998). Sayings such as "a man's home is his castle" indicate that the man is not only dominant in his home, but what occurs there is no one else's business. Extended families are rare, and families often move hundreds or even thousands of miles away from other kin. In urban areas, families commonly know few, if any, of their neighbors well, and therefore are increasingly isolated (Nock 1998). Violence is more likely to occur in families that are socially isolated (U.S. Department of Health and Human Services, Administration on Children, Youth, and Families 2009).

Moreover, many people believe violence is a private matter between family members. Neighbors, co-workers, or even friends and other kin can be hesitant to get involved. "I didn't want to say anything because it's really none of my business" is a common sentiment in Western society. Nicole Brown was repeatedly battered by her husband O. J. Simpson, yet no one spoke up about it until after her death.

As violence occurs, families can become even more isolated from friends, neighbors, and family because of embarrassment or stigma. Victims may be reluctant to seek help and may instead try to keep the abuse hidden.

WHAT DO YOU THINK?

Can you think of examples of patriarchy in the United States that would condone and perpetuate intimate partner violence? Now can you think of examples in less developed countries that would condone and perpetuate violence? How are these examples similar or different?

A Synthesis: Power and Control

Although micro-level and macro-level explanations focus on different factors that contribute to violence, a focus on power and control synthesizes elements of both levels of analysis. This perspective, which admittedly describes perpetrators as men and victims as women, suggests that men who assault their partners are exerting their domination, power, and control over women (Vives-Cases et al. 2009). Likewise, women who feel powerless within their relationships have higher rates of victimization (Filson et al. 2010). Batterers use threats and various forms of physical, sexual, and emotional abuse as a way to exert their dominance and gain control in a relationship, perhaps making up for inadequacies they feel in other domains. The "Power and Control Wheel" depicts behaviors and privileges that batterers use to dominate and control their partners and/or children, and is shown in Figure 13.3.

If you look closely at the Power and Control Wheel, you can see a heterosexual bias—it reflects the power imbalances in male–female relationships, while ignoring the social

Figure 13.3 Power and Control Wheel

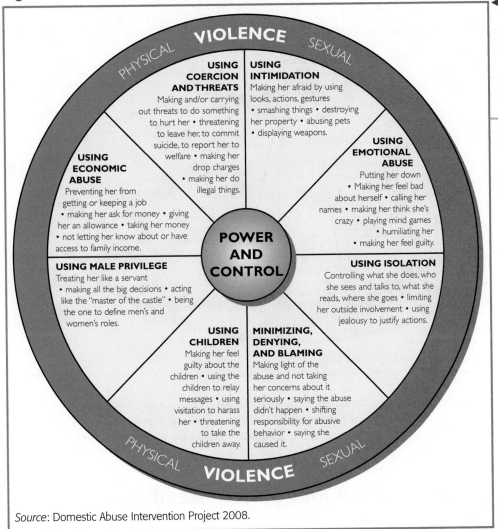

A perpetrator of violence uses many mechanisms to exert power and to control his partner.

Source: Domestic Abuse Intervention Project 2008.

Figure 13.4 **Power and Control Wheel in Lesbian, Gay, Transgender, and Bisexual (LGTB) Relationships**

Power and control are key elements in LGTB violence as well, but the mechanisms may vary from heterosexual relationships.

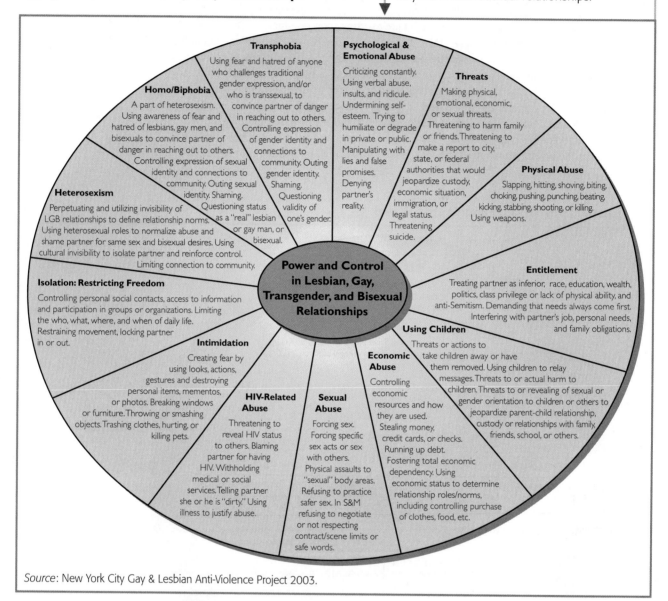

Source: New York City Gay & Lesbian Anti-Violence Project 2003.

and political context experienced by lesbians, gays, transgenders, and bisexuals (LGTBs), including issues such as homophobia or HIV-related abuse. Figure 13.4 illustrates a Power and Control Wheel that may more adequately reflect the realities for those who are not heterosexual (New York City Gay & Lesbian Anti-Violence Project 2003).

Social Policy and Family Resilience

As our society becomes more aware of family violence, this affects our legal and criminal justice systems.

Example: Zero Tolerance in the Legal and Criminal Justice Systems

Throughout the country, state and local governments are taking a tougher stance against violence. **Zero tolerance** is a growing movement that emphasizes tougher laws; more stringent enforcement of those laws; training programs for those who work with victims and offenders, such as physicians or police officers; and a well-coordinated effort to offer victims the protection and services they need. Most programs contain two main features. First, interventions are often concentrated at the misdemeanor level, because these crimes have most often been neglected. By addressing violence at the misdemeanor stage, it is hopeful that more serious injury can be avoided. Second, zero tolerance emphasizes system-wide coordination. Law enforcement, the courts, and social and health services work together to reduce violence and trauma. Together, they identify gaps or duplication in services, and work to better coordinate services in a more efficient and productive manner (Zero Tolerance for Domestic Violence 2003).

Zero tolerance groups are demanding change:

No More . . . Excuses!

No More . . . Tolerance for domestic violence!

No More . . . Minimal sentencing for domestic violence homicides!

No More . . . Restraining order violations going minimally punished!

No More . . . Slap on the hands for offenders!

No More . . . Noneducated domestic violence prosecutors and judges!

No More . . . Excuses for lack of funding! Find funding!

No More . . . Tolerating any excuses!

Begun as a grassroots effort, zero tolerance is taking hold throughout the nation and the world (United Nations Population Fund 2007, 2008). Between 1986 and 2000, the number of shelters, hotlines, and counseling programs specifically serving victims of domestic and partner violence in the United States increased by 50 percent, and the number of legal services programs increased over 300 percent (Tiefenthaler et al. 2005). There are around 1,600 domestic violence shelters in the United States that include emergency shelter services (National Center on Domestic and Sexual Violence 2010). However, because resources tend to be generated at the local rather than federal level, many low-income communities still have few resources or none at all. We can do better.

The zero-tolerance movement is taking hold throughout the world. The United Nations Population Fund (1999), which is the world's largest multilateral source of population assistance, provides billions of dollars in assistance to more than 160 countries, and has recently called for "zero tolerance of violence against women." As the executive director writes,

> It is time that every one of us, individually and collectively, takes a stand to eradicate violence against women in all its manifestations. We must break the culture of violence against women. We must promote zero tolerance of violence against women everywhere.

The United Nations Population Fund sees gender-based violence in all its forms related to women's lack of equality in the world. Beginning with sex selection and female infanticide, and proceeding to rape, forced prostitution, genital cutting, intimate partner violence, and abuses of older women, these manifestations of violence are a result of long-held norms of patriarchy and the devaluation of women socially and politically. They call for zero tolerance.

Conclusion

This chapter illustrates that family problems often have a basis in social structure and cultural norms. The focus of this chapter is violence and abuse among intimates and gender-based violence. It examined dating violence, spouse/partner abuse, child abuse, and elder abuse. Drawing upon social science research and a comparative perspective, we see that many family problems, including violence and abuse, are really *social problems*, not merely personal ones, and therefore require that we examine them in their social, political, and cultural context. Violence among intimates and gender-based abuse have their roots in complex and longstanding traditions of accepting norms promoting violence and male privilege and authority within the family and other social institutions. Violence can also be exacerbated by individual factors such as stress or growing up in and witnessing a violent household.

Key Terms

Child abuse: An attack on a child that results in an injury and violates social norms. (p. 397)

Common couple violence (CCV): Violence that arises out of a specific argument in which at least one partner lashes out physically. (p. 386)

Conflict Tactics Scale (CTS): A violence scale based on people's responses about how they deal with disagreements in relationships. (p. 385)

Cyberstalking: Repeated unwanted attention in the form of e-mail, faxes, bulletin boards, blogs, chat rooms, or other types of media. (p. 387)

Date rape drugs: Used to immobilize a person to facilitate an assault. (p. 392)

Elder abuse: Abuse, neglect, and exploitation of the elderly, often by family members and others close to them. (p. 400)

Gender-based violence: Any act of gender violence that results in or is likely to result in physical, sexual, or psychological harm and suffering to women, including threats of such acts, coercion, or arbitrary deprivations of liberty, whether occurring in public or private life. (p. 381)

Intergenerational transmission of violence: Learning norms and behaviors, including violence, by observing others. (p. 402)

Intimate partner violence: Violence between those who are physically, emotionally, or sexually intimate, such as spouses, partners, or even those who are dating. (p. 384)

Intimate terrorism (IT): Violence that is motivated by a desire to control the other partner. (p. 386)

Medical neglect: Delaying or forgoing a dependent's needed medical, dental, or prescription care. (p. 398)

Mutual violent control (MVC): A violent pattern of behavior in which both partners are controlling and violent. (p. 386)

Neglect: The failure to provide for basic needs for someone who is dependent on you. (p. 397)

Physical abuse: Inflicting physical injury and harm on another person. (p. 398)

Psychological maltreatment: Verbal, mental, or emotional maltreatment that destroys a person's self-esteem. (p. 398)

Sexual abuse: Inappropriate sexual behavior with someone (e.g., a child) for sexual gratification. (p. 398)

Stalking: Obsessive contact or tracking of another person, causing fear. (p. 386)

Trafficking: The illegal recruitment, transport, or sale of human beings into all forms of forced labor and servitude. (p. 382)

Violence among intimates: Physical, economic, sexual, or psychological abuse covering a broad range of relationships. (p. 381)

Violent resistance (VR): Violence associated with self-defense. (p. 386)

Zero tolerance: A growing movement that emphasizes tougher laws; more stringent enforcement of those laws; training programs for those who work with victims and offenders, such as physicians or police officers; and a well-coordinated effort to offer victims the protection and services they need. (p. 407)

Resources on the Internet

National Clearinghouse on Child Abuse and Neglect Information

www.calib.com/nccanch

This website provides information on the prevention, identification, and treatment of child abuse and neglect; it offers statistics and trends on all aspects of child abuse and neglect.

National Coalition Against Domestic Violence

www.ncadv.org

Information and referral center for the public, media, battered women and their children, agencies, and organizations.

National Institute of Justice

www.ojp.usdoj.gov/nij

The National Institute of Justice (NIJ) is the research and development agency of the U.S. Department of Justice and is the only federal agency solely dedicated to researching crime control and justice issues. NIJ provides objective, independent, nonpartisan, evidence-based knowledge and tools to meet the challenges of crime and justice, particularly at the state and local levels.

U.S. Department of Health and Human Services

www.hhs.gov

The U.S. Department of Health and Human Services (DHHS) is the U.S. government's principal agency for protecting the health of all Americans and providing essential human services, especially for those who are least able to help themselves.

Divorce, Repartnering, and Remarriage

CHAPTER 14

CHAPTER OUTLINE

Measuring Divorce 413

Cross-Cultural Comparisons 413

■ **EYE** *on the World:* Comparative Divorce
Rates per 1,000 People *414*

■ **OUR** *Global Community:* Japanese Divorce,
Custody, and Visitation Laws *417*

Historical Trends in the United States 418

Factors Associated with Divorce 419

**The Stations of the Divorce
Experience** 423

Consequences of Divorce for Children 428

Repartnering and Remarriage 431

■ **FAMILIES** *as Lived Experience:* Rebuilding
When Your Relationship Ends *432*

Stepfamily Relationships 435

■ **FAMILIES** *as Lived Experience:* Journey to
Healing *437*

Social Policy and Family Resilience 439

Conclusion 441

Key Terms 441

Resources on the Internet 441

CHAPTER PREVIEW

We talk a lot about the high rate of divorce in the United States. Many people are unaware that divorce is less common today than it was 30 years ago. Nonetheless, the United States still has among the highest rates of divorce in the world. This chapter examines why this is the case and looks at the factors associated with divorce and the implications of divorce. Ending a marriage is a difficult and highly emotional process that affects many people, not just the married couple. In this chapter, you will learn:

- Divorce is measured in many different ways, but the most common way (e.g., "half of all marriages end in divorce") is not the best method

- Cross-cultural and historical trends in divorce

- The macro-level and micro-level factors that are associated with divorce

- Dimensions of the divorce experience and how these differ by sex

- Who has custody of children and who receives child support and alimony

- The short- and long-term consequences of divorce on children

- Issues surrounding repartnering and remarriage

- How common stepfamilies are

- Some of the rewards and challenges associated with stepfamilies

- Initiatives to limit divorce

- Stability of remarriages

What are the effects of divorce on children? That is a complex question and one charged with emotion. When most people think of children and divorce, they imagine how the relationship between parent and child may be affected—yet most children have a kin network that extends beyond simply their parents. They are part of an extended family of aunts, uncles, cousins, and grandparents.

The tie between grandparent and grandchild can be among the closest in this extended kin network. Grandparents can serve as storytellers, confidants, and mentors. Both grandchildren and grandparents themselves derive satisfaction and meaning from these roles. However, what happens when grandparents experience a divorce? How does their divorce affect their relationship with their grandchildren? These are important questions because about one-third of all individuals who had been married and reached age 65 in 2000 experienced a divorce at some point in their lives.

Sociologist Valarie King (2003) used data from a longitudinal study of 538 White rural grandparents living in Iowa to explore how a grandparent's divorce affects his or her relationship with grandchildren. Information was collected directly from grandparents through telephone interviews and mailed questionnaires. King addressed three questions:

1. Does the experience of divorce negatively influence the salience of the grandparent role or involvements with grandchildren?

2. If so, what factors explain the negative influence of divorce on grandparenting?

3. What circumstances moderate the influence of divorce on the grandparent–grandchild relationship?

The results from her analyses indicate that many aspects of grandparenting are negatively associated with having experienced a divorce. Grandparents who had divorced report less contact, engage in fewer shared activities, report feeling less close to their grandchild, are less likely to see themselves as a friend, and report higher levels of conflict within the relationship, compared to grandparents who had not divorced. Most of these differences persisted even when the grandparent remarried.

Why are grandparents who have divorced less involved with their grandchildren? Some of this can be explained by distance. Divorced grandparents tend to live farther away from their grandchild and therefore have less frequent contact. Divorced grandparents also report weaker bonds to their adult children, which may again affect visitation and make it more difficult to sustain strong grandparent–grandchild bonds.

Three factors were found to moderate these relationships. First, the negative effect of grandparental divorce was less for grandmothers than for grandfathers, reflecting their tendency to live closer to their adult child and grandchildren. Second, maternal grandparents tend to be closer than paternal grandparents. Third, a good grandparent–parent relationship can compensate for the negative effects of a grandparent's divorce on the relationship between grandparents and grandchildren. If grandparents and their adult children are close, it is likely that grandparents will have warm and enduring ties with their grandchildren. (King 2003)

A divorce decree may be granted in a matter of minutes by a judge. If you're like many college students, you've seen divorce up close. Family relationships can be irrevocably altered. However, behind those few tense minutes usually lies a long period in which a couple has analyzed, redefined, and reorganized virtually all aspects of their relationship and their lives (Amato 2007; Cartwright and McDowell 2008; Gregson and Ceynar 2009; Wallerstein 2007). Why do couples take years or even decades to move from an unhappy marriage to divorce? It is because most Americans take marriage very seriously and believe that divorce should not be considered a quick or easy reprieve (Martin and Parashar 2006).

This chapter examines the process of divorce, how it unfolds, and its consequences. How does divorce affect children? Since most people eventually remarry after divorce, we will also discuss issues surrounding repartnering. But first, let's begin by examining the prevalence of divorce. Sounds easy, but it really depends on the way that you choose to measure it.

Measuring Divorce

There is a paradox in the United States: although we place a high value on marriage, we also have one of the highest rates of divorce in the world. Other developed countries with which we have much in common pale in comparison.

We commonly hear that "half of all marriages end in divorce." This phrase, however, is somewhat misleading. Some people interpret it to mean that if 100,000 couples married last year, 50,000 divorces were also granted—on the surface it looks as though 50 percent of marriages ended in divorce. But this comparison doesn't really make sense because although these marriages took place in only one year, the divorces are from marriages that may have taken place many years ago. Therefore, this is a misleading comparison and not very useful.

Others use the phrase "half of all marriages end in divorce" to mean that if the current rate of divorce continued over the next several decades, approximately half of all marriages would ultimately end in divorce at some point. Although this could be true, divorce rates fluctuate. For most of history, rates have climbed upward; however, since about 1980, the divorce rate has declined significantly. No one knows what the next 30 years will bring.

How then can we better measure the frequency of divorce? One approach, called the **crude divorce rate**, examines the frequency of divorce per 1,000 people. In the United States in 2009, this amounted to about 3.4 divorces per 1,000 (Tejada-Vera and Sutton 2010). This is a relatively common way of reporting divorce data (for example, by the Centers for Disease Control and Prevention) and can allow for comparisons over time or across countries.

However, the crude divorce rate is problematic. Not all people have married; therefore why should they be included in the statistic? A more useful way to measure the frequency of divorce is to talk about the number of divorces that occur out of every 1,000 married women. This is called a **refined divorce rate**. It also allows us to make historical and international comparisons or to compare the divorce rate state by state. Using the refined divorce rate, there are 16.9 divorces per 1,000 married women in the United States each year (The National Marriage Project 2009). This means that within a year, less than 17 out of 1,000 married women, or less than 2 percent, received a divorce.

These divorce rates are **cross-sectional**, meaning that they reflect rates at only one point in time. However, even though a married woman had a less than 2 percent chance of divorcing last year, she has a far higher chance of divorcing over the *course* of her married life. If only 17 out of 1,000 married women get divorced this year and the remaining 983 did not, they could get divorced the following year, or the year after that, or 15 years later. If the current rate continues, which is unlikely according to family sociologists and demographers, a woman's chances of divorcing are about 50 percent.

Cross-Cultural Comparisons

Is our divorce rate high or low? A question like that is difficult to answer unless you use a comparative perspective—high or low *as compared to what*? As Figure 14.1 shows, the U.S. divorce rate is five times that of Mexico, twice that of China, and 40–50 percent higher than many other developed nations such as Japan or Germany. Russia's divorce rate is even higher (United Nations Statistics Division 2010). The map on pages 414–415 shows the variation in the crude divorce rate around the world. What accounts for such large differences?

Comparative Divorce Rates per 1,000 People

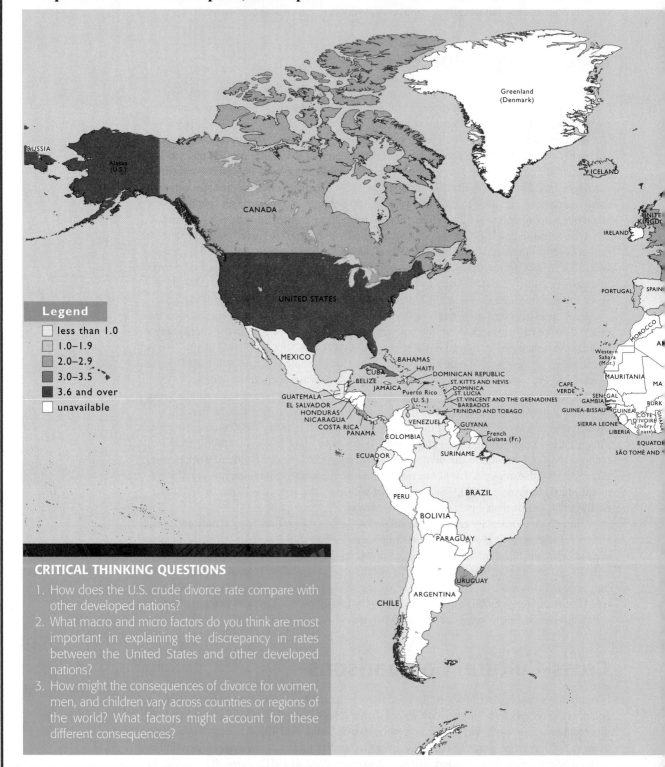

Legend
- less than 1.0
- 1.0–1.9
- 2.0–2.9
- 3.0–3.5
- 3.6 and over
- unavailable

CRITICAL THINKING QUESTIONS

1. How does the U.S. crude divorce rate compare with other developed nations?
2. What macro and micro factors do you think are most important in explaining the discrepancy in rates between the United States and other developed nations?
3. How might the consequences of divorce for women, men, and children vary across countries or regions of the world? What factors might account for these different consequences?

Source: Nugman 2002.

Figure 14.1 **Crude Divorce Rates per 1,000 Population for Selected Countries: 2007–2009**

The chances of divorce in the United States are among the highest in the world.

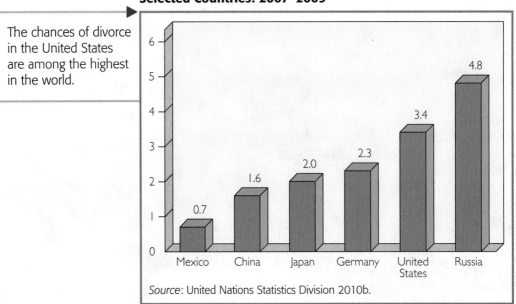

Source: United Nations Statistics Division 2010b.

Divorce rates are related to several factors. First, the *level of socioeconomic development* within a country influences the frequency of divorce. Generally speaking, less developed countries in Africa, Asia, or Central and South America have significantly lower divorce rates than do more developed countries in North America and Europe (United Nations Statistics Division 2010).

China, which has undergone rapid socioeconomic development, has had a surge in the divorce rate, increasing about 50 percent since 2000 (United Nations Statistics Division 2010). The increase is due to many factors, including new social and economic freedom, Western influences, and the decline of parental and political involvement in mate selection. Most Americans may find this unbelievable but, until recently, separating couples in China needed their *work unit's* permission before a divorce could be granted. Permission was rarely given. However, the rules have now changed, and unhappy couples can now visit their local community center and—if both parties agree—the divorce can be issued in only 10 minutes.

A second factor that may influence how rarely or frequently divorce occurs is the *dominant religion* that is practiced. For example, much of Central and South America is dominated by Roman Catholicism, which strictly forbids divorce in all but the most extreme circumstances. In Italy, an industrialized but largely Catholic nation, divorce was illegal until the 1980s and remains rare today. Likewise, in Ireland, the Catholic Church was successful in forbidding divorce until 1997. Religious institutions play a strong role in defining cultural norms toward divorce and other moral issues.

Third, divorce tends to be more restrictive in *patriarchal societies* where women have few legal rights and are considered to be their husband's property (Amato 1994; Greenstein and Davis 2006). In many countries, men are allowed to divorce their wives for almost any reason, yet women are not allowed to initiate divorce except under the most extreme circumstances. In many Muslim countries, for example, husbands can unilaterally divorce their wives by repeating the phrase three times in front of witnesses, "I divorce thee." A wife seeking a divorce, in contrast, must go to a religious court and prove that her husband has failed to support his family or has otherwise had a harmful moral effect on the family (Human Rights Watch 2004).

Women's low status, and particularly their economic dependence on men in patriarchal nations, is a critical factor in predicting divorce rates (Greenstein and Davis 2006; Seccombe and Lee 1986). For example, a study of 71 nations found that those countries in which women had greater access to economic resources had higher divorce rates than nations where women had less access to these resources (Greenstein and Davis 2006). Increased economic activity is one avenue through which women can be independent from their husbands, thereby possibly altering divorce law and customs.

Moreover, in highly patriarchal societies, child custody and spousal support laws are designed to perpetuate male dominance and discourage women from asking for a divorce. In Taiwan, custody of children goes automatically to the father, based on the tradition that children carry on the father's family name. In an exchange to obtain custody of children, some women pay their husbands large sums of money (Chang 1993). In Iran, wives are only entitled to spousal support for three months, despite the very limited economic opportunities available for women. Most divorced women must therefore return to their families for support, often in shame. In India, a woman rarely receives any of the marital assets because these are assumed to belong to her husband and his family. Many Indian women do not even ask for child support out of fear that their husbands will also try to gain custody. The following box, "Our Global Community: Japanese Divorce, Custody, and Visitation Laws," reveals how Japanese laws disregard the rights of noncustodial parents to see their children after a divorce.

One factor associated with divorce rates is the level of patriarchy in a society. For example, in many Muslim cultures, women cannot easily initiate a divorce.

O U R

Global Community

Japanese Divorce, Custody, and Visitation Laws

The laws surrounding divorce, custody, and visitation differ from one country to another and reflect deeply held cultural norms about families. The following illustrates how Japan, a modern developed nation, has approached divorce, custody, and visitation laws.

Divorce has constantly been on the mind of Imelda (not her real name), a 36-year-old Filipino woman who married a Japanese man 7 years ago, but the soft-spoken woman says that despite the nagging loneliness and physical abuse she sometimes has to endure from her husband, she will never leave the man she despises for fear of losing her two children. "I asked my husband for a divorce after my first child was born. He said okay, and told me to leave that night taking only my clothes. I couldn't bear to part from my son who

was then only 10 months old," she explained—so she stayed on.

Imelda is one of a growing number of women and men who are locked in miserable marriages because Japanese laws ignore the individual rights of parents to see their children after a divorce. Joint custody is illegal, and child visitation is not a legal right under Japanese law. The right of children to have access to both parents is ignored. This is why, in many cases, women who want to leave their Japanese husbands do not do so, and their predicament is complicated by the fact that they often face economic hardship raising their children. The situation is particularly difficult for foreign mothers and fathers because they have the added problem of getting legal visas to stay on in the country after a divorce.

(continued)

(continued)

The problems experienced by foreign men and women with Japanese spouses with gaining access to children after separation or divorce were highlighted in 2006 by the Japanese chapter of the Children's Rights Council, a Washington-based organization. Saying the inability to maintain ties with their children was akin to child abduction, several foreign nationals spoke out against a system that they said denied their children the right to see them and the opportunity to develop closer ties with their biological parents. Dale Martin, an Englishman, says he has not seen his 6-year-old daughter for the past 2 years because his Japanese wife refuses to allow it. This, he adds, is despite his telephone calls and letters and a hard-won visitation agreement signed in family courts. "I have no news about her even while living a few hours away from her home. I call this a violation of my daughter's rights to have access to her father," he told the press. Margaret Leyman, an American journalist living in Tokyo, says her Japanese former husband prohibits her son from meeting with her. "My son, who is 12 now, lives with my mother-in-law after the family court decided I was, as a working woman and foreigner, not a responsible mother," she explained. "They have prohibited him from seeing me." In both cases, the foreign spouses signed divorce papers that had, without their knowledge, included the awarding of custody of their children to their estranged husbands or wives.

Japanese laws recognize divorce, granted on mutual consent, on a form signed by both parties. Both Leyman and Martin assumed, in accordance with laws in many Western countries, that custody is a separate issue from divorce and would be treated as such under the Japanese legal system. "I was shocked to realise that I had signed away my right to see my child and also denied my son's right to have a mother as well as enjoy a different culture," recalled Leyman.

In desperation, she tried to get at least visitation rights to her child. However, the concept of visitation rights is not deeply ingrained in the Japanese system. Japanese tradition views children not as individuals with their own rights but as belonging to the family. Even if successful, visitation may only be a couple of hours per month.

Sources: Children's Rights Network of Japan 2006; Kakuchi 2003.

CRITICAL THINKING QUESTIONS

1. Why do you think Japanese custody laws are so much different than those in the United States?
2. Do you think that the custody law is a gender issue? Why or why not?

Historical Trends in the United States

Many people think of divorce as part of the 1960's "me-generation" fallout, but divorce and desertion have been common throughout much of U.S. history (Degler 1980). Legal divorce may have been rare prior to the mid-nineteenth century; however, separation and desertion occurred in its place.

The early colonies recognized adultery, desertion, and usually violence as grounds for divorce; however, because of patriarchal norms, few divorces were granted to wives at their initiation. An early study of marriage and divorce conducted in the mid-1800s examined 29 cases of divorce based on "cruelty" in which the wife was the defendant. In almost every case, the "cruelty" committed was that the wife was attempting to break out of the traditional subordinate role in one way or another (Wright 1889). Half of these cases were based on her refusal to do domestic chores such as keeping her husband's clothes in repair or cooking his meals.

Early feminists spoke in favor of making divorce more available to women as a way to improve women's rights and position in marriage (Degler 1980). They worried that women were locked into destructive marriages, further eroding their emancipation.

Figure 14.2 Crude and Refined Divorce Rates: 1940–2009

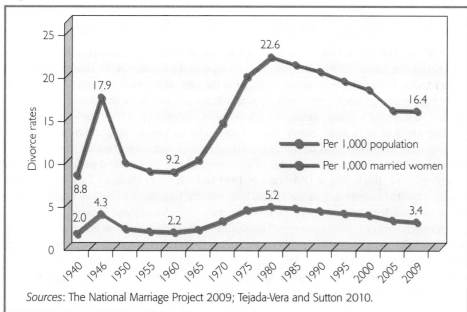

Sources: The National Marriage Project 2009; Tejada-Vera and Sutton 2010.

The divorce rate peaked after World War II, then declined, and peaked again around 1980, then declined yet again.

The divorce rate gradually rose between 1860 and 1940. Then the divorce rate surged in the mid-1940s after World War II ended. It is possible that many couples rushed into marriages during wartime and later faced difficulties they had not imagined in their hurry to marry. In addition, increasing urbanization and geographic mobility broke down traditional ties, and women's greater economic opportunities allowed them to end an unhappy marriage.

Figure 14.2 illustrates the trends in the crude and refined divorce rates in the United States between 1940 and 2009 (Hamilton et al. 2010; Tejada-Vera and Sutton 2010). After the rush of divorces following World War II, the divorce rate fell to around 9 per 1,000 married women. During the 1950s, the divorce rate remained relatively low; however, by the 1960s the divorce rate began to rise again, peaking at approximately 23 divorces per 1,000 married women around 1980. Since then the rate of divorce has declined sharply to 16.4 per 1,000 married women, and 3.4 per 1,000 people. Thus, despite all the attention divorce received in the media, married couples are much less likely to get divorced today than they were a generation ago.

WHAT DO YOU THINK?

Do you think divorce in the United States will stabilize, decrease, or increase over the next decade? How will our changing demographic structure (e.g., an increase in Hispanic groups, delayed marriage and childbearing) and social trends (e.g., economic recession, greater equality between men and women) influence the divorce rate?

Factors Associated with Divorce

If we asked people in the United States why they divorced, we would likely get many different answers that primarily focused on individual attributes or personal problems: *"We grew apart...," "We are just too different...," "She met someone new...," "He doesn't listen to me...."* However, family scholars are interested in the *social patterns* associated with divorce. These patterns include structural factors as well as personal explanations to help us understand why people divorce.

Macro-Level Factors

Let us first examine the structural factors that contribute to divorce.

Changes in Divorce Laws   The frequency of divorce reflects the laws of a particular culture (Kneip and Bauer 2009). Until recently, to be granted a divorce in the United States, one partner had to file suit against the other, blaming the partner for violating marriage vows, or making the marriage intolerable, such as mental cruelty, adultery, or desertion. Being found "at fault" could affect custody arrangements, property settlements, and alimony awards.

Beginning in 1953, states slowly began to amend their laws to support **no-fault divorce** as a way to make divorce less acrimonious, coercive, and restrictive. Instead, couples could simply say that they have irreconcilable differences and that they wished to divorce without assigning blame. Beginning in Oklahoma in 1953 and Alaska in 1962, no-fault divorce laws spread across the country during the 1970s. Utah was the final holdout but eventually enacted no-fault divorce legislation in 1987 (Nakonezny et al. 1995; Vlosky and Monroe 2002).

A high number of divorces occurred immediately after legislation was passed (Nakonezny et al. 1995; Rodgers et al. 1997). This may indicate a backlog of unhappy couples waiting until the legislation went into effect so that they could divorce more easily and without blame. Today, states vary somewhat in certain aspects of their divorce laws (e.g., waiting periods). However, no-fault divorce is available in all 50 states.

Women's Employment   Trends in women's employment opportunities are also correlated with divorce. As we have learned in previous chapters, throughout most of history, married couples were tightly bound together because they needed the labor of one another to survive and support their families. Today, most married women, including those with children, are employed outside the home for pay (Bureau of Labor Statistics 2010b). This change in employment patterns has enabled women to more easily support themselves and end an unhappy marriage. Women who are more self-sufficient, such as those who have higher incomes, or who earn more than half the household income are more likely to divorce than those who are economically dependent (Rogers 2004).

Changing Attitudes Toward Divorce   Cultural views about divorce also influence how frequently a divorce will occur. Divorce itself and divorced people in the United States faced heavy stigma through most of history. For example, the unflattering term *divorcée*, which was applied to women only, had sexually suggestive connotations. It was unlikely that any divorced woman or man would have been elected to a major political office; however, in 1980 Ronald Reagan beat the odds after some discussion of his divorce. And, in the 1996 presidential election, candidate Bob Dole's divorce was barely mentioned. More accepting attitudes toward divorce are probably both a cause and a consequence of an increasing divorce rate.

As divorce became less stigmatized, unhappy couples considered it an appropriate way to end their relationship. Moreover, some people who contemplate marriage see it as only semi-permanent, noting that they could "opt out" if it did not work. One study based on a nationally representative sample of high school seniors found that only 57 percent of boys and 63 percent of girls claim, "It is 'very likely' that I will stay married to the same person for life" (The National Marriage Project 2009).

But this doesn't really mean that people take marriage and divorce lightly. In fact, more people now oppose divorce and believe a divorce should be more difficult to obtain than people did a generation ago. A study by the Pew Research Center (Taylor et al. 2008), based on a representative sample of adults across the United States, found that 45 percent of adults aged 18–29 believe that divorce "should be avoided except in extreme situations" compared to only 32 percent of adults aged 65 and over who feel that way. To repeat, it is *younger*

Figure 14.3   Views About Divorce by Sex, Race/Ethnicity, and Age in Years—Which statement comes closer to your views about divorce?

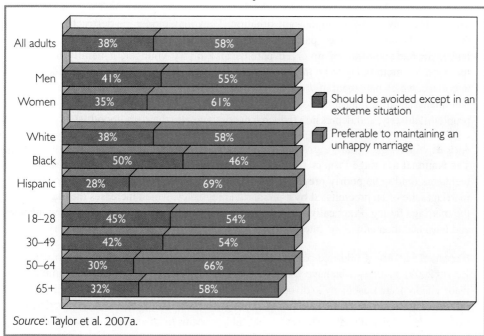

	Should be avoided except in an extreme situation	Preferable to maintaining an unhappy marriage
All adults	38%	58%
Men	41%	55%
Women	35%	61%
White	38%	58%
Black	50%	46%
Hispanic	28%	69%
18–28	45%	54%
30–49	42%	54%
50–64	30%	66%
65+	32%	58%

Men, Blacks, and younger adults are most likely to believe that divorce should be avoided in extreme circumstances.

Source: Taylor et al. 2007a.

adults, not older adults, who want divorce to be more restrictive, perhaps because many of them experienced divorce as children. The researchers also found that Blacks were more likely than Whites or Hispanics to want divorce more restrictive, as shown in Figure 14.3. In fact, a fear of divorce keeps many low-income mothers from marrying in the first place (Edin and Kefalas 2005). In other words, it appears that those people who are at a higher risk for divorce actually want it to be more difficult to get.

Cultural Norms   Other cultural issues may affect divorce. Immigrants to the United States often face new relationship stressors that increase the likelihood of divorce. Some of these stressors revolve around gender expectations, which tend to be more traditional in the country of origin. For example, immigrants from Latin America or the Middle East are more likely to believe that a man's primary responsibility is to earn a living and support the family, and a woman should tend to the home and children. However, after immigrating to the United States, they find less support for these traditional expectations, and it may take both spouses working to make ends meet financially. One study of Iranian immigrants to the United States found women tended to adopt views similar to mainstream America, whereas men's views remained more traditional (Hojat et al. 2000). This difference, coupled with the need for two incomes and women's increased job opportunities, paved the way for potential conflict.

Micro-Level Factors

In addition to these macro-level societal forces that influence divorce rates, specific individual characteristics may also influence the risk of couples divorcing. Naturally, this doesn't mean that all people with these characteristics will divorce; it just means that they are more likely to do so.

Parental Divorce   People whose parents have divorced are also more likely to divorce (Amato and Hohmann-Marriott 2007; Sassler et al. 2009). There are several possible explanations for this. First, adult children model their own parents' behavior. They may learn that divorce is a way out of an unpleasant situation. They may model the destructive behaviors that led to the demise of their parents' marriage, such as poor communication skills or violence. Second, children of divorced parents also marry younger, generally have lower incomes, are more likely to be involved in a nonmarital pregnancy, and are less likely to go to college, which puts them in several higher-risk categories. Third, parental divorce also has potentially negative long-term consequences for children's mental health, such as emotional problems, anxiety, and depression, which can continue into their adulthood.

Age at Marriage   Marrying young increases the likelihood of divorce (Lowenstein 2005; The National Marriage Project 2006). Teen marriages are particularly at high risk because teenagers tend to be poorly prepared for marriage and its responsibilities. Moreover, teen marriages are often precipitated by a premarital pregnancy, which increases the likelihood of the marriage failing. Practically speaking, the young couples are likely to have low incomes and have had their education interrupted, also putting them in a higher risk category.

Parental Status   Child-free couples are more likely to divorce (Bramlett and Mosher 2002; Hewitt 2009). Families who have young preschool-aged children in particular, or families with many children, are least likely to divorce. This, of course, says nothing about the quality of these marriages; people may stay in unfulfilling marriages because they feel it is the appropriate thing to do for their children's sake. The sex of the children seems to affect the likelihood of divorcing as well; families with only boys are less likely to divorce than are families with only girls.

Nonmarital Childbearing   Couples who bear a child or conceive prior to marriage have higher divorce rates than other couples. Part of this may be explained by the fact that a nonmarital pregnancy may encourage people to marry when they may not otherwise have chosen to do so. It may also encourage them to marry before they are financially or emotionally ready. Pregnancy, caring for a newborn, and raising a child put additional strains and stresses on a relationship. Couples who have not yet had the opportunity to truly get to know themselves and their partner as a couple may have a more difficult time transitioning to their role as parents.

Race and Ethnicity   The likelihood of divorce differs among racial or ethnic groups (Clarkwest 2007). Hispanic and Asian groups are least likely to divorce and Blacks are most likely to do so. These differences are likely a combination of structural and cultural factors. For example, the lack of jobs for urban Black males and high rates of unemployment or poverty could make marriage and remarriage less attractive to Black women (Wilson 1996). What might explain the relatively lower rate of divorce among most Hispanic and Asian groups? The most common explanation is a cultural one, focusing on the primacy of the family; the importance of Catholicism among Hispanics, which does not recognize divorce; and greater tolerance for patriarchal norms.

Education   On average, persons with lower levels of education are more likely to divorce than are persons with higher levels of education (Cohn 2009; Heaton 2002). A college degree reduces the risk of divorce, but the relationship is less clearcut for women than it is for men. Some studies suggest that women with very high levels of education are also more likely to divorce, especially later in the marriage, because it contributes to their ability to be economically independent (Heidemann et al. 1998).

Income   Divorce is more common among persons with lower incomes than among those with higher incomes (The National Marriage Project 2009; Taylor et al. 2008). Although certainly not all wealthy couples have happy marriages and not all couples with lower incomes are doomed to an unhappy or unstable union, unemployment, poverty, and financial strains do take a toll and can cause marital conflict, a greater chance of violence, and divorce.

Degree of Similarity Between Spouses   Spouses are more likely to divorce when they are different from one another in key ways, such as age, race, ethnic group, or religion (Bratter and King 2008; Vaaler et al. 2009; Zhang and Van Hook 2009). For example, a large study of over 23,000 married couples found that interracial marriages faced a higher risk for divorce, especially marriages involving a Black husband and a White wife, or a Hispanic husband and a White wife (Zhang and Van Hook 2009). Couples who differ from each other in some of these important ways may have different values, norms, or experiences. They may encounter additional stress from outsiders who disapprove of their marriage. This could lead to greater conflict and less social support.

WHAT DO YOU THINK?

Consider your odds for divorce. Are they high or low? For example, did your parents divorce? Do you plan to have children? What do you think your income will be when you are finished with school? What are your attitudes toward divorce? What type of culture do you live in?

The Stations of the Divorce Experience

Divorce is not simply the ending of a relationship between two people; it alters or even severs many personal and legal ties. A divorce can end relationships with family members; with friends who find themselves taking sides; with neighbors if you have moved away; and with community groups of which you are no longer a member or can no longer afford to join.

The Emotional Dimension

The emotional aspects of divorce begin long before any legal steps are taken and may end long afterward. One or both partners may feel angry, resentful, sad, or rejected. Generally, one spouse initiates the breakup of the marriage (Hewitt et al. 2006). Symbolic interaction theory reminds us here of how the interpretation we attach to events affects its meaning. Initiators have the advantage of preparing emotionally for the separation. A common pattern is that an initiator expresses general discontent at first, but without attributing it to the marriage *per se*. They may try to alter the relationship or their spouse's behavior by suggesting such remedies as a new job, having a baby, or some other substantial change to the nature of the relationship. They may even use the threat of leaving as a way to demand change. The other spouse's reaction—anger, resentment, sadness, resolve, or rejection—shapes his or her emotional response.

However, the labels of "initiator" versus "noninitiator" may really be accidental and random (Hopper 1993). In fact, divorcing spouses sometimes disagree as to who the initiator actually was (Hewitt et al. 2006; Sweeney 2002). Hopper (1993) found that both spouses were generally aware that they had multiple marital problems, experienced discontent and contemplated divorce or separation, and were ambivalent about the best way to resolve their marital problems.

Many factors influence the emotional dimension of a divorce, such as the degree of unhappiness and conflict they experience in the marriage, whether they have young children, their ages, and the amount of time they have been married. Men and women often have different emotional challenges following divorce (Blekesaune 2008). As feminist theory reminds us, society offers men and women different opportunities and constraints that help explain our gendered experiences. For example, women are more likely than men to have financial problems after a divorce, as discussed below (Grall 2009). In contrast, men often have a more difficult time emotionally after a divorce, and in some cases this stress is so extreme that it can lead to increased illness or an early death. One reason for this emotional difficulty is that men tend to have a weaker network of supportive relationships (Chu 2005). Men are also more dependent on marriage, and those who have been in more traditional marriages may find routine household tasks, such as cooking, cleaning, and shopping, to be daunting. Finally, most men lose custody of their children, and for many fathers, this loss is devastating (Bokker et al. 2006; Hawthorne and Lennings 2008).

The Legal Dimension

There is a strong impetus to view family relationships as a private matter, but some aspects are governed by law. The state intervenes to mandate or restrict how family members act toward one another or to define rights or privileges, such as child support, visitation, or payment of alimony. The state is also involved in dividing up assets and property, including the home, cars, savings, and retirement accounts and dividing up debts, including credit cards or loans.

Hiring attorneys to iron out the division of assets and child visitation can cost an average of over $15,000 (Kallen 2008). Because a lawyer represents only his or her client's interests, which are not necessarily in the interests of all parties, both sides usually hire their own representation, increasing the drain on the couple's assets. Some assets are difficult to divide easily. For example, suppose one spouse has earned a college degree while the other has worked full-time at a low-wage job to put his or her partner through school. How can the couple, or the court, divide this asset—the college degree—which translates into real future earning power?

The Parental Dimension

When a divorcing couple has children, they must design and agree upon co-parenting strategies. For example, the issue of custody can be more complicated than you might think.

Many divorcing couples have children, and, therefore, must decide about custody arrangements. Legal custody refers to who has the legal authority to make important decisions. Physical custody refers to where the child will live.

Custody **Legal custody** refers to who has the legal authority to make important decisions concerning the children, such as where they will go to school, in what community or state they will reside, and who will be notified in case of a health emergency or school problem. In the past, legal custody was usually given solely to the parent with whom the child lived, but this is changing. Today, **joint legal custody** is becoming more common; it refers to noncustodial parents (usually fathers) also retaining their legal rights with respect to their children.

Physical custody refers to the place where the children actually reside. This seemingly straightforward concept can actually be difficult to measure when interviewing parents. Mothers are more likely

than fathers to report that children live with the mother, whereas fathers are more likely than mothers to say that the children either live with the father or with both parents (Lin et al. 2004). There is an obvious discrepancy that has not been explained.

The court maintains that living arrangements should be based on the best interests of the child, which theoretically should not discriminate against men or women in any systematic way. Most divorced families have sole physical custody arrangements, where the child formally resides with only one parent and the other parent is awarded visitation. In about 8 of 10 divorces involving children, mothers have physical custody (Grall 2009).

In the past, fathers usually could not obtain custody of children unless the mother was proven to be unfit or there were other extenuating circumstances. Today, the courts are more open; however, generally men do not seek physical custody. A small but growing number of fathers do seek and gain custody, often through mutual agreement with the mother. Their households tend to be better off financially than single-mother households, but they still have lower incomes and twice the poverty rate of families in which children live with both parents (Fields 2004; DeNavas-Walt et al. 2010).

Relative to White men, Black men are less likely to have ever married the mothers of their children (Hamer and Marchioro 2002). Therefore, the circumstances of their custody arrangements are somewhat different. One study found that Black fathers often became custodians of their children by default, often without any real discussion with the mothers. Most fathers were reluctant to accept their children at first but did so because of pressure or because they assumed the situation would be only temporary (Hamer and Marchioro 2002):

> I thought, "hey, she'll go in [into drug rehabilitation center], get cleaned up, and come and get these kids." But no! [laughing] it did not happen that way at all. These kids have been living with me; they are my pride and joy and have been since '94, that's when they came to live with Daddy. But in the beginning I tell you, I did not want any part of it and they [Child Service Workers] had to practically threaten me to do it—they made me realize there was no other place for my kids to go, and my kids had been through a lot of bad things with their mother. I didn't know the extent of it until they was living with me. (p. 121)

About 17 percent of families and courts are deciding on **joint physical custody**, meaning that children spend a near equal portion of time in the homes of both parents, perhaps alternating weeks or days within a week (Lyster 2007; Spruijt and Duindam 2010). It is far more common in dual-earning families and those in which mothers either have high levels of education or have failed to complete high school (Juby et al. 2005). This arrangement requires a tremendous amount of cooperation and, therefore, tends to work best when both parents are willing to facilitate smooth transitions for the children.

Joint physical custody is controversial. Supporters claim that it lightens the economic and emotional responsibilities of single parenthood and that it provides men with the opportunity to routinely care for and nurture their children, which, in turn, is in the child's best interests. They say that joint physical custody is also in the fathers' interests (Bokker et al. 2006) because close relationships with biological children increase fathers' well-being. On the other hand, critics believe that joint physical custody is disruptive to children's routines and school schedules. They claim that it can exacerbate conflict between parents because no two parenting strategies are identical and that it creates loyalty conflicts for children.

The Economic Dimension

Divorce tends to reduce the income of women and children considerably (DeNavas-Walt et al. 2010; Gadalla 2009). A study using a large and nationally representative sample compared men and women's incomes for up to five years during and after divorce (or separation). It found a dramatic drop in women's income and a slight drop in men's income during

TABLE 14.1 Median Income and Percent in Poverty by Family Type, 2009

Married couple households have the highest incomes and are the least likely to live in poverty.

	MEDIAN INCOME	PERCENT IN POVERTY
Married Couple Families	$71,830	6%
Male Householder, No Wife Present	$48,084	17%
Female Householder, No Husband Present	$32,597	30%

Source: DeNavas-Walt et al. 2010.

the divorce year. One in five women became impoverished, as compared to only one in thirteen men (Gadalla 2008). One year later, women's average income was 80 percent of men's, although women remained twice as likely as men to be impoverished. Four years after divorce, women's average income still only reached 85 percent of men's (Gadalla 2008, 2009).

The Census Bureau reports similar findings, as shown in Table 14.1. An average married couple has an annual income of around $72,000, compared to $48,000 for a single male-headed family (no wife present) and only $33,000 for a single female-headed family (no husband present). Female-headed families are nearly twice as likely as male-headed families, and five times as likely as married-couple families, to live in poverty (DeNavas-Walt et al. 2010).

Why such a large income difference? First, women generally retain custody of children. As just mentioned, over 80 percent of single parents are mothers (Grall 2009). Therefore, child-rearing responsibilities have a strong impact upon a single mother's lifestyle. For example, her employment opportunities may be more restricted than those of her ex-husband because the demands of children may force her to alter her work schedule; reduce her ability to work overtime; or limit opportunities for travel, relocation, and further training needed for advancement.

A second reason for divorced women's poor economic situation is the lower wages paid to women generally. Women who work full-time average $36,000 per year—about 80 percent of the wages paid to men in 2009 (Institute for Women's Policy Research 2010), and the gap for Blacks and Hispanics is far higher at 69 percent and 60 percent, respectively.

Third, women are more likely to have intermittent work histories. Some couples had a mutual agreement that, at least when the children were young, the husbands would support the family while the mother stayed home to take care of their children. Not surprisingly, after several years of unemployment, some women cannot reenter the labor force easily or they find that their skills are outdated.

A fourth reason for divorced women's financial difficulties is that many noncustodial parents do not pay child support regularly or pay all that is owed. An ex-spouse may also default on alimony owed. Let's turn to these issues in depth.

Child Support   According to the Census Bureau, only about 54 percent of custodial parents have some type of agreement or court award establishing child support from the noncustodial parent (Grall 2009). Of these custodial parents, only about three-quarters receive any child support at all, and less than half of custodial parents received the full amount on a regular basis (Grall 2009). Moreover, only about one-third of parents paying child support provided health insurance for their children, paid their medical bills, or included health care costs in their child support payments, and thus, custodial parents (usually mothers) end up paying these costs themselves (Grall 2009). Medical bills can easily pull families into poverty (Seccombe and Hoffman 2007).

Millions of families do not have a formal agreement about child support. About 700,000 have a nonlegal informal support agreement, and 5.5 million have no child support agreement at all. It may seem odd that parents fail to have a child support agreement in place. Reasons

Figure 14.4   Reasons No Legal Agreement Established for Custodial Parents: 2008

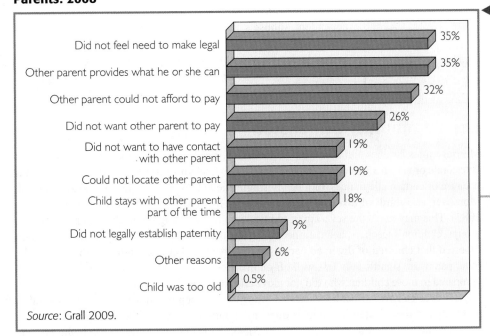

Did not feel need to make legal — 35%
Other parent provides what he or she can — 35%
Other parent could not afford to pay — 32%
Did not want other parent to pay — 26%
Did not want to have contact with other parent — 19%
Could not locate other parent — 19%
Child stays with other parent part of the time — 18%
Did not legally establish paternity — 9%
Other reasons — 6%
Child was too old — 0.5%

Nearly half of custodial parents do not have a legal child support agreement. Many do not feel the need to enforce child support and feel that the noncustodial parent is doing what he or she can.

Source: Grall 2009.

for this are shown in Figure 14.4 and include sentiments such as "did not feel the need to make it legal" (35 percent), "other parent pays what they can" (35 percent), or various other reasons (Grall 2009).

Alimony   One of the most contentious aspects of marital dissolutions may be the award-ing of **alimony**, defined as post-divorce support for a former spouse (Shehan et al. 2002). There are several factors a judge considers when deciding whether to grant alimony. These differ across states, but they usually involve things like the parties' relative ability to earn money, now and in the future; their respective age and health; the length of the marriage; the age of children, if any; the amount of money and property involved; and the conduct of the parties. Generally, alimony is awarded if one spouse has been economically dependent on the other spouse for most of a lengthy marriage (Divorceinfo.com 2006).

The amount and duration of alimony payments can vary substantially. *Permanent alimony* provides payment for an indefinite or unlimited period of time and is designed to main-tain a spouse's standard of living close to that which she or he had prior to the divorce. It may be awarded when the spouse is clearly unable to be self-supporting, such as when she or he is elderly or in poor health. For example, a man who initiates a divorce from his 50-year-old wife who has been a full-time homemaker over the course of their marriage may be required to pay permanent alimony because it is unlikely that she will obtain employment sufficient to support herself. A woman in this situation is often referred to as a **displaced homemaker**.

Gross alimony is a fixed, lump-sum amount that can be paid in one, several, or monthly installments over a short period of time. It is designed to provide compensation for contribu-tions made during the marriage. For example, a judge may require a man who has just com-pleted medical school prior to the divorce to reimburse his wife for the financial costs she incurred putting him through school by paying her a lump sum of money.

Limited duration alimony involves payment over a fixed period of time, mandated by the judge or state statute. Its purpose is to help support the spouse during a period of transition and reorganization to become self-sufficient. For example, a judge may require a husband to pay a specific monthly sum for a few years until all the young children are in school.

Rehabilitative alimony is specifically targeted to improve the dependent spouse's employability. It may be awarded so the spouse can finish school or training. For example, a husband may be required to reimburse his former spouse for the costs associated with obtaining her college degree, including tuition, books, and partial or complete living expenses (Shehan et al. 2002).

The Community Dimension

Marriage joins families and friendship networks; divorce breaks them apart. Relationships can deteriorate or vanish altogether. Divorced people may feel uncomfortable with their old friends because of certain allegiances, or a newly single friend may threaten those who are married. Moreover, two-thirds of divorced mothers move in the first year after a divorce (McLanahan 1983). This may mean the severing of old ties with friends, neighbors, church or community groups, children's teachers, and their networks, and the building of new ones. One recent study reported that children of divorced parents who moved further than an hour's drive from the other parent are significantly less well off on many child mental and physical health measures compared to those children who did not move after divorce (Braver et al. 2003).

Divorce can also affect the extended family. One group that has sought legal protection and captured media attention in their quest to maintain ties with children after a divorce is grandparents (Giles-Sims and Lockhart 2005). Grandparents are important kin who provide unique benefits to children. However, in some divorces, the parent may choose to deny or strictly limit visitation to former in-laws, their children's grandparents.

The Psychic Divorce

As time moves on, most people adjust to the separation and divorce (Gregson and Ceynar 2009; Thomas and Ryan 2008). There is no specific time frame to this adjustment, as some people take many months, whereas others take many years. The psychic divorce refers to the process of regaining psychological autonomy and beginning to feel whole and complete again as a single person. As people experience this phase of the divorce experience, ex-wives and ex-husbands must learn to distance themselves from the still-loved and still-hated aspects of the ex-spouse. Forgiveness is an important predictor of well-being (Bonach et al. 2005), but it often takes years to achieve (Yaben 2009).

Let's now turn to how divorce affects children. About half of all divorce cases occur among families with children. Although presumably at least one of the spouses *chooses* to divorce, children have little choice in the matter.

Consequences of Divorce for Children

What are the effects of divorce on children? Some people try to brush off the effects of their parents' divorce saying, "Hey, I turned out just fine....", but the truth is that many people are deeply affected by their parents' divorce and remain so for many years (Ahrons 2007; Amato 2007; Cartwright and McDowell 2008; Dennison and Koerner 2008). Some factors that influence the consequences of divorce are micro-level ones, such as personal coping skills, or their relationship with their (usually) noncustodial father. Others are more macro in nature, such as their mother's economic situation. Because the interweaving of factors is complex, it may be helpful to distinguish between short- and long-term effects.

Short-Term Effects

The first year or two after a divorce can be particularly tough for both adults and children because of grief and the numerous transitions they face (Ricci 2007). Parents may be distracted and preoccupied with their own distress, thereby making it difficult to be an effective parent and offer the support, nurturance, and discipline that their children need (Buehler and Gerard 2002; Taylor and Andrews 2009). In fact, some parents turn to their children for comfort and support (Afifi et al. 2009).

During this time, children are also grieving the loss of their intact family and are dealing with new feelings and fears (Ricci 2007). They may feel guilty and depressed. Young children are egocentric and often feel that they are responsible for their parents' conflict and divorce—that if they had just behaved better, their parents would not have divorced. During this crisis period, children face many situations with which they must learn to cope. These may include (1) handling parental conflict; (2) weakened parental bonds; (3) coping with a reduced standard of living; and (4) adjusting to many transitions.

Handling Parental Conflict   Sometimes, parents involve children in their disputes by using them as a weapon to hurt the ex-spouse, getting them to take sides in a dispute, or using them to gather information. Parents may communicate their anger and hostility toward one another to their children and demean and ridicule their ex-spouse. During and after a breakup, children have fewer emotional and behavioral problems if their parents can cooperate or at least minimize overt conflict in front of the child (Ahrons 2005; Bing et al. 2009).

Weakened Parental Bonds   During a separation and after a divorce, children most often live with their mothers, and many children see their fathers only sporadically, if at all. Somewhere between 15 and 40 percent of children have not seen their noncustodial parent over the course of a year; the figure is highest for children whose parents never married, and somewhat lower for children whose parents have divorced (Koball and Principe 2002).

Yet, the research continues to show that fathers are extremely important in their children's lives (Booth et al. 2010; Hawkins et al. 2007; Lundberg et al. 2007). Children whose fathers are more involved in their lives are less likely to have behavioral problems, including delinquency and depression (Carlson 2006). Dads matter. They provide important social capital, in addition to love and material support. Moreover, noncustodial fathers who have frequent contact with their children during their younger years often have closer relationships with their children as they mature into adulthood as well (Aquilino 2006).

Why do so many noncustodial fathers fail to see their children regularly? The reasons are more complex than we might first think. Certainly, many fathers *choose* to ignore their children. But the residential parent (generally the mother) is a gatekeeper (Trinder 2008), and she may also interfere with the relationship between father and children by not supporting access, not cooperating in arranging visits, being inflexible about altering visitation schedules, and discouraging children from visiting (Pearson and Thoennes 1998).

Divorce usually brings many transitions to children. Often, the custodial parent can no longer afford the family's home. For children, this may mean making new friends and going to a new school.

A Reduced Standard of Living   As we have discussed, the standard of living for mothers and their children often drops considerably after a divorce. Everyone in the family must adjust to a lower income. Certain types of clothing, outings, vacations, or other aspects of a family's lifestyle that were the norm prior to the divorce may no longer be possible. Given the

severely limited budgets of most divorced families, consumption patterns must change. Teenagers may need to work at after-school jobs to provide basic necessities for themselves or their family.

Adjusting to Transitions   A divorce can cause children to go through many unsettling transitions (Kelly 2007; Sun and Li 2009). If the legal settlement requires that assets be divided, then the family's home may have to be sold, necessitating a move to a new house or apartment. For children, this may mean adjusting to new schools, new neighborhoods, and making new friends. Children must also adapt to a visitation schedule with the noncustodial parent and adjust to seeing him or her in unfamiliar surroundings. Over time, both parents are likely to resume dating; therefore, children will meet their parents' new partners. Cohabitation is common, so many children must also adapt to other adults moving in (and out of) the household (Xu et al. 2006). Finally, since most single parents eventually remarry, children will likely experience stepparent relationships, and possibly stepsibling relationships as well. Using data from a 17-year longitudinal study, Amato and Sobolewski (2001) found that children's psychological well-being declines as the number of family transitions increase.

Long-Term Effects

Although most children adjust adequately over time to the transitions in their lives, some children continue to be plagued by depression, fear of commitment, or behavioral problems (Ängarne-Lindberg et al. 2009; Cartwright 2005; Lindsey et al. 2009; Whitton et al. 2008). Children whose parents divorce are more likely to become pregnant prior to marriage or impregnate someone, drop out of school and have lower academic achievement, experience more behavioral problems and aggression towards peers, use alcohol or drugs, have poor health, are more likely to suffer from depression, and are more likely to be idle or unemployed.

For instance, a study of about 9,000 teens followed for 12 years into adulthood assessed the impact of their parents' divorce on their income and earnings (Sun and Li 2008). Like others, this study also found that children whose parents divorced have achieved, on average, lower educational credentials and lower incomes. Some of this difference may be explained by their own parents' lower levels of education and income as compared to others, but some degree of difference remains, which the researchers attribute to divorce. In particular, they found that those children who were in unstable living situations after the divorce (e.g., first a single-parent household, then a stepparent household) seemed to fare worse than those children whose lives were more stable after the divorce.

Amato and Sobolewski (2001) examined the effect of divorce on adult children's psychological well-being. They found that marital conflict appears to erode children's emotional bonds with their mothers, whereas both divorce and marital conflict erode children's emotional bonds with their fathers. This places adult children at risk for distress, low self-esteem, and general unhappiness. Why does marital conflict potentially harm a child's relationship with both mother and father, but the actual divorce itself seems to have more negative repercussions for the child-father bond? It is probably related to the fact that many children live with their mothers after divorce and see their fathers only sporadically.

These findings certainly do not mean that *all* children from divorced households experience these negative outcomes. Many children whose parents have divorced lead happy, well-adjusted, and successful lives; these studies simply mean that children of divorced parents are more likely to have these problems than are children from families in which parents have not divorced. In fact, many negative outcomes are related to the higher rates of poverty among children growing up in divorced households and are less apt to occur if the family has adequate financial resources.

The Million-Dollar Question

At this point in my life, I'm almost positive that I'll never get married ... I'm just so disillusioned by the whole concept. I don't think my parents' divorce has affected me negatively that much. Their marriage, however, has screwed me up more than I'll probably ever know (Harvey and Fine 2004).

The question that people want answered is: Are children better off when their unhappily married parents remain married or are children better off when their parents divorce? The answer depends on many things, particularly the *severity of the conflict* in the marriage.

Children do not fare well when there is tremendous conflict, violence, name-calling in the home, and when they are put in the middle of their parents' struggles (Cummings et al. 2006; Michael et al. 2007). This is true regardless of whether parents divorce or remain married. In fact, many researchers suggest that it is the amount of conflict rather than a divorce *per se* that causes the most harm to children. For example, Jekielek (1998) examined data on families from the National Longitudinal Surveys of Youth. Looking at 1,640 children between the ages of 6 and 14, she found that children in high-conflict but intact families had lower levels of well-being than did children whose highly conflicting parents divorced. A study by Amato and Booth (1997), which was based on telephone and in-person interviews conducted in 1980 and 1992 with a nationally representative sample, found that of the children who were in families with high marital conflict in 1980, they were actually doing *better* in 1992 if their parents had divorced than if they had stayed together. Likewise, Strohschein (2005) reported that antisocial behavior in highly dysfunctional families actually decreased once the parents divorced.

However, Amato and Booth also found that children from relatively low-conflict families were *worse* off if their parents divorced than if their parents had remained together. These findings suggest that the worst situations for children are to be in either (1) a high-conflict marriage that does not end in divorce or (2) a low-conflict marriage that does end in divorce.

Yet, it appears that most unhappy marriages do not display extreme forms of conflict. In fact, in the longitudinal study by Amato and Booth (1997), only one-quarter of parents who divorced between 1980 and 1992 reported any sort of violence or even reported that they disagreed "often" or "very often" with their spouse. In fact, only 30 percent reported at least two serious quarrels during the previous month. Consequently, the authors conclude that the majority of children whose parents divorce probably experienced relatively low conflict, and therefore would be better off if their parents had stayed together.

Children also must face that their parents are very likely to enter a new relationship. Let's turn to issues surrounding repartnering, remarriage, and stepfamilies.

WHAT DO YOU THINK?

If you had children and then later got divorced, how would you minimize the impact of divorce on your children? Think about both short- and long-term effects. What theoretical perspective introduced in Chapter 1 could help guide you?

Repartnering and Remarriage

When in the throes of a divorce, it can be difficult to think of it as a new beginning—yet for most people, it is exactly that: an opportunity to start over. The majority of divorced individuals do find another life partner. Generally, finding a new partner is the most important factor in improving life satisfaction for both men and women. Compared to divorced persons, remarried individuals have significantly lower rates of both economic and psychological distress and depression. As shown in the box on pages 432–433, "Families as Lived Experience: Rebuilding When Your Relationship Ends," moving on requires a critical level of introspection and analysis.

FAMILIES
as Lived Experience

Rebuilding When Your Relationship Ends

Divorce is a stressful and highly emotional experience. Here, nine divorcing individuals describe a wide range of emotions that they experienced during the process of ending their marriages.

- "Fear was my biggest obstacle. I was afraid of all the changes I had no control over, and at the same time, I was afraid nothing would ever change. My whole life was being influenced by my fears! I was afraid of being alone, and at the same time isolating myself, afraid of never really being loved again and yet pushing love away when it got too close.... I was completely stuck, paralyzed by my own fear.... It wasn't until I admitted my fears, listed them and talked about them openly that they lost their power over me."—Jere

- "In my first marriage, I was the parent taking care of him. In my next love relationship, I would like to have a parent to take care of me and nurture the little girl inside of me. And then in my third love relationship, maybe I can become balanced and have a healthy relationship."—Janice

- "Maria and I had lots of friends and family around all the time. Most weekends we'd have a barbeque or go over to her sister's place or take a picnic with two or three other couples. Since we split up, none of these people ever call me or drop by. How come married people don't seem to want us around when we're single?"—Jose

- "I spent 33 years as a homemaker, raising a large family. I had the security and comfort of upper-middle-class living. When I became a single parent, with responsibility for our youngest child and faced with the task of becoming self-supporting, with few if any marketable skills, I was literally paralyzed with fear."—Joanne

- "I don't know what came over me. I saw his car in the parking lot and I knew he had met his girlfriend and left in her car. I went over and let the air out of all four tires. Then, I went behind the building and waited until they returned so I could watch them find his car with the tires flat. I watched them trying to solve their problem and I felt so good. I've never done anything like that before in my life. Guess I didn't know how angry I could get."—Jean

- "When I was a child, my father continually warned me about getting a "big head" and becoming "stuck on myself." Then, I went to church and learned that I had been born sinful. At school, it was the jocks and the brains that got all the attention. Finally, I married so there would be someone who thought I was worthwhile. It made me feel good that someone cared. But then she became a pro at pointing out my faults. I finally reached a point where I began to believe that I was truly worthless. It was then that I decided to leave the marriage."—Carl

- "After my divorce, looking for ways to meet new people, I took a small part in a little theater production. One night at rehearsal, I suddenly realized that's what I'd been doing in my marriage—reciting lines. I wasn't myself, I was a character in a romantic comedy-tragedy."—Scott

- "I felt many times in my marriage that I was trapped in a prison of love. It was hard to be myself when there were so many demands and expectations placed upon me. When I first separated, I felt even worse. But now, I have found that I can fly. I can be me. I feel as if I have left the chrysalis and have become a butterfly. I feel so free."—Alice

- "I've become aware that living as a single person is an affirmation of strength and self—not an embarrassing admission of failure. I'm more relaxed in the company of others—I'm no longer wasting emotional energy being a social chameleon.

Post-marital guilt, self-doubt, and questions like "Will I ever love again?" are greatly diminished. I am happy as a single person—something I had not thought possible."—Larry

Source: Fisher and Alberti 2006. Reproduced for Karen Seccombe by permission of Impact Publishers, Inc., P.O. Box 6016, Atascadero, CA 93423 USA. Further reproduction prohibited.

CRITICAL THINKING QUESTIONS
1. How might these feelings associated with getting a divorce and rebuilding when the relationship ends differ between men and women?
2. Do you think the process of divorce and rebuilding is different for cohabiting couples or gay and lesbian couples compared to those couples who are legally married?

Persons who are young and married only a short time may find it relatively easy to begin dating again. Dating may be more difficult for older people who have been married for longer periods because they may feel awkward or be unaware of changing dating norms (Remarriage.com 2008). Who should initiate a date? Who does the paying? Should I meet him/her at the restaurant or have them pick me up at my house? Who pays for the babysitter? What sexual expectations will there be? Am I supposed to like her children right away? Are my children supposed to like him right away?

As shown in Chapter 7, the most common way to meet partners is through friends, but as we age, fewer of our friends are single or know others who are single. Consequently, online dating is popular. There are approximately 1,400 online dating sites, the largest being eHarmony with over 20 million users and Match.com with 15 million users (Scott 2009). Nearly half of adults (49 percent) know at least one person who has dated someone they met online (Greenberg 2009), and most have relatively positive things to say about the experience.

Cohabitation and Repartnering

Cohabitation is not just for the young; it is also common among previously married and middle-aged adults (Kreider 2008; U.S. Census Bureau 2010a; Xu et al. 2006). Over half of remarried persons have cohabited with someone prior to remarriage (although not necessarily with the person they married). Children are present in about half of these cohabiting relationships. In fact, the number of people aged 45–54 who are cohabiting (and presumably have been previously married) is close to the number of people aged 15–24 who are cohabiting (and presumably have never been married) (Fields 2004).

Divorced people who cohabit may view the arrangement as an extension of serious dating—it may lead to marriage with that particular partner, or it may not. Yet for some, cohabitation is not simply a precursor to marriage but replaces it altogether.

Remarriage

Remarriage has always been a common feature of family life in the United States primarily because of high rates of widowhood in the past (Phillips 1997). It was difficult to maintain a household as a widow or widower; therefore, a quick remarriage was a fact of life. Today, however, 9 in 10 remarriages occur following a divorce, rather than a death. A remarriage that occurs after a divorce has very different characteristics from a remarriage that occurs after death, primarily because of the fact that the ex-spouse may still have a commanding presence.

Demographic Trends: Who Remarries and When? Most people remarry after a divorce, often quickly. As shown in Table 14.2, 39 percent of women remarry within three years, and three-quarters remarry within 10 years (Bramlett and Mosher 2002). For women, the likelihood of remarriage is lower when they are older at the time of divorce, have a lower income, or are Black.

TABLE 14.2 Probability of Remarriage by Duration of Divorce, Women Aged 15–44

Younger women, those with higher earnings, and Whites are more likely to remarry and do so more quickly.

	1 YEAR	3 YEARS	5 YEARS	10 YEARS
Total	15%	39%	54%	75%
Age at Divorce				
Less than 25	17%	41%	57%	81%
25 and over	14%	37%	51%	68%
Education				
Less than high school	17%	37%	50%	74%
High school	17%	41%	56%	78%
More than high school	13%	36%	53%	71%
Income				
Less than $25,000	14%	30%	42%	62%
$25,000–$49,999	16%	40%	54%	73%
$50,000 or more	17%	46%	65%	87%
Race/Ethnicity				
White	17%	42%	58%	79%
Hispanic	8%	29%	44%	68%
Black	8%	23%	32%	49%

Source: Bramlett and Mosher 2002.

Men and women also have different odds of remarrying (Goodwin et al. 2010; Wu and Schimmele 2005). Men remarry on average within three years, compared to five years for women. For men, age doesn't really affect their likelihood of remarrying, but for women, remarriage declines substantially with age. In fact, fewer than 7 percent of women who divorced between the ages of 50 and 59 remarry within 5 years, compared to 46 percent of men in that age group. Why is the difference so large? Reasons include both micro-level and macro-level factors. Some women simply do not want to remarry. But for others, cultural norms make it more difficult for women to find a partner.

- *Men are able to initiate contact more easily.* They have a lifetime of experience as the initiator in social relationships. Moreover, men tend to have a larger circle of casual friends and acquaintances than do women, and these can be drawn upon to meet potential partners. Their incomes are considerably higher than those of women; therefore, men have more money to treat someone to a dinner, movie, or some other type of date.
- *There is a double standard of aging.* As men age, they are considered to be "distinguished," whereas women are considered to be less attractive as they grow older.
- *The pool of eligible partners is larger for men than it is for women because of cultural norms that allow men to marry younger women.* A 40-year-old male could easily marry a 40-year-old woman or a 30-year-old woman or even a 20-year-old woman without people giving it much thought, but older women are generally not granted the same latitude.
- *Women are more likely than men to have children living with them.* The presence of children tends to decrease one's chances of remarrying. Women may be cautious about bringing someone new into the family, and men may be hesitant to take on the financial and emotional responsibility that comes with a ready-made family.

Satisfaction and Stability of Remarriages   Second and subsequent remarriages are not necessarily happier than first marriages and are actually more likely to end in divorce (Barna 2008; Xu et al. 2006). Thirty-nine percent of remarriages end in divorce within 10 years (Bramlett and Mosher 2002). This may reflect a selection bias; people who remarry obviously consider divorce as an option to end an unhappy relationship. Remarried couples, however, face additional stressors largely related to tension between stepchildren and stepparents or between stepparents on issues related to child rearing or discipline (Kurdek 1999). By 10 years, 43 percent of women who had two or more children at the time of the remarriage divorced again, compared to only 32 percent of women who were childfree (Bramlett and Mosher 2002). In fact, both remarried men and women are more likely to be depressed than are first-time married men and women (LaPierre 2009). A second divorce is also more common among Blacks and Whites than among Hispanics and is more common among younger persons, those earning less income, and those who are not employed.

Since so many couples that remarry or cohabit also have children, let us now turn to the topic of stepfamilies.

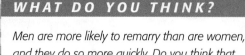

WHAT DO YOU THINK?

Men are more likely to remarry than are women, and they do so more quickly. Do you think that cultural norms affecting sex differences in remarriage rates are changing? Provide evidence for your answer.

Stepfamily Relationships

Stepfamilies are families in which one or both of the adult partners has at least one child, either residing with them or elsewhere. The majority of children first enter a stepfamily through their parent's cohabitation rather than through marriage, although often the parent later marries. Stepfamilies can create an intricate weave of complex relationships. For example, children in stepfamilies can be referred to as (1) siblings (biologically related to same parents); (2) stepsiblings (not biologically related, but parents are married to each other); (3) half-siblings (share one parent biologically); (4) mutual child (a child born to the remarried couple); (5) residential stepchildren (live in the household with the remarried couple more than half of the time); and (6) nonresidential stepchildren (live in the household less than half of the time) (National Stepfamily Resource Center 2007). There are also multiple part-time and full-time living arrangements (Allan et al. 2010; Dupuis 2007). A cross-sectional look reveals that, at a given point in time, about one in six children live in stepfamilies, except among Asian Americans, where the figure is about one in twenty children (Kreider 2008).

Stepfamily relationships receive a lot of bad press. They have been stigmatized as harmful environments for children and adolescents, a view that is shared in many different

TABLE 14.3   Number and Percent of Children Living in Stepfamilies, by Child's Race and Ethnicity

White, Black, and Hispanic children are near equally likely to live in stepfamilies, whereas Asian American children are far less likely to do so.

White, Non-Hispanic	7,029,000	16%
Black	2,077,000	18%
Asian Americans	103,000	5%
Hispanic	2,431,000	17%

Source: Kreider 2008.

Stepfamilies are very common—over one-third of children will live in one by age 18, but the norms in stepfamilies are unclear. Roles are ambiguous and people do not necessarily know what to expect.

cultures (Ganong and Coleman 1997). For examples, views of the "wicked stepmother" are rampant, found from Shakespeare to Cinderella fairy tales, with connotations of cruelty, jealousy, and neglect.

Yet, stepfamilies can also be an enriching experience (Crohn 2006; Michaels 2006; Stewart 2007). For example, children living in stepfamilies gain exposure to new behavior patterns and lifestyles. They also may profit from living with an adult who has different views and is possibly more objective than a biological parent. Children may also benefit from an increased standard of living made possible by two incomes and their parents' greater happiness at being involved in another relationship. Many children live in warm and loving stepfamilies. Stepfamily adoptions are the most common type of adoption in the United States, a testament to the love and commitment that many stepparents and children feel toward one another (Child Welfare Information Gateway 2008; Lamb 2007). Among minority groups, living in a stepfamily is often reported to have significantly positive effects on a child's well-being. Family researchers have found that high-quality relationships with stepfathers may have a positive effect on internalized problems, such as depression or feelings of worth, and on externalizing problems, including impulsivity (White and Gilbreth 2001).

Nonetheless, stepfamilies face considerable challenges (Ganong and Coleman 2004). Despite their prevalence—over one-third of children will be in a stepfamily before reaching age 18 (Parke 2007)—society has not really acknowledged them in any systematic way. What formal rules and rights do stepfamily members have toward one another? Family scientist Jason Hans (2002) notes that stepparents are "legal strangers" to their stepchildren; the law does not protect the relationship during marriage or following a divorce.

Stepfamilies have been referred to as a **normless norm**; they are very common, yet the expectations, obligations, and rules within these families are vague and confusing (Lamanna and Riedmann 1997). Roles in stepfamilies are ambiguous, and people do not know what is expected of them. There is no socially prescribed script for how family members are expected to relate to one another (Stewart 2007). Should a stepparent behave like a biological parent, like a friend, like an uncle, or like someone else entirely? To what extent can stepparents discipline their stepchildren? How are stepparents and stepchildren supposed to feel about one another? What names do children call their stepparent? Indeed, do stepparents and their stepchildren even include one another as part of their "family"? For example, if your father remarries when you are an adult and living away from home, and you see her once a year or so, would you consider his new wife your "stepmom"? Or would you think of her as "my dad's wife"? Would you think of her grown children, whom you may have never met, as your "stepsiblings"? What type of relationship would you likely foster with them?

Being in a new intimate relationship is exciting, but if there are children involved, both men and women may need to make significant adjustments. For example, the privacy that newly partnered couples crave goes out the door—marriage might begin with a group of teenagers living with you! For noncustodial stepparents, the stepchildren may visit on a part-time basis—perhaps every other weekend and several weeks or months at a time in the summer. The presence of stepchildren invariably brings an ex-spouse into the picture. What potential tensions can arise with an "ex" or with your spouse's "ex"? The box on page 437, "Families as Lived Experience: Journey to Healing," offers one woman's story of living in a stepfamily.

Journey to Healing

What is it like to be a stepparent? Here is one woman's story and her journey to a healthy relationship.

I divorced my husband when my daughter was eight years old. When I realized that perhaps one day I would remarry, I remember thinking that I would like to marry a man who already had children. I never thought about what it would mean to be a part of a step or blended family, and just how that would impact my life.

Four years later, I married a man who had two children. My new husband also has an ex-wife, ex-in-laws, plus his ex-wife's long time live-in significant other. The coming together of our family—my daughter, myself, my husband, his children, his ex-wife, her significant other, and her parents—has been a very difficult task.

It is very difficult to form a blending and extended family. Part of the dilemma of blending families is that there are few, if any, cultural guidelines to follow. For example, we know how to behave and what is expected of us when we become in-laws. But we really do not know what our role is with our spouse's ex-spouse. There is no language for these new members of our extended family, nor do we think of them as friends. They may actually be seen as intruders, and a relationship built on this type of foundation can be very draining.

My own story is probably not all that different from the many other women who have married men who have previously been married. It took over eight years for the adults to come together. For years, I felt in the midst of an angry tug of war. My husband's relationship with Jane [his ex-spouse] was based on anger and fighting. I was hurt when my husband was unable to set boundaries for himself and for letting Jane manipulate him. I felt that Jane was trying to control her children in ways that were interfering with my life with my new husband. It seemed that no matter what my husband and Jane did, I had to enter into the picture and would become angry and frustrated as well. The two main issues that I was confronted with were control and anger. And then I had to learn to deal with issues of jealousy. I had no role model, and I was very confused by all the emotions because of having Jane in my life. I think all three of us really had no idea of how to behave: for Jane and my husband to be cordial ex-spouses who share and love their children; for Jane and myself, who had the awkward relationship of having been married to the same man; and even for myself and my husband on how to deal with his ex-wife.

There were no road maps for any of us to follow. The difficulties between the three of us kept growing, and none of us were capable at the time to make the necessary adjustments. I could no longer take having Jane call our home, because most times an argument would ensue. I did not know how to pull myself out of the turmoil. I did something that may sound radical; I sent a note to Jane asking her not to call our home and explained that I could no longer deal with the arguing.

A year later, I came to a halting revelation: I can choose to be married to my husband, and if I do, then his ex-wife must be a part of the picture. I sent another note, this time asking her to simply put the past aside and to begin again as friends. I give Jane much credit because she has been able to do this with dignity.

Our first meeting was for her son's college graduation. The whole family went, myself, my husband, all our children, Jane and her boyfriend, and her parents. Our first few minutes were a bit awkward and then we eased into a relationship. Her boyfriend and I have an inside take on "our family," as we share the sense of being "the in-laws." In the past two years, we have shared several family events. Having been able to succeed at this relationship has been and continues to be a very gratifying and healing experience.

Source: Posner 2002.

CRITICAL THINKING QUESTIONS

1. If remarriage is so common, why are the ensuing relationships so awkward? Why do we not have a common understanding of language, behavior, expectations, and responsibilities?
2. What kinds of issues would cause such tension between the current and ex-wife? Are these issues similar to or different from the issues among current and ex-husbands? Do you think that her action was appropriate? Why or why not?

WHAT DO YOU THINK?

A strengths-based perspective reminds us to build upon the potential advantages of stepfamilies. What kinds of programs or policies are needed to help stepfamilies thrive? What would a program look like for children? What would it look like for adults?

How Do Children Fare in Stepfamilies?

How do children from stepfamilies fare? Although there are many fantastic stories, on average, the news is not particularly encouraging. Just as children from single-parent households face an increased chance of certain negative outcomes, so do many children who live in stepfamilies. In other words, generally the well-being of children in stepfamilies is not significantly better than the well-being of children in divorced single-parent families.

Certainly not all stepchildren experience problems (Wen 2008). Many stepchildren grow up feeling secure in happy homes made possible by their parent's remarriage (Sample 1999). The longer a stepfamily has been together, the more positively children describe the relationship with their stepfathers.

Still, in general, children in stepfamilies earn lower grades in school, complete fewer grades, and score lower on achievement tests than do children who grow up living with both parents (Carlson 2006; Ganong and Coleman 2004). They also have higher rates of depression and emotional problems, particularly when conflict between two households is present. They are also more likely to exhibit behavioral problems such as involvement with alcohol and drugs, nonmarital childbearing, idleness, or being arrested.

In a small study of 15 adolescents, they were interviewed in depth about their experiences during their parents' divorce, remarriage, and creation of stepfamilies. They responded to the divorce largely with resignation. Reactions to the single-parenting phase were divided, with about half expressing negative feelings about their parent's dating. Remarriage and stepfamilies were generally negative events. Adolescents expressed concern about their powerlessness, the disruption resulting in living space, and confusion over relationship expectations and new rules. They felt excluded and resentful about sharing their parent with another person and about their reduced intimacy with their parent (Stoll et al. 2006).

Explanations for Added Risk   Let's be clear, most stepchildren do well in school and do not have emotional, behavioral, or delinquency problems. Having a stepparent may increase the household income and provide a new supportive relationship. However, why do children living in stepfamilies face an increased chance for negative outcomes? Several explanations have been proposed.

- *Stressful Transitions.* Remarriage and repartnering involve many stressful changes and potential conflicts for both adults and their children (Cooper et al. 2009; Magnuson and Berger 2009). These include possibly moving to a new residence and adapting to the parent's new partner, living with new family members, and settling into new routines. These can all contribute to poorer school performance, depression, and behavioral problems.
- *Economic and social capital deprivation.* Children living in stepfamilies and in single-parent families are disadvantaged because of their lower incomes and reduced levels of social capital (connections to other adults or institutions in the community) related to the divorce (Shriner et al. 2009). Remarriage does not fill these deficits completely, perhaps because stepparents are expending resources on their children from a prior union, or because stepparents are not fully invested in their stepchildren (McLanahan and Sandefur 1994; Schwartz and Finley 2006).
- *Parents may be investing time and energy into their new relationships rather than into child rearing.* For example, parents may not spend as much time talking with their children, helping them with their homework, or monitoring their friends and activities as they did prior to the remarriage because they are preoccupied with their new partner (Downey 1995; Pong 1997; Stoll et al. 2006). Also, parents may become less involved in their children's lives when a new child is born into the family (Stewart 2005).

Social Policy and Family Resilience

Children from divorcing families and stepfamilies are at special risk of behavioral and emotional problems, but they can gain remarkable strength from many sources, including neighbors, schools, and peers. Family scientists Kathleen Boyce Rodgers and Hilary Rose (2002) studied over 2,000 seventh-, ninth-, and eleventh-grade adolescents to examine the importance of these other relationships in times of divorce. They report that, although parents are of primary importance to the well-being of children, peers, schools, and neighbors are also critical in helping adolescents navigate risks and develop skills necessary to become productive and healthy adults. Youth clubs, organizations, sports, churches, or peer helper groups in schools may allow adolescents experiencing their parents' divorce to build supportive networks that can counterbalance the other stressors in their lives.

Example: Initiatives to Limit Divorce

There are divergent opinions throughout the world about the costs and benefits of divorce. In many countries, the popular sentiment is that divorce is wrong if children are involved. In other countries the people see divorce as wrong regardless of whether the couple has children. Table 14.4 presents data from the International Social Survey Program (ISSP), a cross-national extension of the General Social Survey. As shown in the table, the percentage of people agreeing with the statement "Parents ought to stay together if they have children" ranges from 26 percent in the Netherlands and 28 percent in Canada to 79 percent in Japan and 81 percent in Poland. In fact, the majority of respondents in the Philippines and Japan agree that the couple ought to stay together even if there are no children involved.

Many people in the United States are also concerned about divorce and its consequences, and the trend is an increasing belief that divorce should be more difficult to obtain (Kapinus and Flowers 2008; Maher 2006; Martin and Parashar 2006). As you have learned in this chapter, the Pew Research Center found that those people who are at a higher risk for divorce—young people and Blacks, for example—actually want it to be more difficult to obtain. But what measures should be taken?

A telephone survey was conducted with a representative sample of adults in Arizona, Louisiana, and Minnesota to assess the degree of support for a number of measures that could lower the divorce rate (Hawkins et al. 2002). The researchers found that about 8 in 10 respondents in all three states believed that premarital counseling is important to making a marriage successful, and 9 in 10 supported counseling if the couple is unable to resolve problems that come up in their marriage. About two-thirds of adults in Arizona and Louisiana and 58 percent of adults in Minnesota believe that long waiting periods would help a couple work out their problems.

Given these attitudes, it is not surprising that many states are funding initiatives to strengthen marriage (as shown in Chapter 8) and passing legislation to make divorce more difficult to obtain. Although major changes may be difficult to enact, such as eliminating no-fault divorce, it has not kept some grassroots or religious groups from trying. There have been a number of successes (Hawkins et al. 2002; Maher 2006). For example, a Georgia law allows no-fault divorce only if both parties agree to the divorce and if no children are involved. Florida has implemented a three-day waiting period for marriage licenses if couples do not seek premarital education. Florida also now requires high schools to offer a marriage education course parallel to driver education. Oklahoma committed $10 million in unspent welfare funds to an initiative to strengthen marriage and reduce divorce by 30 percent by 2010. As mentioned in Chapter 8, former President George W. Bush targeted $1.5 billion toward a Healthy Marriage Initiative to not only encourage people to marry, and to stay married as well.

TABLE 14.4 Attitudes Toward Divorce in 23 Countries

PARENTS OUGHT TO STAY TOGETHER IF THEY HAVE CHILDREN (% agreeing)		COUPLE OUGHT TO STAY TOGETHER EVEN IF NO CHILDREN (% agreeing)	
Netherlands	26%	East Germany	10%
Canada	28%	Netherlands	10%
Austria	28%	New Zealand	12%
East Germany	28%	West Germany	13%
New Zealand	30%	Slovenia	13%
United States	**33%**	Czech Republic	14%
West Germany	36%	Austria	15%
Slovenia	42%	Great Britain	16%
Israel	42%	Israel	16%
Great Britain	42%	Australia	16%
Spain	42%	Canada	16%
Australia	43%	Russia	17%
Russia	45%	Norway	17%
Northern Ireland	45%	Hungary	17%
Norway	48%	Sweden	17%
Ireland	49%	**United States**	**18%**
Sweden	49%	Spain	19%
Hungary	55%	Ireland	20%
Czech Republic	55%	Italy	21%
Italy	58%	Northern Ireland	22%
Philippines	62%	Bulgaria	29%
Japan	79%	Poland	42%
Poland	81%	Philippines	51%
Bulgaria	—	Japan	54%

Note: Questions about divorce with children not asked in Bulgaria.
Source: Smith 1999.

Three states have created a covenant marriage option—Louisiana, Arkansas, and Arizona—that allows couples to select a more rigid set of legal requirements surrounding their marriage and grounds for divorce (Maher 2006; Spaht 2002). Covenant marriage would require (Hawkins et al. 2002):

1. some marriage preparation
2. full disclosure of all information that could reasonably affect the decision to marry
3. an oath of lifelong commitment to marriage
4. acceptance of limited grounds for divorce (e.g., abuse, adultery, addiction, felony imprisonment, separation for two years)
5. marital counseling if problems threaten the marriage

So far, very few couples are choosing covenant marriage. Only about 2 percent of new marriages in Louisiana fall into the covenant category, and about 40–50 percent of spouses who chose the traditional marriage option had never heard of covenant marriage (Sanchez et al. 2002). In Arizona and Arkansas, less than half of 1 percent choose this option (Stritof and Stritof 2006).

Conclusion

The United States has one of the highest rates of divorce in the world, and to understand why this is the case, we must look at structural, historical, cultural, and personal factors. This chapter explored rising and falling divorce rates, divorce policy, and how families cope with a divorce and its aftermath. Divorcing couples face many issues, including the emotional, legal, parental, and economic dimensions.

Children are particularly vulnerable to the hardships associated with divorce, including a greater likelihood of poverty and other behavioral and social problems. Most divorced persons remarry or repartner after the divorce. Stepfamilies, however, have many unique characteristics compared to two-parent biological families and face a number of specific challenges.

Key Terms

Alimony: Post-divorce support for a former spouse. (p. 427)

Cross-sectional divorce rate: A divorce rate at only one point in time. (p. 413)

Crude divorce rate: The number of divorces that occur out of 1,000 people in the population. (p. 413)

Displaced homemaker: A full-time homemaker who is divorced by her husband. (p. 427)

Joint legal custody: Both the custodial and noncustodial parents retain their legal rights with respect to their children. (p. 424)

Joint physical custody: Children spend substantial or nearly equal portions of time in the homes of each parent. (p. 425)

Legal custody: Refers to who has the legal authority to make important decisions concerning a child. (p. 424)

No-fault divorce: A divorce in which the couple can say they have irreconcilable differences and do not wish to assign blame. (p. 420)

Normless norm: Something common enough to be considered normative, but with vague and confusing expectations, obligations, and rules. (p. 436)

Physical custody: The child's legal residence. (p. 424)

Refined divorce rate: The number of divorces that occur out of every 1,000 married women. (p. 413)

Stepfamilies: One or both of the adult partners has at least one child, either residing with them or elsewhere. (p. 435)

Resources on the Internet

Divorce Support

www.divorcesupport.com

This is a Web site devoted to connecting users to the most valuable and comprehensive divorce-related information on the Internet. They offer helpful and supportive information about divorce, child custody, child support, visitation, modifications, separation, alimony, spousal support, divorce laws, statutes, and much more.

National Fatherhood Initiative

www.fatherhood.org

The National Fatherhood Initiative (NFI) was founded in 1994 to stimulate a society-wide movement to confront the growing problem of father absence. NFI's mission is to improve the well-being of children by increasing the number of children growing up with involved, committed, and responsible fathers in their lives. NFI offers a quarterly newsletter and a catalog of books and videos focusing on fatherhood issues.

Parents Without Partners

http://parentswithoutpartners.org

Parents Without Partners (PWP) provides single parents and their children with an opportunity for enhancing personal growth, self-confidence, and sensitivity toward others by offering an environment for support, friendship, and the exchange of parenting techniques. PWP provides free referrals to local PWP chapters, which offer social and educational opportunities for single parents.

Single Parent-Tips

www.singleparent-tips.com

This site offers advice on custody, visitation, dealing with ex-spouses, legal matters, and effective parenting for single parents.

CHAPTER 15

Summing It Up: Families and the Sociological Imagination

CHAPTER OUTLINE

The Sociological Imagination   444

■ **OUR** *Global Community:* HIV/AIDS: Girls Are Very Vulnerable   *449*

■ **EYE** *on the World:* Percentage of Adults (15–49) Estimated To Be Living with HIV/AIDS, 2008 *450*

Using the Sociological Imagination: Themes of the Text Revisited   453

■ **FAMILIES** *as Lived Experience:* "Tommy Johnson" and "Randall Simmons"   *455*

■ **USING** *the Sociological Imagination:* Managing the Stigma of Welfare   *457*

Future Trends: Where Are Families Heading?   463

Conclusion   465

Resources on the Internet   465

CHAPTER PREVIEW

This chapter summarizes the contributions that the sociological imagination can make to our understanding of families. A family is far more than a personal relationship among related individuals; a family is also a powerful social institution inextricably linked with other social institutions. We will revisit the text's five major themes to integrate what we have learned. In this chapter, you will also review:

- The sociological imagination, with its comparative and empirical approaches, as a powerful lens for understanding both the micro and macro aspects of families and personal relationships

- Families as both a social institution and a private personal relationship

- Social inequality with its powerful influence on family life

- Benefits of a strengths-based perspective

- Family policies as they reflect historical, cultural, political, and social factors

- Understanding families in the United States through a comparative perspective

- Trends for the future

John was born in a homeless shelter. His mother Susan was hardly a stereotypical candidate for homelessness. She was 25 years old, a receptionist at a corporation, and was attending trade school. When the company suffered heavy losses, she was fired. Pregnant with John, she quickly headed down the slippery slope into homelessness. All the helping hands that should have been there let her down. The unemployment office refused to give her benefits unless she dropped her trade school classes to concentrate on finding work. Susan was trying hard to find work and believed a college degree would make her more employable. The welfare office caseworkers told her that she was ineligible for cash welfare because she was technically eligible for unemployment benefits, never mind that she wasn't collecting a penny of it. She had to go to soup kitchens for meals. Susan found a few temporary jobs that postponed her eviction, but for only four months. Homelessness is tough for anyone, especially for a pregnant woman. Every 28 days, she had to move from one shelter to another, dragging her belongings with her. She continued to look for work but was caught in the "catch-22" predicament of the homeless. She needed a job to secure a permanent address and phone number, but without a permanent address and phone number, she couldn't land a job. When John was born, the job search was put on hold, and she faced new child care demands that added obstacles to her path out of homelessness.

It is suppertime and Marie, a mother of two young children and one handicapped adult daughter who contracted spinal meningitis as a toddler, surveys the nearly bare shelves in the kitchen—some beans, vegetables, and canned potato soup. The week's meat, which she buys when it is on sale, has been rationed and stretched as far as possible and is now gone. Marie always makes sure the children eat dinner first, although it might be just canned soup, and sometimes she goes hungry for the night. "As long as they get something," she says. Marie has been working for over a decade and a half; she is not on welfare. When she tried to apply for food stamps last year, she was told that she earned one dollar above the income requirement to be eligible. She is a child care provider. She works hard every day to assure the toddlers in her care are safe, well fed, comforted when they cry, and given as much love and stimulation as possible. For her crucial work she brings home so little money she can barely feed and house her own children. The average child care worker makes about $20,000 [in 2009] and usually without health benefits.

(Children's Defense Fund 2002)

The stories of Susan, Marie, and their children are accounts of struggle and hope. Are these just isolated stories? How can we interpret their circumstances? This chapter will synthesize the contributions that a sociological imagination can make to understanding something as common and yet as unique as families. It will review the importance of using a sociological perspective to understand both families as a social institution and the everyday interactions that go on within families. The chapter will then review the basic themes of the text that were introduced in Chapter 1, providing examples from the previous chapters to illustrate and summarize these themes. Finally, the chapter concludes with a look forward. Given what we know about families today, what might we expect in the future?

The Sociological Imagination

Most people think they are experts in understanding the dynamics of the society in which they live. After all, when you experience something every day, what is there not to know? However, the text has asked us to move beyond personal experience to explore general patterns situated in a particular society, culture, or historical period. A sociological imagination shows us that many commonsense assumptions do not hold up when we look at broader social trends, and it brings new insights into the way we live. These insights expose the opportunities, challenges, and constraints in our lives.

As we have seen throughout this text, the social structure we live in, and the social positions we hold, shape our life experiences. Understanding these linkages reminds us that many seemingly personal problems or isolated events are really social in nature and therefore often require broad policy changes for their solution. Moreover, the better we understand the ways in which social structures shape our personal lives, the better we may be able to adjust those social forces to pursue the life we desire. A sociological imagination asks us to step back from our ordinary routines so that we may critically evaluate the strengths and weaknesses of different ways of organizing our lives (Mills 1959).

Susan, Marie, and Their Children

The quandaries of Susan, Marie, and their children described in the opening vignette are not simply personal problems or isolated events. These women and their children are poor or nearly so, but it is not because of laziness or inadequate parenting. On the contrary, Marie is doing socially productive work that millions of families depend on every day. It is not her fault that the pay for child care workers is notoriously low, averaging less than $10 per hour (Bureau of Labor Statistics 2009b; Center for the Child Care Workforce 2010; National Association of Child Care Resource & Referral Agencies 2009), and fails to provide health care benefits. If she left the work she loves to get a higher-paying job with benefits, who then would care for the nation's children? Society depends on someone to do this work, yet balks at paying a living wage for it.

Likewise, Susan had an important and respectable, if low-paying, job as a receptionist. She was also going to school to improve her employment prospects further. Through no fault of her own, she was laid off. She looked for assistance afterwards, but found none. The available programs thwarted her every effort to improve her circumstances, assuring that she would stay in low-paying, dead-end jobs for the rest of her life. Susan refused these benefits, recognizing that they would stifle any chances for upward mobility. However, the result was that she lost her apartment and had to move into a homeless shelter where she later gave birth to her son John.

Instead of placing the blame on Marie and Susan as individuals, let us look deeper within these two women's stories to see what particular insights a sociological imagination can provide.

Jobs, Income, and Poverty

Both Susan and Marie are poor or nearly so. Are these women unique? Unfortunately, no. As shown in earlier chapters, women's incomes are significantly less than men's and have seen little improvement in recent years. Women earn only about 80 percent of what men earn, and the gap is widest among Whites and Asians. The pay gap is even higher for older workers (Bureau of Labor Statistics 2009e). Is this an individual problem or a social one?

The predicaments of Susan and Marie are rooted in the fact that the labor market is highly segregated into "men's" jobs and "women's" jobs (U.S. Department of Labor 2009). Occupations dominated by women, such as child care worker or receptionist, tend to be low paying with little opportunity for advancement. Yet, there is nothing inherent in these occupations that warrant the low wages paid to them. The jobs are respectable and provide a valuable service. Thus, Susan and Marie's low incomes reflect far more than personal inadequacy; they reflect inequalities that are embedded in the social structure.

Poverty is quickly becoming a women's problem, as the popular term *feminization of poverty* suggests. Women are far more likely than men to be impoverished, and single mothers are a particularly vulnerable group. About 30 percent of single mothers live below the poverty line (DeNavas-Walt et al. 2010). If women earned the same pay as men (controlling for the same number of hours, education level, age, union status, and living in the same region of the country), their annual incomes would rise by several thousand dollars and poverty rates would be cut in half.

Millions of families have critical housing needs just like Susan because they cannot afford to pay rent. The demand for assisted housing overwhelms the supply. Because of funding limitations, only one in four households that are eligible for public housing receives any form of federal housing assistance. Most agencies have long waiting lists for public housing, and some no longer accept new applications because of the size of the backlog (Center on Budget and Policy Priorities 2008). Not surprisingly, women and children make up a large and growing segment of the homeless population. According to a 23-city study by the U.S. Conference of Mayors, about 7 percent of people living on the street and 30 percent of people in shelters were part of families (National Coalition for the Homeless 2009). Unemployed women, without social and financial support, find themselves in a precarious situation, made even more difficult by the needs of their children. Nonetheless, it does not have to be this way in a country as wealthy as the United States.

Health Insurance   It is unlikely that Susan, Marie, or their children have health insurance. They are part of the over 50 million Americans who are without health insurance to meet their most basic health care needs (DeNavas-Walt et al. 2010). Millions more are underinsured; their high deductibles or copayments render their insurance virtually useless except in the most catastrophic conditions.

As you have learned, living without health insurance can have serious financial, emotional, and health consequences for the entire family. If even one person within a family is uninsured, all share in the anguish of trying to pay medical bills and suffer the consequences when they cannot. Families without health insurance are more likely to delay or forgo seeking needed medical care. They are twice as likely to postpone seeking medical care, over four times as likely to forgo needed care, and are more than twice as likely to have a needed prescription go unfilled. Children may not get needed immunizations as preventative care.

Is the lack of health insurance a personal issue or a social problem? When nearly 17 percent of Americans find themselves in the precarious situation of being uninsured, Americans must examine the social structure to best understand the problem and to seek solutions to it. With the health care reform passed in 2010 and slowly implemented through 2014, it is likely that Susan, Marie, and their children will reap some benefits. Susan and Marie will now be required by law to have insurance. They will most likely be offered a reduced rate, although it may still be difficult to afford. Marie's place of employment may be required to provide her with insurance or they will have to pay into a fund.

We can better understand the plight of Susan and John, described in the opening vignette, if we apply a sociological imagination. This perspective gives us new insight because it shows us that many so-called personal problems are really social problems, rooted in the social structure.

Nonmarital Childbearing and Child Support
Referring back to the cases of Susan and Marie, both are single mothers. Susan has never been married and had her child out of wedlock. It may be tempting to ask: Isn't Susan responsible for creating her own problem?

A simple answer might be "yes," if we take a cursory look at out-of-wedlock births. However, a sociological analysis digs deeper to uncover the complexity of seemingly simple situations and their solutions. After all, Susan is hardly unique in having a baby outside of marriage.

Today, over one-third of all births occur outside of marriage, a significant increase from just a decade ago. Some women become pregnant and opt for an abortion rather than to carry the child to term. Susan did not want an abortion and chose to have her baby instead. Should we criticize her for that decision?

We tend to associate nonmarital births with teens, but the data in Chapter 10 reveal that the number of teenagers giving birth has declined over the past 20 years. Instead, the largest increases in nonmarital childbearing are occurring among older

> ## *WHAT DO YOU THINK?*
>
> *Identify how this text, and this course in general, has shaped your thoughts about Susan, Marie, and their children. Do you see the situation differently than you would have just a few short months ago?*

women who have completed high school or who have some college behind them. For most women, the pregnancy was unplanned, but some single women are becoming mothers by choice, many feeling that they have been unable to find a suitable partner, but still longing for the benefits associated with motherhood. In other words, having a child outside of marriage is becoming increasingly normative, following the trends in many other developed nations.

As we have discussed, having a child out of wedlock in other countries does not pose the great financial problem that it does in the United States (UNICEF Innocenti Research Centre 2000). Of 22 selected developed countries, rates of poverty among children in single-parent households are highest in the United States. The reason children in other countries are better off is because they and their single mothers are eligible for many programs to help sustain them, including paid maternity leave, child or family allowances, housing subsidies, health insurance, and free or low-cost child care. The United States has a laissez-faire approach; parents are expected to assemble their own assistance. However, U.S. programs are limited, income thresholds are extremely low, and the social service maze can be daunting. The result is that many families, just like Susan and Marie's, fall through the cracks of the safety net.

Finally, it is easy to judge Susan for the choice she made (either to deliberately have a child outside of marriage or to be lax about using birth control), but let us remember that she did not impregnate herself—nor did Marie. Shouldn't we also pose questions for the fathers of their children, most notably, where are they, and why aren't they paying child support?

Susan and Marie are among millions of women who fail to receive support from their children's fathers. As noted in Chapter 14, only about 60 percent of custodial parents have some type of support agreement for their children (Grall 2009). Some of these are legal agreements and some are simply informal agreements between the parties. Among families who did have some sort of agreement, most received only a partial payment or none at all. Yet child support dollars matter tremendously to families like Susan's, Marie's, and millions of others, and can prevent them from slipping into poverty.

A sociological imagination reveals that many seemingly private struggles are really large-scale social problems. When millions of women are paid poverty-level wages, when health insurance is a privilege dependent on the goodwill of employers rather than a right of citizenship, when critical safety nets are missing, and when children receive no or inadequate financial support from their noncustodial parents, these are much more than "Susan's" or "Marie's" problems. These are examples of social problems, and their solutions require broad policy changes in U.S. social structure.

A Comparative Perspective

As we learned in Chapter 1, the sociological imagination uses a comparative perspective to study families. If we want to understand contemporary patterns in the United States, we must compare ourselves to other cultures or to other points in history. Is the U.S. divorce rate high or low? Is its rate of child poverty high or low? Answers to these questions are meaningless unless we ask, "Compared to what?" The U.S. divorce rate is indeed high compared to other countries, but it is much lower than it was 30 years ago. Likewise, the rate of child poverty is much higher than other countries that have universal programs specifically designed to en-hance the lives of children, but it is lower in the United States than it was 40 years ago.

In the past, it was easier to ignore what was happening in the world, but this is no longer the case because societies are becoming more interconnected. New technologies, immigration, commerce across borders, the outsourcing of jobs, and greater ease in world travel and com-munication show us that societies are no longer isolated entities. What happens in one corner of the world affects us all. HIV/AIDS provides a vivid example of this interconnectedness.

HIV/AIDS Chapter 7 discussed the epidemic of HIV/AIDS in the United States, yet as common as this disease is in this country, its prevalence and incidence are dwarfed by what is happening around the globe. The effects of widespread HIV and AIDS ravage many mil-lions of people in many different countries. A United Nations report states that the number of people living with HIV reached 33.4 million in 2008, with little signs of abatement. There were 2.7 million new infections in 2008 alone and 2 million deaths. This brings the number of deaths since 1981—the year of the first documented case—to about 30 million persons (UNAIDS 2009). Men most often contract HIV/AIDS through injecting drugs or from sex with other men. However, the number of women infected is growing quickly, and they most often become infected from heterosexual intercourse.

The HIV/AIDS problem occurs everywhere, but it is particularly acute in sub-Saharan Africa, as shown in the map on pages 450–451. Although the region has just over 10 percent of the world's population, it is home to two-thirds of all people living with HIV—22.4 million. In 2008, nearly 2 million people in sub-Saharan Africa became newly infected, whereas 1.4 million died of AIDS (UNAIDS 2009).

The full impact of AIDS is still not well understood. Its effects come in waves; first the in-fection, followed by opportunistic diseases, then later by a wave of AIDS-related illness, and finally death. However, its effects are still accumulating across families, communities nation-ally and, eventually, internationally. HIV and AIDS are ripping families apart. Millions of chil-dren are orphaned, living a life on the street in which they fight to survive (AVERT.ORG 2010a; UNAIDS 2009). Food scarcities are exacerbated because families can no longer tend to their crops, and by 2020, the epidemic may claim the lives of at least one-fifth of all those working in agriculture in many African countries (Food and Agricultural Organization of the United Nations 2006). Life expectancy has dropped because of the high number of AIDS-related deaths in many countries. In Zimbabwe, the life expectancy at birth declined from 55 years in 1970 to 41 years in 2009 (Population Reference Bureau 2010b). HIV and AIDS are shrouded in stigma, making effective prevention and treatment exceedingly difficult. Even gov-ernments are slow to acknowledge the epidemic because of its stigma.

In many parts of the world, especially sub-Saharan Africa, women suffer from HIV and AIDS at rates that outpace men. In sub-Saharan Africa, women make up 60 percent of adults living with HIV. In some countries, women are twice as likely to be infected as are men (UNAIDS 2009). Women's greater vulnerability not only reflects greater physiological sus-ceptibility in heterosexual transmissions, but reflects patriarchy and women's powerlessness in social, legal, and economic realms as well. Sexual and physical violence are key determi-nants of a country's severity of HIV/AIDS (Khobotlo et al. 2009). According to a recent sur-vey, 47 percent of men and 40 percent of women in Lesotho say women have no right to refuse sex with their husbands or boyfriends (Andersson et al. 2007).

HIV and AIDS are particularly devastating to the younger women and girls in sub-Sa-haran Africa. For example, girls in Kenya aged 15–19 are three times more likely to be in-fected than are boys their age, and girls aged 20–24 are over five times as likely as their male counterparts to be infected. This highlights the vulnerability and exploitation of young girls, as reported in the box on page 449, "Our Global Community: HIV/AIDS: Girls Are Very Vulnerable." Young people lack solid information about HIV/AIDS and misconceptions are

O U R

Global Community

HIV/AIDS: Girls Are Very Vulnerable

In the United States, HIV and AIDS are far more common among men than among women. However, in other parts of the world, the most common victims of HIV and AIDS are heterosexual young women, as this report by UNICEF reveals.

Globally, more men are infected with HIV than women, but women, especially adolescent girls, are catching up. This pattern is especially clear in sub-Saharan Africa, the region most severely affected by HIV/AIDS. More than two-thirds of the newly infected 15- to 19-year-olds in this region are female. In Ethiopia, Malawi, Tanzania, Zambia, and Zimbabwe, for every 15- to 19-year-old boy who is infected, there are 5–6 girls infected in the same age group.

This indicates a "sexual mixing" pattern whereby older men are having sex with young girls. In many countries where economic conditions make it difficult for girls to afford school fees, some seek favors of a *sugar daddy* (an older man who offers compensation in cash or in-kind exchange for sexual favors), engage in transactional sex (exchange sex for money or goods on an occasional basis), or enter sex work (willingly or forced) to pay for school, support their families, or take care of themselves. A study in Botswana found that about one in five out-of-school adolescent girls reported that it is difficult to refuse sex when money and gifts are offered; girls as young as 13 had engaged in sex with sugar daddies.

The age-mixing is fueled by the dangerous myth that having sex with a virgin can "cure" HIV. Many men also assume that younger girls are not yet infected. Cultural norms prevent many girls from taking active steps to protect themselves. In cultures where it is vital for girls to be virgins at marriage, some girls protect their virginity by engaging in unsafe sexual practices such as unprotected anal intercourse.

Biological factors also play an important role. The risk of getting infected during unprotected vaginal intercourse is always greater for women than men; the risk for girls is further heightened because their vaginal tracts are immature and the tissues tear easily. In Kisumu, Kenya, where over a quarter of girls said that they had had sex before age 15, one in twelve contracted the virus before her fifteenth birthday.

Marriage on its own offers no protection against HIV for young women, especially if their husband is much older. Another study in Kisumu, Kenya, reported that as many as half of the women with husbands at least a decade older were infected with HIV; by contrast, no women were infected whose husbands were only three years older or less. Another study of nearly 400 women attending the city's sexually transmitted disease clinic in Pune, India, found the vast majority were married and had never had sex with anyone but their husbands. Lacking the power to negotiate safe sex practices, many young brides may be even more vulnerable to HIV/AIDS and sexually transmitted diseases than unmarried girls.

Interventions to stem HIV must target boys as well as girls. A mutually respectful relationship can free both young men and young women from the dangers of coerced or unwanted sex and enable them to feel comfortable discussing sexual matters and negotiating safety and protection.

Sources: United Nations Children's Fund 2002; UNAIDS 2009.

CRITICAL THINKING QUESTIONS
1. How does patriarchy contribute to a woman's inability to negotiate safe sex and protect herself from HIV/AIDS?
2. How can the spread of HIV/AIDS be stopped in sub-Saharan Africa?

Percentage of Adults (15–49) Estimated To Be Living with HIV/AIDS, 2008

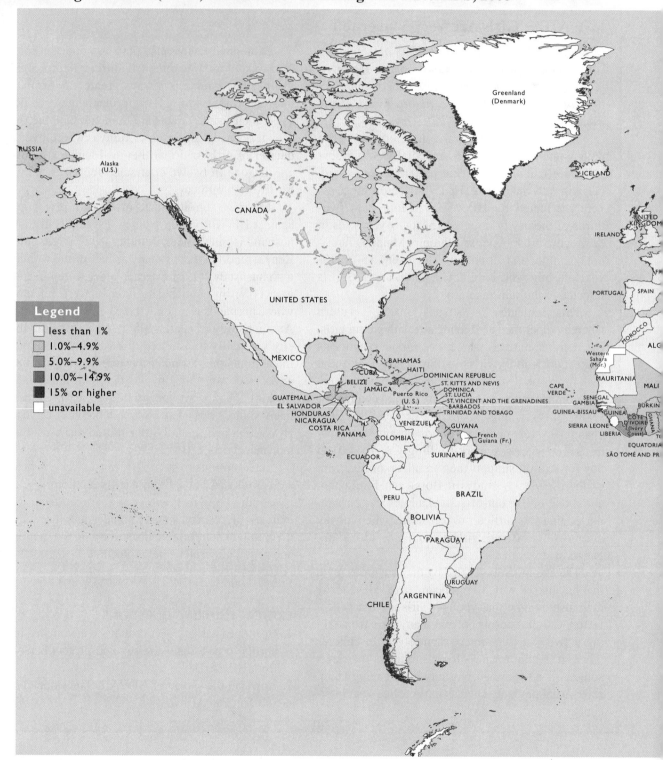

Legend
- less than 1%
- 1.0%–4.9%
- 5.0%–9.9%
- 10.0%–14.9%
- 15% or higher
- unavailable

rampant even in countries with HIV epidemics. In Somalia, only 26 percent of girls have heard of AIDS and only 1 percent know how to avoid infection. Young people are also likely to experiment sexually; boys avoid using condoms and girls are afraid to make them do so. Many young girls have sex with older and infected men, often under coercion or because the man in turn has offered to feed her and her family.

How can a comparative approach help the situation here or in Africa? Although HIV and AIDS remain significant problems in the United States, widespread education efforts have been coupled with important breakthroughs in medical treatment. Fewer Americans are becoming infected, and those who are infected are living longer productive lives. If medical treatment is available in the United States, why is it not made available to those countries that need it the most? Decisions about public health measures are often rooted in politics or quests for profit. Tired of waiting for government action, many private organizations, such as the Bill and Melinda Gates Foundation (created by Microsoft billionaire Bill Gates), have poured many millions of dollars into HIV/AIDS prevention and treatment.

An Empirical Approach

The sociological imagination also uses an empirical approach to study families. Most of us probably have opinions about what families are "supposed" to look like, what they are supposed to do, or how they are "supposed" to behave. Families have several universal functions, as discussed in Chapter 2. Families are associated with the regulation of sexual behavior, reproduction and socialization of children, property and inheritance, economic cooperation, social placement, and intimacy. These may be universal expectations, but precisely how these are implemented differ from society to society based upon religious teachings, cultural customs, or societal laws. For example, is it wrong to have sex outside of marriage? Does it matter whether it is premarital or extramarital sex? Do attitudes differ for women and men?

What can we depend on to help us understand family dynamics? Sociologists and other family scientists do not want to rely only on so-called common sense, personal experience, authority figures, or the sentiment "It's always been that way so it must be right." Instead, they use an empirical approach, in which they answer questions through a systematic collection and analysis of quantitative or qualitative data. The goals of empirical research can either be to (1) describe some phenomenon; (2) assess what factors are associated with the phenomenon; (3) explain the cause-and-effect relationships; or (4) understand the meanings attached to behaviors and situations. Empirical research findings often shatter popular ideas and reveal their underlying misconceptions.

Effects of Divorce on Children   A compelling example of the importance of empirical research can be seen regarding the effects of divorce on children, as discussed in Chapter 14. For several decades the sentiment was that divorce did little harm to children. "Staying together for the sake of the children" became a meaningless phrase, because unhappily married adults argued that their children would be made better off by the divorce. However, as you learned, a large and growing body of empirical research suggests that we may need to rethink this view; children are not necessarily better off when their parents divorce. Children likely experience a significant drop in income and are subject to numerous transitions, such as moving or attending a new school. Although most children adjust adequately over time to the transitions in their lives, some are plagued by depression or other behavioral problems for many years.

Are these problems related to divorce *per se*, or are they a by-product of witnessing parental conflict? We no longer need to guess at the answer. Using empirical data from large and representative samples, researchers have addressed these questions and found some interesting answers. If a marriage contains severe conflict, such as domestic violence, a divorce may indeed be better for the children. However, in cases of relatively low conflict, children benefit when their parents stay together. Therefore, empirical research has demonstrated that previous thinking may have been in error; it is likely that the majority of children whose parents divorce probably would be better off if their parents had stayed together.

Using the Sociological Imagination: Themes of the Text Revisited

Five themes regarding families have run throughout this book. We witnessed how families are more than simply a private relationship; they are also a social institution. We uncovered patterns of social inequality, noting their importance in fully understanding family structure and family dynamics. We incorporated a strengths-based perspective and recognized the need for sound social policies and programs. We emphasized that these family programs and policies do not exist in isolation but reflect historical, cultural, political, and social factors. Finally, we found that understanding families requires a comparative perspective. Let's review these themes, integrating information from the chapters, to see what we have learned.

Theme 1: Families Are Both a Public Social Institution and a Private Personal Relationship

Because families fulfill many of our own personal needs, it is easy to forget that families are based on a set of beliefs and rules organized to meet basic human needs generally. In addition to talking about *your* specific family, we talk about *the* family. Families are a social institution, in much the same way our political, economic, religious, health care, and educational systems are social institutions.

Families can best be understood by examining how they interact with (and are influenced by) other social institutions. Families cannot simply be separated as "havens" from the rest of society. Patterns of education, religious customs, economic systems, and political systems all shape family attitudes, behaviors, and the constraints and opportunities experienced by individual members. For example, education can determine the normative age at which young people marry in a society; religious customs can determine the degree of patriarchy; the economic system can determine the degree of struggle families are likely to experience meeting their basic needs for food, shelter, and clothing; and political systems can determine the degree to which a family experiences an open democracy or lives under tyranny.

In all likelihood, most people do not reflect very often on families as social institutions. Instead, most people focus on their lived day-to-day experiences and think about their families in very individualized terms, failing to see the interconnection to larger social structures.

Chances are, these sisters do not spend a lot of time thinking about their family as a social institution. To them it is simply a personal relationship—a fun one, at that.

Example: Childbirth and Cesarean Sections   As discussed in Chapter 9, one certainly personal and private family experience is childbirth, yet it is also shaped by the health care system and powerful special-interest groups. Many expectant parents write personalized birth plans so that the experience will closely match their expectations. However, in reality, the birthing experience for most women is a highly medicalized and impersonal event, as indicated by the growing rate of surgical births.

The rate of Cesarean sections (C-sections) increased to nearly 33 percent of all U.S. births in 2008 (Hamilton et al. 2010), reflecting a 40 percent increase from the mid-1990s. C-sections are the most frequent operations performed in the United States. The likelihood of having a surgical birth depends on far more than medical necessity; it varies by race and ethnicity, and even by state. For example, Utah, Idaho, Alaska, and New Mexico all have Cesarean rates well below average, while Puerto Rico's rate is nearly 45 percent.

To put these numbers into perspective, leading health organizations, including UNICEF, the World Health Organization (WHO), and the United Nations Population Fund (UNFPA), agree that a C-section rate above 15 percent indicates improper use of the procedure (March of Dimes 2006). Births by C-section involve considerable risk, and thousands of women and babies are injured, maimed, or even die unnecessarily.

Why is the procedure increasing so remarkably in the wake of concerns by leading health organizations? The reasons can be divided into biological and sociocultural categories. With respect to biology, increasing numbers of older women are giving birth, resulting in an increase in some complications including twins or other multiples. However, these factors alone do not account for the high rates of surgical births because most older women deliver their babies vaginally without any complications, as do many mothers of multiples. Moreover, other developed countries also have high numbers of older women giving birth, yet they have significantly lower rates of surgical births. Rather than biology, something else explains the United States' increasing reliance on a surgical procedure that continues to worry leading health officials.

Many people blame doctors for the increase in surgical births. Doctors perform C-sections to ward off lawsuits, to speed up the birthing process, to make more money, or to schedule their workload most efficiently. But they also do it because women are requesting them (Korn 2010). One study based on 157 pregnant women in a New Orleans hospital found that 14.7 percent requested C-sections. "I liked having a Cesarean section because once you get in and have your epidural (anesthetic), it takes 20 minutes," reported one woman, despite the six weeks of often painful recuperation needed (Pope 2004). Many women are quite comfortable with the remedicalization of childbirth, in contrast to the move toward more natural methods promoted in the 1990s.

In all likelihood, most pregnant women do not reflect on the ways that childbirth is shaped by the medical institutions within society. They are generally unaware how something so seemingly private is intertwined with larger social structures. Instead, they focus on their daily personal experience—yet a sociological imagination asks that we be mindful of the social forces operating to shape our personal choices and experiences.

Theme 2: Social Inequality Has a Powerful Influence on Family Life

Social inequality is pervasive throughout the world. Wars have been fought, homes and communities have been ravaged, families have been torn apart, and ethnic groups have been obliterated in battles over valued resources. U.S. society is also highly stratified on the basis of valued resources, notably income, power, and social status. These patterns of social inequality shape all dimensions of family life, as shown in the box on pages 455–456, "Families as Lived Experience: 'Tommy Johnson' and 'Randall Simmons.'" Compare the lifestyles, opportunities, and constraints of Tommy Johnson and Randall Simmons.

FAMILIES

as Lived Experience

"Tommy Johnson" and "Randall Simmons"

How do our financial resources shape our lives? Let's take a look at Tommy Johnson and Randall Simmons.

Profile 1:

Name: Tommy Johnson

Age: 29

Father's Occupation: Janitor

Mother's Occupation: Nurse's Aide

Community When Growing Up: Miami, Florida

Principal Caretakers as a Child: Grandmother, neighbor, older sister

Education: Large public elementary and secondary schools in inner-city Miami. Emphasis on rote learning of basic skills. Security guards patrolled school. Occasional church camp during the summer. Classmates included sons and daughters of domestics, sales clerks, factory workers, and service workers.

Family Activities as a Child: Church, television, visiting family members.

First Job: Age 16—short-order cook at a fast-food restaurant in Miami.

Hobbies: Working on cars.

College: Attended nearby community college. Quit after two semesters to take a full-time job.

First Full-Time Job: Age 19. Sales clerk at auto parts store in Miami.

Current Position: Muffler installer at a national chain shop devoted to installing mufflers and brakes. Has been with the company for three years. Works Tuesday through Saturday, with occasional overtime. Annual earnings approximate $27,000 per year.

Marital Status: Married at age 20. Wife is employed part-time, 20 hours per week as a sales clerk in a discount department store. Annual

earnings approximately $9,000 per year. Three children aged 7, 5, and 2.

Family Activities: Bowling, church, watching television, city league baseball, visiting relatives.

Current Residence: Owns a small three-bedroom mobile home in a trailer park in a lower-income Miami suburb. Comfortably furnished with older and well-worn furniture and appliances. Has two cars, a Ford Escort and a minivan, both over seven years old.

Goals: To someday manage his own auto parts store, send children to vocational college to learn a "good trade," and be a good father and provider to his family.

Profile 2:

Name: Randall Simmons

Age: 29

Father's Occupation: Real Estate Attorney

Mother's Occupation: Homemaker and Community Volunteer

Principal Caretakers as a Child: Mother and governess

Community When Growing Up: Beverly Hills, California

Education: Private elementary and secondary schools devoted to liberal and creative arts. Small student–teacher ratio. Supplemental tutoring in French, piano, clarinet. Fellow students are the sons and daughters of business leaders, physicians, real-estate developers, and ambassadors. Spent summers in camps devoted to educational enrichment, including athletics and horseback riding.

Family Activities as a Child: Riding horses, theater, summer vacations in Europe, winter vacations at a condo in the Caribbean. Parents

(continued)

(continued)

made generous donations to the performing arts community and were granted season tickets for the family to music and dance events at the community theater.

Hobbies: Riding horses (owns two horses, boarded approximately 35 miles from home), golf, gourmet cooking.

College Attended: Bachelor of Arts degree in small, elite private college. Active in a campus fraternity and the college debate team. Attended law school at Stanford University, where father and uncle are alumni.

First Full-Time Job: Age 26—Attorney in large and prestigious law firm in West Los Angeles.

Current Job and Earnings: Attorney in the same law firm. Works approximately 50 hours per week. Annual salary approximates $200,000 per year. Also receives dividends of $150,000 per year from stocks and trust funds established by his wife's parents.

Marital Status: Married at age 27. Wife is a community volunteer. She has a Bachelor of Arts degree in music from the same college as Randall. No children, but would like to have a baby within two or three years. Ideal family size is three children.

Family Activities: International travel, theater, riding horses, golf at the country club.

Current Residence: 3,000-square-foot home in Pacific Palisades area of Los Angeles, located five blocks from a private beach on the Pacific Ocean. Parents helped with the down payment. Interior was professionally designed and furnished. Family has two cars, a late-model BMW and a new Mercedes.

Goals: To make partner in law firm, where he is currently employed, within next five to seven years.

CRITICAL THINKING QUESTIONS

1. How does your life compare to Tommy Johnson and Randall Simmons? Whose life is closer to yours? Can you think of the ways in which income has specifically shaped your personal choices and behaviors?
2. Why is there so little social mobility? For example, why didn't Tommy Johnson go to college and law school? Who or what stopped him from doing so? Do you think it is likely that his children will do so?
3. In a country as "free" and open as the United States, why does income still shape our choices and behaviors?

Social class, sex, race, and ethnicity are master statuses that affect the distribution of income, power, and social status. They also affect the way family members interact and the way in which family members respond. For example, Chapter 6 showed us that multi-generational households are more common among minorities than among Whites and offer many opportunities for emotional and financial support and assistance with childrearing. Despite these benefits, extended families have been branded as deficient rather than as a real source of strength. Instead, the model dominant among Whites, the isolated nuclear family, is posited as the "ideal." Minority youth, in particular, are sensitive to the normative definitions of family and often feel frustrated or embarrassed that their family does not "measure up" to the idealized American family, as shown in Chapter 1 (Pyke 2000a, 2000b).

Conversely, patterns of social inequality are also shaped *by* families. Americans fantasize that they can be anything they want to be, but in reality there is little substantial upward (or downward) social mobility. As shown in Chapter 5, people usually live out their lives in generally the same social class in which they were born. Families pass on their wealth, educational opportunities, and social capital (or their lack of it) to their newest members, and this perpetuates social inequality. For example, former President George W. Bush was accepted to college at

Yale University despite having a C average in high school. Clearly, it was his family background that opened the doors to Yale, which then paved the way for many of his subsequent achievements. What if George W. Bush had been born to a middle-class or working-class family? What wealth, educational opportunities, or social capital would they have to pass on that would have helped him to become President of the United States? What about Barack Obama, you ask, since he is a glowing example of upward social mobility? Although he was raised by a lower-income single mother, he had the good fortune to attend an exclusive prep school in Hawaii on financial aid. This, combined with his keen intelligence and a bit of good luck, propelled him toward new possibilities.

Several theoretical perspectives help interpret the connections between inequality and families, as revealed in Chapter 1, and these have been used throughout this text. One particularly useful perspective for examining the influence that inequality has on family lives is conflict theory, which examines the assumptions, values, and ideologies that are used to justify or explain family dynamics and our understanding of society's role in shaping or helping families. The ideologies of the more powerful groups are presented as the norm, and even persons with less power, status, and wealth begin to agree, failing to see that these ideologies may not really be in their best interest. The following box, "Using the Sociological Imagination: Managing the Stigma of Welfare," describes how even welfare recipients be-

USING
the Sociological Imagination

Managing the Stigma of Welfare

The following looks at the ways that women who receive welfare manage the stigma associated with welfare programs.

Most Americans denigrate welfare recipients and accuse them of being lazy, unmotivated, irresponsible, and content to live off the public dole and take advantage of hardworking taxpayers. Famous author and welfare critic George Gilder (1995) wrote in the *American Spectator*, "On the whole, black or white, these women are slovenly, incompetent, and sexually promiscuous" (p. 25).

Are welfare recipients aware of the deep-rooted stigma surrounding welfare and those who receive it? Interviews with 49 women on welfare revealed that they are very much aware of these hostilities. Rhonda, a 28-year-old woman with one child, summed up the sentiment:

> I heard one girl was going to quit working because all the taxes come to us. Plus, they downgrade us in every kind of way there is. They say we look like slobs, we keep our houses this way and that way. And our children, depending on the way

they're dressed, we're like bad parents and all sorts of things like that.

Many respondents told me that the derogatory comments were very painful, discouraging, or humiliating to hear. Amy, a 23-year-old mother, said:

> It's a very humiliating experience—being on welfare and being involved in the system. You are treated as though you are the scum of the earth—a stupid, lazy, nasty person. How dare you take this money? It's a very unpleasant experience. I'd avoid it at all costs. But unfortunately, I can't avoid it right now.

How do women cope with or manage the stigma of being on welfare? Erving Goffman (1963) suggests that for someone with a known stigma, the basic issue is to manage the tension produced by the fact that people know of the problem. One can hide being on welfare in some contexts, but it is revealed in others such as grocery stores or in the welfare office.

(continued)

(continued)

During the interviews, it became clear that women tend to rely on one or more of four primary strategies for coping with the stigma attached to using welfare: (1) denial that they were on welfare or that they had experienced any stigma; (2) distancing themselves from other recipients; (3) blaming external forces for their own need of welfare; and (4) extolling the importance of motherhood. Few women questioned the dominant views of welfare recipients, and instead, most women believe the stereotypes about welfare and welfare recipients. They denigrated welfare recipients, even referring to other recipients as "they." Virtually every woman then explained that she was different from all the others. For example, Janie sees her situation as unique because she bore a child as a result of a rape and only intends to be on welfare for a short time, although she has been on for two years already. She holds disdain for other recipients:

> There are some people on welfare who don't need to be on welfare. They can go out and get a job. They have nothing better to do than to live off welfare and to live off the system. I'm sorry. I have no sympathy. Look at all the signs on the road, "will work for food." Go down to Day Labor, for crying out loud. They'll pay you more money than you can make in a regular day. It's by choice. Either (1) they don't want to work; (2) they are being supported by others; or (3) they don't give a damn about themselves.

I heard many negative comments about other welfare recipients: "they're breeders…if they don't get themselves stopped they'll keep having babies," "I think a lot of them are on it just to be lazy." Yet, virtually all women believed that their own personal story was somehow unique among women on welfare. Their situations were distinctly different from the others, they claimed. They were victims of unplanned and unfortunate circumstances. They fled intolerable domestic violence. They were victims of rape or incest. They were deserted by men after finding out they were pregnant. They left men who were having affairs or abused their children. They had serious health problems that interfered with their work, or their children were sick. They were on assistance only temporarily while they got on their feet, got a job, got their child into day care, found a job, or got their children's fathers to finally pay the child support owed. What was striking was how few women thought that other welfare recipients might have these problems too. Women perceived that their own use of welfare was caused by factors outside their control, but welfare use by other women, in contrast, was attributed to laziness, personal shortcomings, or other inadequacies.

Given the strong negative messages about welfare and welfare recipients, perhaps it is not surprising that women who receive welfare blame other women for their circumstances. When the dominant ideology is repeated often enough, it becomes "common sense" and the poor and less powerful also internalize it. Poverty and welfare use become personal problems, rather than social ones.

Source: Seccombe 2011.

CRITICAL THINKING QUESTIONS

1. How does the ideology of the prominent group become so powerful that even women on welfare will subscribe to negative stereotypes about women on welfare?
2. Do you think the ideological hegemony operates differently among minorities than it does for Whites? Why or why not?
3. What would it take for the poor and powerless to see their collective interests?

lieve that women who receive welfare are lazy and unmotivated although they vehemently deny that they are like that. A conflict perspective asks that we examine the assumptions, values, and ideologies, which are used to define families, characterize family dynamics, and to create family policy.

Example: Sex and Gender as Dimensions of Social Inequality Of all the issues shaping families, both as a social institution and the lived experiences within families, certainly sex and gender are among the most influential, as you learned in Chapter 4. Regardless of social class, racial or ethnic identity, type of political or economic regime, or any other aspect of the social structure, there are cultural rules that govern the behavior of males and females in every society. These rules begin virtually from the day children are born. Although rigid expectations can be a burden on boys and men too, girls and women suffer from unrelenting sex and gender rules in many parts of the world. From female infanticide at birth, female genital mutilation in childhood, forced child marriages in adolescence, to the legal subjugation of women by their husbands, many women routinely face gross violations of their human rights. Why do these abuses continue? Why do women seemingly not object and change things?

Of course, many women do object. Millions of women are resisting their continued exploitation and are becoming increasingly empowered. They are creating grassroots organizations and joining established human rights organizations. They are sharing their skills with others; they are teaching girls and women how to read and write; and they are lobbying the police, courts, and legislatures for change (Kristof and WuDunn 2009).

Nonetheless, we also know that many women do not actively promote sex and gender equality. Some women feel powerless to do so. Others believe in their subjugation, but should we be surprised? After all, women are socialized into their culture and therefore, like many men, do not really know any other way of being. Cultural norms are powerful. Hence, women may also believe in the religiously based or politically motivated justifications for inequality, and often perpetuate it. To fail to do so means facing a terrible social risk. We saw this in Chapter 4, where at least 100 million women alive today have had their genitals mutilated. One study in Sudan found that 90 percent of women have had their daughter cut or infibulated or planned to do so (Williams and Sobieszczyk 1997). Despite the severe pain and health consequences, these women are willing to inflict the same procedure on their daughters to ensure her prospective husband that she is a virgin. To fail to cut or infibulate their daughters may make the young girls seem different, subject them to ridicule, eliminate marriage prospects, and subject the entire family to scorn. Women mutilate their daughters because their culture tells them that husbands should have all sexual privileges, and over time they come to believe these messages (Gramsci 1971).

Americans like to believe in social mobility, but realistically, what are the odds that these children will grow up to be a CEO of a Fortune 500 company?

Theme 3: An Expanded Strengths-Based Perspective Can Improve Family Resiliency

A family strengths perspective focuses on identifying, creating, mobilizing, advocating, and respecting the resources, assets, wisdom, and knowledge that every person and every family has to help ameliorate problems. It focuses on how members of our society can work together to make families stronger and more resilient. Resiliency is the capacity to rebound from adversity, misfortune, trauma, or other transitional crises and become strengthened and more resourceful.

Individual-level protective factors include individual personality traits and dispositions that enhance a person's ability to be successful. These factors include such traits as insight, independence, supportive relationships, initiative, creativity, humor, and morality.

Family protective factors (FPF) are those characteristics or dynamics that shape the family's ability to endure in the face of risk factors; family recovery factors (FRF) assist families in "bouncing back" from a crisis situation (McCubbin et al. 1997). Key characteristics of resilient families include warmth, affection, cohesion, commitment, clear expectations, shared goals, and emotional support for one another. Resilient families participate in family celebrations, share spiritual connections, have specific traditions, and predictable routines (Saleebey 2009; Walsh 2006).

There are also community factors that help develop resilient youth and foster resiliency among adults (Walsh 2006). These may include organizations such as youth groups or extracurricular activities. They can teach important skills, promote group pride, provide access to mentors, foster inner strength and self-esteem, and provide an avenue to help others.

Finally, national and statewide policies can also strengthen families. Children and adults cannot always go it alone, but often need the assistance of government intervention to really thrive (Seccombe 2002). One study examined the gap in math and science achievement of third- and fourth-graders who lived with a single parent versus those who lived with two parents in 11 different countries (Pong et al. 2003). The researchers found that countries that provided the fewest policies to equalize the resources of parents, such as the United States and New Zealand, had the largest achievement gap between children in single- versus two-parent families. In contrast, those countries with family policies specifically designed to equalize resources between single- and two-parent families were far more successful in decreasing the achievement gap.

Example: Poverty Policy   Poor children are more likely to drop out of school, less likely to graduate from high school, and less likely to attend college. Poor children are also more likely to have health problems and suffer from a wide variety of ailments, both chronic and acute, including asthma, depression, and learning difficulties. Chapter 5 showed you that poverty contributes to poorer nutrition, lower-quality home environment, parental stress, fewer resources for learning, housing problems, and poor-quality neighborhoods, which in turn lead to further negative consequences. Poor children face many obstacles and have many challenges socially, emotionally, and physically.

Yet, despite these, many poor children grow up to be strong, healthy, and happy adults. They thrive even in the face of adversity. How can this be? Some children may have particular personality traits that enhance resiliency. Perhaps they are naturally outgoing, resourceful, or intelligent. Or they may have learned adaptive personality traits, such as ingenuity, or how to ask for needed help. Some children have supportive families that encourage them to do their best, offer resources to the best of their ability, or provide stable routines and predictability to help children make sense of their lives. Children may also have found support in their community, such as a teacher who prodded them to do their best work, a mentor who gave of their time and advice, or a spiritual leader who offered a moral compass.

Yet, despite the value inherent in all these factors, our government has a critical role in helping children in poverty. It is our government that develops nutrition programs such as food stamps or school breakfast and lunch programs that enable poor children to eat nutritious food more regularly. It is our government that ensures poor children's health care needs are attended to. It is our government that ensures poor children receive a cash welfare grant to care for them if the parents are unable to work. Granted, we can argue whether these programs work as intended, whether they are sufficient to meet the problems, and whether other models of care might work better. There are many different views, probably with some legitimate claims on all sides. But who can argue whether family policies are *needed*. Families have a rough road toward resiliency without them.

Theme 4: Family Policies Reflect Historical, Cultural, Political, and Social Factors

The fourth theme emphasizes that family policies do not exist in a vacuum. They reflect historical, cultural, political, and social factors in every society—values about personal responsibility versus collective good, the role of work in our lives, the expectations placed on mothers and fathers to manage the inherent conflicts between their work and family lives, and the level of concern over social inequality (Day 2009; Gilbert and Terrell 2010; Karger and Stoesz 2010).

Countries that develop explicit family policies, such as Sweden, France, or Norway, see the family as the key unit of analysis. Their goal is to strengthen the entire family because they see that as good for all of society. It is in the best interest of all citizens to have well-cared for and well-educated children. In contrast, countries such as the United States develop policies and programs that focus on individual needy members, such as the physically disabled, the juvenile delinquent, a qualifying poor child, or the aged.

The United States has a long history of "rugged individualism" and a distrust of government and its programs. Family policies in the United States reflect and promote the concepts of individualism and self-sufficiency. They tend to be selective, meaning that persons need to meet some eligibility requirement to qualify for benefits, but it is not always clear to the observer why some programs are available to everyone and others are not. Why is access to education a guaranteed "right," but not access to health care? Why does the federal government have a health care program for all elderly, Medicare, but none for children? Why does the government subsidize the cost of college attendance but does little to assist families to pay for preschool? We cannot turn simply to logic to answer these questions; the answers often reflect the success of special interest groups in having their agendas served.

The policies in the United States differ from those in other developed nations. Other countries lean toward universal programs that are available to all persons. As we have learned, not only is the United States the only developed nation without universal health insurance coverage, but it is also virtually the only one without paid maternal/parental leave at childbirth, or a family allowance/child dependency grant. Americans think of these issues in individualistic terms and frown upon government assistance. There is the fear that assistance will make families weak and dependent on the system.

Example: Work and Family   Many family scholars have been writing about the policies needed to reconcile parenthood and employment (Galinsky et al. 2009; Goodman et al. 2009; Voydanoff 2008). As we learned in Chapter 11, not only are single parents employed, but most two-parent families in the United States have both parents employed outside the home for pay (Bureau of Labor Statistics 2010b). Nonetheless, family policies have failed to keep up with the changing needs of families, and family and employment needs often collide with one another. Compared to other developed nations, American mothers and fathers work more hours per week, have less vacation time, and are more likely to report a desire for having more time with the family. Americans receive even maternity leave that is minimal.

Moreover, families in the United States have only a patchwork of child care and early childhood education arrangements, as discussed in Chapter 11, and these are plagued with limited access, variable quality, and high cost. Families' access to child care depends largely on their own private resources and what happens to be available in the community. Quality is uneven and often poor because there is little standardization or oversight. Pay is low, turnover is high, and working conditions are often deplorable. Early childhood education is not a valued occupation, despite its importance to the community, and workers have little incentive to upgrade their skills or provide the highest quality care. Yet, the cost is high because there is little government subsidization. For the most part, parents bear the full brunt of the costs. Head Start programs or welfare-to-work day care subsidies are an exception to this. Other developed countries subsidize their early childhood education programs for all families far more than does the United States.

Chapter 1 identified three approaches that can be used when family and work conflict with one another. The first approach establishes policies that create more family-friendly work environments, such as paid maternity and family leave. A second approach mandates that workers themselves learn specific techniques for handling their conflicts, such as managing their time better. A third approach asks workers to modify the meanings of the situation, suggesting that people face family and work conflicts simply because they want to work more hours or want more money. Policies would focus on increasing personal responsibility and commitments. The second and third approaches dominate social policies in the United States. Family concerns are generally viewed as personal issues or problems, in contrast to many other countries that take a more collective view, reflecting a difference in fundamental values.

Theme 5: Understanding Families in the United States Requires a Comparative Perspective

Finally, the fifth theme focuses on a comparative perspective. Because the world is so interconnected, societies are no longer isolated entities. People can see other ways of doing things and sometimes adopt pieces of another's culture as their own. This is the case for family life as well. Learning how other societies structure families, how they collectively think about families, how they encourage members to interact, and how they deal with the challenges families face can provide insight into our own patterns and family concerns.

Although many problems, such as poverty or HIV/AIDS, are considerably worse in other countries, other problems loom larger in the United States than elsewhere. For example, the U.S. infant mortality rate is among the highest in the developed world, and its life expectancy rate is among the lowest. Many minority babies have trouble surviving even their first year of life. How can a society as richly endowed as the United States have such poor health statistics? Poor health reflects both personal behavior such as obesity and structural factors such as racism or an inadequate health care system. What can we learn from other countries to better understand and help our own?

Example: Teenage Birthrates   The teenage birthrate in the United States remains the highest among developed nations. The United States has a teenage birthrate almost twice as high as the United Kingdom, twice the rate as in Canada, our closest developed neighbor, and nearly 12 times the rate of Japan. It is three times as high as Australia's, four times as high as Germany's, six times as high as France's, and eight times as high as that of the Netherlands (The Annie E. Casey Foundation 2009).

Chapter 10 described the negative consequences of teen pregnancies and births (Advocates for Youth 2009; The Annie E. Casey Foundation 2009). For example, teenage mothers are more than twice as likely to die in childbirth as are older mothers, their infants are twice as likely to be of low birth weight, and nearly three times more likely to die within the first month of life. Teen mothers are also far more likely to be impoverished.

Why are rates of teen births so much lower in other countries? It is arguably due to policies in those countries that include mandatory, medically accurate sex education programs that provide comprehensive information and encourage teens to make responsible choices; easy access to contraceptives and other forms of reproductive health care; the social acceptance of adolescent sexual expression as normal and healthy; and other governmental and social programs that provide needed services such as medical care, education, or other social services (Berne and Huberman 1999; Garner 2009). These countries are successful at curbing teenage pregnancies and births with a combination of education and medical technology. In contrast, the United States places a far greater emphasis on abstinence. The United States could learn ways to curb the number of teens having babies by closely examining the values, policies, and practices of other countries. A comparative perspective shows us that family practices are embedded in a social context. Learning how other societies structure families, how they collectively think about families, and how they deal with the challenges families face can provide insight into our own concerns.

WHAT DO YOU THINK?

Reflect back on material that you have learned in previous chapters. Can you think of other specific examples of each of these five themes? Which theme resonates with you the most? The least?

Future Trends: Where Are Families Heading?

Our study of families shows that they are dynamic and always changing. There is not one type of family that is inherently better (or worse) than others. Families are evolving and emerging to meet societies' needs.

Looking into the future is always a bit of a gamble, but given what we know about the social and demographic forces operating in the United States today and the changing nature of our social institutions, what might we anticipate with respect to the families of the future? The following are a few of my predictions. What do you think?

1. *The age at marriage will continue to rise.* Today, the average age of marriage is about 26 for women and 28 for men. However, I predict that the age of marriage will continue to rise somewhat for several reasons. First, greater educational and employment oppor-

The number of Hispanics in the United States will continue to grow because of higher-than-average birth rates and immigration. Their presence will richly influence American culture.

tunities will continue for women, thus rendering a push toward early marriage less relevant. Second, as the population of unmarried persons increases (because of cohabitation, delayed marriage, or other reasons), there will be greater acceptance of the unmarried.

2. *The rate of cohabitation will increase.* Disapproval of cohabitation is on the decline and is found primarily among older persons or among certain religious groups today. I anticipate that cohabitation will become increasingly common. As younger persons eventually age, they will retain their support of cohabitation, and a new generation will see cohabitation as relatively routine.

3. *The percentage of women and men without children will rise.* The percentage of women between the ages of 40 and 44 who do not have children has more than doubled since 1980. As U.S. society sees more childfree women and men, pronatalism may decline further and more people will see a childfree life as a legitimate option.

4. *The divorce rate will continue to decline slightly.* The divorce rate crested in 1980 and has since declined to less than 17 per 1,000 married women. I anticipate that divorce will continue to decline further somewhat as the children of divorce grow up and marry.

5. *The United States will become more diverse.* Demographers who study population trends predict that within a few decades, minorities will constitute roughly half of the U.S. population.

6. *The rapid growth in the Hispanic population will continue.* Hispanic groups now comprise the largest minority in the United States, eclipsing Blacks. Because the birthrate of Hispanics is higher than average, coupled with immigration, their presence in the United States will continue to grow quickly. Hispanic culture will have a growing influence on U.S. culture and family life.

7. *The rate of mothers working outside the home will likely stabilize.* Today, about two-thirds of married couples with children have both parents working outside the home for pay, either full- or part-time. The early 2000s witnessed a slight decline in the employment rate of mothers of very young children. However, because of the economic recession, women's advancing education, and greater labor market opportunities, I anticipate that the employment of mothers will likely stabilize or may eventually rise again.

8. *The United States will remain highly stratified.* Since 1980, the income and wealth distribution in the United States has become more highly skewed in favor of the wealthy. This seems to be a longstanding trend, and I anticipate that it will continue unless tax policies change substantially.

9. *The elderly population will continue to increase rapidly.* The elderly now constitute one of every eight people, increasing to about one of every five by the middle of this century as the baby-boomers age. This large aging cohort will have a significant effect on U.S. culture and social policies.

10. *The United States will see some challenges to its piecemeal approach to family policy.* Historically, no real special interest group has taken on the task of developing a national family policy. However, this may change slowly, as people become more vocal about what they see as unfair or discriminatory programs or policies. For example, as more middle-income families lost their health insurance, they clamored for change, and health reform was passed in 2010. Likewise, same-sex couples are vocal about marriage laws that they see as discriminatory, and laws in several states have been passed to grant them equal rights. Families are also voicing concern about the costs of child care. However, given U.S. values of rugged individualism, discussions of a more universal approach are bound to be controversial.

Conclusion

This chapter summarizes the contributions that the socio-logical imagination can make to our understanding of families. The five themes that run throughout the book are reviewed, and specific examples from earlier chapters are provided: (1) families are both a public social institution and a private personal relationship; (2) social inequality has a powerful influence on family life; (3) an expanded strengths-based perspective can improve family resiliency; (4) family policies reflect historical, cultural, political, and social factors; and (5) understanding families in the United States requires a comparative perspective. A family is far more than a personal relationship among related individuals; family is also a powerful social institution

inextricably linked with other social institutions. Despite important universal features that are found in families throughout the world, they also reflect historical, politi-cal, and cultural contexts, including power and social in-equality. My goal has been to help you better understand family issues such as mate selection, marriage rituals, gendered expectations, division of household labor, fertil-ity patterns, parent–child relationships, aging and the care of the elderly, family conflict and violence, and divorce and repartnering within these contexts. Only then can we reveal trends that illuminate both the past (where we've been) and the future (where we are going). I wish you good luck in your journey.

Resources on the Internet

Center for Law and Social Policy

www.clasp.org

> The Center for Law and Social Policy is a national nonprofit organization that seeks to improve the economic security of low-income families with children and secure access for low-income persons to the civil justice system. Their work is concentrated on family policy and access to civil legal as-sistance for low-income families. Family policy projects in-clude welfare reform, workforce development, child care, child support enforcement, child welfare, couples and mar-riage policy, and reproductive health and teen parents.

National Coalition for the Homeless

www.nationalhomeless.org

> The mission of the National Coalition for the Homeless is to end homelessness. Toward this end, the organization en-gages in public education, policy advocacy, and grassroots organizing. They focus their work in the following four ar-eas: housing justice, economic justice, health care justice, and civil rights.

UNAIDS

www.unaids.org

> The Joint United Nations Programme on HIV/AIDS (UNAIDS) is the main advocate for global action on the epi-demic. It leads, strengthens, and supports an expanded re-sponse aimed at preventing transmission of HIV, providing care and support, reducing the vulnerability of individuals and communities to HIV/AIDS, and alleviating the impact of the epidemic.

UNICEF

www.unicef.org

> UNICEF works in 158 countries to overcome the obsta-cles that poverty, violence, disease, and discrimination place in a child's path. UNICEF is mandated by the United Nations General Assembly to advocate for the pro-tection of children's rights, to help meet their basic needs, and to expand their opportunities to reach their full poten-tial. Their Web site contains valuable information about children worldwide.

Glossary

Absolute poverty: The lack of resources such as food, housing, and clothing that is life-threatening. (p. 134)

Achieved statuses: Statuses achieved on one's own. (p. 42)

Active listening: A form of communication in which the listener is extremely attentive, with good eye contact and body language, and encourages the person to continue talking. (p. 245)

Activities of daily living (ADL): A common set of measures that gerontologists use to track elders' degree of impairment, such as bathing, dressing, eating, getting into and out of bed, walking indoors, and using the toilet. (p. 372)

Affirmative action: A set of social policies designed to increase opportunities for minority groups and one of the most misunderstood strategies of our time. (p. 179)

Agents of socialization: The people, social institutions, and organizations that teach boys and girls their gendered expectations. (p. 98)

Alimony: Post-divorce support for a former spouse. (p. 427)

Androgyny: Having both masculine and feminine traits in near equal proportion. (p. 95)

Antimiscegenation laws: The banning of marriage between Whites and other races. (p. 229)

Ascribed statuses: Statuses that a person is born with, such as his or her sex, racial and ethnic background, and social class. (pp. 42 and 120)

Assisted reproductive technology (ART): All fertility treatments in which both egg and sperm are handled. (p. 270)

Authoritarian parenting style: Strict, punitive, and not very warm. (p. 297)

Authoritative parenting style: Demand and maintain high levels of control over their children, but also warm and receptive to their children. (p. 297)

Baby bust: Period from the early 1960s through the 1970s when U.S. fertility rates dropped significantly. (p. 264)

Baby-boom generation: Persons born after World War II through the early to mid-1960s. (p. 352)

Bilateral: Descent can be traced through both male and female sides of the family. (p. 54)

Birth centers: Freestanding facilities, usually with close access to, but not affiliated with a hospital; childbirth is approached as a normal, healthy process. (p. 277)

Bisexual: An attraction to both males and females. One who engages in both heterosexual and homosexual relationships. (p. 197)

Bourgeoisie: According to Karl Marx, the capitalist class that owns the means of production. (p. 124)

Bundling: A dating practice in colonial America in which a young man and woman may continue their date by spending the night in a bed together, separated by a wooden board. (p. 75)

Caste system: A system of social stratification that is based on ascribed characteristics one is born with, such as race, ethnicity, or family lineage. (p. 123)

Caucasian: A theoretical racial category comprised of those individuals with relatively light skin. (p. 155)

Centenarians: Persons who are age 100 and older. (p. 355)

Child abuse: An attack on a child that results in an injury and violates social norms. (p. 397)

Child/family allowance: A cash grant from the government for each child. (p. 63)

China's one-child policy: Most families in China are allowed by law to have only one child. (p. 261)

Civil unions: Public recognition of a relationship that is more restrictive than marriage and offers fewer rights and privileges. (p. 214)

Clitoridectomy: A form of genital cutting or mutilation in which the clitoris is cut out of the body. (p. 106)

Closed adoption: All identifying information is sealed and unavailable to all parties. (p. 273)

Cohabitation: Unmarried partners living together. (p. 207)

Common couple violence (CCV): Violence that arises out of a specific argument in which at least one partner lashes out physically. (p. 386)

Communication: An interactive process, using symbols like words and gestures, that includes both sending and receiving messages. (p. 243)

Community factors: Community resources that help develop resilient youth and foster resiliency among adults. (p. 32)

Compadres: Godparents in the Mexican American community who serve as co-parents to children. (p. 79)

Companionate family: A family built upon mutual affection, sexual attraction, compatibility, and personal happiness. (p. 82)

Comparative perspective: Looking at other societies around the world or looking at a culture historically to see how others organize their social life and respond to its challenges. (p. 9)

Concrete operational thought: Piaget's third stage of cognitive development; occurs between the ages of 7 and 11 or 12 when children begin to see the causal connections in their surroundings and can manipulate categories, classification systems, and hierarchies in groups. (p. 292)

Conflict: Members of the group disagree over two or more options to make a decision, solve a problem, or achieve a goal. (p. 250)

Conflict Tactics Scale (CTS): A violence scale based on people's responses about how they deal with disagreements in relationships. (p. 385)

Conflict theory: This theoretical perspective emphasizes issues surrounding social inequality, power, conflict, and social change. (p. 16)

Covenant marriage: A type of marriage that restricts access to divorce, requires premarital counseling, and includes other rules and regulations. (p. 242)

Cross-sectional data: Data collected at only one point in time rather than following trends over time. (p. 132)

Cross-sectional divorce rate: A divorce rate at only one point in time. (p. 413)

Crude divorce rate: The number of divorces that occur out of 1,000 people in the population. (p. 413)

Cult of domesticity: The glorification of women's domestic role. (p. 81)

Cyberstalking: Repeated unwanted attention in the form of e-mail, faxes, bulletin boards, blogs, chat rooms, or other types of media. (p. 387)

Date rape drugs: Used to immobilize a person to facilitate an assault. (p. 392)

Day care centers: Child care provided in nonresidential facilities. (p. 338)

Dementia: Severe memory loss, the most common form of which is Alzheimer's Disease. (p. 372)

Demographic transition: The process in which a society moves from a situation of high fertility rates and low life expectancy, to one of low fertility rates and high life expectancy. (p. 352)

Developmental theory: Families and family members go through distinct stages, each with its own set of tasks, roles, and responsibilities. (p. 7)

Direct financial costs: Out-of-pocket expenses for things such as food, clothing, housing, and education. (p. 267)

Discrimination: Negative behavior towards a racial or ethnic group. (p. 157)

Displaced homemaker: A full-time homemaker who is divorced by her husband. (p. 427)

Doing gender: Housework is so ingrained as women's work that it functions as an area in which gender is symbolically created and reproduced. (p. 331)

Domestic partners: Heterosexual or homosexual unmarried couples in long-term committed relationships. (p. 17)

Double standard: Men have been allowed far more permissiveness in sexual behavior than have women. (p. 203)

Dowry: The financial gift given to a woman's prospective in-laws by her parents. (p. 188)

Early childhood education and care (ECEC): An international term for day care, preschool, and other programs to ensure that all children begin elementary school with basic skills and ready to learn. (p. 341)

Earned Income Tax Credit (EITC): A federal tax credit for low-income working families. (p. 146)

Egalitarian: The expectation that power and authority are equally vested in men and women. (p. 54)

Ego: According to Sigmund Freud, the rational component of personality that attempts to balance the need for immediate gratification with the demands of society. (p. 292)

Elder abuse: Abuse, neglect, and exploitation of the elderly, often by family members and others close to them. (p. 400)

Elderly: Persons who are age 65 and over. (p. 347)

Empirical approach: Answers questions through a systematic collection and analysis of data. (p. 10)

Endogamy: Norms that encourage marriage between people of the same social category. (pp. 43 and 191)

Ethnic cleansing (or genocide): The systematic killing, torturing, or removal of persons with the intention of eliminating a specific racial or ethnic group. (p. 162)

Ethnic group: People who share specific cultural features. (p. 156)

Ethnicity: Representing culture, including language, place of origin, dress, food, religion, and other values. (p. 155)

Ethnocentrism: The assumption that society's way of doing things is always the best way. (p. 10)

Ethnographies: Detailed accounts and interpretations of some aspect of culture. (p. 70)

Exogamy: Norms that encourage marriage between people of different social categories. (pp. 43 and 191)

Extended families: Families that include other family members such as grandparents, uncles, aunts, or cousins, in addition to parents and their children. (p. 168)

Families: Relationships by blood, marriage, or affection, in which members may cooperate economically, may care for any children, and may consider their identity to be intimately connected to the larger group. (p. 5)

Familism: Family relationships are paramount and take precedence over individual needs or wants. (p. 79)

Family allowances: Cash benefits given to families by the government. (p. 310)

Family child care providers: Child care provided in a private home other than the child's home. (p. 338)

Family Medical Leave Act (FMLA): Governmental act that requires employers with over 50 employees working for them (within a 75-mile radius) to provide 12 weeks of unpaid leave to eligible employees (both men and women) to care for themselves or their immediate families with specified medical conditions. (p. 283)

Family of orientation: The family into which you were born. (p. 27)

Family of procreation: The family you make through partnership, marriage, and/or with children. (p. 27)

Family protective factors (FPF): Characteristics or dynamics that shape the family's ability to endure in the face of risk factors. (p. 30)

Family reconstitution: Attempts are made to compile all available information about significant family events and everyday life within a particular family to piece together social history. (p. 70)

Family recovery factors (FRF): Characteristics or dynamics that assist families in "bouncing back" from a crisis situation. (p. 30)

Family systems theory: Family members and the roles they play make up a system, and this system is larger than the sum of its individual members. (p. 17)

Fee-for-service health care system: When you are sick or injured, you must pay for medical care. (p. 325)

Feminist theory: Gender is the central concept for explaining family structure and dynamics. (p. 16)

Fertility rates: Average number of children born to a woman during her lifetime (total); number of children born per 1,000 women aged 15–49 (refined); or number of children born per 1,000 population (crude). (p. 257)

Fictive kin: Nonrelatives whose bonds are strong and intimate. (p. 5)

Food insecurity: Defined by the USDA as just having enough nourishing food available on a regular basis. (p. 143)

Formal care: Care for the elderly that is provided by social service agencies on a paid or volunteer basis. (p. 373)

Formal operational thought: Piaget's fourth stage of cognitive development; children develop capacities for abstract thought and can conceptualize more complex issues or rules that can be used for problem solving. (p. 292)

Gay: Usually refers to homosexual men. (p. 198)

Gemeinschaft: A type of society that emphasizes the intimacy found in primary relationships. (p. 56)

Gender: The culturally and socially constructed differences between males and females found in the meanings, beliefs, and practices associated with femininity and masculinity. (p. 93)

Gender socialization: Teaching the cultural norms associated with being male or female. (p. 98)

Gender-based violence: Any act of gender violence that results in or is likely to result in physical, sexual, or psychological harm and suffering to women, including threats of such acts, coercion, or arbitrary deprivations of liberty, whether occurring in public or private life. (p. 381)

Genocide (or ethnic cleansing): The systematic killing, torturing, or removal of persons with the intention of eliminating a specific racial or ethnic group. (p. 162)

Gerontology: An interdisciplinary science of aging that draws upon biology, medicine, and the social sciences, including sociology, psychology, and family studies. (p. 356)

Gesellschaft: A type of society that is based on largely impersonal secondary relationships. (p. 56)

Global gag rule: Denies U.S. assistance to all organizations that provide abortion services, counsel their patients on their options for abortions, refer their patients for abortion services, or educate their communities about or lobby their governments for safe abortion with their own, non-U.S. funding. (p. 116)

Heterogeneous relationships: Those in which the partners are significantly different from one another on some important characteristic. (p. 191)

Heterosexual: An attraction and preference for sexual relationships with members of the other sex (e.g., a man and a woman). (p. 198)

Hidden curriculum: Informal school curriculum that teaches gender socialization. (p. 100)

Home observation of the measurement of the environment (HOME): A widely used tool that measures maternal warmth and learning experiences provided to the child; is associated with a variety of child outcomes. (p. 121)

Homogeneous relationships: Those in which partners are similar to one another. (p. 191)

Homosexual: Refers to a preference for same-sex sexual and romantic relationships. (p. 198)

Household labor: Generally refers to the unpaid work done to maintain family members and/or a home. (p. 327)

Human agency: The ability of human beings to create viable lives even when they are constrained or limited by social forces. (p. 27)

Id: According to Sigmund Freud, the part of the personality that includes biological drives and needs for immediate gratification. (p. 292)

Immigration: The introduction of people into a new habitat or population, such as Europeans or Mexicans moving to the United States. (p. 80)

Incest taboo: A rule forbidding sexual activity (and marriage) among close family members. (p. 41)

Individualism: The belief that anyone can pull themselves up by their bootstraps and achieve success. Poverty is the result of personal failings. (p. 137)

Individual-level protective factors: Individual personality traits and dispositions that enhance a person's ability to be successful and resilient. (p. 30)

Industrialization: Transforming an economy from a system based on small family-based agriculture to one of large industrial capital. (p. 79)

Infant mortality rate: The number of deaths within the first year of life per 1,000 births in the population. (p. 62)

Infertility: The inability to conceive a child. (p. 270)

Infibulation: The most extreme form of genital cutting or mutilation in which the clitoris and vaginal lips are cut or scraped away, and the outer portion of the vagina is stitched together. (p. 106)

Informal care: Care for the elderly that is unpaid, usually done by someone close to the elder. (p. 373)

Instrumental activities of daily living (IADL): Includes activities such as preparing meals, shopping, managing money, using the telephone, doing housework, and taking medications. (p. 372)

Interethnic marriage: Partners coming from different countries or having different cultural, religious, or ethnic backgrounds. (p. 230)

Intergenerational transmission of violence: Learning norms and behaviors, including violence, by observing others. (p. 402)

Intersexed: A person whose anatomical categories are not easily identifiable. (p. 93)

Intimate partner violence: Violence between those who are physically, emotionally, or sexually intimate, such as spouses, partners, or even those who are dating. (p. 384)

Intimate terrorism (IT): Violence that is motivated by a desire to control the other partner. (p. 386)

Joint legal custody: Both the custodial and noncustodial parents retain their legal rights with respect to their children. (p. 424)

Joint physical custody: Children spend substantial or nearly equal portions of time in the homes of each parent. (p. 425)

Kinkeeper: The person who has the primary responsibility for maintaining family relationships. (p. 367)

Labor market segmentation: Men and women often work in different types of jobs with distinct working conditions and pay. (p. 112)

Legal custody: Refers to who has the legal authority to make important decisions concerning a child. (p. 424)

Lesbian: Homosexual woman. (p. 198)

Life course perspective: Examines how individuals' lives change as they pass through the events in their lives, recognizing that many changes are socially produced and shared among a cohort of people. (p. 17)

Life expectancy: How long a person can expect to live, usually calculated from birth. (p. 352)

Listening: The process of giving thoughtful attention to what we hear. (p. 244)

Living wage: Ordinances that require employers to pay wages that are above federal or state minimum wage levels, usually ranging from 100 to 130 percent of the poverty line. (p. 323)

Long-term care: Assistance for chronic physical or mental conditions that are long-term, and in the case of the elderly, may never go away. (p. 373)

Looking-glass self: According to Cooley, we come to see ourselves as others perceive and respond to us. (p. 293)

Love: An enduring bond based on affection and emotion, including a sense of obligation toward one another. (p. 185)

Machismo: Mexican Americans have a long tradition of masculine authority, which is exercised in the home, in the work place, in sexual prowess, and in the raising of children. (p. 79)

Macro theories: A general framework that attempts to understand societal patterns, such as structural functionalism, conflict theory, and feminist theory. (p. 15)

Marital decline perspective: Suggests the institution of marriage is being threatened by hedonistic pursuits of personal happiness at the expense of a long-term commitment. (p. 233)

Marital resilience perspective: Suggests ending an unhappy marriage is not necessarily cause for alarm because it gives adults another chance at happiness and provides the opportunity to end a child's dysfunctional home life. (p. 233)

Marriage: A legally and socially recognized relationship that includes sexual, economic, and social rights and responsibilities between partners. (p. 221)

Marriage movement: A group of family scholars, therapists, and civic leaders who have come together in hopes of influencing public policy to promote and strengthen traditional marriage. (p. 241)

Marriage premium: People who are married are happier, healthier, and financially better off than those who are not married, including cohabitors. (p. 235)

Matriarchy: A form of social organization in which the norm is that the power and authority in society would be vested in women. (p. 54)

Matrilineal: A descent pattern characterized as having the lineage more closely aligned with women's families rather than men's families. (p. 54)

Matrilocal: The married couple is expected to live with the family of the wife. (p. 55)

Means-tested: People have to be below a certain income to qualify for a social program. (p. 22)

Medicaid: The federal-state health care program for the eligible poor. (pp. 326 and 376)

Medical neglect: Delaying or forgoing a dependent's needed medical, dental, or prescription care. (p. 398)

Medicalization of childbirth: Childbirth viewed as a medical event in need of drugs and technological intervention. (p. 276)

Medicare: A federal/state health care program designed to serve poor persons, regardless of age, and also covering long-term care for the poor. (p. 375)

Meritocracy: A system in which economic and social rewards, such as income, occupation, or prestige, are obtained on individual merit rather than inheritance. (p. 123)

Micro theories: A general framework that focuses on personal dynamics and face-to-face interaction, including social exchange, symbolic interaction, developmental, and family systems theories. (p. 15)

Midwives: Attendants trained to help women give birth and who believe that childbirth is a normal part of life. (p. 276)

Minority group: A category of people who have less power than the dominant group and who are subject to unequal treatment. (p. 156)

Modernization: A process of social and cultural transformation from traditional societies to modern societies that influences all dimensions of social life. (p. 55)

Monogamy: The law or custom that does not permit individuals to have multiple spouses. (p. 45)

Mongoloid: A theoretical racial category representing those individuals who have characteristics such as yellow or brown skin and folds on their eyelids. (p. 155)

Mortality rates: Measures of the number of deaths for a given population. (p. 257)

Mutual violent control (MVC): A violent pattern of behavior in which both partners are controlling and violent. (p. 386)

Nannies/babysitters: Child care provided in the home by a nonrelative. (p. 338)

Neglect: The failure to provide for basic needs for someone who is dependent on you. (p. 397)

Negroid: A theoretical racial category comprised of people with darker skin and other characteristics such as coarse curly hair. (p. 155)

Neolocal: The married couple is expected to establish its own residence and live there independently. (p. 55)

No-fault divorce: A divorce in which the couple can say they have irreconcilable differences and do not wish to assign blame. (p. 420)

Nonregulated couples: Couples who have many negative communication exchanges, such as criticism or defensiveness. (p. 250)

Nonstandard work schedules: Jobs that are part-time, subcontracted, temporary in nature, occur at night, or offer irregular work schedules. (pp. 87 and 323)

Nonverbal communication: Communicating without words, and which includes gestures, expressions, and body language. (p. 243)

Normless norm: Something common enough to be considered normative, but with vague and confusing expectations, obligations, and rules. (p. 436)

Occasional labor: Household tasks that are more time-flexible and more discretionary, such as household repairs, yard care, or paying bills. (p. 327)

Old Age, Survivor, and Disability Insurance (OASDI): A cash pension program for seniors that is known as "Social Security." (p. 358)

Oldest-old cohort: Usually defined as those persons aged 80 and over. (p. 347)

Open adoption: Involves direct contact between the biological and adoptive parents. (p. 273)

Opportunity costs: Lost opportunities for income by working only part-time or not at all because of children. (p. 267)

Patriarchy: A form of social organization in which the norm is that men have a natural right to be in positions of authority over women. (p. 51)

Patricians: During the Roman era, these were landowners, at the top of the stratification system. (p. 72)

Patrilineal: A descent pattern in which lineage is traced exclusively (or at least primarily) through the man's family line. (p. 54)

Patrilocal: A married couple will live with the husband's family. (p. 55)

Permissive parenting style: Having few controls or demands on the child. (p. 297)

Physical abuse: Inflicting physical injury and harm on another person. (p. 398)

Physical custody: The child's legal residence. (p. 424)

Polyandry: The marriage pattern that involves one woman and several husbands. (p. 49)

Polygamy: A law or custom that allows for more than one spouse at a time (gender unspecified). (p. 48)

Polygyny: The marriage pattern in which husbands can have more than one wife. (p. 48)

Poverty threshold: The official U.S. government method of calculating how many people are poor and assessing how that number changes from year to year. (p. 132)

Power: The ability to achieve goals, wishes, and desires even in the face of opposition from others. (p. 124)

Prejudice: Negative attitudes about members of a selected racial or ethnic group. (p. 157)

Preoperational thought: Piaget's second stage of cognitive development; occurs through ages 6 or 7 as the child learns language, symbolic play and symbolic drawing, but does not grasp abstract concepts. (p. 292)

Prestige: The esteem or respect a person is afforded. (p. 124)

Primogeniture: Families during the Middle Ages leaving their wealth or property to the eldest son. (p. 73)

Private adoption: Arranged directly between adoptive parents and the biological birth mother, usually through the assistance of an attorney. (p. 273)

Progressive taxation: Those who earn more pay a higher percentage of their income in taxes. (p. 24)

Proletariat: According to Karl Marx, individuals who must sell their labor to the owners in order to earn enough money to survive. (p. 124)

Pronatalism: A cultural value that encourages child-bearing. (p. 256)

Psychological maltreatment: Verbal, mental, or emotional maltreatment that destroys a person's self-esteem. (p. 398)

Public adoptions: Occur through licensed public agencies. (p. 273)

Qualitative methods: The focus is on narrative description with words rather than numbers to analyze patterns and their underlying meanings. (p. 11)

Quantitative methods: The focus is on collecting data that can be measured numerically. (p. 11)

Race: A category composed of people who share real or alleged physical traits that members of a society deem as socially significant. (p. 155)

Racial (or ethnic) socialization: Teaching minority children about prejudice and discrimination; the coping skills necessary to develop and maintain a strong and healthy self-image. (p. 296)

Racism: The belief that one racial group is superior or inferior to others. (p. 156)

Refined divorce rate: The number of divorces that occur out of every 1,000 married women. (p. 413)

Regulating couples: Couples who generally use communication to promote closeness and intimacy and tend to use constructive rather than negative comments even during arguments. (p. 250)

Relative poverty: The lack of basic resources relative to others in society. (p. 133)

Relative resources perspective: The greater the relative amount or value of resources contributed by a partner, the greater is his or her power within the relationship; can then be translated into bargaining to avoid tasks such as housework that offer no pay and minimal social prestige. (p. 331)

Resiliency: The capacity to rebound from adversity, misfortune, trauma, or other transitional crises and become strengthened and more resourceful. (p. 30)

Role overload: Feeling overwhelmed by many different commitments and not having enough time to meet each commitment effectively. (p. 333)

Role taking: According to Mead, it is the process of mentally assuming the role of another person to understand the world from his or her point of view and to anticipate his or her response to us. (p. 293)

Roles: Behaviors associated with social positions in society. (p. 42)

Routine household labor: Nondiscretionary, routine tasks that are less able to be postponed, such as cooking, washing dishes, or cleaning. (p. 327)

Sandwich generation: Adult children, usually daughters, who are caring for both their parents and their own children. (p. 374)

Sapir-Whorf hypothesis: The idea that language shapes our culture, and at the same time, our culture shapes our language. (p. 248)

Selection effect: People who engage in some behavior (e.g., cohabitation) are different from those who do not. (p. 211)

Selective programs: Persons need to meet some eligibility requirement to qualify for benefits. (p. 22)

Self-care: School-age children who are unsupervised and taking care of themselves. (p. 339)

Self-disclosure: Telling a person something private about yourself that he or she would not otherwise know. (p. 245)

Semi-open adoption: Biological and adoptive families exchange personal information through a social worker or attorney, but have no direct contact. (p. 273)

Sensorimotor intelligence: Piaget's first stage of cognitive development; infants and toddlers understand the world primarily through touch, sucking, listening, and looking. (p. 292)

Separate spheres: A dominant ideology within the nineteenth-century middle and upper-middle classes that suggested that women should stay home to rear the children and take care of the home while husbands should be the sole breadwinners. (p. 81)

Sex: Biological differences and one's role in reproduction. (p. 93)

Sexual abuse: Inappropriate sexual behavior with someone (e.g., a child) for sexual gratification. (p. 398)

Sexual orientation: The sex that one is attracted to. (p. 197)

Sexual scripts: A social construction that provides the norms or rules regarding sexual behavior. (p. 201)

Social capital: The connections, social support, information, and other benefits that are produced through relationships among people. (pp. 156 and 237)

Social class: A system of social stratification that is based both on ascribed statuses and individual achievement. (p. 123)

Social exchange theory: Individuals are rational and their behavior reflects an evaluation of costs and benefits. (p. 16)

Social institution: A major sphere of social life, with a set of beliefs and rules that is organized to meet basic human needs, such as the family, political, or educational systems. (p. 26)

Social mobility: Movement in the stratification system based on individual effort or achievement. (p. 123)

Social stratification: The hierarchical ranking of people within society on the basis of specific coveted resources, such as income and wealth. (p. 123)

Social structure: The organized pattern of social relationships and social institutions that together form the basis of society. (p. 8)

Socialization: The lifelong process through which we acquire the cultural values and skills needed to function as human beings and participate in society. (p. 292)

Socially constructed: Values or norms that are invented or "constructed" in a culture; people learn these and follow the conventional rules. (p. 93)

Socioeconomic status (SES): A vague combination of education, occupation, and income. (p. 125)

Sociological imagination: Reveals general patterns in what otherwise might be thought of as simple random events. (p. 9)

Spillover: The negative (or sometimes positive) moods, experiences, and demands involved in one sphere that carry over or "spill over" into the other sphere. (p. 333)

Spurious: An apparent relationship between two variables that is really caused by a third factor. (p. 211)

Stalking: Obsessive contact or tracking of another person, causing fear. (p. 386)

Statuses: Social positions in a group or society. (p. 42)

Stepfamilies: One or both of the adult partners has at least one child, either residing with them or elsewhere. (p. 435)

Structural functionalist theory: This theoretical perspective suggests that all social institutions, including the family, exist to fill a need in society. (p. 16)

Subsistence economies: Economies in which families use all of what they have, with virtually no surplus of food or other resources. (p. 72)

Superego: According to Freud, it is our conscience, which draws upon our cultural values and norms to help us understand why we cannot have everything we want. (p. 292)

Surrogacy: One woman gives birth for another person (or couple) who then adopts or takes legal custody of the child. (p. 271)

Symbolic interaction: Humans interact not just with words, but also with symbols and meanings. (p. 293)

Symbolic interaction theory: This theoretical perspective focuses on the social interaction between family members and other groups, concerned with the meanings and interpretations that people have. (p. 17)

Temporary Assistance for Needy Families (TANF): The principal cash welfare program, previously known as Aid to Families with Dependent Children (AFDC). (p. 24)

Theory: A general framework, explanation, or tool to understand and describe the real world. (p. 15)

Time availability perspective: Suggests that the division of labor is largely determined by (1) the need for household labor, such as the number of children in the home; and (2) each partner's availability to perform household tasks, such as the number of hours spent in paid work. (p. 331)

Total fertility rate: The average number of births to women. (p. 85)

Trafficking: The illegal recruitment, transport, or sale of human beings into all forms of forced labor and servitude. (p. 382)

Transgender: Persons who feel comfortable expressing gendered traits associated with the other sex. (p. 96)

Transnational family: A family living between two nations, often in search of work that pays a survivable wage. (p. 289)

Transsexuals: Persons who undergo sex reassignment surgery and hormone treatments, either male to female, or female to male. (p. 97)

Triple jeopardy: People who face multiple disadvantages in society (e.g., old, female, and minority). (p. 358)

Universal programs: Social and economic programs that are available to all persons or families. (p. 23)

Verbal communication: The spoken exchange of thoughts, feelings, or other messages. (p. 243)

Violence among intimates: Physical, economic, sexual, or psychological abuse covering a broad range of relationships. (p. 381)

Violent resistance (VR): Violence associated with self-defense. (p. 386)

Wealth: The value of all of a person's or a family's economic assets, including income, real estate, stocks, bonds, and other items of economic worth, minus debt. (p. 124)

Work–family conflict: Inter-role conflict in which the role pressures from the work and family domains are mutually incompatible in some respect. (p. 332)

World systems theory: A perspective that focuses on the economic and political interdependence and exploitation among nations. (p. 57)

Zero tolerance: A growing movement that emphasizes tougher laws; more stringent enforcement of those laws; training programs for those who work with victims and offenders, such as physicians or police officers; and a well-coordinated effort to offer victims the protection and services they need. (p. 407)

Bibliography

All highlighted entries are new to the second edition.

Aardvarc.org. 2008. "Domestic Violence in Gay and Lesbian Relationships." Retrieved 25 March 2010 (www.aardvarc. org/dv/gay.shtml).

AARP. 2005. *Sexuality At Midlife and Beyond: 2004 Update of Attitudes and Behaviors.* Washington, DC.

—. 2007. "Grandparents Devoted To Grandchildren, But Their Support Constrained By Concerns About Their Financial Futures, Questions About Grandkids' Money Values." Retrieved 26 April 2010 (www.aarpfinancial.com/content/ AboutUs/news_template.cfm?).

Abaid, Thoraya Ahmed. 2003. "Women and the United Nations: State of the World Population 2002—People, Poverty, and Possibilities." *Women's International Network* 29(1, Winter): 7.

Abazov, Rafis. 2007. *Culture and Customs of the Central Asian Republics.* Santa Barbara, CA: Greenwood Press.

ABC/Nepal. 2003. "Red Light Traffic: The Trade in Nepali Girls." Retrieved 19 March 2003 (www.hsph.harvard.edu/ Organizations/healthnet/SAsia/repro2/RED_LIGHT_ TRAFFIC).

Abd el Salam, Seham. 1998. "Female Sexuality and the Discourse of Power: The Case of Egypt," Cairo: AUC/MA Thesis.

Abramovitz, Mimi. 1996. *Regulating the Lives of Women: Social Welfare Policy from Colonial Times to the Present, Rev. ed.* Boston, MA: South End Press.

Acevedo, Bianca P. and Arthur Aron. 2009. "Does a Long-Term Relationship Kill Romantic Love?" *Review of General Psychology* 13(1): 59–65.

Acs, Gregory and Pamela Loprest. 2004. *Leaving Welfare: Employment and Well-Being of Families That Left Welfare in the Post-Entitlement Era.* Kalamazoo, MI: W.E. Upjohn Institute for Employment Research.

Acuna, Rodolfo. 2011. *Occupied America: A History of Chicanos, 7th ed.* Boston: Pearson.

Adams, Bert N. 2004. "Families and Family Study in International Perspective." *Journal of Marriage and Family* 66 (December): 1076–88.

Adams, Bert N. and Jan Trost, eds. 2004. *Handbook of World Families.* Thousand Oaks, CA: Sage.

Adams, Michele and Scott Coltrane. 2003. "Boys and Men in Families." Pp. 188–98 in *Families and Society: Classic and Contemporary Readings*, edited by S. Coltrane. Belmont, CA: Wadsworth/Thomson Learning.

Administration on Aging. 2009. "Fact for Features from the Census Bureau." Retrieved 23 April 2010 (www.aoa.gov/ AoARoot/Aging_Statistics/Census_Population/Population/ 2001/factsforfeatures2001.aspx).

—. 2010a. "A Profile of Older Americans: 2009." Retrieved 23 April 2010 (www.aoa.gov/AoARoot/Aging_Statistics/ Profile/2009/4.aspx).

—. 2010b. "Projected Future Growth of the Older Population." Retrieved 29 June 2010. U.S. Department of Health & Human Services (www.aoa.gov/AoARoot/Aging_ Statistics/future_growth/future_growth.aspx).

Advocates for Youth. 2009. "The Facts: Adolescent Childbearing and Educational and Economic Attainment, 2009." Retrieved 1 December 2009 (www.advocates-foryouth.org/PUBLICATIONS/factsheet/fsadlchd. htm).

Afifi, Tamara D., Walid A. Afifi, and Amanda Coho. 2009. "Adolescents' Physiological Reactions to Their Parents' Negative Disclosures About the Other Parent in Divorced and Nondivorced Families." *Journal of Divorce & Remarriage* 50(8, November): 517–40.

Agnes, Flavia. 2001. *Law and Gender Inequality: The Politics of Women's Rights in India.* New York: Oxford University Press.

Ahmed, Sania Sultan and Sally Bould. 2004. "'One Able Daughter is Worth 10 Illiterate Sons': Reframing the Patriarchal Family." *Journal of Marriage and Family* 66(5, December): 1332–41.

Ahrons, Constance R. 2005. *We're Still Family: What Grown Children Say About Their Parents' Divorce.* New York: HarperCollins.

—. 2007. "Introduction to the Special Issue on Divorce and Its Aftermath." *Family Process* 46(1): 3–6.

Ali, Lorraine. 2008. "True or False: Having Kids Makes You Happy." Retrieved 6 March 2010. Newsweek.com (www. newsweek.com/id/143792).

Allan, Graham, Graham Crow, and Sheila Hawker. 2010. *Stepfamilies: A Sociological Review.* New York: Palgrave Macmillan.

Allen, Brenda J. 2004. *Differences Matter: Communicating Social Identity.* Long Grove, IL: Waveland Press.

Allen, Katherine. 1997. "Lesbian and Gay Families." In *Contemporary Parenting*, edited by T. Arendell. Thousand Oaks, CA: Sage Publications.

Altman, Irwin and Joseph Ginat. 1996. *Polygamous Families in Contemporary Society.* Cambridge, England: Cambridge University Press.

Alzheimer's Association. 2010. *Alzheimer's Disease: Facts and Figures.* Chicago.

Amato, Paul R. 1994. "The Impact of Divorce on Men and Women in India and the United States." *Journal of Comparative Family Studies* 25: 207–21.

—. 2004. "Tension Between Institutional and Individual Views of Marriage." *Journal of Marriage and Family* 66 (November): 959–65.

—. 2005. "The Impact of Family Formation Change on the Cognitive, Social, and Emotional Well-Being of the Next Generation." *Marriage and Child Wellbeing: The Future of Children* 15: 75–96.

—. 2007. "Divorce and the Wellbeing of Adults and Children." *National Council on Family Relations Report* 52(4, December): F3–F4, F18.

Amato, Paul R. and Alan Booth. 1997. *A Generation at Risk: Growing up in an Era of Family Upheaval*. Cambridge, MA: Harvard University Press.

Amato, Paul R. and Bryndl Hohmann-Marriott. 2007. "A Comparison of High and Low-Distress Marriages That End in Divorce." *Journal of Marriage and Family* 69: 621–38.

Amato, Paul R. and Juliana M. Sobolewski. 2001. "The Effects of Divorce and Marital Discord on Adult Children's Psychological Well-Being." *American Sociological Review* 66: 900–21.

American Psychological Association. 2009. "Answers to Your Questions for a Better Understanding of Sexual Orientation and Homosexuality." Retrieved 10 April 2010. APA Public Interest (www.apa.org/topics/sorientation.html).

—. 2010. "Elder Abuse and Neglect: In Search of Solutions." Retrieved 30 June 2010. Washington, D.C. (www.apa.org/pi/aging/resources/guides/elder-abuse.aspx).

American Psychological Association Online. 2009. "Answers to Your Questions About Transgender Individuals and Gender Identity." Retrieved 14 August 2009 (www.apa.org/topics/transgender.html).

American Society for Reproductive Medicine. 2009. "Frequently Asked Questions About Infertility." Retrieved 15 December 2009 (www.asrm.org/Patients/faqs.html).

American Society of Plastic Surgeons. 2009a. "2000/2007/2008 National Plastic Surgery Statistics: Cosmetic and Reconstructive Procedure Trends." Retrieved 20 January 2010 (www.plasticsurgery.org/Media/stats/2008-cosmetic-reconstructive-plastic-surgery-minimally-invasive-statistics.pdf).

—. 2009b. "2008 Quick Facts: Percentage Change 2008 vs. 2007." Retrieved 20 January 2010 (www.plasticsurgery.org/Media/stats/2008-quick-facts-cosmetic-surgery-minimally-invasive-statistics.pdf).

—. 2009c. "National Clearinghouse of Plastic Surgery Statistics." Retrieved 19 January 2010 (www.plasticsurgery.org/Media/Statistics.html).

Amnesty International. 2004. "What is Female Genital Mutilation? Section One." In *Female Genital Mutilation—A Human Rights Information Pack*. Retrieved 5 November 2003 (www.amnesty.org/ailib/intcam/femgen/fgm1.htm).

Amnesty International USA. 2010. "Women's Human Rights." Retrieved 15 June 2010 (www.amnestyusa.org/violence-against-women/page.do?id=1011012).

Andersen, Margaret L. and Howard F. Taylor. 2006. *Sociology: Understanding a Diverse Society, 4th ed.* Belmont, CA: Wadsworth Publishing Co.

Anderson, David and Mykol Hamilton. 2006. "Sex Stereotyping and Under-Representation of Female Characters in 200 Popular Children's Picture Books: A 21st Century Update." *Sex Roles* 55(11/12): 757–65.

Anderson, Gillian and Karen Robson. 2006. "Male Adolescents' Contributions to Household Labor as Predictors of Later-Life Participation in Housework." *The Journal of Men's Studies* 14(1, Winter): 1060–65.

Andersson, Neil, Ari Ho-Foster, Steve Mitchell, Esca Scheepers, and Sue Goldstein. 2007. "Risk Factors for Domestic Physical Violence: National Cross-Sectional Household Surveys in Eight Southern African Countries." *BMC Women's Health* 7(11): doi: 10.1186/1472-6874-7-11.

Ängarne-Lindberg, Teresia, Marie Wadsby, and Carina Berterö. 2009. "Young Adults with Childhood Experience of Divorce: Disappointment and Contentment." *Journal of Divorce & Remarriage* 50(3, April): 172–84.

Angel, Jacqueline, Maren A. Jimenez, and Ronald J. Angel. 2007. "The Economic Consequences of Widowhood for Older Minority Women." *The Gerontologist* 47: 224–34.

The Annie E. Casey Foundation. 2009. "Kids Count Indicator Brief: Reducing the Teen Birth Rate." Retrieved 16 February 2010 (www.aecf.org/KnowledgeCenter/Publications.aspx?pubguid={E0E22911-04C9-4C11-A0EB-79FD615297CA}).

APA Task Force on Gender Identity and Gender Variance. 2008. *Report of the Task Force on Gender Identity and Gender Variance*. Washington, DC: American Psychological Association.

Aquilino, William S. 2006. "The Noncustodial Father-Child Relationship from Adolescence Into Young Adulthood." *Journal of Marriage and Family* 68(4): 929–46.

Aranda, Elizabeth. 2003. "Global Case Work and Gendered Constraints: The Case of Puerto Rican Transmigrants." *Gender and Society* 17: 609–26.

Archibold, Randal C. 2010. "Arizona Enacts Stringent Law on Immigration." Retrieved 30 June 2010. New York Times (www.nytimes.com/2010/04/24/us/politics/24immig.html?pagewanted=print).

Arditti, Joyce A. 2006. "Editor's Note." *Family Relations* 55(3): 263–65.

Arendell, Terry. 2000. "Conceiving and Investigating Motherhood: The Decade's Scholarship." *Journal of Marriage and the Family* 62(4, November): 1193–207.

Aries, Philippe. 1962. *Centuries of Childhood: A Social History of Family Life*. New York: Vintage Books.

Arliss, Laurie P. 1991. *Gender Communication*. Englewood Cliffs, NJ: Prentice Hall.

Artis, Julie E. 2007. "Maternal Cohabitation and Child Well-Being Among Kindergarten Children." *Journal of Marriage and the Family* 69: 222–36.

Asante, Molefi K., Yoshitaka Miike, and Jing Yin. 2007. *The Global Intercultural Reader*. New York: Routledge.

Ashford, Lori and Donna Clifton. 2005. *Women of Our World*. Population Reference Bureau: Available online (www.prb. org/pdf05/womenofourworld2005.pdf).

Assisted Senior Living. 2009. "The Cost of Assisted Living." Retrieved 26 April 2010 (www.assistedseniorliving.net/ ba/facilty-costs.cfm/).

Aubrey, Jennifer Stevens and Kristin Harrison. 2004. "The Gender-Role Content of Children's Favorite Television Programs and Its Link to Their Gender-Related Perceptions." *Media Psychology* 6(2): 111–46.

Aubry, Tim, Bruce Tefft, and Nancy Kingsbury. 2006. "Behavioral and Psychological Consequences of Unemployment in Blue-Collar Couples." *Journal of Community Psychology* 18(2, February): 99–109.

August, Diane and Timothy Shanahan. 2006. *Developing Literacy in Second-Language Learners*. Mahwah, NJ: Lawrence Erlbaum.

Aumann, Kerstin and Ellen Galinsky. 2009. *The State of Health in the American Workforce: Does Having an Effective Workplace Matter?* 2008 National Study of the Changing Workforce. New York: Families and Work Institute.

Avellar, Sarah and Pamela J. Smock. 2005. "The Economic Consequences of the Dissolution of Cohabiting Unions." *Journal of Marriage and Family* 67(May): 315–27.

AVERT.ORG. 2008. "Stories." Retrieved 11 September 2008 (www.avert.org/stories/htm).

—. 2010a. "AIDS Orphans." Retrieved 30 June 2010 (www. avert.org/aidsorphans.htm).

—. 2010b. "How Many Gay People Are There?" Retrieved 14 February 2010 (www.avert.org/gay-people.htm).

Axinn, June and Mark J. Stern. 2008. *Social Welfare: A History of the American Response to Need, 7th ed.* Boston: Allyn & Bacon.

Baca Zinn, Maxine, D. Stanley Eitzen, and Barbara Wells. 2011. *Diversity in Families, 9th ed.* Boston, MA: Pearson.

Bachman, Jerald G., Lloyd D. Johnston, and Patrick M. O'Malley. 1993. *Monitoring the Future: Questionnaire Responses from the Nation's High School Seniors, 1991*. Ann Arbor, MI: Institute for Social Research.

—. 2001. *Monitoring the Future: Questionnaire Responses from the Nation's High School Seniors, 2000*. Ann Arbor, MI: Institute for Social Research.

—. 2009. *Monitoring the Future: Questionnaire Responses from the Nation's High School Seniors, 2008*. Ann Arbor, MI: Institute for Social Research.

Bade, Robin and Michael Parkin. 2011. *Foundations of Economics & MyEconLab Student Access Code Card Package, 5th ed.* Upper Saddle River, NJ: Prentice Hall.

Bailey, Eric J. 2008. *Black America, Body Beautiful*. Westport, CT: Praeger Publishers.

Bailey, J. Michael and Richard C. Pillard. 1991. "A Genetic Study of Male Sexual Orientation." *Archives of General Psychiatry* 48: 1089–96.

Bailey, J. Michael, Richard C. Pillard, Michael C. Neale, and Yvonne Agyei. 1993. "Heritable Factors Influence Sexual Orientation in Women." *Archives of General Psychiatry* 50: 217–23.

Baker, Kaysee and Arthur A. Raney. 2007. "Equally Super? Gender-Role Stereotyping of Superheroes in Children's Animated Programs."*Mass Communication & Society* 10(1): 25–41.

Bales, Kevin and Ron Soodalter. 2009. *The Slave Next Door: Human Trafficking and Slavery in America Today*. Berkeley, CA: University of California Press.

Bandura, Alfred. 1977. *Social Learning Theory*. New York: General Learning Press.

Barna, George. 2008 March. "New Marriage and Divorce Statistics." Retrieved 26 April 2010. The Barna Group, Ltd. (www.barna.org).

Barnett, Melissa A., Laura V. Scaramella, Tricia K. Neppl, Lenna Ontai, and Rand D. Conger. 2010. "Intergenerational Relationship Quality, Gender, and Grandparent Involvement." *Family Relations* 59(1, February): 28–44.

Baron, Naomi S. 2008. *Always On: Language in an Online and Mobile World*. New York: Oxford University Press.

Barr, Simone C. and Helen A. Neville. 2008. "Examination of the Link Between Parental Racial Socialization Messages and Racial Ideology Among Black College Students." *Journal of Black Psychology* 34(2): 131–55.

Bass, Brenda L., Adam B. Butler, Joseph G. Grzywacz, and Kirsten D. Linney. 2009. "Do Job Demands Undermine Parenting? A Daily Analysis of Spillover and Crossover Effects." *Family Relations* 58(2, April): 201–15.

Baum, Katrina, Shannan Catalano, Michael Rand, and Kristina Rose. 2009. *Stalking Victimization in the United States*. Bureau of Justice Statistics No. NCJ 224527. Washington, DC: U.S. Department of Justice.

Baumrind, Diana. 1966. "Effects of Authoritative Parental Control on Child Behavior." *Child Development* 37(4): 887–907.

—. 1968. "Authoritarian Versus Authoritative Parental Control." *Adolescence* 3: 255–72.

Baumrind, Diana and A. E. Black. 1967. "Socialization Practices Associated with Dimensions of Competence in Preschool Boys and Girls." *Child Development* 38(2): 291–327.

Beah, Ismael. 2007. *A Long Way Gone*. New York: Sarah Crichton Books.

Bearak, Barry. 2010a. "Gay Couple in Malawi Get Maximum Sentence of 14 Years in Prison." Retrieved 23 May 2010 (www.nytimes.com/2010/05/21/world/africa/21malawi. html).

—. 2010b. "Malawi: Prosecutors State Case Against Gay Couple." Retrieved 21 February 2010. New York Times (www.nytimes.com/2010/02/19/world/africa/19briefs-Malawi.html).

Becker, Gary. 1981. *A Treatise on the Family*. Cambridge, MA: Belknap.

Becker, Jill B., Karen J. Berkley, Nori Geary, Elizabeth Hampson, James P. Herman, and Elizabeth A. Young, eds. 2008. *Sex Differences in the Brain: From Genes to Behavior*. New York: Oxford University Press.

Bee, Helen L. and Denise A. Boyd. 2007. *The Developing Child, 11th ed.* Boston: Pearson.

Beebe, Steven A., Susan J. Beebe, and Mark V. Redmond. 2011. *Interpersonal Communication Relating to Others, 6th ed.* Boston, MA: Allyn & Bacon.

Beebe, Steven A. and John T. Masterson. 2006. *Communicating in Small Groups: Principles and Practices, 8th ed.* Boston: Allyn & Bacon.

Beecher, Catherine E. 1869. *The American Woman's Home*. Reprint Services Corporation.

Belsky, Jay, Martha Weinraub, Margaret Owen, and Jean F. Kelly. 2001. "Quantity of Child Care and Problem Behavior." Presented at the Biennial Meeting of the Society for Research on Child Development, Minneapolis, MN.

Bem, Sandra L. 1975. "The Measurement of Psychological Androgyny." *Journal of Personality and Social Psychology* 31: 634–43.

—. 1981. *Bem Sex-Role Inventory*. Mountain View, CA: Consulting Psychologists Press, Inc.

Bentley, Keisha C., Valerie N. Adams, and Howard C. Stevenson. 2009. "Racial Socialization: Roots, Processes, & Outcomes." In *Handbook of African American Psychology*, edited by Helen A. Neville, Brendesha M. Tynes and Shawn O. Utsey. Thousand Oaks, CA: Sage Publications.

Berardo, Felix M. 1998. "Family Privacy: Issues and Concepts." *Journal of Family Issues* 19(1): 4–19.

Berardo, Felix M. and Donna H. Berardo. 2000. Widowhood. Pp. 3255–61 in *Encyclopedia of Sociology*. 2nd ed. Edited by Edgar F. Borgatta and Rhonda J. V. Montgomery. New York: Macmillon.

Bergemann, Annette and Regina T. Riphahn. 2009. *Female Labor Supply and Parental Leave Benefits: The Causal Effect of Paying Higher Transfers for a Shorter Period of Time*. Bonn, Germany: Institute for the Study of Labor.

Berger, Peter. 1977. *Facing Up to Modernity: Excursions in Society, Politics, and Religion*. New York: Basic Books.

Bergmann, Barbara R. 1996. *Saving Our Children From Poverty: What the United States Can Learn From France*. New York: Russell Sage Foundation.

Berlin, Lisa J., Jean M. Ispa, Mark A. Fine, Patrick S. Malone, Jeanne Brooks-Gunn, Christy Brady-Smith, Catherine Ayoub, and Yu Bai. 2009. "Correlates and Consequences of Spanking and Verbal Punishment for Low-Income White, African American, and Mexican American Toddlers." *Child Development* 80(5): 1403–20.

Bernard, Jessie. 1972. *The Future of Marriage*. New York: World Pub.

—. 1973. *The Future of Marriage*. New York: Bantam.

Berne, Linda and Barbara Huberman. 1999. *European Approaches to Adolescent Sexual Behavior and Responsibility*. Washington, DC: Advocates for Youth.

Berns, Roberta M. 2001. *Child, Family, School, Community: Socialization and Support, 5th ed.* New York: Thomson Learning.

Bernstein, Basil. 1960. "Language and Social Class: A Research Note." *British Journal of Sociology (London)* 11(3): 271–76.

—. 1973. *Class, Codes, and Control, Vol. 1*. London: Routledge & Kegan Paul.

Bernstein, Robert and Tom Edwards. 2008. "An Older and More Diverse Nation by Midcentury" (Press Release). Retrieved 22 August 2008. U.S. Census Bureau (www.census.gov/Press-Release/www.releases/archives/population/012496.html).

Bertrand, Marianne and Sendhil Mullainathan. 2004. "Are Emily and Greg More Employable Than Lakisha and Jamal? A Field Experiment on Labor Market Discrimination." *American Economic Review* 94 (September): 991–1013.

Beverly, Brenda, Teena M. McGuinness, and Debra J. Blanton. 2008. "Communication Challenges for Children Adopted from the Former Soviet Union." *Language, Speech, and Hearing Services in Schools* 39: 1–11.

Bhat, Aparna, Aatreyee Sen, and Uma Pradhan, eds. 2005. *Child Marriages and the Law in India*. New Delhi: Human Rights Law Network.

Bianchi, Suzanne M. and Melissa A. Milkie. 2010. "Work and Family Research in the First Decade of the 21st Century." *Journal of Marriage and Family* 72(3 June).

Bianchi, Suzanne M., John Robinson, and Melissa A. Milkie. 2006. *Changing Rhythms of American Family Life*. New York: Russell Sage Foundation.

Biblarz, Timothy J. and Evren Savci. 2010. "Lesbian, Gay, Bisexual, and Transgender Families." *Journal of Marriage and Family* 72(3, June).

Biblarz, Timothy J. and Judith Stacey. 2010. "How Does the Gender of Parents Matter?" *Journal of Marriage and Family* 72(1, February): 3–22.

Biddulph, Steve and Paul Stanish. 2008. *Raising Boys: Why Boys Are Different—and How to Help Them Become Happy and Well-Balanced Men*. Berkeley, CA: Celestial Arts.

Bidwell, Lee D. Millar and Brenda J. Vander Mey. 2000. *Sociology of the Family: Investigating Family Issues*. Needham Heights: Allyn & Bacon.

Bierman, Alex, Elana Fazio, and Melissa Milkie. 2006. "A Multifaceted Approach to the Mental Health Advantage of Married Women: Assessing How Explanations Vary by Outcome Measures and Unmarried Group." *Journal of Family Issues* 27: 554–82.

Billingsley, Andrew. 1968. *Black Families in White America*. Englewood Cliffs, NJ: Prentice-Hall, Inc.

Bing, Nicole M., W. M. Nelson, III, and Kelly L. Wesolowski. 2009. "Comparing the Effects of Amount of Conflict on Children's Adjustment Following Parental Divorce." *Journal of Divorce & Remarriage* 50(3, April): 159–71.

Bittman, M., P. England, L. Sayer, N. Folbre, and G. Matheson. 2003. "When Does Gender Trump Money? Bargaining and Time in Household Work." *American Journal of Sociology* 109: 186–214.

Blackless, Melanie, Anthony Charuvastra, Amanda Derryck, Anne Fausto-Sterling, Karl Lauzanne, and Ellen Lee. 2000. "How Sexually Dimorphic Are We? Review and Synthesis." *American Journal of Human Biology* 12: 151–166.

Blair, Sampson Lee and Michael P. Johnson. 2000. "Parents and Family Structure: An Examination of Ethnic-Based Variations in Children's Household Labor." Paper presented at the 2000 American Sociological Association meetings in Washington, D.C.

Blassingame, John W. 1972. *The Slave Community: Plantation Life on the Antebellum South*. New York: Oxford University Press.

Blee, Kathleen and Ann Tickamyer. 1995. "Racial Differences in Men's Attitudes About Women's Gender Roles." *Journal of Marriage and the Family* (February): 1–10.

Blekesaune, Morten. 2008. "Partnership Transitions and Mental Distress: Investigating Temporal Order." *Journal of Marriage and Family* 70(4, October): 879–90.

Block, Jennifer. 2008. *Pushed: The Painful Truth About Childbirth and Modern Maternity Care*. Cambridge, MA: Da Capo Press.

Blood, Robert O. and Donald M. Wolfe. 1960. *Husbands and Wives: The Dynamics of Married Living*. New York: Free Press.

Blumenthal, David. 2006. "Employer-Sponsored Health Insurance in the United States—Origins and Implications." *New England Journal of Medicine* 355(1, 6 July): 82–88.

Blyth, Dale A. and Eugene C. Roelkepartian. 1993. *Healthy Communities, Healthy Youth*. Minneapolis: Search Institute.

Bogenschneider, Karen. 2006. *Family Policy Matters: How Policymaking Affects Families and What Professionals Can Do*. New York: Lawrence Erlbaum.

Bokker, Lon Paul, Roy C. Farley, and William Bailey. 2006. "The Relationship Between Custodial Status and Emotional Well-Being Among Recently Divorced Fathers." *Journal of Divorce and Remarriage* 44(3/4): 83–98 (DOI: 10.1300/J087vol44n03_06).

Bonach, Kathryn, Esther Sales, and Gary Koeske. 2005. "Gender Differences in Perceptions of Coparenting Quality Among Expartners." *Journal of Divorce and Remarriage* 43(1/2): 1–28.

Bonvillain, Nancy. 2007. *Women and Men: Cultural Constructs of Gender, 4th ed.* Boston: Pearson.

—. 2010. *Cultural Anthropology, 2nd ed.* Boston: Pearson.

Booth, Alan, Ann C. Crouter, and Mari Clements. 2001. *Couples in Conflict*. Mahwah, NJ: Lawrence Erlbaum Associates.

Booth, Alan, Mindy E. Scott, and Valarie King. 2010. "Father Residence and Adolescent Problem Behavior: Are Youth Always Better Off in Two-Parent Families?" *Journal of Family Issues* 31(5): 585–605.

Boss, Pauline G., William J. Doherty, Ralph LaRossa, Walter R. Schumm, and Suzanne K. Steinmetz, eds. 2008. *Sourcebook of Family Theories and Methods: A Contextual Approach*. New York: Springer Publishing Co.

Bouchard, Genevieve, Jolene Boudreau, and Renee Herbert. 2006. "Transition to Parenthood and Conjugal Life: Comparisons Between Planned and Unplanned Pregnancies." *Journal of Family Issues* 27: 1512–31.

Boucher, Debora, Catherine Bennett, Barbara McFarlin, and Rixa Freeze. 2009. "Staying Home to Give Birth: Why Women in the United States Choose Home Birth." *Journal of Midwifery & Women's Health* 54(2, March–April): 119–26.

Bradley, Nicki. 2006. "Authoritative Parenting: An Overview." In *Parenting Advice*. Retrieved 29 November 2009. Families.com (Parenting.families.com/blog/authoritative-parenting-an-overview).

Bramlett, Matthew D. and William D. Mosher. 2002. "Cohabitation, Remarriage, Divorce, and Remarriage in the United States." National Center for Health Statistics. *Vital Health Statistics* 23(22).

Branden, Nathaniel. 2008. *The Psychology of Romantic Love: Romantic Love in an Anti-Romantic Age*. New York: Tarcher Press.

Brandolini, Andrea and Timothy M. Smeeding. 2006. "Patterns of Economic Inequality in Western Democracies: Some Facts on Levels and Trends." *PS: Political Science and Politics* 39(1): 21–26.

Bratter, Jenifer L. and Rosalind B. King. 2008. ""But Will It Last?": Marital Instability Among Interracial and Same-Race Couples." *Family Relations* 57(2): 160–71.

Braund, Kathryn E. Holland. 1990. "Guardians of Tradition and Handmaidens to Change: Women's Role in Creek Economic and Social Life During the Eighteenth Century." *American Indian Quarterly* 14(Summer): 239–58.

Braver, Sanford L., Ira M. Ellman, and William V. Fabricius. 2003. "Relocation of Children After Divorce and Children's Best Interests: New Evidence and Legal Considerations." *Journal of Family Psychology* 17.

Bremner, Jason, Carl Haub, Marlene Lee, Mark Mather, and Eric Zuehlke. 2009. *World Population Highlights: Key Findings from PRB's 2009 World Population Data Sheet*. Population Bulletin No. 64 (3). Washington, DC: Population Reference Bureau.

Breslau, Naomi, Nigel S. Paneth, and Victoria C. Lucia. 2004. "The Lingering Academic Deficits of Low Birth Weight Children." *Pediatrics* 114(4, October): 1035–40.

Brettell, Caroline B. and Carolyn F. Sargent. 2009. *Gender in Cross-Cultural Perspective, 5th ed.* Boston: Pearson.

Briere, John and Carol E. Jordan. 2009. "Childhood Maltreatment, Intervening Variables, and Adult Psychological Difficulties in Women." *Trauma, Violence, & Abuse* 10(4): 375–88.

Briggs, Sarah. 2006. "Confessions of a 'Helicopter Parent'." Retrieved 5 January 2010. Experience.com (www. experience. com/alumnus/channel?channel_id=parents_survival_guide&page_id=helicopter_parents).

Broderick, Carlfred and James Smith. 1979. "The General Systems Approach to the Family." Pp. Vol. 2, pp. 112–29 in *Contemporary Theories About the Family*, edited by Wesley R. Burr, Reuben Hill, F. Ivan Nye and Ira Reiss. Englewood Cliffs, NJ: Prentice Hall.

Bronte-Tinkew, Jacinta, Jennifer Carrano, Allison Horowitz, and Akemi Kinukawa. 2008. "Involvement Among Resident Fathers and Links to Infant Cognitive Outcomes." *Journal of Family Issues* 29: 1211–44.

Brooks-Gunn, Jeanne and Elisabeth Hirschhorn Donahue. 2008. "Introducing the Issue." In *Children and Electronic Media*. 3–10. Retrieved 22 November 2009. The Future of Children/Princeton-Brookings (www.futureofchildren.org).

Brooks-Gunn, Jeanne and Greg J. Duncan. 1997. "The Effects of Poverty on Children." *The Future of Children (Children and Poverty)* 7(2, Summer/Fall): 55–71.

Brooks-Gunn, Jeanne and Lisa B. Markman. 2005. "The Contribution of Parenting to Ethnic and Racial Gaps in School Readiness." *The Future of Children* 15(1): 138–67.

Brown, Heidi. 2009. "U.S. Maternity Leave Benefits Are Still Dismal." Retrieved 16 December 2009. Forbes.com (www. forbes.com/2009/05/04/maternity-leave-laws-forbes-woman-wellbeing-pregnancy.html?feed=rss_news).

Brown, Mackenzie. 2008. "The State of Our Unions." Retrieved 22 February 2010. Redbook (www.redbookmag.com/love-sex/advice/types-of-marriages?click=main_sr).

Brown, Tony N., Emily E. Tanner-Smith, Chase L. Lesane-Brown, and Michael E. Ezell. 2007. "Child, Parent, and Situational Correlates of Familial Ethnic/Race Socialization." *Journal of Marriage and Family* 69(1, February): 14–25.

Browning, Edgar K. 2008. *Stealing from Each Other: How the Welfare State Robs Americans of Money and Spirit*. New York: Praeger Publishers.

Bryant-Davis, Thema, Haewoon Chung, and Shaquila Tillman. 2009. "From the Margins to the Center." *Trauma, Violence, & Abuse* 10(4): 330–57.

Bucx, Freek, Frits van Wel, Trudie Knun, and Louk Hagendoorn. 2008. "Intergenerational Contact and the Life Course Status of Young Adult Children." *Journal of Marriage and Family* 70(1): 144–56.

Budrys, Grace. 2005. *Our Unsystematic Health Care System: Second Edition*. New York: Rowman & Littlefield.

Buehler, Cheryl and Jean M. Gerard. 2002. "Marital Conflict, Ineffective Parenting, and Children's and Adolescent's Maladjustment." *Journal of Marriage and Family* 64: 78–92.

Buhle, Mari Jo, Teresa Murphy, and Jane Gerhard. 2009. *Women and the Making of America, Combined Volume*. Boston: Pearson.

Bunting, Madeleine. 2005. *Willing Slaves: How the Overwork Culture is Ruling Our Lives*. New York: HarperCollins.

Bureau of Labor Statistics. 2008. "Married Parents' Use of Time Summary." Retrieved 31 December 2009 (www.bls. gov/news.release/atus2.nr0.htm).

—. 2009a. *Employment and Earnings, 2009 Annual Averages and the Monthly Labor Review*. Washington, DC: U.S. Department of Labor.

—. 2009b. "Characteristics of Minimum Wage Workers: 2008." *U.S. Department of Labor*, 11 March. Retrieved 1 July 2009 (www.bls.gov/cps/minwage2008.pdf).

—. 2009c. "Employment Characteristics of Families Summary" (Economic News Release). Retrieved 17 June 2009 (data. bls.gov/cgi-bin/print.pl/news.release/famee.nr0.htm).

—. 2009d. "The Employment Situation: June 2009" (Press Release). Retrieved 3 August 2009. U.S. Department of Labor (www.bls.gov/news.release/pdf/empsit.pdf).

—. 2009e. "Women in the Labor Force: A Datebook (2009 Edition)" (Report 1018). *U.S. Department of Labor*, September. Retrieved 17 May 2010 (www.bls.gov/cps/wlf-databook2009.htm).

—. 2010a. Economic News Release: Regional and State Employment and Unemployment Summary (http://data. bls.gov/cgi-bin/print.pl/news.release/laus.nr0.htm).

—. 2010b. "Employment Situation News Release." Retrieved 5 March 2010. Washington, D.C./U.S. Department of Labor (www.bls.gov/news.release/empsit.htm).

—. 2010c. "Labor Force Statistics from the Current Population Survey." Retrieved 16 June 2010. U.S. Department of Labor (data.bls.gov/cgi-bin/surveymost).

—. 2010d. "More Than 75 Percent of American Households Own Computers" (V. 1, No.4). In *Office of Publications & Special Studies, Focus on Prices and Spending*. Retrieved 26 May 2010. U.S. Department of Labor (www.bls.gov/opub/focus/volume1_number4/cex_1_4.htm).

Bures, Regina M., Tanya Koropeckyj-Cox, and Michael Loree. 2009. "Childlessness, Parenthood, and Depressive Symptoms Among Middle-Aged and Older Adults." *Journal of Family Issues* 30(5): 670–87.

Burgess, Ernest W. and Harvey J. Locke. 1945. *The Family: From Institution to Companionship*. New York: American Book Company.

Burke, Tod, Michael L. Jordan, and Stephen S. Owen. 2002. "A Cross-National Comparison of Gay and Lesbian Domestic Violence." *Journal of Contemporary Criminal Justice* 18(3, August): 231–57.

Burton, C. Emory. 1992. *The Poverty Debate*. Westport, CT: Praeger.

Busby, Dean M., Thomas B. Holman, and Eric Walker. 2008. "Pathways to Relationship Aggression Between Adult Partners." *Family Relations* 57 (January): 72–83.

Buss, David M., Todd K. Shackelford, Lee A. Kirkpatrick, and Randy J. Larson. 2001. "A Half Century of Mate Preferences: The Cultural Evolution of Values." *Journal of Marriage & the Family* 63: 491–503.

Butterfield, Alice K., Cynthia J. Rocha, and William H. Butterfield. 2010. *The Dynamics of Family Policy.* Chicago, IL: Lyceum Books.

Cahill, Sean, Ken South, and Jane Spade. 2000. *Outing Age: Public Policy Issues Affecting Gay, Lesbian, Bisexual, and Transgender Elders.* The Policy Institute of the National Gay and Lesbian Task Force Foundation.

California Work and Family Coalition. 2010. "Basics of California's Paid Family Leave Program." Retrieved 24 May 2010 (www.paidfamilyleave.org/learn/basics.html).

Calvert, Sandra L. 2008. "Children as Consumers: Advertising and Marketing." In *Children and Electronic Media.* 205–34. Retrieved 22 November 2009. The Future of Children/Princeton-Brookings (www.futureofchildren.org).

Cambron, M. Janelle, Linda K. Acitelli, and Jeremy W. Pettit. 2009. "Explaining Gender Differences in Depression: An Interpersonal Contingent Self-Esteem Perspective." *Sex Roles* 61(11–12): 751–61.

Campbell, Jacquelyn C., Nancy Glass, Phyllis W. Sharps, Kathryn Laughon, and Tina Bloom. 2007. "Intimate Partner Homicide." *Trauma, Violence, & Abuse* 8(3): 246–69.

Campbell, Jacquelyn C., Linda Rose, Joan Kub, and Daphne Nedd. 1998. "Voices of Strength and Resistance: A Contextual and Longitudinal Analysis of Women's Responses to Battering." *Journal of Interpersonal Violence* 13: 743–62.

The Canadian Encyclopedia. 2010. "Family Allowance." Retrieved 26 June 2010 (www.thecanadianencyclopedia. com/index.cfm?PgNm=TCE&Params=A1ARTA0002718).

Cancian, Francesca M. 1987. *Love in America: Gender and Self-Development.* New York: Cambridge University Press.

—. 1989. "Love and the Rise of Capitalism." Pp. 12–25 in *Gender in Intimate Relations: A Microstructural Approach,* edited by Barbara J. Risman and Pepper Schwartz. Belmont, CA: Wadsworth Publishing Company.

Cantor, Marjorie H., Mark Brennan, and R. Andrew Shippy. 2004. *Caregiving Among Older Lesbian, Gay, Bisexual, and Transgender New Yorkers.* New York: National Gay and Lesbian Task Force Policy Institute.

Capizzano, Jeffrey and Gina Adams. 2004. "Children in Low-Income Families Are Less Likely to Be in Center-Based Child Care" (No. 16 in "Snapshots of America's Families III"). Retrieved 11 July 2005. Urban Institute (www.urban. org/urlprint.cfm?ID=8701).

Carlson, Marcia J. 2006. "Family Structure, Father Involvement, and Adolescent Behavioral Outcomes." *Journal of Marriage and Family* 68(1): 137–54.

Carr, Deborah. 2004. "The Desire to Date and Remarry Among Older Widows and Widowers." *Journal of Marriage and the Family* 66: 1051–68.

Carroll, Joseph. 2007. "Most Americans Approve of Interracial Marriages." Retrieved 21 February 2010. Gallup Poll (www.gallup.com/search/default.aspx?q=interracial+ marriage&s=p=1).

Carter, Wendy Y. 2006. "Attitudes Toward Pre-Marital Sex, Non-Marital Childbearing, Cohabitation, and Marriage Among Blacks and Whites" (NSFH Working Paper No. 61). Retrieved 8 July 2006. Center for Demography and Ecology, University of Wisconsin-Madison (www.ssc. wisc.edu/cdc/nsfhwp/nsfh61.pdf).

Cartwright, Claire. 2005. "You Want to Know How It Affected Me? Young Adults' Perceptions of the Impact of Parental Divorce." *Journal of Divorce and Remarriage* DOI: 10.1300/J087v44n03_08: 125-43.

Cartwright, Claire and Heather McDowell. 2008. "Young Women's Life Stories and Accounts of Parental Divorce." *Journal of Divorce & Remarriage* 49(1–2, June): 56–77.

Cassidy, Margaret and Gary R. Lee. 1989. "The Study of Polyandry: A Critique and Synthesis." *Journal of Comparative Family Studies* 20: 1–11.

Cassidy, Tina. 2007. *Birth: The Surprising History of How We Are Born.* New York: Grove Press.

CBS News/New York Times Poll. 2009. Retrieved 24 June 2009. PollingReport.com (www.pollingreport.com/prioriti. htm).

Center for Families, Work, and Well-Being. 2001. "Response to Extension of Parental Leaves." Retrieved 19 October 2001 (www.worklifecanada.ca/index.shtml).

Center for Substance Abuse Prevention. 2007. *Fetal Alcohol Spectrum Disorders Among Native Americans.* Washington, DC: U.S. Department of Health & Human Services.

Center for the Child Care Workforce. 2010. "Wage Data Fact Sheet: 2010." Retrieved 30 June 2010 (www.ccw.org/ storage/ccworkforce/documents/all%20data_web% 28final%29.pdf).

Center on Budget and Policy Priorities. 2006. "New Estate Tax 'Compromise' Even Costlier Than Previous One." Retrieved 27 June 2006 (www.cbpp.org/policy-points6- 23-06.htm).

—. 2008. "Policy Basics: Introduction to Public Housing." Retrieved 4 July 2010 (www.cbpp.org/cms/index.cfm? fa=view&id=2528).

Centers for Disease Control and Prevention. 2003. "HIV/STD Risks in Young Men Who Have Sex with Men Who Do Not Disclose Their Sexual Orientation—Six US Cities, 1994–2000." *Morbidity and Mortality Weekly Report* 52: 81–85.

—. 2007. "Sexual Violence: Fact Sheet." Retrieved 17 August 2007 (www.cdc.gov/ncipc/factsheets/svfacts.htm).

—. 2008a. "Intimate Partner Violence: Risk and Protective Factors." Retrieved 12 July 2009 (www.cdc.gov/ ViolencePrevention/intimatepartnerviolence/ riskprotectivefactors.html).

—. 2008b. "Youth Risk Behavior Surveillance—United States, 2007." *Morbidity and Mortality Weekly Report* 57(SS-4).

—. 2009a. "Basic Information: HIV." Retrieved 18 February 2010 (`www.cdc.gov/hiv/topics/basic/index.htm).

—. 2009b. "Assisted Reproductive Technology (ART) Report: National Summary." Retrieved 15 December 2009 (apps. nccd.cdc.gov/ART/NSR.aspx?SelectedYear=2007).

—. 2009c. "Assisted Reproductive Technology: Home." In *Division of Reproductive Health*. Retrieved 16 November 2009 (www.cdc.gov/ART/).

—. 2009d. "Breastfeeding: Frequently Asked Questions (FAQs)." Retrieved 22 November 2009 (www.cdc.gov/breastfeeding/faq/index.htm).

—. 2009e. "Cases of HIV Infection and AIDS in the United States and Dependent Areas, by Race/Ethnicity, 2003–2007." In *HiV/AIDS Surveillance Supplemental Report*. Retrieved 14 August 2009 (www.cdc.gov/hiv/topics/surveillance/resources/reports/2009supp_vol14no2/).

—. 2009f. "Deaths Among Persons with AIDS Through December 2006." Retrieved 21 February 2010 (www.cdc.gov/hiv/topics/surveillance/resources/reports/2009supp_ vol14no3/default.htm).

—. 2009g. "Intimate Partner Violence: Consequences." Retrieved 25 March 2010 (www.cdc.gov/Violence Prevention/intimatepartnerviolence/consequences.html).

—. 2009h. "Suicide: Facts at a Glance." Retrieved 1 July 2010 (www.cdc.gov/ViolencePrevention).

—. 2009i. "What is HPV?" Retrieved 1 June 2010 (www.cdc.gov/hpv/whatishpv.html).

—. 2010a. "Chlamydia—CDC Fact Sheet." Retrieved 1 June 2010 (www.cdc.gov/std/chlamydia/stdfact-chlamydia.htm).

—. 2010b. "Genital Herpes—CDC Fact Sheet." Retrieved 1 June 2010 (www.cdc.gov/std/Herpes/STDFact-Herpes.htm).

—. 2010c. "Questions and Answers on the Use of HIV Medications to Help Prevent the Transmission of HIV." Retrieved 2 June 2010 (www.cdc.gov/hiv/topics/treatment/resources/qa/art.htm).

Centers for Disease Control and Prevention, National Center for Environmental Health. 2006. "General Lead Information: Questions and Answers." Retrieved 19 March 2006 (www.cdc.gov/nceh/lead/faq/about.htm).

Centers for Disease Control and Prevention and The Merck Company Foundation. 2007. "The State of Aging and Health in America 2007." Retrieved 4 June 2010 (www.cdc.gov/aging/data/stateofaging.htm).

Central Intelligence Agency. 2010. "The World Factbook." Retrieved 23 April 2010 (www.cia.gov/library/publications/the-world-factbook/geos/us.html).

Centre des Liaisons Europeennes et Internationales de Securite Sociale. 2006. "The French Social Security System." Retrieved 15 January 2006 (www.cleiss.fr/docs/regimes/regime_france/an_3.html).

Chang, Winnie. 1993. "Unequal Terms." *Free China Review* 43(11): 26–31.

Cheah, Charissa S. L., Christy Y. Y. Leung, Madiha Tahseen, and David Schultz. 2009. "Authoritative Parenting Among Immigrant Chinese Mothers of Preschoolers." *Journal of Family Psychology* 23(3): 311–20.

Cherlin, Andrew J. and Frank F. Furstenberg. 1986. *The New American Grandparent: A Place in the Family, A Life Apart*. New York: Basic Books.

ChicagoLegalNet.com. 2003. ChicagoLegalNet.com. Available online (chicagolegalnet.com/FMLA.htm).

Child Labor Public Education Project. 2010. "Welcome to the Child Labor Public Education Project." Retrieved 1 June 2010 (www.continuetolearn.uiowa.edu/laborctr/child_labor/).

Child Welfare Information Gateway. 2006. "Long-Term Consequences of Child Abuse and Neglect." Retrieved 30 June 2010 (www.childwelfare.gov/pubs/factsheets/long_term_consequences.cfm).

—. 2008. "Stepparent Adoption: Factsheet for Families." Retrieved 13 April 2010 (www.childwelfare.gov/pubs/f_step.cfm).

Children's Defense Fund. 1994. *Wasting America's Future: The Children's Defense Fund Report on the Cost of Child Poverty*. Washington, DC: Children's Defense Fund.

—. 2002. *The State of Children in America's Union: A 2002 Action Guide to No Child Left Behind*. Washington, DC.

—. 2005. "Defining Poverty and Why It Matters for Children." (www.childrensdefensefund.org).

—. 2008. *The State of America's Children 2008*. Washington, DC.

__. 2010. "About Us: Nathan Cabrera." Retrieved 20 August 2010 (www.childrensdefense.org/newsroom/real-children-real-stories/beat-the-odds/nathan-cabrera.html).

Children's Rights Network of Japan. 2006. "Child Custody." Retrieved 6 June 2006 (www.crnjapan.com/custody/en/).

Childs, Erica Chito. 2005. *Navigating Interracial Borders: Black-White Couples and Their Social Worlds*. New Brunswick, NJ: Rutgers University Press.

Christie-Mizell, C. André, Erin M. Pryor, and Elizabeth Grossman, R. B. 2008. "Child Depressive Symptoms, Spanking, and Emotional Support: Differences Between African American and European American Youth." *Family Relations* 57 (July): 335–50.

Christopher, F. Scott and Susan Sprecher. 2000. "Sexuality in Marriage, Dating, and Other Relationships: A Decade Review." *Journal of Marriage and the Family* 62(4): 999–1017.

Chu, Judy. 2005. "Adolescent Boys' Friendships and Peer Group Culture." *New Directions for Child and Adolescent Development* 2005(107): 7–22.

Chun, Hyunbae and Injae Lee. 2001. "Why Do Married Men Earn More: Productivity or Marriage Selection?" *Economic Inquiry* 13: 307–19.

Claffey, Sharon T. and Kristin D. Mickelson. 2009. "Division of Household Labor and Distress: The Role of Perceived Fairness for Employed Mothers." *Sex Roles* 60(11–12, June): 819–31.

Clarkwest, Andrew. 2007. "Spousal Dissimilarity, Race, and Marital Dissolution." *Journal of Marriage and Family* 69(3, August): 639–53.

The Clearinghouse on International Developments in Child, Youth, & Family Policies. 2001. "New 12 Country Study Reveals Substantial Gaps in U.S. Early Childhood Education and Care Policies." Retrieved 28 July 2003. Columbia University (www.childpolicyintl.org/issuebrief/issuebrief1.htm).

—. 2005. "Section 1.2: Early Childhood Education and Care." Retrieved 17 January 2006. New York/Columbia University (www.childpolicyintl.org/ecec.html).

—. 2009. "France." Retrieved 8 August 2009 (www.childpolicyintl.org/countries/france.html).

Cline, Foster W. and Jim Fay. 1990. *Parenting with Love and Logic: Teaching Children Responsibility*. Colorado Springs, CO: Pinon Press.

Clopper, Cynthia G. and David B. Pisoni. 2004. "Some Acoustic Cues for the Perceptual Categorization of American English Regional Dialects." *Journal of Phonetics* 32: 111–40.

CNN.com. 2003. "Supreme Court Strikes Down Texas Sodomy Law." Retrieved 5 July 2006 (www.cnn.com/2003/LAW/06/26/scotus.sodomy/).

CNN. 2010. "CNN Pilot Demonstration." Retrieved 30 June 2010 (i2.cdn.turner.com/cnn/2010/images/05/13/expanded_results_methods_cnn.pdf).

Cobb, Nancy. 2007. *Adolescence*. New York: McGraw-Hill Higher Education.

Cockerham, William C. 1997. *This Aging Society*. Upper Saddle River, NJ: Prentice Hall.

Cockrell, Stacie, Cathy O'Neill, and Julia Stone. 2008. *Babyproofing Your Marriage: How to Laugh More and Argue Less As Your Family Grows*. New York: HarperCollins.

Cohen, Carl and James Sterba. 2003. *Affirmative Action and Racial Preference: A Debate*. Oxford, U.K.: Oxford University Press.

Cohen, Elizabeth. 2009. "Mom Won't Be Forced to Have C-Section." Retrieved 2 March 2010. CNNhealth.com (www.cnn.com/2009/HEALTH/10/15/hospitals.ban.vbacs.index.html.)

Cohen, Robin A. and Michael A. Martinez. 2009. "Early Release of Estimates from the National Health Interview Survey, 2008." Retrieved 19 June 2010. National Center for Health Statistics (www.cdc.gov/nchs/nhis.htm).

Cohn, D'Vera. 2009. "Public Has Split Verdict on Increased Level of Unmarried Household." Retrieved 25 October 2009. Pew Research Center (pewsocialtrends.org/pubs/729/out-of-wedlock-births-public-sees-costly-to-society).

Coker, Tumaini R., Marc N. Elliott, David E. Kanouse, Jo Anne Grunbaum, David C. Schwebel, Janice Gilliland, Susan R. Tortolero, Melissa F. Peskin, and Mark A. Schuster. 2009. "Perceived Racial/Ethnic Discrimination Among Fifth-Grade Students and Its Association with Mental Health." *American Journal of Public Health* 99(5, May): 878–84.

Cole, Kristen. 2003. "Census Study: Whites Less Likely Than Blacks to Live with Extended Family" (Press Release).

Brown University News Service. Retrieved 28 June 2006 (www.brown.edu/Administration/News_Bureau/2003-04/03-033.html).

Coleman-Jensen, Alisha and Mark Nord. 2010. "Food Insecurity in Households with Children Increased in 2008." *USDA, ERS, Amber Waves* 8(1, March): 8.

CollegeBoard. 2009. "2009–10 College Prices." Retrieved 14 December 2009 (www.collegeboard.com/student/pay/add- it-up/4494.html).

Coltrane, Scott. 1997. *Family Man: Fatherhood, Housework, and Gender Equity*. New York: Oxford University Press.

—. 2000. "Research on Household Labor: Modeling and Measuring the Social Embeddedness of Routine Family Work." *Journal of Marriage and the Family* 62 (November): 1208–33.

Colwell, Eric W. and Malinda Lindsey. 2005. "Preschool Children's Pretend and Physical Play and Sex of Peer Play Partner." *Sex Roles* 52: 497–509.

Commission on Family and Medical Leave. 1996. "A Workable Balance: Report to Congress on Family and Medical Leave Policies." Retrieved February 2000. Washington, DC (www.dol.gov/dol/esa/fmla.htm).

Commonwealth Fund Commission on a High Performance Health System. 2009. *The Path to a High Performance U.S. Health System: A 2020 Vision and the Policies to Pave the Way*. New York: Commonwealth Fund.

Conger, Rand D. and Katherine J. Conger. 2008. "Understanding the Processes Through Which Economic Hardship Influences Families and Children." Pp. 64–81 in *Handbook of Families and Poverty*, edited by D. Russell Crane and Timothy B. Heaton. Thousand Oaks, CA: Sage Publications.

Conley, Dalton. 2009. *Elsewhere, U.S.A.: How We Got from the Company Man, Family Dinners, and the Affluent Society to the Home Office, BlackBerry Moms, and Economic Anxiety*. New York: Pantheon.

Coontz, Stephanie. 1997. *The Way We Really Are: Coming to Terms with America's Changing Families*. New York: Basic Books.

—. 2000. *The Way We Never Were: American Families and the Nostalgia Trap*. New York: Basic Books.

—. 2004. "The World Historical Transformation of Marriage." *Journal of Marriage and Family* 66(4, November): 974–79.

—. 2005. *Marriage, a History: From Obedience to Intimacy, or How Love Conquered Marriage*. New York: Penguin.

—. 2006. "Three 'Rules' That Don't Apply." *Newsweek*, 5 June, p. 49.

—. 2007. "The Paradoxical Origins of Modern Divorce." *Family Process* 46 (March): 7–16.

Cooper, Carey E., Sara S. McLanahan, Sarah O. Meadows, and Jeanne Brooks-Gunn. 2009. "Family Structure Transitions and Maternal Parenting Stress." *Journal of Marriage and Family* 71(3, August): 558–74.

Corsaro, William A. 1997. *A Sociology of Childhood*. Thousand Oaks, CA: Pine Forge Press.

Cott, Nancy F. 2002. *Public Vows: A History of Marriage and the Nation*. Cambridge, MA: Harvard University Press.

Cott, Nancy. 1997. *The Bonds of Womanhood: "Woman's Sphere" in New England, 1780–1935, 2nd ed.* New Haven, CT: Yale University Press.

Covel, Simona. 2003. "The Heart Never Forgets." *American Demographics*, July 1.

Covenant Marriage Movement. 2008. "Home Page." Retrieved 22 February 2010 (www.covenantmarriage.com/index.php).

Covey, Herbert C. and Paul T. Lockman. 1996. "Narrative References of Older African American Living Under Slavery." *Social Science Journal* 3: 23–37.

Cowan, Philip A., Carolyn P. Cowan, Marsha K. Pruett, Kyle D. Pruett, and Jessie J. Wong. 2009. "Promoting Fathers' Engagement With Children: Preventive Interventons for Low-Income Families." *Journal of Marriage and Family* 71(3rd ed.): 663–79.

Craig, Lyn. 2006. "Does Father Care Mean Fathers Share? A Comparison of How Mothers and Fathers in Intact Families Spend Time with Children." *Gender and Society* 20: 259–81.

Crawford, James. 1999. *Bilingual Education: History, Politics, Theory, and Practice, 4th ed.* Los Angeles: Bilingual Education Services.

Creighton, Mathew J., Hyunjoon Park, and Graciela M. Teruel. 2009. "The Role of Migration and Single Motherhood in Upper Secondary Education in Mexico." *Journal of Marriage and Family* 71(5, December): 1325–39.

Crissey, Sarah R. 2005. "Race/Ethnic Differences in the Marital Expectations of Adolescents: The Role of Romantic Relationships." *Journal of Marriage and Family* 67(3): 697–709.

Crohn, Helen M. 2006. "Five Styles of Positive Stepmothering from the Perspective of Young Adult Stepdaughters." *Journal of Divorce and Remarriage* 46(1): 119–34.

Crompton, Rosemary. 2006. "Class and Family." *Sociological Review* 54(4): 658–77.

Cruz, J. Michael. 2003. " 'Why Doesn't He Just Leave?': Gay Male Domestic Violence and the Reasons Victims Stay." *The Journal of Men's Studies* 11(3): 309–23.

Cruz, Serena. 2004. "Statements of Multnomah County Commissioners About Gay Marriage. Personal Statement." *The Oregonian* [Portland, OR] 5 March, A: 17.

Cui, Ming, M. Brent Donnellan, and Rand D. Conger. 2007. "Reciprocal Influences Between Parents' Marital Problems and Adolescent Internalizing and Externalizing Behavior." *Developmental Psychology* 43(6): 1544–52.

Cummings, E. Mark, Alice C. Schermerhorn, Davies, Marcie C. Goeke-Morey, and Jennifer S. Cummings. 2006. "Interparental Discord and Child Adjustment: Prospective Investigations of Emotional Security as an Explanatory Mechanism." *Child Development* 77(1): 132–52.

Cummings, Jason L. and Pamela Braboy Jackson. 2008. "Race, Gender and SES Disparities in Self-Assessed Health 1974–2004." *Research on Aging* 2: 137–67.

Cunningham-Burley, Sarah. 2001. "The Experience of Grandfatherhood." Pp. 92–96 in *Later Life: Connections and Transitions*, edited by Alexis J. Walker, Margaret Manoogian-O'Dell, Lori A. McGraw and Diana L. G. White. Thousand Oaks, CA: Pine Forge Press.

D'Aluisio, Faith and Peter Menzel. 1996. *Women in the Material World*. Berkeley, CA: University of California Press.

Dahl, Gordon and Enrico Moretti. 2003. "The Demand for Sons: Evidence from Divorce, Fertility, and Shotgun Marriage," National Bureau of Economic Research, September. Unpublished draft.

Daly, Kerry J. 2001. "Deconstructing Family Time: From Ideology to Lived Experience." *Journal of Marriage and Family* 63: 283–94.

Data Lounge. 2004. "City of San Francisco Sues California." Retrieved 22 February 2004 (www.datalounge.com/datalounge/news/record.html?record=21216).

Datner, Elizabeth M, Douglas J. Wiebe, Colleen M. Brensinger, and Deborah B. Nelson. 2007. "Identifying Pregnant Women Experiencing Domestic Violence in an Urban Emergency Department." *Journal of Interpersonal Violence* 12(1): 124–35.

Davis, F. James 1991. *Who Is Black? One Nation's Definition*. University Park, PA: Pennsylvania State University Press.

Davis, Kelly D., W. Benjamin Goodman, Amy E. Pirretti, and David M. Almeida. 2008. "Nonstandard Work Schedules, Perceived Family Well-Being, and Daily Stressors." *Journal of Marriage and Family* 70 (November): 991–1003.

Davis, Shannon N. and Theodore N. Greenstein. 2004. "Cross-National Variations in the Division of Household Labor." *Journal of Marriage and Family* 66 (December): 1260–71.

Dawley, Katy. 2003. "Origins of Nurse-Midwifery in the United States and Its Expansion in the 1940s." *Journal of Midwifery & Women's Health* 48(2, March/April): 86–95.

Day, Phyllis J. 2009. *A New History of Social Welfare, 6th ed.* Boston: Allyn & Bacon.

de Jonge, A., B. van der Goes, A. Ravelli, M. Amelink-Verburg, B. Mol, J. Nijhuis, J. Bennebroek Gravenhorst, and S. Buitendijk. 2009. "Perinatal Mortality and Morbidity in a Nationwide Cohort of 529688 Low-Risk Planned Home and Hospital Births." *BCOG: An International Journal of Obstetrics & Gynaecology* 116(9): 1177–84.

De Lew, Nancy, George Greenbery, and Kraig Kinchen. 1992. "A Layman's Guide to the U.S. Health Care System." *Health Care Financing Review* 14: 151–65.

DeFrain, John. 2008. "Creating a Strong Family: Looking at Life From a Family Strengths Perspective." In *NebGuide G1883*. Retrieved 12 October 2009. University of Nebraska-Lincoln Extension, Institute of Agriculture and Natural Resources (elkhorn.unl.edu/epublic/live/g1883/build/g1883.pdf).

Degler, Carl N. 1980. *At Odds: Women and the Family in America from the Revolution to the Present*. New York: Oxford University Press.

—. 1983. *Out of Our Past.* Harper Perennial.

Del Castillo, Richard G. 1984. *La Familia: Chicano Families in the Urban Southwest, 1848 to the Present.* Notre Dame, IN: University of Notre Dame Press.

DeLamater, John J. and Morgan Sill. 2010. "Sexual Desire in Later Life." *Journal of Sex Research.* 42: 138–149.

DeLeire, Thomas and Ariel Kalil. 2005. "How Do Cohabiting Couples with Children Spend Their Money?" *Journal of Marriage and Family* 67 (May): 286–95.

Delsol, Catherine, Gayla Margolin, and Richard S. John. 2003. "A Typology of Maritally Violent Men and Correlates of Violence in a Community Sample." *Journal of Marriage and Family* 65(3, August): 635–51.

DeMaris, Alfred, Michael L. Benson, Greer L. Fox, Terrence Hill, and Judy Van Wyk. 2003. "Distal and Proximal Factors in Domestic Violence: A Test of an Integrated Model." *Journal of Marriage and Family* 65: 652–67.

Demetriou, Danielle. 2010. "'Fathering School' Opens for Japan's Time-Pressed Salarymen Parents." Retrieved 23 May 2010 (www.telegraph.co.uk/news/worldnews/asia/japan/7101692).

Demo, David H. and Martha J. Cox. 2000. "Families with Young Children: A Review of Research in the 1990s." *Journal of Marriage and the Family* 62 (November): 876–95.

Demos, John. 1970. *A Little Commonwealth: Family Life in Plymouth Colony.* New York: Oxford University Press.

—. 1986. "The Rise and Fall of Adolescence." In *Past, Present, and Personal.* New York: Oxford University Press.

DeNavas-Walt, Carmen, Bernadette D. Proctor, and Jessica C. Smith. 2010. *Income, Poverty, and Health Insurance Coverage in the United States: 2009.* Technical Report No. P60-238(RV). Washington, DC: U.S. Census Bureau.

Dennison, Renee Peltz and Susan Silverberg Koerner. 2008. "A Look at Hopes and Worries About Marriage: The Views of Adolescents Following a Parental Divorce." *Journal of Divorce and Remarriage* 48(3/4): 91–107.

Derne, Steve. 2003. "Arnold Schwarzenegger, Ally McBeal, and Arranged Marriages: Globalization's Effect on Ordinary People in India." *Contexts* 2(1): 12–18. Reprinted. Pp. 146–153 in *Globalization: The Transformation of Social Worlds,* edited by D. S. Eitzen and M. Baca Zinn. Belmont, CA: Wadsworth Publishing Co., 2006.

DeVito, Joseph A. 2011. *Essentials of Human Communication, 7th ed.* Boston: Allyn & Bacon.

DeWolfe, Chris and Tom Anderson, 2009. "Founders of MySpace, Interviewed by Charlie Rose." The Charlie Rose Show, PBS. Aired February 3, 2009.

Dhaher, Enas A., Rafael T. Mikolaczyk, Annette E. Maxwell, and Alexander Krämer. 2010. "Attitudes Toward Wife Beating Among Palestinian Women of Reproductive Age From Three Cities in West Bank." *Journal of Interpersonal Violence* 25(3): 518–37.

Diekman, Amanda B. and Sarah K. Murnen. 2004. "Learning to Be Little Women and Little Men: The Inequitable Gender Equality of Nonsexist Children's Literature." *Sex Roles: A Journal of Research,* March.

Dilworth-Anderson, Peggye. 2001. "Extended Kin Networks in Black Families." Pp. 104–06 in *Families in Later Life: Connections and Transitions,* edited by A. J. Walker, M. Manoogian-O'Dell, L. A. McGraw and D. L. White. Thousand Oaks, CA: Pine Forge Press.

Divine, Robert A., T. H. H. Breen, George M. Frederickson, R. Hal Williams, Ariela J. Gross, and H. W. A. Brands. 2011. *America Past and Present, Combined Volume, 9th ed.* Boston: Pearson.

Divorceinfo.com. 2006. "Alimony in Divorce." Retrieved 6 June 2006 (www.divorceinfo.com/alimony.com).

Dodson, Lisa and Jillian Dickert. 2004. "Girls' Family Labor in Low-Income Households: A Decade of Qualitative Research." *Journal of Marriage and Family* 66: 318–32.

Domestic Abuse Intervention Project. 2008. *Power and Control Wheel.* Retrieved 4 September 2010 (www.theduluthmodel.org/pdf/PhyVio.pdf).

Domhoff, G. William. 2005. *Who Rules America: Power, Politics, and Social Change.* New York: McGraw-Hill.

Dorr, Rheta Louise Childe. 1970. *Susan B. Anthony: The Woman Who Changed the Mind of a Nation.* New York: AMS Press.

Doss, Brian D., Galena K. Rhoades, Scott M. Stanley, and Howard J. Markham. 2009. "The Effect of the Transition to Parenthood on Relationship Quality: An Eight-Year Prospective Study." *Journal of Personality and Social Psychology* 96: 601–19.

Downey, Douglas B. 1995. "Understanding Academic Achievement Among Children in Stephouseholds: The Role of Parental Resources, Sex of Stepparent, and Sex of Child." *Social Forces* 73: 875–94.

Dr. Phil.com. 2009. "Advice-Spanking Research." Retrieved 26 March 2010 (www.drphil.com/articles/article/256).

Drago, Robert. 2009. "The Parenting of Infants: A Time-Use Study." *Monthly Labor Review* 132(10, October): 33–43.

Dubas, Judith Semon. 2001. "How Gender Moderates the Grandparent-Grandchild Relationship: A Comparison of Kin-Keeper and Kin-Selector Theories." *Journal of Family Issues* 22 (May): 478–92.

Dumas, Tara M., Heather Lawford, Thanh-Thanh Tieu, and Michael W. Pratt. 2009. "Positive Parenting in Adolescence and Its Relation to Low Point Narration and Identity Status in Emerging Adulthood: A Longitudinal Analysis." *Developmental Psychology* 45(6, November): 1531–44.

Dunn, Daniel M. and Lisa J. Goodnight. 2011. *Communication: Embracing Difference.* Boston: Allyn & Bacon.

Dupuis, Sara B. 2007. "Examining Remarriage: A Look at Issues Affecting Remarried Couples and the Implications Towards Therapeutic Techniques." *Journal of Divorce & Remarriage* 48(1–2, December): 91–104.

Durkheim, Emile. 1897 (reprinted 1967). *Suicide.* New York: Houghton Mifflin, 1967.

Duvall, Evelyn and Brent C. Miller. 1985. "Stage-Critical Family Development Tasks." In *Marriage & Family Development, 6th ed.* New York: Harper & Row.

Duxbury, Linda, Sean Lyons, and Christopher Higgins. 2008. "Too Much to Do, and Not Enough Time: An Examination of Role Overload." Pp. 125–40 in *Handbook of Work-Family Integration: Research, Theory, and Best Practices*, edited by Karen Korabik, Donna S. Lero and Denise L. Whitehead. Amsterdam: Elsevier.

Dye, Jane Lawler 2005. *Fertility of American Women: June 2004*. U.S. Census Bureau.

—. 2008. *Fertility of American Women: 2006*. Current Population Reports No. P20-558. Washington, DC: U.S. Census Bureau.

Dykstra, Pearl A. and Aafke E. Komter. 2006. "Structural Characteristics of Dutch Kin Networks." Pp. 21–43 in *Family Solidarity in the Netherlands*, edited by Pearl A. Dykstra, Matthijs Kalmijn, Trudie C. Knijn, Aafke E. Komter, Aart C. Liefbloer and Clara H. Mulder. Amsterdam: Dutch University Press.

Eastwick, Paul W. and Eli J. Finkel. 2008. "Sex Differences in Mate Preferences Revisited: Do People Know What They Initially Desire in a Romantic Partner?" *Journal of Personality and Social Psychology* 94(2, February): 245–64.

Economic and Social Council. 2010. 14 April. *Despite Drops in Mortality, Rise in Life Expectancy, Efforts to Combat HIV/AIDS Have Not Profoundly Altered Course of Epidemic, Population Commission Told*. United Nations. Retrieved 20 June 2010 (www.un.org/News/Press/docs/2010/pop982.htm).

The Economist. 2006. "Don't Fence Us Out." *The Economist*, 1–7 April, pp. 25–26.

Economist.com. 2004. "Ever Higher Society, Ever Harder to Ascend." Retrieved 24 June 2006 (www.economist.com/world/na/PrinterFriendly.cfm?story_id=3518560).

Edin, Kathryn and Maria Kefalas. 2005. *Promises I Can Keep: Why Poor Women Put Motherhood Before Marriage*. Berkeley, CA: University of California Press.

Edin, Kathryn and Rebecca Joyce Kissane. 2010. "Poverty and the American Family: A Decade in Review." *Journal of Marriage and Family* 72(3, June).

Eggebeen, David J. 2005. "Cohabitation and Exchanges of Support." *Social Forces* 83(3): 1097–110.

Ehrenreich, Barbara. 2001. *Nickel and Dimed: On (Not) Getting By in America*. New York: Henry Holt and Co.

Eitzen, D. Stanley and Kelly Eitzen Smith. 2009. *Experiencing Poverty: Voices from the Bottom*. Upper Saddle River, NJ: Prentice Hall.

Elder, Jr., Glen H. 1998. "The Life Course and Human Development." Pp. 939–91 in *Handbook of Child Psychology*, Vol. 1, 5th ed., edited by R. M. Lerner. Theoretical Models of Human Development. New York: Wiley.

—. 1999. *Children of the Great Depression: Social Change in Life Experience. 25th Anniversary Edition*. Boulder, CO: Westview Press (Originally published in 1974, University of Chicago Press).

Elder, Glen H., Jr., Rand D. Conger, E. Michael Foster, and Monika Ardelt. 1992. "Families Under Economic Pressure." *Journal of Family Issues* 13: 5–37.

Eliot, Lise. 2009. *Pink Brain, Blue Brain: How Small Differences Grow Into Troublesome Gaps—And What We Can Do About It*. New York: Houghton Mifflin.

Ellis, Albert. 1963. *The Origins and Development of the Incest Taboo*. New York: Lyle Stewart.

Elwert, Felix and Nicholas A. Christakis. 2006. "Widowhood and Race." *American Sociological Review* 71(1): 16–41.

Ember, Carol R. and Melvin R. Ember. 2011. *Cultural Anthropology, 13th ed.* Boston: Pearson.

Employee Benefit Research Institute. 2009. "Domestic Partner Benefits: Facts and Background." Retrieved 26 October 2009 (www.ebri.org/pdf/publications/facts/0209fact.pdf).

—. 2010. *Notes*. Technical Report No. V. 31, No. 6. Retrieved 14 June 2010 (www.ebri.org/pdf/notespdf/EBRI_Notes_06-June10.Inc-Eld.pdf).

Encyclopedia of Surgery. 2009. "Sex Reassignment Surgery." Retrieved 21 February 2010 (www.surgeryencyclopedia.com/Pa-St/Sex-Reassignment-Surgery.html).

Engels, Friedrich. 1902, original 1884. *The Origin of the Family*. Chicago: Charles H. Kerr and Co.

England, Pam and Rob Horowitz. 1998. *Birthing From Within*. Albuquerque, NM: Partera Press.

England, Paula and Su Li. 2006. "Desegregation Stalled." *Gender & Society* 20(5th): 657–77, 5th ed.

Entertainment Software Association. 2010. "Industry Facts." Retrieved 16 April 2010 (www.theesa.com/facts/index.asp).

Epel, Orna Baron, Giora Kaplan, and Mika Moran. 2010. "Perceived Discrimination and Health-Related Quality of Life Among Arabs and Jews in Israel: A Population-Based Survey." *BMC Public Health 2010* 10: 282.

Erens, Bob, Sally McManus, Alison Prescott, and Julia Field. 2003. *National Survey of Sexual Attitudes and Lifestyles II: Reference Tables and Summary Report*. London: National Centre for Social Research.

Erera, Pauline Irit. 2002. *Family Diversity: Continuity and Change in the Contemporary Family*. Thousand Oaks, CA: Sage Publications.

Estes, Carroll L. and Associates. 2001. *Social Policy and Aging: A Critical Perspective*. Thousand Oaks, CA: Sage.

Ethnicmajority.com. 2006. "Demographics: African, Hispanic, and Asian American Demographics." Retrieved 19 March 2006 (www.ethnicmajority.com/demographics_home.htm).

Evans, Gary W., Carrie Gonnella, Lyscha.A. Marcynyszyn, L. Gentile, and N. Salpekar. 2005. "The Role of Chaos in Poverty and Children's Socioemotional Adjustment." *Psychological Science* 16(7, July): 560–65.

Evertsson, Marie and Magnus Nermo. 2004. "Dependence Within Families and the Division of Labor: Comparing Sweden and the United States." *Journal of Marriage and Family* 66 (December): 1272–86.

Fagan, Jay. 2009. "Relationship Quality and Changes in Depressive Symptoms Among Urban, Married African Americans, Hispanics, and Whites." *Family Relations* 58(3, July): 259–74.

Faragher, John Mack, Mari Jo Buhle, Daniel Czitrom, and Susan H. Armitage. 2009. *Out of Many, Combined Volume, 6th ed.* Boston: Pearson.

Farley, John E. 2010. *Majority-Minority Relations, 6th ed.* Upper Saddle River, NJ: Prentice Hall.

Farr, Kathryn. 2005. *Sex Trafficking: The Global Market in Women and Children.* New York: Worth Publishers.

Farrell, Betty G. 1999. *Family: The Making of an Idea, an Institution, and a Controversy in American Culture.* Boulder, CO: Westview Press.

Federal Hospital Insurance and Federal Supplementary Medical Insurance Trust. 2009. *2009 Annual Report of the Board of Trustees.*

Federal Interagency Forum on Child and Family Statistics. 2009. *America's Children: Key National Indicators of Well-Being, 2009.* Washington, DC: U.S. Government Printing Office.

Federal Writers Project. 1936. "Slave Narrative Collection." Pp. 321–23 in *America's Families: A Documentary History, 1982,* edited by D. Scott and B. Wishy. New York: Harper Collins.

Felmlee, Diane H. and Anna Muraco. 2009. "Gender and Friendship Norms Among Other Adults." *Research on Aging* 31(3, 1 May): 318–44.

Felson, Richard B. and Paul-Philippe Pare. 2005. "The Reporting of Domestic Violence and Sexual Assault by Nonstrangers to the Police." *Journal of Marriage and Family* 67(3): 597–610.

Fenigstein, Allan and Matthew Preston. 2007. "The Desired Number of Sexual Partners as a Function of Gender, Sexual Risks, and the Meaning of 'Ideal.'" *Journal of Sex Research* 44(1): 89–95.

Fenstermaker Berk, S. 1985. *The Gender Factory: The Apportionment of Work in American Households.* New York: Plenum Press.

Few, A. L. and P. Bell-Scott. 2002. "Grounding Our Feet and Hearts: Black Women's Coping Strategies and the Decision to Leave." *Women & Therapy, Special Edition: Violence in the Lives of Black Women* 25(3/4): 59–77.

Few, April L. and Karen H. Rosen. 2005. "Victims of Chronic Dating Violence: How Women's Vulnerabilities Link to Their Decisions to Stay." *Family Relations* 54 (April): 265–79.

Fields, Jason. 2003. "Children's Living Arrangements and Characteristics: March 2002." In *Current Population Reports P20-547.* U.S. Census Bureau, U.S. Department of Commerce.

—. 2004. *America's Families and Living Arrangements: 2003.* Technical Report No. P20-553. Washington, DC: U.S. Census Bureau, November.

Fields, Jason and Lynne M. Casper. 2001. "America's Families and Living Arrangements: March 2000." In *Current Population Reports, P20-537.* Washington, DC: U.S. Census Bureau.

Filson, Jennifer, Emilio Ulloa, Cristin Runfola, and Audrey Hokoda. 2010. "Does Powerlessness Explain the Relationship Between Intimate Partner Violence and Depression?" *Journal of Interpersonal Violence* 25(3): 400–15.

Fincham, Frank D. and Steven H. Beach. 2010. "Marriage in the New Millennium: A Decade in Review." *Journal of Marriage and Family* 72(3, June).

Fingerman, Karen L. 2004. "The Role of Offspring and In-Laws in Grandparents' Ties to Their Grandchildren." *Journal of Family Issues* 25: 1026–49.

Finley, Gordon E., Sandra D. Mira, and Seth J. Schwartz. 2008. "Perceived Paternal and Maternal Involvement: Factor Structures, Mean Differences, and Paternal Roles." *Fathering* 6(1, Winter): 62–82.

Fisher, Allen P. 2003. "A Critique of the Portrayal of Adoption in College Textbooks and Readers on Families, 1998–2001." *Family Relations* 52: 154–60.

Fisher, Bonnie S., Francis T. Cullen, and Michael G. Turner. 2000. *The Sexual Victimization of College Women.* Technical Report No. NCJ 182369. Washington, DC: U.S. Department of Justice, National Institute of Justice.

Fisher, Bruce and Robert E. Alberti. 2006. *Rebuilding: When Your Relationship Ends, 3rd ed.* Atascadero, CA: Impact Publishers.

Fisher, Helen. 2004. *Why We Love: The Nature and Chemistry of Romantic Love.* New York: Owl Books.

—. 2010. *Why Him? Why Her?: How to Find and Keep Lasting Love.* New York: Henry Holt and Company.

Fisher, Helen and Jr. Thomson, J. Anderson. 2007. "Lust, Romance, Attraction, Attachment: Do the Side-Effects of Serotonin-Enhancing Antidepressants Jeopardize Romantic Love, Marriage and Fertility?" Pp. 245–83 in *Evolutionary Cognitive Neuroscience,* edited by Steven M. Platek, Julian P. Keenan and Todd K. Shackelford. Cambridge, MA: MIT Press.

The Fistula Foundation. 2010. "Fistula Fast Facts and Frequently Asked Questions." Retrieved 16 June 2010 (www.fistulafoundation.org/aboutfistula/faqs.html).

Fitzpatrick, Laura. 2009. "A Brief History of China's One Child Policy." *Time,* 27 July. Retrieved 9 November 2009 (www.time.com/time/world/article/0,8599,1912861,00.html).

Flack, Jr., William F., Kimberly A. Daubman, Marcia L. Caron, Jenica A. Asadorian, Nicole R. D'Aureli, Shannon N. Gigliotti, Anna T. Hall, Sarah Kiser, and Erin R. Stine. 2007. "Risk Factors and Consequences of Unwanted Sex Among University Students: Hooking up, Alcohol, and Postraumatic Symptoms." *Journal of Interpersonal Violence* 22: 139–57.

Flaherty, Sr. Mary Jean, Loma Facteau, and Patricia Garver. 1994. "Grandmother Functions in Multi-Generational Families: Exploratory Study of Black Adolescent Mothers and Their Infants." Pp. 195–203 in *The Black Family: Essays and Studies, 5th ed.,* edited by R. Staples. Belmont, CA: Wadsworth.

Flaks, David K., Ida Ficher, Frank Masterpasqua, and Gregory Joseph. 1995. "Lesbians Choosing Motherhood: A Comparative Study of Lesbian and Heterosexual Parents and Their Children." *Developmental Psychology* 31(1): 105–25.

Fleck, Carole. 2009. "Grandparents Help Out." Retrieved 4 December 2009. AARP Bulletin Today (bulletin.aarp.org/ yourmoney/personalfinance/articles/more_grandparents_ giving_money_to_kids_.html).

Flexner, Eleanor. 1959. *Century of Struggle*. Cambridge: Harvard University Press.

Flood, Michael and Bob Pease. 2009. "Factors Influencing Attitudes to Violence Against Women." *Trauma, Violence, & Abuse* 10(2): 125–42.

Florida Coalition Against Domestic Violence. 2001. "History of the Battered Women's Shelter/Movement." Retrieved 20 March 2003 (www.fcadv.org/history.html).

Forger, Nancy G., Greta J. Rosen, Elizabeth M. Waters, Dana Jacob, Richard B. Simerly, and Geert J. de Vries. 2004. "Deletion of Bax Eliminates Sex Differences in the Mouse Forebrain." *PNAS* 101(37, 14 September): 13666–71.

Frech, Adrianne and Kristi Williams. 2007. "Depression and the Psychological Benefits of Entering Marriage." *Journal of Health and Social Behavior* 48(2): 149–63.

Fredrix, Emily. 2008. "NOT-SUCH-BABY 'BOOMERANGS' Adults Returning to Nest Often Deplete." *Oakland Tribune* (Oakland, CA), 22 March.

Frias, Sonia M. and Ronald J. Angel. 2005. "The Risk of Partner Violence Among Low-Income Hispanic Subgroups." *Journal of Marriage and Family* 67(3): 552–64.

Friedan, Betty. 1963. *The Feminine Mystique*. New York: Dell.

Frisco, Michelle and Kristi Williams. 2003. "Perceived House-work Equity, Marital Happiness, and Divorce in Dual-Earner Households." *Journal of Family Issues* 24: 51–73.

Frum, David. 2000. *How We Got Here: The 70's*. New York: Basic Books.

Fry, Richard and D'Vera Cohn. 2010. "New Economics of Marriage: The Rise of Wives." Retrieved 20 January 2010 (pewresearch.org/pubs/1466/economics-marriage-rise-of-wives).

Fry, Richard and Jeffrey S. Passel. 2009. "Latino Children: A Majority Are U.S.-Born Offspring of Immigrants." Retrieved 20 January 2010. Pew Hispanic Center (pewhispanic.org/reports/report.php?ReportID=110).

Fryar, Cheryl D., Rosemarie Hirsch, Kathryn S. Porter, Benny Kottiri, Debra J. Brody, and Tatiana Louis. 2007. "Drug Use and Sexual Behaviors Reported by Adults: United States, 1999–2002." Centers for Disease Control and Prevention, 384. Hyattsville, MD: National Center for Health Statistics, 28 June.

Fulfer, Jamie L., Jillian J. Tyler, Natalie Choi, J. S., Jill A. Young, Steven J. Verhulst, Regina Kovach, and J. Kevin Dorsey. 2007. "Using Indirect Questions to Detect Intimate Partner Violence." *Journal of Interpersonal Violence* 22(2): 238–49.

Furstenberg, Frank F., Jr. 2007. "Should Government Promote Marriage?" *Journal of Policy Analysis and Management* 26(4): 956–60.

Gadalla, Tahany M. 2008. "Gender Differences in Poverty Rates After Marital Dissolution: A Longitudinal Study." *Journal of Divorce and Remarriage* 49(3/4): 225–38.

—. 2009. "Impact of Marital Dissolution on Men's and Women's Incomes: A Longitudinal Study." *Journal of Divorce & Remarriage* 50(1, January): 55–65.

Galinsky, Ellen, Kerstin Aumann, and James T. Bond. 2009. *Times Are Changing: Gender and Generation at Work and at Home*. New York: Families and Work Institute.

Gallagher, Sally K. 1994. "Doing Their Share: Comparing Patterns of Help Given by Older and Younger Adults." *Journal of Marriage and the Family* 56: 567–78.

Gallagher, Sally K. and Naomi Gerstel. 2001. "Connections and Constraints: The Effects of Children on Caregiving." *Journal of Marriage and the Family* 63: 265–75.

Gallup News Service. 2007. "Whites, Blacks, Hispanics Assess Race Relations in the U.S." Retrieved 7 April 2008 (www.gallup.com/poll/28312/Whites-Blacks-Hispanics-Assess-Race-Relations-US.aspx).

Gallup Poll. 2001. "What's the Best Arrangement for Today's Families?" (www.gallup.com/tuesday briefing.asp).

Galtry, Judith and Paul Callister. 2005. "Assessing the Optimal of Parental Leave for Child and Parental Well-Being: How Can Research Inform Policy." *Journal of Family Issues* 26: 219–46.

Galvin, Kathleen M., Carma L. Bylund, and Bernard J. Brom-mel. 2008. *Family Communication: Cohesion and Change, 7th ed.* Boston: Allyn & Bacon.

Ganong, Lawrence H. and Marilyn Coleman. 1997. "How Society Views Stepfamilies." *Marriage and Family Review* 26: 85–106.

—. 2004. *Stepfamily Relationships: Development, Dynamics, and Interventions*. New York: Kluwer Academic.

García-Coll, Cynthia T. 1990. "Developmental Outcome of Minority Parents: A Process-Oriented Look into Our Beginnings." *Child Development* 61(2): 270–89.

Gardner, Margo and Jeanne Brooks-Gunn. 2009. "Adolescents' Exposure to Community Violence: Are Neighborhood Youth Organizations Protective?" *Journal of Community Psychology* 37: 520–25.

Gardner, Margo, Jodie Roth, and Jeanne Brooks-Gunn. 2008. "Adolescents' Participation in Organized Activities and Developmental Success Two and Eight Years After High School: Do Sponsorship, Duration, and Intensity Matter?" *Developmental Psychology* 44(3): 814–30.

Garfinkel, Irwin, Timothy M. Smeeding, and Lee Rainwater. 2010. *The American Welfare State: Laggard or Leader*. Oxford, UK: Oxford University Press.

Garner, Richard. 2009. "The Big Question: Why Are Teenage Pregnancy Rates So High, and What Can Be Done About It?" Retrieved 8 July 2010. The Independent (www.independent.co/uk).

Garrod, Andrew, Lisa Smulyan, Sally I. Powers, and Robert Kilkenny. 2008. *Adolescent Portraits: Identity, Relation-ships, and Challenges, 6th ed.* Boston: Allyn & Bacon.

Gates, Gary J. 2006 October. *Same-Sex Couples and the Gay, Lesbian, Bisexual Population: New Estimates from the American Community Survey*. Los Angeles, CA: The Williams Institute.

Gazamarian, Julie A. 2000. "Violence and Reproductive Health: Current Knowledge and Future Research Directions." *Maternal and Child Health Journal* 4(2): 80.

Gentleman, Amelia. 2008. "India Nurtures Business of Surrogate Motherhood." Retrieved 20 December 2009. New York Times (travel.nytimes.com/2008/03/10/world/asia/10surrogate.html?sq=women&st=nyt&scp=19&pagewanted=all).

Gerson, Kathleen. 2001. "Dilemmas of Involved Fatherhood." pp. 324–39 in *Shifting the Center: Understanding Contemporary Families*, edited by Susan J. Ferguson. Mountain View, CA: Mayfield Publishing Company.

Gerson, Michael. 2009. "Today's Singles, Lost Without a Courtship Narrative." Retrieved 4 February 2010. washingtonpost.com (www.washingtonpost.com/wp-dyn/content/article/2009/09/15/AR2009091502981.html).

Gettleman, Jeffrey. 2010. "Kenyan Police Disperse Gay Wedding." Retrieved 21 February 2010. New York Times (www.nytimes.com/2010/02/13/world/africa/13kenya.html).

Giele, Janet Z. 1996. "Decline of the Family: Conservative, Liberal, and Feminist Views." In *Promises to Keep: Decline and Renewal of Marriage in America*, edited by David Popenoe, Jean Bethke Elshtain, and David Blankenhorn. Lanham, MD: Rowman and Littlefield.

Gierveld, Jenny de Jong, Marjolein Broese van Groenou, Adriaan W. Hoogendoorn, and Johannes H. Smit. 2008. "Quality of Marriages in Later Life and Emotional and Social Loneliness." *The Journals of Gerontology: Series B* 64B(4): 497–506.

Gilbert, Dennis and Joseph A. Kahl. 1993. *The American Class Structure: A New Synthesis, 4th ed.* Belmont, CA: Wadsworth.

Gilbert, Neil and Paul Terrell. 2010. *Dimensions of Social Welfare Policy, 7th ed.* Boston: Pearson Education Inc.

Gilder, George. 1995. "Welfare Fraud Today." *The American Spectator*, 5 September, p. B6.

Giles-Sims, Jean and Charles Lockhart. 2005. "Grandparents' Visitation Rights Using Culture to Explain Cross-State Variation." *Journal of Divorce and Remarriage* 44(3/4): 1–16 (DOI: 10.1300/J087vol44n03_01).

Girschick, Lori B. 2008. *Transgender Voices: Beyond Women and Men*. Lebanon, NH: University Press of New England.

Glenn, Norval D. 1998. "The Course of Marital Success and Failure in Five American 10-Year Marriage Cohorts." *Journal of Marriage and the Family* 60: 569–76.

Glick, Jennifer E. and Jennifer Van Hook. 2002. "Parent's Coresidence with Adult Children: Can Immigration Explain Race and Ethnic Variation?" *Journal of Marriage and the Family* 64: 240–53.

Glynn, Keva, Heather Maclean, Tonia Forte, and Marsha Cohen. 2009. "The Association Between Role Overload

and Women's Mental Health." *Journal of Women's Health (Larchmont)* 18(2, February): 217–23.

Goffman, Erving. 1963. *Stigma*. Englewood Cliffs, NJ: Prentice Hall.

Goldman, Jill, Marsha K. Salus, Deborah Wolcott, and Kristie Y. Kennedy. 2003. "A Coordinated Response to Child Abuse and Neglect: The Foundation for Practice" (Child Abuse and Neglect User Manual). Retrieved 30 June 2010. Washington, DC/Government Printing Office (www.child-welfare.gov/pubs/usermanuals/foundation/foundation.pdf).

Goldscheider, Frances and Calvin Goldscheider. 1994. "Leaving and Returning Home in 20th Century America." *Population Bulletin* 48(4): 1–35.

Goldsmith, Scott, Jane Angvik, Lance Howe, Alexandra Hill, and Linda Leask. 2004. "The Status of Alaska Natives Report 2004." Retrieved 19 March 2006. Institute for Social and Economic Research (www.iser.uaa.alaska.edu/Home/ResearchAreas/AlaskaNativeStudies.htm).

Gonzalez-Lopez, Gloria. 2003. "De Madres a Hijas: Gendered Lessons on Virginity Across Generations of Mexican Immigrant Women." Pp. 217–40 in *Gender and U.S. Immigration: Contemporary Trends*, edited by P. Hondagneu-Sotelo. Berkeley, CA: University of California Press.

—. 2004. "Fathering Latina Sexualities: Mexican Men and the Virginity of Their Daughters." *Journal of Marriage and the Family* 66: 1118–30.

Goode, William J. 1959. "The Theoretical Importance of Love." *American Sociological Review* 24: 38–47.

—. 1963. *World Revolution and Family Patterns*. New York: Free Press.

—. 1993. *World Changes in Divorce Patterns*. New Haven, CT: Yale University Press.

Goodman, Catherine Chase and Merril Silverstein. 2006. "Grandmothers Raising Grandchildren: Ethnic and Racial Differences in Well-Being Among Custodial and Coparenting Families." *Journal of Family Issues* 27: 1605–26.

Goodman, Ellen. 2003. "Cloe's First Fourth." *Boston Globe*, 3 July, p. A13.

Goodman, W. Benjamin, Ann C. Crouter, and The Family Life Project Key Investigators. 2009. "Longitudinal Associations Between Maternal Work Stress, Negative Work-Family Spillover, and Depressive Symptoms." *Family Relations* 58 (July): 245–58.

Goodwin, Paula Y., William D. Mosher, and Anjani Chandra. 2010. *Marriage and Cohabitation in the United States: A Statistical Portrait Based on Cycle 6 (2002) of the National Survey of Family Growth*. Technical Report No. Vital Health Stat 23 (28). National Center for Health Statistics.

Goodwin, Robin. 2009. *Changing Relations: Achieving Intimacy in a Time of Social Transition*. New York: Cambridge University Press.

Gorchoff, Sara M., Oliver P. John, and Ravenna Helson. 2008. "Contextualing Change in Marital Satisfaction During Middle Age: An 18-Year Longitudinal Study." *Psychological Science* 19(11): 1194–200.

Gordon, Linda. 1979. "The Struggle for Reproductive Freedom: Three Stages of Feminism." Pp. 107–36 in *Capitalist Patriarchy and the Case for Socialist Feminism*, edited by Z. Eisenstein. New York: Monthly Review Press.

—. 1994. *Pitied But Not Entitled*. New York: Free Press.

—. 2001. *The Great Arizona Orphan Abduction*. Cambridge, MA: Harvard University Press.

Gornick, Janet C., Presser, and Caroline Ratzdorf. 2009. "Outside the 9-to-5." *The American Prospect* 20(5): 21–24.

Gornick, Janet C., Alexandra Heron, and Ross Eisenbrey. 2007. *The Work-Family Balance: An Analysis of European, Japanese, and U.S Work-Time Policies*. Technical Report No. Briefing Paper #189. Washington, DC: Economic Policy Institute.

Gottman, John M., James A. Coan, Sybil Carrere, and Catherine Swanson. 1998. "Predicting Marital Happiness and Stability from Newlywed Interactions." *Journal of Marriage and the Family* 60: 5–22.

Gottman, John M. 1994. *Why Marriages Succeed or Fail*. New York: Simon & Schuster.

Gottman, John and Julie Schwartz Gottman. 2008. *And Baby Makes Three: The Six-Step Plan for Preserving Marital Intimacy and Rekindling Romance After Baby Arrives*. New York: Three Rivers Press.

Goulbourne, Harry, Tracey Reynolds, John Solomos, and Elisabetta Zontini. 2010. *Transnational Families: Ethnicities, Identities, and Social Capital (Relationships and Resources)*. New York: Routledge.

Goyer, Amy. 2006. "Intergenerational Relationships: Grandparents Raising Grandchildren." Retrieved 29 October 2007. AARP.org (www.aarp.org/research/international/perspectives/nov_05_grandparents.html).

Graff, E.G. 2004. "Gay & Lesbian Advocates & Defenders." *The Oregonian*, 14 February, pp. A-5.

Grall, Timothy S. 2009. *Custodial Mothers and Fathers and Their Child Support: 2007*. Current Population Reports No. P60-237. Washington, DC: U.S. Census Bureau.

Gramsci, Antonio. 1971. *Selected Readings from the Prison Notebooks of Antonio Gramsci*. Translated by Q. Hoare and G. N. Smith. New York: International Publishers.

Granger, Robert C. 2008. *After-School Programs and Academics: Implications for Policy, Practice, and Research*. Social Policy Report No. Vol. XXII, Number 2. Society for Research in Child Development.

Grant, Jaime M. 2009. *Outing Age: Public Policy Issues Affecting Gay, Lesbian, Bisexual, and Transgender Elders*. National Gay and Lesbian Task Force Policy Institute.

Gray, John. 1992. *Men Are from Mars, Women Are from Venus: A Practical Guide for Improving Communication and Getting What You Want in Your Relationships*. New York: Thorsons.

Gray, Ronald F., Alka Indurkhya, and Marie C. McCormick. 2004. "Prevalence, Stability, and Predictors of Clinically Significant Behavior Problems in Low Birth Weight Children at 3, 5, and 8 Years of Age." *Pediatrics* 114(3, September): 736–43.

Graybill, Wilson H., Clyde V. Kiser, and Pascal K. Whelpton. 1958. *The Fertility of American Women*. New York: Wiley & Sons.

Green, Rayna. 2010. "The Pocahontas Perplex: The Image of Indian Women in American Culture." Pp. 159–64 in *Native American Voices, 3rd ed.*, edited by S. Lobo, S. Talbot and T. L. Morris. Boston: Pearson.

Greenberg, Kenneth. 2009. "Half of Americans Know Someone Who Has Dated a Person They Met Online, According to New Study From People Media." Retrieved 22 January 2010. PRWeb.com (www.prweb.com/printer/2758114.htm).

Greenfield, Emily A. and Nadine F. Marks. 2004. *Linked Lives: Adult Children's Distress and Their Parents' Well-Being*. Center for Democracy and Ecology No. CDF Working Paper No. 2004-27. Madison, WI: University of Wisconsin-Madison.

Greenstein, Robert. 2005. "The Earned Income Tax Credit: Boosting Employment, Aiding the Working Poor." Retrieved 28 March 2008. Center on Budget and Policy Priorities (www.cbpp.org/7-19-05eic.htm).

Greenstein, Theodore N. and Shannon N. Davis. 2006. "Cross-National Variations in Divorce: Effects of Women's Power, Prestige and Dependence." *Journal of Comparative Family Studies* 37: 253–73.

Gregson, Joanna and Michelle L. Ceynar. 2009. "Finding 'Me' Again: Women's Postdivorce Identity Shifts." *Journal of Divorce & Remarriage* 50(8, November): 564–82.

Griffith, Wendy. 2006. "A Look at India's Arranged Marriages." Retrieved 24 July 2006. CBN.com (www.cbn.com/cbnnews/news/050323c.aspx).

Grogger, Jeffrey. 2009. "Speech Patterns and Racial Wage Inequality." Working Paper Series 08.13, Harris School of Public Policy, University of Chicago, September.

Grossman, Arnold H. and Anthony R. D'Augelli. 2006. "Transgender Youth: Invisible and Vulnerable." *Journal of Homosexuality* 51(1): 111–28.

Gupta, Giri Raj. 2005. "Forum on Child Marriage in Developing Countries." Forum Presented at the U.S. Department of State, 14 September.

Gurian, Michael. 1999. *The Good Son: Shaping the Moral Development of Our Boys and Young Men*. New York: Putnam.

Gurko, Miriam. 1974. *The Ladies of Seneca Falls: The Birth of the Woman's Rights Movement*. New York: MacMillan Publishing Co., Inc.

Gurunath, Vatsala. 2009. "Amniocentesis: Sex Determination or Sex Termination?" Retrieved 15 June 2010. Oneindia (living.oneindia.in/health/pregnancy/amniocentesis.html).

Gutman, Herbert. 1976. *The Black Family in Slavery and Freedom, 1750-1925*. New York: Pantheon.

Hadley, Jack. 2007. "Insurance Coverage, Medical Care Use, and Short-Term Health Changes Following an Unintentional Injury or the Onset of a Chronic Condition." *Journal of the American Medical Association* 297(10, 14 March): 1073–84.

Hagerty, Barbara Bradley. 2008. "Some Muslims in U.S. Quietly Engage in Polygamy." Retrieved 15 June 2010. NPR.org (www.npr.org/templates/story/story.php?storyID=90857818).

Hall, Carl T. 2002. "Pediatricians Endorse Gay, Lesbian Adoption 'Children Deserve to Know Their Relationships With Both Parents Are Stable, Legally Recognized'." Retrieved 13 July 2006. San Francisco Chronicle (www.sfgate.com/ cgi-bin/article.cgi?file=/chronicle/archive/2002/02/04/MN227427).

Hall, Mark A., Mary Anne Bobinski, and David Orentlicher. 2008. *Health Care Law and Ethics, 7th ed.* New York: Aspen.

Hamer, Jennifer and Kathleen Marchioro. 2002. "Becoming Custodial Dads: Exploring Parenting Among Low-Income and Working-Class African American Fathers." *Journal of Marriage and the Family* 64: 116–29.

Hamilton, Brady E., Joyce A. Martin, and Stephanie A. Ventura. 2006. "Births: Preliminary Data for 2005. Health E-Stats." Retrieved 27 November 2006. Centers for Disease Control and Prevention (www.cdc.gov/nchs/products/pubs/pubd/hestats/prelimbirths05/prelimbirths05.htm).

—. 2009. "Births: Preliminary Data for 2007." Vol. 57, No. 12. Retrieved 18 August 2009. Hyattsville, MD/National Center for Health Statistics (www.cdc.gov/nchs/data/nvsr/nvsr57/nvsr57_12.pdf).

—. 2010. *Births: Preliminary Data for 2008.* National Vital Statistics Reports No. Vol. 58, No. 16. Washington, DC: National Center for Health Statistics.

Han, Shin-Kap and Phyllis Moen. 1999. "Work and Family Over Time: A Life Course Approach." *The Annals of the American Academy of Political and Social Sciences* 562: 98–110.

Han, Wen-Jui, Christopher Ruhm, Jane Waldfogel, and Elizabeth Washbrook. 2009. "Public Policies and Women's Employment After Childbearing." *National Bureau of Economic Research* (Working Paper No. 14660). Retrieved 22 November 2009. Cambridge, MA (www.nber.org/papers/w14660).

Hancock, Ange-Marie. 2004. *The Politics of Disgust: The Public Identity of the Welfare State.* New York: New York University Press.

Hans, Jason D. 2002. "Stepparenting After Divorce: Stepparents' Legal Position Regarding Custody, Access, and Support." *Family Relations* 51(4): 301–07.

Hansen, Chris. 2002. "The Cost of Raising a Child." Retrieved 25 June 2003 (http://familyguardian.betterthanyours.com/Subjects/Parenting/Articles/CostofChild.htm).

Hardy, Melissa A. and Kim Shuey. 2000. "Retirement." Pp. 2401–10 in *Encyclopedia of Sociology, 2nd ed.,* edited by Edgar F. Borgatta and Rhonda J. Montgomery. New York: Macmillan.

Hartog, Hendrik. 2000. *Man and Wife in America: A History.* Cambridge, MA: Harvard University Press.

Harvard School of Public Health. 2001. "Dating Violence Against Adolescent Girls Linked with Teen Pregnancy, Suicide, and Other Health Risk Behaviors" (www.harvard.edu/press/releases/press07312001.html).

Harvey, David L. and Michael H. Reed. 1996. "The Culture of Poverty: An Ideological Analysis." *Sociological Perspectives* 39: 465–95.

Harvey, Elizabeth. 1999. "Short-Term and Long-Term Effects of Early Parental Employment on Children of the National Longitudinal Survey of Youth," *Developmental Psychology* 35(2): 445–459.

Harvey, John H. and Mark Fine. 2004. *Children of Divorce: Stories of Loss and Growth.* Mahwah, NJ: Lawrence Erlbaum Associates.

Hasson, Yael. 2009. *Gender Mainstreaming in Sweden: Lessons for Israel.* Tel Aviv: Women's Budget Forum.

Hastings, Deborah. 2000. "Register Ranks Ultra Rich: Social Register Keeps Track of Who's Who in the Upper Crust." The Detroit News (www.detnews.com/2000/nation/0006/11/a07-72601.htm).

Haub, Carl. 2010. "Japan's Demographic Future." Retrieved 23 May 2010. Population Reference Bureau (www.prb.org/Articles/2010/japandemography.aspx).

Haub, Carl and Mary Mederios Kent. 2009. *2009 World Population Data Sheet.* Washington, DC: Population Reference Bureau.

Hawkins, Alan J., Kimberly R. Lovejoy, Erin K Holmes, Victoria L. Blanchard, and Elizabeth B. Fawcett. 2008. "Increasing fathers' Involvement in Child Care with a Couple-Focused Intervention During the Transition to Parenthood." *Family Relations* 57(1): 49–59.

Hawkins, Alan J., Steven L. Nock, Julia C. Wilson, Laura Sanchez, and James D. Wright. 2002. "Attitudes About Covenant Marriage and Divorce: Policy Implications From a Three-Stage Comparison." *Family Relations* 51: 166–75.

Hawkins, Daniel N., Paul R. Amato, and Valarie King. 2007. "Nonresident Father Involvement and Adolescent Well-Being: Father Effects or Child Effects?" *American Sociological Review* 72(6, December): 990–1010.

Hawthorne, Bruce and C.J. Lennings. 2008. "The Marginalization of Nonresident Fathers: Their Postdivorce Roles." *Journal of Divorce and Remarriage* 49(3/4): 191–209.

Hays, Jeffrey. 2010. "One-Child Policy in China." Retrieved 23 May 2010. Facts and Details (factsanddetails.com/china.php?itemid=128&catid=4&subcatid=15).

Hays, Sharon. 1996. *The Cultural Contradictions of Motherhood.* New Haven: Yale University Press.

—. 2001. "The Mommy Wars: Ambivalence, Ideological Work, and the Cultural Contradictions of Motherhood." Pp. 305–23 in *Shifting the Center: Understanding Contemporary Families, 2nd ed.,* edited by S. J. Ferguson. Mountain View, CA: Mayfield Publishing Company.

—. 2003. *Flat Broke with Children: Women in the Age of Welfare Reform.* New York: Oxford University Press.

He, Wan, Manisha Sengupta, Victoria A. Velkoff, and Kimberly A. DeBarros. 2005. *65+ in the United States: 2005.*

Current Population Reports: Special Studies, P23-209. Washington, DC: U.S. Census Bureau.

Heaton, Tim B. 2002. "Factors Contributing to Increasing Marital Stability in the United States." *Journal of Family Issues* 23-3 (April): 392–409.

Hefling, Kimberly. 2004. "Benefits Cited as More US Women Over 40 Give Birth." The Associated Press. *The Oregonian*, 27 November, pp. A-2.

Heidemann, Bridget, Olga Suhomlinova, and Angela O'Rand. 1998. "Economic Independence Economic Status, and Empty Nest in Midlife Marital Disruption." *Journal of Marriage and the Family* 60: 219–31.

Helgeson, Vicki. 2009. *Psychology of Gender, 3rd ed.* Boston: Pearson.

Helms, Heather M., Christine M. Proulx, Mary Maguire Klute, Susan M. McHale, and Ann M. Crouter. 2006. "Spouses' Gender-Typed Attributes and Their Links with Marital Quality: A Pattern-Analytic Approach." *Journal of Social and Personal Relationships* 23 (December): 843–64.

Helpguide.org. 2010. "Assisted Living Facilities for Seniors: Exploring Services and Options." Retrieved 26 April 2010 (Helpguide.org/elder/assisted_living_facilities.htm).

Hendrick, Susan S. and Clyde Hendrick. 1992. *Romantic Love.* Newbury Park, CA: Sage Publications.

The Henry J. Kaiser Family Foundation. 2010a. *Medicare: A Primer.*

—. 2010b. *Summary of Coverage Provisions in the Patient Protection and Affordable Care Act and the Health Care and Education Reconciliation Act of 2010.*

Heron, Melonie, Donna L. Hoyert, Sherry L. Murphy, and Jiaquan Xu. 2009. *Deaths: Final Data for 2006.* National Vital Statistics Reports No. V. 57, No. 14. Centers for Disease Control and Prevention.

Herrnstein, Richard and Charles Murray. 1994. *The Bell Curve: Intelligence and Class Structure in American Life.* New York: Free Press.

Hertz, Rosanna and Nancy L. Marshall. 2001. *Working Families: The Transformation of the American Home.* Berkeley, CA: University of California Press.

Hesketh, Therese, Li Lu, and Zhu Wei Xing. 2005. "The Effect of China's One-Child Family Policy After 25 Years." *New England Journal of Medicine* 353(11, 15 September): 1171–76.

Hewitt, Belinda. 2009. "Which Spouse Initiates Marital Separation When There Are Children Involved?" *Journal of Marriage and Family* 71(2): 362–72.

Hewitt, Belinda, Mark Western, and Janeen Baxter. 2006. "Who Decides? The Social Characteristics of Who Initiates Marital Separation." *Journal of Marriage and Family* 68: 1165–77.

Heyman, Kathleen M., Patricia M. Barnes, and Jeannine S. Schiller. 2009. "Early Release of Selected Estimates Based on Data from the 2008 National Health Interview Survey." Retrieved 19 June 2010. Centers for Disease Control and Prevention (www.cdc.gov/nchs/nhis/about200906.htm).

Hickman, Lisa N. 2006. "Who Should Care for Our Children? The Effects of Home Versus Centre Care on Child Cognition and Social Adjustment." *Journal of Family Issues* 27(5): 652–84.

Hill, E. Jeffrey, Chongming Yang, Alan J. Hawkins, and Maria Ferris. 2004. "A Cross-Cultural Test of the Work/Family Interface in 48 Countries." *Journal of Marriage and Family* 17: 1300–16.

Hill, Robert B. 1972. *The Strengths of Black Families.* New York: Emerson Hall Publishers.

Hill, Shirley. 2002. "Teaching and Doing Gender in African American Families." *Sex Roles* 47(11/12): 493–506.

Hill, Shirley A. 2005. *Black Intimacies.* Lanham, MD: AltaMira Press.

Hine, Darlene Clark, William C. Hine, and Stanley Harrold. 2011. *The African American Odyssey, 5th ed.* Upper Saddle River, NJ: Prentice Hall.

Hines, Melissa. 2005. *Brain Gender.* New York, NY: Oxford University Press.

Hirsch, Jennifer S. 2003. *A Courtship After Marriage: Sexuality and Love in Mexican Transnational Families.* Berkeley, CA: University of California Press.

Hirschman, Charles and Nguyen Huu Minh. 2002. "Tradition and Change in Vietnamese Family Structure in the Red River Delta." *Journal of Marriage and Family* 64: 1063–79.

Hochschild, Arlie. 1989. *The Second Shift: Working Parents and the Revolution at Home.* New York: Viking.

—. 1997. *The Time Bind: When Work Becomes Home and Home Becomes Work.* New York: Metropolitan Books.

Hoefer, Michael, Nancy Rytina, and Brian C. Baker. 2010. "Estimates of the Unauthorized Immigrant Population Residing in the United States: January 2009." In *Population Estimates.* Retrieved 30 June 2010. Department of Homeland Security Office of Immigration Statistics (www.dhs.gov/xlibrary/assets/statistics/publications/ois_ill_pe_2009.pdf).

Hoffman, Saul D. 2006. "By the Numbers: The Public Cost of Teen Childbearing." Retrieved 30 November 2006. The National Campaign to End Teenage Pregnancy (www.teenpregnancy.org/costs/national.asp).

Hohmann-Marriott, Bryndl E. 2006. "Shared Beliefs and the Union Stability of Married and Cohabiting Couples." *Journal of Marriage and Family* 68: 1015–28.

Hojat, Mohammadreza, Reza Shapurian, Danesh Foroughi, Habib Nayerahmadi, Mitra Farzneh, Mahmood Shafieyan, and Mohin Parsi. 2000. "Gender Differences in Traditional Attitudes Toward Marriage and the Family: An Empirical Study of Iranian Immigrants in the United States." *Journal of Family Issues* 21: 419–34.

Holcomb, Pamela A., Karen Tumlin, Robin Koralek, Randy Capps, and Anita Zuberi. 2003. *The Application Process for TANF, Food Stamps, Medicaid and SCHIP: Issues for Agencies and Applicants, Including Immigrants and Limited English Speakers.* U.S. Department of Health and Human Services Office of the Secretary; Office of the Assistant Secretary for Planning and Evaluation; the Urban Institute.

Holcombe, Emily, Kristin Peterson, and Jennifer Manlove. 2009. *Ten Reasons to Still Keep the Focus on Teen Childbearing*. Child Trends Research Brief, March.

Holmberg, Diane, Karen L. Blair, and Maggie Phillips. 2010. "Women's Sexual Satisfaction as a Predictor of Well-Being in Same-Sex Versus Mixed-Sex Relationships." *Journal of Sex Research* 47(1, January): 1–11.

Holmes, Thomas H. and Richard H. Rahe. 1967. "The Social Readjustment Rating Scale." *Journal of Psychosomatic Research* 11: 213–18.

Honberg, Ron. 2003. "Almost 25% Homeless Are Kids." Retrieved 3 September 2003. NAMI: The Nation's Voice in Mental Illness (web.nami.org/update/update1.htm).

Honore, Carl. 2008. *Under Pressure: Rescuing Our Children From the Culture of Hyperparenting*. London: Orion Publishing.

Hook, Jennifer L. 2006. "Care in Context: Men's Unpaid Work in 20 Countries, 1965–2003." *American Sociological Review* 71(4, August): 639–60.

Hopper, Joseph. 1993. "The Rhetoric of Motives in Divorce." *Journal of Marriage and the Family* 55: 801–13.

Horn, Wade F. and Tom Sylvester. 2006. "Father Facts: Research Notes." Retrieved 16 July 2006. National Fatherhood Initiative, Fatherhood Online (www.fatherhood.org/fatherfacts_rsh.asp).

Houser, Ari N. 2007. "Long-Term Care Trends: Women & Long-Term Care Research Report." Retrieved 19 March 2008 (www.aarp.org/research/longtermcare/trends/fs77r_ltc.html).

Hu, Mandy. 2005. *Selling Us Short: How Social Security Privatization Will Affect Lesbian, Gay, Bisexual, and Transgender Americans*. Washington, DC: National Gay and Lesbian Task Force Policy Institute.

Hughes, Diane and Deborah Johnson. 2001. "Correlates in Children's Experiences of Parents' Racial Socialization Behaviors." *Journal of Marriage and Family* 63(4, November): 981–95.

Hughes, Mary Elizabeth and Linda J. Waite. 2009. "Marital Biography and Health at Mid-Life." *Journal of Health and Social Behavior* 50(3): 344–58.

Human Rights Campaign. 2009. "Parenting Laws: Joint Adoption." Retrieved 2 March 2010 (www.hrc.org/state_laws).

—. 2010. "Domestic Partners." Retrieved 16 April 2010 (www.hrc.org/issues/marriage/domestic_partners.asp).

Human Rights Watch. 2001. "Sacrificing Women to Save the Family? Domestic Violence in Uzbekistan." In *Women's Human Rights: Domestic Violence in Uzbekistan*. Retrieved 19 March 2003 (www.hrw.org/women/domesticviolence.php?country=Uzbekistan).

—. 2004. "Divorced From Justice: Women's Unequal Access to Divorce in Egypt." Retrieved 8 April 2010 (hrw.org/reports/2004/egypt1204/index.htm).

—. 2009. "Time to Tear Down the Wall of Caste." Retrieved 15 June 2010 (www.hrw.org/en/news/2009/10/09/time-tear-down-wall-caste).

—. 2010a. "EU: Remain Firm on Mladic." Retrieved 28 June 2010 (www.hrw.org/en/news/2010/06/11/eu-remain-firm-mladic).

—. 2010b. "Iraqi Kurdistan: Girls and Women Suffer the Consequences of Female Genital Mutilation." Retrieved 18 June 2010 (www.hrw.org/en/news/2010/06/16/iraqi-kurdistan-girls-and-women-suffer-consequences-female-genital-mutilation).

Hunter, Andrea G. 1997. "Counting on Grandmothers: Black Mothers' and Fathers' Reliance on Grandmothers for Parenting Support." *Journal of Family Issues* 18: 251–69.

Hurst, Charles. 2010. *Social Inequality: Forms, Causes, and Consequences, 7th ed.* Upper Saddle River, NJ: Prentice Hall.

Huston, Ted and Heidi Melz. 2004. "The Case for (Promoting) Marriage: The Devil is in the Details." *Journal of Marriage and Family* 66: 943–58.

Hutchinson, Courtney. 2010. "Birth Rates Rise Among Women Over 40, CDC Finds." Retrieved 30 June 2010. ABC News (abcnews.go.com/Health/Wellness/cdc-birth-rates-middle-aged-mothers-rise/story?id=10298740).

Hyman, Batya. 2000. "The Economic Consequences of Child Sexual Abuse for Adult Lesbian Women." *Journal of Marriage and the Family* 62: 199–211.

IIPS (International Institute for Population Sciences) and ORC Macro. 2000. *India: National Family Health Survey (NFHS-2) 1998–99*. Mumbai: IIPS.

Indiamarks.com. 2009. "The Culture of Arranged Marriages in India." Retrieved 28 May 2010 (www.indiamarks.com/guide/The-Culture-of-Arranged-Marriages-in-India/961/).

Ingraham, Chrys. 1999. *White Weddings: Romancing Heterosexuality in Popular Culture*. New York: Routledge.

Institute for American Values. 2000. "The Marriage Movement: A Statement of Principles, 2000." Retrieved 5 July 2005 (marriagemovement.org).

Institute for Family Policies. 2008. *Report on the Evolution of the Family in Europe*.

Institute for Women's Policy Research. 2010. *Fact Sheet: The Gender Wage Gap: 2009*. Technical Report No. IWPR #C350. Washington, DC.

Internal Revenue Service. 2009. "EITC Thresholds and Tax Law Updates." Retrieved 4 December 2009 (www.irs.gov/indivduals/article/0,id=150513,00.html).

—. 2010. *Publication 503: Child and Dependent Care Expenses*.

The International Foundation for Androgynous Studies. 2004. "Gender Traits Test." Retrieved 3 July 2007 (Androgyne.0catch.com/gentest1.htm).

International Humanist and Ethical Union. 2010. "The Dalit FAQ." Retrieved 15 June 2010 (www.iheu.org/dalitfaq).

Ishii-Kuntz, Masako. 2003. "Balancing Fatherhood and Work: Emergence of Diverse Masculinities in Contemporary

Japan." Pp. 198–216 in *Men and Masculinities in Contemporary Japan: Dislocating the Salaryman Doxa*, edited by James E. Roberson and Nobue Suzuki. New York: Routledge.

—. 2004a. "Asian American Families: Diverse History, Contemporary Trends, and the Future." Pp. 369–84 in *Handbook of Contemporary Families*, edited by Marilyn Coleman and Lawrence H. Ganong. Newbury Park, CA: Sage Publications.

—. 2004b. "Fathers' Involvement and School-Aged Children's Sociability: A Comparison Between Japan and the United States."*Japanese Journal of Family Sociology* 16(1): 83–93.

—. 2004c. "Men's Participation in Housework Among Dual-Earner Families." Pp. 201–14 in *Structure and Change in Contemporary Japanese Families: Quantitative Analyses of National Family Research*, edited by Hiroyuki Watanabe, Naoko Shimazaki, and Akihide Inaba. Tokyo: University of Tokyo Press.

—. 2006. "Child Caring Fathers in Japan and the U.S.A." *Annual Report of the Institute for International Studies* 9: 125–36.

Ishii-Kuntz, Masako, Katsuko Makino, Kuniko Kato, and Michiko Tsuchiya. 2004. "Japanese Fathers of Preschoolers and Their Involvement in Child Care." *Journal of Marriage and Family* 66 (August): 779–91.

Ivy, Diana K. and Phil Backlund. 2008. *Genderspeak: Personal Effectiveness in Gender Communication, 4th ed.* Boston: Pearson/Allyn & Bacon.

Jacobs, Julie N. and Michelle L. Kelley. 2006. "Predictors of Paternal Involvement in Childcare in Dual-Earner Families with Young Children." *Fathering* 4(1): 23–47.

Jansson, Bruce S. 2008. *The Reluctant Welfare State: A History of American Social Welfare Policies, 6th ed.* Belmont, CA: Brooks/Cole.

Jasinski, Jana L., Jennifer K. Wesely, James D. Wright, and Elizabeth E. Mustaine. 2010. *Hard Lives, Mean Streets: Violence in the Lives of Homeless Women*. Boston: Northeastern.

Jayson, Sharon. 2005. "Hyphenated Names Less-and-Less Used." *USA Today* (www.usatoday.com/life/2005-05-30-name-change_x.htm), 30 May.

Jekielek, Susan M. 1998. "Parental Conflict, Marital Disruption, and Children's Emotional Well-Being." *Social Forces* 76: 905–36.

Jessop, Carolyn and Laura Palmer. 2008. *Escape*. New York: Broadway.

—. 2010. *Triumph: Life After the Cult—A Survivor's Lessons*. New York: Broadway.

Joe, Jennie R., Shannon Sparks, and Lisa Tiger. 1999. "Changing American Indian Marriage Patterns: Some Examples from Contemporary Western Apaches." Pp. 5–21 in *Till Death Do Us Part: A Multicultural Anthology on Marriage*, edited by Sandra Lee Browning and R. Robin Miller. Greenwich, CT: JAI Press.

John, Robert. 1988. "The Native American Family." Pp. 325–66 in *Ethnic Families in America: Patterns and Variations, 3rd ed.*, edited by C. Mindel, R. Habenstein and R. Wright, Jr. New York: Elsevier.

Johnson, C.A. and S.M. Stanley, eds. 2001. *The Oklahoma Marriage Initiative Statewide Baseline Survey*. Available from the Bureau for Social Research, Oklahoma State University, 306 HES, Stillwater, OK 74078-6117.

Johnson, Christine A., Scott M. Stanley, Norval D. Glenn, Paul R. Amato, Steve L. Nock, Howard J. Markman, and M. Robin Dion. 2002. *Marriage in Oklahoma: 2001 Baseline Statewide Survey on Marriage and Divorce*. Bureau for Social Research. Stillwater, OK: Oklahoma State University.

Johnson, Dana. 2009. "Adopting an Institutionalized Child: What Are the Risks?" Retrieved 16 December 2009. Association for Research in International Adoption (www.adoption-research.org/risks.htm).

Johnson, Julia Overturf. 2005. *Who's Minding the Kids? Child Care Arrangements: Winter 2002*. Current Population Reports No. P70-101. Washington, DC: U.S. Census Bureau.

Johnson, Michael P. 2000. "Conflict and Control: Images of Symmetry and Asymmetry in Domestic Violence." In *Couples in Conflict*, edited by Alan Booth, Ann C. Crouter, and Mari Clements. Hillsdale, NJ: Erlbaum.

—. 2008. *A Typology of Domestic Violence: Intimate Terrorism, Violent Resistance, and Situational Couple Violence*. Boston: Northeastern University Press.

Johnson, Michael P. and Kathleen J. Ferraro. 2000. "Research on Domestic Violence in the 1990's: Making Distinctions." *Journal of Marriage and the Family* 62: 948–63.

Johnson, Michael P. and Janel M. Leone. 2005. "The Differential Effects of Intimate Terrorism and Situational Couple Violence." *Journal of Family Issues* 26(3): 322–49.

Joint United Nations Programme on HIV/AIDS and World Health Organization. 2009 November. *AIDS Epidemic Update*. Technical Report No. UNAIDS/09.36E/JC1700E.

Jolivet, Muriel. 1997. "The Ten Commandments of the Mother." Pp. 77–105 in *Japan: The Childless Society*, edited by M. Jolivet. London: Routledge.

Jones, Janine M. 2007. "Exposure to Chronic Community Violence: Resilience in African American Children." *Journal of Black Psychology* 33(2): 125–49.

Jones, Jo. 2008. *Adoption Experiences of Women and Men and Demand for Children to Adopt by Women 18–44 Years of Age in the United States, 2002*. Vital and Health Statistics No. Series 23, Number 27. Atlanta, GA: Centers for Disease Control and Prevention.

Jones, Rachel K., Lawrence B. Finer, and Susheela Singh. 2010. *Characteristics of U.S. Abortion Patients, 2008*. New York: Guttmacher Institute.

Joseph, Elizabeth. 1997. "Polygamy: The Ultimate Feminist Lifestyle." Retrieved 26 October 2008. Polygamy.com (www.polygamy.com/articles/templates/?a=10&z=3).

Joshi, Pamela and Karen Bogen. 2007. "Nonstandard Schedules and Young Children's Behavioral Outcomes

Among Working Low-Income Families." *Journal of Marriage and Family* 69 (February): 139–56.

Juby, Heather, Celine Le Bourdais, and Nicole Marcil-Gratton. 2005. "Sharing Roles, Sharing Custody? Couples' Characteristics and Children's Living Arrangements at Separation." *Journal of Marriage and Family* 67(1, February): 157–72.

Kageyama, Y. 1999. "A Tale of Two Drugs Irks Japan's Women." *The Oregonian*, 11 February, pp. A-6.

Kaiser Commission on Medicaid and the Uninsured. 2010. *The Uninsured and the Difference Health Insurance Makes*. Washington, DC: The Henry J. Kaiser Family Foundation.

Kaiser Family Foundation and Health Research & Educational Trust. 2010. *Employer Health Benefits: 2010 Summary of Findings*.

Kaiser Family Foundation. 2001. "Inside-OUT: A Report of the Experiences of Lesbians, Gays, and Bisexuals in America and the Public's Views on Issues and Policies Related to Sexual Orientation." Retrieved October 27, 2002 (www.kff.org/content/2001/3193/LGBChartpack.pdf).

—. 2009. *The Uninsured: A Primer: Key Facts About Americans Without Health Insurance*. Washington, DC: Kaiser Commission on Medicaid and the Uninsured.

—. 2010. April 5. *Summary of Coverage Provisions in the Patient Protection and Affordable Care Act and the Health Care and Education Reconciliation Act of 2010*.

Kakuchi, Suvendrini. 2003. "Women: Foreign Spouses in Japan Seek Easier Child Custody Laws." *International Divorce Law Office: Japanese Divorce and Custody Laws*. Retrieved 8 May 2003 (http://dwp.bigplanet.com/leidyb/japanesedivorceand custodylaw/).

Kaleidoscope. 2003. "Latinos/Hispanics." Retrieved 30 June 2008 (cnnc.uncg.edu/pdfs/latinoshispanics.pdf).

Kalil, Ariel and Kathleen M. Ziol-Guest. 2008. "Parental Employment Circumstances and Children's Academic Progress." *Social Science Research* 37(2): 500–15.

Kallen, Craig G. 2008. "How to Save On the Cost of A Divorce." *Woman's Divorce*. Retrieved 23 December 2008 (www.womansdivorce.com/cost-of-a-divorce.html).

Kamerman, Sheila. 2003. "Welfare States, Family Policies, and Early Childhood Education, Care and Family Support." In *Consultation Meeting on Family Support Policy in Central and Eastern Europe*. Budapest, Hungary: UNESCO and the Council of Europe, 3–5 September.

Kamerman, Sheila and Shirley Gatenio. 2002. "Tax Day: How Do America's Child Benefits Compare?" In *Issue Brief*. Retrieved 15 July 2002. Columbia University/The Clearinghouse on International Developments in Child, Youth, & Family Policies (www.childpolicyintl.org/issuebrief/issuebrief4.htm).

Kamo, Yoshinori and Ellen E. Cohen. 1998. "Division of Household Work Between Partners: A Comparison of Black & White Couples." *Journal of Comparative Family Studies* 29(1): 131.

Kane, Emily W. 2006. " 'No Way My Boys Are Going to Be Like That!' " *Gender & Society* 20(2): 149–76.

Kapinus, Carolyn A. and Daniel R. Flowers. 2008. "An Examination of Gender Differences in Attitudes Toward Divorce." *Journal of Divorce and Remarriage* 49(3/4): 239–57.

Karger, Howard and David Stoesz. 2010. *American Social Welfare Policy, 6th ed.* Boston: Pearson.

Karraker, Meg Wilkes. 2008. *Global Families: Volume II in the "Families in the 21st Century" Series*. Boston: Allyn & Bacon.

Kaschak, Ellyn. 2002. *Intimate Betrayal: Domestic Violence in Lesbian Relationships*. New York: Routledge.

Kashiwase, Haruna. 2002. "Shotgun Weddings a Sign of the Times in Japan." Retrieved 21 April 2003. Population Today, Population Reference Bureau. Available online (www.prb.org).

Kaufman, Gayle and Hiromi Taniguchi. 2006. "Gender and Marital Happiness in Later LIfe." *Journal of Family Issues* 27: 737–57.

Kaufman, Joan and Edward Zigler. 1987. "Do Abused Children Become Abusive Parents?" *Journal of Orthopsychiatry* 57: 186–92.

Keen, Cathy. 2005. "UF Study: Women Increasingly Pick Husbands' Surnames Over Their Own." Retrieved 10 July 2007. University of Florida News (news.ufl.edu/2005/11/16/married-names/).

Keenan, Nancy. 2008. *Speech at NARAL's San Francisco Power of Choice Luncheon*. San Francisco, CA, 6 March.

Kelleher, Ann and Laura Klein. 2011. *Global Perspectives, 4th ed.* New York: Longman.

Kellough, J. Edward. 2006. *Understanding Affirmative Action: Politics, Discrimination, and the Search for Justice*. Washington, DC: Georgetown University Press.

Kelly, Erin L., Samantha K. Ammons, Kelly Chermack, and Phyllis Moen. 2010. "Gendered Challenge, Gendered Response." *Gender & Society* 24(3): 281–303.

Kelly, Joan B. 2007. "Children's Living Arrangements Following Separation and Divorce: Insights from Empirical and Clinical Research." *Family Process* 46(1): 35–52.

Kelly, Maura. 2009. "Women's Voluntary Childlessness: A Radical Rejection of Motherhood?" *WSQ: Women's Studies Quarterly* 37(3–4, Fall/Winter): 157–72.

Kelly, Melissa. 2008. "Active Listening: Steps and Instructions." Retrieved 28 September 2008. About.com (712educators.about.com/cs/activelistening/a/activelistening_2.htm).

Kendall, Diana. 2002. *The Power of Good Deeds: Privileged Women & the Social Reproduction of the Upper Class*. Lanham, MD: Rowman and Littlefield Publishers.

Kendig, Sarah M. and Suzanne M. Bianchi. 2008. "Single, Cohabitating, and Married Mothers' Time with Children." *Journal of Marriage and Family* 70(5, December): 1228–40.

Kennedy, Tracy L. M., Aaron Smith, Amy Tracy Wells, and Barry Wellman. 2008. *Networked Families*. Washington, DC: Pew Internet & American Life Project.

Kenney-Benson, Gwen A., Eva M. Pomerantz, Allison M. Ryan, and Helen Patrick. 2006. "Sex Differences in Math Performance: The Role of Children's Approach to Schoolwork." *Developmental Psychology* 42(1, January): 11–26.

Kerchoff, A. C. and K. E. Davis. 1962. "Value Consensus and Need Complementarity in Mate Selection." *American Sociological Review* 27: 295–303.

Khobotlo, Motlalepula, Relebohile Tshehlo, John Nkonyana, Mahlape Ramoseme, Mokete Khobotle, Abhimanyu Chitoshia, Mikaela Hildebrand, and Nicole Fraser. 2009. *Lesotho: HIV Prevention Response and Modes of Transmission Analysis*. Maseru: Lesotho National AIDS Commission.

Kibria, Nazli. 1993. *The Family Tightrope: The Changing Lives of Vietnamese Americans*. Princeton, NJ: Princeton University Press.

—. 1997. "The Construction of 'Asian American': Reflections on Intermarriage and Ethnic Identity Among Second-Generation Chinese and Korean Americans." *Ethnic and Racial Studies* 20: 523–44.

Kiecolt, K. Jill. 2003. "Satisfaction with Work and Family Life: No Evidence of a Cultural Reversal." *Journal of Marriage and Family* 65: 23–35.

Kim, Jinseok and Karen A. Gray. 2008. "Leave or Stay?: Battered Women's Decision After Intimate Partner Violence." *Journal of Interpersonal Violence* 23(10): 1465–82.

Kim, Mikyoung, Kyoung-Nan Kwon, and Mira Lee. 2009. "Psychological Characteristics of Internet Dating Service Users: The Effect of Self-Esteem, Involvement, and Sociability on the Use of Internet Dating Services." *Cyberpsychology & Behavior* 12(4, August): 445–49.

Kimura, Doreen. 2002. "Sex Differences in the Brain." *Scientific American.Com*, 15 May. Retrieved 23 June 2006 (www.sciam.com/print_version.cfm?articleID=00018E9D-879D-1D06-8E49809EC5).

Kindlon, Dan and Michael Thompson. 2000. *Raising Cain: Protecting the Emotional Life of Boys*. New York: Ballantine Books.

King, Valarie. 2003. "The Legacy of a Grandparent's Divorce: Consequences for Ties Between Grandparents and Grandchildren." *Journal of Marriage and Family* 65: 170–83.

King, Valarie, Kathleen Mullan Harris, and Holly E. Heard. 2004. "Racial and Ethnic Diversity in Nonresident Father Involvement." *Journal of Marriage and Family* 66: 1–21.

King, Valarie and Mindy E. Scott. 2005. "A Comparison of Cohabiting Relationships Among Older and Younger Adults." *Journal of Marriage and Family* 67 (May): 271–85.

Kinsella, Kevin and Wan He. 2009. *An Aging World: 2008*. U.S. Census Bureau, International Population Reports No. P95/09-1. Washington, DC: U.S. Government Printing Office.

Kinsella, Kevin and David R. Phillips. 2005. *Global Aging: The Challenge of Success*. Population Bulletin No. Vol. 60, No. 1. Washington, DC: Population Reference Bureau.

Kinsella, Kevin and Victoria A. Velkoff. 2001. *An Aging World: 2001*. U.S. Census Bureau No. P95-011. Washington, DC: U.S. Government Printing Office.

Kinsey, Alfred, Wardell B. Pomeroy, and Clyde E. Martin. 1953. *Sexual Behavior in the Human Female*. Philadelphia, PA: Saunders.

Kishor, Sunita. 2005. "Domestic Violence Measurement in Demographic and Health Surveys: The History and the Challenges." UN Division for the Advancement of Women in collaboration with the Economic Commission for Europe and the World Health Organization (www.un.org/womenwatch/daw/egm/vaw-stat-2005/docs/expert-papers/Kishor.pdf).

Kloss, Heinz. 1998. *The American Bilingual Tradition (Language in Education)*. Washington, DC: Center for Applied Linguistics.

Kneip, Thorsten and Gerrit Bauer. 2009. "Did Unilateral Divorce Laws Raise Divorce Rates in Western Europe?" *Journal of Marriage and Family* 71(3): 592–607.

Knobloch-Fedders, Lynne M. and Roger M. Knudson. 2009. "Marital Ideals of the Newly-Married: A Longitudinal Analysis." *Journal of Social and Personal Relationships* 26(2–3): 249–71.

Knodel, John, Vu Manh Loi, Rukmalie Jayakody, and Vu Tuan Huy. 2004. *Gender Roles in the Family: Change and Stability in Vietnam*. PSC Research Report 04-559. Ann Arbor, MI: Population Studies Center at the Institute for Social Research, University of Michigan.

Knoester, Chris and David J. Eggebeen. 2006. "The Effects of the Transition to Parenthood and Subsequent Children on Men's Well-Being and Social Participation." *Journal of Family Issues* 27: 1532–60.

Koball, Heather and Desiree Principe. 2002. *Do Nonresident Fathers Who Pay Child Support Visit Their Children More?* New Federalism: National Survey of America's Families No. Series B, No. B-44. The Urban Institute.

Koerner, Ascan F. and Mary Anne Fitzpatrick. 2002. "Nonverbal Communication and Marital Adjustment and Satisfaction: The Role of Decoding Relationship Relevant and Relationship Irrelevant Affect." *Communication Monographs* 69: 33–51.

Kohn, Melvin L., Atsushi Naoi, Carrie Schoenbach, Carmi Schooler, and Kazimierz M. Slomczynski. 1990. "Position in the Class Structure and Psychological Functioning in the United States, Japan, and Poland." *American Journal of Sociology* 95(4): 864–1008.

Kohn, Melvin L. 1977. *Class and Conformity: A Study in Values, 2nd ed.* Chicago: University of Chicago Press.

—. 2006. *Change and Stability: A Cross-National Analysis of Social Structure and Personality*. Boulder, CO: Paradigm Publishers.

Kontula, Osmo and Elina Haavio-Mannila. 2009. "The Impact of Aging on Human Sexual Activity and Sexual Desire." *Journal of Sex Research* 46(1, January): 46–56.

Korn, Peter. 2010. "Natural Birth? Nope, C-Section Rates on Rise." Retrieved 2 March 2010 (www.portlandtribune.com/news/story.php?story_id=126644252863826200).

Kornbluh, Karen, Katelin Isaacs, and Shelley Waters Boots. 2004. *Workplace Flexibility: A Policy Problem*. Work & Family Program: Issue Brief #1. Washington, DC: New America Foundation.

Koropeckyj-Cox, Tanya. 2002. "Beyond Parental Status: Psychological Well-Being in Middle & Old Age." *Journal of Marriage and Family* 64: 957–71.

Koropeckyj-Cox, Tanya and Gretchen Pendell. 2007a. "Attitudes About Childlessness in the United States." *Journal of Family Issues* 28(8): 1054–82.

—. 2007b. "The Gender Gap in Attitudes About Childlessness in the United States." *Journal of Marriage and Family* 69(4): 899–915.

Koropeckyj-Cox, Tanya, Amy Mehraban Pienta, and Tyson H. Brown. 2007. "Women of the 1950s and the "Normative" Life Course: The Implications of Childlessness, Fertility Timing, and Marital Status for Psychosocial Well-Being in Late Midlife." *International Journal of Aging and Human Development* 64: 299–330.

Koss, Mary P. and Sarah L. Cook. 1993. "Facing the Facts: Date and Acquaintance Rape Are Significant Problems for Women." In *Current Controversies in Family Violence*, edited by Richard J. Gelles and Donileen R. Loseke. Newbury Park, CA: Sage Publications.

Koss, Mary P., Christine Gidyzc, and Nadine Wisniewski. 1987. "The Scope of Rape: Incidence and Prevalence in a National Sample of Higher Education Students." *Journal of Consulting and Clinical Psychology* 55: 162–70.

Kraditor, Aileen S. 1965. *The Ideas of the Woman Suffrage Movement: 1890–1920*. Garden City: Anchor Books.

Kramer, Laura. 2007. *The Sociology of Gender: A Brief Introduction, 2nd ed*. New York: Oxford University Press.

Kreider, Rose M. 2008. *Living Arrangements of Children: 2004*. Technical Report No. P70-114. Washington, DC: U.S. Census Bureau.

Kreider, Rose M. and Diana B. Elliott. 2009. "America's Families and Living Arrangements: 2007." In *Current Population Reports, P20-561*. U.S. Census Bureau, September. Washington, DC.

Kristof, Nicholas D. and Sheryl WuDunn. 2009. *Half the Sky: Turning Oppression into Opportunity for Women World-wide*. New York: Knopf.

Kroska, Amy. 2003. "Investigating Gender Differences in the Meaning of Household Chores and Child Care." *Journal of Marriage and Family* 65: 456–73.

Kubler-Ross, Elisabeth. 1969. *On Death and Dying*. New York: Macmillan.

Kulikoff, Allan. 2000. *From British Peasants to Colonial American Farmers*. Chapel Hill, NC: University of North Carolina Press.

Kurchinka, Mary Sheedy. 1998. *Raising Your Spirited Child*. New York: Harper Perennial.

Kurdek, Lawrence A. 1999. "The Nature and Predictions of the Trajectory of Change and Marital Quality for Husbands and Wives Over the First 10 Years of Marriage." *Developmental Psychology* 35: 1283–96.

—. 2003. "Differences Between Gay and Lesbian Cohabiting Couples." *Journal of Social Personal Relationships* 20: 411–36.

—. 2004. "Are Gay and Lesbian Cohabiting Couples Really Different from Heterosexual Married Couples?" *Journal of Marriage and the Family* 6(4): 880–900.

—. 2005. "What Do We Know About Gay and Lesbian Couples?" *Current Directions in Psychological Science* 14(5): 251–54.

—. 2006. "Differences Between Partners from Heterosexual, Gay, and Lesbian Cohabiting Couples." *Journal of Marriage and the Family* 68(2): 509–28.

—. 2007. "Avoidance Motivation and Relationship Commitment in Heterosexual, Gay Male, and Lesbian Partners." *Personal Relationships* 13: 521–35.

—. 2008. "A General Model of Relationship Commitment: Evidence from Same-Sex Partners." *Personal Relationships* 15: 391–405.

—. 2009. "Assessing the Health of a Dyadic Relationship in Heterosexual and Same-Sex Partners." *Personal Relationships* 16: 117–27.

La Leche League International. 2010. *The Womanly Art of Breastfeeding*. New York: Ballantine Books.

Labov, William. 1966. *The Social Stratification of English in New York City*. Washington, DC: Center for Applied Linguistics.

—. 1972. *Language in the Inner City*. Philadelphia: University of Pennsylvania Press.

Ladner, Joyce A. 1998. *The Ties That Bind: Timeless Values for African American Families*. New York: John Wiley.

LaFraniere, Sharon. 2009. "Chinese Bias for Baby Boys Creates a Gap of 32 Million." *New York Times*, 11 April. Retrieved 23 May 2010. NYTimes.com (www.nytimes.com/2009/04/ 11/world/asia/11china.html?r=1&page wanted=print).

Lamanna, Mary Ann and Agnes Riedmann. 1997. *Marriages and Families: Making Choices in a Diverse Society*, 6th ed. Belmont, CA: Wadsworth.

Lamb, Kathleen A. 2007. "'I Want to Be Just Like Their Real Dad.' " *Journal of Family Issues* 28(9): 1162–88.

Lamont, Michele. 2003. "Who Counts as 'Them?': Racism and Virtue in the United States and France." *Contexts* 2(4): 36–41.

Landale, Nancy S. 2002. "Contemporary Cohabitation: Food For Thought." Pp. 33–40 in *Just Living Together*, edited by Alan Booth and Ann Crouter. Mahwah, NJ: Lawrence Erlbaum.

Landsburg, Steven E. 2003. "Oh, No: It's a Girl! Do Girls Cause Divorce?" *Slate*, 2 October. Retrieved 2 October 2003.

Lane, Shelley D. 2010. *Interpersonal Communication: Competence and Contexts*. Boston: Allyn & Bacon.

Langer, Gary, Cheryl Arnedt, and Dalia Sussman. 2004. "Primetime Live Poll: American Sex Survey." Retrieved 9 June 2007 (abcnews.go.com/print?id=156921).

LaPierre, Tracey A. 2009. "Marital Status and Depressive Symptoms Over Time: Age and Gender Variations." *Family Relations* 58(4, October): 404–16.

Lareau, Annette. 2003. *Unequal Childhoods: Class, Race, and Family Life*. Berkeley, CA: University of California Press.

Lareau, Annette and Dalton Conley, eds. 2008. *Social Class: How Does It Work?* New York: Sage Publications.

LaRossa, Ralph. 1997. *The Modernization of Fatherhood: A Social and Political History*. Chicago: University of Chicago Press.

LaRossa, Ralph, Charles Jaret, Malati Gadgil, and G. Robert Wynn. 2000. "The Changing Culture of Fatherhood in Comic-Strip Families: A Six-Decade Aanalysis." *Journal of Marriage and the Family* 62: 375–87.

Laughlin, Lynda and Joseph Rukus. 2009. "Who's Minding the Kids in the Summer? Child Care Arrangements for Summer 2006." Presentation. Presented at the Annual Meeting of the Population Association of America, April 30–May 2, 2009, Detroit, MI.

Lavee, Yoav and Ruth Katz. 2002. "Division of Labor, Perceived Fairness, and Marital Quality: The Effect of Gender Ideology." *Journal of Marriage and Family* 64: 27–39.

Le Mare, Lucy, Karyn Audet, and Karen Kurytnik. 2007. "A Longitudinal Study of Service Use in Families of Children Adopted from Romanian Orphanages." *International Journal of Behavioral Development* 31: 242–51.

Leaper, Campbell and Carly K. Friedman. 2006. "The Socialization of Gender." Pp. 561–87 in *The Handbook of Socialization: Theory and Research*, edited by John E. Grusec and Paul D. Hastings. New York: Guilford Press.

Lee, Gary R., Marion C. Willets, and Karen Seccombe. 1998. "Widowhood and Depression: Gender Differences." *Research on Aging* 20: 611–30.

Lee, Gary R. and Alfred DeMaris. 2007. "Widowhood, Gender, and Depression." *Research on Aging* 29(1): 56–72.

Lee, John A. 1973. *The Colors of Love: An Exploration of the Ways of Loving*. Don Mills, Ontario: New Press.

—. 1974. "The Styles of Loving." *Psychology Today* (October): 46–51.

—. 1988. "Love-Styles." Pp. 38–67 in *The Psychology of Love*, edited by Robert J. Sternberg and Michael L. Barnes. New Haven, CT: Yale University Press.

Lee, Jennifer and Min Zhou. 2004. *Asian American Youth: Culture, Identity and Ethnicity*. New York: Routledge.

Lee, Kristin Schultz, Paula A. Tufis, and Duane F. Alwin. 2010. Separate Spheres or Increasing Equality? Changing Gender Beliefs in Postwar Japan. *Journal of Marriage and Family* 72(1 February): 184-201.

Lee, Sharon M. Edmonston, Barry. 2005. *New Marriages, New Families: U.S. Racial and Hispanic Intermarriage Population Bulletin*, vol. 60, no. 2. Washington, DC: Population Reference Bureau.

Lee, Yun-Suk and Linda J. Waite. 2005. "Husbands' and Wives' Time Spent on Housework: A Comparison of Measures." *Journal of Marriage and Family* 67(May): 328–36.

Leeder, Elaine. 2004. *The Family in Global Perspective: A Gendered Journey*. Thousand Oaks, CA: Sage Publications, Inc.

Lenski, Gerhard. 1984. *Power & Privilege: A Theory of Social Stratification*. Chapel Hill: University of North Carolina Press.

Leonard, Lori. 2000. "Interpreting Female Genital Cutting: Moving Beyond the Impasse." *Annual Review of Sex Research* 11: 158–91.

Leonhardt, David. 2007. "He's Happier, She's Less So." In *Nytimes.Com. New York Times*, 26 September. Retrieved 27 September 2007 (www.nytimes.com/2007/09/26/business/26leonhardt.html).

Lerman, Robert I. 2002. "Married and Unmarried Parenthood and Economic Well-Being: A Dynamic Analysis of a Recent Cohort." Retrieved 27 June 2005 (www.urban.org/exoert.cfm?ID=RobertLerman).

Leserman, Jane and Douglas A. Drossman. 2007. "Relationship of Abuse History to Functional Gastrointestinal Disorders and Symptoms." *Trauma, Violence, & Abuse* 8(3): 331–43.

Levin, Diane E. and Jean Kilbourne. 2008. *So Sexy So Soon: The New Sexualized Childhood and What Parents Can Do to Protect Their Kids*. New York: Ballantine Books.

Levine, Judith A., Clifton R. Emery, and Harold A. Pollack. 2007. "The Well-Being of Children Born to Teen Mothers." *Journal of Marriage and the Family* 69(1): 105–22.

LeVine, Robert A. 1977. "Child Rearing as a Cultural Adaptation." In *Culture and Infancy*, edited by P. Leiderman, S. Tulken, and A. Rosenfeld. New York: Academic Press.

—. 1988. "Human Parental Care: Universal Goals, Cultural Strategies, Individual Behavior." In *Parental Behavior in Diverse Societies*, edited by R. LeVine, P. Miller, and M. West. San Francisco: Jossey-Bass.

Lewin, Tamar. 2005. "3 New Studies Assess Effects of Child Care." Retrieved 5 January 2010. NYTimes.com (www.nytimes.com/2005/11/01/national/01child.html?_r=1&pagewanted=print).

Lewis, Oscar. 1966. "The Culture of Poverty." *Scientific American*, pp. 19–25.

Lewontin, Richard C. 2006. "Confusion About Human Races" (Web Forum Organized by the Social Science Research Council). Retrieved 18 August 2008 (Raceandgenomics.ssrc.org/Lewontin/printable.html).

Lin, I-Fen, Nora Cate Schaeffer, Judith A. Seltzer, and Kay L. Tuschen. 2004. "Divorced Parents' Qualitative and Quantitative Reports of Children's Living Arrangements." *Journal of Marriage and Family* 66 (May): 385–97.

Lin, I-Fen, Noreen Goldman, Maxine Weinstein, Yu-Hsuan Lin, Tristan Gorrindo, and Teresa Seeman. 2003. "Gender Differences in Adult Children's Provision of Support to Their Elderly Parents in Taiwan." *Journal of Marriage and the Family* 65(1): 184–200.

Lindau, Stacy T., L. Philip Schumm, Edward O. Laumann, Wendy Levinson, Colm A. O'Muircheartaigh, and Linda J. Waite. 2007. "A Study of Sexuality and Health Among Older Adults in the United States." *New England Journal of Medicine* 357 (23 August): 762–74.

Linden, Michael. 2009. "Turning Point: The Long Term Effects of Recession-Induced Child Poverty." Retrieved 21 January 2010. First Focus Campaign for Children (www.firstfocus.net/Download/TurningPoint.pdf).

Lindsey, Eric W., Jessica Campbell Chambers, James M. Frabutt, and Carol Mackinnon-Lewis. 2009. "Marital Conflict and Adolescents' and Aggression: The Mediating and Moderating Role of Mother-Child Emotional Reciprocity." *Family Relations* 58(5, December): 593–606.

Lindsey, Linda. 2011. *Gender Roles: A Sociological Perspective, 5th ed.* Upper Saddle River, NJ: Prentice Hall.

Lino, Mark. 2010. *Expenditures on Children by Families, 2009.* U.S. Department of Agriculture, Center for Nutrition Policy & Promotion, Miscellaneous Publication No. 1528-2009.

Lino, Mark and Andrea Carlson. 2009. *Expenditures on Children in Families, 2008.* Washington, DC: U.S. Department of Agriculture, Center for Nutrition Policy & Promotion, Publication No. 1528-2008.

Livingston, Gretchen, Susan Minushkin, and D'Vera Cohn. 2008. "Hispanics and Health Care in the United States: Access, Information and Knowledge." In *Pew Hispanic Center.* Retrieved 22 August 2008. Washington, DC (pewhispanic.org/reports/report.php?ReportID=91).

Lloyd, Sally A., April L. Few, and Katherine R Allen. 2009. *Handbook of Feminist Family Studies.* Thousand Oaks, CA: Sage Publications.

Lobe, Jim. 2003. "Bush Charged with Leading 'Secret War' Against Reproductive Freedom." Retrieved 20 December 2003. Common Dreams Newscenter (www.commondreams.org/headlines03/0123-02.htm).

Lobo, Susan, Steve Talbot, and Traci L. Morris. 2010. *Native American Voices, 3rd ed.* Upper Saddle River, NJ: Prentice Hall.

Loeb, Susanna, Margaret Bridges, Daphna Bassok, Bruce Fuller, and Russell W. Rumberger. 2007. "How Much Is Too Much? The Influence of Preschool Centers on Children's Social and Cognitive Development." *Economics of Education Review* 26(1, February): 52–66.

Logan, T. K. and Robert Walker. 2009. "Partner Stalking." *Trauma, Violence, & Abuse* 10(3): 247–70.

Lopez, Mark Hugo and Susan Minushkin. 2008. *2008 National Survey of Latinos: Hispanics See Their Situation in U.S. Deteriorating: Oppose Key Immigration Enforcement Measures.* Washington, DC: Pew Hispanic Center.

Lovell, Philip and Julia B. Isaacs. 2010. *Families of the Recession: Unemployed Parents & Their Children.* Washington, DC: First Focus Campaign for Children.

Lowenstein, Ludwig F. 2005. "Causes and Associated Features of Divorce as Seen by Recent Research." *Journal of Divorce and Remarriage* 42(3/4): 153–71 (DOI: 10.1300/J087vol42n03_09).

Ludwig, Jens and Susan Mayer. 2006. "Culture and the Intergenerational Transmission of Poverty: The Prevention Paradox." *The Future of Children* 16: 176–96.

Luft, Joe. 1969. "Of Human Interaction." In *Palo Alto.* Retrieved 30 June 2008. Cited by Tim Borchers, 1999, *Self-Disclosure.* Allyn & Bacon (www.abacon.com/commstudies/interpersonal/indisclosure.html).

Luft, Joe and Harry Ingram. 1955. *The Johari Window, a Graphic Model of Interpersonal Awareness.* Proceedings of the western training laboratory in group development. Los Angeles: UCLA.

Lundberg, Shelly, Sara McLanahan, and Elaina Rose. 2007. "Child Gender and Father Involvement in Fragile Families." *Demography* 44(1): 79–92.

Lung and Asthma Information Agency. 2000/3. "Asthma and Social Class." Retrieved 28 August 2003. London/Public Health Sciences Dept., St. George's Hospital Medical School (www.sghms.ac.uk/depts/laia/laia.htm).

Luo, Michael. 2009. "Job Woes Exacting a Toll on Family Life." *The New York Times,* 12 November. Retrieved 30 December 2009. NYTimes.com (www.nytimes.com/2009/11/12/us/12families.html?_r=1&pagewanted=print).

Lustig, Myron W. and Jolene Koester. 2010. *Intercultural Competence: Interpersonal Communication Across Culture, 6th ed.* Boston: Allyn & Bacon.

Lyster, Mimi E. 2007. *Building a Parental Agreement That Works.* Berkeley, CA: Nolo Publishers.

Maas, Carl, Todd I. Herrenkohl, and Cynthia Sousa. 2008. "Review of Research on Child Maltreatment and Violence in Youth." *Trauma, Violence, & Abuse* 9(1): 56–67.

Maccoby, Eleanor E. 1998. *The Two Sexes: Growing up Apart, Coming Together.* Cambridge, MA: Harvard University Press.

Maccoby, Eleanor E. and Carol. N. Jacklin. 1974. *The Psychology of Sex Differences.* Stanford, CA: Stanford University Press.

Mackie, Gerry. 2000. "Female Genital Cutting: The Beginning of the End." Pp. 253–82 in *Female "Circumcision" in Africa: Culture, Controversy, and Change,* edited by B. Shell-Duncan and Y. Hernlund. Boulder, CO: Lynne Reinner.

Mackie, Vera, ed. 2010. *Gender in Japan: Power and Public Policy.* New York: Routledge.

MacPhee, David, Janet Fritz, and Janet Miller-Heyl. 1996. "Ethnic Variations in Personal Social Networks and Parenting." *Child Development* 67: 3278–95.

Madden, Mary and Amanda Lenhart. 2006. *Online Dating: Americans Who Are Seeking Romance Use the Internet to Help Them in Their Search, but There is Still Widespread Public Concern About the Safety of Online Dating.* Washington, DC: Pew Internet & American Life Project.

Madden, Mary and Lee Rainie. 2006. *Not Looking for Love: The State of Romance in America.* Pew Internet & American Life Project.

Magnuson, Katherine and Lawrence M. Berger. 2009. "Family Structure States and Transitions: Associations with Children's Well-Being During Middle Childhood." *Journal of Marriage and Family* 71(3, August): 575–91.

Maher, Bridget E. 2006. "Why Marriage Should Be Privileged in Public Policy." Retrieved 6 June 2006. Family Research Council (www.frc.org/index.cfm?i=IS03D1).

Mallinson, Christine and Robin Dodsworth. 2009. "Revisiting the Need for New Approaches to Social Class in Variationist Sociolinguistics." *Sociolinguistic Studies* 3(2): 253–78.

Mammen, Kristin. 2009. "Fathers' Time Investments in Children: Do Sons Get More?" *Journal of Population Economics*, 10.1007/s00148-009-0272-5.

Manganello, Jennifer A. 2008. "Teens, Dating Violence, and Media Use." *Trauma, Violence, & Abuse* 9(1): 3–18.

Manning, Wendy D. and Susan Brown. 2006. "Children's Economic Well-Being in Married and Cohabiting Parent Families." *Journal of Marriage and Family* 68(2): 345–62.

Manning, Wendy D., Monica A. Longmore, and Peggy C. Giordano. 2007. "The Changing Institution of Marriage: Adolescents' Expectations to Cohabit and to Marry." *Journal of Marriage and Family* 69(3, August): 559–75.

Manpower Inc. 2009. "About Manpower." Retrieved 4 August 2009 (www.manpower.com/about/about.cfm).

Manzoli, Lamberto, Paolo Villari, Giovanni M. Pirone, and Antonio Boccia. 2007. "Marital Status and Mortality in the Elderly: A Systematic Review and Meta-Analysis." *Social Science and Medicine* 64: 77–94.

March of Dimes. 2006. "C-Section: Medical Reasons." Retrieved 15 June 2006 (www.marchofdimes.com/pnhec/240_1031.asp).

Marindin, Hope. 1987. *The Handbook for Single Adoptive Parents*. Chevy Chase, MD: National Council for Single Adoptive Parents.

Markey, Charlotte N. and Patrick M. Markey. 2009. "Correlates of Young Women's Interest in Obtaining Cosmetic Surgery." *Sex Roles* 61(3–4, August): 158–66.

Marks, Jaime L., Chun Bun Lam, and Susan M. McHale. 2009. "Family Patterns of Gender Role Attitudes." *Sex Roles* 61(3–4, August): 221–34.

Marland, Hillary and Anne Marie Rafferty. 2005. *Midwives, Society, and Childbirth*. Oxford, England: Taylor and Francis Publishers.

The Marriage Movement. 2004. "Can Government Strengthen Marriage? Evidence from the Social Sciences." Retrieved 5 July 2005. National Fatherhood Initiative, Institute for Marriage and Public Policy, and Institute for American Values (www.marriagemovement.org/gov/gov_print.htm).

Marsiglio, William and Joseph H. Pleck. 2005. "Fatherhood and Masculinities." Pp. 249–69 in *The Handbook of Studies on Men and Masculinities*, edited by Michael S. Kimmel, Robert W. Connell, and Jeff Hearn. Thousand Oaks, CA: Sage Publications.

Marsiglio, William, Kevin Roy, and Greer Litton Fox, eds. 2005. *Situated Fathering: A Focus on Physical and Social Spaces*. Lanham, MD: Rowman and Littlefield Publishers.

Martin, Carol Lynn and Richard A. Fabes. 2001. "The Stability and Consequences of Same-Sex Peer Interactions." *Developmental Psychology* 37: 431–46.

Martin, Joyce A., Brady E. Hamilton, Paul D. Sutton, Stephanie J. Ventura, Fay Menacker, and Martha L. Munson. 2005. *Births: Final Data for 2003*. Technical Report No. 54 (2). Centers for Disease Control and Prevention.

Martin, Steven P. and Sangeeta Parashar. 2006. "Women's Changing Attitudes Toward Divorce, 1974–2002: Evidence for an Educational Crossover." *Journal of Marriage and Family* 68(1, February): 29.

Marx, Karl and Friedrich Engels. 1971, original 1867. *Manifesto of the Communist Party*. New York: International Publishers (Original work published 1867).

Massey, Douglas S. and Garvey Lundy. 2001. "Use of Black English and Racial Discrimination in Housing Markets." *Urban Affairs Review* 36(4): 452–69.

Mather, Mark. 2010. *Data Brief: U.S. Children in Single-Mother Families*. Population Reference Bureau.

Mathews, T. J. and Brady E. Hamilton. 2009. *Delayed Childbearing: More Women Are Having Their First Child Later in Life*. Technical Report No. NCHS Data Brief, no. 21. Hyattsville, MD: National Center for Health Statistics.

Max, Wendy, Dorothy P. Rice, Eric Finkelstein, Robert A. Bardwell, and Steven Leadbetter. 2004. "The Economic Toll of Intimate Partner Violence Against Women in the United States." *Violence and Victims* 19(3): 259–72.

Mays, Vickie M., Susan D. Cochran, and Namdi W. Barnes. 2007. "Race, Race-Based Discrimination, and Health Outcomes Among African Americans." *Annual Review of Psychology* 58: 24.1–24.25.

McCool, William F. and Sara A. Simeone. 2002. "Birth in the United States: An Overview of Trends Past and Present." *Nursing Clinics of North America* 37(4, December): 735–46.

McCubbin, Hamilton I., Marilyn A. McCubbin, Anne I. Thompson, Sae-Young Han, and Chad T. Allen. 1997. "Families Under Stress: What Makes Them Resilient." Commemorative Lecture. Washington, DC: AAFCS, 22 June.

McDonald, Steve, Nan Lin, and Dan Ao. 2009. "Networks of Opportunity: Gender, Race, and Job Leads." *Social Problems* 56(3, August): 385–402.

McDowell Group. 2003. "Areas of Expertise." Retrieved 19 March 2006 (www.mcdowellgroup.net/pages/areaexpert/aknative.html).

McElvaine, Robert S. 1993. *The Great Depression: America, 1929–1941*. New York: Times Books.

McLanahan, Sara. 1983. "Family Structure and Stress: A Longitudinal Comparison of Two-Parent and Female-Headed Families." *Journal of Marriage and the Family* 45: 347–57.

McLanahan, Sara and Gary Sandefur. 1994. *Growing up with a Single Parent: What Hurts, What Helps*. Cambridge, MA: Harvard University Press.

McLoyd, Vonnie C. 1990. "The Impact of Economic Hardship on Black Families and Children: Psychological Distress,

Parenting, and Socioemotional Development." *Child Development* 61: 311–46.

McLoyd, Vonnie C., Ana Mari Cauce, David Takeuchi, and Leon Wilson. 2000. "Marital Processes and Parental Socialization in Families of Color: A Decade Review of Research." *Journal of Marriage and the Family* 62(4, November): 1070–93.

Mead, Margaret. 1935. *Sex and Temperament in Three Primitive Societies*. New York: Morrow.

—. 1949. *Male and Female: A Study of the Sexes in a Changing World*. New York: Morrow.

Mead, Sara. 2006. "Evidence Suggests Otherwise: The Truth About Boys and Girls." Retrieved 17 June 2010. Education Sector (www.educationsector.org/research/research_ show.htm?doc_id=378705).

Media Awareness Network. 2008. "Video Games—Gender Stereotyping." Retrieved 22 August 2008 (www.media-awareness.ca/english/parents/video_games/concerns/gender_videogames).

Medora, Nilufer P. 2003. "Mate Selection in Contemporary India." Pp. 209–30 in *Mate Selection Across Cultures*, edited by Raeann R. Hamon and Bron B. Ingoldsby. Thousand Oaks, CA: Sage Publications.

MedPAC. 2010. *Report to the Congress: Medicare Payment Policy*. Washington, DC: Medicare Payment Advisory Commission.

Melzer, Scott A. 2002. "Gender, Work, and Intimate Violence: Men's Occupational Violence Spillover and Compensatory Violence." *Journal of Marriage and Family* 64(4): 820–33.

Merriam-Webster Online. 2010. "Love." Retrieved 22 January 2010 (www.merriam-webster.com/dictionary/love).

Merrill, Gary S. and Valerie A. Wolfe. 2000. "Battered Gay Men: An Exploration of Abuse, Help Seeking, and Why They Stay." *Journal of Homosexuality* 39(2): 1–30.

Messner, Michael A. 2009. *It's All for the Kids: Gender, Families, and Youth Sports*. Berkeley, CA: University of California Press.

MetLife Mature Market Institute. 2009. *Market Survey of Long-Term Care Costs: The 2009 MetLife Market Survey of Nursing Home, Assisted Living, Adult Day Services, and Home Care Costs*.

Miall, Charlene E. and Karen March. 2005. "Open Adoption as a Family Form: Community Assessments and Social Support." *Journal of Family Issues* 26: 380–410.

Michael, Kerry C., Aurora Torres, and Eric A. Seemann. 2007. "Adolescents' Health Habits, Coping Styles and Self-Concept Are Predicted by Exposure to Interparental Conflict." *Journal of Divorce & Remarriage* 48(1–2, December): 155–74.

Michael, Robert T., John Gagnon, Edward O. Laumann, and Gina Kolata. 1994. *Sex in America: A Definitive Survey*. New York: Little, Brown and Company.

Michaels, Marcia. 2006. "Factors That Contribute to Stepfamily Success: A Qualitative Analysis." *Journal of Divorce and Remarriage* 44(3/4): 53–65.

Microsoft Encarta Online Encyclopedia. 2004. "Affirmative Action." Retrieved 17 January 2004 (encarta.msn.com).

Milkie, Melissa A., Marybeth J. Mattingly, Kei M. Nomaguchi, Suzanne M. Bianchi, and John P. Robinson. 2004. "The Time Squeeze: Parental Statuses and Feelings About Time With Children." *Journal of Marriage and Family* 66 (August): 739–61.

Milkman, Ruth. 1976. "Women's Work and the Economic Crisis: Some Lessons from the Great Depression." *Review of Radical Political Economics* 8: 73–97.

Miller, Nancy B., Virginia L. Smerglia, D. Scott Gaudet, and Gay C. Kitson. 1998. "Stressful Life Events, Social Support, and the Distress of Widowed and Divorced Women." *Journal of Family Issues* 19: 181–203.

Mills, C. Wright. 1959. *The Sociological Imagination*. New York: Oxford University Press.

Mindel, Charles H. 1980. "Extended Familism Among Urban Mexican-Americans, Anglos, and Blacks." *Hispanic Journal of Behavioral Sciences* 2: 21–34.

Ministry of Health and Social Affairs. 2005. "Swedish Family Policy." *Government of Sweden*, April. Retrieved 15 June 2010. Stockholm (www.famratt.com/pdf/eng_sv_ familjepolitik.pdf).

Ministry of Integration and Gender Equality. 2009. "The Swedish Government's Gender Equality Policy." *Government of Sweden*, August. Retrieved 15 June 2010. Stockholm (www.sweden.gov.se/content/1/c6/13/07/15/8a48ffb6.pdf).

Ministry of Internal Affairs and Communications. 2009. *Statistical Yearbook of Japan 2009*.

Mintz, Steven. 2003. "Introduction: The Contemporary Crisis of the Family." Retrieved 5 July 2005. Council on Contemporary Families (www.contemporaryfamilies.org/public/fact1.php).

—. 2004. *Huck's Raft: A History of American Childhood*. Cambridge, MA: Belknap Press.

Mintz, Steven and Susan Kellogg. 1989. *Domestic Revolution: A Social History of Family Life*. New York: Free Press.

Miracle, Tina, Andrew Miracle, and Roy Baumeister. 2003. *Human Sexuality: Meeting Your Basic Needs*. Upper Saddle River, NJ: Prentice Hall.

Mirande, Alfredo. 1985. *The Chicano Experience: An Alternative Perspective*. Notre Dame, IN: University of Notre Dame Press.

Mishel, Lawrence, Jared Bernstein, and Sylvia Allegretto. 2007. *The State of Working America: 2006/2007*. Washington, DC: Economic Policy Institute.

Mitchell, Katherine Stamps, Alan Booth, and Valarie King. 2009. "Adolescents With Nonresident Fathers: Are Daughters More Disadvantaged Than Sons?" *Journal of Marriage and Family* 71(3, August): 650–62.

Moen, Phyllis, Jungmeen Kim, and Heather Hofmeister. 2001. "Couples' Work/Retirement Transitions, Gender, and Marital Quality." *Social Psychology Quarterly* 64(1, March): 55–71.

Monserud, Maria A. 2008. "Intergenerational Relationships and Affectual Solidarity Between Grandparents and Young Adults." *Journal of Marriage and Family* 70(1): 182–95.

Morgan, Leslie and Suzanne Kunkel. 1998. *Aging: The Social Context*. Thousand Oaks, CA: Pine Forge Press.

Morgan, Lewis Henry. [1851] 1962. *League of the Ho-de-No-Sau-Ne, or Iroquois*. New York: Corinth Press.

Morin, Rich and Paul Taylor. 2008. "Revisiting the Mommy Wars: Politics, Gender and Parenthood." Retrieved 9 March 2010. Pew Research Center (pewsocialtrends.org/pubs/709/politics-gender-parenthood).

Morrissey, Taryn W. 2008. "Familial Factors Associated with the Use of Multiple Child-Care Arrangements." *Journal of Marriage and the Family* 70 (May): 549–63.

Mossaad, Nadwa. 2010. "The Impact of the Recession on Older Americans." Retrieved 23 April 2010. Population Reference Bureau (www.prb.org/Articles/2010/recessionolderamericans.aspx).

Moynihan, Daniel P. 1965. "Office of Policy Planning and Research." In *The Negro Family: The Case for National Action*. U.S. Department of Labor, Office of Policy Planning and Research. Washington DC.

Mulsow, Miriam, Yvonne M. Caldera, Marta Pursley, Alan Reifman, and Aletha C. Huston. 2002. "Multilevel Factors Influencing Maternal Stress During the First Three Years." *Journal of Marriage and Family* 64 (November): 944–56.

Muraco, Anna. 2006. "Intentional Families: Fictive Kin Ties Between Cross-Gender, Different Sexual Orientation Friends." *Journal of Marriage and Family* 68 (December): 1313–25.

Murdock, George. 1949. *Social Structure*. New York: Macmillan.

—. 1957. "World Ethnographic Sample." *American Anthropologist* 59: 664–87.

—. 1967. *Ethnographic Atlas*. Pittsburgh: University of Pittsburgh Press.

Murkoff, Heidi, Sandee Hathaway, and Arlene Eisenberg. 2003. *What to Expect the First Year, 2nd ed.* New York: Workman Publishing.

Murkoff, Heidi and Sharon Mazel. 2008. *What to Expect When You're Expecting, 4th ed.* New York: Workman Publishing.

Murray, Charles. 1984. *Losing Ground: American Social Policy, 1950–1980*. New York: Basic Books.

Myers, Scott M. 2006. "Religious Homogamy and Marital Quality: Historical and Generational Patterns, 1980–1997." *Journal of Marriage and Family* 68(2): 292–304.

Nagae, Miyoko and Barbara L. Dancy. 2010. "Japanese Women's Perceptions of Intimate Partner Violence (IPV)." *Journal of Interpersonal Violence* 25(4): 753–66.

Nakonezny, Paul A., Robert D. Shull, and Joseph Lee Rodgers. 1995. "The Effect of No-Fault Divorce Law on the Divorce Rate Across the 50 States and Its Relation to Income, Education, and Religiosity." *Journal of Marriage and the Family* 57: 477–88.

NARAL Pro-Choice America Foundation. 2010. *Insurance Coverage for Contraception: A Proven Way to Protect and Promote Women's Health*. Naral.org.

National Adoption Information Clearinghouse. 2002. "Single Parent Adoption: What You Need to Know." Retrieved 11 June 2003. U.S. Department of Health & Human Services: Administration for Children & Families (www.calib.com/naic/pubs/factsheets.cfm).

National Alliance for Caregiving and AARP. 2009. *Caregiving in the U.S.: Executive Summary*.

National Association of Child Care Resource & Referral Agencies. 2009. "What Child Care Providers Earn." Retrieved 23 December 2009 (www.naccrra.org/randd/child-care-workforce/what-providers-earn).

National Campaign to Prevent Teen and Unplanned Pregnancy. 2009. "National Campaign Analysis: Preliminary 2007 Teen Birth Data." Retrieved 1 December 2009 (www.thenationalcampaign.org/resources/birthdata/analysis.aspx).

National Center for Education Statistics. 2009. "Status Dropout Rates by Race/Ethnicity." In *Student Effort and Educational Progress: Elementary/Secondary Persistence and Progress*. Retrieved 20 February 2010 (nces.ed.gov/programs/coe/2009/section3/indicator20.asp).

—. 2010. "Digest of Education Statistics: 2009." Retrieved 19 June 2010 (nces.ed.gov/programs/digest/d09/).

National Center for Health Statistics. 2002. "Cohabitation, Marriage, Divorce, and Remarriage in the United States." Retrieved 30 June 2005. Hyattsville, MD/Department of Health and Human Services (www.cdc.gov/nchs/data/series/sr_23/sr23_022.pdf).

—. 2005. *Health, United States, 2005: With Chartbook on Trends in the Health of Americans*. Hyattsville, MD.

—. 2009. *Health, United States, 2008: With Chartbook*. Hyattsville, MD.

—. 2010. *Health, United States, 2009: With Special Feature on Medical Technology*. Hyattsville, MD.

National Center on Domestic and Sexual Violence. 2010. "Domestic Violence Shelters in the U.S.—2005." Retrieved 14 June 2010 (www.ncdsv.org).

National Center on Elder Abuse. 2006. *Fact Sheet: Abuse of Adults Aged 60+ 2004 Survey of Adult Protective Services*. Washington, DC.

—. 2010. "Frequently Asked Questions." Retrieved 12 June 2010 (www.ncea.aoa.gov/NCEAroot/Main_Site/FAQ/Questions.aspx).

National Child Care Information and Technical Assistance Center. 2010. *United States Child Care Statistics*.

National Coalition Against Domestic Violence. 2005. "Dating Violence Facts." Retrieved 1 June 2006. Washington, DC.

—. 2009. "Domestic Violence Facts." Retrieved 23 September 2009 (www.ncadv.org/files/DomesticViolenceFact-Sheet(National).pdf).

National Coalition for the Homeless. 2009. "How Many People Experience Homelessness?" Retrieved 9 November 2009 (www.nationalhomeless.org/factsheets/How_Many.html).

National Conference of State Legislatures. 2010. "Same Sex Marriage, Civil Unions and Domestic Partnerships." Retrieved 20 February 2010 (www.ncsl.org/IssuesResearch/HumanServices/SameSexMarriage/tabid/16430/Default.aspx).

National Family Caregivers Association. 2008. "Caregiving Depression-Symptoms and Hope." Retrieved 20 March 2008 (www.nfcares.org/improving_caregiving/depression.cfm).

National Institute of Justice and Centers for Disease Control and Prevention. 1998. "Prevalence, Incidence, and Consequences of Violence Against Women: Findings From the National Violence Against Women Survey" (Research In Brief) (www.ojp.usdoj.gov/nii/pubs-sum/172837. htm).

National Institute of Mental Health. 2009. "Eating Disorders." Retrieved 21 November 2009 (ww.nimh.nih.gov/health/topics/eating-disorders/index.html).

National Institute on Media and the Family. 2009. "Fact Sheet: Media's Effect On Girls: Body Image And Gender Identity." Retrieved 16 April 2010 (www.mediafamily.org/facts/ facts_mediaeffect.shtml).

The National Marriage Project. 2007. *The State of Our Unions 2007: The Social Health of Marriage in America*. Piscataway, NJ: Rutger University.

—. 2009. *The State of Our Unions: Marriage in America 2009*. Charlottesville, VA: University of Virginia.

National Opinion Research Center (NORC). 2009. "Mnemonic Index." Retrieved 24 June 2009 (www.norc.org/GSS+ Website/Browse+GSS+ Variables/Mnemonic+Index/).

National Stepfamily Resource Center. 2007. "Frequently Asked Questions." Retrieved 28 September 2007 (www.stepfamiles.info/faqs/faqs.php).

National Women's Education Center, Japan. 2009. "NWEC Summary Statistics Women and Men in Japan 2009." Retrieved 15 June 2010 (www.nwec.jp/en/program/research.html).

Nemeth, Danielle. 2000. "The 19th Amendment is Ratified." Retrieved 10 August 2005. David M. Koeller (campus.northpark.edu/history/WebChron/USA/19Amend.CP.html).

Neuman, Lawrence W. 2009. *Understanding Research*. Boston: Pearson.

New Deal Network. (2003). "Always Lend a Helping Hand: Sevier County Remembers the Depression." Available online (http://newdeal.feri.org/sevier/index.htm). Retrieved 5 January 2007. Interviews compiled by honors English students at Richfield High School, Sevier County, Utah. Sevier County (Utah) Oral History Project Collection, 1997, Utah State Historical Society.

New York City Gay & Lesbian Anti-Violence Project. 2003. "Building Safer Communities for Lesbian, Gay, Transgender, Bisexual and HIV-Affected New Yorkers."

New York Times/CBS News. 2008. *The Presidential Race: Midsummer.* July 7–14. Retrieved 16 August 2008 (www.usaelectionpolls.com/2008/polls/pdfs/cbs-new-york-times-july7to14-2008.pdf).

Newman, Katherine S. 2008. *Chutes and Ladders: Navigating the Low-Wage Labor Market*. New York: Russell Sage Foundation.

Newport, Frank and Elizabeth Mendes. 2009. "About One in Six U.S. Adults Are Without Health Insurance." Retrieved 1 July 2010. Gallup (www.gallup.com/poll/121820/one-six-adults-without-health-insurance.aspx).

NHS Knowledge Service. 2009. "Home Birth 'Safe as in Hospital.' " Retrieved 16 December 2009 (www.nhs.uk/news/2009/04April/Pages/HomeBirthSafe.aspx).

NICHD Early Child Care Research Network. 1999. "Study Finds That Child Care Does Impact Mother-Child Interaction" (Press Release for "Child Care and Mother-Child Interaction in the First 3 Years of Life," *Developmental Psychology* 35(6): 1399-1413.

___. 2005. "Duration and Developmental Timing of Poverty and Children's Cognitive and Social Development from Birth Through Third Grade." *Child Development* 76(4, July): 795–810.

Nock, Steven L. 1998. *Marriage in Men's Lives*. New York: Oxford University Press.

Nock, Steven L., James D. Wright, and Laura A. Sanchez. 1999. "America's Divorce Problem." *Society* 36: 43–52.

Nolan, Patrick and Gerhard Lenski. 1999. *Human Societies: An Introduction to Macrosociology*. New York: McGraw-Hill.

Nomaguchi, Kei M. 2009. "Change in Work-Family Conflict Among Employed Parents Between 1977 and 1997." *Journal of Marriage and Family* 71(1, February): 15–32.

Nomaguchi, Kei M. and Melissa A. Milkie. 2003. "Costs and Rewards of Children: The Effects of Becoming a Parent on Adults' Lives." *Journal of Marriage and Family* 65: 356–74.

Nomaguchi, Kei M. and Suzanne M. Bianchi. 2004. "Exercise Time: Gender Differences in the Effects of Marriage, Parenthood, and Employment." *Journal of Marriage and Family* 66 (May): 413–30.

Nord, Mark, Margaret Andrews, and Steven Carlson. 2009. *Household Food Security in the United States, 2008*. Technical Report No. Economic Research Service, Economic Research Report 83. Washington, DC: U.S. Department of Agriculture.

NPR Online. 2001. "Poverty in America." In *NPR/Kaiser/Kennedy School Poll*. Retrieved 1 December 2005 (www.npr.org/programs/specials/poll/poverty).

Nugman, Gulnar. 2002. "World Divorce Rates." Retrieved 6 June 2006 (www.divorcereform.org/gul.html).

Nye, F. Ivan. 1979. "Choice, Exchange, and the Family." Pp. 1–41 in *Contemporary Theories About the Family*, Vol. 2., edited by Wesley R. Burr, Reuben Hill, F. Ivan Nye and Ira L. Reiss. New York: Free Press.

Obama, Barack. 2007. *The Audacity of Hope: Thoughts on Reclaiming the American Dream*. New York: Vintage Books.

Office of Minority Health. 2008. "Suicide and Suicide Prevention 101." Retrieved 30 June 2010. U.S. Department of Health & Human Services (minorityhealth.hhs.gov/templates/browse.aspx?lvl=3&lvlID=136).

—. 2009. "American Indian/Alaska Native Profile." Retrieved 30 June 2010. U.S. Department of Health & Human Services (minorityhealth.hhs.gov/templates/browse.aspx?lvl=2&lvlID=52).

Official Journal of the European Communities. 1998. "Council Directive 97/81/EC of 15 December 1997 Concerning the Framework Agreement on Part-Time Work Concluded by UNICE, CEEP and the ETUC." Retrieved 5 January 2010. Eur-Lex (eur-lex.europa.eu/LexUriServ/LexUriServ.do?uri=CELEX: 31997L0081: EN: HTML).

Ogburn, William F. 1964. *On Cultural and Social Change: Selected Papers*. Chicago: University of Chicago Press.

Ogunwole, Stella U. 2006. *We the People: American Indians and Alaska Natives in the United States*. Technical Report No. CENSR-28. Washington, DC: U.S. Census Bureau.

O'Hare, William P. 1995. "3.9 Million U.S. Children in Distressed Neighborhoods." *Population Today* 22: 4–5.

Oklahoma Marriage Initiative. 2005. "Frequently Asked Questions." Retrieved 5 July 2005 (www.okmarriage.org/MarriageAdviseQuestionsDetail.asp?id=10).

—. 2010. "Home Page: Building Better Marriages in Oklahoma." Retrieved 18 May 2010 (www.okmarriage.org/).

Oláh, Livia S. and Eva M. Bernhardt. 2003. "Coresidential Paternal Roles in Three Countries: Sweden, Hungary, and the United States." Retrieved 1 May 2003 (www.suda.su.se/SRRD/srrd126.doc).

Oliver, Melvin L. and Thomas M. Shapiro. 2006. *Black Wealth/White Wealth: A New Perspective on Racial Inequality, 2nd Ed.* New York: Routledge.

Onion, Amanda. 2005. "Scientists Find Sex Differences in Brain." *ABC News: Technology & Science*, 19 January. Retrieved 23 June 2006 (abcnews.go.com/Technology/Health/story?id=424260&page=1).

Orenstein, Peggy. 1994. *School Girls*. New York: Anchor Books.

Organisation for Economic Co-Operation and Development. 2007. *Babies and Bosses: Reconciling Work and Family Life: A Synthesis of Findings for OECD Countries*. Paris: OECD.

Orshansky, Mollie. 1965. "Counting the Poor: Another Look at Poverty." *Social Security Bulletin* 28: 3–29.

Osborne, Cynthia. 2005. "Marriage Following the Birth of a Child Among Cohabiting and Visiting Parents." *Journal of Marriage and Family* 67(1, February): 14–26.

Osborne, Cynthia, Wendy D. Manning, and Pamela J. Smock. 2007. "Married and Cohabiting Parents' Relationship Stability: A Focus on Race and Ethnicity." *Journal of Marriage and Family* 69: 1345–66.

Osmond, Marie Withers and Barrie Thorne. 1993. "Feminist Theories: The Construction of Gender in Families and Society." Pp. 591–622 in *Sourcebook of Family Theories and Methods: A Contextual Approach*, edited by Pauline G. Boss, William J. Doherty, Ralph LaRossa, Walter R. Schumm and Suzanne K. Steinmetz. New York: Plenum.

Otnes, Cele and Elizabeth H. Pleck. 2003. *CInderella Dreams: The Allure of the Lavish Wedding*. Berkeley, CA: University of California Press.

Oyez Project. 1978. *Regents of the University of California v. Bakke*. Retrieved 20 August 2010 (www.oyez.org/cases/1970-1979/1977/1977_76_811).

Pai, Manacy and Anne E. Barrett. 2007. "Long-Term Payoffs of Work? Women's Past Involvement in Paid Work and Mental Health in Widowhood." *Research on Aging* 29(5): 436–56.

The Paid Family Leave Collaborative. 2009. "On Fifth Anniversary of California's Successful Paid Family Leave Law, Congresswoman Woolsey & Advocates Call for More Progress on State and Federal Level." Retrieved 24 May 2010 (www.paidfamilyleave.org/press_release09.pdf).

Pailhe, Ariane and Anne Solaz. 2008. "Time With Children: Do Fathers and Mothers Replace Each Other When One Parent Is Unemployed?" *European Journal of Population* 24(2): 211–36.

Parasuraman, Saroj and Jeffrey H. Greenhaus. 1997. *Integrating Work and Family: Challenges and Choices for Changing World*. Westport, CT: Quorum.

Pardo, Tamara. 2008. "Growing up Transgender: Research and Theory." In *Research Facts and Findings*. Retrieved 14 August 2009. ACT for Youth Center of Excellence (www.actforyouth.net/documents/GrowingUpTransPt1_March08.pdf).

Parke, Mary. 2007. "Are Married Parents Really Better for C hildren? What Research Says About the Effects of Family Structure on Child Well-Being." In *Couples and Married Research and Policy Brief (May 2003)*. Retrieved 14 April 2010. Center for Law and Social Policy (www.clasp.org/admin/site/publications_states/files/0086.pdf).

Parker, Kim. 2009. "The Harried Life of the Working Mother." Retrieved 25 October 2009. Pew Research Center (pewsocialtrends.org/pubs/745/the-harried-life-of-the-working-mother).

Parker-Pope, Tara. 2007. "Does Flex Time Lead to Better Health?" *New York Times Online*, 13 December (Well.blogs.nytimes.com/2007/12/13/does-flex-time-lead-to-better-health/).

—. 2010. "Is Marriage Good for Your Health?" Retrieved 23 May 2010. NYTimes.com (www.nytimes.com/2010/04/18/magazine/18marriage-t.html?pagewanted=print).

Parrenas, Rhacel. 2005. *Children of Global Migration: Transnational Families and Gendered Woes*. Palo Alto, CA: Stanford University Press.

Parsons, Talcott. 1937. *The Structure of Social Action*. New York: McGraw-Hill.

—. 1951. *The Social System*. Glencoe, IL: Free Press.

Parsons, Talcott and Robert F. Boles. 1955. *Family, Socialization, and Interaction Process*. New York: Free Press.

Partenheimer, David. 2001. "Same-Sex Peers Reinforce Sex Role Behavior in Social Activities, Study Finds." (Press Release). Retrieved 6 December 2003. American Psychological Association (www.apa.org/releases/same-sex.html).

—. 2003. "Race Has Powerful Effects on Children's Perceptions of Occupations, Study Finds" (Press Release). Retrieved 6 January 2004. American Psychological Association (www.apa.org/releases/race_jobs.html).

—. 2005. "Do Opposites Attract or Do Birds of a Feather Flock Together?" (Press Release). Retrieved 21 June 2005. American Psychological Association (www.apa.org/releases/attraction.html).

Passel, Jeffrey S. and D'Vera Cohn. 2009a. *A Portrait of Unauthorized Immigrants in the United States*. Washington, DC: Pew Hispanic Center.

—.2009b. *Mexican Immigrants: How Many Come? How Many Leave?* Washington, DC: Pew Hispanic Center.

Passel, Jeffrey S., Wendy Wang, and Paul Taylor. 2010. "Marrying Out: One-in-Seven New U.S. Marriages is Interracial or Interethnic." Retrieved 1 July 2010. Pew Research Center (pewresearch.org/pubs/1616/american-marriage-interracial-interethnic).

Patrikar, Seema R., Col RajVir Bhalwar, Col Amitava Datta, and Dashrath R. Basannar. 2008. "Gender Inequality: Is the National Population Policy's Objective of Two Child Norm Heading the Correct Way?" *Medical Journal Armed Forces India* 64(221–223).

Patterson, Charlotte J. and Paul D. Hastings. 2007. "Socialization in the Context of Family Diversity." Pp. 328–51 in *Handbook of Socialization: Theory and Research*, edited by J. E. Grusec and P. D. Hastings. New York: The Guilford Press.

Paul, Annie Murphy. 2006. "The Real Marriage Penalty." *New York Times Magazine*, 19 November, pp. 22–23.

Pawelski, James G., Ellen C. Perrin, Jane M. Foy, Carole E. Allen, James E. Crawford, Mark Del Monte, Miriam Kaufman, Jonathan D. Klein, Karen Smith, Sarah Springer, J. Lane Tanner, and Dennis L. Vickers. 2006. "The Effects of Marriage, Civil Union, and Domestic Partnership Laws on the Health and Well-Being of Children." *Pediatrics*, 118: 349–64.

Pearson, Jessica and Nancy Thoennes. 1998. "Programs to Increase Fathers' Access to Their Children." Pp. 220–52 in *Fathers Under Fire*, edited by I. Garfinkel, S. S. McLanahan, D. R. Meyer, and J. A. Seltzer. New York, NY: Russell Sage Foundation.

Pearson, Quinn M. 2008. "Role Overload, Job Satisfaction, Leisure Satisfaction, and Psychological Health Among Employed Women." *Journal of Counseling & Development* 86(1): 57–63.

Pedersen, Willy and Hans W. Kristiansen. 2008. "Homosexual Experience, Desire and Identity Among Young Adults." *Journal of Homosexuality* 54(1–2): 68–102.

Pelham, Brett W. 2010. "Rest Eludes Nearly 30% of Americans." Retrieved 2 March 2010. Gallup Poll (www.gallup.com/poll/125471/rest-eludes-nearly-americans.aspx?version=print).

Peplau, Letitia A. and Kristin P. Beals. 2004. "The Family Lives of Lesbians and Gay Men." Pp. 233–48 in *Handbook of Family Communication*, edited by Anita L. Vangelisti. Mahwah, NJ: Lawrence Erlbaum Associates.

Perkins, Daniel F. and Kate Fogarty. 2005. "Active Listening: A Communication Tool." In *FCS2151, One of a Series of the Family, Youth, and Community Sciences Department, Florida Cooperative Extension Service, Institute of Food and Agricultural Sciences, University of Florida*. Retrieved 29 September 2008 (Edis.ifas.ufl.edu/he361).

Perry-Jenkins, Maureen, Abbie E. Goldberg, Courtney P. Pierce, and Aline G. Sayer. 2007. "Shift Work, Role Overload, and the Transition to Parenthood." *Journal of Marriage and the Family* 69: 123–38.

Perry-Jenkins, Maureen, Rena L. Repetti, and Ann C. Crouter. 2000. "Work and Family in the 1990s." *Journal of Marriage and the Family* 62(4, November): 981–98.

Peters World Atlas. 2001. Niagara Falls, NY: USA New International Publisher.

The Pew Forum on Religion and Public Life. 2009. "Brides, Grooms Often Have Different Faiths." Retrieved 18 May 2010 (pewforum.org/Brides-Grooms-Often-Have-Different-Faiths.aspx).

Pew Global Attitudes Project. 2009. February 12. *The Global Middle Class: Views on Democracy, Religion, Values, and Life Satisfaction in Emerging Nations*. Washington, DC: Pew Research Center.

Pew Hispanic Center. 2006. *The State of American Public Opinion on Immigration in Spring 2006: A Review of Major Surveys (Fact Sheet)*. Washington, DC.

—. 2008. "Statistical Portrait of Hispanics in the United States, 2006." Retrieved 22 August 2008 (pewhispanic.org/factsheets/factsheet.php?FactsheetID=35).

—. 2009. "Between Two Worlds: How Young Latinos Come of Age in America." Retrieved 20 January 2010 (pewhispanic.org/files/reports/117.pdf).

—. 2010a. "Statistical Portrait of Hispanics in the United States, 2008." Retrieved 29 June 2010 (pewhispanic.org/factsheets/factsheet.php?FactsheetID=58).

—.2010b. *Hispanics and Arizona's New Immigration Law*. Technical Report No. Fact Sheet.

Pew Research Center. 2007. "Generation Gap in Values, Behaviors: As Marriage and Parenthood Drift Apart, Public is Concerned About Social Impact." Retrieved December 15, 2007 (http://pewresearch.org/pubs/526/marriage-parenthood).

—. 2008. "Religion in America: Non-Dogmatic, Diverse, and Politically Relevant." Retrieved 24 June 2008 (pewresearch.org/pubs/876/religion-america-part-two).

—. 2009. "Problems and Priorities." Retrieved 24 June 2009. PollingReport.com (www.pollingreport.com/prioriti.htm).

—. 2010. *Millennials: Confident. Connected. Open to Change.* Retrieved 24 February 2010(pewsocialtrends.org/pubs/751/millennials-confident-connected-open-to-change).

Pew Research Center for the People and the Press. 2009. "Majority Continues to Support Civil Unions." Retrieved 20 February 2010 (people-press.org/report/553/same-sex-marriage).

Pfeffer, Carla A. 2010. "'Women's Work?' Women Partners of Transgender Men Doing Housework and Emotion Work." *Journal of Marriage and Family* 72(1, February): 165–83.

PFLAG. 2009. "Get Support: Welcome to TNET!" Retrieved 14 February 2010 (Community.pflag.org/Page.aspx?pid=380).

Phillips, Julie A. and Megan M. Sweeney. 2005. "Premarital Cohabitation and Marital Disruption Among White, Black, and Mexican American Women." *Journal of Marriage and Family* 67 (May): 296–314.

Phillips, Roderick. 1997. "Stepfamilies from a Historical Perspective." Pp. 5–18 in *Stepfamilies: History, Research and Policy*, edited by Irene Levin and Marvin Sussman. New York: Haworth.

Pineo, Peter. 1961. "Disenchantment in the Later Years of Marriage." *Marriage and Family Living* 23: 3–11.

Pinquart, Martin and Silvia Sorensen. 2005. "Ethnic Differences in Stressors, Resources, and Psychological Outcomes of Family Caregiving: A Meta-Analysis." *The Gerontologist* 45: 90–106.

Planty, Michael, William Hussar, Thomas Snyder, Grace Kena, Angelina KewalRamani, Jana Kemp, Kevin Bianco, Rachel Dinkes, Katie Ferguson, Andrea Livingston, and Thomas Nachazel. 2009. *The Condition of Education 2009*. National Center for Education Statistics, Institute of Education Sciences No. NCES 2008-081. Washington, DC: U.S. Department of Education.

Poelmans, Steven, Olena Stepanova, and Aline Masuda. 2008. "Positive Spillover Between Personal and Professional Life: Definitions, Antecedents, Consequences, and Strategies." Pp. 141–56 in *Handbook of Work-Family Integration: Research, Theory, and Best Practices*, edited by K. Korabik, D. S. Lero, and D. L. Whitehead. Amsterdam: Elsevier.

Pollock, Linda A. 1983. *Forgotten Children: Parent-Child Relations from 1500 to 1900*. New York, NY: Cambridge University Press.

—. 1987. *Lasting Relationship: Parents & Children Over Three Centuries*. Hanover, NH: University Press of New England.

Pong, Suet-Ling, Jaap Dronkers, and Gillian Hampden-Thompson. 2003. "Family Policies and Children's School Achievement in Single-Versus Two-Parent Families." *Journal of Marriage and Family* 65(3): 681–99.

Poortman, Anne-Rigt and Tanja van der Lippe. 2009. "Attitudes Toward Housework and Child Care and the Gendered Division of Labor." *Journal of Marriage and Family* 71(3, August): 526–41.

Pope, John. 2004. "Controlling Childbirth." *New Orleans Times-Picayune*, 22 September.

Popenoe, David. 2005. "Marriage and Family: What Does the Scandinavian Experience Tell Us?" In *The State of Our Unions 2006*. National Marriage Project.

—. 2007. "Essay: The Future of Marriage in America." In *The State of Our Unions: The Social Health of Marriage in America*. New Brunswick, NJ: The National Marriage Project.

—. 2008. *Cohabitation, Marriage and Child Well-Being: A Cross-National Perspective*. National Marriage Project. Piscataway, NJ: Rutgers, The State University of New Jersey, 08/11/10.

Population Reference Bureau. 2010a. "Data Comparisons by Topic: Ever-Married Females Ages 15–19 (%)." Retrieved 18 May 2010 (www.prb.org/Datafinder/Topic/Bar.aspx?sort=v&order=d&variable=34).

—. 2010b. "World Population Highlights: Key Findings from PRB's 2009 World Population Data Sheet." Retrieved 23 May 2010 (www.prb.org/Publications/PopulationBulletins/2009/worldpopulationhighlights2009).

—. 2010c. 2010 World Population Fact Sheet. Retrieved 20 August 2010. (www.prb.org/pdf10/10wpds_eng.pdf).

Porter, Kirk H. 1971. *A History of Suffrage in the United States*. New York: AMS Press.

Posner, Patti. 2002. "One Family's Journey to Healing." Stepfamily Network (www.stepfamily.net).

Powell, Alvin. 2005. "A New Comfort Zone? Fewer Women Keeping Names on Marriage." *Harvard University Gazette*. Retrieved 10 July 2007 (www.news.harvard.edu/gazette/2004/08.26/11-namechange.html).

Premi, Mahendra K. 2002. "The Girl Child: Some Issues for Consideration." Paper presented at the Symposium on Sex Ratio in India, organized by IIPS and the Ford Foundation, Mumbai.

Presser, Harriet B. 2003. *Working in a 24/7 Economy: Challenges for American Families*. New York: Russell Sage Foundation.

Presser, Harriet B., Janet C. Gornick, and Sangeeta Parashar. 2008. "Nonstandard Work Schedules in Twelve European Countries: A Gender Perspective." *Monthly Labor Review* 131(2): 83–103.

Project NoSpank. 2007. "VENEZUELA: Second Latin American country to ban corporal punishment." Retrieved 24 October 2010. (www.nospank.net/n-r42r.htm).

Prokos, Anastasia H., Irene Padavic, and S. Ashley Schidt. 2009. "Nonstandard Work Arrangements Among Women and Men Scientists and Engineers." *Sex Roles* 61(9-10): 653–66.

Pyke, Karen. 2000a. "Ideology of 'Family' Shapes Perception of Immigrant Children." Minneapolis, MN: National Council on Family Relations.

—. 2000b. "'The Normal American Family' as an Interpretive Structure of Family Life Among Grown Children of Korean and Vietnamese Immigrants." *Journal of Marriage and the Family*, 62: 240–45.

Quick, Heather E. and Phyllis Moen. 1998. "Gender, Employment, and Retirement Quality: A Lifecourse

Approach to the Differential Experiences of Men and Women." *Journal of Occupational Health Psychology* 3: 44–64.

Raj, Anita, Saggurti Niranjan, Donta Balaiah, and Jay G. Silverman. 2009. "Prevalence of Child Marriage and Its Effect on Fertility and Fertility-Control Outcomes of Young Women in India: A Cross-Sectional, Observational Study." *The Lancet* 373(9678, 30 May): 1883–89.

Ramirez, Jr., Artemio and Kathy Broneck. 2009. " 'IM Me': Instant Messaging as Relational Maintenance and Every-day Communications." *Journal of Social and Personal Relationships* 26(2–3): 291–314.

Rani, Manju and Sekhar Banu. 2009. "Attitudes Toward Wife Beating." *Journal of Interpersonal Violence* 24(8): 1371–97.

Rank, Mark R. 2003. "As American as Apple Pie: Poverty and Welfare." *Contexts* 2(3, Summer): 41–49.

Rankin, Nancy. 2002. "The Parent Vote." Pp. 251–64 in *Taking Parenting Public*, edited by S. A. Hewlett, N. Rankin and C. West. Lanham, MD: Rowman & Littlefield.

Ray, Rebecca, Janet C. Gornick, and John Schmitt. 2009. *Parental Leave Policies in 21 Countries: Assessing Generosity and Gender Equality*. Washington, DC: Center for Economic and Policy Research.

Reese, Leslie, Helen Garnier, Ronald Gallimore, and Claude Goldenberg. 2000. "Longitudinal Analysis of the Antecedents of Emergent Spanish Literacy and Middle-School English Reading Achievement of Spanish-Speaking Students." *American Educational Research Journal* 37(3): 633–62.

Reeves, Terrance and Claudette Bennett. 2003. *The Asian and Pacific Islander Population in the United States: March 2002*. Current Population Reports No. P20-540. Washington, DC: U. S. Census Bureau.

Reiss, Ira L. 1960. "Toward a Sociology of the Heterosexual Love Relationship." *Marriage and Family Living* 22: 139–45.

Reitzes, Donald C. and Elizabeth J Mutran. 2004. "The Transition to Retirement: Stages and Factors That Influence Retirement Adjustment." *International Journal of Aging and Human Development* 59(1): 63–84.

Remarriage.com. 2008. "Remarriage Issues: General Findings." Retrieved 4 September 2008 (www.remarriage.com/Remarriage-Factsw/Likelihood-of-Marriage.html).

Resolve: The National Infertility Association. 2010. "Frequently Asked Questions About Infertility." Retrieved 24 May 2010 (www.resolve.org).

Reyes, J. Roberto. 2003. "Couple Formation Practices in Spain." Pp. 175–90 in *Mate Selection Across Cultures*, edited by R. R. Hamon and B. B. Ingoldsby. Thousand Oaks, CA: Sage Publications, Inc.

Ricci, Isolina. 2007. "Divorce from the Kids' Point of View: From Damage Control to Empowerment." *National Council on Family Relations Report* 52(4, December): F11–F12; F19.

Richters, Juliet, Richard de Visser, Chris Rissel, and Anthony Smith. 2006. "Sexual Practices at Last Heterosexual Encounter and Occurrence of Orgasm in a National Survey." *The Journal of Sex Research* 43(3): 217–26.

Ristock, Janice. 2009. *Intimate Partner Violence in LGBTQ Lives*. New York: Routledge.

Rockquemore, Kerry Ann and Tracey Laszloffy. 2005. *Raising Biracial Children*. Lanham, MD: AltaMira Press.

Rodgers, Joseph Lee, Paul A. Nakonezny, and Robert D. Shull. 1997. "Feedback: The Effect of No-Fault Divorce Legislation on Divorce Rates: A Response to a Reconsideration." *Journal of Marriage and the Family* 59: 1026–30.

Rodgers, Kathleen Boyce and Hilary A. Rose. 2002. "Risk and Resiliency Factors Among Adolescents Who Experience Marital Transitions." *Journal of Marriage and Family* 64 (November): 1024–37.

Rodgers, Roy H. and James M. White. 1993. "Family Development Theory." Pp. 225–54 in *Sourcebook of Family Theories and Methods: A Contextual Approach*, edited by Pauline G. Boss, William J. Doherty, Ralph LaRossa, Walter R. Schumm and Suzanne K. Steinmetz. New York: Plenum Press.

Rodriguez, Michael, Jeanette M. Valentine, John B. Son, and Marjani Muhammad. 2009. "Intimate Partner Violence and Barriers to Mental Health Care for Ethnically Diverse Populations of Women." *Trauma, Violence, & Abuse* 10(4): 358–74.

Roer-Strier, Dorit and Dina Ben Ezra. 2006. "Intermarriages Between Western Women and Palestinian Men: Multidirectional Adaptation Processes." *Journal of Marriage and Family* 68(1): 41–55.

Rogers, Stacy J. 2004. "Dollars, Dependency, and Divorce: Four Perspectives on the Role of Wives' Income." *Journal of Marriage and Family* 66 (February): 59–74.

Rohall, David E., Melissa A. Milkie, and Jeffrey W. Lucas. 2011. *Social Psychology: Sociological Perspectives, 2nd ed.* Boston: Allyn & Bacon.

Rohner, Ronald P., and Robert A. Veneziano. 2001. The Importance of Father Love: History and Contemporary Evidence. *Review of General Psychology* 5(4 December): 382-405.

Rooks, Judith. 1997. *Midwifery and Childbirth in America*. Philadelphia: Temple University Press.

Rosenberg, Matt. 2009. "China's One Child Policy." Retrieved 9 November 2009. About.com (geography.about.com/od/populationgeography/a/onechild.htm).

Rosenfeld, Michael J. 2008. *The Age of Independence: Interracial Unions, Same-Sex Unions and the Changing American Family*. Cambridge, MA: Harvard University Press.

Ross, Catherine E. and Marieke Van Willigen. 1996. "Gender, Parenthood, and Anger." *Journal of Marriage and the Family* 58: 572–84.

Ross, Emma. 2005. "Genes Affect Woman's Orgasm, Study Shows." *The Oregonian* (Portland, OR), 8 June, A, p. 15.

Rossell, Christine H. and Keith Baker. 1996. "The Educational Effectiveness of Bilingual Education." *Research in the Teaching of English* 30(1): 7–69.

Rossi, Alice S. 1968. "Transition to Motherhood." *Journal of Marriage and the Family* 30: 26–39.

Rothman, Barbara Katz. 1991. *In Labor: Women and Power in the Birthplace*. New York: W.W. Norton and Co.

Roudi-Fahimi, Farzaneh. 2010. "Child Marriage in the Middle East and North Africa." Retrieved 18 May 2010. Population Reference Bureau (www.prb.org/Articles/2010/menachildmarriage.aspx).

Rouse, Cecelia Elena and Lisa Barrow. 2006. "U.S. Elementary and Secondary Schools: Equalizing Opportunity or Maintaining the Status Quo?" *The Future of Children* 16(2): 99–123.

Rowe, Gretchen and Mary Murphy. 2008. *Welfare Rules Databook: State TANF Policies as of July 2006*. Washington, DC: The Urban Institute.

Roxburgh, Susan. 2005. "Parenting Strains, Distress, and Family Paid Labor: A Modification of the Cost-of-Caring Hypothesis." *Journal of Family Issues* 26: 1062–81.

Rubin, Lillian B. 1976. *Worlds of Pain*. New York: Basic Books.

—. 1994. *Families on the Fault Line: America's Working Class Speaks About the Family, the Economy, and Ethnicity*. New York: Harper Collins.

Rush, Sharon E. 2000. *Loving Across the Color Line: A White Adoptive Mother Learns About Race*. Lanham, MD: Rowman & Littlefield.

Saad, Lydia. 2004. "Romance to Break Out Nationwide This Weekend." Retrieved 25 September 2008. Gallup Poll (www.gallup.com/poll/10609/Romance-Break-Nationwide-Weekend.aspx).

—. 2008. "By Age 24, Marriage Wins Out." Available online (www.gallup.com/poll/109402/Age-24-Marriage-Wins.aspx).

—. 2009. "Republicans Move to the Right on Several Moral Issues." Retrieved 14 February 2010. Gallup Poll (www.gallup.com/poll/118546/republicans-veer-right-several-moral-issues.aspx).

Sabol, William J., Heather C. West, and Matthew Cooper. 2009. "Prisoners in 2008." Retrieved 21 February 2010. Bureau of Justice Statistics, U.S. Department of Justice (bjs.ojp.usdoj.gov/content/pub/pdf/p08.pdf).

Saleebey, Dennis. 2009. *The Strengths Perspective in Social Work Practice, 5th ed.* Boston: Allyn & Bacon.

Saltzman, Linda E., Christopher H. Johnson, Brenda C. Gilbert, and Mary M. Goodwin. 2003. "Physical Abuse Around the Time of Pregnancy: An Examination of Prevalence and Risk Factors in 16 States." *Maternal and Child Health Journal* 7: 31–42.

Saluter, Arlene. 1996. *Marital Status and Living Arrangements: March 1995 (Update)*. Current Population Reports. U.S. Census Bureau.

Salverda, Wiemer, Brian Nolan, and Timothy M. Smeeding, eds. 2009. *Oxford Handbook of Economic Inequality*. Oxford, UK and New York: Oxford University Press.

Samandari, Ghazeleh and Sandra L. Martin. 2010. "Homicide Among Pregnant and Postpartum Women in the United States: A Review of the Literature." *Trauma, Violence, & Abuse* 11(1): 42–54.

Sample, Neal. 1999. "What I Felt Like Being Adopted" (www.stepfamilynetwork.net/Adoption.htm).

Sanchez, Laura, Steven Nock, and James D. Wright. 2002. "Social and Demographic Factors Associated with Couples' Choice Between Covenant and Standard Marriage in Louisiana." Available online (www.bgsu.edu/organizations/cfdr/research/pdf/2002/2002_06.pdf).

Sandberg, John F. and Sandra L. Hofferth. 2001. "Changes in Children's Time with Parents: United States." *Demography* 38: 423–36.

Sands, Roberta G. and Robin S. Goldberg-Glen. 2000. "Factors Associated with Stress Among Grandparents Raising Their Grandchildren." *Family Relations* 49: 97–105.

Santelli, John S., Mark Orr, Laura D. Lindberg, and Daniela C. Diaz. 2009. "Changing Behavioral Risk for Pregnancy Among High School Students in the United States: 1991–2007." *Journal of Adolescent Health* 44(7): 25–32.

Sapir, Edward. 1949. *Selected Writings of Edward Sapir in Language, Culture, and Personality, David G. Mandelbaum, Ed.* Berkeley, CA: University of California Press.

Sarkadi, Anna, Robert Kristiansson, Frank Oberklaid, and Sven Bremberg. 2008. "Fathers' Involvement and Children's Developmental Outcomes: A Review of Longitudinal Studies." *Acta Paediatrica* 97: 153–58.

Sassler, Sharon. 2010. "Partnering Across the Life Course: Sex, Relationships, and Mate Selection." *Journal of Marriage and Family* 72(3, June).

Sassler, Sharon, Anna Cunningham, and Daniel T. Lichter. 2009. "Intergenerational Patterns of Union Formation and Relationship Quality." *Journal of Family Issues* 30(6): 757–86.

Saul, Stephanie. 2009. "Building a Baby, with Few Ground Rules." Retrieved 20 December 2009. New York Times (www.nytimes.com/2009/12/13/us/13surrogacy.html?_r=1&pagewanted=print).

Savage, Howard Allen, and Peter J. Fronczek. 1993. *Who Can Afford to Buy a House in 1991?* Washington, DC: Housing and Household Economic Statistics Division, U.S. Census Bureau.

Sax, Leonard. 2006. *Why Gender Matters: What Parents and Teachers Need to Know About the Emerging Science of Sex Differences*. New York: Doubleday.

Scaramella, Laura V., Tricia K. Neppl, Lenna L. Ontai, and Rand D. Conger. 2008. "Consequences of Socioeconomic Disadvantage Across Three Generations." *Journal of Family Psychology* 22(5): 725–33.

Schaefer, Richard T. 2011. *Racial and Ethnic Groups, Census Update, 12th ed.* Upper Saddle River, NJ: Prentice Hall.

Schaie, K. Warner and Glen H. Elder, Jr. 2005. *Historical Influences on Lives and Aging*. New York: Springer Publishing Co.

Schieber, Sylvester J. 2008. *Beyond the Golden Age of Retirement*. University of Michigan Retirement Research Center Policy Brief No. 6.

Schiebinger, Londa and Shannon K. Gilmartin. 2010. "Housework is an Academic Issue." In *Academe Online*. Retrieved 1 June 2010. American Association of University Professors (www.aaup.org/AAUP/pubsres/academe/2010/JF/feat/schlie.htm).

Schilt, Kristen. 2006. "Just One of the Guys? How Transmen Make Gender Visible at Work." *Gender & Society* 20(4, August): 465–90.

Schmalzbauer, Leah. 2004. "Searching for Wages and Mothering from Afar: The Case of Honduran Transnational Families." *Journal of Marriage and Family* 66 (December): 1317–31.

Schoenborn, Charlotte A. and Patricia F. Adams. 2010. *Health Behaviors of Adults: United States, 2005–2007*. National Center for Health Statistics. Vital Health Statistics 10(245).

Schor, Juliet B. 2002. "Time Crunch Among American Parents." Pp. 83–102 in *Taking Parenting Public*, edited by S. A. Hewlett, N. Rankin, and C. West. Lanham, MD: Rowman & Littlefield.

Schwartz, Karyn. 2007. "Spotlight on Uninsured Parents: How a Lack of Coverage Affects Parents and Their Families" (Kaiser Low-Income Coverage and Access Survey). *The Kaiser Commission on Medicaid and the Uninsured*, June. Menlo Park, CA/The Henry J. Kaiser Family Foundation.

Schwartz, Seth J. and Gordon E. Finley. 2006. "Father Involvement, Nurturant Fathering, and Young Adult Psychosocial Functioning." *Journal of Family Issues* 27(5): 712–31.

Science Daily. 2006. "Transgender Experience Led Stanford Scientist to Critique Gender Difference." Retrieved 21 November 2006 (www.sciencedaily.com/releases/2006/07/060714174545.htm).

ScienceBlog.com. 1999. "New Longitudinal Study Finds That Having A Working Mother Does No Significant Harm To Children" (www.scienceblog.com/community/older/1999/A/199900447.html).

Scott, Donald M. and Bernard W. Wishy. 1982. *America's Families: A Documentary History*. New York: Harper & Row Publishers.

Scott, Megan K. 2009. "Multitaskers Say One Online Dating Site Won't Do." Retrieved 22 January 2010. Fall River, MA: The Herald News (www.heraldnews.com/lifestyle/x545172880/Multitaskers-say-one-online-dating-site-wont-do).

Sears, William and Martha Sears. 2001. *The Attachment Parenting Book: A Commonsense Guide to Understanding and Nurturing Your Baby*. New York: Little, Brown.

Seccombe, Karen. 1991. "Assessing the Costs and Benefits of Children: Gender Comparisons Among Childfree Husbands and Wives." *Journal of Marriage and the Family* 53: 191–202.

———. 2002. " 'Beating the Odds' Versus 'Changing the Odds': Poverty, Resilience, and Family Policy." *Journal of Marriage and Family* 64: 384–94.

———. 2007. *Families in Poverty*. Boston: Allyn & Bacon.

———. 2011. *So You Think I Drive a Cadillac?: Welfare Recipients' Perspectives on the System and Its Reform*. Needham Heights, NJ: Allyn & Bacon.

Seccombe, Karen and Gary R. Lee. 1986. "Female Status, Wives' Autonomy and Divorce: A Cross-Cultural Study." *Family Perspectives* 20: 241–49.

Seccombe, Karen and Kim A. Hoffman. 2007. *Just Don't Get Sick: Access to Health Care in the Aftermath of Welfare Reform*. Piscataway, NJ: Rutgers University Press.

Sedlak, Andrea J. and Diane D. Broadhurst. 1998. "Executive Summary of the Third National Incidence Study of Child Abuse and Neglect" (www.casanet.org/library/abuse/stabuse.htm).

Seegobin, Winston and Kristen M. Tarquin. 2003. "Mate Selection in Trinidad and Tobago." Pp. 61–75 in *Mate Selection Across Cultures*, edited by R. R. Hamon and B. B. Ingoldsby. Thousand Oaks, CA: Sage Publications, Inc.

Seiler, William J. and Melissa L. Beall. 2011. *Communication: Making Connection, 8th ed.* Boston: Allyn & Bacon.

Seltzer, Judith A. 2004. "Cohabitation and Family Change." Pp. 57–78 in *Handbook of Contemporary Families*, edited by M. Coleman and L. H. Ganong. Thousand Oaks, CA: Sage Publications, Inc.

Senanayake, Pramilla. 1999. "Global Challenges in Ending Gender-Based Violence." Retrieved 19 March 2003. International Planned Parenthood Federation. Available online (www.ippf.org/resource/gbv/chogm99/global.htm).

Serbin, Lisa, Diane Poulin-Dubois, Karen A. Colburne, Maya G. Sen, and Julie A. Elchstedt. 2001. "Gender Stereoptyping in Infancy: Visual Preferences for and Knowledge of Gender-Stereotyped Toys in the Second Year." *International Journal of Behavioral Development* 25(1): 7–15.

Shanhong, Luo and Eva C. Klohnen. 2005. "Assortative Mating and Marital Quality in Newlyweds: A Couple-Centered Approach." *Journal of Personality and Social Psychology* 88: 304–26.

Shehan, Constance L., Felix M. Berardo, Erica Owens, and Donna H. Berardo. 2002. "Alimony: An Anomaly in Family Social Science." *Family Relations* 51: 308–16.

Shelton, Beth Anne. 1992. *Women, Men, and Time: Gender Differences in Paid Work, Housework, and Leisure*. Greenwood Press.

Shepard, Judy. 2009. *The Meaning of Matthew: My Son's Murder in Laramie, and a World Transformed*. New York: Hudson Street Press.

Sherman, Arloc. 2009. "Income Gaps Hit Record Levels in 2006, New Data Show Rich-Poor Gap Tripled Between 1979 and 2006." Retrieved 9 November 2009. Washington, DC: Center for Budget and Policy Priorities (www.cbpp.org/cms/index.cfm?fa=view&id=2789).

Sherman, Arloc and Aviva Aron-Dine. 2007. "New CBO Data Show Income Inequality Continues to Widen: After-Tax Income for Top 1 Percent Rose by $146,000 in 2004." Retrieved 1 October 2007. Center on Budget and Policy Priorities (www.cbpp.org/1-23-07inc.htm).

Shin, Hyon B. and Robert A. Kominski. 2010. *Language Use in the United States: 2007*. Technical Report No. ACS-12. Washington, DC: U.S. Census Bureau.

Shriner, Michael, Ronald L. Mullis, and Bethanne M. Schlee. 2009. "The Usefulness of Social Capital Theory for Understanding the Academic Improvement of Young Children in Stepfamilies Over Two Points in Time." *Journal of Divorce & Remarriage* 50(7, October): 445–58.

Sickels, Robert J. 1972. *Race, Marriage, and the Law.* Albuquerque, NM: University of New Mexico Press.

Siefert, Kristine, Colleen Heflin, Mary Corcoran, and David R. Williams. 2004. "Food Insufficiency and Physical and Mental Health in a Longitudinal Survey of Welfare Recipients." *Journal of Health and Social Behavior* 45: 171–86.

Simon, Rita J. and Howard Alstein. 2000. *Adoption Across Borders: Serving the Children in Transracial and Intercountry Adoptions.* Lanham, MD: Rowman & Littlefield.

Simon, Rita J. and Rhonda M. Roorda. 2009. *In Their Siblings' Voices: White Non-Adopted Siblings Talk About Their Experiences Being Raised with Black and Biracial Brothers and Sisters.* New York: Columbia University Press.

Simon, Robin W. 2008. "Life's Greatest Joy?: The Negative Emotional Effects of Children on Adults." *Contexts* 7: 40–45.

Simons, Ronald L., Leslie G. Simons, Callie H. Burt, Holli Drummund, Eric Stewart, Gene H. Brody, Frederick X. Gibbons, and Carolyn Cutrona. 2006. "Supportive Parenting Moderates the Effect of Discrimination Upon Anger, Hostile View of Relationships, and Violence Among African American Boys." *Journal of Health and Social Behavior* 47(December): 373–89.

Simpson, Gaynell Marie and Claudia Lawrence-Webb. 2009. "Rethinking Relationships Between Divorced Mothers and Their Children: Capitalizing on Family Strengths." *Journal of Black Studies* 39(6): 825–47.

Simpson, George Eaton and Milton J. Yinger. 1985. *Racial and Cultural Minorities: An Analysis of Prejudice and Discrimination, 4th ed.* New York: Harper & Row.

Sinclair, Upton. 1906, reprinted 1981. *The Jungle.* New York: Bantam.

Singh, Susheela, Jacqueline E. Darroch, Lori S. Ashford, and Michael Vlassoff. 2009. *Adding It Up: The Costs and Benefits of Investing in Family Planning and Maternal and Newborn Health.* New York: Guttmacher Institute and United Nations Population Fund.

Skogrand, Linda, Nikki DeFrain, John DeFrain, and Jean E. Jones. 2007. *Surviving and Transcending a Traumatic Childhood: The Dark Thread.* New York & London: Hayworth Press/Taylor & Francis.

Slavin, Robert E., Nancy Madden, Margarita Calderón, Anne Chamberlain, and Anne Hennessy. 2010. *Reading and Language Outcomes of a Five-Year Randomized Evaluation of Transitional Bilingual Education.* Institute of Education Sciences, U.S. Department of Education.

Small, Wolf Joanne. 2007. *The Adoption Mystique: A Hard-Hitting Expose of the Powerful Negative Social Stigma That Permeates Child Adoption in the United States.* Bloomington, IN: Authorhouse.

Smedley, Brian D., Adrienne Y. Stith, and Alan R. Nelson, eds. 2002. *Unequal Treatment: Confronting Racial and Ethnic Disparities in Health Care.* Washington, DC: National Academy Press.

Smith, Alison J. 2004. "Who Cares? Fathers and the Time They Spend Looking After Children" (Sociology Working Paper No. 2004-05). *Department of Sociology, University of Oxford.* Oxford, England (www.nuff.ox.ac.uk/users/smith/2004-05).

Smith, Dan. 1997. *The State of War and Peace Atlas.* Myriad Editions Ltd.

Smith, Earl and Angela Hattery. 2009. *Interracial Relationships in the 21st Century.* Durham, NC: Carolina Academic Press.

Smith, Gregory C., Susan E. Savage-Stevens, and Ellen S. Fabian. 2002. "How Caregiving Grandparents View Support Groups for Grandchildren in Their Care." *Family Relations* 51(3): 274–81.

Smith, Judith, Jeanne Brooks-Gunn, and Pamela Klebanov. 1997. "Consequences of Growing Up Poor for Young Children." In *Consequences of Growing Up Poor*, edited by Greg J. Duncan and Jeanne Brooks-Dunn. New York: Russell Sage Foundation.

Smith, Lynne, Patrick C.L. Heaven, and Joseph Ciarrochi. 2008. "Trait Emotional Intelligence, Conflict Communication Patterns, and Relationship Satisfaction." *Personality and Individual Differences* 44(6, April): 1314–25.

Smith, Sandi W. and Steven Wilson. 2009. *New Directions in Interpersonal Communication Research.* Newbury Park, CA: Sage Publications.

Smith, Suzanne R., Raeann R. Hamon, J. Elizabeth Miller, and Bron B. Ingoldsby. 2009. *Exploring Family Theories, 2nd ed.* New York: Oxford University Press.

Smith, William L. 1999. *Families and Communes: An Examination of Nontraditional Lifestyles.* Newbury Park, CA: Sage Publications.

Social Register. 2003. New York: Social Register Association.

Social Security Online. 2010. "Electronic Fact Sheet Update 2010" (SSA Publication No. 05-10003). Retrieved 4 June 2010 (www.socialsecurity.gov/pubs/10003.html).

Society for Research in Child Development. 2008. *Improving After-School Programs in a Climate of Accountability.* Social Policy Report Brief No. 22 (2).

Solarz, Andrea, ed. 2008. *Lesbian Health: Current Assessments and Directions for the Future.* Washington, DC: National Academies Press.

Soto, Mauricio. 2009. "How Is the Financial Crisis Affecting Retirement Savings?" Retrieved 30 April 2010. (www.urban.org/publicaions/901206.html). Washington, DC/Urban Institute.

Southern Poverty Law Center. 2010. "Active U.S. Hate Groups." Retrieved 28 June 2010 (www.splcenter.org/get-informed/hate-map).

Spaht, K. 2002. "Why Covenant Marriage May Prove Responsive to the Culture of Divorce." Pp. 59–67 in *Revitalizing the Institution of Marriage for the 21st Century: An Agenda for Strengthening Marriage*, edited by Alan J. Hawkins, Lynn D. Wardle, and David Coolidge. New York: Praeger.

Spock, Benjamin, Dr. 2004. "Gay and Lesbian Parents" (Webpage). In *Dr. Spock*. Retrieved 25 May 2006 (www. drspock.com/article/0,1510,4028,00.html).

Spruijt, Ed and Vincent Duindam. 2010. "Joint Physical Custody in The Netherlands and the Well-Being of Children." *Journal of Divorce & Remarriage* 51(1, January): 65–82.

Stacey, Judith and Timothy J. Biblarz. 2001. "(How) Does the Sexual Orientation of Parents Matter?" *American Sociological Review* 66(2, April): 159–83.

Stack, Peggy Fletcher. 1998. "Globally, Polygamy is Commonplace." Retrieved 21 April 2003. The Salt Lake Tribune. Available online (polygamy.com/other-globally-polygamy-18-commonplace.htm).

Stack, Steven and J. Ross Eshleman. 1998. "Marital Status and Happiness: A 17-Nation Study." *Journal of Marriage and the Family* 60: 527–36.

Stalking Resource Center. 2009. *Stalking Fact Sheet*. Washington, DC: National Center for Victims of Crime.

Steinberg, Stephen. 1981. *The Ethnic Myth: Race, Ethnicity, and Class in America*. Boston, MA: Beacon Press.

Stephens, William N. 1963. *The Family in Cross-Cultural Perspective*. New York: Holt, Rinehart, and Winston.

Sterba, James P. 2009. *Affirmative Action for the Future*. Ithaca, NY: Cornell University Press.

Sterk-Elifson, Claire. 1994. "Sexuality Among African American Women." Pp. 99–127 in *Sexuality Across the Life Course*, edited by A. Rossi. University of Chicago Press.

Sternberg, Robert J. 1986. "A Triangular Theory of Love." *Psychological Review* 93(2): 119–35.

Sternberg, Robert J. and Karen Sternberg, eds. 2008. *The New Psychology of Love*. New Haven, CT: Yale University Press.

Stevens, Daphne Pedersen, Krista Lynn Minnotte, Susan E. Mannon, and Gary Kiger. 2007. "Examining the 'Neglected Side of the Work-Family Interface.'" *Journal of Family Issues* 28(2): 242–62.

Stevens, Jacqueline. 1999. *Reproducing the State*. Princeton, NJ: Princeton University Press.

Stevenson, Betsey and Justin Wolfers. 2007. "The Paradox of Declining Female Happiness." bpp.wharton.upenn.edu/ betseys/papers/Paradox%20of%20declining%20female% 20happiness.pdf.

Stevenson, Michelle L., Tammy L. Henderson, and Eboni Baugh. 2007. "Vital Defenses." *Journal of Family Issues* 28(2): 182–211.

Stewart, Susan D. 2005. "How the Birth of a Child Affects Involvement with Stepchildren." *Journal of Marriage and Family* 67(2, May): 461.

—. 2007. *Brave New Stepfamilies*. Thousand Oaks, CA: Sage Publications.

Stockard, Janice E. 2002. *Marriage in Culture*. Orlando, FL: Harcourt Brace.

Stoll, Barre M., Genevieve L. Arnaut, Donald K. Fromme, and Jennifer A. Felker-Thayer. 2006. "Adolescents in Stepfamilies." *Journal of Divorce and Remarriage* 44(1): 177–89.

Stombler, Mindy, Dawn M. Baunach, Elisabeth O. Burgess, Denise Donnelly, Wendy Simonds, and Elroi J. Windsor, eds. 2010. *Sex Matters: The Sexuality and Society Reader, 3rd ed.* New York: Prentice Hall.

Stone, Pamela. 2008. *Opting Out? Why Women Really Quit Careers and Head Home*. Berkeley, CA: University of California Press.

Strach, Patricia. 2007. *All in the Family: The Private Roots of American Public Policy*. Palo Alto, CA: Stanford University Press.

Strathern, Andrew and Pamela J. Stewart. 2011. *Kinship in Action: Self and Group*. Boston: Pearson.

Straus, Murray A. 1980. "Social Stress and Marital Violence in a National Sample of American Families." *Annals of the New York Academy of Sciences* 347: 229–50.

Straus, Murray A. and Mallie J. Paschall. 2009. "Corporal Punishment by Mothers and Development of Children's Cognitive Ability: A Longitudinal Study of Two Nationally Representative Age Cohorts." *Journal of Aggression, Maltreatment & Trauma* 48: 459–83.

Straus, Murray, A., Richard J. Gelles, and Suzanne K. Steinmetz. 1980. *Behind Closed Doors: Violence in the American Family*. New York: Anchor Books.

Strayhorn, Joseph M. and Jillian C. Strayhorn. 2009. "Religiosity and Teen Birth Rate in the United States." *Reproductive Health* 6(14): doi: 10.1186/1742-4755-6-14.

Strazdins Lyndall, Mark Clements, and Rosemary J. Korda. 2006. "Unsociable Work? Nonstandard Work Schedules, Family Relationships and Children's Well-Being." *Journal of Marriage and the Family* 68(2): 394–410.

Stritof, Sheri and Bob Stritof. 2006. "Covenant Marriage Statistics." Retrieved 6 June 2006. About.com (marriage. about. com/cs/covenantmarriage/ a/covenant_3.htm).

Strohschein, Lisa. 2005. "Parental Divorce and Child Mental Health Trajectories." *Journal of Marriage and Family* 67(5, December): 1286.

Strom, Robert D., Steven D. Heeder, and Paris S. Strom. 2005. "Performance of Black Grandmothers: Perceptions of Three Generations of Females." *Educational Gerontology* 31(3, March): 187–205.

Strong-Jekely, Lara. 2006. Letter to the Editor. Brain, Child, p. 2. Budapest, Hungary, Winter.

Sudarkasa, Niara. 1999. "Interpreting the African Heritage in Afro-American Family Organization." Pp. 59–73 in *American Families: A Multicultural Reader*, edited by S. Coontz, M. Parson and G. Raley. New York: Routledge.

Sukel, Kayt. 2008. "The Unexpected Dependent: When Retirement Is Not for You Alone." Retrieved 4 December 2009. AARP Bulletin Today (Bulletin.aarp.org/yourworld/family/articles/the_unexpected_dependent, html).

Sullivan, Oriel and Scott Coltrane. 2008. "Men's Changing Contribution to Housework and Child Care" (Discussion Paper Prepared for 11th Annual Conference of the Council on Contemporary Families, April 25–26, 2008). Retrieved 31 December 2009 (www.contemporary-families.org/subtemplate.php?t=briefingPapers&ext=menshousework).

Sun, Yongmin and Yuanzhang Li. 2008. "Stable Postdivorce Family Structures During Late Adolescence and Socioeconomic Consequences in Adulthood." *Journal of Marriage and Family* 69(742–762).

—. 2009. "Postdivorce Family Stability and Changes in Adolescents' Academic Performance." *Journal of Family Issues* 30(11): 1527–55.

Suro, Roberto. 2006. "A Developing Identity: Hispanics in the United States." In *Carnegie Reporter. Carnegie Foundation*, Spring. New York.

Swanbrow, Diane. 2002. "Study Finds American Men Doing More Housework." In *News and Information Services*. Retrieved 25 March 2009. (www.umich.edu/~urecord/0102 Mar25_02/16.htm). Ann Arbor/University of Michigan.

Swedberg, Richard. 2007. *Principles of Economic Sociology*. Princeton, NJ: Princeton University Press.

Sweeney, Megan M. 2002. "Remarriage and the Nature of Divorce." *Journal of Family Issues* 23(3): 410–40.

Szasz, Margaret Connell. 1985. "Native American Children." In *American Childhood: A Research Guide and Historical Handbook*, edited by J. M. Hawes and N. R. Hiner. Westport, CT: Greenwood Press.

Szinovacz, Maximiliane E. 1998. "Grandparents Today: A Demographic Profile." *The Gerontologist* 38: 37–52.

Szinovacz, Maximiliane E. and Paula Harpster. 1993. "Employment Status, Gender Role Attitudes, and Marital Dependence in Later Life." *Journal of Marriage and the Family* 49: 927–40.

Tach, Laura and Sarah Halpern-Meekin. 2009. "How Does Premarital Cohabitation Affect Trajectories of Marital Quality?" *Journal of Marriage and Family* 71(2, May): 298–317.

Tafoya, Sonya M., Hans Johnson, and Laura E. Hill. 2004. *Who Chooses to Choose Two?* New York and Washington, DC: Russell Sage Foundation and Population Reference Bureau.

Tamis-LeMonda, Catherine S., Niobe Way, Diane Hughes, Hiro Yoshikawa, Ronit Kahana Kalman, and Erika Y. Niwa. 2008. "Parents' Goals for Children: The Dynamic Co-Existence of Individualism and Collectivism in Cultures and Individuals." *Social Development* 17: 183–209.

Tannen, Deborah. 1994. *Gender and Discourse*. New York: Oxford University Press.

Tapestry against Polygamy. 2006. Home page. Retrieved 14 March 2006 (www.polygamy.org).

Taylor, Paul, Cary Funk, and April Clark. 2007a. *From 1997 to 2007: Fewer Mothers Prefer Full-Time Work*. Washington, DC: Pew Research Center.

—. 2007b. Generation Gap in Values, Behaviors: As Marriage and Parenthood Drift Apart, Public is Concerned About Social Impact. Washington, D.C.: Pew Research Center, 1 July.

Taylor, Paul, Cary Funk, and Peyton Craighill. 2006. *Are We Happy Yet?* Technical Report No. 13 February. Washington, DC: Pew Research Center.

Taylor, Paul, Rakesh Kochhar, Rich Morin, Wendy Wang, Daniel Dockterman, and Jennifer Medina. 2009. *America's Changing Workforce: Recession Turns a Graying Office Grayer*. Washington, DC: Pew Research Center.

Taylor, Paul, Rich Morin, D'Vera Cohn, Richard Fry, Rakesh Kochhar, and April Clark. 2008. *Inside the Middle Class: Bad Times Hit the Good Life*. Washington, DC: Pew Research Center.

Taylor, Paul, Jeffrey Passel, Richard Fry, Richard Morin, Wendy Wang, Gabriel Velasco, and Daniel Dockterman. 2010. "The Return of the Multi-Generational Family Household." Retrieved 4 April 2010. Pew Research Center (pewresearch.orgs/pubs/1528/multi-generational-family-household).

Taylor, Raymond and Beth Andrews. 2009. "Parental Depression in the Context of Divorce and the Impact of Children." *Journal of Divorce & Remarriage* 50(7, October): 472–80.

Teachman, Jay D. 2002. "Childhood Living Arrangements and the Intergenerational Transmission of Divorce." *Journal of Marriage & Family* 64: 717–29.

—. 2004. "The Childhood Living Arrangements of Children and the Characteristics of Their Marriages." *Journal of Family Issues* 25(1): 86–111.

Tejada-Vera, Betzaida and Paul D. Sutton. 2010. *Births, Marriages, Divorces, and Deaths: Provisional Data for July 2009*. Technical Report No. National Vital Statistics Reports, Vol. 58, No. 15. Hyattsville, MD: National Center for Health Statistics.

Telzer, Eva H. and Heidie A. Vazquez Garcia. 2009. "Skin Color and Self-Perceptions of Immigrant and U.S.-Born Latinas." *Hispanic Journal of Behavioral Sciences* 31(3): 357–74.

Tenthani, Raphael. 2010. "Gay Malawi Couple Sentenced to 14 Years in Prison." Retrieved 23 May 2010. AOL News (www.aolnews.com/ca/article/gay-couple-sentenced-to-14-years-in-malawi/19484837).

Territo, Leonard and George Kirkham. 2010. *International Sex Trafficking of Women & Children*. Flushing, NY: Loose-leaf Law Publications, Inc.

TheKnot.com. 2010. "Engagement Rings." Retrieved 2 June 2010 (wedding.theknot.com/engagement-rings.aspx).

Thigpen, Jeffry W. 2009. "Early Sexual Behavior in a Sample of Low-Income, African American Children." *Journal of Sex Research* 46(1, January): 67–79.

Thomas, Adam and Isabel Sawhill. 2002. "For Richer or For Poorer: Marriage as an Antipoverty Strategy." *Journal of Policy Analysis and Management* 21: 4.

Thomas, Cindy and Marilyn Ryan. 2008. "Women's Perception of the Divorce Experience: A Qualitative Study." *Journal of Divorce & Remarriage* 49(3–4, September): 210–24.

Thornton, Arland and Linda Young-DeMarco. 2001. "Four Decades of Trends in Attitudes Toward Family Issues in the United States: The 1960s Through the 1990s." *Journal of Marriage and the Family* 63: 1009–37.

Tiefenthaler, Jill, Amy Farmer, and Amandine Sambira. 2005. "Services and Intimate Partner Violence in the United States: A County-Level Analysis." *Journal of Marriage and Family* 67(3): 565–78.

Tierney, John. 2003. "Iraqi Marriage Bedevils Americans." New York Times News Service. *The Oregonian*, 28 September, p. A-2.

Tjaden, Patricia and Nancy Thoennes. 2000. "Extent, Nature, and Consequences of Rape Victimization: Findings from the National Violence Against Women Survey" (Report NCJ 181867). *National Instiute of Justice*. Washington, DC (www.ojp.usdoj.gov/nij/pubssum/181867.htm).

—. 2006. "Extent, Nature, and Consequences of Rape Victimization: Findings from the National Violence Against Women Survey" (Report NCJ 210346). *National Instiute of Justice*. Washington, DC (www.ncjrs.gov/pdffiles1/nij/210346.pdf).

Tonnies, Ferdinand. 1963. *Community and Society,* translated by C. P. Loomis. New York: Harper and Row.

Trask, Bahira Sherif and Raeann R. Hamon. 2007. *Cultural Diversity and Families*. Thousand Oaks, CA: Sage Publications.

Trenholm, Sarah. 2008. *Thinking Through Communication*. Boston: Allyn & Bacon.

Trinder, Liz. 2008. "Maternal Gate Closing and Gate Opening in Postdivorce Families." *Journal of Family Issues* 29(10): 1298–324.

Tubbs, Stewart L. and Sylvia Moss. 2008. *Human Communication: Principles and Contexts, 11th ed.* New York: McGraw-Hill.

U.S. Census Bureau. 2006. *The 2006 Statistical Abstract: The National Data Book*. www.census.gov/compendia/statab/income_expenditures_wealth.

—. 2008a. *American Community Survey: California S1002. Grandparents.*

—. 2008b. "Table SF1. Percent Childless and Births Per 1,000 Women in the Last Year: Selected Years, 1976 to 2006." In *Fertility of American Women*. Retrieved 7 March 2010 (www.census.gov/population/www/socdemo/fertility.html).

—. 2009a. "America's Families and Living Arrangements: 2008." Retrieved 1 July 2009 (www.census.gov/population/www/socdemo/hh-fam/cps2008.html).

—. 2009b. "American Indian and Alaska Native Heritage Month: November 2009" (Press Release). Retrieved 20 January 2010 (www.census.gov/Press-Release/www/releases/archives/facts_for_features_special_editions/014346.html).

—. 2009c. *Table MS-2. Estimated Median Age at First Marriage, by Sex: 1890 to the Present*. Technical Report No. Current Population Survey, March and Annual Social and Economic Supplements, 2009 and earlier. Washington, DC.

—. 2009d. "A Child's Day: 2006 (Selected Indicators of Child Well-Being)." Retrieved 2 June 2010 (www.census.gov/population/www/socdemo/2006_detailedtables.html).

—. 2009e. "Who's Minding the Kids? Child Care Arrangements: Summer 2006: Detailed Tables." Retrieved 1 July 2009 (www.census.gov/population/www/socdemo/child/tables-2006.html).

—. 2010a. "America's Families and Living Arrangements: 2009." Retrieved 21 February 2010 (www.census.gov/population/www/socdemo/hh-fam/cps2009.html).

—.2010b. *Asian/Pacific American Heritage Month: May 2010*. Washington, DC: U.S. Department of Commerce.

—. 2010c. "Labor Force, Employment, & Earnings: Labor Force Status." In *2010 Statistical Abstract*. Washington, DC.

—. 2010d. *International Data Base*. (www.census.gov/ipc/www/idbnew.html). Washington, DC.

U.S. Census Bureau Population Division. 2009. "Analytical Document: Table 1. Projections and Distribution of the Population by Race and Hispanic Origin for the United States: 2010 to 2050." In *2009 National Population Projections (Supplemental)*. Retrieved 30 June 2010 (www.census.gov/population/www/projections/analytical-document09.pdf).

U.S. Conference of Mayors. 2008. *A Status Report on Hunger and Homelessness in America's Cities: A 25-City Survey*. Washington, DC.

U.S. Department of Health and Human Services. 2009. "Temporary Assistance for Needy Families (TANF) Caseload Data 2008." Retrieved 14 April 2009 (www.acf.hhs.gov/programs/ofa/data-reports/caseload/caseload_current.htm).

U.S. Department of Health and Human Services, Administration for Children & Families. 2006. "Children Home Alone and Babysitter Age Guidelines." Retrieved 17 July 2006 (www.nccic.org/poptopics/homealone.html).

—. 2009. "Child Maltreatment 2007." Retrieved 26 March 2010. Washington, DC: Government Printing Office (www.acf.hhs.gov/programs/cb/pubs/cm07/cm07/pdf).

—. 2010. "Child Mistreatment 2008." *Administration on Children, Youth, and Families, Children's Bureau*. Retrieved 7 June 2010 (www.acf.hhs.gov/programs/cb/stats_research/index.htm#can).

U.S. Department of Health and Human Services, Office of Women's Health. 2008. "Date Rape Drugs: Frequently

Asked Questions." Retrieved 28 March 2010 (www. womenshealth.gov/faq/date-rape-drugs.cfm).

U.S. Department of Homeland Security. 2010. "2009 Yearbook of Immigration Statistics." Retrieved 3 July 2010 (www. dhs.gov/files/statistics/publications/yearbook.shtm).

U.S. Department of Housing and Urban Development. 2010. "Final FY 2010 Fair Market Rent Documentation System." Retrieved 17 May 2010 (www.huduser.org/ portal/datasets/fmr/fmrs/docsys.html&data=fmr10).

U.S. Department of Justice, Bureau of Justice Statistics. 2007. "Homicide Trends in the U.S.: Intimate Homicide." Retrieved 10 October 2008 (www.ojp.usdoj.gov/bjs/ homicide/intimates.htm).

U.S. Department of State. 2006. "Immigrant Visas Issued to Orphans Coming to the U.S." Retrieved 13 July 2006 (Travel.state.gov/family/adoption/stats/stats_451.html).

—. 2009. "Trafficking in Persons Report 2009." Retrieved 25 March 2010 (www.state.gov/g/tip/rls/tiprpt/2009/).

—. 2010a. "Total Adoptions to the United States." Retrieved 9 November 2009 (Adoption.state.gov/news/total_chart. html?css=print).

—. 2010b. "About Us." *Under Secretary for Democracy and Global Affairs/Office To Monitor and Combat Trafficking in Persons*. Retrieved 12 June 2010 (www.state.gov/g/tip/ c16465.htm).

U.S. Equal Employment Opportunity Commission. 2010. "Charges of Discrimination FY1997-FY2009." Retrieved 18 January 2010 (www1.eeoc.gov//eeoc/statistics/ enforcement/sex.cfm?renderforprint=1).

Uebelacker, Lisa A., Emily S. Courtnage, and Mark A. Whisman. 2003. "Correlates of Depression and Marital Dissatisfaction: Perceptions of Marital Communication Style." *Journal of Social and Personal Relationships* 20 (December): 757–69.

Uhlenberg, Peter. 2009. "Children in an Aging Society." *The Journals of Gerontology: Series B* 64B(4): 489–96.

Uhlenberg, Peter and James B. Kirby. 1998. "Grandparenthood Over Time: Historical and Demographic Trends." Pp. 23–39 in *Handbook on Grandparenthood*, edited by M. E. Szinovacz. Westport CT: Greenwood.

Umaña-Taylor, Adriana J., Edna C. Alfaro, Mayra Y. Bámaca, and Amy B. Guimond. 2009. "The Central Role of Familial Ethnic Socialization in Latino Adolescents' Cultural Orientation." *Journal of Marriage and Family* 71(1, February): 46–60.

Umaña-Taylor, Adriana J., Ani Yazedjian, and Mayra Y. Bámaca-Gómez. 2004. "Developing the Ethnic Identity Scale Using Eriksonian and Social Identity Perspectives." *Identity: An International Journal of Theory and Research* 4(1): 9–38.

Umberson, Debra. 2006. "Parents, Adult Children, and Immortality." *Contexts* 5(4, Fall): 48–53.

Umberson, Debra, Tetyana Pudrovska, and Corinne Reczek. 2010, forthcoming. "Parenthood and Well-Being Over the Life Course." *Journal of Marriage and Family*.

UNAIDS. 2009. "AIDS Epidemic Update." Retrieved 17 June 2010 (www.unaids.org/en/KnowledgeCentre/HIVData/ EpiUpdate/EpiUpdArchive/2009/default.asp).

UNAIDS and World Health Organization. 2009. *AIDS Epidemic Update*. Technical Report No. UNAIDS/09.36E/JC1700E.

Ungar, Michael. 2008. "Resilience Across Cultures." *British Journal of Social Work* 38(2): 218–35.

UNICEF Innocenti Research Centre. 2000. *A League Table of Child Poverty in Rich Nations Innocenti Report Card No.1.* www.unicef-icdc.org/cgi-bin/unicef/main.sql?menu=/ publications/menu.html&testo=download_insert. sql?ProductID=226. Accessed December 5, 2005.

United Nations. 2000. *The World's Women 2000 Trends and Statistics*. New York.

—. 2000a. Retrieved 21 February 2009 (www.census.gov/ipc/ www/idbnew.html).

United Nations Children's Fund. 2002. *Young People and HIV/AIDS: Opportunity in Crisis*. United Nations Children's Fund, Joint United Nations Programme on HIV/AIDS, and World Health Organization.

—. 2006. *The State of the World's Children: Excluded and Invisible*. Retrieved 11 June 2007 (www.unicef.org/ sowc06/index.php).

—. 2009. Child Protection from Violence, Exploitation and Abuse: Child Marriage. Retrieved 18 November 2009 (www.unicef.org/protection/index_earlymarriage.html).

United Nations Population Division. 2009. "World Population Prospects: The 2008 Revision Population Database." Retrieved 15 June 2010 (esa.un.org/unpp/index.asp? panel=7).

United Nations Population Fund. 1999. "UNFPA Executive Director Dr. Nafis Sadik to Address Global Videoconfer- ence, Calls for 'Zero Tolerance of Violence Against Women' " (Press Release). Retrieved 23 March 2003 (www.unfpa.org/news/pressroom/1999/iwd99rel.htm).

—. 2007. *Programming to Address Violence Against Women: Ten Case Studies*.

—. 2008. "About UNFPA." Retrieved 14 June 2010 (www. unfpa.org/public/about).

—. 2010. *Giving Birth Should Not Be a Matter of Life and Death*.

—. 2010b. *Family Planning and Poverty Reduction: Benefits for Families and Nations*.

United Nations Statistics Division. 2005. "Table 5c—Maternity Leave Benefits." In *Statistics and Indicators on Women and Men*. Retrieved 14 January 2006 (unstats.un.org/unsd/ demographic/products/indwm/ww2005/tab5c.htm).

—. 2010a. "Statistics and Indicators on Women and Men: Table 5g. Maternity Leave Benefits." Retrieved 3 May 2010 (unstats.un.org/unsd/demographic/poducts/indwm/ tab5g.htm).

—. 2010b. Marriage and Divorce. Retrieved 2 April 2010. (us- tats.un.org/unsd/demographic/sconcerns/mar/default.htm).

University of Michigan News Service. 2002. "People Who Give, Live Longer: U-M Study Shows." University of

Michigan (www.umich.edu/4.7Enewsinfor/Release2002/ Nov02/r11112026.html).

USA.gov. 2010. "Grandparents Raising Grandchildren" (www. usa.gov/Topics/Grandparents.shtml).

USDA Center for Nutrition Policy and Promotion. 2009. "Official USDA Food Plans: Costs of Food at Home at Four Levels, U.S. Average, May, 2009." Retrieved 12 July 2009. U.S. Department of Agriculture (www.cnpp. usda.gov).

Uttal, Lynet. 1999. "Using Kin for Child Care: Embedment in the Socioeconomic Networks of Extended Families." *Journal of Marriage and the Family* 61: 845–57.

Vaaler, Margaret L., Christopher G. Ellison, and Daniel A. Powers. 2009. "Religious Influences on the Risk of Marital Dissolution." *Journal of Marriage and Family* 71(4, October): 917–34.

van Dulmen, Manfred H.M. 2003. "The Development of Intimate Relationships in the Netherlands." Pp. 191–206 in *Mate Selection Across Cultures*, edited by Raeann R. Hamon and Bron B. Ingoldsby. Thousand Oaks, CA: Sage Publications, Inc.

Vanden Boogart, Matthew R. 2006. "Discovering the Social Impacts of Facebook on a College Campus." M.Sc. Thesis, as cited in Baron, *Always On,* p. 97, Kansas State University.

Vandivere, Sharon, Kathryn Tout, Jeffrey Capizzano, and Martha Zaslow. 2003. "Left Unsupervised: A Look at the Most Vulnerable Children." In *Child Trends Research Brief.* Retrieved 27 July 2003 (www.childtrends.org).

Vedantam, Shankar. 2006. "Male Scientist Writes of Life as Female Scientist." Retrieved 21 November 2006. washingtonpost.com (www.washingtonpost.com/wp-dyn/content/article/2006/07/12/AR2006071201883.html).

Velkoff, Victoria A. and Paul A. Kowal. 2007. *Population Aging in Sub-Saharan Africa: Demographic Dimensions 2006.* U.S. Census Bureau International Population Report P95/07-1. Washington, DC: U.S. Government Printing Office.

Ventura, Stephanie J. 2009. *Changing Patterns of Nonmarital Childbearing in the United States.* Technical Report No. NCHS Data Brief, no. 18. Hyattsville, MD: National Center for Health Statistics.

Veroff, Joseph, Elizabeth Douvan, and Richard A. Kulka. 1981. *The Inner American.* New York: Basic Books.

Vincent, Wilson, John L. Peterson, and Dominic J. Parrott. 2009. "Differences in African American and White Women's Attitudes Towards Lesbians and Gay Men." *Sex Roles* 61(9–10, November): 599–606.

Viruell-Fuentes, Edna A. 2007. "Beyond Acculturation: Immigration, Discrimination, and Health Research Among Mexicans in the United States." *Social Science and Medicine* 65(7, October): 1524–35.

Vives-Cases, Carmen, Diana Gil-González, and Mercedes Carasco-Portiño. 2009. "Verbal Marital Conflict and Male Domination in the Family as Risk Factors of Intimate Partner Violence." *Trauma, Violence, & Abuse* 10(2): 171–80.

Vlosky, Denise Ashbaugh and Pamela A. Monroe. 2002. "The Effective Dates of No-Fault Divorce Laws in the 50 States." *Family Relations* 51: 317–24.

Voydanoff, Patricia. 2004. "Community as a Context for the Work-Family Interface." *Organizational Management Journal* 1(1): 49–54.

—. 2008. "A Conceptual Model of Work-Family Interface." Pp. 37–56 in *Handbook of Work-Family Integration: Research, Theory, and Best Practices*, edited by K. Korabik, D. S. Lero, and D. L. Whitehead. Burlington, MA: Elsevier.

Vrangalova, Zhana and Ritch C. Savin-Williams. 2010. "Correlates of Same-Sex Sexuality in Heterosexually Identified Young Adults." *Journal of Sex Research* 47(1, January): 92–102.

Wage and Hour Division, U.S. Department of Labor. 2010. "Minimum Wage Laws in the States—January 1, 2010." Retrieved 6 March 2010 (www.dol.gov/whd/minwage/america.htm).

Wagner, Marsden. 2008. *Born in the USA: How a Broken Maternity System Must Be Fixed to Put Women and Children First.* Berkeley, CA: University of California Press.

Waite, Linda J. and Kara Joyner. 2001. "Emotional and Physical Satisfaction with Sex in Married, Cohabiting, and Dating Sexual Unions." Pp. 239–69 in *Sex, Love, and Health in America*, edited by E. Laumann and R. Michael. Chicago: University of Chicago Press.

Waite, Linda J. and Maggie Gallagher. 2000. *The Case for Marriage.* New York: Doubleday.

Waldfogel, Jane. 2006. *What Children Need.* Cambridge, MA: Harvard University Press.

Walker, Alexis J., Margaret Manoogian-O'Dell, Lori A. McGraw, and Diana L.G. White. 2001. *Families in Later Life: Connections and Transitions.* Thousand Oaks, CA: Pine Forge Press.

Walker, Eric C., Thomas B. Holman, and Dean M. Busby. 2009. "Childhood Sexual Abuse, Other Childhood Factors, and Pathways to Survivors' Adult Relationship Quality." *Journal of Family Violence* 24(6, August): 397–406.

Wall, Elissa and Lisa Pulitzer. 2008. *Stolen Innocence: My Story of Growing Up in a Polygamous Sect, Becoming a Teenage Bride, and Breaking Free of Warren Jeffs.* New York: William Morrow.

Wall, Helena M. 1990. *Fierce Communion: Family and Community in Early America.* Cambridge, MA: Harvard University Press.

Wall, L. Lewis. 2006. "Obstetric Vesicovaginal Fistula as an International Public Health Problem." *Lancet* 368(9542, 30 September): 1201–09.

Wallace, Danielle M. 2007. " 'It's A M-A-N Thang': Black Male Gender Role Socialization and the Performance of Masculinity in Love Relationships." *The Journal of Pan African Studies* 1(7, March): 11–22.

Waller, Maureen and Sara McLanahan. 2005. " 'His' and 'Her' Marriage Expectations: Determinants and Consequences." *Journal of Marriage and Family* 67: 53–67.

Waller, Willard. 1937. "The Rating and Dating Complex." *American Sociological Review* 2: 727–34.

Wallerstein, Immanuel. 1974. *The Modern World System: Capitalist Agriculture and the Origin of the European World Economy in the Sixteenth Century.* New York: Academic Press.

—. 1980. *The Modern World System II: Mercantilism and the Consolidation of the European World-Economy, 1600–1750.* New York: Academic Press.

Wallerstein, Judith S. 2007. "Adult Children of Divorce Speak Out." *National Council on Family Relations Report* 52(4, December): F12–F13; F19.

Wallis, Claudia. 2003. "The Thing About Thongs." Essay. *Time*, 6 October, p. 94.

Walsh, Froma. 2006. *Strengthening Family Resilience, 2nd ed. (Guilford Family Therapy Series).* New York: Guilford Press.

Walsh, Wendy A., Jean Dawson, and Marybeth J. Mattingly. 2010. "How Are We Measuring Resilience Following Childhood Maltreatment? Is the Research Adequate and Consistent? What Is the Impact on Research, Practice, and Policy?" *Trauma, Violence, & Abuse* 11(1): 27–41.

Walzer, Susan. 1998. *Thinking About the Baby: Gender and Transitions Into Parenthood.* Philadelphia: Temple University Press.

Wang, Wendy and Rich Morin. 2009. "Recession Brings Many Young Adults Back to the Nest." Retrieved 4 April 2010. Pew Research Center (pewsocialtrends.org/ pubs/748/ recession-brings-many-young-adults-back-to-the-nest).

Ward, Jane. 2010. "Straight Dude Seeks Same: Mapping the Relationship Between Sexual Identities, Practices, and Cultures." In *Sex Matters: The Sexuality and Society Reader, 3rd ed.*, edited by M. Stombler, D. M. Baunach, E. O. Burgess, D. Donnelly, W. Simonds and E. J. Windsor. New York: Prentice Hall.

Ward, Russell and Glenna Spitze. 2007. "Nestleaving and Coresidence by Young Adult Children." *Research on Aging* 29(3): 257–77.

Wardhaugh, Ronald. 2010. *An Introduction to Sociolinguistics.* New York: Wiley-Blackwell.

Ware, Helen. 1979. "Polygyny: Women's Views in a Transitional Society, Nigeria 1975." *Journal of Marriage and the Family* 41: 185–95.

Warner, Judith. 2005. *Perfect Madness: Motherhood in the Age of Anxiety.* New York: Penguin Group USA.

Watkins, Tom H. 1993. *The Great Depression: America in the 1930's.* New York: Little, Brown and Company.

Weatherford, Doris. 1986. *Foreign and Female: Immigrant Women in America, 1840–1930.* New York: Schocken Books.

Weaver, Hilary N. 2009. "The Colonial Context of Violence." *Journal of Interpersonal Violence* 24(9): 1552–63.

Weber, Max. 1925, reprinted 1947. *The Theory of Social and Economic Organization.* New York: Free Press.

The Wedding Report, Inc. 2010. "Cost of Wedding." Retrieved 21 February 2010 (Costofwedding.com).

Weigel, Daniel J., Kymberley K. Bennett, and Deborah Ballard-Reisch. 2006. "Roles and Influence in Marriage: Both Spouses Perceptions Contribute to Marital Commitment." *Family and Consumer Sciences Research Journal* 35: 74–92.

Weininger, Elliot B. and Annette Lareau. 2009. "Paradoxical Pathways: An Ethnographic Extension of Kohn's Findings on Class and Childrearing." *Journal of Marriage and Family* 71(3, August): 680–95.

Welch, Charles E., III and Paul C. Glick. 1981. "The Incidence of Polygamy in Contemporary Africa: A Research Note." *Journal of Marriage and the Family*, 191–93.

Wells, John. 1982. "Alcohol: The Number One Drug of Abuse in the United States." *Athletic Training* Fall: 172.

Welter, Barbara. 1966. "The Cult of True Womanhood: 1820–1860." *American Quarterly* Summer: 151–74.

—. 2002. *Women's Rights in the United States, 1619–1995.* Krieger Publishing Company.

Wen, Ming. 2008. "Family Structure and Children's Health and Behavior." *Journal of Family Issues* 29(11): 1492–519.

Werner, Emmy E. 1994. "Overcoming the Odds." *Developmental and Behavioral Pediatrics* 15: 131–36.

—. 1995. "Resilience in Development." *American Psychological Society* 4: 81–85.

Werner, Emmy E. and Ruth S. Smith. 1989. *Vulnerable but Invincible: A Longitudinal Study of Resilient Children and Youth.* New York: Adams, Bannister, Cox.

—. 1992. *Overcoming the Odds.* Ithaca, NY: Cornell University Press.

West, Candace and Don H. Zimmerman. 1987. "Doing Gender." *Gender and Society* 1: 125–31.

West, Candace M., ed. 2003. *Violence in the Lives of Black Women: Battered, Black, and Blue.* New York: Haworth Press.

Westley, Sidney B. 2002. *Assessing Women's Well-Being in Asia.* Asia-Pacific Population & Policy No. 61. Honolulu: East-West Center, Population and Health Studies, April.

Westman, Jack C. 1998. "Grandparenthood." In *Parenthood in America.* Proceedings of the Parenthood in America conference held in Madison, Wisconsin, April 19–21, 1998. Available online: parenthood.library.wisc.edu/ Westman/ Westman-grandparenthood.html.

Weston, Kath. 1991. *Families We Choose: Lesbians, Gays, Kinship.* New York: Columbia University Press.

White, James M. and David M. Klein. 2008. *Family Theories, 3rd ed.* Thousand Oaks, CA: Sage Publications.

White, Lynn and Joan G. Gilbreth. 2001. "When Children Have Two Fathers: Effects of Relationships with Stepfathers and Noncustodial Fathers on Adolescent Outcomes." *Journal of Marriage and the Family* 63: 155–67.

White, Lynn and Stacy J. Rogers. 2000. "Economic Circumstances and Family Outcomes: A Review of 1990's." *Journal of Marriage and Family* 62: 1035–51.

White, Rebecca M.B., Mark W. Roosa, Scott R. Weaver, and Rajni L. Nair. 2009. "Cultural and Contextual Influences on Parenting in Mexican American Families." *Journal of Marriage and Family* 71(1, February): 61–79.

Whitehead, Barbara Dafoe. 2004. "Testimony Before the Committee on Health, Education, Labor and Pensions Subcommittee on Children and Families." U.S. Senate: Washington, DC, 28 April.

Whitehead, Barbara Dafoe and David Popenoe. 2002. "Why Men Won't Commit." In *The State of Our Unions: The Social Health of Marriage in America*. The National Marriage Project.

—. 2003. "Sidebar: Did a Family Turnaround Begin in the 1990s?" In *The State of Our Unions: The Social Health of Marriage in America 2003*. Retrieved 17 June 2010. National Marriage Project (www.virginia.edu/marriageproject/pdfs/print_familyturnaround.pdf).

—. 2004. *The Marriage Kind: Which Men Marry and Why*. Piscataway, NJ: National Marriage Project.

—. 2005. "Marriage and Family: What Does the Scandinavian Experience Tell Us?" In *The State of Our Unions: The Social Health of Marriage in America 2005*. Retrieved 9 August 2005. National Marriage Project (marriage.rutgers.edu/Publications/Print/PrintSOOU2005.htm).

Whitehead, Denise L. 2008. "Historical Trends in Work-Family: The Evolution of Earning and Caring." Pp. 13–36 in *Handbook of Work-Family Integration: Research, Theory, and Best Practices*, edited by Karen Korabik, Donna S. Lero, and Denise L. Whitehead. Burlington, MA: Elsevier.

Whitton, Sarah W., Galena K. Rhoades, Scott M. Stanley, and Howard J. Markman. 2008. "Effects of Parental Divorce on Marital Commitment and Confidence." *Journal of Family Psychology* 22(5, October): 789–93.

Whoriskey, Peter. 2009. "GM to Build More Cars Overseas." Retrieved 9 March 2010 (extracted from cbsnews.com). www.washingtonpost.com (www.cbsnews.com/stories/2009/05/08/politics/washingtonpost/main5001058.shtml).

Wilkenfeld, Britt, Kristin Anderson Moore, and Laura Lippman. 2008. "Neighborhood Support and Children's Connectedness" (Child Trends Fact Sheet). The Annie E. Casey Foundation.

Wilkinson, Doris Y. 1997. "American Families of African Descent." In *Families in Cultural Context: Strength and Challenges in Diversity*, edited by Mary Kay DeGenova. Mountain View, CA: Mayfield Publishing Company.

Willetts, Marion C. 2006. "Union Quality Comparisons Between Long-Term Heterosexual Cohabitation and Legal Marriage." *Journal of Family Issues* 27: 110–27.

Williams, Erica and Nicholas Johnson. 2009. "How Much Would a State Earned Income Tax Credit Cost in 2010?" Retrieved 3 May 2010. Center on Budget and Policy Priorities (www.cbpp.org/cms/index.cfm?fa=view&id=2992).

Williams, Lindy and Teresa Sobieszczyk. 1997. "Attitudes Surrounding the Continuation of Female Circumcision in the Sudan: Passing the Tradition to the Next Generation." *Journal of Marriage and the Family* 59: 966–81.

Williams, Norma. 1990. *The Mexican American Family: Tradition and Change*. Dix Hills, NY: General Hall.

Willie, Charles Vert. 1983. *Race Ethnicity and Socioeconomic Status: A Theoretical Analysis of Their Interrelationship*. Lanham, MD: Rowman and Littlefield Publishers.

Willie, Charles Vert and Richard J. Reddick. 2003. *A New Look at Black Families*. Lanham, MD: AltaMira Press.

Wilmoth, Janet and Gregor Koso. 2002. "Does Marital History Matter? Marital Status and Wealth Outcomes Among Preretirement Adults." *Journal of Marriage and the Family* 64: 254–68.

Wilson, Stephan M., Lucy W. Ngige, and Linda J. Trollinger. 2003. "Connecting Generations: Kamba and Maasai Paths to Marriage in Kenya." Pp. 95–118 in *Male Selection Across Cultures*, edited by R. Raeann R. Hamon and Bron B. Ingoldsby. Thousand Oaks, CA: Sage Publications, Inc.

Wilson, William Julius. 1987. *The Truly Disadvantaged: The Inner City, the Underclass, and Public Policy*. Chicago: University of Chicago Press.

—. 1996. *When Work Disappears: The World of the New Urban Poor*. New York: Alfred A. Knopf.

Winslow, Sarah. 2005. "Work-Family Conflict, Gender, and Parenthood, 1977–1997." *Journal of Family Issues* 26(6): 727–55.

Wolff, Jennifer L. and Judith D. Kasper. 2006. "Caregivers of the Frail Elderly: Updating a National Profile." *The Gerontologist* 46(3): 344–56.

Wolin, Steven and Sybil Wolin. 1993. *The Resilient Self*. New York: Villiard Books.

Wood, Julia T. 2009. *Gendered Lives: Communication, Gender, and Culture, 8th ed*. Boston: Wadsworth/Cengage Learning.

World Health Organization. 2009. "Gender, Women, and Health: Sexual Violence." Retrieved 18 August 2009 (www.who.int/gender/violence/sexual_violence/en/index.html).

—. 2010a. "10 Facts on Obstetric Fistula." Retrieved 16 June 2010 (www.who.int/features/factfiles/obstetric_fistula/en/index.html).

—. 2010b. "Female Genital Mutilation" (Media Centre Fact Sheet). Retrieved 17 June 2010 (www.who.int/mediacentre/factsheets/fs241/en/index.html).

World Values Survey. 1994. *World Values Survey, 1990–1993*. Ann Arbor, MI: Inter-University Consortium for Political and Social Research.

Wright, Carroll. 1889. *A Report on Marriage and Divorce in the United States 1867–1886*. Washington DC: Bureau of Labor.

Wu, Zheng and Christoph M. Schimmele. 2005. "Repartnering After First Union Disruption." *Journal of Marriage and Family* 67 (February): 27–36.

Xu, Xiaohe, Clark D. Hudspeth, and John P. Bartkowski. 2006. "The Role of Cohabitation in Remarriage." *Journal of Marriage and Family* 68(2): 261–74.

Yaben, Sagrario Yarnoz. 2009. "Forgiveness, Attachment, and Divorce." *Journal of Divorce & Remarriage* 50(4, May): 282–94.

Yadav, K.P. 2006. *Child Marriage in India*. New Delhi: Adhyahan.

Yang, Sarah. 2009. "Studies Link Maternity Leave with Fewer C-Sections and Increased Breastfeeding" (Press Release). Retrieved 24 May 2010. University of California Berkeley (Berkeley.edu/news/media/releases/2009/01/05_maternity.shtml).

Yao, Li and Stephanie A. Robert. 2008. "The Contributions of Race, Individual Socioeconomic Status, and Neighborhood Socioeconomic Context on the Self-Rated Health Trajectories and Mortality of Older Adults." *Research on Aging* 30(2): 251–73.

Yates, Michael D. 2009. *In and Out of the Working Class*. Winnipeg, MB: Arbeiter Ring.

Yeung, Wei-jun Jean, Miriam R. Linver, and Jeanne Brooks-Gunn. 2002. "How Money Matters for Young Children's Development: Parental Investment and Family Processes." *Child Development* 73: 1861–79.

Yorburg, Betty. 2002. *Family Realities: A Global View*. Upper Saddle River, NJ: Pearson Education Inc.

Yount, Kathryn M. 2002. "Like Mother, Like Daughter? Female Genital Cutting in Minia, Egypt." *Journal of Health and Social Behavior* 43 (September): 336–58.

—. 2005. "Resources, Family Organization, and Domestic Violence Against Married Women in Minya, Egypt." *Journal of Marriage and Family* 67(3): 579–96.

Zero Tolerance for Domestic Violence. 2003. Retrieved 23 March 2003 (www.co.contra-costa.ca.us/depart/cao/DomViol/ztdv%20overview%20for%20website).

Zhang, Yuanting and Jennifer Van Hook. 2009. "Marital Dissolution Among Interracial Couples." *Journal of Marriage and Family* 71(1, January): 95–107.

Zhou, Min. 2006. "Divergent Origins and Destinies: Children of Asian Immigrants." Pp. 109–28 in *Narrowing the Achievement Gap: Strategies for Educating Latino, Black, and Asian Students*, edited by Susan J. Paik and Herbert J. Walberg. New York: Springer Publishing Co.

Zhou, Min and Carl L. Bankston, III. 1998. *Growing Up American: How Vietnamese Children Adapt to Life in the United States*. New York: Russell Sage Foundation.

Zhou, Min and James V. Gatewood, eds. 2007. *Contemporary Asian America: A Multidisciplinary Reader, 2nd ed.* New York: New York University Press.

Zimmerman, Shirley L. 2001. *Family Policy: Constructed Solutions to Family Problems*. Thousand Oaks, CA: Sage.

Name Index

A

Abaid, T. A., 115
Abazov, R., 173
Abd el Salam, S., 107
Abramovitz, M., 17
Acevedo, B. P., 43, 221
Acs, G., 26
Acuña, R., 78
Adams, B. N., 291
Adams, G., 339
Adams, M., 104
Adams, P. F., 235
Afifi, T. D., 394, 429
Agnes, F., 59
Ahmed, S. S., 291
Ahrons, C. R., 428, 429
Alberti, R. E., 433
Ali, L., 298
Allan, G., 435
Allen, B., 5
Allen, B. J., 248
Altman, I., 48
Amato, P. R., 212, 241, 412, 416, 422, 428, 430, 431
Anderson, D., 100
Anderson, G., 332
Anderson, M. L., 197
Anderson, T., 246
Anderson, T. J., 194
Andersson, N., 448
Andrews, B., 429
Ängarne-Lindberg, T., 429
Ange, R. J., 389
Angel, J., 364
Angel, R. J., 387, 388
Anthony, Susan B., 83
Aquilino, W. S., 429
Aranda, E., 289
Archibold, R. C., 154
Arditti, J. A., 155
Arendell, T., 298
Aries, P., 73
Arliss, L. P., 247
Aron, A., 43, 221
Artis, J. E., 212
Asante, M. K., 250
Ashford, L., 107
Aubrey, J. S., 103
August, D., 166

Aumann, K., 330, 334
Avellar, S., 211
Avon-Dine, A., 126
Axinn, J., 22

B

Baca Zinn, M., 27
Bachman, J. G., 189
Backlund, P., 247
Bade, R., 133
Bailey, E. J., 104
Bailey, J. M., 198
Baker, K., 166
Bandura, A., 402
Bankston, C. L., III, 174
Banu, S., 403
Barna, G., 435
Barnett, M. A., 367
Baron, N., 246
Barr, S. C., 296
Barres, B., 97, 111
Barrett, A. E., 364
Barrow, L., 293
Bass, B. L., 332
Bauer, G., 420
Baum, K., 386
Baumrind, D., 297
Beach, S. H., 234
Beall, M. L., 243
Beals, K. P., 213
Bearak, B., 199, 200
Becker, G., 16, 331
Becker, J. B., 96
Bee, H. L., 293, 294
Beebe, S. A., 244, 250
Beecher, C. E., 81
Bell-Scott, P., 387, 389
Belsky, J., 340
Ben Ezra, D., 231
Bennett, C., 170, 174
Bentley, K. C., 296
Berardo, D. H., 363
Berardo, F. M., 363
Bergemann, A., 281
Berger, L. M., 438
Berger, P., 9, 56
Bergman, B., 26
Berlin, L. J., 295
Bernard, J., 237, 300

Berne, L., 462
Berns, R. M., 295, 296
Bernstein, B., 248
Bernstein, R., 150
Bertrand, M., 156
Beverly, B., 276
Bhat, A., 188
Bianchi, S. M., 232, 233, 303, 335
Biblarz, T. J., 213, 274, 307
Biddulph, S., 105
Bidwell, L. D. M., 86
Bierman, A., 235
Billingsley, A., 167
Bing, N. M., 429
Bittman, M., 331
Black, A. E., 297
Blair, S. L, 332
Blassingame, J. W., 78
Blee, K., 232
Blekesaune, M., 423
Block, J., 278
Blood, R. O., 78, 331
Blumenthal, D., 326
Blyth, D. A., 32
Bogen, K., 324
Bogenschneider, K., 22, 33
Bokker, L. P., 424, 425
Boles, R. F., 16, 42
Bonvillain, N., 41, 43, 95, 98
Booth, A., 389, 429, 431
Boss, P. G., 5
Bouchard, G., 279
Bould, S., 291
Boyd, D. A., 293, 294
Bradley, N., 297
Bramlett, M. D., 422, 433, 435
Branden, N., 43, 221
Brandolini, A., 133, 134
Bratter, J. L., 423
Braund, K. E. H., 74
Braver, S. L., 428
Bremner, J., 257
Breslau, N., 143
Brettell, C. B., 51
Briere, J., 400, 402
Briggs, S., 335
Broderick, C., 17
Broneck, K., 246
Bronte-Tinkew, J., 302
Brooks-Gunn, J., 145, 294, 297

Brown, H., 365
Brown, M., 242
Brown, S., 212
Brown, T. N., 150, 296
Browning, E. K., 24, 141
Bryant-Davis, T., 394
Bucx, F., 364
Buehler, C., 429
Buhle, M. J., 72, 74, 79, 81
Bunting, M., 336
Bures, R. M., 272
Burgess, E., 82, 232
Burke, T., 389
Burton, C. E., 142
Busby, D. M., 397, 402
Buss, D. M., 189, 190, 191
Butterfield, A. K., 22

C

Cahill, S., 362
Callister, P., 281
Calvert, S. L., 294
Cambron, M. J., 95
Campbell, J. C., 384, 394
Cancian, F. M., 81, 195, 196
Cantor, M. H., 374
Capizzano, J., 339
Carlson, M. J., 429, 438
Carr, D., 364
Cartwright, C., 412, 428, 429
Cassidy, M., 49
Cassidy, T., 276
Ceynar, M. L., 412, 428
Chang, W., 417
Cheah, C. S. L., 297
Childs, E. C., 178, 230
Christakis, N. A., 363
Christie-Mizell, C. A., 397
Christopher, F. S., 105
Chu, J., 424
Chun, H., 236
Claffey, S. T., 330
Clarkwest, A., 422
Clifton, D., 106
Cline, F. W., 335
Clopper, C. G., 248
Cobb, N., 293
Cockerham, W. C., 358
Cockrell, S., 278
Cohen, C., 179
Cohen, E., 278
Cohen, E. C., 232
Cohen, R. A., 121
Cohn, D., 100, 101, 155, 422
Cohn, D'V., 154, 163

Coker, T. R., 158
Cole, K., 168
Coleman, M., 436, 438
Coleman-Jensen, A., 121
Coltrane, S., 104, 300, 327, 330, 334
Colwell, E. W., 102
Conger, K. J., 146
Conger, R. D., 146
Conley, D., 121, 334
Cook, S. L., 392
Cooley, C. H., 293
Coontz, S., 17, 34, 69, 84, 185, 186, 228, 241, 317
Cooper, C. E., 438
Corsaro, W. A., 76
Cott, N., 76, 81, 207
Covel, S., 196
Covey, H. C., 169
Cowan, P. A., 301
Cox, M. J., 279
Craig, L., 298, 329
Creighton, M. J., 289
Crissey, S. R., 227
Crompton, R., 294, 295
Cruz, J. M., 389
Cruz, S., 214
Cui, M., 146
Cummings, E. M., 431
Cummings, J. L., 372
Cunningham-Burley, S., 297

D

Dahl, G., 92, 99
D'Aluisio, F., 137
Daly, K. J., 335
Dancy, B. L., 403
Datner, E. M., 387
D'Augelli, A. R., 96
Davis, F. J., 155
Davis, K. D., 323, 333
Davis, K. E., 194
Davis, S. N., 328, 329, 416, 417
Dawley, K., 276, 277
Day, P. J., 22, 32, 33, 461
DeFrain, J., 30
Degler, C. N., 74, 76, 82, 417
De Jonge, A., 278
DeLamater, J. J., 237, 361
Del Castillo, R. G., 79
DeLeire, T., 212
De Lew, N., 378
Delsol, C., 392
DeMaris, A., 364, 392
Demetriou, D., 262
Demo, D. H., 279

Demos, J., 69, 75
DeNavas-Walt, C., 128, 132, 164, 168, 171, 174, 235, 236, 238, 305, 325, 358, 364, 425, 426, 445
Dennison, R. P., 428
Derne, S., 43, 187
DeVito, J. A., 243
DeWolfe, C., 246
Dhaher, E. A., 403
Dickert, J., 332
Diekman, A. B., 99, 100
Dilworth-Anderson, P., 369
Divine, R. A., 79, 80
Dodson, L., 332
Dodsworth, R., 248
Domhoff, G. W., 126
Donahue, E. H., 294
Dorr, R. L. C., 83
Doss, B., 267, 298
Douvan, E., 232
Downey, D. B., 438
Drago, R., 279
Drossman, D. A., 393
Dubas, J. S., 367
Duindam, V., 425
Dumas, T. M., 297
Dunn, D. M., 243
Dupuis, S. B., 435
Durkheim, E., 9
Duvall, E., 17
Duxbury, L., 333
Dye, J. L., 112, 270
Dykstra, P. A., 366

E

Eastwick, P. W., 196
Edin, K., 87, 122, 146, 226, 227, 236, 242, 323, 421
Edmonston, B., 230
Edwards, T., 150
Eggebeen, D. J., 211, 267, 279
Ehrenreich, B., 120, 141
Eitzen, D. S., 121
Elder, G. H., Jr., 17, 321
Eliot, L., 93, 96, 98
Elliott, D. B., 208, 305, 306, 307, 308, 309
Ellis, A., 41
Elwert, F., 363
Ember, C. R., 9, 40, 41, 43, 55
Ember, M. R., 10, 40, 41, 43, 55
Engels, F., 16, 42
England, P., 9, 278
Epel, O. B., 158
Erens, B., 198
Erera, P. I., 307

Estes, C. L., 356, 357
Evans, G. W., 143
Evertsson, M., 331

F

Fabes, R. A., 101
Fagan, J., 235
Faragher, J. M., 77, 79, 80, 82
Farley, J. E., 155, 171
Farr, K., 384
Farrell, B. G., 75
Fay, J., 335
Felson, R. B., 394
Fenigstein, A., 204
Fenstermaker Berk, S., 331
Ferraro, K. J., 387
Few, A. L., 387, 389, 390
Fields, J., 307, 309, 425, 433
Filson, J., 405
Fincham, F. D., 234
Fine, M., 431
Finkel, E. J., 196
Finley, G. E., 330, 438
Fisher, A. P., 272, 273
Fisher, B. S., 391
Fisher, B., 433
Fisher, H., 194
Fitzpatrick, L., 261
Fitzpatrick, M. A., 243
Flack, W. F., Jr., 391
Flaherty, M. J., Sr., 169
Flaks, D. K., 308
Fleck, C., 365
Flexner, E., 83
Flood, M., 404
Flowers, D. R., 439
Fogarty, K., 245
Frech, A., 235
Fredrix, E., 365, 366
Freud, S., 292
Frias, S. M., 387, 388, 389
Friedan, B., 264
Friedman, C. K., 99
Frisco, M., 240
Fronczek, P. J., 55
Frum, D., 166
Fry, R., 100, 101, 163
Fryar, C. D, 204
Fulfer, J. L., 385
Furstenberg, F. F., Jr., 241

G

Gadalla, T. M., 425, 426
Galinsky, E., 321, 330, 334, 461

Gallagher, M., 235
Gallagher, S. K., 268
Galtry, J., 281
Galvin, K. M., 243, 245
Ganong, L. H., 436, 438
Garcia-Coll, C. T., 290
Gardner, M., 145, 294
Garfinkel, I., 133, 134
Garner, R., 462
Garrod, A., 293
Gatenio, S., 310, 311, 312
Gates, G. J., 198
Gatewood, J. V., 171
Gazamarian, J. A., 387
Gelles, R. J., 387, 402
Gentleman, A., 271
Gerard, J. M., 429
Gerson, M., 196, 301
Gerstel, N., 268
Gettleman, J., 199
Giele, J., 20, 22
Gierveld, J. d. J., 360
Gilbert, D., 125, 129
Gilbert, N., 22, 32, 461
Gilbreth, J. G., 436
Gilder, G., 457
Giles-Sims, J., 428
Gilmartin, S. K., 327, 328
Ginat, J., 48
Girschick, L. B., 96
Glenn, N., 361
Glick, J. E., 168
Glick, P., 48
Glynn, K., 333
Goffman, E., 457
Goldberg-Glen, R. S., 308
Goldman, J., 400, 403
Goldscheider, C., 55
Goldscheider, F., 55
Goldsmith, S., 177
Gonzalez-Lopez, G., 201, 202
Goode, W. J., 56, 194
Goodman, C. C., 308
Goodman, E., 173
Goodman, W. B., 332, 461
Goodnight, L. J., 243
Goodwin, P. Y., 434
Goodwin, R., 240
Gorchoff, S. M., 267
Gordon, L., 16, 69, 82
Gornick, J. C., 87, 323, 338
Gottman, J., 250, 278
Gottman, J. S., 278
Goulbourne, H., 58
Goyer, A., 310
Graff, E. G., 215

Grall, T. S., 303, 424, 425, 426, 427, 447
Gramsci, A., 459
Granger, R. C., 294
Grant, J. M., 361, 362
Gray, J., 246
Gray, K. A., 394
Gray, R. F., 143
Graybill, W. H., 270
Green, R., 74
Greenberg, K., 191, 433
Greenfield, E. M., 364
Greenhaus, J. H., 33
Greenstein, R., 146
Greenstein, T. N., 328, 329, 416, 417
Gregson, J., 412, 428
Griffith, W., 187, 221
Grogger, J., 248
Grossman, A. H., 96
Gupta, G. R., 188
Gurian, M., 99
Gurko, M., 83
Gurunath, V., 59
Gutman, H., 77, 78, 169

H

Haavio-Mannila, E., 361
Hadley, J., 326
Hall, C. T., 274
Hall, M. A., 271
Halpern-Meekin, S., 211
Hamilton, B. E., 44, 112, 164, 263, 264, 265, 266, 267, 278, 303, 304, 454
Hamilton, M., 100
Hammer, J., 425
Hamon, R. R., 5
Han, S.-K., 371
Han, W.-J., 291
Hancock, A.-M., 22, 141
Hans, J., 436
Hansen, C., 269
Hanson, K., 268, 269
Hardy, M. A., 358
Harpster, P., 371
Harrison, K., 103
Hartog, H., 111
Harvey, D. L., 142
Harvey, J. H., 431
Hasson, Y., 63
Hastings, D., 127
Hastings, P. D., 307
Hattery, A., 178
Haub, C., 257, 262
Hawkins, A. J., 242, 301, 439, 440
Hawkins, D. N., 429

Hawthorne, B., 424
Hays, J., 261
Hays, S., 122, 300
He, W., 347, 353, 358, 363
Heaton, T. B., 239, 422
Hefling, K., 267
Heideman, B., 422
Helgeson, V., 95, 98
Helms, H. M., 240
Hendrick, C., 194, 196
Hendrick, S. S., 194, 196
Heron, M., 352
Herrnstein, R., 142
Hesketh, T., 261, 262
Hewitt, B., 422, 423
Heyman, K. M., 121
Hickman, L. N., 340
Hill, R. B., 167
Hill, S., 104, 167, 202, 203
Hine, D. C., 77
Hines, M., 96
Hirsch, J. S., 104
Hirschman, C., 40
Hochschild, A., 233, 316, 328
Hoefer, M., 154
Hoffert, S. L., 298
Hoffman, K. A., 142, 426
Hoffman, S. D., 303
Hohmann-Marriott, B. E., 211, 422
Hojat, M. R. S., 421
Holcomb, P. A., 25
Holcombe, E., 304
Holmberg, D., 240
Honberg, R., 130
Honore, C., 335
Hook, J. L., 327
Hopper, J., 423
Horn, W. F., 303
Horowitz, R., 278
Horton, C., 293
Houser, A. N., 374
Hu, M., 362
Huberman, B., 462
Hughes, D., 296
Hughes, M. E., 220, 235
Hunter, A. G., 168
Hurst, C., 121, 123, 130
Huston, T., 241
Hutchinson, C., 267
Hyman, B., 400

I

Ingraham, C., 225
Ingram, H., 245
Isaacs, J. B., 142

Ishii-Kuntz, M., 61, 262
Ivy, D. K., 247

J

Jacklin, C. N., 99
Jackson, P. B., 372
Jacobs, J. N., 298
Jansson, B. S., 22
Jasinski, J. L., 129
Jayson, S., 110
Jekielek, S. M., 431
Jessop, C., 48
Joe, J. R., 74
John, R., 73
Johnson, C. A., 240, 251
Johnson, D., 276, 296, 386
Johnson, J. O., 339
Johnson, M. P., 332, 386, 387, 393, 394
Johnson, N., 146
Jolivet, M., 61
Jones, J. M., 69
Jones, R. K., 122
Jordan, C. E., 400, 402
Joseph, E., 48
Joshi, P., 324
Joyner, K., 236

K

Kageyama, Y., 61
Kahl, J. A., 125, 129
Kalil, A., 87, 212, 323
Kallen, C. G., 424
Kamerman, S., 22, 310, 311, 312
Kamo, Y., 232
Kane, E. W., 104
Kapinus, C. A., 439
Karger, H., 22, 32, 461
Karraker, M. W., 40, 291
Kaschak, E., 389
Kashiwase, H., 61
Kaspar, J. D., 372
Katz, R., 330
Kaufman, G., 240
Kaufman, J., 399
Keen, C., 110
Keenan, N., 256
Kefalas, M., 87, 122, 146, 226, 227, 236, 323, 421
Kelley, M. L., 298
Kellogg. S., 78
Kellough, J. E., 179
Kelly, E., 317
Kelly, J. B., 429
Kelly, M., 245, 271

Kendall, D., 126
Kennedy, T. L., 294
Kenney-Benson, G. A., 100
Kent, M. M., 257
Kerchoff, A. C., 194
Khobotlo, M., 448
Kibria, N., 174
Kiecolt, K. J., 316
Kilbourne, J., 102
Kim, J., 394
Kim, M., 193
Kimura, D., 96
Kindlin, D., 105
King, R. B., 423
King, V., 210, 301, 303, 412
Kinsella, K., 347, 353, 370, 371
Kinsey, A., 198
Kirby, J. B., 367
Kirkham, G., 384
Kishor, S., 385
Kissane, R. J., 242
Klein, D. M., 15
Klohnen, E. C., 239
Kneip, T., 420
Knobloch-Fedders, L. M., 221
Knodel, J., 327
Knoester, C., 279, 2267
Knudson, R. M., 221
Koball, H., 429
Koerner, A. F., 243, 428
Koester, J., 250
Kohn, M., 121, 295
Kohn, M. L., 129
Kominski, R. A., 170
Komter, A., 366
Kontula, O., 361
Korn, P., 278, 454
Kornbluh, K., 336
Koropeckyj-Cox, T., 270, 272
Koso, G., 236
Koss, M. P., 392
Kowal, P. A., 352
Kraditor, A. S., 83
Kramer, L., 93
Kreider, R. M., 208, 305, 307, 308, 309, 433, 435
Kristiansen, H. W., 198
Kristoff, N. D., 381, 382, 459
Kroska, A., 327
Kubler-Ross, E., 363
Kulikoff, A., 74
Kulka, R. A., 232
Kunkel, S., 360, 370
Kurchinka, M. S., 291
Kurdek, L. A., 213, 307, 435

L

Labov, W., 248
Ladner, J. A., 167
LaFraniere, S., 261
Lamanna, M. A., 436
Lamb, K. A., 436
Lamont, M., 158, 162
Landale, N. S., 211
Landsburg, S. E., 92, 99
Lane, S. D., 244, 245, 250
LaPierre, T. A., 435
Lareau, A., 121, 294, 295
LaRossa, R., 4, 300
Laszloffy, T., 179
Laughlin, L., 339
Lavee, Y., 330
Lawrence-Webb, C., 169
Leaper, C., 99
Lee, G. R., 49, 364, 417
Lee, I., 236
Lee, J., 173, 194
Lee, K. S., 61, 262
Lee, S. M., 230
Lee, Y.-S., 298, 327
Leeder, E., 34, 35, 187,
    221, 225
LeMare, L., 276
Lenhart, A., 191, 192, 193, 196
Lennings, C. J., 424
Lenski, G., 72
Leonard, L., 106
Leone, J. M., 386, 393
Leonhardt, D., 237
Lerman, R. I., 236
Leserman, J., 393
Levin, D. E., 102
Levine, J. A., 303
LeVine, R. A., 289
Lewin, T., 340
Lewis, O., 142
Lewontin, R. C., 155
Li, S., 9
Li, Y., 429
Lin, I.-F., 425
Lindau, S. T., 237, 361
Lindsey, L., 93
Lindsey, M., 102, 429
Lino, M., 122, 267, 268
Livingston, G., 164
Lloyd, S. A., 5, 16
Lobe, J., 116
Lobo, S., 73
Locke, H., 82, 232
Lockhart, C., 428

Lockman, P. T., 169
Loeb, S., 340
Logan, T. K., 386
Lopez, M. H., 154
Loprest, P., 26
Lovell, P., 142
Lowenstein, L. F., 422
Ludwig, J., 142
Luft, J., 245
Lundberg, S., 429
Lundy, G., 248
Luo, M., 87, 323
Lustig, M. W., 250
Lyster, M. E., 425

M

Maas, C., 400
Maccoby, E. E., 99, 101
Mackie, G., 60, 106
MacPhee, D., 175
Madden, M., 191, 192, 193, 196
Magnuson, K., 438
Maher, B. E., 439, 440
Mallinson, C., 248
Mammen, K., 330
Manganello, J. A., 390
Manning, W. D., 212, 232
Manzoli, L., 235
March, K., 273
Marchioro, K., 425
Marindin, H., 274
Markey, C. N., 110
Markey, P. M., 110
Markham, L. B., 297
Marks, J. L., 98
Marks, N. F., 364
Marsiglio, W., 300
Martin, C. L., 101
Martin, J. A., 263
Martin, S. L., 387
Martin, S. P., 412, 439
Martinez, M. A., 121
Marx, K., 16, 123
Massey, D. S., 248
Masterson, J. T., 250
Mather, M., 306, 307
Mathews, T. J., 112, 265
Max, W., 394
Mayer, S., 142
Mays, V. M., 158
McCool, W. F., 277
McCubbin, H. I., 30, 460
McDonald, S., 156
McDowell, H., 412, 428

McElvaine, R. S., 83
McLanahan, S., 237, 438
McLoyd, V. C., 121, 168
Mead, G. H., 293
Mead, M., 17, 189
Mead, S., 100, 104
Medora, N. P., 187
Melz, H., 241
Melzer, S., 393
Menzel, P., 137
Merrill, G. S., 390
Messner, M. A., 104
Miall, C. E., 273
Michael, K. C., 431
Michaels, M., 436
Mickelson, K. D., 330
Milkie, M. A., 232, 233, 268, 335
Milkman, R., 83
Miller, B. C., 17
Miller, N. B., 364
Mills, C. W., 9, 445
Mindel, C. H., 79
Minh, N. H., 40
Mintz, S., 34, 77, 78, 80, 241, 242
Minushkin, S., 154
Miracle, T., 201
Mishel, L., 137, 140, 168
Mitchell, K. S., 303
Moen, P., 371, 372
Monroe, P. A., 420
Monserud, M. A., 367
Moretti, E., 92, 99
Morgan, L., 360, 370
Morgan, L. H., 41
Morin, R., 317, 365
Morrissey, T. W., 336
Mosher, W. D., 422, 433, 435
Moss, S., 243
Mossaad, N., 365
Moynihan, D. P., 167
Mullainathan, S., 156
Mulsow, M., 279
Muraco, A., 5
Murdock, G., 72, 96
Murnen, S. K., 99, 100
Murphy, M., 26
Murray, C., 20, 142
Mutran, E. J., 367
Myers, S. M., 240

N

Nagae, M., 403
Nakonezny, P. A., 420
Nemeth, D., 83

Nermo, M., 331
Neuman, L. W., 10
Neville, H. A., 296
Newman, K. S., 141
Nissel, A., 179
Nock, S. L., 242, 404
Nolan, P., 72
Nomaguchi, K. M., 268, 332, 335
Nord, M., 121, 143
Nye, F. I., 16

O

Obama, B., 179
Ogburn, W., 257
Ogunwole, S. U., 175, 176
O'Hare, W. P., 145
Olah, L., 63
Oliver, M. L., 168
Orenstein, P., 100
Orshansky, M., 132
Osborne, C., 212, 307
Osmond, M. W., 16
Otnes, C., 225

P

Pai, M., 364
Pailhe, A., 330
Palmer, L., 48
Parashar, S., 412, 439
Parasuraman, S., 33
Pardo, T., 96
Pare, P.-P., 394
Parker, K., 237, 330, 334, 335, 336, 338
Parker-Pope, T., 220, 236, 251
Parkin, M., 133
Parrenas, R., 58
Parsons, T., 16, 42
Partenheimer, D., 101, 220, 239
Paschall, M. J., 380
Passel, J. S., 154, 155, 163, 177, 178
Patrikar, S. R., 59
Patterson, C. J., 307
Paul, A. M., 232
Pawelski, J. G., 307
Pearson, J., 429
Pearson, Q. M., 333
Pease, B., 404
Pedersen, W., 198
Pelham, B. W., 335
Pendell, A. M., 272
Peplau, L. A., 213
Perkins, D. F., 245
Perry-Jenkins, M., 324, 341

Pfeffer, C. A., 96
Phillips, D. R., 353
Phillips, J. A., 211
Phillips, R., 433
Piaget, J., 292
Pillard, R. C., 198
Pisoni, D. B., 248
Planty, M., 167
Pleck, E. H., 225
Pleck, J. H., 300
Poelmans, S., 334
Pollock, L. A., 73
Pong, S.-L., 32, 438, 460
Poortman, A.-R., 298, 327
Popenoe, D., 20, 62, 63, 68, 69, 196, 207, 209, 235
Porter, K. H., 83
Posner, P., 437
Powell, A., 110
Premi, M. K., 59
Presser, H. B., 87, 88, 129, 323
Preston, M., 204
Principe, D., 429
Prokos, A. H., 323
Pulitzer, L., 48
Pyke, K., 29, 85, 174, 456

Q

Quick, H., 372

R

Rainie, L., 196
Raj, A., 188
Ramirez, A., Jr., 246
Rani, M., 403
Rank, M. R., 132
Rankin, N., 335, 338
Ray, R., 284
Reddick, R. J., 167
Reed, M. R., 142
Reese, L., 166
Reeves, T., 170, 174
Reiss, I. L., 194
Reitzes, D. C., 367
Reyes, J. R., 184
Ricci, I., 429
Richters, J., 204, 205
Riedman, A., 436
Riphahn, R. T., 281
Ristock, J., 389
Robert, S. A., 372
Robson, K., 332
Rockquemore, K. A., 179

Rodgers, J. L., 420
Rodgers, K. B., 439
Rodgers, R. H., 17
Rodriguez, M., 394
Roelkepartian, E. C., 32
Roer-Strier, D., 231
Rogers, S. J., 146, 420
Rohall, D. E., 293
Rohner, R. O.., 303
Rooks, J., 277
Rose, H., 439
Rosen, K. H., 387, 390
Rosenberg, M., 261
Rosenfeld, M. J., 230
Ross, C. E., 298
Ross, E., 204
Rossell, C. H., 166
Rossi, A., 279
Rothman, B. K., 278
Roudi-Fahimi, F., 221
Rouse, C. E., 293
Rowe, G., 26
Roxburgh, S., 298
Rubin, L. B., 121, 122, 331
Rukus, J., 339
Rush, S. E., 159
Ryan, M., 428

S

Saad, L., 196, 200, 201
Sabol, W. J., 227
Saleebey, D., 29, 460
Saltzman, L. E., 387
Saluter, A., 168
Salverda, W., 133, 134
Samandari, G., 387
Sample, N., 438
Sanchez, L., 440
Sandberg, J. F., 298
Sandefur, G., 438
Sands, R. G., 308
Santelli, J. S., 304
Sapir, E., 248
Sargent, C. F., 51
Sarkadi, A., 302
Sassler, S., 207, 422
Saul, S., 271
Savage, H. A., 55
Savci, E., 213
Savin-Williams, R. C., 198
Sawhill, I., 236
Sax, L., 297
Scaramella, L. V., 146
Schaefer, R. T., 155, 171

Schaie, K. W., 17
Schieber, S. J., 370
Schiebinger, L., 327, 328
Schilt, K., 96
Schimmele, C. M., 434
Schmalzbauer, L., 289, 290
Schoenborn, C. A., 235
Schor, J. B., 330
Schwartz, K., 326
Schwartz, S. J., 438
Scott, D. M., 77, 78
Scott, M. E., 210
Scott, M. K., 191, 433
Sears, M., 278
Sears, W., 278
Seccombe, K., 22, 32, 88, 122, 129, 131, 141, 142, 143, 226, 268, 281, 300, 324, 417, 426, 458, 460
Seegobin, W., 184
Seiler, W. J., 243
Seltzer, J. A., 207, 208, 209, 210
Senanayake, P., 381
Serbin, L., 99
Shanahan, T., 166
Shanhong, L., 239
Shapiro, T. M., 168
Shehan, C. L., 428
Shelton, B. A., 331
Shephard, J., 308
Sherman, A., 126, 131, 146
Shin, H. B., 170
Shriner, M., 438
Shuey, K., 358
Siefert, K., 122
Sill, M., 237, 361
Silverstein, M., 308
Simeone, S. A., 277
Simon, R. J., 273
Simons, R. L., 297
Simpson, G. E., 155
Simpson, G. M., 169
Sinclair, U., 80, 81
Singh, S., 115
Skogrand, L., 30
Slavin, R. E., 166
Smedley, B. D., 158
Smeeding, T. M., 133, 134
Smith, A. J., 301
Smith, E., 178
Smith, G. C., 310
Smith, J., 17, 143
Smith, K. E., 121
Smith, R. S., 30
Smith, S. R., 15
Smith, S. W., 243

Smock, P. J., 211
Sobieszczyk, T., 106, 459
Sobolewski, J. M., 430
Solarz, A., 362
Solaz, A., 330
Soto, M., 365
Spaht, K., 242
Spitz, G., 365
Spock, B., 307
Sprecher, S., 105
Spruijt, E., 425
Stacey, J., 274, 307
Stack, S., 48
Stanish, P., 105
Stanley, S. M., 251
Steinberg, S., 81
Steinmetz, S. K., 387, 402
Stephens, W. N., 41, 48, 49
Sterba, J., 179
Stern, M. J., 22
Sternberg, K., 43, 221
Sternberg, R. J., 43, 194, 221
Stevens, D. P., 334
Stevens, J., 111
Stevenson, B., 237
Stevenson, M. L., 169
Stevenson, T.H.C., 124
Stewart, P. J., 40
Stewart, S. D., 436, 438
Stockard, J., 44, 45, 49, 51, 55
Stoesz, D., 22, 32, 461
Stoll, B. M., 438
Stombler, M., 196
Strach, P., 22
Strathern, A., 40
Straus, M. A., 380, 385, 387, 402, 403
Strayhorn, J. C., 122
Strayhorn, J. M., 122
Strazdins, L., 129
Stritof, B., 440
Stritof, S., 440
Strohschein, L., 431
Strom, R. D., 169
Strong-Jekely, L., 141, 333
Sudarkasa, N., 78
Sukel, K., 365
Sullivan, O., 330
Sun, Y., 429
Suro, R., 150
Sutton, P. D., 413, 419
Swanbrow, D., 63
Swedberg, R., 141
Sweeney, M. M., 211, 423
Sylvester, T., 303

Szasz, M. C., 74
Szinovacz, M. E., 367, 371

T

Tach, L., 211
Tafoya, S. M., 178
Tamis-LeMonda, C. S., 296
Taniguchi, H., 240
Tannen, D., 247
Tarquin, K. M., 184
Taylor, H. F., 197, 336
Taylor, P., 128, 231, 232, 233, 234, 235, 268, 272, 317, 320, 365, 366, 420, 421, 422
Taylor, R., 429
Teachman, J. D., 238
Tejada-Vera, B., 413, 419
Telzer, E. H., 158
Tenthani, R., 200
Terrell, P., 22, 32, 461
Territo, L., 384
Thigpen, J. W., 196
Thoennes, N., 429
Thomas, A., 236
Thomas, C., 428
Thompson, M., 105
Thorne, B., 16
Tickamyer, A., 232
Tiefenthaler, J., 407
Tierney, J., 225
Tonnies, F., 56
Trask, B. S., 5
Trenholm, S., 247, 248
Trinder, L., 429
Trost, J., 291
Tubbs, S. L., 243

U

Uebelacker, L. A., 247
Uhlenberg, P., 367, 370
Umaña-Taylor, A. J., 150, 289, 296

V

Vaaler, M. L., 423
Vanden Boogart, M. R., 246
van der Lippe, T., 298, 327
Vander Mey, B. J., 86
Vandivere, S., 404
van Dulmen, M. H. M., 185
Van Hook, J., 168, 423
Van Willigen, M., 298
Vazquez Garcia, H. A., 158

Velkoff, V. A., 352, 370, 371
Vedantam, S., 98, 111
Veneziano, R. A., 303
Ventura, S. J., 306
Veroff, J., 232
Vincent, W., 201
Viruell-Fuentes, E. A., 158
Vives-Cases, C., 405
Vlosky, D. A., 420
Voydanoff, P., 332, 461
Vrangalova, Z., 198

W

Wagner, M., 208, 276
Waite, L. J., 220, 235, 236, 298, 327
Waldfogel, J., 291
Walker, A. J., 367, 402
Walker, R., 386
Wall, E., 48
Wall, H. M., 75
Wallace, D. M., 104
Waller, M., 237
Waller, W., 82
Wallerstein, I., 57
Wallerstein, J., 412
Walsh, F., 30, 32, 460
Walsh, W. A., 400
Walzer, S., 279, 280
Wang, W., 365
Ward, J., 198
Ward, R., 365
Ware, H., 48
Warner, J., 22, 280, 298
Watkins, T. H., 83

Weatherford, D., 81
Weaver, H. N., 394
Weber, M., 71, 124
Weigel, D. J., 240
Weininger, E. B., 121, 294, 295
Welch, C., 48
Wells, J., 73
Welter, B., 75
Wen, M., 438
Werner, E. E., 30
West, C., 16, 311, 387
Westley, S. B., 60
Westman, J. C., 369
Weston, K., 213
White, J. M., 15, 17
White, L., 146, 436
White, R. M. B., 289
Whitehead, B. D., 20, 68, 69, 196, 235
Whitehead, D. L., 317, 332
Whitton, S. W., 429
Whoriskey, P., 321
Wilkenfeld, B., 145
Wilkinson, D. Y., 78, 169
Williams, E., 146
Williams, K., 235, 240
Williams, L., 106, 459
Williams, N., 79
Willie, C. V., 167
Wilmoth, J., 236
Wilson, S., 243
Wilson, S. M., 184
Wilson, W. J., 21, 87, 141, 146, 236, 422
Winslow, S., 332
Wishy, B. W., 77, 78

Wohlin, S., 30
Wolfe, D. M., 78, 331
Wolfe, V. A., 390
Wolfers, J., 237
Wolff, J. L., 372
Wood, J. T., 247
Wright, C., 417
Wu, Z., 434
WuDunn, S., 381, 382, 459

X

Xu, X., 211, 352, 433, 435

Y

Yaben, S. Y., 428
Yadav, K. P., 188
Yang, S., 281
Yao, L., 372
Yates, M. D., 129
Yeung, W. J., 121, 145
Yinger, M. J., 155
Yorburg, B., 70, 71
Yount, K. M., 106, 403

Z

Zhang, Y., 423
Zhou, M., 171, 173, 174
Zigler, E., 399
Zimmerman, D. H., 16, 141, 331
Zimmerman, S. L., 63
Ziol-Guest, K. M., 87, 323

Subject Index

Note: Page numbers followed by "f" or "t" refer to figures or tables, respectively.

A

Absolute poverty, 134
Abuse. *See* Child abuse; Elder abuse;
 Intimate partner violence; Violence
Achieved statuses, 42
Active listening, 245
Activities of daily living (ADLs), 372
Adoptions, 272–276
 closed, 273
 by gays and lesbians, 274
 international, 274–276
 open, 273
 private, 273
 public, 273
 semi-open, 273
 single-parent, 274
 transracial, 273–274
Affirmative action, 179–180
African American English (AAE), 248
African Americans, in colonial
 America, 77–78. *See also* Black
 families
Agents of socialization, 98
Aging. *See also* Grandparenthood
 economics of, 357–359
 of gay and lesbian elders, 361–362
 health and, 372–375
 patterns of, in United States, 354–356
 population over 65 in 2008, world
 comparison of, 348–349
 population over 65 in 2010, world
 comparison of, 350–351
 retirement, 369–372
 theories of, 356–357
 widowhood, 362–364
 worldwide demographics of,
 347–353
Aging couples, 359–360
 marital satisfaction of, 360–361
 relationships with children and
 grandchildren, 364–369
 sexuality and, 361
AIDS. *See* HIV/AIDS
Alaska Native families, 175. *See also*
 Families
 contemporary, 176–177
Alimony, 427–428

 gross, 427
 limited duration, 427–428
 permanent, 427
 rehabilitative, 428
Alzheimer's disease, 373
American Indian families, 175. *See also*
 Families
 contemporary, 175–176
 family life of, 73–74
Angel Plan, 262–263
Antimiscegenation laws, 229–230
Arizona, immigration law of, 153–154
Ascribed statuses, 42, 120
Asian American families, 170. *See also*
 Families
 contemporary, 171–174
 generational tension and, 174
Assisted reproductive technology
 (ART), 266, 270–271
Authoritarian parenting styles, 297
Authoritative parenting styles, 297

B

Baby-boom generation, 353
Baby bust, 264
Babysitters, 338
Bereavement and grief, process of, 363
Bhutan, poverty in, case example,
 136–137
Bilateral descent pattern, 54
Birth centers, 277
Bisexual orientation, 198
Black families, 166–168. *See also*
 African Americans; Families
 contemporary, 168
 extended families and, 168–170
Boomerang generation, 365–366
Bourgeoisie, 124
Broken homes, 304
Bundling, 75

C

Caste systems, class systems vs., 123
Caucasian, 155
Centenarians, 355
Cesarean sections, 278, 454

Child abuse
 consequences of, 400
 defined, 396–397
 factors contributing to, 399–400
 types of, 397–399, 397f
Child allowance, in Sweden, 63
Childbearing, nonmarital, 233,
 446–447
Childbirth, 276, 454
 contemporary, 277–278
 medicalization of, 276–277, 278
Child care
 effect of mother's employment on,
 340–341
 preschool-aged children, 338–339
 primary arrangements for, 339f
 school-aged children, 339–340
Childfree, voluntarily, 271–272
Child labor, 318
Child marriage, in India, 188
Child poverty, in single-parent families,
 306t
Children
 aging couples' relationships with,
 364–369
 cohabitation and, 211–212
 effects of divorce on, 412, 428–431,
 452–453
 household labor and, 331–332
 preschool-aged, child care and,
 338–339
 rewards and costs of, 267–269
 school-aged, child care and,
 339–340
 stepfamily relationships and, 438
Child support, 426–427, 446–447
China, one-child policy of, 260–262
Civil unions, same-sex marriage vs.,
 214–216
Class. *See* Social class
Clitoridectomy, 106
Closed adoptions, 273
Cognitive development perspective,
 292–293
Cohabitation, 207–208
 attitudes toward, 209, 210f, 232
 children and, 211–212
 demographics of, 208–209, 208t

Cohabitation, (*continued*)
  gay and lesbian commitment and, 213–214
  marriage and, 209–211
  repartnering and, 433
Colonial America
  African Americans and slavery in, 77–78
  courtship and partnering in, 75
  family life in, 74–79
  family size in, 76
  household structure in, 75
  Mexicans in, 78–79
  parenting in, 76–77
  relationships of husband and wives in, 76
Comic strip families, 4
Common couple violence (CCV), 386
Communication
  conflict and, 250–251
  cultural differences in, 248–250
  defined, 243
  electronic, 246
  embracing differences in, 246–248
  listening and, 244–245
  marriage and, 242–251
  nonverbal, 243–244
  problem solving and, 250–251
  race, ethnicity in, 248
  self-disclosure and, 245–246
  social class and, 248
  verbal, 243
Community factors, resiliency and, 32
Compadres, 79
Companionate family, 82
Comparative perspective, of families, 9–10
Concrete operational thought, 292
Conflict, communication and, 250
Conflict Tactics Scale (CTS), 385
Conflict theory, 16
Contraceptive use, 115f
Courtship
  changing nature of, in United States, 189–191
  in India, 187–188
  love and, 185–187
  mate selection and, 185–193
  in United States, 188–193
Covenant marriage, 242, 440
Cross-sectional data, defined, 132
Cross-sectional divorce rate, 413
Crude divorce rate, 413
  in United States, 419f
C-sections. *See* Cesarean sections

Cult of domesticity, 81
Cultural norms, as cause of violence, 404
Custody
  joint legal, 424
  joint physical, 425
  legal, 424
  physical, 424–425
Cyberstalking, 387

D

Date rape drugs, 392
Dating
  meeting places for, 191–193, 192t, 193t
  online, 191–193, 192t
  origins of, 188–189
  rating and, 189
  violence, 390–392
Day care centers, 338
Dementia, 372–373
Demographic transition, defined, 352
Depression. *See* Great Depression, coming of age in
Descent, patterns of, 54–55
Developmental theory, 17
Discrimination, 157, 158
Displaced homemaker, 427
Disposable workforce, 324–325
Divorce, 412–413
  attitudes toward, in 23 countries, 440t
  community dimension of, 428
  cross-cultural comparisons of, 413–418
  economic dimension of, 425–428
  effects of, on children, 412, 428–431, 452–453
  historical trends in United States for, 418–419
  initiatives to limit, 439–440
  Japanese, 417–418
  macro-level factors associated with, 419–421
  measuring, 413
  micro-level factors associated with, 421–423
  no-fault, 420
  psychic, 428
  remarriage and, 431–435
  repartnering after, 431–433
Divorcee
  emotional dimension of, 423–424
  legal dimension of, 424
  parental dimension of, 424–425
Domesticity, cult of, 81

Domestic partner benefits, 8
Domestic partners, 7
Dowry, 188

E

Early childhood education and care (ECEC), 341–342
Earned Income Tax Credit (EITC), 146
Ego, 292
Elder abuse, defined, 400–401
Electronic communication, 246
Empirical approach, 10–15
Endogamy, 43, 191
Ethnic cleansing, 162
Ethnic group, 156
Ethnic groups, prevalence of, across world, 160–161
Ethnic intermarriage, 228–231
Ethnicity
  child abuse and, 398, 398t
  communication and, 248
  defined, 155–156
  grandparenting and, 367–369
  intimate partner violence and, 387–389
  socialization and, 296
Ethnic socialization, 296
Ethnocentrism, 10
Exogamy, 43, 191
Experiments, 14t
Extended families, Black families and, 168–170

F

Families. *See also* Aging couples; Asian American families; Black families; Hispanic families; Interracial families
  changes in contemporary American, 18–19
  comic strip, 4
  comparative perspective of, 9–10
  defined, 5
  empirical approach to, 10–15
  functions of, 40–43
  future trends for, 463–464
  implications of gender for, 111–114
  importance of definitions of, 5–8
  in India, 58–60
  in Japan, 60–62
  in major types of societies, 71t
  social change and, 17–18
  as social institutions, 26–27

sociological imagination of, 8–9
themes regarding, 453–463
theories of, 15–17, 15f
unemployment and, 321–323
using Social Security for young,
337–338
Familism, 79
Family allowances, 310–312
Family change
causes of, 20f
conservative perspective of, 20–21
feminist perspective of, 21–22
liberal perspective of, 21
as political issue, 19–22
Family child care providers, 338
Family history, reasons for studying, 68–71
Family leaves, 281–284
Family life
in colonial America, 74–79
in early European society, 72–73
effect of social inequality on, 28
in horticultural and agrarian societies,
72–73
as hunter-gatherers, 72
of Native Americans, 73–74
in nineteenth century America, 79–82
in twentieth century America, 82–86
Family life styles, attitudes toward, by
age group, 6t
Family Medical Leave Act (FMLA),
283–284
Family members, as agents of
socialization, 98–99
Family of orientation, 27
Family of procreation, 27
Family patterns, modernization and, 55–57
Family planning, 114–116
Family policy
family values and, 24–26
means-tested programs, 22
as reflection of historical, cultural,
political, and social factors, 32–33
selective programs, 22
state and, 22–26
universal policy and, 22
Family privacy norms, as cause of
violence, 404
Family protective factors (FPF),
resiliency and, 30–32, 459–460
Family recovery factors (FRF),
resiliency and, 30–32
Family strengths perspective, 459
Family systems theory, 17
Family values, family policy and, 24–26
Fatalism, poverty and, 142

"Fathering" parenting style, 297–298,
300–303
as activity, 301–303
as identity, 300–301
Fee-for-service health care system, 325
Female genital cutting, 105–106
Feminist theory, 16
Feminization of poverty, 445–446
Fertility rates
in China, 260–262
in Japan, 262–263
teenage, in United States, 304f
in United States, 263–265
Fictive kin, 5
Fistulas, 52–53
Focus groups, 14t
Formal care, 373
Formal operational thought, 292

G

Gay couples, lesbian couples vs.,
213–214
Gay elders, 361–362
Gay families, 307–308
Gays, 198
adoptions by, 274
attitudes toward, 199–201
intimate relationships of, 212–214
Gemeinschaft, 56
Gender. *See also* Women
defined, 93
differences in, and loving, 195–196
as dimension of social inequality,
459
implications for families of,
111–114
incongruence between sex and,
96–97
median weekly earnings of full-time
workers by educational attainment
and, 113t
social construction of, 93
socialization and, 297
sources of learning about, 98–104
Gender-based violence, 381–384
Gender gap, power of education and,
107, 108–109
Gender socialization, 98
effect of race, ethnicity, and class on,
104
Genocide, 162
Gerontology, 356
Gesellscchaft, 56
Global gag rule, 116

Grandchildren
aging couples' relationships with,
364–369
grandparents raising, 308–310
Grandparenthood, 366–369
contemporary, 267
racial and ethnic differences of,
367–369
sex differences of, 367
Great Britain, social class in, 124–125
Great Depression, coming of age in, 85
Great Recession
families and, 87–88
life in, 321–326
Grief and bereavement, process of, 363
Gross alimony, 427

H

Health, aging and, 372–375
Health insurance, in United States,
325–326, 446
Heterogeneous relationships, 191
Heterosexual couples, homosexual
couples vs., 213
Heterosexual orientation, 198
Hidden curriculum, 100
Hispanic families. *See also* Families
bilingual education and, 164–166
contemporary, 163–164
cultures of, 162–163
HIV/AIDS, 205–207, 448–452
Home observation of the measurement
of the environment (HOME), 121
Homogeneous relationships, 191
Homosexual couples, heterosexual
couples vs., 213
Homosexual orientation, 198
Household labor
child care, 329–330
children and, 331–332
defined, 327
explanations for division of, 331
housework, division of, 327–329, 328f,
329t
occasional, 327
renegotiating, 330
routine, 327
Human agency, 27

I

Id, 292
Immigration
Arizona's law on, 153–154

Immigration (*continued*)
illegal, 153–155
United States and, 80–82, 151–155
Incest taboo, 41
In-depth interviews, 14t
India
age structure of, 62t
birthrates in, 59f
child marriage in, 188
concept of love in, 187–188
courtship and mate selection in, 187–188
educational statistics, 60t
families in, 58–60
infant mortality in, 62f
marriage in, 187–188
Individual-level protective factors, resiliency and, 30
Industrialization, 55–57
in nineteenth America, 79–80
Infant mortality rates
comparative, 12–13
defined, 62
in United States, 10, 62f
Infertility, 270–271
Informal care, 373–374
Information, rules of, 17
Inheritance, patterns of, 54–55
Instrumental activities of daily living (IADLs), 372
Interethnic families, 177–179
Interethnic marriage, 230–231
Intergenerational transmission of violence, 399, 402
International adoptions, 274–276
Interracial families, 177–179
Intersexed individuals, 93
Intimate partner violence, 384–386
consequences of, 393–394
coping with, 292–293
defining and measuring, 384–386
factors associated with, 392–393
frequency of, 387–389
racial and ethnic differences in, 387–389
Intimate terrorism (IT), 386
Iraq, marriages, 224–225

J

Japan
age structure of, 62t
birthrates in, 59f
divorce in, 417–418
educational statistics, 60t

families in, 60–61
fertility rates in, 262–263
infant mortality in, 62f
Johari window, 245
Joint legal custody, 424
Joint physical custody, 425

K

Kinkeepers, 367
Kinship, patterns of, 54–55

L

Labor market segmentation, 112
Legal custody, 424
Lesbian, gay, transgender, and bisexual (LGTB) relationships, Power and Control Wheel in, 406f
Lesbian couples, gay couples vs., 213–214
Lesbian elders, 361–362
Lesbian families, 307–308
Lesbians, 198
adoptions by, 274
attitudes toward, 199–201
intimate relationships of, 212–214
Life expectancy, 352
Limited duration alimony, 427–428
Listening
active, 245
communication and, 244–245
Living wage, 323
Long-term care, 3–373
formal, 373
informal, 373–374
strains of, 374–375, 375t
Looking-glass self, 293
Love, 193–195
concept of, in India, 187–188
sex differences and, 195–196
Luxembourg Income Study (LIS), 136

M

Machismo, 79
Macro theories, 15
Marital decline perspective, 233
Marital resilience perspective, 233–234
Marriage, 41
age at, 239–240
attitudes of U.S high school seniors toward, 7t, 231f
attitudes toward, 231–233
benefits of, 234–236

ceremonies, 221–226
cohabitation and, 209–211
communication and, 242–251
comparative patterns of, 46–47
covenant, 242
defined, 221
delaying, 228
differences in, 43–51
happiness and, 238–239
"his" and "hers," 237–238
in India, 187–188
interethnic, 230–231
in Iraq, 224–225
love and, 185–186
patterns of kinship, descent, and inheritance of, 54–55
patterns of power and authority of, 51–54
patterns of residence of, 55
percentage of women aged 20–24 were married/in union before age 18 across world, 222–223
racial intermarriage, 228–231
rates, 226–228
religious faith and, 240
same-sex, vs. civil unions, 214–216, 215t, 231
satisfaction with gender relations and, 240
sex and, 236–237
sexual relationship and, 240
as source of social capital, 237
universality of, 220–221
Marriage movement, 241–242
Marriage premium, 233
Masculinity, pitfalls of, 104–105
Mass media, as agent of socialization, 103
Maternity leaves, 281–284
benefits of, 282–284
Mate selection
courtship and, 185–193
in India, 187–188
in United States, 188–193
Matriarchy, 54
Matrilineal descent pattern, 54–55
Matrilocal residence, 55
Means-tested programs, family policy and, 22
Medicaid, 326
Medicalization of childbirth, 276–277, 278
Medical neglect, 398
Medicare, 375–378
Meritocracy, 123

Micro theories, 15
Middle class, in United States, 128
Midwives, 276, 277
Minority group, defined, 156
Modernization theory, 55–57
Mongoloid, 155
Monogamy, 45–48
Mortality rates, 257
"Mothering" parenting style, 297–300
    as activity, 298–303
    as identity, 298
Mutual violent control (MVC), 386

N

Nannies, 338
Native Americans. *See* American Indian
    families
Neglect, 397
Negroid, 155
Neolocal residence, 55
Nineteenth Amendment, 83
No-fault divorce, 420
Nonmarital childbearing, 233
Nonmarital sex, 232
Nonregulated couples, 250
Nonstandard work schedules, 323–324
Nonverbal communication, 243–244
Normless norm, 436

O

Observations, 14t
Occasional household labor, 327
Occupational structures, changes in,
    320–321
Oklahoma Marriage Initiative,
    251–252
Old Age, Survivor, and Disability
    Insurance (OASDI), 358–359
Oldest-old cohort, 347
One-child policy, of China, 260–262
Online dating, 191–193, 192t
Open adoptions, 273
Operational thought
    concrete, 292
    formal, 292

P

Parenthood
    sex differences in transition to,
        279–280
    transition to, 278–279
Parenting

comparative view of, 289–291
costs of, 268–269
recent trends in, 291–292
rewards of, 268, 270
socialization and, 292–303
Parenting contexts
    cohabiting families, 307
    grandparents raising grandchildren,
        308–310
    lesbian and gay families, 307–308
    single parents, 304–307
    teen parents, 303–304
Parenting styles, 297–303
    authoritarian, 297
    authoritative, 297
    "fathering," 297–298, 300–303
    "mothering," 297–300
    permissive, 297
Parents, decisions for becoming,
    267–276
Part-time work, 323–324, 336–338
Patriarchy, 51–52
    as cause of violence, 403–404
    in India, 59
    as institutional sex discrimination,
        105–107
    in Western nations, 107–110
Patricians, 72–73
Patrilineal descent pattern, 54
Patrilocal living arrangement, 40
Patrilocal residence, 55
Peers, as agents of socialization, 101
Permanent alimony, 427
Permissive parenting styles, 297
Physical abuse, 398
Physical custody, 424–425
Polyandry, 49–51
Polygamy, 48
Polygyny, 48–49
Population, worldwide fertility rates and,
    257–260
Poverty
    in Bhutan, case example, 136–137
    causes of, 137–142
    combating, 146
    comparative studies of, 133–137
    consequences of, 142–146
    culture of, 142
    families in, 131–146
    fatalism and, 142
    feminization of, 445–446
    policies, 460
    relative vs. absolute, 133–136
    social structural approach, 141–142
    status by age, for U.S., 134f

status by race and Hispanic origin, for
    U.S., 134f
    U.S. demographics of, 133
Poverty threshold, 132–133
Power, patterns of
    egalitarian, 52
    matriarchy, 54
    patriarchy, 51–52
Power and Control Wheel, 405–406, 405f
Prejudice, 157
Preoperational thought, 292
Primogeniture, 73
Private adoptions, 273
Progressive taxation, 24
Proletariat, 124
Pronatalism, 256
Psychoanalytic perspective, 292
Psychological maltreatment, 398
Public adoptions, 273
Purchasing power parity, comparative
    look, 138–139

Q

Qualitative methods, 11
Quantitative methods, 11

R

Race
    child abuse and, 398, 398t
    communication and, 248
    defined, 155
    grandparenting and, 367–369
    intimate partner violence and, 387–389
    single parents by, 305t
    socialization and, 296
Racial intermarriage, 228–231
Racial socialization, 296
Racism, 156–159, 158
    elements of, 157
Rape, college students and, 390–391
Rating and dating, 189
Recession. *See* Great Recession, families
    and
Refined divorce rate, 413
    in United States, 419f
Regulating couples, 250
Rehabilitative alimony, 428
Relative poverty, 133
Remarriage, 431–435
    demographics of, 433–434
    satisfaction and stability of, 435
Repartnering, 431–433
Research methods, summary of, 14t

Residence, patterns of, 54–55
Resiliency, family, 459
   factors affecting, 29–32
   social policy and, 114–116
Retirement
   around the world, 370
   sex differences in, 371–372
Role overload, 333
Roles, 42
Role taking, 293
Routine household labor, 327
Rules of information, 17

S

Safety net policies, U.S. vs. other
   developed countries, 23t
Same-sex marriage, 231
   attitudes toward, 216t
   civil unions vs., 214–216
Same-sex relationships, violence in,
   389–392
Sapir-Whorf hypothesis, 248–250
Schools, as agent of socialization,
   100–101
Secondary analysis, 14t
Selection effect, 211
Selective programs, family policy and,
   22
Self-care, 339–340
Self-concept, 293
Self-disclosure, communication and,
   245–246
Semi-open adoptions, 273
Sensorimotor intelligence, 292
Separate spheres, 81
Sex. *See also* Gender
   defined, 93
   as dimension of social inequality, 459
   incongruence between gender and,
    96–97
   marriage and, 236–237
   nonmarital, 232
Sex differences, 95–96
Sex discrimination, patriarchy as
   institutional, 105–107
Sexual abuse, 398
Sexual aggression, college students and,
   390–391
Sexuality, 196–197
   aging couples and, 361
Sexually transmitted infections (STIs),
   205–206
Sexual orientation, 197–198
   causes of, 198–199

Sexual scripts, 201
   components of male and female,
    203–204
   double standard in, 204–205
   race, ethnicity, social class, sex, and,
    201–203
Sexual trafficking, 382–384
Shelter movement, 395–396
Single-parent adoptions, 274
Single parents, 304–307
   child poverty and, 306
   by race, 305t
   by type, 305f
Slavery, in colonial America, 77–78
Social capital, 156
   defined, 237
   marriage as source of, 237
Social change
   families and, 17–18
   modernization theory, 55–57
   in 1960s and 1970s America, 86
   world systems theory, 57–58
Social class
   caste systems vs., 123–124
   communication and, 248
   conceptualizations of, 123–124
   family relationships and, 121–122
   in Great Britain, 124–125
   socialization and, 294–296
   in United States, 125–130
Social construct, gender and, 93–95
Social exchange theory, 16
Social inequality, 454–459
Socialization, 292–303
   agents of, 98, 99t, 293–294
   ethnic, 296
   gender, 98
   gender and, 297
   racial, 296
   social class and, 294–296
   theoretical approaches to, 292–293
Social mobility, 123
   in United States, 130–131
Social policy, family resiliency and,
   114–116
Social Security, 358–359
   for young families with children,
    337–338
Social stratification, defined, 123. *See
   also* Social class
Social structure, 8
Socioeconomic status (SES), 125
Sociological imagination, 8–9,
   444–445
   example of, 445–447

   use of comparative perspective,
    447–452
   use of empirical approach, 452–453
   using, for revisiting themes of book,
    453–463
Spillover, 333–334
Spousal privilege, 214
Spurious, defined, 211
Stalking, 386
Standard American English (SAE), 248,
   249
Statuses, 42
Stepfamily relationships, 435–438
   children and, 438
Strauss, M., 385
Stress, as cause of violence, 402–403
Structural functional theory, 16
Superego, 292
Surrogacy, 271
Surveys, 14t
Sweden
   age structure of, 62t
   birthrates in, 59f
   educational statistics, 60t
   families in, 62–63
   infant mortality in, 62f
   status of women in, 64f
Symbolic interaction theory, 166, 293

T

Teenage birthrates, 19, 462–463
Teen parents, 303–304
Temporary Assistance for Needy
   Families (TANF), 24
Temporary work, 323–324
Theories, family, 15–17, 15f
Time crunch, 334–336, 335t
Total fertility rate, 85–86
Toys, as agent of socialization,
   100–101
Trafficking, sexual, 382–384
Transgender individuals, 96
Transnational families, 289–290
Transracial adoptions, 273–274
Transsexual individuals, 97
Triple jeopardy, 358

U

Underclass, in United States, 129–130
Unemployment, families and, 321–323
United Kingdom. *See* Great Britain
United States
   birthrates in, 59f

changes in contemporary American families, 18–19
courtship and mate selection in, 188–193
crude divorce rates in, 419f
family life in colonial period, 74–79
family life in nineteenth century, 79–82
family life in twentieth century, 82–86
fertility rates in, 263–265, 263f, 264f
historical divorce trends in, 418–419
immigration and, 80–82, 151–152
increasing diversity in, 151–155
infant mortality in, 10, 62f
middle class in, 128
number of uninsured in, 325t
patterns of aging in, 354–356
poverty rate of, 137, 140t
refined divorce rates in, 419f
requirement for understanding families in, 33–34
social change in 1960s and 1970s in, 86
social class in, 125–130
social mobility in, 130–131
underclass in, 129–130
upper class in, 125–128
upper middle class in, 128
working class in, 128–129
working poor in, 129

Universal programs
family policy and, 23
in other developed countries, 25
Upper class, in United States, 125–128
Upper middle class, in United States, 128

V

Verbal communication, 243
Violence. *See also* Child abuse; Elder abuse
among intimates, 381
common couple, 386
consequences of, 393–394
coping with, 394–395
dating, 390–391
factors associated with, 392–393
gender-based, 381–384
intimate partner, 384–386
intimate terrorism, 386
macro-level societal and cultural causes of, 403–404
micro-level individual causes of, 402–403
mutual violence control, 386
power and control synthesis as cause of, 405–406
in same-sex relationships, 389–390
violent resistance, 386

Violent resistance (VR), 386
Voluntarily child-free, 271–272

W

Welfare programs, 24–26
Widowhood, 362–364
Women. *See also* Gender
changing of last names and, 110–111
cosmetic surgery and, 110, 110t
earnings of, vs. men, 112t
labor force trends for, 318–320
most prevalent occupations for employed, 113t
power of education and, 107, 108–109
Work
changing economy and, 317–321
full-time, or part-time penalty, 336–338
juggling, and family life, 332–338
Work–family conflict, 332–333
Working class, in United States, 128–129
Working poor, in United States, 128
World systems theory, 57–58

Z

Zero tolerance, 407

Credits